Ethnic Museums
and Heritage Sites
in the United States

Ethnic Museums and Heritage Sites in the United States

VICTOR J. DANILOV

McFarland & Company, Inc., Publishers
Jefferson, North Carolina, and London

Victor J. Danilov is the author of numerous
works on museums of all kinds, including
Sports Museums and Halls of Fame Worldwide (McFarland 2005)

LIBRARY OF CONGRESS CATALOGUING-IN-PUBLICATION DATA

Danilov, Victor J.
Ethnic museums and heritage sites in the United States / Victor J. Danilov.
p.   cm.
Includes bibliographical references and index.

ISBN 978-0-7864-3916-4
softcover : 50# alkaline paper ∞

1. Minorities — Museums — United States — Directories.
2. Historical museums — United States — Directories.
3. Ethnological museums and collections — United States — Directories.
4. Museums — United States — Directories.
5. Historic sites — United States — Directories.
6. Heritage tourism — United States — Directories.
I. Title.
E184.A1D265   2009   305.80074'73 — dc22   2008038248

British Library cataloguing data are available

On the cover: *clockwise from top left* Museum of Jewish Heritage
(photograph by Thomas Hinton; courtesy Museum of Jewish Heritage);
Windmill Island Municipal Park, Holland, Michigan (courtesy
Windmill Island Municipal Park); Venetian mask ©2008 Shutterstock;
Castille de San Felipe del Morro (courtesy San Juan National Historic Site
and National Park Service); antique Russian samovar ©2008 Shutterstock

Manufactured in the United States of America

*McFarland & Company, Inc., Publishers
Box 611, Jefferson, North Carolina 28640
www.mcfarlandpub.com*

To the millions of immigrants
who helped to make the
United States what it is today

Table of Contents

Preface   1

Introduction: Celebrating America's Ethnic Heritage   3

Ethnic Museums and Heritage Sites

Preface

The United States is known as a nation of immigrants — with nearly everyone coming from another country or being a descendant of someone from elsewhere in the world (with the possible exception of American Indians, known as Native Americans). America has been called a melting pot for the assimilation of these many different cultures. Yet, many individuals retain their ethnic interests and are proud of their heritage. They want to preserve and further the understanding and appreciation of their ethnic history, culture, and art. And this often results in ethnic museums, art galleries, historic sites, and related facilities with cultural collections, exhibits, and programs.

In addition to these facilities established and operated by ethnic groups, America has a great number of other museums, galleries, and historic and prehistoric sites with ethnic historical and cultural content established by non-ethnic founders, such as individual collectors, independent nonprofit museums, foundations, colleges and universities, and city, county, state, and federal governments. This book — the first comprehensive study of ethnically oriented museums and museum-like facilities — presents an overview of both the ethnic-operated museums and those other places interpreting ethnic history and culture. Selected site visits and talks and correspondence with ethnic museum and historic site officials, as well as ethnic studies, websites, directories, books, articles, and other research sources, have been helpful in this project.

More than 1,100 museums, art galleries, historic and prehistoric sites, and such other ethnically oriented facilities as halls of fame, sculpture displays, botanic gardens, and Internet "museums without walls" are described in this study — and there probably are others. At least 622 are facilities founded and operated by ethnic groups.

There are 478 non-ethnic public institutions that could be called ethnically related. Some are small with limited collections, exhibits, hours, staffs, and attendances, while others are sizeable or major institutions comparable to any of our nation's best museums and related facilities.

They tell the historical and cultural stories of 55 ethnic groups and a multicultural category. Nearly one out of every four places is devoted to Native American history, culture, or art. African American facilities rank second, followed by Jewish, German, Spanish, and Hispanic sites. Thirty-one museums are multicultural, having collections and exhibits of a number of ethnic cultures.

The general public probably has not heard of most of the ethnic museums, but there are some that are well known, have extensive collections and exhibits, and attract large attendances. The latter include such places as the United States Holocaust Memorial Museum in Washington, D.C., and Ellis Island Immigration Museum in New York City, both with approximately 3.4 million visitors each year, and the National Museum of the American Indian, Smithsonian Institution,

1

Washington, with more than two million. Some of the nation's leading natural history, anthropology, and archaeological museums, including the Smithsonian Institution's National Museum of Natural History in Washington, and American Museum of Natural History in New York City, also have ethnically related cultural collections and exhibits.

These museums — as well as numerous historic and prehistoric sites — preserve and interpret the history and culture of ethnic groups, increasing knowledge and pride among various ethnic peoples and helping others to better understand and appreciate the nation's ethnic history, cultures, and contributions. The ethnically oriented facilities also fill the gaps to be found in many mainstream museums, and play a cultural role far beyond their numbers and recognition.

Introduction: Celebrating America's Ethnic Heritage

Among America's most overlooked and underappreciated types of museums and historic sites are those devoted to ethnic history, culture, and related fields. They range from small storefront museums and galleries with limited offerings manned by volunteers to major museums with extensive collections, exhibits, and staffs, as well as historic and prehistoric sites of archaeological, ethnological, or historical significance.

Most of these ethnic institutions and sites are called museums, but they also go by many other names, such as cultural center, gallery, visitor center, historic house, arts center, institute, interpretative center, hall of fame, shrine, and botanical garden. They also can be part of libraries, archives, research centers, and college and university study centers. Some facilities are specialized, being dedicated to such diverse subjects as art, folk costumes, Judaica, sports, the Holocaust, fashion, firefighting, slave relics, Buffalo Soldiers, racist memorabilia, botanical gardens, and sites pertaining to exceptional individuals and historic events. Historic and prehistoric sites — sometimes known as monuments, memorials, landmarks, and historic parks — also often are of ethnic historical importance.

This study includes two types of ethnic facilities — *ethnic* museums, galleries, historic sites, and other facilities founded or operated by ethnic individuals, organizations, religious groups, and colleges, and *ethnically related* facilities with collections and exhibits of ethnic materials and historic and prehistoric sites established and operated by non-ethnic individual collectors and independent museums, organizations, colleges and universities, and city, county, state, and federal government agencies. Ethnic groups are interested in preserving and furthering understanding and appreciation of their history, culture, arts, and accomplishments, while ethnically related museums and historic and prehistoric sites seek to preserve historical, cultural, and artistic objects and to educate the general public about ethnic history, fine art, archaeological sites, and ethnological artifacts.

In addition to their own buildings, ethnic museums are located at such places as ethnic cultural centers, churches and synagogues, historic houses and sites, Indian reservations, and recycled facilities like former stores, banks, schools, churches, factories, libraries, and firehouses. Ethnically related facilities usually are at natural history, anthropology, ethnographic, and archaeology museums; specialized art museums; some local museums; public and campus libraries; historic parks; government cultural complexes; and historic and prehistoric sites. A few are "museums without walls," providing exhibit and educational services only over the Internet, and several others with museum names really are not museums, but suppliers of traveling ethnic exhibitions to museums. This study also includes some museums that are being planned or already are under development.

The United States has more than 1,100 ethnic and ethnically related museums, galleries, historic sites, and other facilities. This book describes 622 facilities founded and operated by ethnic groups and 478 others by non-ethnic governing bodies. They include 107 museums honoring individuals, 199 historic sites, 86 prehistoric sites, 12 botanical gardens, 2 museums with planetariums, and 30 non-ethnic museums with extensive ethnic collections or exhibits. They represent 55 ethnic groups and a multicultural category. The ethnic group with the largest number is Native Americans, with 302 museums and sites. African Americans are second with 189; followed by Jewish, 112; German, 66; Spanish, 60; Hispanic, 56; and multicultural, 31.

The oldest operating ethnic museum in the nation is the Hampton University Museum, an African American museum founded in 1868 in Hampton, Virginia. Among the other early museums founded by ethnic groups are the Vesterheim Norwegian-American Museum, Decorah, Iowa, 1877; Jewish Historical Society, which has a Center for Jewish History, New York City, 1892; the Jewish Museum and the Hispanic Society of America, New York, 1904; and Japan Society Gallery, New York City, 1907. Early ethnic historic sites include such places as the 1000–1450 Taos Pueblo, the oldest continuously inhabited community in the nation, Taos, New Mexico; 1610 Palace of the Governors (built by the Spanish and now part of the Museum of New Mexico), the nation's oldest continuously occupied public building, Santa Fe, New Mexico; and 1610–28 San Miguel Mission Church, the oldest church still in use in the United States, Santa Fe, New Mexico.

Most of the early ethnically related museums and sites were museums of archaeology and anthropology and government-established historic and prehistoric sites. They include such museums with ethnic collections and exhibits as the National Museum of Natural History, Smithsonian Institution, Washington, D.C., 1846 (opened in 1910); Peabody Museum of Archaeology and Ethnology, Harvard University, Cambridge, Massachusetts, and Peabody Museum of Natural History, Yale University, New Haven, Connecticut, 1866; American Museum of Natural History, New York City, 1869; University of Pennsylvania Museum of Archaeology and Anthropology, Philadelphia, 1887; Bishop Museum (also a cultural museum), Honolulu, 1889; and the Field Museum, Chicago, 1893.

Among the other early ethnically related museums are the Sheldon Jackson Museum, Sitka, Alaska, 1887; Phoebe Apperson Hearst Museum of Anthropology, University of California at Berkeley, 1901; and Southwest Museum of the American Indian, Los Angeles, and Museum of Indian Arts and Culture/Laboratory of Anthropology, Santa Fe, New Mexico, 1907. Many of the early state historical societies traced American Indian history and ethnic immigration and settlement with museums and historic sites, including the Minnesota Historical Society, 1849; Colorado Historical Society, 1879; and Arizona Historical Society, 1884.

Early historic and prehistoric sites with American Indian museums or visitor centers established by the federal government include such sites as the Casa Grande Ruins National Monument, Coolidge, Arizona, 1892; El Morro National Monument, Ramah, New Mexico, 1906; Chaco Culture National Historical Park, Nageezi, New Mexico, 1907; Sitka National Historical Park, Sitka, Alaska, 1910; Mesa Verde National Park, Mesa Verde, Colorado, 1917; and Grand Canyon National Park, Grand Canyon, Arizona, 1919.

These ethnic and ethnically related facilities were followed by such institutions as the Museum of the American Indian (which became the George Gustav Heye Center, a branch of the National Museum of the American Indian), New York City, 1916; Sheldon Museum and Cultural Center, Haines, Alaska, 1924; Schomburg Center for Research in Black

The Vesterheim Norwegian-American Museum in Decorah, Iowa, is one of the oldest ethnic museums in the United States. Started as collections in 1877, it is one of the largest and most comprehensive museums devoted to a single ethnic group. In addition to extensive collections and exhibits, it has 16 historic buildings downtown and structures at two other sites. This photograph shows the Norwegian house exhibit in the 1877 Arlington House, a former elegant hotel that now is the museum's main building. *Courtesy Vesterheim Norwegian-American Museum.*

Culture, New York City, 1925; American Swedish Historical Museum, Philadelphia, 1926; Little Norway, Blue Mounds, Wisconsin, 1926; China Institute Gallery, New York City, 1926; Howard University Gallery of Art, Washington, D.C., 1928; Antelope Valley Indian Museum, Lancaster, California, 1928; American Swedish Institute, Minneapolis, 1929; and Heard Museum and Pueblo Grande Museum and Archaeological Park, Phoenix, 1929.

The 1930s and early 1940s produced such museums as Tantaguidgeon Indian Museum, Uncasville, Connecticut, 1930; Polish Museum of America, Chicago, and Smoki Museum, Prescott, Arizona, 1935; Wheelwright Museum of the American Indian, Santa Fe, New Mexico, 1937; Osage Nation Tribal Mu-

seum, Pawhuska, Oklahoma, 1938; and George Washington Carver Museum, part of the Tuskegee Institute National Historic Site, Tuskegee, Alabama, 1941.

Accelerated Development After World War II

It was not until after World War II that the ethnic museum movement greatly expanded. Among those museums founded during the remainder of the century are the Museum of Russian Culture, San Francisco, 1948; Ukrainian National Museum, Library, and Archive, Chicago, 1952; Queen Sofia Spanish Institute (formerly Spanish Institute), New York City, 1954; Asian Art Museum of San

Francisco, Chong-Moon Lee Center for Asian Art and Culture (formerly Avery Brundage Collection), 1966; Martin Luther King, Jr., Center for Nonviolent Social Change, Atlanta, Georgia, 1968; Indian Museum of North America at Crazy Horse Memorial, South Dakota, 1972; National Czech and Slovak Museum and Library, Cedar Rapids, Iowa, 1974; Basque Museum and Cultural Center, Boise, Idaho, 1985; National Civil Rights Museum, Memphis, Tennessee, 1991; and Skirball Cultural Center, Los Angeles, 1996.

New museums continue to be established at a rapid pace in the twenty-first century. They include the National Hispanic Cultural Center, Albuquerque, New Mexico, 2000; Italian American Museum, New York City, 2001; National Museum of the American Indian, Smithsonian Institution, Washington, D.C., 2004; National Underground Railroad Freedom Center, Cincinnati, 2005; Arab American National Museum, Dearborn, Michigan, 2005; Rosa Parks Library and Museum, Montgomery, Alabama, 2005; Maltz Museum of Jewish Heritage, Beechwood, Ohio, 2005; and Sky City Cultural Center and Haak'u Museum, Pueblo of Ácoma, New Mexico, 2006.

Many other ethnic museums and related facilities are being planned, developed, or expanded. Among the more than dozen being planned or developed are the National Museum of African American History and Culture at the Smithsonian Institution, Washington, D.C.; Texas Czech Museum and Cultural Center, La Grange, Texas; National Museum

Thousands of visitors attended the 2004 opening of the National Museum of the American Indian, part of the Smithsonian Institution, on the Mall in Washington, D.C. The 258,000-square-foot museum, which has the world's largest collection of Indian cultural materials, has nearly 1 million objects of aesthetic, religious, and historical significance and everyday articles. It also has a branch museum in New York City and a center for collections, library, and archives in Suitland, Maryland. *Courtesy National Museum of the American Indian, Smithsonian Institution, and photographer Katherine Fogden.*

of American Jewish History, Philadelphia; George Washington Carver Memorial and Cultural Center, Fulton, Missouri; and Swiss Center of North America, New Glarus, Wisconsin.

Others places are being expanded or relocated to larger facilities, including the Contemporary Jewish Museum, San Francisco; August Wilson Center for African American Culture, Pittsburgh; Mizel Museum, Denver; Puyallup Tribal Museum, Tacoma, Washington; Cuban Museum, Coral Gables, Florida; Illinois Holocaust Museum and Education Center, Skokie, Illinois; and Museum of African Art, Long Island City, New York.

Some ethnic museums, however, have closed for lack of interest or support, such as the Stewart Indian Museum in Caron City, Nevada, and Tekakwitha Fine Arts Center in Sisseton, South Dakota. Others are closed temporarily because of hurricane or earthquake damage, renovation, or relocation. Damage from Hurricane Katrina forced the New Orleans African-American Museum of Art, Culture, and History and the Black Arts National Diaspora in New Orleans to close in 2005, while the Mission San Miguel Arcángel in San Miguel had to close to make repairs after the 2003 California earthquake.

Size and Popularity of Ethnic Offerings

Although many ethnic museums are relatively small (less than 10,000 square feet), some are quite large, as are many of the ethnically related facilities. Two of the largest Native American museums are the Mashantucket Pequot Museum and Research Center, built by the Pequot tribe in Mashantucket, Connecticut, which covers 308,000 square feet, and National Museum of the American Indian, Smithsonian Institution, Washington, D.C., with 258,000 square feet (it also operates two other facilities: George Gustav Heye Center in New York City and Cultural Re-

sources Center in Suitland, Maryland). Among the other large facilities are the United States Holocaust Memorial Museum, Washington, D.C., 265,000 square feet; Simon Wiesenthal Center and its Museum of Tolerance, 165,000 square feet; National Underground Railroad Museum Freedom Center, Cincinnati, 158,000 square feet; Heard Museum, Phoenix, 130,000 square feet; and Charles H. Wright Museum of African American History, Detroit, 120,000 square feet.

Some of the largest outdoor ethnically related historic or prehistoric sites are the El Malpais National Monument and El Malpais National Conservation Area, Grants, New Mexico, 377,277 acres; Canyons of the Ancients National Monument, Dolores, Colorado, 164,000 acres; and Ute Mountain Tribal Park, Towaoc, Colorado, 125,000 acres.

A number of ethnically oriented museums and sites have multiple sites, including the Heard Museum in Phoenix with branch museums in Scottsdale and Surprise, Arizona; National Museum of the American Indian, Smithsonian Institution in Washington, D.C., with an exhibition center in New York City and a cultural resources center in Suitland, Maryland; the Abbe Museum in Bar Harbor, Maine, sites in a national park and the town; and the Hopewell Culture National Historical Park in Chillicothe, Ohio, consisting of five Native American mound locations. The Hebrew Union College — Jewish Institute of Religion has museums at three of its four locations (New York, Cincinnati, and Los Angeles). Several museums are located in cultural complexes with other museums, including the Red Earth Indian Center in Omniplex in Oklahoma City and the Sioux Indian Museum in the Journey Museum Complex in Rapid City, South Dakota.

The collections of ethnic artifacts, art, and other objects at most ethnic museums range from a few thousand to 25,000, while those at anthropology, ethnographic, archaeological, and other non-ethnic museums usually are much more extensive. Among the museums with large ethnically oriented collections are the Bishop Museum, Honolulu, 3 million; Anasazi Heritage Center, Dolores, Colorado, 3 million; Peabody Museum of Anthropology and Ethnology, Cambridge, Massachusetts, nearly 2.5 million; University of Pennsylvania Museum of Archaeology and Anthropology, Philadelphia, 1.5 million; Burke Museum of Natural History, Seattle, 1 million; National Museum of the American Indian, Smithsonian Institution, Washington, D.C., nearly 1 million; Palace of the Governors, Santa Fe, New Mexico, over 400,000; and Southwest Museum of the American Indian, Los Angeles, the Field Museum, Chicago, and Institute for American Indian Studies, Washington Green, Connecticut, 250,000 each.

The United States Holocaust Memorial Museum in Washington, D.C., has the largest annual attendance of any of the ethnically oriented museums, with nearly 3.4 million visitors (although the multicultural Ellis Island Immigration Museum, with figures combined with the adjacent Statue of Liberty National Memorial in New York City, total slightly over 3.4 million).

Other museums and sites with large attendances include The Alamo, San Antonio, 2.5 million; National Museum of the American Indian, Smithsonian Institution, Washington, D.C., over 2 million; San Juan National Historic Site, Old San Juan, Puerto Rico, 2 million; San Antonio Missions National Historical Park, San Antonio, 1.4 million; Cabrillo National Monument, San Diego, 1.1 million; Indian Museum of North America at Crazy Horse Memorial, Crazy Horse, South Dakota, 1 million; Martin Luther King, Jr., Historic Site and Preservation District, Atlanta, 900,000; Arthur M. Sackler Gallery, Smithsonian Institution, Washington, D.C., 625,000; Mesa Verde National Park, Mesa Verde, Colorado, 623,000; Charles H. Wright Museum of African American History, Detroit, Martin Luther King, Jr., Center for Nonviolent Social Change, Atlanta, and

Freer Gallery of Art, Smithsonian Institution, Washington, D.C., 600,000 each; Seattle Asian Art Museum, Seattle, 500,000; and National Museum of African Art, Smithsonian Institution, Washington, D.C., 300,000.

Some ethnically related museums and sites have larger total attendances, but it is not known how many visitors actually visit their ethnic offerings. This includes such places as the National Museum of Natural History, Smithsonian Institution, Washington, D.C., over 5.5 million; Grand Canyon National Park, Grand Canyon, Arizona, 5 million; American Museum of Natural History, New York City, 4 million; and the Field Museum, Chicago, 1.2 million.

Native American Museums and Heritage Sites

Native American museums, cultural centers, galleries, and historic and prehistoric sites dominate the ethnic museum world. With 302 ethnically oriented facilities, nearly one out of every four museums and sites containing ethnic collections or exhibits is Native American. Most of the museums — sometimes called cultural or visitor centers — were founded by American Indian tribes. Others resulted from private collections of artifacts and art, college and university studies and research programs, and independent, government, and other initiatives. Nearly all the American Indian historic and prehistoric sites were established by state and federal agencies.

Most of the tribal museums are located on Indian reservations. The Osage Nation Tribal Museum, founded in 1938 in Pawhuska, Oklahoma, is the oldest continually operated tribal museum in North America. The largest and most costly tribal museum is the 308,000-square-foot Mashantucket Pequot Museum and Research Center, which opened in 1998 in Mashantucket, Connecticut, at a cost of $193.4 million. Among the many other tribal museums are the Navajo Nation

Museum, Window Rock, Arizona; Agua Caliente Cultural Museum, Palm Springs, California; Makah Cultural and Research Center, Neah Bay, Washington; Seneca-Iroquois National Museum, Salamanca, New York; Oneida Nation Museum, Oneida, Wisconsin; Shoshone-Bannock Tribal Museum, Pocatello, Idaho; and the Museum at Warm Springs, Warm Springs, Oregon.

Some tribal museums are specialized, such as the Menominee Logging Camp Museum, which has the largest collection of artifacts from Wisconsin's logging era, near Keshena, Wisconsin, and Jicarilla Apache Arts and Crafts Museum, which features the basketry, beadwork, leatherwork, and other arts and crafts for which the tribe is known, in Dulce, New Mexico. A number of tribes have multiple facilities, including the Cherokee Heritage Center in Tahlequah, Oklahoma, which consists of the Cherokee National Museum and two historic village reconstructions; the Eastern Band of the Cherokee, which operates the Museum of the Cherokee and the Oconaluftee Indian Village in Cherokee, North Carolina; and the Pueblo of Ácoma's Sky City Cultural Center and Haak'u Museum in Arizona.

Some multi-tribal museums and cultural centers present an overview of Native American history and culture. They include the Indian Pueblo Cultural Center, which traces the history and accomplishments of the Pueblo people, Albuquerque, and the Gallup Cultural Center, with 25 historical dioramas, Gallup, New Mexico. Among the other broad-based American Indian facilities are the National Hall of Fame for Famous American Indians, which honors 41 outstanding Native Americans with sculptured busts, and Indian City U.S.A.,

The world's largest Native American museum is the 308,000-square-foot Mashantucket Pequot Museum and Research Center in Mashantucket, Connecticut. The $193.4 million complex, which opened in 1998, depicts 18,000 years of Indian and natural history, with the emphasis on the Mashantucket Pequot Tribal Nation. *Courtesy Mashantucket Pequot Museum and Research Center.*

which interprets the lives, cultures, and religions of seven Indian tribes in partial replicas of tribal villages, both in Anadarko, Oklahoma.

A number of Native American museums are named in honor of tribal chiefs and other outstanding figures. Among the tribal museums are the Tahonteeskee Cherokee Courthouse Museum, named for the chief who founded the nation, Gore, Oklahoma; George

W. Brown, Jr., Ojibwa Museum and Cultural Center, which honors a prominent tribal elder, Lac du Flambeau, Wisconsin; and Shako:wi Cultural Center, named for Richard Chrisjohn, a long-time representative of the Oneida tribe, whose native name was Shako:wi, Oneida, New York. Although not named for a person, the San Ildefonso Pueblo Museum near Santa Fe, New Mexico, is dedicated to Maria Martinez, the tribe's noted black-on-black style potter

American Indian leaders also are honored at such non-tribal facilities as Black Kettle Museum, named for the leader of the Southern Cheyenne killed in 1868 in the unprovoked attack on his peaceful village by Lieutenant Colonel George Armstrong Custer and his troops at the Washita Battlefield National Historic Site near Cheyenne, Oklahoma; Chief Plenty Coups Museum State Park, named for the last chief of the Crow tribe, near Pryor, Montana; Sacajawea State Park and Interpretive Center, honoring the Shoshone guide and interpreter for the Lewis and Clark expedition, near Pasco, Washington; and Crazy Horse Memorial, a tribute to the Oglala Sioux leader that is the world's largest sculpture and the site of the Indian Museum of North America, Crazy Horse, South Dakota.

Many diverse Native American museums have been founded by non-tribal parties, such as the private nonprofit Marin Museum of the American Indian, with collections and exhibits of Native American history, culture, and art, Novato, California; Amerind Foundation Museum, devoted to the study, preservation, and interpretation of historic and prehistoric Native American cultures, Dragoon, Arizona; Wheelwright Museum of the American Indian, a museum founded by a wealthy Bostonian and a Navajo medicine man which features changing exhibitions of historic and contemporary Native American art, Santa Fe, New Mexico; Mt. Kearsarge Indian Museum Education and Cultural Center, containing exhibits on the Indian way of life and replicas of Native American dwellings, Warner, New

Hampshire; and Plains Indian Museum, which focuses on the history, traditions, and art of the Plains Indians and is one of five museums at the Buffalo Bill Historical Center, Cody, Wyoming.

Some Native American museums were started by individuals with collections of Native American artifacts or art, including the Antelope Valley Indian Museum, initiated near Lancaster, California, in 1928 by artist Howard Arden Edwards; Abbe Museum in Acadia National Park near Bar Harbor, Maine, begun by Dr. Robert Abbe in 1928; Heard Museum, founded in Phoenix in 1929 by collectors Dwight and Maie Heard; Mitchell Museum of the American Indians, created in 1977 by John and Betty Mitchell in Evanston, Illinois; Eiteljorg Museum of American Indians and Western Art, founded in Indianapolis in 1985 by businessman and art collector Harrison Eiteljorg; and Schingoethe Center for Native American Cultures, established in 1989 at Aurora University in Aurora, Illinois, by Herbert and Martha Schingoethe. A number of colleges and universities have museums related to Native American studies and research centers, including the Center of Southwest Studies at Fort Lewis College, Durango, Colorado, and the Museum of the Native American Resource Center, University of North Carolina at Pembroke.

Numerous American Indian museums and historic sites have been established by government agencies and historical societies. The Totem Heritage Center in Ketchikan, Alaska, and the Native American Museum in Terre Haute, Indiana, are city facilities. In California, the state operates the California State Indian Museum in Sacramento and a network of regional Indian museums. The Museum of Indian Arts/Laboratory of Anthropology in Santa Fe, New Mexico, is part of the state's Museum of New Mexico's branch museum system. The Ute Indian Museum in Montrose, Colorado, and the Mille Lacs Indian Museum near Onamia, Minnesota, are among the museums operated by state historical societies.

Some state historic sites also have museums, such as the Black Hawk State Historic Site near Rock Island, Illinois, and Indian Grinding Rock State Historic Site near Pine Grove, California.

One of the nation's leading and largest Native American museums is the federally operated National Museum of the American Indian, located at the Smithsonian Institution's mall complex in Washington, D.C. The National Park Service is responsible for most of the federal government's Native American museums and historic and prehistoric sites. They are located at national parks, national monuments, national historical parks, and national historic sites such as Mesa Verde National Park, Mesa Verde, Colorado; Little Bighorn Battlefield National Monument, near Crow Agency, Montana; and Nez Percé National Historical Park, Spalding, Idaho.

The Indian Arts and Crafts Board in the Department of the Interior operates three regional museums (Sioux Indian Museum, Rapid City, South Dakota; Museum of the Plains Indians, Browning, Montana; and Southern Plains Indian Museum, Anadarko, Oklahoma) to display and promote Indian arts and crafts. A number of Native American archaeological sites also are preserved and interpreted by the Bureau of Land Management, including the Canyons of the Ancients National Monument near Dolores, Colorado, and by the U.S. Forest Service, such as the Chimney Rock Archaeological Area near Pagosa Springs, Colorado.

Numerous ethnically related archaeological, anthropological, natural history, and art museums also have collections and exhibits of American Indian history, culture, and art. Among such facilities are the Peabody Museum of Archaeology and Ethnology, which has one of the most comprehensive records of human cultural history in the Western Hemisphere, Harvard University, Cambridge, Massachusetts; Maxwell Museum of Anthropology, featuring collections and exhibits of Southwest native cultures, University of New Mexico, Albuquerque; Gilcrease Museum, with many Native American artworks and artifacts among its extensive American West collection, Tulsa; the Field Museum, containing 250,000 artifacts and numerous exhibits pertaining to native cultures of North America, Chicago; and Houston Museum of Natural History, which has a 12,000-square-foot exhibit on the indigenous peoples of the Americas, Houston.

African American Museums and Heritage Sites

Of the 189 African American museums and historic sites in this study, 107 are museums and galleries, 51 honor individuals, and 31 are historic sites. Nearly every large American metropolitan area has an African American museum, cultural center, historic house, or historically significant site. Most were started by African American individuals or groups interested in conveying and building pride in black ethnic history, culture, or achievements. Some are devoted to such diverse specialized areas as art, music, sports, civil rights, firefighting, fashion, slavery, western settlement and cowboys, Buffalo Soldiers, African arts, and racist memorabilia. Others are museums and historic sites operated by city, state, or federal government agencies.

The first African American museum was the Hampton University Museum, founded in 1868 in Hampton, Virginia. It features collections and exhibits about African American history and culture dating from 1607. It was not until the first half of the twentieth century that other African American institutions were being founded, including the Schomburg Center for Research in Black Culture, New York City, 1925; Tuskegee National Historic Site and its George Washington Carver Museum, Tuskegee Institute, Tuskegee, Alabama, 1941; Clark Atlanta University Galleries, Atlanta, 1942; and Fisk University Galleries, Nashville, Tennessee, 1949. They were followed by such places as the African American Museum, Cleveland, 1953; DuSable Museum of African-American History, Chicago, 1961; National Museum of African Art, Smithsonian Institution, Washington, D.C., 1964; Charles H. Wright Museum of African American History, Detroit, 1965; Museum of Afro-American History, Boston, 1966; and Studio Museum in Harlem, New York City, and Anacostia Museum and Center for African American History and Culture, Smithsonian Institution, Washington, D.C., 1967.

The assassination of Dr. Martin Luther King, Jr., in 1968 and the Civil Rights Movement resulted in the founding of the Martin Luther King, Jr., Center for Nonviolent Social Change and the Martin Luther King National Historic Site and Preservation District in Atlanta in 1968 and 1980. They also influenced the founding of such facilities as the National Afro-American Museum and Cultural Center, Wilberforce, Ohio, 1972; National Civil Rights Museum, Memphis, Tennessee, 1991; Birmingham Civil Rights Institute, Birmingham, Alabama, and National Voting Rights Museum and Institute, Selma, Alabama, 1992; National Underground Railroad Freedom Center, Cincinnati, 1995; and Civil Rights Memorial Center and Rosa Parks Library and Museum, both in Montgomery, Alabama, 2005.

Among the largest and best attended African American museums, galleries, and related facilities are the Martin Luther King, Jr., National Historic Site and Preservation District, which contains Dr. King's neighborhood, birthplace, boyhood home, church, and gravesite, with 900,000 visitors annually, Atlanta; Charles H. Wright Museum of African American History, a 120,000-square-foot historical and cultural museum, Detroit, and Martin Luther King, Jr., Center for Nonviolent Social Change, located at the national historical site in Atlanta, both with approximately 600,000 visitors; National Underground Railroad Freedom Center, a new $110 million complex with 158,000 square feet,

Cincinnati; and the Smithsonian Institution's National Museum of African Art, featuring objects of African art, wood, metal, ceramic, ivory, and fiber, Washington, D.C., having an estimated annual attendance of 300,000.

Many of the new African American museums during the latter half of the twentieth and early twenty-first centuries were founded and operated by governments. Among the municipal museums are the Afro-American Historical and Cultural Museum (now the African American Museum in Philadelphia); Smith Robertson Museum and Cultural Center, Jackson, Mississippi; and Alexandria Black History Museum, Alexandria, Virginia. States have founded such facilities as the Banneker-Douglas Museum, Annapolis, Maryland; Black Archives Research Center and Museum at Florida A&M University in Tallahassee, Florida; and Alabama State Black Archives, Research Center, and Museum at Alabama A&M University, Normal, Alabama. States also have such historic sites as Scott Joplin State Historic Site, St. Louis; Fort Gadsden State Historic Site, near Sumatra, Florida; and Colonel Allensworth State Historic Park, near Earlimart, California.

In addition to the National Museum of African Art and the Anacostia Museum and Center for African American History and Culture, the federal government's Smithsonian Institution is planning to add the National Museum of African American History and Culture in Washington, D.C. The National Park Service operates such African American historic sites as the Martin Luther King, Jr., National Historic Site and Preservation District, Atlanta; Tuskegee Institute National Historic Site, Tuskegee, Alabama; Boston African American National Historic Site, Boston; Booker T. Washington National Monument, Hardy, Virginia; and Nicodemus National Historic Site, Nicodemus, Kansas.

Many African American museums, galleries, and research centers also are located at colleges and universities. They include such places as Avery Research Center for African

American History and Culture, College of Charleston, Charleston, South Carolina; Howard University Museum and Howard University Gallery of Art, Washington, D.C.; and Amsted Research Center Art Gallery, Tulane University, New Orleans. Libraries also frequently are sites of African American collections and exhibits, such as the Schomberg Center for Research in Black Culture, New York City; African American Museum and Library at Oakland, Oakland, California; and Afro-American Historical Society Museum, Jersey City, New Jersey.

In addition to the civil rights and historic site museums, a considerable number of other African American facilities are specialized, including the African American Museum of the Arts, DeLand, Florida; African American Firefighter Museum, Los Angeles; Negro Leagues Baseball Museum, Kansas City, Missouri; Slave Relic Museum, Walterboro, South Carolina; Black Fashion Museum, Washington, D.C.; Buffalo Soldiers National Museum, Houston; African American Hall of Fame Museum, Peoria, Illinois; National Great Blacks in Wax Museum, Baltimore; and Jim Crow Museum of Racist Memorabilia, Ferris State University, Big Rapids, Michigan. Some places called museums actually are not museums in the usual sense, such as Internet "museums without walls" like the Black Heritage Museum of Arlington, Virginia, and sometimes traveling exhibition services such as the Museum of Black Innovations and Inventions in Brooklyn, New York.

Two New Orleans museums — the New Orleans African American Museum of Art, Culture, and History and the Black Arts National Diaspora — have closed temporarily because of damage inflicted by Hurricane Katrina in 2005 and are seeking to reopen. Others are being expanded or relocated, such as the August K. Wilson Center for African American Culture, Pittsburgh, and Museum of African Art, Long Island City, New York. A number of facilities also are under development or in planning in other parts of the nation, includ-

ing the National Museum of African American History and Culture, Washington, D.C.; International African American Museum, Charleston, South Carolina; and George Washington Carver Memorial and Culture Center, Fulton, Missouri.

Jewish Museums and Heritage Sites

The United States has at least 112 Jewish museums, galleries, collection exhibit areas, and historic sites. Approximately one-fourth are located in synagogues and temples and devoted to Judaica collections, while about one-eighth are dedicated to the Holocaust. Nearly a dozen are housed in Jewish community centers, and most Jewish colleges, universities, and seminaries have museums or galleries relating to Jewish history, culture, religion, or art.

The American Jewish Historical Society, which operates the Center for Jewish History in New York City, was founded in 1892 and is the oldest national ethnic historical organization in the nation. It was followed in 1904 by The Jewish Museum, which began with a gift of Jewish ceremonial art objects to the Jewish Theological Seminary, under whose auspices it still operates in New York City.

Among the other early Jewish museums and galleries were the Temple Museum of Religious Art, Cleveland, 1950; B'nai B'rith Klutznick National Jewish Museum, Washington, D.C., 1957; National Museum of American Jewish Military History, Washington, D.C., 1958; Holocaust Awareness Museum and Education Center, Philadelphia, 1959; Jewish Museum of Maryland, Baltimore, 1960; Los Angeles Museum of the Holocaust, Los Angeles, 1961; Judah L. Magnes Museum, Berkeley, California, and Judaica Museum of Central Synagogue, New York City, 1962; Sherwin Miller Museum of Jewish Art, Tulsa, 1966; and Spertus Museum, Chicago, 1968.

Many other facilities were founded thereafter, including such places as the Yeshiva University Museum, New York City, 1973;

National Museum of American Jewish History, Philadelphia, 1976; Mizel Museum, Denver, 1982; Museum of Jewish Heritage — A Living Memorial to the Holocaust, New York City, 1984; Roder Shaland Biblical Botanical Garden, Pittsburgh, 1987; United States Holocaust Memorial Museum, Washington, D.C., and Museum of Tolerance, Los Angeles, 1993; Jewish Museum of Florida, Miami Beach, 1995; Skirball Cultural Center, Los Angeles, 1996; and Maltz Museum of Jewish Heritage, Beechwood, Ohio, 2005.

The largest and best attended Jewish museum is the 265,000-square-foot United States Holocaust Memorial Museum in Washington, D.C. It has nearly 1.4 million visitors a year. Other museums with large attendances include the Skirball Cultural Center in Los Angeles, with 370,000 visitors; Museum of Tolerance, part of the Simon Wiesenthal Center in Los Angeles, 250,000; The Jewish Museum, New York City, 223,000; and Museum of Jewish Heritage — A Living Memorial to the Holocaust, New York City, 125,000.

The Skirball Cultural Center in Los Angeles is one of four museums that are part of the Hebrew Union College — Jewish Institute of Religion. The others are in New York City, Cincinnati, and Jerusalem. Among the other Jewish colleges, universities, and seminaries with museums or galleries are the Yeshiva University, New York City; Hampshire College, Amherst, Massachusetts; Jewish Theological Seminary, New York City; and Spertus Institute of Jewish Studies, Chicago.

Most Jewish museums and galleries are devoted to Jewish history, culture, art, and life. They include such places as the B'nai B'rith Klutznick National Jewish Museum, Washington, D.C.; The Jewish Museum, New York City; National Museum of American Jewish History, Philadelphia; William Breman Jewish Heritage Museum, Atlanta; Center for Jewish History, New York City; Judah L. Magnes Museum, Berkeley, California; and Museum of the Southern Jewish Experience, Jackson, Mississippi.

Many museums and exhibits, however, are specialized, such as those with collections of religious ceremonial artifacts and materials of Judaism. They generally occupy a part of synagogues and temples, such as the Temple Judea Museum of Keneseth Israel in Elkins Park, Pennsylvania, and Harold and Vivian Beck Museum of Judaica at the Beth David Congregation in Miami. The Judaica Museum of Central Synagogue in New York City has some of its exhibits in the synagogue and others in a community house across the street, while the Beth Ahabah Museum and Archives is in a historic building adjoining the Congregation Beth Ahabah in Baltimore.

An increasing number of Jewish museums are dedicated to the Holocaust. The Holocaust Awareness Museum and Education Center, founded in Philadelphia in 1959, was the nation's first Holocaust museum. Since then, numerous others have opened in other cities, including the Los Angeles Museum of the Holocaust; Museum of Jewish Heritage — A Living Memorial to the Holocaust, New York City; Dallas Holocaust Museum and Center for Education and Tolerance; Holocaust Memorial Center, Farmington Hills, Michigan; and United States Holocaust Memorial Museum, Washington, D.C.

Some Jewish museums and galleries feature only art — and they often are located at Jewish community centers. They include such galleries as the Chase/Freedom Gallery and Ann Randall Gallery at the Greater Hartford Jewish Community Center, West Hartford, Connecticut; Janice Charach Epstein Gallery, Jewish Community Center of Metropolitan Detroit, West Bloomfield, Michigan; and Koret Gallery, Albert L. Schultz Jewish Community Center, Palo Alto, California.

Among the other Jewish specialized museums and sites are such places as the Temple Museum of Religious Art, Cleveland; National Museum of American Jewish Military History, Washington, D.C.; Jewish Sports Hall of Fame, Commack, New York; Jewish Children's Museum, Brooklyn, New York; Touro

Synagogue Historic Site, Newport, Rhode Island; Eldridge Street Project, New York City; and Jewish Women's Archive, which offers exhibits on the Web about outstanding Jewish women, Brookline, Massachusetts.

German Museums and Heritage Sites

German museums, galleries, and historic sites range from typical ethnic museums devoted to German history and culture to utopian and religious colonies. Among the 66 facilities in the book also are such varied places as historical societies of Germans from Russia, Amish and Mennonite heritage centers, outdoor living-history museums, German Moravian sites, early utopian communities, and German-dominated museums in cities with large German populations.

Some German museums are mainly historical in nature, having collections and exhibits on the history and culture of Germans, often with an emphasis on local immigration, settlement, and contributions. Among these museums are two early sites — Sophienburg Museum and Archives, founded in 1926 in New Braunfels, Texas, and Vereins Kirche Museum, established in Fredericksburg, Texas, in 1935 in a replica of an 1847 German building. Others include the German Heritage Museum, Cincinnati; German Culture Museum, Walnut Creek, Ohio; German Heritage Museum, Roberts Cove, Louisiana; and newly formed DANK Chicago Museum, Chicago.

A number of museums are dedicated to Germans from particular sections of Germany or elsewhere, such as the Society of the Danube Swabians Museum, Des Plaines, Illinois; Texas Wendish Heritage Museum, Giddings, Texas; Bukovina Society Headquarters-Museum, Ellis, Kansas; Heimat Museum (Danube-Swabian culture), Lake Villa, Illinois; Germans from Russia Heritage Society Library and Archives, Bismarck, North Dakota; and American Historical Society of Germans from Russia museums, libraries, and

research centers in Lincoln, Nebraska; Fresno, California; and other areas. The Goschenhoppen Folklife Library and Museum, in Green Lane, Pennsylvania, depicts Pennsylvania Dutch (German) culture prior to 1870, an era of handmade furniture and textiles, while Pennsylvania German Cultural Heritage Center at Kutztown University in Kutztown, Pennsylvania, seeks to preserve and interpret Pennsylvania Dutch history, folklore, and traditions.

Among the living-history museums with costumed interpreters and demonstrators are the Landis Valley Museum, presenting German material, culture, and heritage from 1740 through 1940, Lancaster, Pennsylvania; Historic Sauder Village, with historic structures, craft demonstrations, and collections of artifacts that depict German-oriented rural life in northwest Ohio in the late 1800s, Archbold, Ohio; and Old Salem, a re-creation of the eighteenth-century Moravian Church town of Salem founded in 1766, Winston-Salem, North Carolina.

Many museums and visitor centers interpret Amish, Mennonite, and Moravian history, life, and beliefs in sections of the country where they have settled. As immigrants, they came largely from Germany to find religious freedom and a better life. The Amish Village near Strasburg, Pennsylvania, offers guided tours that interpret the history and culture of Old Order Amish living in Lancaster County, while the Illinois Amish Interpretive Center in Arcola tells the story of the Old Order Amish and features artifacts from the local community.

Among the many Mennonite facilities are the Kauffman Museum and Mennonite Library and Archives at Bethel College, which describe how Mennonites came to America's central plains in the 1870s and contain many of the early records, North Newton, Kansas; Illinois Mennonite Heritage Center, which interprets the faith and life of Mennonites in the state, near Metamora; Mennonite Heritage Museum, a tribute to the German Mennonite families that left Russia in 1874 and settled in the area, Goessel, Kansas; and Mennonite Settlement Museum, devoted to early Mennonite immigrant village life in Hillsboro, Kansas.

Some places seek to further public understanding of both the Amish and Mennonite ways of life, including the Amish and Mennonite Heritage Center, near Berlin, Ohio; Menno-Hoff Mennonite-Amish Visitors Center, Shipshewana, Indiana; and Mennonite Information Center and Biblical Tabernacle Reproduction, Lancaster, Pennsylvania. The People's Place Quilt Museum in Intercourse, Pennsylvania, features antique Amish and Mennonite quilts and other decorative arts.

In addition to the eighteenth-century Moravian Church town at Old Salem living-history museum in North Carolina, a number of other museums interpret the Moravian faith. The Moravian Museum of Bethlehem in Pennsylvania traces the history, culture, and religious traditions of the German Moravians who settled in the area, and the Moravian Historical Society in Nazareth, Pennsylvania, tells the story of the Moravian Church and its contributions to American history and culture.

Germans have been involved in a number of utopian community efforts in America that now are historic sites. The first was Harmonie, a communal settlement in western Pennsylvania founded by a group of Separatists from the German Lutheran Church led by Johann George Rapp in the early 1800s. However, the group moved to Harmonie on the Wabash (now New Harmony, Indiana) in 1814, only to return to Pennsylvania to found Oekonomie in 1824. The settlers developed a peaceful agricultural and industrial society, but many left when Rapp died and the community was dissolved and its holdings sold in 1905. The site now is known as Old Economy Village, a national historic landmark containing 17 restored structures in Ambridge. The New Harmony site also has become a historic site with 25 buildings from the Harmonist period.

Another early German communal col-

ony was the Bethel German Colony in Bethel, Missouri. It was formed in 1844 by followers of charismatic religious leader Wilhelm Keil, who later took some of the settlers to form a new colony in the Willamette Valley of the Oregon Territory. But both communal colonies were disbanded in 1879 after Keil's death. Much of Bethel remains as it did over 150 years ago, with more than 30 original structures. It also has a visitor center with artifacts and exhibits on the colony's history.

The Amana Colonies in Amana, Iowa, also began as a communal community in 1855, but later discontinued the communal way of life. However, church life continues with its spiritualistic pattern and simple worship in unadorned meeting houses. It was founded by members of the Community of True Inspiration, part of the Piestist and Spiritualist Movement within the Lutheran Church in Germany. The site now consists of seven closely-knit villages and tells the community's story at the Amana Heritage Museum and four specialized museums.

Three other early villages founded by Germans in the eighteenth and nineteen centuries now are state historic sites. The Schoenbrunn Village State Memorial near New Philadelphia, Ohio, is the site of the first town in Ohio. It began as a Moravian mission to the Delaware Indians in 1772 by missionary David Zeisberger of the German Protestant sect whose beliefs included pacifism. The village later was destroyed by hostile Indians, but 17 log structures have been reconstructed and the site has a visitor center and costumed interpreters. The Zoar Village State Memorial in Zoar, Ohio, was a communal community founded in 1817 by a group of German religious dissenters called the Society of Separatists of Zoar who sought refuge from religious persecution. The site has 10 restored buildings from the early period. The Deutschheim State Historic Site in Hermann, Missouri, commemorates the founding Germans, who were the most systematic and best organized of Missouri's seven German settlement societies. It contains four mid–1800s structures with furnishings and decorative arts of the period, gardens, and a museum with exhibits on the history and culture of the settlement.

Some early German-founded cities in the United States still are heavily oriented along German historical and cultural lines. These include eighteenth-century Germantown, Pennsylvania, which has the Germantown Historical Society with many exhibits and artifacts relating to its founding by German settlers; and Frankenmuth, Michigan, founded in 1845 and known as Michigan's Little Bavaria, with the Frankenmuth Historical Museum featuring many artifacts and archival materials from the nineteenth century and exhibits describing the German-American influence on the community.

Among the other German-oriented cities are New Ulm, Minnesota, one of America's most Germanic communities that was founded in 1854 by German immigrants and still has a distinctly German appearance and atmosphere (with its story being told at the Brown County Historical Society); and Hermann, Missouri, a city founded by German settlers that now has the Historic Hermann Museum, housed in an 1871 German school building that was the only privately owned public schoolhouse in the state when opened and the only one to conduct classes in both German and English (it contains artifacts, memorabilia, and exhibits related to the city's German past and later development).

Spanish Museums and Heritage Sites

Of the 60 Spanish museums and historic sites in this study, 52 are historic sites and most are early missions and presidios (forts) in Texas, California, and the Southwest. The historic missions and forts were established largely as part of Spanish exploration, conquest, and settlement in the sixteenth through eighteenth centuries. Even the Spanish museums with collections and exhibits are primarily related to the Spanish colonial period in the United States.

The oldest Spanish historic site on American soil is in Puerto Rico. The San Juan National Historic Site includes three sixteenth- to nineteenth-century Spanish forts, bastions, powder houses, and three-fourths of the city wall at Old San Juan. The three forts are the 1539 to 1787 Castille de San Felipe del Morro (known as El Morro), 1634 to 1790 San Cristóbal, and San Juan de la Cruz (also called El Cañuelo). More than 2 million visit the site annually.

Many of the mainland's early museums and historic sites are in the St. Augustine, Florida; Santa Fe, New Mexico; and California coastal areas, which were among the first Spanish settlements in the nation. Some of the oldest facilities are in or near St. Augustine, founded in 1565 and the oldest city in America. They include the Colonial Spanish Quarter Museum, a re-created 1700s Spanish colonial village; Oldest House Museum Complex, featuring an early 1700s house on a site that has been occupied since the 1600s; and two restored Spanish forts built as part of the outer defenses to St. Augustine and the site of the first European battle for control of the New World — the Castillo de San Marcos National Monument, a 1672 to 1695 fort, and Fort Matanzas National Monument, a fort built in 1742.

In the Southwest, Santa Fe was the Spanish capital for the territory in the early seventeenth century. It is where many early Spanish buildings still remain. They include the 1610 Palace of the Governors, now a museum and the nation's oldest continuously occupied public building; 1610 to 1628 San Miguel Mission Church, the oldest church still in use in the United States; ca. 1780 Santuario de Nuestra Señora de Guadalupe, believed to be the oldest shrine in the nation honoring the Virgin of Guadalupe; and the Cathedral Basilica of St. Francis of Assisi, which began as a small Franciscan parish in San Gabriel in 1598 and had five other sites before becoming a cathedral in 1886. Two other Spanish historical museums in the Santa Fe area are the 1700 to 1885 El Rancho de las Golondrinas, a living-history ranch museum, and the Museum of Spanish Colonial Art, which contains Spanish colonial art forms produced in New Mexico and southern Colorado since the region was colonized by Spain in 1598.

A number of other historic Spanish missions and other structures are in New Mexico. They include the 1613 San Augustin de la Isleta Mission, rebuilt in 1692 to 1693 following a fire, Isleta Pueblo; four 1622 to 1672 mission ruins at the Salinas Pueblo Missions National Monument, near Mountainair; 1629 San Estéban del Rey Mission, the largest Spanish mission in the Southwest, Ácoma Pueblo; 1706 San Filipe de Neri Church and Old Town, Albuquerque; ca. 1772 San Francisco de Asis Mission Church, an impressive early Franciscan church, Ranchos de Taos; 1804 La Hacienda de los Martinez, a fortress-like trading post, Taos; and 1815 to 1826 Old San Miguel Mission, with massive walls and huge vigas and supporting arches, Socorro.

Among the historic missions in Arizona are the ruins of three Spanish colonial missions (two founded in 1691 and the third in 1757) at the Tumacácori National Historical Park, near Nogales, and the 1692 Mission San Xavier del Bac, known as the White Dove of the Desert, on the Tohono O'odham Indian Reservation, south of Tucson.

The largest concentration of Spanish colonial resources is located at the San Antonio Missions National Historical Park in San Antonio. It includes four seventeenth- and eighteenth-century frontier missions and an early aqueduct, dam, ranch, flour mill, and several miles of irrigation ditches. Three of the missions were transferred from eastern Texas in 1731 during turbulent Indian times and territorial competition with the French. They included the 1690 Mission San Francisco de la Espada (formerly San Francisco de los Tejas), 1716 Mission San Juan Capistrano, and 1731

to 1755 Mission Nuestra Señora de la Purísima Concepción. The only mission founded at the site is the 1720 Mission San José y San Miguel de Aguayo. The Alamo, where Texans fought the Mexican army in 1836, originally was the Mission San Antonio de Valero, founded with its protecting presidio in 1718.

The oldest Spanish mission in Texas is the Ysleta Mission (originally the Mission Nuestra Señora del Carmen), founded in 1681 to serve Tigua Indian refugees after the Pueblo Revolt of 1680. It is one of two Spanish missions (the other being the Nuestra Señora de la Limpia Concepción del Socorro Mission in Socorro, Texas) that first were located on the Mexican side of the Rio Grande River, but became part of Texas when the river channel changed. The Mission Tejas State Park near Weches, Texas, has a commemorative representation of the 1690 Mission San Francisco de los Tejas that was moved to San Antonio in 1731. Other historic Texas missions include the restored 1749 to 1830 Mission Nuestra Señora del Espíritu Santo de Zuñiga at Goliard State Park near Goliard, 1757 Mission Santa Cruz de San Sabá near Menard, and 1777 San Elizario Presidio Chapel (to serve the Spanish military garrison) near San Elizario.

Spanish presidios often were built near missions to protect and support them. Among the surviving forts and sites are the restored 1749 Presidio la Bahía, near Goliard, Texas; 1752 site of the presidio at Tubac Presidio State Historic Park, Tubac, Arizona; 1757 Presidio San Luis de las Amarillas, near Menard, Texas; and 1782 structures at the El Presidio de Santa Barbara State Historic Site, Santa Barbara, California.

The greatest concentration of Spanish colonial missions is in California, where 21 missions were built during the eighteenth and nineteenth centuries to establish Spain's claim to the region and to Christianize sometimes hostile Indians. Father Junípero Serra headed the effort and established nine of the early missions. The first mission was the 1769 Mission San Diego de Alcala, which later became a basilica, in San Diego, and the last was the 1823 Mission San Francisco Solano, now part of the Sonoma State Historic Park in Sonoma.

Most of the California missions have been partially or totally restored. They include such sites as the 1776 Mission San Francisco de Asis (known as Mission Dolores), the oldest intact building in San Francisco; 1777 Mission Santa Clara de Asis, the only mission to become part of a university (Santa Clara University), Santa Clara; 1786 Mission Santa Barbara, considered among the most beautiful of the missions, Santa Barbara; 1798 Mission San Luis Rey, the largest of the missions, Oceanside; and 1816 Mission San Antonio de Pala, the only mission of the 21 that still primarily serves Indians (on the Pala Indian Reservation), Pala.

The oldest Spanish religious site in America is the Ancient Spanish Monastery of St. Bernard de Clairvaux Cloisters, built in the Province of Segovia, Spain, in 1133 to 1141 and occupied by Cistencian monks until the 1830s. In 1925, newspaper publisher William Randolph Hearst purchased the cloisters and the outbuildings and planned to reassemble them in the United States. However, his financial problems almost immediately forced him to sell much of the monastery collection at auction and for the structure's stones to remain in a Brooklyn warehouse for 26 years. After Hearst's death in 1952, the monastery stones were sold and converted into a tourist attraction and then a church in New York City. In 1964, the monastery stones were obtained by Bishop Henry Louttit, moved to Florida, and then purchased for the parish of St. Bernard de Clairvaux in North Miami Beach. It now is called the Ancient Spanish Monastery of St. Bernard de Clairvaux Cloisters and functions like a museum with religious artifacts and examples of Spanish art and culture.

Other Spanish museums and historic sites range from El Pueblo de Los Angeles Historical Monument in Los Angeles, Queen Sofia Spanish Institute (formerly the Spanish Institute) in New York City, and Basque Museum and Cultural Center in Boise, Idaho, to museums and historic sites honoring Spanish explorers, artists, and government and religious leaders. The El Pueblo de Los Angeles Historical Monument commemorates the oldest section of Los Angeles, near where Spanish and Mexican settlers first established a farming community in 1781. It has 27 historic buildings and four museums. California also has numerous historic Spanish ranches, including the Rancho los Cerritos Historic Site and Rancho los Alamitos, located in Long Beach on the remains of a 167,000-acre land grant given to José Manuel Perez Nieto in the late seventeenth century. The Spanish Institute, founded in 1954, seeks to promote public understanding of Spanish culture and its influence in America, while the Basque Museum and Cultural Center, opened in 1985, interprets the history and culture of Basques from the western Pyrenees of Spain and their lives in this country.

The Cabrillo National Monument in San Diego honors Juan Rodriguez Cabrillo, the Spanish explorer who led the first European expedition to land on the West Coast in 1542. The Serra Museum, also in San Diego, commemorates the site where Father Junípero Serra and Captain Gaspar de Portola established the first mission and military outpost in California in 1769. Three sites honor Francisco Vásquez de Coronado, who explored the Southwest and searched in vain for the fabled Cities of Cibola in 1540 to 1541—the Coronado National Monument, Hereford, Arizona; Coronado State Memorial, near Bernalillo, New Mexico; and Coronado-Quivira Museum, Lyons, Kansas. Another early Spanish leader, Juan de Oñate, first governor of New Mexico and former governor of the San Juan Pueblo, is honored at the Oñate Monument and Visitor Center in Alcalde, New Mexico. Museums also are devoted to two contemporary Spanish figures—artist Salvador Dalí at the Salvador Dalí Museum in St. Petersburg, Florida, and cellist Pablo Casals at the Pablo Casals Museum in Old San Juan, Puerto Rico.

Hispanic Museums and Heritage Sites

Hispanic museums, galleries, and historic sites fall into two categories — those that are multicultural (including several or more Central and South American and Caribbean cultures) and those that are devoted to a single country (such as Mexican, Puerto Rican, and Cuban). Altogether they number about 56 museums, galleries, and historic sites, with 21 being broad-based Hispanic facilities, 18 Puerto Rican, 15 Mexican, and 2 Cuban. Spanish and Portuguese facilities, which account for an additional 61, are treated separately and are not included.

The first Hispanic heritage center in the nation was the Hispanic Society of America, a free museum and reference library founded in New York City in 1904 for the study of the arts and cultures of Spain, Portugal, and Latin America. It still has collections and exhibits of the Iberian Peninsula and Latin America from prehistoric times to the present. The El Museo del Barrio, which was started by Puerto Ricans in New York City in 1969, has evolved into a major institution of art and culture for all of the Caribbean and Latin America. Another center that emphasized Latino cultural arts was the Mission Cultural Center for Latino Arts, founded in San Francisco in 1977.

The 1990s produced the greatest growth of Hispanic facilities, including the Museo de las Americas, Denver, 1991; Museo de las Américas, San Juan, Puerto Rico, 1992; National Hispanic Cultural Center, Albuquerque, and El Museo Latino, Omaha, 1993; and Museum of Latin American Art, Long Beach, California, 1996.

Among the other Hispanic museums and galleries — most of which emphasize works of art by Hispanics — are the newly opened Museo Alameda, one of the largest Latino museums, San Antonio; Fonda del Sol Visual Arts Center, Washington, D.C.; Casa de Unidad Cultural Arts and Media Center, Detroit; Latino Heritage Museum, Brooklyn, New York; Latino Museum of History, Art, and Culture, Los Angeles; La Raza Galeria Posada, Sacramento; and La Casa de la Raza, Santa Barbara, California. The Millicent Rogers Museum of Northern New Mexico, founded in 1956 in Taos, New Mexico, is one of the rare ethnically related museums to feature both Hispanic and Native American cultural materials and art.

Most Puerto Rican museums, galleries, and historic sites are located in Puerto Rico. One of the earliest was the Luis Muñoz Rivera Library and Museum, a 1916 historic home site in Barranquitas honoring the liberal politician, journalist, orator, and writer. In 1940, the Museum of History, Anthropology, and Arts was founded at the University of Puerto Rico in San Juan and was the first to interpret Puerto Rico's historic, anthropological, and artistic legacy. It was followed in 1947 by the establishment of the San Juan National Historic Site in Old San Juan that preserves and interprets three 1500s–1800s Spanish forts, including the fortress known as El Morro that attracts 2 million visitors annually.

Other ethnically oriented museums in Puerto Rico include the Museo de Arte de Ponce, Ponce, founded in 1959; Museum of Contemporary Art of Puerto Rico, Santurce; Museum and Center for Humanistic Studies at Turabo University, Gurabo; Museo de Arte Religious Porta Coeli, San German; Museo Fuerte Conde de Mirasol de Vieques, Vieques; and Popular Arts Museum, San Juan. In addition to preserving the Luis Muñoz Rivera birthplace and mausoleum, Puerto Rico has museums honoring Pablo Casals, the Spanish-born cellist and humanist who lived in Puerto Rico, in Old San Juan and Dr. José Celso Barbosa, noted physician, humanitarian, and political leader, in Bayamon. The only Puerto Rican cultural center and museum in mainland United States (besides the Puerto Rican–founded El Museo del Barrio in New York City) is the Puerto Rican Cultural Center Juan Antonio Corretjer in Chicago, honoring the prominent poet, journalist, and political activist.

Other historic sites in Puerto Rico include the Caparra Museum and Historic Park, site of the first colonization of Puerto Rico, Guaynabo; Casa Blanca Museum, a museum of domestic life during the first three centuries of Spanish colonization located at the site of the ca. 1521 home built by explorer Juan Ponce de León, San Juan; and Hacienda Buena Vista, a restored 1833 mansion and coffee plantation, near Ponce.

Mexican museums and galleries are most numerous in California. In addition to the Mission Cultural Center for Latino Arts, founded in San Francisco in 1977 and which emphasizes Chicano art, the state is the site of the Plaza de la Raza Museum and Boathouse Gallery, Los Angeles, 1969; and The Mexican Museum, San Francisco, 1975. The National Museum of Mexican Art (formerly Mexican Fine Arts Center Museum), established in Chicago in 1982, is the nation's largest Latino arts museum.

Other Mexican museums and galleries include the Mexic-Arte Museum, Austin, Texas; Musee Chicano, Phoenix; Chicano Humanities and Arts Council Gallery, Denver; and Mexico-Cárdenas Museum near Waxhaw, North Carolina, which praises General Lazario Cárdenas, Mexican president in 1934–1940, for his commitment to helping the country's indigenous peoples.

Among the Mexican historic sites are the ca. 1780 Santuario de Nuestra Señora de Guadalupe, believed to be the oldest shrine in the nation honoring the Virgin of Guadalupe, patron saint of Mexico, Santa Fe, New Mexico; El Pueblo de Los Angeles Historical Monument, where Mexican and Spanish settlers established a farming community in 1781 that later became Los Angeles; The Alamo, where the Mexican army under General Antonio López de Santa Anna overwhelmed defenders at a former mission in San Antonio in 1836 in an attempt to crush the Texan Revolution; Petaluma Adobe State Historic Park, near Petaluma, California, which preserves the 1836–1846 adobe house of Mexican General Mariano Guadalupe Vallejo, who became one of the wealthiest and most influential men in early California; and Pancho Villa State Park, which marks the site and has historical exhibits in Columbus, New Mexico, where Mexican soldiers led by General Francisco "Pancho" Villa attacked an American border town and military camp in an armed incursion in 1916.

The Cuban Museum of Arts and Culture, founded by Cuban exiles in Coconut Grove, Florida, to preserve and interpret their cultural heritage, has moved to nearby Coral Gables and has changed its name to simply the Cuban Museum. It is developing a new facility that also will have programs pertaining to Cuban culture in freedom. In New York City, the Center for Cuban Studies, which seeks to further normalization of relations between Cuba and United States, contains an art gallery with works by Cuban artists.

Other European Facilities

The United States has at least 46 other groups of ethnically oriented museums, galleries, historic sites, and related facilities. Nearly three-quarters interpret the history, culture, art, and other aspects of European cultures. The others are devoted mainly to Asian cultures. Sixteen cultures have 10 to 19 museum-like facilities, and a multicultural category has 31. They range from small storefront operations to large museums operated by the Smithsonian Institution.

Some of the best known museums are among those in these cultural groups, such as the Asian Society Museum, New York City; Yale Center of British Art, New Haven, Connecticut; Bishop Museum, Honolulu; Asian Art Museum of San Francisco, Chong-Moon Lee Center of Asian Art and Culture, San Francisco; Ellis Island Immigration Museum, New York City; and Freer Gallery of Art and Arthur M. Sackler Gallery, Smithsonian Institution, Washington, D.C.

There are many other exceptional ethnic museums whose names and reputations are not as familiar, including the National Czech and Slovak Museum and Library, Cedar Rapids, South Dakota; Danish Immigrant Museum, Elk Horn, Iowa; Seattle Asian Art Museum, Seattle; Japanese American National Museum, Los Angeles; American Swedish Historical Museum, Philadelphia; Vesterheim Norwegian-American Museum, Decorah, Iowa; and Polish Museum of America, Chicago.

Thirty-three European cultures have 313 ethnic museums, galleries, and historic sites in the United States, including the 126 Spanish and German facilities mentioned earlier. The Scandinavian countries have 48 museums, galleries, and historic sites, with nearly one-third being Swedish. The New Sweden Historical Society, founded in 1925 in New Sweden, Maine, later opened the New Sweden Museum that documents the lives of early Swedish settlers in the area. The oldest and largest Swedish museum is the American Swedish Historical Museum, established in Philadelphia in 1926. It has 12 galleries dedicated to preserving and promoting the history and contributions of Swedes and Swedish Americans. Among the other Swedish museums are the American Swedish Institute, Minneapolis, 1929; Bishop Hill Heritage Museum, Bishop Hill, Illinois, 1962; Swedish American Museum Center, Chicago, 1976; and New Sweden Farmstead Museum, Bridgeton, New Jersey, 1983.

Among the Swedish historic sites are the Bishop Hill State Historic Site, which preserves 15 buildings from a Swedish communal community founded in Illinois by religious dissidents in 1846, and the 1698–99 Holy Trinity (Old Swedes) Church, the nation's oldest church in Wilmington, Delaware, that is still standing as originally built and used for religious services. The Sail Loft Museum in Wilmington is devoted to the history and craftsmanship of the *Kalmar Nyckel*, a replica of the Swedish tall ship that landed nearly in 1638.

One of the nation's oldest ethnic museums is the Vesterheim Norwegian-American Museum, founded as collections at Luther College in Decorah, Iowa, in 1877. It is one of the largest and most comprehensive museums in the nation dedicated to a single immigrant group. It consists of 16 historic buildings that almost occupy a square downtown block and two sites outside the city.

Among the other 10 Norwegian facilities are the Norwegian-American Historical Association Archives, Northfield, Minnesota, 1925; Little Norway, featuring 14 original log buildings of Norse architecture, Blue Mounds, Wisconsin, 1926; and Heritage Hjemkomst Interpretive Center, with replicas of a Viking ship and a Norwegian stave church and exhibits about local Norwegian heritage, Moorhead, Minnesota, 1986. The Runestone Museum, a local history museum with a Viking orientation in Alexandria, Minnesota, has the controversial Kensington Runestone with drawings about a 1362 Viking visit, fourteenth-century Viking implements, a 28-foot Viking statue, and a three-fourths replica of the Viking ship *Snorri*.

The Danes have two museums — the Danish Immigrant Museum, founded in Elk Horn, Iowa, in 1983, which depicts the life, culture, and diversity of Danish American immigrants and their descendants, and the Elverhoj Museum of History and Art in Solvang, California. Two Danish historic sites are located in St. Croix on the U.S. Virgin Islands — Christiansted National Historic Site, which protects historic structures and interprets the Danish way of life and economy on the islands between 1733 and 1917, and Whim Museum, housed in a 1751 mansion on one of the most prosperous sugar plantations on St. Croix Island in the seventeenth through nineteenth centuries.

The Finns also have two museums — the Finnish American Heritage Center at Finlandia University in Hancock, Michigan, consisting of a museum, art gallery, theater, and archive, and the Finnish-American Historical

Society of the West in Portland, Oregon, dedicated to preserving the cultural heritage of Finnish settlers in the American West. The influence of Icelandic settlers in North Dakota's early days is shown at the Pioneer Heritage Center at Icelandic State Park near Cavalier.

Some Scandinavian museums and cultural centers have collections and exhibits representing all the Nordic countries. The 11 facilities include the Scandinavia House: The Nordic Center in New York City; Nordic Heritage Museum, Seattle; Scandinavian Heritage Center, Minot, North Dakota; and Scandinavian Cultural Center and Scandinavian Immigrant Experience Collection at Pacific Lutheran University, Tacoma, Washington. The Scandia Museum, a local history museum in Scandia, Kansas, traces the history of the town and features artifacts of the Swedish, Norwegian, and Danish homesteaders who settled there in 1857.

The French have 16 museums, galleries, and historic sites (and 13 others are Acadian, dealing primarily with the history and culture of French settlers forced out of Canada and now known largely as Cajuns). The Huguenot Historical Society in New Paltz, New York, preserves and interprets the history and houses of Huguenot refugees who fled northern France because of political and religious persecution and founded New Paltz in 1677. Sainte Marie Among the Iroquois, a county park, is a re-creation of the 1657 French mission that once stood along Onondaga Lake in Liverpool, New York.

Other French-oriented facilities include Isle a la Cache Museum in Romeoville, Illinois, where French voyageurs traded for furs with Potawatomi Indians in the late eighteenth century; French Art Colony, a regional multi-arts center in Gallipolis, Ohio, that preserves French culture through the fine arts; Franco-American Collection at Lewiston-Auburn College of the University of Southern Maine in Lewiston, with historical materials pertaining to Franco-American history and culture in the state and region; and Napoleonic Society of America, which has exhibits about the life and times of Emperor Napoleon Bonaparte, Clearwater, Florida.

French historic sites include the Felix Vallé House State Historic Site, which preserves three early houses in a village settled by French Canadians in the late 1740s, Ste. Genevieve, Missouri; French Azilum Historic Site, where a group of French exiles settled in 1793, near Towanda, Pennsylvania; and French Legation Museum, a restored 1840–41 house with original furnishings built for a French official in the Republic of Texas, but who never lived there, Austin, Texas.

Most of the Acadian sites are in Louisiana, although several are in Maine. The Acadians originally were French settlers forced to leave Acadie (now Nova Scotia) in Canada by the British in 1755–85. The history and culture of the Acadians in Louisiana are presented at such places as the Museum of the Acadian Memorial and St. Martinville Cultural Heritage Center, St. Martinville; Vermilionville and Acadian Village, living-history museums and villages, Lafayette; Acadian Museum, Erath; Cajun Music Hall of Fame, Eunice; and three cultural centers at the Jean Lafitte National Historical Park and Preserve in Eunice, Lafayette, and Thibodaux. In Maine, the Acadian Village in Van Buren is a re-created early Acadian village, and the Tante Blanche Historic Museum in St. David contains Acadian and French-Canadian historical exhibits and artifacts.

Russian and Ukrainian museums and galleries are located at 21 sites, not including the Germans from Russia historical societies in the German section. The Russian museums include the Museum of Russian Culture, San Francisco; Museum of Russian Art, Minneapolis; and Museum of Russian Icons, Clinton, Massachusetts. The 1842 Russian Bishop's House in Sitka, Alaska, is one of the few surviving examples of Russian colonial architecture in North America. Among the 14 Ukrainian museums and galleries are The Ukrainian Museum, New York City; Ukrainian National

Museum of Chicago and Ukrainian Institute of Modern Art, Chicago; Ukrainian American Archives and Museum of Detroit; Ukrainian Museum-Archives, Cleveland; Ukrainian-American Museum and Archives, Warren, Michigan; and Ukrainian Diocesan Museum at St. Basil College Seminary in Stamford, Connecticut.

The Czechs and the Slovaks — which now have separate countries — have 19 facilities, many of which include both cultures. The National Czech and Slovak Museum and Library in Cedar Rapids, Iowa, is the nation's largest and most comprehensive museum interpreting Czech and Slovak history and culture. Small displays incorporating both cultures can be found at Sokol cultural, educational, and gymnastic sites in such cities as Cleveland, Omaha, and St. Paul. Among the Czech museums are the Wilber Czech Museum, Wilbur, Nebraska; Czech Memorial Museum, Jennings, Kansas; Burleson County Czech Heritage Museum, Caldwell, Texas; and House of Memories Museum at the Wilson Czech Opera House, Wilson, Kansas. The Czech Center New York is a cultural center with art exhibitions and performing arts operated by a Czech ministry. Slovak museums include the National Slovak Society of the USA Museum, McMurray, Pennsylvania; Slovak Cultural Center Library and Museum, Winter Park, Florida and Baine/Cincebeau Collection of Slovak Folk Dress and Folk Art, Rochester, New York.

The Polish and Dutch each have 12 museums, galleries, and related sites. The Polish Museum of America, founded in Chicago in 1935, and the Polish American Cultural Center and Museum, established in Philadelphia in 1981, have the most extensive collections and exhibits on Polish his-

tory, culture, and achievements. Holland, Michigan, has the most Dutch-oriented facilities, including the Holland Museum, Windmill Island Municipal Park and Little Netherlands Museum, Dutch Village theme park, and two historic houses. Another major Dutch center is the Pella Historical Village, an open-air museum with more than 20 historic buildings around a courtyard in Pella, Iowa, which resembles a village in the Netherlands.

The Windmill Island Municipal Park in Holland, Michigan, features the restored ca. 1761 DeZwaan windmill. The ethnically oriented park also has seventeenth-century-style Dutch architecture, a Dutch carousel and drawbridge, floral garden, and the Little Netherlands Museum in the windmill with an exhibit on old Holland. *Courtesy Windmill Island Municipal Park.*

Other European cultures with numerous cultural facilities are the Swiss, with eight (not including 13 Mennonite and Amish sites listed under German); British, nine (including Scottish and Welsh); Italian and Lithuanian, six each; and Hungarian, five. Three of the Swiss museums — Swiss Historical Village, Chalet of the Golden Fleece, and Swiss Center of North America (now under development)— are in New Glarus, Wisconsin. Among the British sites are the Yale Center for British Art at Yale University, New Haven, Connecticut; St. John's Episcopal Church and Museum at the oldest continuous English-speaking parish in the nation, Hampton, Virginia; Scottish Tartans Museum, a Scottish heritage center devoted primarily to tartans and Highland dress, Franklin, North Carolina; and Welsh-American Heritage Museum, Oak Hill, Ohio.

Italian museums include such places as the American Italian Museum, New Orleans; Garibaldi-Meucci Museum, Staten Island, New York; and National Italian American Sports Hall of Fame, Chicago, while among the Lithuanian facilities are the American Lithuanian Cultural Archives, Putnam, Connecticut; Lithuanian Museum of Art, Lemont, Illinois; and Lithuanian Museum and Balzekas Museum of Lithuanian Culture, Chicago. Hungarian history, culture, and art are displayed at the Museum of the American Hungarian Foundation in New Brunswick, New Jersey, and Hungarian Heritage Museum, in Cleveland, while folk art is featured at the Hungarian Folk-Art Museum in Port Orange, Florida. Other European nationalities with cultural exhibit facilities are Albanian, Austrian, Croatian, Greek, Irish, Latvian, Macedonian, Portuguese, Romanian, Serbian, and Slovenian.

Asian Museums and Heritage Sites

The 55 Asian museums, galleries, botanical gardens, and historic sites include 16 museums and galleries with exhibits displaying and interpreting the history, culture, or art of Asia. The first was the Freer Gallery of Art, founded in 1906 at the Smithsonian Institution in Washington, D.C. It is connected by an underground tunnel to the Arthur M. Sackler Gallery, established in 1982. They have world-renowned collections of art from China, Japan, Korea, India, South and Southeast Asia, and the Near East. A comprehensive collection of Asian art also is located at the Asian Art Museum of San Francisco, Chong-Moon Lee Center for Asian Art and Culture, started in 1966 by noted collector Avery Brundage. Among the other Asian cultural facilities are the Pacific Asia Museum, Pasadena, California; Seattle Asian Art Museum, Seattle; and Asia Society Museum and Asian American Arts Centre, New York City.

In addition to museums, galleries, and historic sites, Chinese and Japanese botanical gardens are located in a number of cities. One of the earliest Chinese cultural facilities in the nation was the China Institute Gallery, dedicated to traditional Chinese art, founded in New York City in 1926, while one of the newest and largest is Forbidden Gardens, an outdoor museum that replicates some of China's major historic sites in scaled versions in Katy, Texas. Among the other Chinese museums are the Museum of Chinese in the Americas, New York City; Chinese Historical Society of America Museum, San Francisco; Chinese American Museum, Los Angeles; and San Diego Chinese Historical Museum. A number of Chinese historical sites are preserved in California and Oregon, including the 1863 Oroville China Temple, Oroville, California; and 1887 Kam Wah Chung & Co. Museum, John Day, Oregon. The New York Chinese Scholar's Garden is one of the attractions at the Staten Island Botanical Garden on Staten Island, New York.

The most prominent of the six Japanese museums in the nation is the Japanese American National Museum, devoted to the history, culture, and experiences of Americans of Japanese ancestry, in Los Angeles. Among the others are the Japan Society Gallery, founded in

1907 in New York City; Japanese Cultural Center of Hawaii, Honolulu; and Noguchi Museum, Long Island City, New York. Two museums have Japanese gardens — Morikami Museum and Japanese Gardens in Delray Beach, Florida; and Hammond Museum and Japanese Stroll Garden in North Salem, New York. The oldest Japanese residential gardens in the Western Hemisphere are located at the Hakone Gardens in Saratoga, California. Japanese gardens also can be seen at such public botanical gardens as the Brooklyn Botanical Garden Japanese Hill-and-Pond Garden, opened in 1915, and Chicago Botanic Garden's Elizabeth Hubert Malott Japanese Garden, Glencoe, Illinois.

Cambodian, Korean, and Tibetan museums also interpret the history, culture, or art of those countries. The two Cambodian museums — Cambodian American Heritage Museum and Killing Fields Memorial in Chicago and Cambodian Cultural Museum and Killing Fields Memorial in White Center, Washington — emphasize the Khmer Rouge's killing fields atrocities in which 2 million perished in the 1970s. The Korean American Museum in Los Angeles interprets the history, culture, and accomplishments of Korean Americans, while the Korean Cultural Center, operated by a Korean government ministry in Los Angeles, is devoted to the cultural heritage of Korea. The Jacques Marchais Museum of Tibetan Art on Staten Island, New York has exhibits on Tibetan art and culture.

Other Ethnic Facilities

The 16 Hawaiian ethnically oriented museums, historic sites, and botanical gardens range from a fifteenth-century historic site that was a place of refuge for ancient lawbreakers and defeated warriors to the Bishop Museum, the islands' oldest, largest, and most extensive museum, founded in Honolulu in 1889 and named for a Hawaiian princess. The place of refuge is located at Pu'uhonua o Hōnaunau

National Historical Park in Honaunau. It is one of a number of historic sites predating Hawaii's statehood. Other historic sites include Pu'ukohola Heiau National Historic Site, the site of a 1790–91 temple associated with the founding of the Hawaiian kingdom, near Kawaihae; ca. 1838 Hulihe'e Palace, vacation home of Hawaiian royalty, Kailua-Kona; ca. 1847 Queen Emma Summer Palace, Honolulu; 1874 Ali'iolani Hale and King Kamehameha V — Judiciary History Center of Hawaii, historic home of Hawaii's Supreme Court, Honolulu; and 1882 'Iolani Palace, residence of Hawaii's last two monarchs, Honolulu.

In addition to the Bishop Museum, the premier cultural and natural history museum in the Pacific, Hawaii has such historical museums as the Bailey House Museum, Wailuku; Kauai Museum, Lihue; Lyman Museum and Mission House, Hilo; and Hawaii's Plantation Village, an outdoor museum and botanical garden, Waipahu. The plants of Hawaii and Polynesia are featured at the National Tropical Botanical Garden, based in Kalaheo, which has four gardens and three preserves in Hawaii and one in south Florida. The Honolulu Botanical Gardens include five different tropical gardens on the island of Oahu, and the Hawaii Tropical Botanical Garden features over 2,000 species of tropical plants on the big island of Hawaii.

Five other facilities in the Pacific region interpret the history, culture, or art of those island inhabitants sometimes known as the Oceanic Peoples. The most elaborate is the Polynesian Cultural Center, a cultural entertainment park in Laie, Hawaii, with re-created villages, exhibits, performances and hands-on activities pertaining to the South Pacific islands. Among the United States territory island museum sites are the Jean P. Haydon Museum, Fagatogo, American Samoa; Commonwealth of the Northern Mariana Islands Museum of History and Culture, Saipan; Guam Museum, Adelup, Guam; and Isla Center for the Arts at the University of Guam, Mangilao, Guam.

The restored Great Hall of Ellis Island is part of the Ellis Island Immigration Museum in New York City's lower harbor. Twelve million immigrants passed through the old processing center between its opening in 1892 and closing in 1954. The multicultural museum is devoted to the history of the immigration entry center and stories of the immigrants. *Courtesy Ellis Island Immigration Museum and National Park Service.*

Another group — called Arctic Peoples — is centered principally in Alaska. Among the 12 native historical and cultural facilities (beyond those in the Native American section) are the Alaska Native Heritage Center and Alaska Heritage Museum, Anchorage; Alutiiq Museum and Archaeological Repository and Baranov Museum, Kodiak; Inupiat Heritage Center, Barrow; Yupiit Piciryarait Cultural Center and Museum, Bethel; Sheldon Jackson Museum, Sitka; and Simon Paneak Memorial Museum, Anaktuvuk Pass. Two collegiate museums and study centers also are devoted to Arctic history and culture — Peary-Macmillan Arctic Museum and Arctic Studies Center at Bowdoin College in Brunswick, Maine, and Jensen Arctic Museum at Western Oregon University in Monmouth.

Among the other ethnic museums are the Arab American National Museum, which opened in 2005 in Dearborn, Michigan; Kurish Museum, Brooklyn, New York; Armenian Cultural Foundation Library and Museum, Arlington, Massachusetts; and Armenian Library and Museum of America, Watertown, Massachusetts. The Rosicrucian Order also operates the Rosicrucian Egyptian Museum, featuring ancient Egyptian history, culture, and art, in San Jose, California.

Some ethnically related museums are

multicultural, focusing on more than a single ethnic group. Included among the 31 such places are the Ellis Island Immigration Museum, with exhibits about the over 12 million immigrants processed at the Ellis Island entry point in 1892 to 1954, New York City; Old World Wisconsin, an outdoor museum containing 67 nineteenth- and early twentieth-century buildings of early immigrants who settled in the state, Eagle, Wisconsin; Mathers Museum of World Cultures, containing ethnological, historical, and archaeological collections and exhibits at Indiana University, Bloomington; Bowers Museum, featuring the traditional arts and cultures of many nations, Santa Ana, California; University of Texas Institute of Texan Cultures, offering cultural exhibits and programs of ethnic groups who have settled in the state, San Antonio; Museum of International Folk Art, which has the world's largest collection of folk art from 100 countries, Santa Fe, New Mexico; and UCLA Fowler Museum of Cultural History, displaying and interpreting the material culture, archaeology, and art of various continents, Los Angeles.

Some of the nation's leading archaeological, anthropological, and nature history museums also have extensive ethnic collections and exhibits. They include such museums as the American Museum of Natural History, with seven cultural halls featuring ethnic artifacts, New York City; Milwaukee Public Museum, which has a simulated village of 1875 to 1925 houses and shops of 33 European cultures and an Indian gallery, Milwaukee; and University of Pennsylvania Museum of Archaeology and Anthropology, containing 1.5 million archaeological and ethnological materials in its collections and 25 long-term exhibits on the cultural heritage of the ancient and more contemporary regions of the world, Philadelphia.

Ethnically oriented museums, galleries, historic sites, and related facilities have come a long way since their beginning in the 1800s. Although some founded by ethnic groups still are staffed only by volunteers or have relatively poor collections, exhibits, or attendances, most are operated more professionally, have thematic exhibits as well as collections of artifacts and memorabilia on display, and are better attended. They also play a greater role in preserving and interpreting the history, culture, and art of ethnic Americans. Some even have become major institutions in the museum world. At the same time, the number of museums with ethnic collections and exhibits and historic and prehistoric sites of ethnic significance operated by non-ethnic groups, such as private nonprofits, colleges and universities, and city, county, state, and federal governments, have increased dramatically in number, quality, and popularity.

These ethnically oriented museums and related facilities fill a need — to better understand the history, culture, and contributions of America's immigrants and their homelands and descendants. Some institutions may be small, have limited offerings and hours, and only a volunteer staff, but nearly all instill greater pride and knowledge of their histories and cultures among ethnic peoples and provide greater insight and appreciation among others. The United States may be a melting pot, but it still is a nation of people of many nationalities who treasure their origins and cultures.

Ethnic Museums
and Heritage Sites

ACADIAN (*also see* French)

Museums and Galleries

Acadian Cultural Center. The Acadian Cultural Center in Lafayette, Louisiana, is one of three facilities that interpret the region's Acadian culture in the Jean Lafitte National Historical Park and Preserve. The Acadian people, known today as Cajuns, originally were French settlers in Acadie (now Nova Scotia), Canada, who were forced to leave by the British in 1755 through 1785. The cultural center tells the story of those who came to the Mississippi Delta region. Exhibits interpret the history, language, music, and architecture of Acadians and artifacts reflect their past and present life.

Acadian Cultural Center, Jean Lafitte National Historical Park, 501 Fisher Rd., Lafayette, LA 70508. Phone: 337/232-0789. Fax: 337/232-5740. Web site: *www.nps.gov/iela/ielaweb.htm*. Hours: 8–5 daily; closed Christmas and Mardi Gras. Admission: free.

Acadian Museum. The Acadian Museum in Erath, Louisiana, seeks to preserve the history and culture of the Cajuns — those French Acadians who came to the Mississippi Delta after being driven from Canada by the British in the mid–nineteenth century. The museum, located in the historic Old Bank of Erath building, has three rooms with exhibits and artifacts pertaining to Acadian history, Cajun settlement in Vermilion Parish, and development of Erath. It also operates an annex at Lake Peigneur.

Acadian Museum, 203 S. Broadway, Erath, LA 70533. Phone: 337/937-5468. Fax: 337/235-4382. Web site: *www.acadianmuseum.com*. Hours: 1–4 Mon.–Fri.; closed Sat.–Sun. and major holidays. Admission: free.

Acadian Village (Lafayette). Acadian Village near Lafayette, Louisiana, is a living-history museum with a re-created bayou town depicting the 1800s lifestyle of Cajuns in the southern portion of the state. The museum has eight original and three re-constructed buildings from the nineteenth century around a pond, surrounded by 10 acres of gardens and woodlands. The Mississippi Valley Missionary Museum, housed in a log cabin resembling a frontier mission of the region, also is located on the grounds. It contains Native American artifacts and scenes illustrating missionary experiences among the tribes of the region drained by the Mississippi River and its tributaries.

Acadian Village, 200 Greenleaf Dr., Lafayette, LA 70506. Phones: 337/981-2389 and 800/962-9133. Fax: 337/988-4554. Hours: 10–5 daily; closed major holidays. Admission: adults, $7; seniors, $6; children 6–14, $4; children under 6, free.

Acadian Village (Van Buren). Maine also has an open-air Acadian Village in an area where French Acadians settled after being forced by the British to leave Nova Scotia in the nineteenth century. The re-created village in Van Buren has such original and replica buildings as a railroad station, general store, church, schoolhouse, blacksmith shop, and historic houses.

Acadian Village, U.S. Rte. 1, PO Box 165, Van Buren, ME 04785. Phone: 207/868-5042. Fax: 207/868-2691. Web site: *http://themainelink.com/acadianvillage*. Hours: June 15–Sept. 15 —12–5 daily; closed reminder of year. Admission: adults, $5; children 5–15, $3; children under 5, free.

Bayou Folk Museum. See Kate Chopin House and Bayou Folk Museum in Museums Honoring Individuals section.

Cajun Music Hall of Fame and Museum. More than 40 musicians and others who have made significant contributions to Cajun music are honored at the Cajun Music Hall of Fame and Museum in Eunice, Louisiana. In addition to photographs and biographical sketches of honorees, the museum displays vintage musical instruments, old records, and memorabilia.

Cajun Music Hall of Fame and Museum, 248 S. C. C. Duson Dr., Eunice, LA 70535. Phone: 337/457-6534. Web site: *www.isue.edu/acadgate/caiunmus. htm.* Hours: Apr.–Oct.— 9–5 Tues.–Sat.; remainder of year— 8:30–4:30 Tues.–Sat.; closed Sun.–Mon. and major holidays. Admission: free.

Museum of the Acadian Memorial. See Acadian Memorial in Historic Sites section.

Prairie Acadian Cultural Center. The Prairie Acadian Cultural Center, one of three Acadian cultural centers in the Jean Lafitte National Historical Park and Preserve, tells the story of French-Canadians who settled in the prairie region of southwest Louisiana after being driven from Nova Scotia by the British in the eighteenth century. The history, language, music, architecture, and everyday life of Acadians, now known as Cajuns, are presented at the cultural center in Eunice.

Prairie Acadian Cultural Center, Jean Lafitte National Park and Preserve, 250 W. Park Ave., Eunice, LA 70535. Phone: 337/457-7700. Fax: 337/457-0061. Web site: *www.nps.gov/jela/prairie-acadian-cul tural-center-eunice.htm.* Hours: 8–5 Tues.–Fri.; 8–6 Sat.; closed Sun.–Mon. Admission: free.

St. Martinville Cultural Heritage Center. Two museums with a common theme— the story of people uprooted from their homelands who started new lives in Louisiana — are housed in the St. Martinville Cultural Heritage Center in St. Martinville. See separate listings for the Museum of the Acadian Memorial and the African American Museum. Also located near the center is the famous Evangeline Oak tree where Acadian Evangeline waited in vain for Gabriel in Longfellow's epic poem *Evangeline.*

St. Martinville Cultural Heritage Center, 123 S. New Market St., St. Martinville, LA 70682. Phone: 337/394-2250. Web site: *www.cityofsaintmartinville. com/english/attractions/attractioms/htm.* Hours: 10–4 daily. Admission: adults, $2; children under 12, $1.

Vermilionville. Vermilionville in Lafayette, Louisiana, is a 23-acre living-history museum and folklife village that re-creates the 1765 through 1890 Acadiana period of southern Louisiana. The museum features five original eighteenth- and nineteenth-century houses and an outhouse and six replicated buildings of the period. It has three sections — Festive Area with a visitor center modeled after a Creole plantation house, a cooking school building that re-creates slave quarters, and a per-

formance center fashioned after an old cotton gin; Folklife Area, where spinning, quilting, and textile crafts are demonstrated in the Beau Basin House; and a third section containing largely historic houses.

Vermilionville, 300 Fisher Rd., Lafayette, LA 70508. Phones: 337/233-4077 and 866/992-2968. Fax: 337/223-1694. E-mail: *vville@bellsouth.net.* Web site: *www.vermilionville.org.* Hours: 10–4 Tues.–Sun.; closed Mon. and major holidays. Admission: adults, $8; seniors, $6.50; students 6–18, $5; children under 6, free.

Wetlands Acadian Cultural Center. The history of Acadians who settled along the bayous and in the swamps and wetlands of southeastern Louisiana is presented at the Wetlands Acadian Cultural Center in the Jean Lafitte National Historical Park and Preserve in Thibodaux, Louisiana. The cultural center relates the origins, migration, settlement, and contemporary culture of Cajuns in the area.

Wetlands Acadian Cultural Center, Jean Lafitte National Historical Park and Preserve, 314 St. Mary St., Thibodaux, LA 70301. Phone: 985/448-1375. Fax: 985/448-1425. Web site: *www.nps.gov/jela/wetlands-acadian-cultural-center.htm.* Hours: 9–8 Mon.; 9–6 Tues.–Thurs.; 9–5 Fri.–Sun.; closed Christmas and Mardi Gras. Admission: free.

Museums Honoring Individuals

Kate Chopin House and Bayou Folk Museum. The Kate Chopin and Bayou Folk Museum is located in the 1809 two-story Louisiana-style house in Cloutierville where the Creole writer and her husband and six children lived from 1880 to 1884. It became the Bayou Folk Museum in 1965. In her writings, Chopin was know for her intriguing plots, vivid descriptions of Louisiana scenes, and realistic portrayals of Cajun and Creole characters and society. The house still contains items that belonged to Chopin, but the emphasis is on the educational, religious, social, and economic life of the bayou country. A doctor's office, blacksmith shop, and agricultural equipment can be seen behind the house.

Kate Chopin House and Bayou Folk Museum, 243 State Hwy. 495, Cloutierville, LA (mailing address: PO Box 2248, Natchitoches, LA 71457). Phone: 337/379-2233. Fax: 337/378-0055. Hours: 10–5 Mon.–Sat.; 1–5 Sun.; closed major holidays. Admission: adults, $5; students over 12, $3; children 6–12, $2; children under 6, free.

Tante Blanche Historic Museum. The Tante Blanche Historic Museum in St. David, Maine, is named for Marguerite-Blanche Thibodeau, heroine of the 1797 Black Famine in St. John Valley who was known as Tante (Aunt) Blanche. She helped the sick, poor, and starving during a snowbound winter following a flood and drought that destroyed all the crops. The Madawaska Centennial Log Cabin Museum, containing Acadian and French-Canadian historical exhibits and artifacts, was renamed in her honor by the Madawaska Historical Society.

Tante Blanche Historic Museum, Madawaska Historical Society, U.S. Rte. 1, St. David, ME (mailing address: PO Box 99, Madawaska, ME 04756). Phone: 207/728-4272. Hours: June–Aug.—10:30–3:30 Mon.–Fri.; closed remainder of year. Admission: free.

Historic Sites

Acadian Memorial. The Acadian Memorial in St. Martinville, Louisiana, honors the 3,000 men, women, and children who found refuge in Louisiana after the British expelled them from Acadie (now Nova Scotia) in Canada in the mid–eighteenth century. The memorial contains the names of all the Acadian immigrants on a Wall of Names, an eternal flame, a wall-size mural, and a multimedia research center. The Museum of the Acadian Memorial is located in the adjacent St. Martinville Cultural Heritage Center. It traces the Acadian history and features the Acadian Odyssey Quilt and images from the Claude Picard Deportation Series at the Grand-Pre National Historic Site in Nova Scotia.

Acadian Memorial, 121 S. New Market St., PO Box 379, St. Martinville, LA 70582-4523. Phone: 337/394-2258. Fax: 337/394-2280. E-mail: *info@acadiamemorial.org*. Web site: *www.acadiamemorial.org*. Hours: 10–4 daily; closed major holidays. Admission: adults, $2; children under 12, $1.

Museum of the Acadian Memorial, St. Martinville Cultural Center, 123 S. New Market St., St. Martinville, LA 70582-4523. Phone: 337/394-2258. Fax: 337/394-2280. E-mail: *info@acadiamemorial.org*. Web Site: *www.acadiamemorial.org*. Hours: 10–4 daily. Admission: adults, $2; children under 12, free

Longfellow-Evangeline State Historic Site. The Longfellow-Evangeline State Historic Site in St. Martinville, Louisiana, tells the story of the French-speaking people of the Bayou Teche area. It was the meeting place of exiled French aristocrats fleeing the French Revolution and of Acadians of Nova Scotia seeking refuge after the British expulsion from Canada. The 157-acre park received its name from the legend that the area was the site of Henry Wadsworth Longfellow's ill-fated Acadian lovers Evangeline and Gabriel in his epic poem *Evangeline*. Among the highlights at Louisiana's first state park are Masion Olivier, a ca. 1815 raised Creole cottage built by plantation owner Charles

DuCozel Olivie and where Louis Arceneaux (who is said to have served as the prototype for Gabriel in Longfellow's poem) is believed to have lived later; a cabin; and farmstead illustrating Acadian lifestyle in the nineteenth century; and a visitor center with exhibits on the history, culture, and everyday life of the Acadian and native-born Creole people of the area.

Longfellow-Evangeline State Historic Site, 1200 N. Main St., St. Martinville, LA 70582. Phones: 337/394-3754 and 888/677-2900. Fax: 337/394-3553. E-mail: *longfellow@crt.state.la.us*. Web site: *www.lastateparks.com/longfell/longfell.htm*. Hours: 9–5 daily; closed New Year's Day, Thanksgiving, and Christmas. Admission: adults, $2; seniors and children under 13, free.

AFRICAN AMERICAN

Museums and Galleries

Acacia Collection Gallery. The Acacia Collection Gallery in Savannah, Georgia, is an Internet gallery that displays artifacts, crafts, and rarities in material culture relating to African American history in North America. Each artifact was made and used by African Americans. The gallery features the Judith Wragg Chase and Louise Alston Graves Charleston Old Slave Mart Collection.

Acacia Collection Gallery, Savannah, GA. E-mail: *info@acaciacollection.com*. Web site: *www.acaciacollectionffl.com/gallery/gallery.html*.

African American Collection of Maine. The African American Collection of Maine is part of the Jean Byers Sampson Center for Diversity in Maine at the University of Southern Maine in Portland. It contains documents, books, serials, artifacts, records, and photographs pertaining to African Americans primarily in Maine.

African American Collection of Maine, Jean Byers Sampson Center for Diversity in Maine, Glickman Family Library, University of Southern Maine, 314 Forest Ave., Portland, ME 04104-9301. Phone: 207/780-4269. E-mail: *bocks@usm.maine.edu*. Hours: 1–5 Mon., Wed., and Fri.; closed remainder of week and major holidays. Admission: free.

African-American Cultural Center. The African-American Cultural Center in Decatur, Illinois, seeks to promote the study and celebration of African-American culture. It has a beginning collection of artifacts, artwork, photographs, books, and research materials relating to the African American experience. The center is a project of the African-American Cultural and Genealogical Society Museum of Illinois.

African-American Cultural Center, African-American Cultural and Genealogical Society Museum of Illinois, 314 N. Main St., Decatur, IL 62523. Phone: 217/429-7458. Web site: *www.african-americancultural.org*. Hours: 12–3 Mon.–Tues. and Fri.–Sat.; closed Wed.–Thurs., Sun., and major holidays. Admission: free.

African American Firefighter Museum. The African American Firefighter Museum in Los Angeles, California, is dedicated to collecting, conserving, and sharing the heritage of African American firefighters. It is housed in the restored Fire Station 30, one of two segregated stations in Los Angeles between 1924 and 1955. The facility still has the original apparatus floor titles, poles, and kitchen out-building dating back to 1913 when the station opened.

African American Firefighters Museum, 1401 S. Central Ave., Los Angeles, CA 90021. Phone: 213/744-1730. Fax: 213/744-1731. Web site: *www.aaffmuseuim.org*. Hours: 10–2 Tues. and Thurs.; 10–4 Sun.; closed remainder of week. Admission: free.

African American Hall of Fame Museum. In addition to honoring outstanding black individuals, the African American Hall of Fame Museum in Peoria, Illinois, has collections and exhibits on African-American life and culture.

African American Hall of Fame Museum, 309 S. DuSable St., Peoria, IL 61605. Phone: 309/673-2206. Hours: 10–2 Mon.–Fri.; closed Sat.–Sun. and major holidays. Admission: free.

African-American Heritage Center. The African-American Heritage Center in Pensacola, Florida, features exhibits and performances relating to the history and culture of African Americans.

American Heritage Center, 200 E. Church St., Pensacola, FL 32502. Phone: 850/469-1299. Web site: *www.africanamericanheritagesociety.org*. Hours: by appointment. Admission: free.

African American Historical Museum and Cultural Center. Exhibits on the history of African Americans and Africans in the United States, with the emphasis on Iowa, are presented at the African American Historical Museum and Cultural Center in Cedar Rapids, Iowa.

African American Historical Museum and Cultural Center, 55 12th Ave., S.E., PO Box 1626, Cedar Rapids, IA 52406. Phone: 319/862-2101. Fax: 319/862-2105. E-mail: *info@blackiowa.org*. Web site: *www.blackiowa.org*. Hours: 10–4 Mon.–Sat.; closed Sun. and major holidays. Admission: adults, $4; children, $2.50.

African American Museum (Cleveland). The African American Museum in Cleveland, Ohio, was founded in 1953 to preserve and disseminate information on the contributions of individuals of African descent. It now also features exhibits on the history, culture, and art of the African American experience.

African American Museum, 1765 Crawford Rd., Cleveland, OH 44106. Phone: 216/791-1700. Fax: 216/791-1774. E-mail: *ourstory@aamcleveland.org*. Web site: *www.aamcleveland.org*. Hours: 10–3 Tues.–Fri.; 11–3 Sat.; closed Sun.–Mon. and major holidays. Admission: adults, $4; seniors, $3.50; children under 18, $3.

African American Museum (Dallas). The African American Museum in Dallas, Texas, began as part of the Bishop College Special Collections in 1974 and now operates independently in Fair Park. It is devoted to African American artistic, cultural, and historical materials. The museum has four galleries, one of the largest black folk art collections in the nation, and uses a variety of visual art forms and historical documents to portray the African American experience in Dallas, the Southwest, and throughout the United States.

African American Museum, 3536 Grand Ave, Fair Park, PO Box 150157, Dallas, TX 75315-0157. Phone: 214/565-9026. Fax: 214/421-8204. Web site: *www.aamdallas.org/illformatioll.htm*. Hours: 12–5 Tues.–Fri.; 10–5 Sat.; 1–5 Sun.; closed Mon., New Year's Day, Independence Day, Thanksgiving, and Christmas. Admission: free.

African American Museum (Hempstead). The heritage of African Americans and their contributions to the region and nation are presented in exhibits and programs at the African American Museum on Long Island in Hempstead, New York.

African American Museum, 110 N. Franklin St., Hempstead, NY 11550. Phone: 516/572-0730. Web site: *www.aamooflollgislalld.org*. Hours: 10–5 Thurs.–Sat.; 1–5 Sun.; closed Mon.–Wed. and major holidays. Admission: donation.

African American Museum (St. Martinville). The African American Museum in the St. Martinville Cultural Heritage Center in St. Martinville, Louisiana, tells of the arrival, struggles, adaptations, and contributions of African Americans in Louisiana, as well as the rise and fall of slavery. It contains exhibits, artifacts, and a 26-foot mural depicting the trades and accomplishments of the area's free people of color.

African American Museum, St. Martinville Cultural Heritage Center, 125 S. New Market St., PO Box 646, St. Martinville, LA 70582. Phone: 337/394-2250. Fax: 337/394-2265. E-mail: *stmchc@bellsouth.net*. Web site: *www.africanamericanmuseumla.org*. Hours: 10–4 daily. Admission: heritage center —

adults, $2; children under 12, $1; museum — donation.

African American Museum and Library at Oakland. The African American Museum and Library at Oakland seeks to discover, preserve, and share the historical and cultural experiences of African Americans in California. It also hosts original and traveling exhibitions that highlight the history and culture of African Americans. The museum, a public-private partnership that also has an extensive library and archives, is located at the former Charles A. Greene Library, a historic branch of the Oakland Public Library.

African American Museum and Library at Oakland, 659 14th St., Oakland, CA 94612. Phone: 510/637-9299. Fax: 510/637-0204. E-mail: *rmoss@oaklandlibrary.org*. Web site: *www.oaklandlibrary.org*. Hours: 12–5:30 Tues.–Sat.; closed Sun.–Mon. and major holidays. Admission: free.

African American Museum in Philadelphia. The African American Museum in Philadelphia, founded in 1976 as the Afro-American Historical and Cultural Museum as part of the nation's bicentennial celebration, was the first institution funded and built by a major municipality to preserve, interpret, and exhibit the heritage of African Americans. The museum has four galleries and an auditorium presenting exhibits and programs anchored by one of the museum's three dominant themes — African Diaspora, Philadelphia story, and contemporary narrative.

African American Museum in Philadelphia, 701 Arch St., Philadelphia, PA 19106. Phone: 215/574-0380. Fax: 215/574-3110. E-mail: *hharrison@aarnpnuseum.org*. Web site: *www.aamprnuseum.org*. Hours: 10–5 Tues.–.Sat.; 12–5 Sun.; closed Mon., New Year's Day, Easter, Thanksgiving, and Christmas. Admission: adults, $8; seniors, students, children, and handicapped, $6.

African American Museum of the Arts. The African American Museum of the Arts in DeLand, Florida, is devoted to the visual, literary, and performing arts and culture of African and Caribbean Americans. It has collections of paintings, sculptures, masks, and photographs.

African American Museum of the Arts, 325 S. Clara Ave., PO Box 1319, DeLand, FL 32721. Phone: 386/736-4004. Fax: 386/736-4088. E-mail: *info@africanmuseumdeland.org*. Web site: *www.africanmuseumdeland.org*. Hours: 10–4 Wed.–Sat.; closed Sun.–Tues. and major holidays. Admission: free.

African Art Museum of Maryland. The African Art Museum of Maryland, housed in the historic Oakland Mansion in Columbia, is devoted to traditional African art, including sculpture, textiles,

masks, jewelry, musical instruments, and household items. It also organizes guided tours to Africa with an opportunity to use traditional masks and drums.

African Art Museum of Maryland, 5430 Vantage Point Rd., Columbia, MD 21044-7105. Phone: 410/730-7105. Fax: 410/730-3407. E-mail: *africanartmuseum@erols.com*. Web site: *www.africanartmuseum.org*. Hours: 10–4 Tues.–Fri.; 12–4 Sun.; closed Mon., Sat., and major holidays. Admission: adults, $2; seniors and children, $1.

African Art Museum of the SMA Fathers. The African Art Museum of the SMA Fathers in Tenafly, New Jersey, is one of five museums around the world founded and maintained by the Society of African Missions (SMA), an international Roman Catholic missionary organization that serves the people of Africa. It is devoted solely to the arts of Africa, containing sub–Saharan sculpture, painting, costumes, textiles, decorative arts, religion, and folklore.

African Art Museum of the SMA Fathers, Society of African Missions, 23 Bliss Ave., Tenafly, NJ 07670. Phone: 201/894-8811. Fax: 201/541-1280. E-mail: *smausa-e@smafathers.org*. Web site: *www.smafathers.org/museum*. Hours: 9–5 daily; closed national and religious holidays. Admission: free.

African Cultural Center. The African Cultural Center in Washington, D.C., seeks to promote African history and culture and informational and cultural exchange among peoples of African descent through exhibits, tours, performances, lectures, discussions, classes, workshops, and radio and television programs. It has a museum, art gallery, library, and archives.

African Cultural Center, 731 Rock Creek Church Rd., N.W., Washington, DC 20010. Phone: 202/882-7465. Hours: varies. Admission: free.

Afro-American Cultural Center. Visual arts exhibits, musical and theatrical programs, and various community events are presented at the Afro-American Cultural Center in Charlotte, North Carolina. The center is located in a historic former black church, the Little Rock African Methodist Episcopal Zion Church.

Afro-American Cultural Center, 401 N. Myers St., Charlotte, NC 28202. Phone: 704/374-1565. Fax: 704/374-9273. Web site: *www.aacc-charlotte.org*. Hours: 10–6 Tues.–Sat.; 1–5 Sun.; closed Mon. and major holidays. Admission: Tues.–Sat., $5; Sun., free.

Afro-American Cultural Foundation Museum. The Afro-American Cultural Foundation in Mount Vernon, New York, seeks to preserve African American history and culture, study the problems of racism, and recognize the contributions of African

Americans. The foundation operates a museum and sponsors traveling exhibitions, lectures, seminars, research, and a speaker's bureau. The museum was founded in honor of noted black businesswoman Madam C. J. Walker.

Afro-American Foundation Museum, 19 Fiske Pl., Suite 204–206, Mt. Vernon, NY 10550. Phone: 914/665-0784. Hours: varies. Admission: free.

Afro American Historical Association of Fauquier County. The Afro American Historical Association of Fauquier County in The Plains, Virginia, is a virtual museum that provides three historical museum programs and an archive on the history and culture of African Americans over the Internet.

Afro American Historical Association of Fauquier County, 4243 Loudoun Ave., PO Box 340, The Plains, VA 20198-0340. Phone: 540/253-7488. Fax: 540/253-5126. E-mail: *aaha@infionline.net*. Web site: *www.afro-americanfva.org*. Hours: 10–3 Mon.–Sat.; Sun. and evenings by appointment. Cost: free.

Afro-American Historical Society Museum. The Afro-American Historical Society Museum in Jersey City, New Jersey, was founded in 1977 to develop a greater appreciation for the historic and cultural heritage of African Americans. It obtained a permanent location on the second floor of the Greenville Public Library in 1984 and now presents permanent and changing exhibits toward that goal.

Afro-American Historical Society Museum, 1841 Kennedy Blvd., Jersey City, NJ 07305. Phone: 201/547-5262. Fax: 201/547-5392. Web site: *www.citvofjerseycity.org/docs/afroam.shtml*. Hours: mid–June–Aug.—12–5 Mon.–Fri.; closed Sat.–Sun.; remainder of year—10–5 Mon.–Sat.; closed Sun. and major holidays. Admission: free.

Alabama State Black Archives, Research Center, and Museum. The primary purpose of the Alabama State Black Archives, Research Center, and Museum on the Alabama A&M University campus in Normal is to create a repository of source materials on African American history and culture. In doing so, the state-funded facility acquires and preserves such materials, makes the materials available to scholars and others for educational and cultural purposes, and exhibits the materials to enhance public awareness of African American history and culture. It also organizes traveling exhibitions and makes the materials available on loan.

Alabama State Black Archives, Research Center, and Museum, Alabama A&M University, James H. Wilson Bldg., PO Box 595, Normal, AL 35762. Phone: 256/851-5846. Fax: 256/851-5338. Web site: *www.aamu.ed/pr/stateblackarchives/sba.htm*. Hours: 9–4:30 Mon.–Fri. when university in session; varies

at other times; closed Sat.–Sun. and major holidays. Admission: free.

Albany Civil Rights Movement Museum at Old Mt. Zion Church. The Albany Civil Rights Movement Museum at Old Mt. Zion Church in Albany, Georgia, commemorates the 1960s Civil Rights Movement in the city and southwest Georgia with exhibits and programs on the struggle. It contains memorabilia, photographs, and archives of the movement and presents changing exhibitions. The museum is located at the former Mt. Zion Church in the historic Freedom District near downtown that includes the Thronateeska Heritage Center.

Albany Civil Rights Movement Museum at Old Mt. Zion Church, 326 Whitney Ave., PO Box 6036, Albany, GA 31701. Phone: 229/432-1698. Fax: 229/432-2150. E-mail: *mtzion@surfsouth.com*. Web site: *www. albany@civilrights.org*. Hours: 10–4 Wed.–Sat.; 2–5 Sun.; closed Mon.–Tues. and major holidays. Admission: adults, $4; seniors and children, $3.

Alexandria Black History Museum. The municipally operated Alexandria Black History Museum, located in the nine-acre Alexandria African American Heritage Park in Alexandria, Virginia, seeks to enrich the lives of the city's residents and visitors, foster tolerance and understanding among all cultures, and stimulate appreciation of the diversity of the African American experience. It exhibits local and regional history. The museum also incorporates the Robert H. Robinson Library, initially constructed in 1940 following a sit-in at the segregated Alexandria Library.

Alexandria Black History Museum, 902 Wythe St., Alexandria, VA 22314. Phone: 703/838-4358. Fax: 703-706-3999. E-mail: *black.history@ci.alexandria.va.ns*. Web site: *www.alexblackhistorv.org*. Hours: 10–4 Tues.–Sat.; closed Sun.–Mon. and major holidays. Admission: free.

American Jazz Museum. The American Jazz Museum in Kansas City, Missouri, celebrates the artistic, historic, and cultural contributions of jazz. The museum, which shares the complex with the Negro Leagues Baseball Museum in a historic district, features interactive exhibits, music, and educational programs about such jazz legends as Louis Armstrong, Duke Ellington, Ella Fitzgerald, Count Basie, Charlie Parker, and Big Joe Turner. It also has a working jazz club, the Blue Room, and the Gem Theater, a 500-seat performing arts center.

American Jazz Museum, 1616 E. 18th St., Kansas City, MO 64108-1610. Phone: 815/474-8463. Fax: 816/474-0074. Email: *jimoore@kcjazz.org*. Web site: *www.americanjazzmuseum.com*. Hours: 9–6 Tues.–Sat.; 12–6 Sun.; closed Mon. Admission: adults, $6; children under 12, $2.50.

America's Black Holocaust Museum. The America's Black Holocaust Museum in Milwaukee, Wisconsin, was founded in 1988 to inform the public of the injustices suffered by African Americans and to enable visitors to rethink their assumptions about race and racism. Among the exhibits are the forced migration of blacks from Africa from an African American perspective; the lives of eighteenth- and nineteenth-century African Americans and how their experiences shaped American history, culture, and politics; and historical firsts for African Americans in Wisconsin.

America's Black Holocaust Museum, 2233 N. 4th St., Milwaukee, WI 53212. Phone: 414/264-2500. Fax: 414/2640112. E-mail: *abhmwi@aol.com.* Web site: *www.blackholocaustmuseum.org.* Hours: 9–5 Tues.–Sat.; closed Sun.–Mon. (except for groups of 25 or more by appointment on Sun.), New Year's Day, Independence Day, Thanksgiving, and Christmas. Admission: adults, $5; seniors, $4; students 5–17, $3; children under 5, free.

Amistad Research Center Art Gallery. The Amistad Research Center at Tulane University in New Orleans, Louisiana, is the nation's largest independent archives specializing in the history of African Americans and other ethnic groups. It has an extensive collection of manuscripts, photographs, oral histories, books, periodicals, and works of art on such African American areas as slavery, race relations, civil rights movement, and community development.

The center displays examples of African and African American art from its collection in an art gallery. The collection includes such items as African textiles, raffia pile cloth, beaded objects, masks, carved figures, musical instruments, sacred containers, and basketry, and African American works of late nineteenth- and early twentieth-century art and contemporary art.

Amistad Research Center Art Gallery, Tulane University, Tilton Memorial Hall, 16823 St. Charles Ave., New Orleans, LA 70118. Phone: 504/865-5535. Fax: 504/865-5580. Web site: *www.amistadresearchcenter. org.* Hours: 9–4 Mon.–Fri.; closed Sat.–Sun. and major holidays. Admission: free.

Anacostia Museum and Center for African American History and Culture. The Anacostia Museum and Center for African American History and Culture is one of the Smithsonian Institution museums in Washington, D.C. It began as a neighborhood museum in 1967 and later expanded its mission to include African American materials from throughout the nation.

The museum explores American history, society, and creative expression from an African American perspective. In addition to such exhibits and programs at the museum, it operates an On-line Academy that is a virtual learning environment with links to resources, information on artifacts in the collections, and video presentations by leading scholars on topics relating to the discovery, interpretation, and preservation of African American history and material culture.

Anacostia Museum and Center for African American History and Culture, 1901 Fort Pl., Washington, DC 20020-0004. Phone: 202/287-3306. Fax: 202/287-3183. Web site: *anacostia.si.edu.* Hours: 10–5 daily; closed Christmas. Admission: free.

Apex Museum. The Apex Museum in Atlanta, Georgia, tells about the early African American pioneers in Atlanta, the slavery period, and black achievers in the arts, sciences, business, athletics, and other fields. It has a replica of the Yates and Milton Drug Store, one of Atlanta's first black businesses, and offers video presentations in the Trolley Theater about African American experiences.

Apex Museum, 135 Auburn Ave., Atlanta, GA 30303. Phone: 404/523-2739. Fax: 404/523-3248. E-mail: *apexmuseum@aol.com.* Web site: *www.apex-museum.org.* Hours: 10–5 Tues.–Sat.; 1–5 Sun. (only in February, June, July, and August); closed Mon. and major holidays. Admission: adults, $4; seniors and students, $3; children under 4, free.

August Wilson Center for African American Culture. See Museums Honoring Individuals section.

Avery Research Center for African American History and Culture. The Avery Research Center for African American History and Culture at the College of Charleston in Charleston, South Carolina, collects, preserves, and documents the history and culture of African Americans in South Carolina. It has several galleries where it presents exhibits from its collections, art exhibitions, and temporary displays. Regional art features sweetgrass baskets, handwoven fish nets, and materials showing the relationship between West Africa and the Sea Islands of Georgia, Florida, and the Carolinas. The center also circulates traveling exhibitions based on its collections to schools and community groups.

Avery Research Center for African American History and Culture, College of Charleston, 125 Bull St., Charleston, SC 29424 (mailing address: 66 George St., Charleston, SC 29424). Phone: 843/953-7609. Fax: 843/953-7607. Web site: *www.cofc.edu/~avery. rsc.* Hours: 12–5 Mon.–Fri.; closed Sat.–Sun. and college holidays. Admission: free.

Banneker-Douglass Museum. See Museums Honoring Individuals section.

Beck Cultural Exchange Center. The Beck Cultural Exchange Center in Knoxville, Tennessee, contains information, photographs, and documents on the history and culture of African Americans in the Knoxville area. It displays photographs from its collections on a rotating basis, features outstanding local African Americans in a stairway exhibit, and devotes a room to the life of Judge William H. Hastie, the first African American federal judge and first black governor of the Virgin Islands.

Beck Cultural Exchange Center, 1927 Dandridge Ave., Knoxville, TN 37915-1997. Phone: 865/524-8461. Fax: 865/524-8462. E-mail:*beckcenter@knoxlib.org*. Web site: *www.discoveret.org/beckcec/contact.htm*. Hours: 10–6 Tues.–Sat.; closed Sun.–Mon. and major holidays. Admission: free

Birmingham Civil Rights Institute. The Birmingham Civil Rights Institute in Birmingham, Alabama, encourages communication and reconciliation of human rights issues worldwide and serves as a depository for civil rights archives and documents. As part of the mission, it has an exhibit area that traces segregation and the Civil Rights Movement. Exhibits describe segregation from 1920 to 1954, violence and intimidation that reinforced segregation, the Civil Rights Movement from 1955 to 1963, the walk to freedom in the 1960s, local and national achievements on the road to racial justice, and human rights struggles internationally.

Birmingham Civil Rights Institute, 520 16th St., N., Birmingham, AL 35203. Phones: 205/328-9696 and 866/328-9696. Fax: 205/323-5219. E-mail: *bcri@bcri.org*. Web site: *www.bcri.org*. Hours: 10–5 Tues.–Sat.; 1–5 Sun.; closed Mon. and major holidays. Admission: adults, $9; seniors, $5; college students, $4; children under 18, free; free on Sun.

Black American West Museum and Heritage Center. The story of African American pioneers who helped shape the American West is told at the Black American West Museum and Heritage Center in Denver, Colorado. The museum shows how blacks played a role in settling and developing the West. Exhibits contain artifacts, photographs, and other historical materials on African Americans in fur trading, homesteading, mining, ranching, military service, and other fields in the region. The museum is located in the former home and office of Dr. Justina L. Ford, Colorado's first black female licensed physician.

Black American West Museum and Heritage Center, 3091 California St., Denver, CO 80205. Phone: 303/292-2566. Fax: 303/382-1981. E-mail: *director@blackamericanwest.org*. Web site: *www.blackamericanwest.org*. Hours: May–Sept.—10–5 daily; remainder of year—10–2 Wed.–.Fri.; 10–5 Sat.–Sun.; closed Mon.–

Tues. and major holidays. Admission: adults, $6; seniors, $5.50; children 5–12, $4.

Black Archives of Mid-America. The Black Archives of Mid-America, a collaboration with the Kansas City Public Library funded by the Missouri State Library, features documents, books, periodicals, photographs, oral histories, and artifacts in the history of African Americans in the Midwest, the nation, and other countries. The emphasis is on African American experiences and accomplishments in the Kansas City area from the late 1700s to the 1920s. The facility, housed in the former firehouse of the all-black Hose Reel Company No. 11, functions as a museum as well as an archive. It has exhibits on such topics as the Buffalo Soldiers and Kansas City jazz, as well as collections of materials from such achievers as scientist George Washington Carver, choreographer Alvin Alley, and author Langston Hughes.

Black Archives of Mid-America, 2033 Vine St., Kansas City, MO 64108. Phone: 816/483-1300. Web site: *www.blackarchives.org*. Hours: 9–4:30 Mon.–Fri.; Sat. by appointment; closed Sunday and major holidays. Admission: adults, $2; children, free.

Black Archives Research Center and Museum. The Black Archives Research Center and Museum, founded by the state of Florida and located in the 1907 Carnegie Library building at Florida A&M University in Tallahassee, contains materials relevant to the history of African Americans and black people worldwide. The archives contain more than a half million documents and the museum has thousands of artifacts from throughout the world, including a 500-piece Ethiopian Christian cross collection, rare African books and maps, and materials relating to ancient and modem Africa and periods of slavery, reconstruction, and Jim Crow.

Exhibits about the history of racism and discrimination are on permanent display, while special exhibits are presented on such topics as black education, blacks in the military, the black church, and black women. The archives-museum also has a mobile unit displaying historical materials on the contributions of African Americans that travels throughout Florida and adjacent states.

Black Archives Research Center and Museum, Florida A&M University, Carnegie Library, Martin Luther King Jr. Blvd. and Gamble St., Tallahassee, FL 32307. Phone: 850/599-3020. Web site: *www.famu.edu*. Hours: 9–4 Mon.–Fri.; closed Sat.–Sun. and major holidays. Admission: free.

Black Arts National Diaspora. In 2005 Hurricane Katrina destroyed the home of the Black Arts National Diaspora in New Orleans, Louisiana. The museum, which specializes in contemporary

African art from around the world, now is closed while it seeks a new site. It had over 300 contemporary paintings, woodcarvings, and sculptures from Brazil, Ghana, Haiti, Ivory Coast, and the Americas.

Black Arts National Diaspora, formerly at 4008 Odin St., New Orleans, LA 70126-2249. Phone: 504/949-2263. Fax: 504/949-6052. Web site: *www.handinc.org*. Hours and admission still to be determined.

Black Fashion Museum. The Black Fashion Museum in Washington, D.C., features antique and recent garments that have been designed or worn by people of color. It also seeks to identify and honor people of the African Diaspora who have made significant contributions to the fashion industry.

Black Fashion Museum, 2007 Vermont Ave., N.W., Washington, DC 20004. Phone: 202/667-0744. Fax: 202/667-4379. E-mail: *bfmdc@aol.com*. Hours: by appointment. Admission: adults, $2 suggested donation; seniors and children, $1 suggested donation.

Black Heritage Museum. The principal mission of the Black Heritage Museum in Miami, Florida, is to promote racial harmony in Dade County by increasing awareness and understanding of black culture and heritage. The museum has art and artifacts of the black heritage from around the world, including collections relating to Afro-Cuban art, black heritage dolls and music, the black church, and Dr. Martin Luther King, Jr.

Black Heritage Museum, 15801 S.W. 102nd Ave., PO Box 570327, Miami, FL 33257-0327. Phone and fax: 305/252-3535. E-mail: *bikheru@bellsouth.net*. Hours: varies; closed New Year's Day, Easter, and Christmas. Admission: free.

Black Heritage Museum of Arlington, Virginia. The Black Heritage Museum of Arlington, Virginia, is a museum without walls. The museum currently is being developed to celebrate the African American journey to freedom in Arlington County. The core of the project is the story of Freedmen's Village. A model of the village has been part of a co-sponsored exhibit on slave life at Arlington House, the Robert E. Lee Memorial at Arlington National Cemetery. The museum also sponsors a lecture series, oral history program, walking tour, and a Web site.

Black Heritage Museum of Arlington, Virginia, 951 S. George Mason Dr., Suite 204, Arlington, VA 22204. Phone: 703/271-8700. Web site: *www.arlingtonblackheritage.org*. Hours and admission: still to be determined.

Black History Museum and Cultural Center of Virginia. The home of the Black History and Cultural Center of Virginia in Richmond is a restored 1832 house that historically has served numerous other African American organizations. The museum has more than 5,000 artifacts and documents. It features a permanent exhibit on the history of the predominately black Jackson Ward district and offers changing art, history, and cultural exhibitions. Among the temporary shows have been exhibitions on prominent African American leaders, basketball star Michael Jordan, and Bill "Bojangles" Robinson.

Black History Museum and Cultural Center of Virginia, 3 E. Clay St., Richmond, VA 23219. Phone: 804/780-9093. Fax: 804/780-9107. E-mail: *blackhist@aol.com*, Web site: *www.blackhistorymuseum.org*. Hours: 10–5 Tues.–Sat.; closed Sun.–Mon. and major holidays. Admission: adults, $5; seniors and students over 12, $3; children under 13, $2.

Black Legends of Professional Basketball. The Black Legends of Professional Basketball in Detroit, Michigan, is a small, private museum that honors outstanding African American basketball players from the 1900 to 1960 period. The museum, operated by Dr. John Kline, a psychologist and former Globetrotter, contains photographs, posters, and uniforms of the early black players.

Black Legends of Professional Basketball, 8900 E. Jefferson Ave., Suite 1523, PO Box 02384, Detroit, MI 48202. Phone: 313/822-8208. Fax: 313/579-0495. E-mail: *blackkline@aol.com*. Hours: Sept.–Mar.— 9–5 Mon.–Fri.; 9–1 Sat.; closed Sun. and major holidays; remainder of year — 9–5 Mon.–Fri.; closed Sat.–Sun. and major holidays. Admission: free.

Brazos Valley African American Museum. The Brazos Valley African American Museum opened in 2006 in Bryan, Texas. It is devoted to African American history and culture, and features a collection of artifacts, photographs, and other materials from founders Willie and Mell Pruitt, retired educators.

Brazos Valley African American Museum, 500 E. 20th St., Bryan, TX 77803. Phone: 979/775-3961. Hours: 1–5 Tues.–Fri.; 10–4 Sat.; 2–5 Sun.; closed Mon. and major holidays. Admission: adults, $5; seniors, $4; students, $2; children under 5, free.

Buffalo Soldiers National Museum. The Buffalo Soldiers National Museum in Houston, Texas, is devoted to the African American men and women who have fought in the nation's great wars. The nickname Buffalo Soldiers was given to frontier black servicemen by Cheyenne warriors in 1867 and gradually became a generic term for all African American soldiers. The term, which translates to wild buffalo in Cheyenne, was given out of respect for the fierce fighting ability of the black 10th Cavalry.

The museum, founded by military historian and Vietnam War veteran Paul J. Matthews, is the only one dedicated primarily to preserving the legacy and honor of black soldiers in the nation. It contains artifacts, documents, videos, prints, and memorabilia relating to the history and achievements of African Americans who served in various wars.

Buffalo Soldiers National Museum, 1834 Southmore, Houston, TX 77004. Phone: 713/942-8920. Fax: 713/942-8912. E-mail: *matthews@buffalosoldier museum.com*. Web site: *www.buffalosoldiermuseum. com*. Hours: 10–5 Mon.–Fri., 10–4 Sat.; closed Sun. and major holidays. Admission: $2 per person.

Calaboose African American History Museum. The Calaboose African American History Museum, housed in the 1873 former county jail building in San Marcos, Texas, has exhibits pertaining to local and national aspects of African American history. In addition to displays on San Marcos area history and African American achievements, the museum has had exhibits on Buffalo Soldiers (who helped settle the Texas frontier), Tuskegee airmen, World War II, civil rights, Ku Klux Klan, and Eddie Durham, local jazz great. The museum also offers several outreach programs, including a Traveling Trunk program that goes to schools and community groups and festivals.

Calaboose African American History Museum, 200 Martin Luther King Dr., San Marcos, TX 78666 (mailing address: 1421 W. Hopkins St., San Marcos, TX 78666). Phone: 512/393-8421. Web site: *www. sanmarcosarts/calaboose.htm*. Hours: 1–5 Sat. and by appointment. Admission: $3 donation.

California African American Museum. The California African American Museum is a combination art and history museum in Exposition Park in Los Angeles, California. Although the site of numerous exhibitions of art, the museum's major permanent exhibit is on the history of African Americans in the settlement of the West. It begins by chronicling the African American journey from West Africa to the West Coast of America, examining artifacts from West Africa that demonstrate the art, history, and culture of the regions. It follows with exhibits on the southern legacy of blacks, the great migration west, and the art and cultural contributions of African Americans to opening the western frontier.

California African American Museum, 600 State Dr., Exposition Park, Los Angeles, CA 90037. Phone: 213/744-7432. Fax: 213/744-2050. Web site: *www.caa museum.org*. Hours: 10–4 Wed.–Sat.; 11–5 first Sun. of month; closed Mon.–Tues., New Year's Day, Thanksgiving, and Christmas. Admission: free.

Caribbean Cultural Center. See Hispanic Museums and Galleries section.

Central Pennsylvania African American Museum. The Central Pennsylvania African American Museum in Reading, Pennsylvania, is located in the 1837 Bethel African Methodist Episcopal Church building, one of the terminal sites of the Underground Railroad that southern slaves used to reach freedom in the north before the Civil War. The museum has collections and exhibits that document the history and culture of African Americans, with emphasis on local and regional black history and culture.

Central Pennsylvania African American Museum, 119 N. 10th St., Reading, PA 19605. Phone: 610/371-8713. Fax: 610/371-8739. Web site: *www.homestead. com/cpaam*. Hours: 1–4 Sat. and by appointment. Admission: adults, $3; seniors, $2; children under 12, $1.50.

Charles H. Wright Museum of African American History. The Charles H. Wright Museum of African American History in Detroit, Michigan, is one of the largest and most popular African American historical museums in the world. The 120,000-square-foot museum serves approximately 600,000 visitors annually. Originally founded in 1965 as the International Afro-American Museum, the museum grew with city support and evolved into its present form with extensive exhibits and programs on black history, life, and culture in 1997. It is named for major supporter Dr. Charles H. Wright, an obstetrician and gynecologist, and located in Detroit's cultural center.

The museum has collections of art, artifacts, photographs, and other materials pertaining to African and African American culture. Its core exhibit is And Still We Rise, a journey through African American history and culture. The museum also has an interactive three-dimensional dictionary-style exhibit that introduces young children to interesting persons, places, events, ideas, and objects to better understand the histories and cultures of Africa. Among the recent changing exhibits have been exhibitions on black stereotypes in American material culture, African American professional football players, images of South African human rights, and mixed media paintings and stained glass by black artists.

Charles H. Wright Museum of African American History, 315 E. Warren Ave., Detroit, MI 48201. Phone: 315/404-5800. Fax: 312/404-5855. E-mail: *info@maah-detroit.org*. Web site: *www.maah-detroit. org*. Hours: 9:30–3 Tues.–Thurs.; 9:30–5 Fri.–Sat.; 1–5 Sun.; closed Mon. and major holidays. Admission: adults, $8; seniors and children 3–12, $5; children under 3, free.

Chattanooga African American Museum. The Chattanooga African American Museum, housed in a restored historic building in Chattanooga, Tennessee, has displays ranging from Africa and the slave trade to the history and experiences of African Americans in the Chattanooga area. A mural at the entrance shows a thriving city of East Africa in the twelfth century, followed by a replica of a Bushman's hut, a model of a stucco church in Ethiopia, and a multimedia presentation on how Africans were enslaved and brought to America. Other exhibits depict how Africans came to Chattanooga to work as servants and laborers, rather than plantation field hands, with many later starting businesses and entering the professions. Some also founded towns around Chattanooga.

Chattanooga African American Museum, 200 E. Martin Luther King Blvd., PO Box 11493, Chattanooga, TN 37403. Phones: 423/266-8658 and 423/267-1628. Fax: 423/267-1076. E-mail: *caam@ bellsouth.net*. Web site: *www.caamhistory.com*. Hours: 10–5 Mon.–Fri., 12–4 Sat.; closed Sun. and major holidays. Admission: adults, $5; seniors and students over 12, $3; children 6–12, $2; children under 6, free.

Civil Rights Memorial Center. The Southern Poverty Law Center opened the Civil Rights Memorial Center across the street from its headquarters in Montgomery, Alabama, in 2005. The new facility and the Civil Rights Memorial, the black granite memorial designed by Maya Lin in the plaza adjacent to the center, honor the memory and achievements of those who lost their lives during the Civil Rights Movement of the 1950s and 1960s. The center contains exhibits and information about the Civil Rights Movement, its martyrs, and contemporary social justice issues. It also has a Wall of Tolerance, containing names of people who have pledged to take a stand against hate, injustice, and intolerance.

Civil Rights Memorial Center, Southern Poverty Law Center, 403 Washington Ave., Montgomery, AL 36104. Phone: 334/956-8200. Web site: *www.splcen ter.org*. Hours: 9–4:30 Mon.–Fri.; 10–4 Sat.; closed Sun. and major holidays. Admission: adults, $2; children under 17, free.

Clark Atlanta University Art Galleries. The Clark Atlanta University Art Galleries, located in Trevor Arnett Hall on the Morehouse College campus in Atlanta, Georgia, has one of the largest and most historically significant collections of art by African Americans. It has over 1,000 works, including an African art collection. Much of the art is from the 1942 to 1970 period when the university hosted an annual national exhibition for African American artists who were excluded from most cultural insti-

tutions because of segregation. Among the artists represented are Jacob Lawrence, Elizabeth Catlett, Romare Bearden, John Biggers, Lois Mailou Jones, and John Wilson.

Clark Atlanta University Art Galleries, Clark Atlanta University, Trevor Arnett Hall, Atlanta, GA 30314 (mailing address: 223 James P. Brawley Dr., S.W., Atlanta, GA 30314). Phone: 404/880-6102. Fax: 404/880-6968. E-mail: *tdunkley@cau.edu*. Web site: *www.cau.edu/artgalleries*. Hours: 11–4 Tues.–Fri.; 12–4 Sat.; closed Sun.–Mon. and major holidays. Admission: donation.

Delta Blues Museum. A former railroad station in Clarksdale, Mississippi, has been converted into the Delta Blues Museum, which celebrates the world of blues music. The exhibits use photographs, instruments, artifacts, and words to inform visitors of the culture and people of the blues, while the music of Muddy Waters, Robert Johnson, and John Lee Hooker can be heard throughout the galleries.

Delta Blues Museum, 1 Blues Alley, PO Box 459, Clarksdale, MS 38614. Phone: 662/627-6820. Fax: 662/627-7263. E-mail: *info@deltabluesmuseum.org*. Web site: *www.deltabluesmuseum.org*. Hours: Mar.–Oct.—9–5 Mon.–Sat.; remainder of year—10–5 Mon.–Sat.; closed Sun. and major holidays. Admission: adults, $7; children 6–12, $5; children under 6, free.

Diggs Gallery of Winston-Salem State University. The Diggs Gallery of Winston-Salem State University in Winston-Salem, North Carolina, presents changing exhibitions of African American and African artists. The gallery seeks to further greater understanding, tolerance, and celebration of a diverse global community through art.

Diggs Gallery of Winston-Salem State University, Winston-Salem State University, 601 Martin Luther King Jr. Dr., Winston-Salem, NC 27110-0003. Phone: 336/750-2458. Fax: 336/750-2463. Hours: 11–5 Tues.–Sat.; closed Sun.–Mon. and major holidays. Admission: free.

DuSable Museum of African American History. The DuSable Museum of African American History in Chicago, Illinois, is one of the oldest museums in the nation devoted to the preservation and interpretation of the historical experiences and achievements of African Americans. Founded in 1961, the museum was renamed in 1969 in honor of Jean Baptist Pointe DuSable, a Haitian fur trader who was the first permanent settler in the city, and recently named a new wing for the late mayor Harold Washington.

The museum, located in Washington Park on Chicago's South Side, presents exhibits of African and African American art, history, and culture. Among the recent displays have been exhibitions on African American music pioneers, African quilts, the Civil Rights Movement, and black inventors. The museum also has a gallery for small-scale community-oriented exhibitions.

DuSable Museum of African American History, 740 W. 56th St., Chicago, IL 60637. Phone: 773/947-0600. Fax: 773/947-0677. E-mail: *awright@dusablemuseum.org.* Web site: *www.dusablemuseum.org.* Hours: 10–5 Tues.–Sat.; 12–5 Sun.; closed Mon. and major holidays. Admission: adults, $3; seniors and students over 13, $2; children 6–13, $1; children under 6, free.

Fisk University Galleries. Fisk University in Nashville, Tennessee, has two art galleries — Carl Van Vechten Gallery and Aaron Douglas Gallery — housed in the 1888 Van Vechten neo–Romanesque building. The galleries present exhibitions from its collection of African American paintings, sculpture, graphics, and photographs, as well as other works.

Fisk University Galleries, Vechten Bldg., 1000 17th St., N., Nashville, TN 37208-3051. Phone: 615/329-8720. Fax: 615/329-8544. E-mail: *galleries@fisk.edu.* Web site: *www.fisk.edu/gallery.* Hours: June–Aug.— 10–5 Tues.–Fri.; closed Sat.–Mon.; remainder of year—10–5 Tues.–Fri.; 1–5 Sat.–Sun.; closed Mon. and major holidays. Admission: free.

Freetown Village Living History Museum. Freetown Village Living History Museum is being planned for Indianapolis, Indiana. It will depict the history and culture of African Americans in Indianapolis in the 1870s, with the focus on the old Fourth Ward, the oldest black settlement in the city. Currently, museum organizers have several exhibits on African American experiences in Indianapolis and the state in the museum office at the Madame Walker Theatre Center.

Freetown Village Living History Museum, Madame Walker Theatre Center, 625 Indiana Ave., Indianapolis, IN 46202. Phone: 317/631-1870. Fax: 317/631-0224. Web site: www.freetown.org. Hours: by appointment. Admission: free.

Freewoods Farms. Freewoods Farms in Burgess, South Carolina, is the nation's only operating African American living history museum. The museum, founded by O'Neal Smalls, a recently retired professor of law at the University of South Carolina, replicates an African American farming community in South Carolina between 1865 and 1900. The 40-acre working farm contains such relocated historic buildings as a farmhouse, smoke house, four barns (including two tobacco barns and a grain barn), and a building in which sugar cane is cooked

over a wood fire to make syrup. In addition to syrup, the farm produces sweet potatoes and collard greens.

Freewoods Farms, 9515 Freewoods Rd., Burgess, SC 29576. Phone: 843/650-9139. Hours: by appointment. Admission: free.

Greater Flint Afro-American Hall of Fame. Outstanding African American athletes from the area are enshrined annually into the Greater Flint Afro-American Hall of Fame in Flint, Michigan. Started in 1985, the program includes an induction ceremony and the placement of plaques (with a photograph and highlights of an athlete's achievements) on the lower level of the Flint Public Library.

Greater Flint Afro-American Hall of Fame, Flint Public Library, 1025 E. Kearsley St., Flint, MI 48502 (mailing address: 605 Josephine St., Flint, MI 48503). Phones: 810/232-7111 and 810/767-6621. Fax: 810/249-2633. Hours: 9–9 Mon.–Thurs.; 9–6 Fri.–Sat.; closed Sun. and major holidays. Admission: free.

Great Plains Black Museum. The Great Plains Black Museum in Omaha, Nebraska, focuses on African American history west of the Mississippi River. It tells of the role of African Americans in the development of the American West, with exhibits on settlers, cowboys, women, and other aspects of the experience. The museum, which is housed in the historic Nebraska Telegraph Building, also has collections or exhibits on the Underground Railroad and black military, jazz, athletic, and other accomplishments.

Great Plains Black Museum, 2213 Lake St., Omaha, NE 68110. Phone: 402/345-2212. Fax: 402/345-2256. Hours: 10–2 Mon.–Fri.; other times by appointment; closed Sat.–Sun. and major holidays. Admission: donation.

Greenville Cultural Exchange Center. The Greenville Cultural Exchange Center in Greenville, South Carolina, is a museum and cultural center dedicated to African American history in the area. The center, located in a converted two-story house, displays memorabilia, photographs, and information, including contributions of local African Americans. The principal exhibit is devoted to the the Rev. Jesse Jackson, who is a native of Greenville, a former aide to Dr. Martin Luther King, Jr., and founder of People United to Save Humanity.

Greenville Cultural Exchange Center, 700 Arlington St., Greenville, SC 39601-3206. Phone: 854/232-9162. Hours: 10–5 Tues.– Sat.; other times by appointment. Admission: donation.

Hampton University Museum. Founded in 1868, the Hampton University Museum in Hampton, Virginia, is the oldest African American museum in the United States and one of the earliest in Virginia. The museum, which has collections dating from 1607, contains over 9,000 objects, including African American fine arts; traditional African, Native American, Hawaiian, Pacific Islands, and Asian art; and items relating to the history of the United States. In addition, the university's archives have one of the largest and most comprehensive collections of materials on the history and culture of African Americans. The museum is housed in the renovated Huntington Building, which has 10 galleries devoted to permanent and changing exhibits.

Hampton University Museum, Hampton University, Huntington Bldg., Hampton, VA 23668. Phone: 757/727-5398. Fax: 757/727-5170. E-mail: *museum@hamptonu.edu*. Web site: *www.hamptonu.edu/museum*. Hours: 8–5 Mon.–Fri.; 12–4 Sat.; closed Sun. and major holidays. Admission: free.

Harrison Museum of African American Culture. The history, culture, and achievements of African Americans — especially in southwestern Virginia — are presented at the Harrison Museum of African American Culture in Roanoke, Virginia. The museum is housed in the renovated 1916 Harrison School, the first public high school for black students which now also houses a cultural center. The museum's collections include memorabilia, photographs, objects, and oral histories related to the African American experience in Roanoke Valley, as well as African and contemporary art.

Harrison Museum of African American Culture, 523 Harrison Ave., N.W., Roanoke, VA 24016. Phone: 540/345-4818. E-mail: *webmaster@harrisonmuseum.org*. Web site: *www.harrisonmuseum.org*. Hours: 1–5 Tues.–Sat. (also to 7 Thurs.); closed Sun.–Mon. and major holidays. Admission: free.

Harvey W. Lee, Jr., Memorial Gallery. See Museums Honoring Individuals section.

Howard County Center of African-American Culture. The Howard County Center of African-American Culture in Columbia, Maryland, promotes greater awareness of African American history in the county. It has collections and exhibits of artifacts, memorabilia, murals, and recordings of spirituals, jazz, and rap.

Howard County Center of African-American Culture, 5434 Vantage Point Rd., Columbia, MD 21045. Phone: 410/715-1921. Fax: 410/715-8755. E-mail: *hccaacmd@juno.com*. Hours: 12–5 Tues.–Fri.; 12–4 Sat.; Sun. by appointment; closed Mon. and major holidays. Admission: free.

Howard University Gallery of Art. The Howard University Gallery of Art in Washington, D.C., was established in 1928 to "make revolving exhibitions of contemporary arts and crafts available for visitation and study to students." Since then, the gallery has developed into a study and research facility with a permanent collection — including an array of paintings, sculptures, drawings, and prints by African Americans — and produced numerous changing exhibitions of national and international artists, augmented by selections from its collection.

Howard University Gallery of Art, Howard University, Childers Hall, 2455 6th St., N.W., Washington, DC 20059. Phone: 202/806-7070. Fax: 202/806-6503. Web site: *www.howard.edu/library/art*. Hours: 9:30–4:30 Mon.–Fri.; 12:30–6 Sat.–Sun.; reduced hours in summer; closed major holidays. Admission: free.

Howard University Museum. The Howard University Museum is a teaching museum in Washington, D.C., that collects, preserves, and interprets artifacts and documents pertaining to the university and the history and culture of people of African descent. The museum is part of the Moorland-Spingarn Research Center, which has one of the largest and most comprehensive repositories of documentation of Africans in Africa, the Americas, and elsewhere in the world. The research center contains 175,000 bound volumes; tens of thousands of journals, periodicals, and newspapers; more than 17,000 feet of manuscript and archival collections; 1,000 audio tapes; hundreds of artifacts; and 100,000 prints, photographs, maps, and other graphic materials.

Howard University Museum, Moorland-Spingarn Research Center, Howard University, 500 Howard Pl., Washington, DC 20059. Phone: 202/806-7240. Fax: 202/896-6405. Web site: *www.founders.howard.edu/moorland-spingarn/museum.htm*. Hours: 9–4:30 Mon.–Fri.; closed Sat.–Sun. and major holidays. Admission: free.

Idaho Black History Museum. The Idaho Black History Museum in Boise seeks to inform people of all races about the history and culture of African Americans, with special emphasis on blacks in Idaho. The museum, housed in the historic former St. Paul Baptist Church building, presents exhibits and provides educational and outreach programs on African American history and culture.

Idaho Black History Museum, 508 Julia Davis Dr., Boise, ID 83702. Phone: 208/433-0017. E-mail: *museum@ibhm.org*, Web site: *www.ibhm.org*. Hours: June–Aug.—10–4 Tues.–Sat.; 12–4 Sun.; closed Mon.; remainder of year—11–4 Wed.–Sat.; 12–4 Sun.; closed Mon.–Tues. and major holidays. Admission: donation.

International African American Museum. A $60 million International African American Museum is being proposed for Charleston, South Carolina.

The museum would be devoted to the history, culture, and experiences of African Americans, with the emphasis on Charleston and South Carolina. The museum would be located on a city-owned site adjacent to the South Carolina Aquarium. The Charleston City Council has made a $250,000 planning grant for the project. A steering committee has been appointed to plan and raise funds for the museum.

International African American Museum, c/o Carolee Williams, Special Projects, City of Charleston, 75 Calhoun St., Charleston, SC 29401. Phone: 843/724-3776. E-mail: *iaam@ci.charleston.sc.us*. Web site: *www.charlestoncity.info/iaam*. Hours and admission: still to be determined.

International Afro-American Sports Hall of Fame. Outstanding black athletes are enshrined in the International Afro-American Sports Hall of Fame, located on the fourth floor of the Old Wayne County Building in Detroit, Michigan. The hall of fame, founded in 1982 by former Negro Leagues ballplayer Elmer Anderson, features plaques, photographs, memorabilia, and equipment of such athletes as Joe Louis, Althea Gibson, Satchel Page, Dave Bing, Jackie Robinson, Muhammad Ali, Oscar Robinson, and Hank Aaron.

International Afro-American Sports Hall of Fame, Old Wayne County Bldg., 600 Randolph St., PO Box 27615, Detroit, MI 48227 (mailing address: 15419 N. Gate Blvd., Suite 202, Oak Park, MI 48237). Phones: 313/862-5034 and 248/968-0767. Hours: 9–5 Mon.–Fri.; closed Sat.–Sun. and major holidays. Admission: free.

I. P. Stanback Museum and Planetarium. See Museums Honoring Individuals section.

Jacqueline House African American Museum. Exhibits and programs of African American history and culture are presented at the Jacqueline House African American Museum in Vicksburg, Mississippi. The museum has over 20,000 artifacts, manuscripts, photographs, books, and other materials in its collections.

Jacqueline House African American Museum, 1325 Main St., Vicksburg, MS 39183. Phone: 601/623-0941. Hours: 10–5 Sat.; other times by appointment. Admission: adults, $1; children, 50¢.

James E. Lewis Museum of Art. See Museums Honoring Individuals section.

Jim Crow Museum of Racist Memorabilia. The Jim Crow Museum of Racist Memorabilia at Ferris State University in Big Rapids, Michigan, collects, preserves, and exhibits materials related to racial segregation, civil rights, and anti-black caricatures. The museum has such early to mid–twen-

tieth century artifacts and segregation memorabilia as Ku Klux Klan objects, pro-segregation signs, brochures, posters, musical records, magazines, Civil Rights Movement materials, and over 3,000 anti-black caricature items. It is an educational, teaching, and research resource that seeks to further racial understanding and healing.

Jim Crow Museum of Racist Memorabilia, Ferris State University, 820 Campus Dr., ASC 2180, Big Rapids, MI 49307. Phone: 231/591-5873. Fax: 231/591-2541. E-mail: *thorpj@ferris.edu*. Web site: *www.ferris.edu/jimcrow*. Hours: 8–5 Mon.–Fri. by appointment; closed Sat.–Sun. and national holidays. Admission: free.

Kansas African American Museum. The Kansas African American Museum, located in the historic former First Calvary Baptist Church building in downtown Wichita, seeks to foster community among the diverse groups living in the area. It has collections of art, artifacts, music, and other materials and presents exhibits on the history, culture, and contributions of African Americans in Wichita and Kansas.

Kansas African American Museum, 601 N. Water St., Wichita, KS 67203. Phone: 316/362-7651. Fax: 316/265-6953. E-mail: *tkaam@aol.com*. Web site: *www.thekansasafricanamericanmuseum.org*. Hours: 10–5 Tues.–Fri.; 2–6 Sun.; closed Mon., Sat., and major holidays. Admission: donation.

Legacy Museum of African-American History. The Legacy Museum of African-American History in Lynchburg, Virginia, presents changing exhibitions and programs on local African American history and culture from the first arrival of blacks in central Virginia to the present. The exhibitions focus on such subjects as the civil rights struggle, health and medicine, education, business, and contributions of African Americans to society, politics, and the arts.

Legacy Museum of African-American History, 403 Monroe St., Lynchburg, VA 24504. Phone 434/845-3455. Fax: 434/845-9809. E-mail: *legacymuseum@intelos.net*. Web site: *www.legacymuseum.org*. Hours. 12–4 Wed.–Sat.; 2–45 Sun.; closed Mon.–Tues. and major holidays. Admission: adults, $2; children, $1.

Lucy Craft Laney Museum of Black History and Conference Center. See Museums Honoring Individuals section.

Mattye Reed African Heritage Center. See Museums Honoring Individuals section.

Melvin B. Tolson Black Heritage Center. See Museums Honoring Individuals section.

Motown Historical Museum. The Motown Historical Museum in Detroit, Michigan, traces the history and achievements of the Motown Record Corporation and its founder, Berry Gordy, Jr., known for the recordings by many outstanding African American singers, including Diana Ross and the Supremes, Michael Jackson and the Jackson 5, Stevie Wonder, Martin Gaye, and Smokey Robinson. It is housed in the first headquarters and studio of the recording company, known as Hitsville USA. The company was founded in 1959 and became the largest independent record company by the mid–1970s.

Motown Historical Museum, 2648 W. Grand Blvd., Detroit, MI 48208-1237. Phone: 313/875-2264. Fax: 313/875-2267. E-mail: *rterry@motownmuseum.com*. Web site: *www.motownmuseum.org*. Hours: 10–6 Tues.–Sat.; closed Sun.–Mon. and major holidays. Admission: adults, $8; seniors, $7; children under 12, $5.

Museum of African American Art (Los Angeles). Traditional and contemporary art of African Americans, as well as Africa, the Caribbean, and South America, comprises the collections and exhibitions of the Museum of African American Art in Los Angeles, California. The museum is tucked away on the third floor of the Robinsons-May store.

Museum of African American Art, 4005 Crenshaw Blvd., Los Angeles, CA 90008. Phone: 323/294-7071. Fax 323/294-7084. Hours: 11–6 Thurs.–Sat.; 12–5 Sun.; closed Mon.–Wed. Admission: free.

Museum of African American Art (Tampa). The Museum of African American Art in Tampa, Florida, exhibits African American art dating from the early nineteenth century to the Harlem Renaissance and beyond. Its collection includes works by such artists as Edward Bannister, Romare Bearden, Elizabeth Catlett, Jacob Lawrence, and Henry O. Tanner. The museum opened in 1991 after acquiring the Barnett-Aden Collection.

Museum of African American Art, 1305 N. Florida Ave., Tampa, FL 33602-2917. Phone: 813/272-2466. Fax: 813/272-2325. Hours: 10–4:30 Tues.–Sat.; closed Sun.–Mon. and major holidays. Admission: adults, $4; seniors and children 5–15, $2.50; children under 5, free.

Museum of African-American Culture. The Museum of African-American Culture in the historic Mann-Simons Cottage in Columbia, South Carolina, preserves antebellum life and the role and culture of African Americans. In addition to exhibits, it offers performing arts presentations.

Museum of African-American Culture, 1403 Richland St., Columbia, SC 29201. Phone: 803/252-1770. Hours: 10:15–3:15 Tues.–Fri.; 10:15–1:15 Sat.; closed Sun.–Mon. and major holidays. Admission: adults, $3; seniors, students, and children, $1.

Museum of African Art. The Museum of African Art has temporary facilities in Long Island City, New York, until it moves into its new permanent home in New York City in 2009–10. Meanwhile, it is organizing temporary exhibitions at various off-site venues rather than presenting exhibitions at its site. The new 90,000-square-foot museum will have 16,000 square feet of gallery space for classic and contemporary African art and sculpture in a new building at Fifth Avenue and East 110th Street on the northeastern corner of Central Park.

Museum of African Art, 36-01 43rd St., Long Island City, NY 11101. Phone: 718/784-7700. Fax: 718/784-7718. E-mail *museum@africanart.org*. Web site: *www.africanart.org*. Hours and admission: office and store —10–6 Mon.–Fri.; closed Sat.–Sun. and major holidays; galleries — closed, but exhibitions presented at various off-site locations.

Museum of African Culture. The Museum of African Culture in Portland, Maine, is devoted to sub–Saharan African tribal arts. The museum, which formerly was known as the Museum of African Tribal Art, has over 1,500 pieces in its collection, with approximately 150 being on permanent display with audio and video footage of ceremonies and festivals from Africa. The collection includes elaborately carved masks, wooden and bronze figures, textiles, utilitarian objects, and ceramic, bone, ivory, and composite artifacts. The oldest mask dates to 1600, while some ivory flutes and clay vessels are up to 2000 years old and many bronzes go back 1000 years.

Museum of African Culture, 122 Spring St., #1, Portland, ME 04101. Phone: 207/871-7188. Fax: 207/773-1197. E-mail: *africart@maine.rr.com*. Web site: *www.tribalartmuseum.com*. Hours: 10:30–5 Tues.–Fri.; 12:30–5 Sat.; closed Sun.–Mon., New Year's Day, Easter, Thanksgiving, and Christmas. Admission: adults, $5 donation.

Museum of Afro-American History. The Museum of Afro-American History in Boston, Massachusetts, preserves and interprets the contributions of people of African descent in New England from the colonial period through the nineteenth century. In telling the story, the museum has preserved four historic sites and two Black Heritage Trails in Boston and Nantucket.

In Boston, the historic sites are the 1806 African Meeting House, the oldest extant black church building in the nation, and the adjacent 1835 Abiel Smith School, the nation's first publicly funded grammar school for African American children. The school features exhibits and a museum store open year around. On the island of Nantucket, the sites are the Higginbotham House, built after the land was purchased in 1774, and the restored nineteenth-century African Meeting House, which is open for scheduled tours during July and August and by appointment other times. Guided walking tours also are given of two Black Heritage Trails, highlighting African American life during the eighteenth and nineteenth centuries on Boston's Beacon Hill and 10 sites on the island of Nantucket.

Museum of Afro-American History, 46 Joy St., Boston, MA 02114 (mailing address: 14 Beacon St., Suite 719, Boston, MA 02108). Phone: 617/725-0022. Fax: 612/720-5225. E-mail: *history@afroammuseum. org.* Web site: *www.afroammuseum.org.* Hours: 10–4 Mon.–Sat.; closed Sun. and major holidays. Admission: donation.

Museum of Black Innovations and Inventions. The Museum of Black Innovations and Inventions in Brooklyn, New York, is not a museum, but a traveling exhibition service. It has developed and circulated the "Black Inventors" exhibit, which features a multimedia presentation with patent designs, letters, photographs, posters, and videos documenting the innovations of African American inventors and scientists.

Museum of Black Innovations and Inventions, 271 Cadman Plaza East, Suite 21158, Brooklyn, NY 11202. Web site: *www.blackinventions101.com.*

Museum of Contemporary African Diasporan Arts. The Museum of Contemporary African Diasporian Arts, formerly located in a building owned by the Bridge Street AWME Church in the Bedford-Stuyvesant section of Brooklyn, New York, has moved to a new location — the 80 Arts-James E. Davis Building in the Fort Greene community of Brooklyn. The museum seeks to increase public awareness of the art and culture of people of African descent as it relates to contemporary urban issues through exhibitions, public programs, interactive school and family tours, and community outreach initiatives.

Museum of Contemporary African Diasporan Arts, 80 Arts-James E. Davis Bldg., 80 Hansen Pl., Brooklyn, NY 11217. Phone: 718/230-0492. Fax: 718/230-0246. E-mail: *info@mocada.org.* Web site: *www.mocada.org.* Hours: 11–6 Wed.–Sat.; closed Mon.–Tues. Admission: adults, $4 suggested donation; students, $3 suggested donation; children under 6, free.

Museum of the National Center of Afro-American Artists. The Museum of the National Center of Afro-American Artists in Boston, Massachusetts, presents historical and contemporary exhibitions in painting, sculpture, graphics, photography, and decorative arts. Among the resources of the museum are African, Afro-Latin, Afro-Caribbean, and African American collections and an extensive slide archive.

Museum of the National Center of Afro-American Artists, 300 Walnut Ave., Boston, MA 02119. Phone: 617/442-8614. E-mail: *bgaither@mfa.org.* Web site: *www.ncaaa.org.* Hours: 1–5 Tues.–Sun.; closed Mon. and major holidays. Admission: adults, $4; seniors and students, $3.

National African-American Archives and Museum. The National African-American Archives and Museum in Mobile, Alabama, contains exhibits and collections on African American history and culture. It displays art, biographies, historical items, and such other materials as memorabilia of baseball slugger Hank Aaron. The archives and museum are housed in the former Davis Avenue Branch of the Mobile Public Library, which was the only library for African Americans in Mobile from 1932 to the mid–1960s.

National African-American Archives and Museum, 5654 Martin Luther King Jr. Ave., Mobile, AL 36603. Phone: 251/433-8511. Fax: 251/433-4265. Hours: 8–4 Mon.–Fri.; 10–2 Sat.; closed Sun. and major holidays. Admission: free.

National Afro-American Museum and Cultural Center. The National Afro-American Museum and Cultural Center in Wilberforce, Ohio, aims to educate the public about African American history and culture from African origins to the present by collecting, preserving, and interpreting material evidence of the black experience.

The museum's permanent exhibit, *From Victory to Freedom: Afro-American Life in the Fifties,* chronicles the trends, struggles, and social changes that occurred after World War II to the passage of the Voting Rights Act of 1965. In addition to artifacts and photographs, the exhibit uses life-sized scenes and settings, such as a barber shop, beauty salon, and church interior with recorded voices and gospel music, to convey this crucial period in American history. This major exhibit is supplemented by changing exhibitions on such topics as the legacy of American slavery, African American dance in history and art, and dolls from the museum's collection. The museum is located on the grounds of the former Wilberforce University campus and adjacent to Central State University.

National Afro-American Museum and Cultural Center, 1350 Brush Row Rd., PO Box 578, Wilberforce, OH 45384. Phones: 937/376-4944 and 800/752-2605. Fax: 937/376-2007. E-mail: *webmaster@ohiohistory.org.* Web site: *www.ohiohistorv.org/ places/afroam.* Hours: 9–5 Tues.–Sat.; 1–5 Sun.; closed Mon. and major holidays. Admission: adults, $4; students and children 6–12, $1.50; children under 6, free.

National Civil Rights Museum. The National Civil Rights Museum — the first comprehensive exhibit tracing America's Civil Rights Movement — is located in the former Lorraine Motel and adjacent buildings at the site in Memphis, Tennessee, where Dr. Martin Luther King, Jr., was slain in 1968. The museum uses artifacts, photographs, and other materials to document civil rights and associated segregationist activities from 1619 to 2000, including Dr. King's role and assassination.

National Civil Rights Museum, 450 Mulberry St., Memphis, TN 38103. Phone: 901/521-9599. Fax: 901/521-9740. Email: *contact@civilrightsmuseum.org*. Web site: *www.civilrightsmuseum.org*. Hours: 9–5 Mon. and Wed.–Sat.; 1–5 Sun.; closed Tues., New Year's Day, Thanksgiving, and Christmas. Admission: adults, $12; seniors and students, $10; children 4–17, $8.50; children under 4, free; free after 3 on Mon.

National Great Blacks in Wax Museum. More than 100 leading African American figures are featured in the Great Blacks in Wax Museum in Baltimore, Maryland. The museum, founded by Drs. Elmer and Joanne Martin and located in a renovated fire station, shows black experiences and contributions from early history through the Civil Rights Movement. In addition to wax depictions of such individuals as Booker T. Washington, Dr. Martin Luther King, Jr., Malcolm X, Ida Wells-Barnett, Dr. Charles G. Woodson, and Bessie Coleman, the museum has exhibits of segregation scenes, black inventions, and other topics.

National Great Blacks in Wax Museum, 1601-03 E. North Ave., Baltimore, MD 21213-1409. Phone: 410/563-3404. Fax 410/675-5040. E-mail: j*imartin@greatblacksinwax.org*. Web site: *www.greatblacksinwax.org*. Hours: 9–5 Tues.–.Sat.; 12–6 Sun.; closed Mon., New Year's Day, Thanksgiving, and Christmas. Admission: adults, $6.80; seniors and college students, $6.30; children 12–17, $4.80; children 2–11, $4.55; children under 2, free.

National Museum of African American History and Culture. One of the nation's newest developing major African American museums is the National Museum of African American History and Culture, which will join the array of Smithsonian Institution museums on the Mall in Washington, D.C. Legislation establishing the museum was passed in 2003 and five acres near the Washington Monument were selected for its site in 2006.

The estimated cost of the museum is $300 million to $500 million. It is likely to become the largest and most expensive African American museum in the nation. The new museum will be the only national museum devoted exclusively to the documentation of African American life, art, history, and culture. It will cover such areas as slavery, post–Civil War Reconstruction, the Harlem Renaissance, and the Civil Rights Movement.

National Museum of African American History and Culture, Smithsonian Institution, Washington, DC 20013. Phone: 202/633-4820. E-mail: *nmaahcinfo@si.edu*. Web site: *www.nmaahc.si.edu*. Hours: still to be determined. Admission: free.

National Museum of African Art. The National Museum of African Art, one of the Smithsonian Institution museums on the Mall in Washington, D.C., features the diverse artistic expressions found throughout Africa from ancient to contemporary times. It is one of three black museums that are part of the Smithsonian, the other two being the Anacostia Museum and Center for African American History and Culture in the neighborhood and the National Museum of African American History and Culture now under development on the Mall (see separate listings). Collections and exhibits at the African art museum range from painting, printmaking, and sculpture to masks, figures, musical instruments, ceramics, textiles, furniture, and tools.

National Museum of African Art, Smithsonian Institution, 950 Independence Ave., S.W., Washington, DC 20560-7012 (mailing address: MRC 708, PO Box 37012, Washington, DC 20013-7012). Phone: 202/633-4600, Ext. 277. Fax: 202/357-4879. E-mail: *nmafaweb@nmafa.si.edu*. Web site: *www.nmafa.si.edu*. Hours: 10–5:30 daily; closed Christmas. Admission: free.

National Underground Railroad Freedom Center. The National Underground Railroad Freedom Center in Cincinnati, Ohio, is a $110 million complex that tells how an estimated 100,000 enslaved southern black people in the early 1800s sought freedom in the North through the Underground Railroad, which was not a railroad but a system operated by abolitionists and free blacks that enabled slaves to escape to safety in free states and Canada. The general story of freedom also is woven through the Underground Railroad at the 158,000-square-foot facility, which has three pavilions.

Among the exhibits are *From Slavery to Freedom*, tracing the rise of slavery and the development of the Underground Railroad; *ESCAPE! Freedom Seekers and the Underground Railroad*, an interactive display for young children about the Underground Railroad and some of the leaders during that period; *Brothers of the Borderland*, relating the story of the Underground Railroad heroes in Ripley, Ohio; *The Struggle Today*, depicting the challenges faced by African Americans since the end of slavery and the struggles for freedom throughout the world; and *The Hall of Everyday Freedom Heroes*, describing in-

The story of enslaved black people escaping from the South to the North in the early 1800s is told in this building, housing the National Underground Railroad Freedom Center in Cincinnati, Ohio. An estimated 100,000 slaves sought freedom through the Underground Railroad, an escape system operated by abolitionists and free blacks. *Courtesy National Underground Railroad Freedom Center.*

dividuals who have helped shape freedom in the world throughout history. Three animated films also address the fragile nature of freedom throughout human history. The museum's principal artifact is a 21×30-foot two-story log slave pen built in Kentucky in 1830 to house slaves being shipped to auction.

National Underground Railroad Freedom Center, 50 E. Freedom Way, Cincinnati, OH 45202-3413. Phones: 513/333-7500 and 877/648-4838. Web site: *www.freedomcenter.org*. Hours: 11–5 Tues.–Sun.; closed Mon., Thanksgiving, and Christmas. Admission: adults, $12; seniors and students over 12, $10; children 6–12, $8; children under 6, free.

National Voting Rights Museum and Institute. The National Voting Rights Museum and Institute, located at the foot of the historic Edmund Pettus Bridge in Selma, Alabama, was organized by participants and supporters of the Voting Rights Movement of the 1960s. It documents the struggles and accomplishments of those Americans dedicated to the attainment and retention of equal treatment under the law; serves as a depository of

source materials on the history of voting rights in America; and describes the pivotal events leading to the signing of the Voting Rights Act of 1965.

National Voting Rights Museum and Institute, 1012 Water Ave., PO Box 2516, Selma, AL 36702. Phone: 334/418-0800. Fax: 334/418-0278. E-mail: *vorimus@aol.com*. Web site: *www.voterights.org*. Hours: 9–5 Mon.–Fri.; 10–3 Sat.; Sun. by appointment; closed Thanksgiving and Christmas. Admission: adults, $6; seniors and students, $4.

NCCU Art Museum. The NCCU Art Museum at North Carolina Central University in Durham, North Carolina, features the works of African American artists from the nineteenth and twentieth centuries and a selection of objects from the African continent. Among the prized holdings are the works of Harlem Renaissance artists. The collections include paintings by Robert S. Duncanson, Henry O. Tanner, and William H. Johnson and sculptures by Selma H. Burke and Richard Hunt. Five temporary exhibitions featuring the works of emerging and established artists are presented each year.

NCCU Art Museum, North Carolina Central University, 1801 Fayetteville St., PO Box 10555, Durham, NC 27703. Phone: 919/530-6211. Fax: 919/560-5649. E-mail: *krodgers@wpo.nccu.edu*. Web site: *www.nccu.edu/artmuseum*. Hours: June–Aug.— 8:30–4 Mon.-Fri.; closed Sat.–Sun.; remainder of year — 9–5 Tues.-Fri.; 2–5 Sun.; closed Mon., Sat., and major holidays. Admission: free.

Negro Leagues Baseball Museum. The rich history of African American baseball is celebrated at the Negro Leagues Baseball Museum in Kansas City, Missouri. The museum, which shares the site with the Jazz Museum, contains multimedia and other exhibits with hundreds of artifacts, photographs, memorabilia, and equipment from the late 1800s through the 1960s. The museum focuses on players and other individuals who made significant contributions to the black leagues and those that made the transition to major league baseball, including such stars as Jackie Robinson, Larry Doby, Ernie Banks, Minnie Minoso, Elston Howard, Hank Thompson, and Monte Irwin.

Negro Leagues Baseball Museum, 1616 E. 18th St., Kansas City, MO 64108. Phone: 816/221-1920. Fax: 816/221-8424. Hours: 9–6 Tues.–Sat.; 12–6 Sun.; closed Mon. and major holidays. Admission: adults, $6; children 5–11, $2.50; children under 5, free.

New Orleans African-American Museum of Art, Culture, and History. The New Orleans African-American Museum of Art, Culture, and History is located in the historic Villa Meilleur complex in the Tremé neighborhood near the French Quarter in New Orleans, Louisiana. It focuses on the development of African American culture in New Orleans and serves as a site for presenting visual and performing arts. Exhibits cover such diverse topics as voodoo, Mardi Gras, Indians, and jazz. The museum is closed indefinitely because of damage caused by Hurricane Katrina in 2005.

New Orleans African-American Museum of Art, Culture, and History, 1418 Gov. Nicholls St., New Orleans, LA 70116. Phone: 504/565-7497. Hours: closed indefinitely.

Northeast Louisiana Delta African American Heritage Museum. The Northeast Louisiana Delta African American Heritage Museum in Monroe preserves and promotes African American contributions and culture through exhibits and educational, artistic, and cultural events.

Northeast Louisiana Delta African American Heritage Museum, 503 Plum St., Monroe, LA 71202 (mailing address: PO Box 168, Monroe, LA 71210-0168). Phone: 318/323-1167. Fax: 218/323-8954. Web site: www.nldaahm.com. Hours:10–4 Tues.–Sat.; Sun. by appointment: closed Mon. and major holidays. Admission: adults, $2; students and children, $1.

Oran Z Pan African Black Facts and Wax Museum. The Oran Z Pan African Black Facts and Wax Museum in Los Angeles, California, displays wax figures, artifacts, memorabilia, photographs, and other materials related to black experiences throughout the world. Among the wax figures are Frederick Douglass, Malcolm X, Sojourner Truth, George Washington Carver, Harriet Tubman, and Thurgood Marshall. The museum also depicts historical eras and scenes using a wide range of artifacts and memorabilia.

Oran Z Pan African Black Facts and Wax Museum, 3742 W. Martin Luther King Blvd., Los Angeles, CA 90008. Phone: 323/299-8829. Web site: *www.oransblackmuseum.com*. Hours: 11–4 Tues.; by appointment remainder of week. Admission: adults, $10; children, $5.

Ozarks Afro-American Heritage Museum. Quilts, textiles, furniture, farm implements, and other artifacts and antiques made by blacks in the area are featured at the Ozarks Afro-American Heritage Museum in Ash Grove, Missouri. The museum was started in 2002 by Father Moses Berry, a priest of the Orthodox Church America, to honor the historical contributions of African Americans in southwestern Missouri. Most of the objects were preserved by Berry family ancestors, who settled in the area in 1872. Nearby is a historic cemetery, owned by the Berry family since 1875, that was dedicated to the burial of "Slaves, Paupers and Indians," who were excluded from other burial places for many years.

Ozarks Afro-American Heritage Museum, 107 W. Main St., PO Box 265, Ash Grove, MO 65604. Phone: 417/672-3104. Web site: www.oaahm.org. Hours: 9–1 Tues.–Thurs.; 10–2 Sat.; other times by appointment; closed major holidays. Admission: donation.

Pinellas County African American History Museum. Artifacts, memorabilia, and funds are being collected for the establishment of a Pinellas County African American History Museum in Clearwater, Florida. Meanwhile, the materials are being stored and displayed at Heritage Village-Pinellas County Historical Museum.

Pinellas County African American History Museum, c/o Randolph Lightfoot, President, 14099 Belcher Rd. S., Largo, FL 33771. Phone: 727/588-6342. E-mail: *rlight06@aol.com*. Hours and admission: still to be determined.

Ralph Mark Gilbert Civil Rights Museum. See Museums Honoring Individuals section.

Reflections in Black Museum. The Reflections in Black Museum in Northfield, Ohio, is a traveling exhibition service rather than an operating museum that can be visited. It has developed and circulates *African American History on Wheels*, consisting of several traveling exhibits about the accomplishments of African Americans. The exhibits seek to educate and inspire visitors through exhibits about the accomplishments of black inventors, political leaders, war heroes, sports figures, singers and musicians, and civil rights leaders.

Reflections in Black Museum, PO Box 670794, Northfield, OH 44067. Phone: 330/468-6917. Web site: *www.reflectionsinblackmuseum.com.*

Reginald F. Lewis Museum of Maryland African American History and Culture. See Museums Honoring Individuals section.

Rhode Island Black Heritage Society. The Rhode Island Black Heritage Society, which was inspired by the spirit of the 1960s Civil Rights Movement, is committed to the preservation of art, culture, and the role that African Americans have had in influencing the history of the state. The society, located in Providence, furthers understanding of the African American experience through its library, publications, conferences, tours, musical events, plays, and museum exhibits and related activities. The museum features artifacts, art works, documents, and photographs, with the emphasis on Rhode Island, but also including Africa, Caribbean Islands, and Cape Verde Islands.

Rhode Island Black Heritage Society, 65 Weyboset St., Providence, RI 02903. Phone: 401/751-3490. Fax: 401/751-0040. E-mail: *blkheritage@netzero.net.* Web site: *www.providenceri.com/ri-blackheritage.* Hours: 10–4 Mon.–Fri.; Sat. by appointment; closed Sun. and major holidays. Admission: free.

River Road African American Museum. The River Road African American Museum in Donaldsonville, Louisiana, is devoted to the history and culture of African Americans in the rural communities along the Mississippi River between Baton Rouge and New Orleans. The museum, which gives tours, focuses on the lives and contributions of black slaves who once lived and worked on plantations along the Mississippi River. It also offers tours of historic sites along River Road.

River Road African American Museum, 406 Charles St., PO Box 266, Donaldsonville, LA 70346. Phone: 225/474-5553. E-mail: *kathe@africanamericanmuseums.org.* Web site: *www.africanamericanmuseum.org.* Hours: 10–5 Wed.–Sat.; 1–5 Sun.; closed Mon.–Tues. and major holidays. Admission: $4 donation.

San Francisco African American Historical and Cultural Society. The San Francisco African American Historical and Cultural Society seeks to inform African Americans and the general public about the history and culture of San Francisco's African American community. It serves as a cultural center by documenting and presenting the African American experience, providing a forum for discussion of relevant issues, fostering the study and appreciation of African and African American history and culture, and instilling a sense of pride in African Americans and their heritage. The society no longer operates a museum and gallery at the Fort Mason complex, but has a library, archives, and listening room to hear taped lectures, speeches, and music by leading African Americans at its downtown offices.

San Francisco African American Historical and Cultural Society Museum, 762 Fulton St., 2nd Floor, San Francisco, CA 94102. Phone: 415/292-6172. Hours: 12–5 Wed.–Sun.; closed Mon.–Tues. and major holidays. Admission: adults, $2 suggested donation; children, $1 suggested donation.

Schomburg Center for Research in Black Culture. See Museums Honoring Individuals section.

Seminole Nation Museum. See Native American Museums and Galleries section.

Slave Relic Museum. The Slave Relic Museum in Walterboro, South Carolina, collects, preserves, and interprets African American artifacts, documents, photographs, and memorabilia of the slavery period. In telling the history and culture of enslaved Africans at that time, the museum displays slave collars, chains, spiked ankle shackles, and other such other materials as quilts, dolls, and diaries.

Slave Relic Museum, 208 Carn St., Walterboro, SC 29488. Phone: 843/549-9130, Web site: *www.slaverelics.org.* Hours: 9:30–5 Mon.–Thurs.; 10–3 Sat.; closed Fri., Sun., and major holidays. Admission: adults, $6; children, $5.

Smith Robertson Museum and Cultural Center. See Museums Honoring Individuals section.

Southern University Museums of Art. Southern University Museum of Art has two locations — on the main campus in Baton Rouge, Louisiana, and at a branch campus in Shreveport. The Baton Rouge museum, housed in the Martin L. Harvey Auditorium building, has four galleries devoted to African art and four to African American art, with the foyers and stage displaying both African and African American art. The African galleries feature art from such countries as Cameroon, Congo, Ivory Coast, Mali, and Nigeria, while the African American galleries contain works by master artists, Louisiana artists, and faculty and staff, and serves as the site for special exhibitions. The Shreveport branch presents more than 2,000 pieces of African and African American art from the museum's collections and special exhibitions at its Metro Center campus.

Southern University Museum of Art, Martin L. Harvey Hall, G. Leon Nettervile Dr., Baton Rouge, LA 70813. Phone: 225/771-4513. Fax: 225/771-4498. Web site: *www.sus.edu/suma*. Hours: 10–5 Tues.–Fri.; 10–4 Sat.; closed Sun.–Mon. and major holidays. Admission: free.

Southern University Museum of Art at Shreveport, Metro Center Campus, 610 Texas St., Shreveport, LA 71101. Phone: 318/676-5520. Fax: 318/676-7734. Web site: *www.sus.edu/suma*. Hours: 10–5 Tues.–Fri.; 10–4 Sat.; closed Sun.–Mon. and major holidays. Admission: free.

Spelman College Museum of Fine Art. The Spelman College Museum of Fine Art in Atlanta, Georgia, emphasizes works by and about women of the African Diaspora. The museum, which has collections of nineteenth- and twentieth-century American, African American, and European works, is located in the Camille Olivia Hanks Cosby Academic Center. The center also houses the Women's Research and Resource Center, archives, media center, and academic classrooms and offices.

Spelman College Museum of Art, 350 Spelman Lane, S.W., Box 1526, Atlanta, GA 30314-4399. Phone: 404/270-5607. Fax 404/270-5980. E-mail: *museum@spelman.edu*. Web site: *www.museum.spelman.edu*. Hours: 10–4 Tues.–Fri.; 12–4 Sat.; closed Sun.–Mon., college breaks, and national holidays. Admission: $3 suggested donation.

Stax Museum of American Soul Music. Visitors can listen and dance to popular soul music and see artifacts, memorabilia, videos, and interactive exhibits at the Stax Museum of American Soul Music in Memphis, Tennessee. The museum, operated by a music recording studio, also presents changing exhibitions on soul music. Among the star performers highlighted in the exhibits are Aretha Franklin, James Brown, Ray Charles, Ike and Tina Turner, Sam Cooke, and the Jackson family.

Stax Museum of American Soul Music, 926 E. McLemore Ave., Memphis, TN 28105. Phones: 901/942-7685 and 888/942-7685. Fax 901/507-1463. Web site: *www.soulsvilleusa.com*. Hours: Mar.–Oct.—9–4 Mon.–Sat.; 1–4 Sun.; remainder of year—10–4 Mon.–Sat.; 1–4 Sun.; closed New Year's Day, Easter, Thanksgiving, and Christmas. Admission: adults, $9; seniors, $8; children 9–12, $6; accompanied children under 9, free.

Stephens African American Museum. Paints, prints, drawings, and sculptures by African American artists and black history featuring national and local historical documents and memorabilia are presented at the Stephens African American Museum in Shreveport, Louisiana.

Stephens African American Museum, 2810 Lindholm St., Shreveport, LA 71108. Phone: 318/635-2147. Fax: 318/636-0504. Hours: 9–2 Mon.–Fri.; 1–4 Sat.; closed Sun., Easter, Independence Day, and Christmas. Admission: adults, $2; seniors, $1.75; students and children, $1.

Studio Museum in Harlem. The Studio Museum in Harlem in New York City is a fine arts museum that specializes in the art and artifacts of black Americans and of the African Diaspora. It has collections of nineteenth- and twentieth-century African American art, traditional and contemporary African art, and Caribbean art, and presents changing exhibitions of black art, history, and culture.

Studio Museum in Harlem, 144 W. 125th St., New York, NY 10027, Phone: 212/864-4500. Fax: 212/864-4800. Web site: *www.studiomuseum,org*. Hours: 12–6 Wed.–Fri.; 10–6 Sat.; 12–6 Sun.; closed Mon.–Tues. and major holidays. Admission: adults, $7 suggested donation; seniors and students over 11, $3 suggested donation; children under 12, free.

Texas Southern University Museum. Historical and contemporary African American and African art are featured at the Texas Southern University Museum in Houston, Texas. Although originally proposed in 1949, it was not until 2000 that the museum opened in the renovated Fairchild Building. It now is the permanent home of the huge *Web of Life* mural by John Biggers on the beauty and complexity of African American people. It is complimented by terra cotta sculptures by art students and serves as the introduction to changing exhibitions of African American and African art.

Texas Southern University Museum, Fairchild Bldg., 3100 Cleburne St., Houston, TX 77004. Phone: 713/313-7120. Fax: 713/313-7342. E-mail: *turner_nl@tsu.edu*. Web site: *www.tsu.edu/about/history/museum.asp*. Hours: 10–5 Tues.–Fri.; 12–5 Sat.–Sun.; closed Mon. and national holidays. Admission: free.

Tougaloo College Art Gallery. Tougaloo College in Tougaloo, Mississippi, has an art gallery at the site of an old cotton plantation with an antebellum mansion. It has collections of African American and African art from the seventeenth to twenty-first centuries, archives that include civil rights documents, and a program of changing exhibitions.

Tougaloo College Art Gallery, 500 W. County Line Rd., Tougaloo, MS 39174. Phone: 601/977-7743. Fax: 601/977-7714. E-mail: *art@pop.tougaloo.edu*. Web site: *www.tougaloo.edu/art*. Hours: temporarily closed for renovation.

Tubman African American Museum. See Museums Honoring Individuals section.

United States National Slavery Museum. A major museum on slavery is being planned as the centerpiece of the 2,100-acre Celebrate Virginia, a commercial, recreational, and tourist-oriented project in Fredericksburg, Virginia. The museum, which will be called the United States National Slavery Museum, will be located a short distance from where slaves first entered the country and near where several Civil War battles were fought over whether to set them free. It will occupy a 39-acre bluff overlooking the Rappahannock River.

The museum, which will have 100,000 square feet of permanent and temporary exhibit space, will take visitors through time — beginning with Africa as the cradle of civilization through the Middle Passage on slave ships to the slave resistance movement, Civil War, and the continuing struggle for equality. It also will have a comprehensive library and archives with materials on slavery and the pursuit of freedom. While in the developmental stage, the museum is offering traveling exhibitions, such as *Reflections on American Slavery* (featuring artifacts from the museum's collections) and *Slavery in America: A More Complete Story*.

United States National Slavery Museum, 1320 Central Park Blvd., Suite 251, Fredericksburg, VA 22401. Phone: 540/548-8818. Fax: 540/548-8977. E-mail: *ddaniels@museum.org*. Web site: *www.usnationalslaverymuseum.org*. Hours and admission: still to be determined.

Walker African American Museum and Research Center. The Walker African American Museum and Research Center in Las Vegas, Nevada, is located in a temporary facility while planning a new 10,000-square-foot home. It has collections of documents, artifacts, and memorabilia about African Americans in Nevada from the 1800s to the present and presents changing exhibitions on the history and culture of African Americans. It intends to have a museum area, art gallery, genealogy research center, and gift and sweet shop at the new location.

Walker African American Museum and Research Center, 705 W. Van Buren Ave., Las Vegas, NV 89106. Phones: 702/649-2238 and 702/399-5400. Hours: by appointment. Admission: adults, $2; children, $1.

Weeksville Heritage Center. See Historic Sites section.

Western States Black Research and Educational Center. The Western States Research and Educational Center in Los Angles, California, has the largest collection of materials relating to the African American experience in the western United States. The diverse collection, assembled over a 40-year period by Dr. Mayme A. Clayton, a retired university librarian, consists of rare and out-of-print books, manuscripts, documents, films, music, photographs, and memorabilia. The materials express the history of African American life and letters in the West between 1790 and the present. An exhibition of some items is presented every three or four months.

Western States Black Research and Educational Center, 3617 Montclair St., Los Angeles, CA 90018. Phone: 323/737-3292. Fax: 323/737-2842. Hours: 10–6 Mon.–Sat.; closed Sun. and major holidays. Admission: varies.

Worcester African Cultural Center. Masks, figurative sculptures, textiles, and contemporary art from the entire African continent are exhibited at the Worcester African Cultural Center in Worcester, Massachusetts. The cultural center, located in a historic former manufacturing building, has a gallery and a performing arts center.

Worcester African Cultural Center, 33 Canterbury St., Worcester, MA 01610. Phone 508/757-7727. Fax: 508/792-4988. E-mail: *amareno@african-museum.com*. Web site: *www.african-museum.com*. Hours: 10–5 Wed.–Sat.; Sun. by appointment; closed Mon.–Tues. and major holidays. Admission: adults, $5.50; seniors, students, and children 3–16, $3.50; children under 3, free.

Zora Neale Hurston National Museum of Fine Arts. See Museums Honoring Individuals section.

Museums Honoring Individuals

Anne Spencer Memorial. The house in which Anne Spencer, an acclaimed African American lyric poet of the Harlem Renaissance period of the 1920s, lived for 72 years now is a memorial in her honor. It contains her Victorian furnishings, samples of her writings, photographs, other family materials, and the garden her husband, Edward, built as inspiration for her poetry.

Anne Spencer Memorial, 1313 Pierce St., Lynchburg, VA 24501. Phone: 804/845-1313. Hours: by appointment. Admission: adults, $5; seniors, $4; students, $3: children, $2.

A. Philip Randolph Pullman Porter Museum. The A. Philip Randolph Pullman Porter Museum in Chicago, Illinois, is a tribute to the founding president of the Brotherhood of Sleeping Car Porters and the contributions made by African Americans to America's labor movement. Randolph fought to improve the working conditions and pay for black porters who worked on Pullman railroad cars and obtained the first union collective bargaining agreement with a major United States company in 1937. The museum tells the story of Randolph and the Pullman porters union and their impact on African American employment and the labor movement.

A. Philip Randolph Pullman Porter Museum, 10406 S. Maryland Ave., Chicago, IL 60628 (mailing address: PO Box 6276, Chicago, IL 60680-6276). Phone: 773/928-3935. Fax: 773/928-8372. E-mail: *blhmuseum-website@yahoo.com*. Web site: *www.aphili prandolphmuseum.com*. Hours: summer — varies, but generally 11–4 Thurs.–Sat.; closed winter and major holidays. Admission: $5 per person.

Arna Bontemps African American Museum. The Arna Bontemps African American Museum in Alexandria, Louisiana, honors the noted black poet and author who wrote over 20 books, plays, and anthologies and was considered the leading authority on the Harlem Renaissance. He was part of a core of young black writers who led the New Negro movement. The museum is located in the house in which he was born in 1902. Racism forced the family to move to California six years later, but he always considered it his home and frequently returned to learn more about his family heritage. The museum contains his collected writings and many of his furnishings, and the former dining room has become a community room where a Junior Writing Guild meets weekly.

Arna Bontemps African American Museum, 1327 3rd St., Alexandria, LA 71301. Phone: 318/473-4692. Fax: 318/473-4675. Web site: *www.amabontempsmu seum.com*. Hours: 10–4 Tues.–Fri.; 10–2 Sat.; closed Sun.–Mon. and major holidays. Admission: free.

August Wilson Center for African American Culture. The African-American Cultural Center of Greater Pittsburgh was renamed in 2006 for August Wilson, the Pulitzer Prize–winning playwright from Pittsburgh, Pennsylvania. The center, now named the August Wilson Center for African American Culture, also began construction on a new 85,000-square-foot, three-story home in downtown Pittsburgh. In addition to exhibits on African American art and culture, the new center will showcase black contributions in music, theater, dance, science, athletics, business, and other fields. One gallery will be devoted largely to African American cultural history in western Pennsylvania, while another will feature changing exhibitions of works by African American visual artists and those of African descent.

August Wilson Center for African American Culture, corner of Liberty Ave. and 10th St., Pittsburgh, PA 15219 (mailing address: Regional Enterprise Tower, 425 6th Ave., Suite 1750, Pittsburgh, PA 15219). Phone 412/258-2700. Fax: 412/258-2701. E-mail:

info@africanaculture.org. Web site: *www.africanacul ture.org*. Hours and admission: still to be determined.

Banneker-Douglass Museum. The state-operated Banneker-Douglass Museum, named for scientist-astronomer Benjamin Banneker and abolitionist Frederick Douglass, is dedicated to preserving Maryland's African American heritage and serving as the state's official repository of African American material culture. The museum, housed in the old Mt. Moriah A.M.E. Church building in Annapolis, contains artifacts, art, photographs, historical documents, rare books, and other materials related to black history and life in Maryland. Both Banneker and Douglass were born in Maryland.

Banneker-Douglass Museum, 84 Franklin St., Annapolis, MD 21401. Phone: 410/216-6180. Hours: 10–3 Tues.–Fri.; 12–4 Sat.; closed Sun.–Mon. and major holidays. Admission: free.

Benjamin Banneker Historical Park and Museum. The Benjamin Banneker Historical Park and Museum in Oella, Maryland, honors the nation's first African American man of mathematics and science at his homestead and farm. He also is known for helping to survey the site for the formation of the District of Columbia in 1790, publishing an almanac from 1791 through 1802, and defending the intellectual equality of the Negro in correspondence with Thomas Jefferson. The 142-acre park contains a variety of trails, an archaeological site, and a museum with exhibits on the life and times of Banneker and changing community exhibitions.

Benjamin Banneker Historical Park and Museum, 300 Oella Ave., Oella, MD 21228. Phone: 410/887-1081. Web site: *www.thefriendsofbanneker.org*. Hours: 10–4 Tues.–Sat.; closed Sun.–Mon. and national holidays. Admission: $3 suggested donation.

Booker-Thomas Museum. The Booker-Thomas Museum in Lexington, Mississippi, is named for founder Fannye Thomas Booker, who wanted to show the way of life she had known as a child, including the country store her family operated. It contains an assortment of artifacts and memorabilia that show a disappearing way of life. The collection includes such items as cut glass, iron beds, old record players, cast-iron pots, farming equipment, and even a 100-year-old church pulpit and four pews.

Booker-Thomas Museum, Tchula Rd., Lexington, MS 39095. Phone: 662/831-2322. Hours: by appointment. Admission: donation.

Carter G. Woodson Home National Historic Site. The home of Dr. Carter G. Woodson, the noted historian who founded the Association for the Study of Afro-American Life and History and

Black History Month, is a national historic site in Washington, D.C. Born the son of former slaves, he realized early the important role of African Americans in the nation's history and committed his life to research and dissemination of the African American past. He has written or co-authored 22 books and become known as the "father of African-American history."

In 1915, Dr. Woodson began the association to collect historical and sociological data, publish books, promote the study of African American life and history, and encourage racial harmony through the organization and work of clubs and schools. The organization now conducts and promotes research and study of the black person's role in world history. Dr. Woodson began the first of the Black History Month observances in 1926, and the association's publishing arm still is responsible for the publication and circulation of the popular history month kits.

The decaying Woodson red-brick Victorian row house, which also served as the association's headquarters from 1923 until the 1970s, was declared to be one of the nation's 11 most endangered historic places in 2001. The National Park Service acquired the house in 2005 and it now is closed while being rehabilitated and restored.

Carter G. Woodson Home National Historic Site, 1538 9th St., N.W., Washington, DC (mailing address: c/o Mary McLeod Bethune Council House, 1318 Vermont Ave., N.W., Washington, DC 20005). Phone: 202/673-2402. Fax: 202/673-2414. Web site: *www.nps.gov/cawo.* Hours and admission: site is closed temporarily for renovation.

Charlotte Hawkins Brown Museum. The Charlotte Hawkins Brown Museum is named for the founder of the former Alice Freeman Palmer Memorial Institute, a boarding school for African Americans in Sedalia, North Carolina. Twelve buildings still remain from the school at the state's first historic site honoring its African American heritage. The museum describes Dr. Brown's contributions to African American education in exhibits and audiovisual presentations.

Charlotte Hawkins Brown Museum, Charlotte Hawkins Brown Memorial State Historic Site, 6136 Burlington Rd., PO Box B, Sedalia, NC 27342. Phone: 336/449-4846. Fax: 336/449-0176. Web site: *www.ah.der.state.nc.us/sections/hs/chb/main.htm.* Hours: Apr.–Oct.— 9–5 Mon.–Sat.; closed Sun. and major holidays; remainder of year —10–4 Tues.–Sat.; closed Sun.–Mon. and major holidays. Admission: free.

Coach Eddie G. Robinson Museum. In 1999, the Louisiana Legislature authorized the creation of the Coach Eddie G. Robinson Museum at Grambling State University in honor of the late legendary coach who is the only collegiate football coach to win more than 400 games. He retired in 1997 after coaching for 56 years at Grambling State University. The museum, which opened and then closed for further development and lack of funds, featured exhibits of artifacts, memorabilia, photographs, and other materials that reflected the life and coaching career of Robinson.

Coach Eddie G. Robinson Museum, Grambling State University, Stadium Support Facility, Grambling, LA 71245. Phones: 318/274-3811 and 800/569-4714. Hours and admission: still to be determined.

Frederick Douglass Museum (Rochester). Efforts are under way in Rochester, New York, to develop a museum honoring Frederick Douglass, the ex-slave who became a leader in the abolitionist movement, who lived and worked in Rochester for 25 years before moving to Washington. A building has been found in downtown Rochester (36 King St.) as a likely site while the fundraising proceeds. While living in Rochester from 1847 to 1872, Douglass published an anti-slavery newspaper, served as an adviser to President Abraham Lincoln, and worked with Susan B. Anthony for the abolitionist cause and the women's suffrage movement. The house in which Douglass and his family lived was one of the stops on the Underground Railroad that helped southern blacks to escape to freedom. It was destroyed by fire in 1872. An earlier Rochester museum project honoring Douglass, called the Frederick Douglass Museum and Cultural Center, failed in 2000 after one year of operation.

Frederick Douglass Museum (information not available).

Frederick Douglass Museum (Washington). The first home of African American leader and abolitionist Frederick Douglass in Washington, D.C., now is the Frederick Douglass Museum. He purchased the three-story house in 1871 and two years later added an adjoining structure. He and his family moved to Cedar Hill in 1877, but the house remained in the family until 1920.

The property and two adjoining houses now are occupied by the Caring Institute, an organization that promotes selflessness and public service and honors caring people in its Museum and Hall of Fame for Caring Americans. The Douglass house has been restored to the period when the family lived there. Visitors can see some of Douglass's personal items, including his original desk, photographs of him and his family, and a drawing by grandson Joseph Douglass, a concert violinist.

Frederick Douglass Museum, 320 A St., N.E., Washington, DC 20002. Phone: 202/547-4273. Fax: 202/547-4510. E-mail: *rdb@caring-institute.org.* Web site: www.nahc.org. Hours: Mon.–Fri. by appointment; closed major holidays. Admission: free.

George Washington Carver Memorial and Culture Center. A former elementary school that Dr. George Washington Carver dedicated and was named for him in Fulton, Missouri, is being recycled as the George Washington Carver Memorial and Culture Center. The public school for black children was opened in 1937, closed in the 1980s during school consolidation, and was acquired in 1989 for the cultural center. In addition to honoring Dr. Carver, the center will seek to provide historical, educational, cultural, and social services to the community and have a historical display of African American artifacts and memorabilia from the area.

George Washington Carver Memorial and Culture Center, 906 Westminster Ave., PO Box 344, Fulton, MO 65251. Phone: 573/642-2619. E-mail: *george@coin.org.* Hours and admission: still to be determined.

George Washington Carver Museum. The George Washington Carver Museum at the Tuskegee Institute in Tuskegee, Alabama, focuses on Dr. Carver's far-reaching career in agriculture, chemurgy, chemistry, and the development and growth of Tuskegee Institute. It contains Dr. Carver's personal memorabilia, manuscripts, and awards; natural history collections; paintings; needleworks; and artifacts and furnishings of Tuskegee Institute. The museum, which is housed in the institute's former laundry, is part of the Tuskegee Institute National Historic Site.

George Washington Carver Museum, Tuskegee Institute, 1212 Montgomery Rd., PO Drawer 10, Tuskegee, AL 36088. Phones: 334/727-6390 and 334/727-3200. Fax: 334/727-4597. Web sites: *www.nps.gov* and *http://bama.ua.edu/~almuseum/g_gwen.htm.* Hours: 9–4:30 daily; closed New Year's Day, Thanksgiving, and Christmas. Admission: free.

George Washington Carver Museum and Cultural Center. The George Washington Carver Museum and Cultural Center in Austin, Texas, is named for the noted African American botanist who advocated soil-enriching crops and developed over 300 derivative products from peanuts and 118 from sweet potatoes. The museum and center, part of the Austin Parks and Recreation Department, was the first neighborhood black history museum in Texas. It presents changing exhibitions and has permanent galleries on the history and evolution of Juneteenth, history of African Americans in the Austin area, and leading African American scientists and inventors.

George Washington Carver Museum and Cultural Center, 1165 Angelina St., Austin, TX. 78702. Phone:

512/974-4926. Fax: 512/974-3699. Web site: *www.ci.austin.tx.us/carver/location.htm.* Hours: 9:30–6 Mon., Wed., and Fri.; 9:30–8 Tues. and Thurs.; 1–5 Sat.; closed Sun. and major holidays. Admission: free.

Harriet Beecher Stowe Slavery to Freedom Center. The 1807 Georgian brick house in Washington, Kentucky, that once was the residence of Harriet Beecher Stowe, the anti-slavery author of *Uncle Tom's Cabin,* now is the site of the Harriet Beecher Stowe Slavery to Freedom Center. Beecher and her sister and father lived in the house from 1832 to 1835 while her Congregationalist minister father taught at the Lane Theological Seminary and she and her sister founded the Western Female Institute in nearby Cincinnati, Ohio. It was during that time that she witnessed a slave auction that influenced her life and the writing of the anti-slavery book.

The center contains slave documents and shackles, various other artifacts, copies of *Uncle Tom's Cabin* and other books written by Stowe, and photographs of Stowe and her family. Behind the museum is a small two-level brick structure with vertical slits (likely gun slits) — known as the Indian Fort — that helped early settlers ward off Indians.

Harriet Beecher Stowe Slavery to Freedom Museum, Old Main St., PO Box 184, Washington, KY 41096. Phone: 606/759-4860. Web site: *www.washingtonkentucky.com/museums/beecherstowe.html.* Hours: Mar.–Dec.—12–4 Sat.; closed remainder of week and year, but guided tours offered Mon.–Fri. by appointment through the Washington Visitor Center, 2215 Old Main St., 606/759-7411. Admission: $1.

Harriet Tubman Home. The frame house in Auburn, New York, where Harriet Tubman, known as the Moses of her people for helping over 300 slaves escape to the North on the Underground Railroad, lived at the turn of the twentieth century has been restored and now serves as a memorial to her life and work. Tubman escaped from a Maryland slave plantation in 1849, became a leading abolitionist, and served as a nurse, laundress, and spy with federal forces operating in South Carolina in the Civil War. The house was restored in 1953 under the auspices of the African Methodist Episcopal Zion Church.

Harriet Tubman Home, 180 South St., Auburn, NY 13201. Phone: 315/252-2081. E-mail: *hthome@localnet.com.* Hours: Feb.–Oct.—10–4 Tues.–Fri.; 10–3 Sat.; and remainder of year by appointment; closed Sun.–Mon. and major holidays. Admission: donation.

Harriet Tubman Museum and Educational Center. The life of Harriet Tubman, the former slave known for her role in the Underground Railroad and the abolitionist movement, is celebrated in the county of her birth and early years at the Harriet

Tubman Museum and Educational Center in Cambridge, Maryland. The storefront museum features exhibits and programs on her life and offers tours of places in Dorchester County where she lived, prayed, and worked. Efforts are under way to find a larger site for the museum.

Harriet Tubman Museum and Educational Center, 424 Race St., PO Box 1164, Cambridge, MD 21613. Phone: 410/228-0401. Web site: *www.harriet tubmanmuseum.org.* Hours: 10–2 Tues.–Fri. and alternate Mon. and Sat.; closed Sun. and major holidays. Admission: free.

Harvey W. Lee, Jr., Memorial Gallery. The Harvey W. Lee, Jr., Memorial Gallery, a component of the Mary McLeod Bethune Fine Arts Center at Bethune-Cookman College in Daytona Beach, Florida, honors a long-time professor of art at the college. The gallery has a permanent collection of African art and frequently presents changing exhibitions of works by local African American artists.

Harvey W. Lee, Jr., Memorial Gallery, Mary McLeod Bethune Fine Arts Center, Bethune-Cookman College, 1151 Lincoln St., Daytona Beach, FL 32114. Phone: 386/255-1401, Ext. 2711. Hours: 9–5 Mon.–Fri.; closed Sat.–Sun. and major holidays. Admission: free.

Howard Thurman House. The Rev. Howard Thurman, a nationally known theologian and author of 22 books, was the first African American to hold the post of dean (of Marsh Chapel) at a predominately white university (Boston University). He was the first black in Florida to pass the high school entrance examination. He also is remembered for leading a delegation to India, meeting Mahatma Gandhi, and then giving a sermon and writing a book, *Jesus and the Disinherited,* about Gandhi and his philosophy of nonviolent resistance that helped Dr. Martin Luther King, Jr., to shape his philosophy and leadership in the Civil Rights Movement. The ca. 1888 frame house in Daytona Beach, Florida, where Thurman was born and lived as a youth with his grandmother, now is a historic house with many of the original furnishings, photographs, and other materials.

Howard Thurman House, 614 Whitehall St., Daytona Beach., FL 32114. Phones: 386/822-7598 and 386/258-7514. Web site: *www.nps.gov/travel/civil rights/f2.htm.* Hours: by appointment. Admission: free.

I. P. Stanback Museum and Planetarium. The I. P. Stanback Museum and Planetarium at South Carolina State University in Orangeburg is named for Isreal Pinkney Stanback, a businessman, philanthropist, and first African American chairman of the university's board of trustees. The museum has

African and African American art collections and exhibits and an 82-seat planetarium with a 40-foot dome. It is one of the few museums with art and science offerings. Its holdings include contemporary African American art and photographs, bronze statuary from Benin, and over 200 works from the Cameroons and parts of West Africa.

I. P. Stanback Museum and Planetarium, South Carolina State University, 300 College St., N.E., PO Box 7636, Orangeburg, SC 29117. Phones: 803/536-7174 and 803/536-8711. Fax: 803/536-8309. E-mail: *starman@scsu.edu.* Web site: *www.dracp.scsu.edu.* Hours: museum — 9–4:30 Mon.–Fri.; closed Sat.–Sun.; planetarium — 3 and 4 every 2nd Sun. Admission: museum — free; planetarium — adults, $2; seniors and children, $1.

James E. Lewis Museum of Art. The James E. Lewis Museum of Art at Morgan State University in Baltimore, Maryland, is devoted largely to African American and African art. It is named for a former director, who was a sculptor, archaeologist, and art historian, in recognition of his role in the museum's growth and development. The museum, housed in the Carl J. Murphy Fine Arts Center, has a wide variety of nineteenth- and twentieth-century works that encompass American, Asian, European, and traditional African arts.

James E. Lewis Museum of Art, Morgan State University, 242 Carl J. Murphy Fine Arts Center, 1700 E. Coldspring Lane, Baltimore, MD 21251. Phones: 443/885-3030 and 443/885-3333. Fax: 443/885-8258. E-mail: *gtenabe@moac.morgan.edu.* Web site: *www.morgan.edu.* Hours: 10–4 Tues.–Fri.; 11–4 Sat.; 12–4 Sun.; closed Mon., Easter, Thanksgiving, and Christmas. Admission: free.

Jim Beckwourth Museum. Jim Beckwourth was an African American mountain man who roamed the American West and became an Indian war chief during the nineteenth century. The museum in his name near Portola, California, is housed in an 1850s log cabin he built as a trading post and hotel in Sierra Valley and from which he guided immigrant trains over the mountain pass he discovered and was named for him. The museum has exhibits on his life and serves as a trading post. Beckwourth was born in 1798 to a plantation owner and a slave woman. He was educated, emancipated, and apprenticed to a blacksmith before heading west, where he served as a mountain man, guide, interpreter, member of the Blackfoot tribe, and Crow Indian war chief. He left California in 1858 and spent the rest of his life in the Rockies and reportedly died among the Crows.

James Beckwourth Museum, 2081 Rocky Point Rd., PO Box 2367, Portola, CA 96122. Phone: 530/832-4888. Hours: Memorial Day–Labor Day —

1–4 Sat.–Sun.; closed Mon.–Fri.; remainder of year — by appointment. Admission: free.

John G. Riley Center/Museum of African American History and Culture. The John G. Riley Center/Museum of African American History and Culture in Tallahassee, Florida, is located in the restored 1890 John Gilmore Riley historic home in what once was a thriving black neighborhood. It is the last vestige of the accomplishments of an entire group of people — the African American middle class — that emerged in the area in the latter part of the nineteenth century.

Riley was the first African American principal of Lincoln High School in Tallahassee. His home was one of six owned by African Americans and others rented by blacks in the neighborhood east of downtown before being disrupted by a parkway expansion in the 1950s. The museum preserves and interprets the cultural and educational history of African Americans in the city and state from the Reconstruction era through the Civil Rights Movement. Its program components seek to develop an awareness and appreciation of the contributions of African Americans in Florida's history.

John G. Riley Center/Museum of African American History and Culture, 419 E. Jefferson St., Tallahassee, FL 32301 (mailing address: PO Box 4261, Tallahassee, FL 32315). Phone: 850/681-7881. Fax: 850/386-4368. E-mail: *staff@rileymuseum.org*. Web site: www.rileymuseum.org. Hours: 10–4 Mon.–Fri.; closed Sat.–Sun. and major holidays. Admission: adults, $2; members, $1.50.

Julee Cottage. Julee Cottage in Pensacola, Florida, is dedicated to the memory of Julee Panton, the legendary "free woman of color" who owned the 1804 cottage — one of the oldest houses in Pensacola and the only surviving one in the city reminiscent of the Creole cottages of the French Quarter in New Orleans. Panton became known for helping to purchase the freedom of enslaved blacks and assisting them in their lives.

The cottage is one of 11 buildings in Historic Pensacola Village operated by the University of West Florida. Many of the village's collection of 150,000 southeastern historical artifacts and archives are displayed in the historic structures. The Julee Cottage features an exhibit on African American history in west Florida, spanning the period from the slave era to modern times.

Julee Cottage, Historic Pensacola Village, 120 Church St., Pensacola, FL 32501 (mailing address: PO Box 12866, Pensacola, FL 32591). Phone: 850/595-5985. Fax: 850/595-5989. E-mail: *rbrosnaham@historicpensacola.org*. Web site: *www.historicpensacola.org*. Hours: June–mid–Aug.—10–4 Mon.–Sat.;

closed Sun.; remainder of year —10–4 Mon.–Fri.; closed Sat.–Sun. and state holidays. Admission: adults, $6; seniors and military, $5; children 4–16, $2.50; children under 4, free.

Lois E. Woods Museum. Art from 46 tribes in 14 African countries is exhibited at the Lois E. Woods Museum at Norfolk State University in Norfolk, Virginia. The museum was made possible by the Woods family in honor of the mother, who encouraged and assisted her collector son, John S. Woods, now director of the museum in the Lyman B. Brooks Library. John began collecting African and African American art and memorabilia as a child. In addition to giving early encouragement to her son, Lois E. Woods and her husband later contributed to the collection.

Lois E. Woods Museum, Norfolk State University, Lyman B. Brooks Library, 2401 Corfew Ave., Norfolk, VA 23504 (mailing address: 700 Park Ave., Norfolk, VA 23504). Phone: 757/823-2006. Fax: 757/823-2899. Web site: *www.nsu.edu/resources/woods/index.htm*. Hours: 9–5 Mon.–Fri.; other times by appointment; closed major holidays. Admission: free.

Lucy Craft Laney Museum of Black History and Conference Center. The Lucy Craft Laney Museum of Black History and Conference Center in Augusta, Georgia, seeks to further the legacy of Mrs. Laney, an educator who devoted her life to providing educational services to African American children. She began offering instruction in a church basement, eventually growing into a private school with over 1,000 students. One of her students was Mary McLeod Bethune, who developed into the nation's leading black educator. The museum, located in the restored Laney home in the historic Walker District of Augusta, focuses on the history and contributions of African Americans in the Augusta and central Savannah River areas. The facility also has a computer center, period garden, and conference center.

Lucy Craft Laney Museum of Black History and Conference Center, 1116 Phillips St., Augusta, GA 30901. Phone: 706/724-3576. Fax: 706/724-3576. E-mail: *info@lucycraftlaneymuseum.com*. Web site: *www.lucycraftmuseum.com*. Hours: 9–5 Tues.–Fri.; 10–4 Sat.; 2–5 Sun.; closed Mon. and major holidays. Admission: adults, $3; students and children 6–17, $1; children under 6, free.

Marian Anderson Birthplace and Marian Anderson Residence/Museum. A historic district named for Marian Anderson, the great contralto, in Philadelphia, Pennsylvania, includes her birthplace and former residence (now a museum). Anderson was born in 1897 in the small house that now features a room with information and memorabilia about her childhood, and she lived in the house from 1924 to 1990. The museum contains memorabilia, music, photographs, newspaper clippings, and other materials about her life and career. The site was opened in 1998 by the Marian Anderson Historical Society. Anderson was the first African American to become a permanent member of the Metropolitan Opera Company in 1955, and the first African American to perform in the White House in Washington. In 1958, she served as an alternate delegate to the United Nations.

Marian Anderson Birthplace, 1833 Marian Anderson Pl., and Marian Anderson Residence/Museum, 762 S. Marian Anderson Way, Philadelphia, PA 19146 (mailing address: Marian Anderson Historical Society, 752 S. Marian Anderson Way, Philadelphia, PA 19146-1822.). Phone: 215/732-9505. Fax: 215/732-1247. Web site: *www.mariananderson.org.* Hours: by appointment. Admission: adults, $10 donation; seniors and children under 12, $5 donation.

Marian Anderson Studio. The studio cottage where contralto Marian Anderson practiced during most of her professional life is now part of the Danbury Museum and Historical Society complex in downtown Danbury, Connecticut. The studio originally was located at Marianna Farm in Danbury, where Anderson and her husband, architect Orpheus "King" Fisher, lived for more than 50 years.

After Anderson's death, the property was sold and the historical society bought and moved the studio to its collection of seven other historical buildings — partly with funding from the Daughters of the American Revolution. It was in 1939 that the DAR barred Anderson from performing at its Constitution Hall, which had a "whites only" policy. The studio tells of Anderson's life and career and contains many of her concert gowns, a baby grand piano, and vintage record covers, magazine covers, photos, and programs. Guided tours are offered of the Anderson studio and other historical buildings in the complex.

Marian Anderson Studio, Danbury Museum and Historical Society, 43 Main St., Danbury, CT 06810. Phone: 203/7435200. Fax: 203/743-1131. E-mail: *dmhs@danburyhistorical.org.* Web site: *www.danbury historical.org.* Hours: Tues.-Thurs. by appointment. Admission: adults, $6; seniors, $5; students, $2; children under 5, free.

Martin Luther King, Jr., Center for Nonviolent Social Change. The Martin Luther King, Jr., Center for Nonviolent Change in Atlanta, Georgia, was established by Dr. King's widow, Coretta Scott King, as the living memorial and institutional guardian of his legacy. The center, located in the

Martin Luther King, Jr., National Historic Site, develops and disseminates programs to further Dr. King's philosophy and methods of nonviolence, human relations, service to mankind, and related teachings.

The 1895 house where Dr. King was born and his tomb are located at the site, which also has furnishings of the King family, personal effects of Dr. King, a manuscript collection, memorabilia donated by the public, and works by artists in memory of Dr. King. The center has a Freedom Hall and Walk, eternal flame, chapel, library, and archival and museum materials pertaining to Dr. King, black history, and the Civil Rights Movement. Permanent and temporary exhibits are presented. More than 650,000 people visit the King Center annually.

Martin Luther King, Jr., Center for Nonviolent Social Change, 449 Auburn Ave., N.E., Atlanta, GA 30312. Phone: 404/526-8900. Fax: 404/526-8932. E-mail: *information@thekingcenter.org.* Web site: *www.thekingcenter.org.* Hours: June–Aug.— 9–6 daily; remainder of year — 8:30–5:30 Mon.–Sat.; 9–8 Sun.; closed national holidays. Admission: free.

Mary McLeod Bethune Home. The former home of Mary McLeod Bethune, founder of Bethune-Cookman College in Daytona Beach, Florida, is a memorial to Mrs. Bethune, one of the best known African American leaders from the 1920s through World War II. The fifteenth child of parents who were former slaves, Bethune became a missionary and educator who opened a school for African American girls that merged with the Cookman Institute for Boys to form Bethune-Cookman College in 1923.

She became a major figure in education and civil rights, served as advisor to five American presidents, and was appointed director of Negro affairs in the National Youth Administration in 1936 by President Franklin D. Roosevelt. The two-story frame house on the campus was her home until her death in 1955. The house, which became a national historic landmark, still has all her furnishings and is maintained as a museum with artifacts, citations, and photographs, with an attached building serving as an archive for the Bethune papers. Her gravesite also is on the property.

Mary McLeod Bethune Home, Bethune-Cookman College, 640 Mary McLeod Bethune Blvd., Daytona Beach, FL 32114. Phone: 386/255-1401, Ext. 372. Hours: Sept.–May — 9–4 Mon.–Fri.; closed Sat.–Sun. and major holidays; June–Aug.— by appointment. Admission: free.

Mary Walker Memorial Museum. Mary Walker, a former slave who became the nation's oldest student, is memorialized at the Mary Walker Memorial Museum in Chattanooga, Tennessee. She was 117 years old when she learned reading, writing, and arithmetic in the Chattanooga-area literacy movement. She was 121 when she died. The museum, housed in a replica plantation house that has re-created slave quarters, tells the Mary Walker story and has exhibits on the literacy and civil rights movements and the contributions of African Americans during and after the Civil War.

Mary Walker Museum, 3031 Wilcox Blvd., Chattanooga, TN 37411. Phone: 423/629-7651. Fax: 423/267-2414. Hours: by appointment. Admission: donation.

Mattye Reed African Heritage Center. More than 30 African nations, New Guinea, and Haiti are represented in the collections and exhibits at the Mattye Reed African Heritage Center at North Carolina Agricultural and Technical State University in Greensboro. The center, which has over 3,500 art and craft works, is named for the wife of a faculty member who started the museum with her extensive collection of African arts and crafts.

Mattye Reed African Heritage Center, North Carolina A&T State University, Greensboro, NC 27411. Phone: 336/334-3209. Fax: 336/334-4378. Hours: 10–5 Tues.–Fri.; 1–5 Sat.; closed Sun.–Mon. and major holidays. Admission: free.

Melvin B. Tolson Black Heritage Center. The Melvin B. Tolson Black Heritage Center at Langston University in Langston, Oklahoma, is named for the prominent African American modernist poet and playwright who taught at the university and was poet laureate of Liberia. The center, located in Sandford Hall, features African and African American history, culture, and art exhibits. Langston is one of the many towns established by blacks who migrated from the South to the North and West after slavery.

Melvin B. Tolson Black Heritage Center, Langston University, Sandford Hall, PO Box 1600, Langston, OK 73050. Phone: 405/466-3239. Hours: late Aug.–mid–May — 8–5 Mon.–Fri. (also to 10 Tues. and Thurs.); 2–10 Sun.; closed Sat., major holidays, and remainder of year. Admission: free.

Newsome House Museum and Cultural Center. The elegant 1899 Victorian residence of J. Thomas Newsome, a highly regarded black attorney, journalist, churchman, and civic leader in Newport News, Virginia, has become a center of African American history and culture. The restored Queen Anne house was the hub of the local black community from which Newsome led the fight for social justice within the commonwealth during the early twentieth century. The museum contains collections and exhibits of local African American history and culture, Anderson Johnson folk art, and Newsome family personal papers.

Newsome House Museum and Cultural History, 2803 Oak Ave., Newport News, VA 23607. Phones: 757/247-2360 and 757/247-2380. Fax: 757/928-6754. E-mail: *mkayaselcuk@nngov.com.* Web site: *www.newsomehouse.org.* Hours: Apr.–Dec.—10–4 Wed.–Sat.; 1–5 Sun.; closed Mon.–Tues. and major holidays; remainder of year—10–4 Mon. and Thurs.–Sat.; 1–5 Sun.; closed Tues.–Wed. Admission: free.

Paul Laurence Dunbar State Monument. The Italianate turn-of-the-century house that was the home of writer and poet Paul Laurence Dunbar in Dayton, Ohio, now is a state monument. Dunbar, who was known as the "poet laureate of African Americans," gave voice to the social dilemma of disenfranchised people of his day and became a proclaimer of black dignity. It was the first state monument to honor an African American.

Dunbar produced a body of work that included novels, plays, short stories, lyrics, and more than 400 published poems. He was ill most of his life, and died of tuberculosis at the age of 34 in 1906. The Dunbar house has been renovated and restored to furnishings and wallpapers of the period, and a visitor center with interpretive panels chronicling Dunbar's life has added to the site. The memorial also is part of the Dayton Aviation Heritage National Historical Park that honors Wilbur and Orville Wright and Dunbar (see separate listing).

Paul Laurence Dunbar State Monument, 219 Paul Laurence Dunbar St., PO Box 1872, Dayton, OH 45401. Phones: 937/224-7061 and 800/860-0148. Fax: 937/224-4256. E-mails: *paul33@sbcglobal.net* and *lsci@ohiohistory.org.* Web site: *www.ohiohistory.org/places/dunbar.* Hours: Memorial Day weekend–Labor Day — 9–5 Wed.–Sat.; 12–5 Sun.; closed Mon.–Tues.; Apr.–late May — 9–5 Sat.–Sun.; closed Mon.–Fri.; early Sept.–Oct.— 9:30–5 Sat.–Sun.; closed Mon.–Fri. and remainder of year. Admission: adults, $6; children 6–12, $3; children under 5, free.

Paul Robeson Art Gallery. The art gallery at the Paul Robeson Campus Center at Rutgers University in Newark, New Jersey, is named for the noted African American stage and movie actor and singer. It features changing artworks and photography exhibitions.

Paul Robeson Art Gallery, Rutgers University–Newark, Paul Robeson Campus Center, 350 Dr. Martin Luther King, Jr. Blvd., Newark, NJ 07102. Phone: 973/353-1610. Fax: 973/353-5912. E-mail: *galleryr@andromeda.rutgers.edu.* Web site: *www.andromeda.rutgers.edu/artgallery.* Hours: 11–5 Tues. and Thurs., 1–6 Wed.; closed Fri.–Mon. and major holidays. Admission: free.

Paul Robeson Cultural Center. The Paul Robeson Cultural Center at Pennsylvania State University in University Park honors the African American stage and movie actor and singer. The center exhibits African, African American, and Caribbean works in its gallery, as well as art by Asian Pacific, Hispanic-Latino, Native American, Alaskan Islands, and multicultural artists. Its library features books by and about African Americans and includes materials on black people of the Caribbean, Latin America, and Africa. Speakers, films, plays, and musical presentations also are offered at the center.

Paul Robeson Cultural Center, Pennsylvania State University, HUB-Robeson Center, University Park, PA 16802. Phone: 814/865-3776. Web site: *www.sa.psu.edu/prcc/facilities.shtml*. Hours: Sept.–May— 7:30 A.M.–11 P.M. Mon.–Fri.; 1–4 Sat.; closed Sun. and major holidays; June–Aug.— varies. Admission: free.

Peter Mott House and Museum. The Peter Mott House and Museum in the historically African American community of Lawnside, New Jersey, was a safe house on the Underground Railroad for southern blacks seeking freedom in the nineteenth century. Mott, a free black man who was a plasterer, farmer, and ordained minister, purchased the two-story frame house for $100 in 1844. It has been restored and opened as a historic house museum by the Lawnside Historical Society, which conducts tours of the house. Parts of the hand-built lath-and-plaster walls by Mott were retained during restoration to show his workmanship.

Peter Mott House and Museum, 26 King St., PO Box 608, Lawnside, NJ 08045-0508. Phone: 856/546-8850. E-mail: *lhs@petermotthouse.org*. Web site: *www.petermotthouse.org*. Hours: 12–3 Sat.; closed remainder of week. Admission: $2 per person.

Prudence Crandall Museum. The Prudence Crandall Museum in Canterbury, Connecticut, was the site of New England's first academy for black girls in 1833 and 1834. It was opened by Prudence Crandall, who began an academy in 1832 at the request of the community to educate the daughters of wealthy local families. It was extremely successful until Sarah Harris, a 20-year-old black woman, was admitted. The admittance led white parents to withdraw their daughters. Crandall then announced she was reopening the school for "young ladies and little misses of color."

More than 20 young black women from throughout New England enrolled as students. The state of Connecticut responded by passing the Black Law, which made it illegal for Crandall to operate her school. When she persisted, he was arrested and faced trial, but the case was dismissed. However, a mob attack on the academy in 1834 forced the school to close four years before the Black Law was repealed. The museum, housed in the 1805 Prudence Crandall house, now tells the story and features three period rooms with changing exhibitions.

Prudence Crandall Museum, Rts. 14 and 169, Canterbury Green, PO Box 58, Canterbury, CT 06331-0058. Phone: 860/546-9916. Fax: 860/546-7803. E-mail: *cmdll@snet.net*. Web site: *www.chc.state.ct.us/crandall%20musewn.htm*. Hours: Apr.–mid–Dec.— 10–4:30 Wed.–Sun.; closed Mon.–Tues., remainder of year, and major holidays. Admission: adults, $3; seniors and children 6–17, $2; children under 6, free.

Ralph Mark Gilbert Civil Rights Museum. The Ralph Mark Gilbert Civil Rights Museum in Savannah, Georgia, is named in honor of Dr. Ralph Mark Gilbert, an NAACP leader and father of Savannah's Civil Rights Movement. It is devoted to the history of the movement, and conducts African American historical tours.

Ralph Mark Gilbert Civil Rights Museum, 460 Martin Luther King, Jr., Blvd., Savannah, GA 31401. Phone: 912/231-8900. Fax: 912/234-2577. Web site: *www.savannahcivilrightsmuseum.com*. Hours: 9–5 Mon.–Sat.; closed Sun. and major holidays. Admission: adults, $4; seniors, $3; students, $2.

Reginald F. Lewis Museum of Maryland African American History and Culture. Maryland's African American history and culture are presented in the new Reginald F. Lewis Museum of Maryland African American History and Culture in Baltimore. The museum, which opened in 2005 near the city's inner harbor with state support, is named for the entrepreneur and philanthropist who served as chairman and chief executive officer of TLC Beatrice International, the largest company owned by an African American in the nation. It is dedicated to sharing the courageous journeys toward freedom and self-determination made by African Americans in Maryland.

Reginald F. Lewis Museum of Maryland African American History and Culture, 830 E. Pratt St., Baltimore, MD 21202. Phone: 443/263-1800. Web site: *www.africanamericanculture.org*. Hours: 10–5 Tues.– Sun.; closed Mon. and major holidays. Admission: adults, $8; seniors and college students, $6; children under 7, free.

Rosa Parks Library and Museum. The Rosa Parks Library and Museum in Montgomery, Alabama, is dedicated to the African American seamstress who launched the pivotal event in the Civil Rights Movement in 1955 by refusing to yield her seat on a public bus to a white man. That courageous act resulted in the Montgomery bus boycott that led to the Civil Rights Movement and the banning of bus service segregation. The museum, located at the site where Mrs. Parks made her historic stand, occupies the first floor of the building that also contains Troy University's Montgomery Campus Library. The exhibits describe the work of Mrs. Parks and other early civil rights workers and include a replica of the bus in which Mrs. Parks was sitting that eventful day in 1955.

Rosa Parks Library and Museum, 251 Montgomery St., Montgomery, AL 36604. Phone: 334/241-8615. Web site: *http://montgomery.troy.edu/rosaparks/museum.* Hours: 9–5 Mon.–Fri.; 9–3 Sat.; closed Sun. and major holidays. Admission: adults and children over 12, $5.50; children under 13, $3.50.

Schomburg Center for Research in Black Culture. The Schomburg Center for Research in Black Culture, a part of the New York Public Library system, is a national research library devoted to collecting, preserving, and providing access to resources documenting the experiences of peoples of African descent throughout the world. It is named for Arturo Alfonso Schomburg, the Puerto Rican-born black scholar and bibliophile whose personal collection began the center in 1926 and who later served as curator.

The center now has five divisions with over 5 million items, including art objects, audio and video tapes, books, manuscripts, motion picture films, newspapers, periodicals, photographs, prints, recorded music discs, and sheet music. The center interprets its collections through exhibitions, publications, and educational, scholarly, and cultural programs. It includes an extensive traveling exhibition program on the history and culture of African descent peoples.

Schomburg Center for Research in Black Culture, New York Public Library, 515 Malcolm X Blvd., New York, NY 10037-1891. Phone: 212/491-2200. Web site: *www.nypl.org/research/hours/schours.htm.* Hours: hours vary with divisions, but all closed Sun.–Mon. and major holidays. Admission: free.

Scott Joplin State Historic Site. The restored home in St. Louis, Missouri, where renowned ragtime composer Scott Joplin and his bride, Belle Hayden, lived in the early twentieth century now is a national historic landmark and a state historic site. Joplin was living in one of the flats in the two-story row house in 1902 — one of his most productive years — when eight of his compositions, including *The Entertainer,* were published. The historic structure contains exhibits on Joplin's life and work and a music room with a player piano and piano rolls that enable visitors to listen to ragtime jazz as Joplin played it.

Scott Joplin State Historic Site, 2658 Delmar Blvd., St. Louis, MO 63103. Phone: 314/340-5790. Hours: 10–4 Mon.–Sat.; 12–5 Sun.; closed major holidays. Admission: adults, $2.50; children 6–12, $1.50; children under 6, free.

Smith Robertson Museum and Cultural Center. The city-operated Smith Robertson Museum and Cultural Center, which got its name from the former school building in which it is housed in Jackson, Mississippi, uses art, artifacts, and photography to increase public understanding and awareness of the historical experiences and cultural expressions of people of African descent. The school was the first public school built for African Americans in Jackson, opening in 1894 and then being burned, replaced, and expanded before closing in 1971. The school was named for Smith Robinson, a former slave who became a barber, political leader, and the first black alderman in Jackson.

Smith Robertson Museum, 528 Bloom St., Jackson, MS 39202-4005. Phone: 601/960-1457. Fax: 601/960-2070. Web site: *www.jacksonms.gov/visitors/museums/smithrobertson.* Hours: 8–5 Mon.–Fri.; closed Sat.–Sun. and school holidays and vacations. Admission: free.

Tubman African American Museum. The Tubman African American Museum in Macon, Georgia, is dedicated to the spirit of Harriet Tubman, a leading abolitionist who helped more than 300 slaves escape to the North on the Underground Railroad. But it is more than a personal tribute. The museum seeks to educate people about African American art, history, and culture. It has 14 galleries, including the Noel Collection of African Art, with 2,000-year-old Nok figures, beaded Yoruba wall panels, and Benin bronzes. Other galleries feature such diverse topics as local African American history, cuisines of Africa and America, and African American military leaders.

Tubman African American Museum, 340 Walnut St., Macon, GA (mailing address: PO Box 6671, Macon, GA 31208). Phone: 478/743-8544. Fax: 478/743-9063. E-mail: *cpickard@tubmanmuseum. com.* Web site: *www.tubmanmuseum.com.* Hours: 9–5 Mon.–Sat.; 2–5 Sun.; closed major holidays. Admission: adults and children over 12, $5; children under 13, $3.

W. C. Handy Museum and Library. The W. C. Handy Museum and Library in Florence, Alabama, honors the African American composer and musician known as the "father of the blues." Handy, who was born in the Florence house in 1873, wrote more than 150 secular and sacred musical compositions, including *Memphis Blues, Saint Louis Blues,* and *Yellow Dog Blues.* He was the first to codify and publish songs in what became the blues. He created his own blues form by combining spirituals of the South with chant melodies and rhythms from Africa. In 1918, he opened a publishing firm in New York and operated it through two onsets of blindness. The second became permanent. The museum-library contains Handy's personal papers, trumpet, piano, handwritten sheet music, library, furnishings, citations, photographs, and memorabilia.

W. C. Handy Birthplace, Museum, and Library, 620 W. College St., Florence, AL 35630 (mailing address: 217 Tuscaloosa St., Florence, AL 35630). Phone: 256/760-6434. Fax: 256/760-6382. E-mail: *bbroach@florenceal.org*. Hours: 10–4 Tues.–Sat.; closed Sun.–Mon. and major holidays. Admission: adults, $2; children, 50¢.

Wright-Dunbar Interpretive Center. The Wright-Dunbar Interpretive Center at the Dayton Aviation Heritage National Historical Park in Dayton, Ohio, interprets the lives and contributions of aviation pioneers Wilbur and Orville Wright and the gifted African American writer and poet Paul Laurence Dunbar (see Paul Lawrence Dunbar State Monument). The center is housed in two renovated buildings that are historically associated with both the Wright brothers and Dunbar. The Wright brothers' printing office was located at the site in 1890–95 and Dunbar's newspaper, *The Dayton Tattler,* was printed there. Dunbar was an internationally acclaimed writer whose works ranged from novels, plays, and short stories to lyrics and poems. The national historical park consists of four separate units — the interpretive center, Huffman Prairie Flying Field, Carillon Park, and the Dunbar State Memorial.

Wright-Dunbar Interpretive Center, Dayton Aviation Heritage National Historical Park, 30 S. Williams St., Dayton, OH 45407 (mailing address: Wright-Dunbar Inc., 1105 W. 3rd St., Dayton, OH 45407). Phones: 937/225-7705 and 937/443-0249. Fax: 937/443-0207. Web site: *www.wright-dunbar. org*. Hours: 8:30–5 daily. Admission: free.

Zora Neale Hurston House. Zora Neale Hurston was a Harlem Renaissance author who was born in the historically black town of Eatonville, Florida, was educated and became a best-selling author in New York, and later continued her writing and worked for a newspaper in Fort Pierce, Florida. The Zora Neale Hurston House, a one-story, concrete-block structure in Fort Pierce, is the only known residence associated with her life that still exists. It now is a private home and visitors may only walk or drive by. A branch library also has been named in Hurston's honor in Fort Pierce. See separate listing for Zora Neale Hurston National Museum of Fine Arts in her hometown of Eatonville.

Zora Neale Hurston House, 1734 School Court St., Fort Pierce, FL 34949. Not open to the public.

Zora Neale Hurston National Museum of Fine Arts. The Zora Neale Hurston National Museum of Fine Arts honors the gifted Harlem Renaissance writer and cultural anthropologist in her hometown of Eatonville, Florida, the oldest incorporated African American town in the nation. She was widely regarded as the most significant interpreter of southern American life during the 1920s and 1930s. Among her novels were *Tell My Horse, Their Eyes Were Watching God,* and the autobiographical *Dusk Tracks on a Road.* Despite her successes in the 1930s and 1940s, she died nearly penniless in a welfare home in 1960.

The museum displays the works of emerging and established artists of African descent in four exhibitions each year. The Zora Neale Hurston Memorial Park also has been established in her honor in Eatonville, and an annual arts and humanities festival that celebrates African American culture is held in her memory in the community. Also see separate listing for Zora Neale Hurston House, which tells of her experiences as a reporter in Fort Pierce, Florida.

Zora Neale Hurston National Museum of Fine Arts, 227 E. Kennedy Blvd., Eatonville, FL 32751. Phone: 407/647-3307. Hours: 9–4 Mon.–Fri.; closed Sat.–Sun. and major holidays. Admission: free.

Zora Neale Hurston Memorial Park, 11 People St., Eatonville, FL 32751. Phone: 407/623-1166. Hours: open 24 hours. Admission: free.

Historic Sites

Battle of Fort Wagner, Morris Island. The second 1863 Civil War battle for Fort Wagner on Morris Island at the entrance to the Charleston, South Carolina, harbor was led by the 54th Massachusetts Colored Infantry, the first major American unit comprised of African Americans. They stormed Fort Wagner after the first assault by Union troops had failed. The black soldiers fought valiantly and entered the heavily fortified Confederate stronghold, only to be driven back with heavy losses, as portrayed in the motion picture *Glory.*

Although the attack failed, the battle against almost hopeless odds proved the valor of the black troops if given the chance. It also resulted in additional African Americans joining the army and giving a North a further numerical advantage over the South. Fort Wagner finally was taken by Union forces when Confederates abandoned it after 58 days of heavy shelling. The fort now is underwater.

Fort Wagner, Morris Island, Charleston, SC. Now underwater.

Booker T. Washington National Monument. The Booker T. Washington National Monument in Hardy, Virginia, honors the African American educator who was born in slavery and founded Tuskegee Institute in Alabama in 1881. It is located on the site of the Burroughs Plantation, a tobacco farm, which was his birthplace and early home. Washington became an important and controversial African American leader at a time when increasing racism in the nation made it necessary for blacks to adjust to a new era of legalized oppression. The site is a living-history farm with plantation equipment and exhibits on black history and the life and times of Washington.

Booker T. Washington National Monument, 12130 Booker T. Washington Hwy., Hardy, VA 24101. Phone: 540/721-2094. Fax: 540/721-8311. Web site: *www.nps.gov/bowa.* Hours: 9–5 daily; closed New Year's Day, Thanksgiving, and Christmas. Admission: free.

Boone Hall Plantation. The historic Boone Hall Plantation in Mt. Pleasant, South Carolina, contains a 1680s Slave Street with nine original slave row houses. The plantation's primary commodities were rice and pecans. Brick slave quarters dating to the 1740s and the plantation house built in the 1930s are open to the public. One of the slave cabins was used in Alex Haley's movie *Queen* starring Halle Berry. The working plantation's current farming operation — known as Boone Hall Farms — produces strawberries, peaches, tomatoes, and other fruits and vegetables.

Boone Hall Plantation, 1235 Long Point Rd., Mt. Pleasant, SC 29464. Phone: 843/884-4371. Fax: 843/884-0475. Hours: May–Oct.— 8:30–6:30 Mon.–Sat.; 1–5 Sun.; remainder of year — 9–5 Mon.–Sat.; 1–4 Sun.; closed major holidays. Admission: adults, $14.50; seniors, $13; children 6–12, $7; children under 6, free.

Boston African American National Historic Site. Fifteen pre–Civil War structures relating to Boston's nineteenth-century African American community are part of the Boston African American National Historic Site in the heart of the city's Beacon Hill neighborhood. National Park Service rangers offer tours of the 1.6-mile Black Heritage Trail that begins at Augustus Saint-Gaudens' 1897 memorial to Robert Gould Shaw and African American Massachusetts 54th Regiment, the first black regiment to be recruited in the North during the Civil War.

Among the historic structures along the trail are the 1806 African Meeting House, the oldest standing African American church in the United States, and the 1834 Abiel Smith School, the nation's first schoolhouse to educate black children. Both are open to the public, but other buildings are privately owned.

Boston African American National Historic Site, 14 Beacon St., Suite 503, Boston, MA 02108. Phone: 617/742-5415. Fax: 617/720-0848. E-mail: *boaf@nps. gov.* Web site: *www.nps.gov/boaf.* Hours: 10–4 Mon.–Sat.; closed Sun., New Year's Day, Thanksgiving, and Christmas. Admission: free.

Central High School National Historic Site. Little Rock Central High School in Little Rock, Arkansas, was the site of the highly publicized local school confrontation following the 1954 Supreme Court decision integrating public schools. It was the first important test for the implementation of the *Brown v. Board of Education of Topeka* decision. The school now is a national historic site, and a visitor center, across the street from the school in a former gas station, traces and interprets the Little Rock school crisis.

In 1957, nine African American tried to enroll in the all-white Central High School and were turned away by a threatening and shouting crowd of whites. It was followed by Governor Orval Faubus calling out the National Guard to preserve order and prevent the students' enrollment. It was only after President Dwight D. Eisenhower federalized the Arkansas National Guard and sent a detachment of the 101st Airborne Division to protect the nine black students that they were able to attend the school. After an initial hostile reception, they were accepted with respect by other students and followed by the enrollment of other black students.

Central High School National Historic Site Visitor Center, 2125 Daisy L. Gatson Bates Dr., Little Rock, AR 72202. Phone: 501/374-1957. Fax: 501/376-4728. E-mail: *chsc_visitor_center@nps.gov.* Web site: *www. centralhigh57.org* and *www.nps.gov/chsc.* Hours: 9–4:30 Mon.–Sat.; 1–4:30 Sun.; closed New Year's Day, Thanksgiving, and Christmas. Admission: free.

Colonel Allensworth State Historic Park. The Colonel Allensworth State Historic Park near Earlimart, California, was the site of the only California town that was founded, financed, and governed by African Americans. The small farming community was started in 1908 by Colonel Allen Allensworth, a Civil War navy officer and later Baptist minister and army chaplain, and a group of others determined to live and work without prejudice and to improve the economic and social status of African Americans.

The town became a thriving community of 200 African Americans, but a number of uncontrollable circumstances, including a drop in the water table and the 1930s Depression, caused the demise of the town. The site now is coming back to life as a state historic park with continuing restoration and special events. About 20 wooden buildings have been restored to their 1911 to 1914 style, including the library, schoolhouse, and Allensworth's home. A visitor center features a film about the site and an annual rededication ceremony reaffirms the vision of Allensworth and the black pioneers.

Colonel Allensworth State Historic Park, County Rd. J22, Star Rte. 1, Box 148, Earlimart, CA 93219. Phone: 661/849-3433. Fax: 661/849-8412. Web site: *www.parks.ca.gov/?page_id=583*. Hours: park — open 24 hours; visitor center —10–4 daily. Admission: free.

Dade Battlefield State Historic Site. The Dade Battlefield State Historic Site near Bushnell, Florida, is where the second Seminole War began in 1835 when Seminole Indians and escaped African American slaves who lived with the Seminoles ambushed pursuing federal troops and took the lives of Major Francis L. Dade and all but three of his 108 men. Dade's mission was to move the Indians west of the Mississippi and to return the fugitive slaves to their owners.

The slaves had escaped from Georgia and the Carolinas and many had been free for more than a generation. They used their superior knowledge of the Everglades swamps to put up a fierce struggle, but federal forces and militias from several states eventually overpowered them and the Seminoles. After the seven-year Seminole War ended in 1842, many of the defeated Indians and African Americans were forced to march to the new territory of Oklahoma. The first Seminole War of 1817 to 1818 also was caused partly by the harboring of runaway slaves. The historic battle site now has a visitor center that tells the story of the Dade battlefield and the Seminole wars.

Dade Battlefield State Historic Site, 7200 County Rd., 603 S. Battlefield Dr., Bushnell, FL 33513. Phone: 352/7934781. Fax: 352/793-4230. E-mail: *chuck.wicks@dep.state.us.fl.* Web site: *www.florida stateparks.org.* Hours: site — 8–sunset daily; visitor center — 9–5 daily. Admission: vehicle, $2; pedestrian or bicyclist, $1.

Fort Gadsden State Historic Site. During the War of 1812, the British built a fort along the Apalachicola River southwest of present-day Sumatra, Florida, with the permission of Spanish authorities. It served as a base for the recruitment of Indians and blacks against the United States. After the war, the British commander left the fort — together with substantial arms and 700 kegs of gunpowder — to a group of free blacks, escaped slaves, and Indians. The post, which became known as the Negro Fort, attracted more African American settlers who farmed and traded along the river.

General Andrew Jackson became alarmed at the Negro Fort's expanding activities and built another fort, Fort Scott, nearby to watch over the other fort. A conflict soon broke out between the two sides that involved artillery and federal gunboats. During one artillery exchange, an artillery shot from attacking American gunboats struck the Negro Fort's powder magazine and blew up the fort, killing 270 people.

In 1818, General Jackson, while leading a force down the Apalachicola River to destroy Seminole Indian villages, directed Lt. James Gadsden of the Engineer Corps to built a fortification at the site as a supply base. Despite Spanish protests, the fort, called Fort Gadsden, was maintained until Florida was ceded to the United States. During the Civil War, it became a Confederate fort. The historic site still has the earthworks marking the fort's location, and an interpretive center features a miniature replica of Fort Gadsden and six exhibits on the site's history.

Fort Gadsden State Historic Site, County Rd. 129 off Hwy. 65, PO Box 157, Sumatra, FL 32335. Phone: 904/670-8616. Hours: 9–5 daily. Admission: free.

Fort Mose State Historic Site. Fort Mose State Historic Site, located in Anastasia State Park two miles north of the Castillo de San Marcos National Monument in St. Augustine, Florida, is a national historic landmark that was the first legally sanctioned free black settlement in North America. By the late 1600s, black slaves learned they could escape their British masters and find freedom in Spanish Florida if they embraced Catholicism and pledged to serve the Spanish crown. Many adopted Spanish names and customs. In 1738, the governor in Spanish Florida granted the blacks a plot of land where they could build their own settlement and a fort that became Fort Mose, an earthen-walled enclosure with Indian-type thatched huts and a population of about 100 inhabitants. In exchange for the land, the Spanish felt that the black militia could protect the northern approaches to Castillo de San Marcos and St. Augustine.

In 1740, British General James Oglethorpe captured Fort Mose and the inhabitants fled to St. Augustine. But a few weeks later Francisco Menendez, leader of the Fort Mose community, retook the fort. However, the battle destroyed the fort and it was not rebuilt until 1752. The former enslaved Africans from English colonies lived there until 1763 when the First Treaty of Paris gave Florida to Great Britain and the inhabitants of Fort Mose and most residents of Spanish St. Augustine relocated to Cuba. The fort fell into ruin and eventually disappeared. It was not until the middle of the twentieth century that researchers bound evidence of the fort in a marsh and uncovered the story of Fort Mose. Although there is no public access to the actual fort site because of the marsh, the 34-acre historic site does have a newly opened visitor center with exhibits and artifacts.

Fort Mose State Historic Site, Anastasia State Park, Saratoga Blvd. (off U.S. Rte. 1), St. Augustine, FL 32084. Phone: 904/461-2033. Hours: 8–sundown daily. Admission: free.

Frederick Douglass National Historic Site. The 1877 to 1895 home of Frederick Douglass in Washington, D.C., is a national historic site. Douglass, a former slave who became the nation's leading nineteenth-century African American spokesman, was an abolitionist who sought to abolish slavery and to further human, equal, and civil rights for all oppressed peoples. He lived in the 20-room brick home on Cedar Hill during the last 17 years of his life. National Park Service rangers conduct tours of the historic site, which contains many of Douglass' original furnishings and personal items. An earlier Douglass home in Washington is a historic house museum, and efforts are under way to open a museum in his honor in Rochester, New York, where he lived and worked for 25 years.

Frederick Douglass National Historic Site, 1411 W St., S.E., Washington, DC 20020. Phone: 202/426-5961. Fax: 202/426-0880. Web site: *www.nps.gov/frdo*. Hours: mid–Apr.–mid–Oct.— 9–5 daily; remainder of year — 9–4 daily; closed New Year's Day, Thanksgiving, and Christmas. Admission: free; guided tour, $2.

George Washington Carver National Monument. The site in Diamond, Missouri, where scientist George Washington Carver was born into slavery between 1861 and 1864 now is a national monument in his honor. The one-room cabin of his birth no longer exists, but the 210-acre park contains the 1881 home of the farm owners and other things associated with his boyhood. The site also has a museum devoted to Dr. Carver's life and career, an interactive exhibit area for students, a nature trail, and a statue of Carver as a boy.

Dr. Carver joined the Tuskegee Institute faculty in 1896 and spent the rest of his life teaching, conducting research, and promoting diversification among southern farmers, especially the adoption of peanuts, soybeans, and other soil-enriching crops. The George Washington Carver Museum

on the campus is part of the Tuskegee Institute National Historic Site in Alabama (see separate listing).

George Washington Carver National Monument, 5646 Carver Rd., Diamond, MO 64840-8314. Phone: 417/325-4151. Fax: 417/325-4231. E-mail: *gwca superintendent@nps.gov*. Web site: *www.nps.gov/gwca*. Hours: 9–5 daily; closed New Year's Day, Thanksgiving, and Christmas. Admission: free.

Hampton Plantation State Historic Site. The Hampton Plantation State Historic Site in McClellanville, South Carolina, offers a look at the life and craftsmanship of African American slaves in the eighteenth century. The 322-acre rice plantation was homesteaded by the Horry family, French Huguenots who fled to the South to escape religious persecution in their homeland. They built their two-story Georgian grand mansion in 1750 and had 320 slaves by 1760. African American craftsmanship of that period can be seen in the house structure, and guided tours interpret slave life at that time. The house is unfurnished with cutaway sections to show its architectural and construction details.

Hampton Plantation State Historic Site, 1950 Rutledge Rd., McClellanville, SC 29458. Phone: 843/546-9361. Fax: 843/527-4995. E-mail: *hampton_plantation_sp@scprt.com*. Web site: *www.southcarolinaparks.com*. Hours: site — 9–6 daily; mansion — Memorial Day–Labor Day: 11–4 daily; remainder of year: 1–4 Thurs.–Mon. Admission: adults, $4; children 6–15, $3; children under 6, free.

Harpers Ferry National Park. Harpers Ferry, at the confluence of the Potomac and Shenandoah rivers in West Virginia, is known for many things — the first successful application of interchangeable manufacture, the arrival of the first successful American railroad, the largest surrender of federal troops during the Civil War, and the education of former slaves in one of the earliest integrated schools in the nation. But it is best known for the attack on the federal arsenal on October 16, 1859, by abolitionist John Brown, who seized the armory with 18 others, including five African Americans, in an ill-fated effort to incite a slave insurrection. But the plan failed when no slaves joined the group.

After a two-day battle and several deaths, Brown and his party surrendered. He then was tried for treason and criminal conspiracy, found guilty, and executed by hanging. The abortive plan received sympathetic responses in the North, struck terror in the South, further embittered the sections, and hastened the start of the Civil War.

Harpers Ferry National Historical Park, Fillmore St., PO Box 65, Harpers Ferry, WV 25425. Phone: 304/535-6029. Fax: 404/535-6244. Web site: *www.*

nps.gov/hafe. Hours: 8–5 daily; closed New Year's Day, Thanksgiving, and Christmas. Admission: $6 per car or $4 per person.

Historic Seabrook Village. Historic Seabrook Village in Midway, Georgia, is a unique African American living-history museum. The 104-acre community was established through federal land grants made possible by General William T. Sherman's 1865 Field Order 15, a policy that came to be known as "40-acres-and-a-mule." Freedmen settled as landowners on the same lands where they once worked as slaves. Seabrook portrays African American history and culture in the rural Georgia coastal area from 1865 to 1930.

The village contains eight restored structures, including a one-room schoolhouse, and seven others are about to be added. In addition to the buildings, furniture, artifacts, and memorabilia, Seabrook programs offer hands-on experiences in turn-of-the-century history, such as grinding corn into meal and grits and washing clothes on a scrub board.

Historic Seabrook Village, 660 Trade Hill Rd., Midway, GA 31320. Phone: 912/884-7008. Fax: 912/884-7005. Email: *fortmorris@coastalnow.net.* Web site: *www.seabrookvillage.org.* Hours: 10–4 Tues.–Thurs.; other times by appointment. Admission: adults, $5; seniors, $2.50; children 6–18, $2; children under 6, free.

Historic Stagville. Historic Stagville near Durham, North Carolina, once was among the largest plantations in the South. By 1860, the Bennehan-Cameron families owned almost 30,000 acres and nearly 900 slaves. Today, Historic Stagville consists of only 71 acres in three tracts, but still contains the 1787 Bennehan House, four 1860 two-story slave houses, a pre–Revolutionary War yeoman farmer's house, a massive timber-framed barn, and the family cemetery. It now also has a modern visitor center. The site was donated to the state in 1976 by the Liggett and Myers Tobacco Company.

Historic Stagville, 5828 Old Orchard Rd., PO Box 71217, Durham, NC 27722-1217. Phone: 919/620-0120. Fax: 919/620-0422. E-mail: *stagville@sprynet. com.* Web site: *www.ah.dcr.stte.nc.us/sections/do/stageville/default.htm.* Hours: 10–4 Tues.–Sat.; closed Sun.–Mon and major holidays. Admission: free.

Laurel Valley Village. Laurel Valley Village near Thibodaux, Louisiana, is a rural life museum at the site of the largest surviving nineteenth- and twentieth-century sugar plantation in the United States. Sugar was the plantation's major crop from 1832 until well into the twentieth century, although rice, cotton, and potatoes also were grown there. The plantation, which reached its height in 1893

through 1926, was started about 1790 by Etienne Boudreaux, an Acadian who obtained a Spanish land grant. About 60 of the plantation's 105 buildings still remain, including 26 shotgun houses from the 1840s where slaves lived. A 1906 school, a store, and five houses have been restored. The remains of an 1845 sugar refinery, which closed in the 1920s, and early farm equipment also can be seen at the village.

Laurel Valley Village, 595 Hwy. 308, PO Box 1847, Thibodaux, LA 70301. Phone: 985/446-8111. Web site: *www.thibodauxchamber.com/community/local places.htm.* Hours: 10–3 Mon.–Fri.; 11–3 Sat.–Sun. Admission: free; guided tour, $3.

Maggie L. Walker National Historic Site. The Maggie L. Walker National Historic Site in Richmond, Virginia, commemorates the life of an African American businesswoman and community leader who was the first woman in the United States to charter and serve as president of a bank. In 1901, Maggie Lena Walker said the African American community in Richmond needed a savings bank founded and operated by blacks to achieve economic empowerment. Two years later she founded the St. Luke Penny Savings Bank and now it thrives as the Consolidated Bank and Trust Company, the oldest continually operated African American bank in the nation. The restored 28-room red brick house where Walker and her family lived from 1904 to 1934 has become a national historic site. It contains the original furnishings and many of Walker's personal belongings. A nearby visitor center offers a video and exhibits on her life, the bank, and the Jackson Ward neighborhood.

Maggie L. Walker National Historic Site, 600 N. 2nd St.. Richmond, VA 23219 (mailing address: 3215 E. Broad St., Richmond, VA 23223). Phone: 804/771-2017. Fax: 804/771-2226. E-mail: *cynthia_mac leod@nps.gov.* Web site: *www.nps.gov/mama.* Hours: 9–5 Mon.–Sat.; closed Sun., New Year's Day, Thanksgiving, and Christmas. Admission: free.

Martin Luther King, Jr., National Historic Site and Preservation District. The birthplace, boyhood home, church, and grave of Dr. Martin Luther King, Jr., are part of a national historic site and preservation district in his honor in Atlanta, Georgia. The historic site and district are located in the residential section of Sweet Auburn, the center of black Atlanta.

Dr. King was born in 1929 in the upstairs bedroom of the Rev. and Mrs. Martin Luther King, Sr. He spent his boyhood in a two-story Victorian home with his parents and grandparents, served as co-pastor with his father of the Ebenezer Baptist Church, and was buried in a tomb at the historic site. He became a national civil rights leader as he preached, marched, and led rallies and boycotts about love, equality, and non-violence. His life was ended by assassination in 1968. Visitors can take a walking tour of the historic district, tour Dr. King's birthplace and church, see a film and exhibits on his life at a visitor center, and attend interpretive programs on the community and the Civil Rights Movement. The historic site and preservation district have an annual attendance of 900,000.

Martin Luther King, Jr., National Historic Site, 450 Auburn Ave., N.E., Atlanta, GA 30312. Phone: 404/331-5190. Fax: 404/730-3112. Web site: *www. nps.gov/malu.* Hours: mid–June–mid-Aug.–9–6 daily; remainder of year — 9–5 daily; closed New Year's Day, Thanksgiving, and Christmas. Admission: free.

Mary McLeod Bethune Council House National Historic Site. The Mary McLeod Bethune Council House National Historic Site in Washington, D.C., is located in an 1876 three-story Victorian townhouse, known as the Council House. It is where noted African American educator Mary McLeod Bethune lived from 1943 to 1950 and the organization she founded, the National Council of Negro Women, had its offices. Bethune, one of 17 children born to former slaves in South Carolina in 1885, started an African American girls school that became part of the combined Bethune-Cookman College, of which she was the long-time president (see separate listing). She also served as director of the Division of Negro Affairs in the National Youth Administration, minority adviser to President Franklin D. Roosevelt, and vice president of the National Association for the Advancement of Colored People.

The historic house now features changing exhibitions on various aspects of African American women's history and has a carriage house that serves as home to the National Archives for Black Women's History. The archives contain Bethune's papers and those of other black women leaders, early files of the National Council of Negro Women, and other materials documenting the history of African American women in the United States.

Mary McLeod Bethune Council House National Historic Site, 1318 Vermont Ave., N.W., Washington, DC 20005. Phone: 202/673-2402. Fax: 202/673-2414. Web site: *www.nps.gov/mamc.* Hours: 10–4 Mon.–Sat.; closed Sun. and major holidays. Admission: free.

Mayhew Cabin and Historical Village. The 1850s Allen and Barbara Mayhew log cabin that served as a stop on the Underground Railroad for escaping southern slaves is preserved at the Mayhew Cabin and Historical Village, an open-air museum with 20 historical buildings and numerous artifacts in Nebraska City, Nebraska. The fleeing slaves were hidden in a hand-dug cave that became known as John Brown's Cave. Mrs. Mayhew's brother, John Henri Kagi, who spent considerable time at the homestead, was the secretary of war for the radical abolitionist movement led by John Brown and was killed in 1859 in the Harpers Ferry federal arsenal raid led by Brown. Brown later was executed for treason and criminal conspiracy (see separate listing for Harpers Ferry National Historical Park).

Mayhew Cabin and Historical Village, 2012 4th Corso (Bus. Hwy. 2), Nebraska City, NE 68410-2602. Phone: 402/873-3115. Fax: 402/721-0109. E-mail: *mayhewcabin@hotmail.com.* Web site: *www.mayhewcabin.com.* Hours: late Apr.–Oct.—11–5 Mon.–Sat., 12–5 Sun.; closed remainder of year. Admission: adults, $6; seniors, $5; children 3–12, $3; children under 3, free.

Melrose Plantation Home Complex. The Melrose Plantation Home Complex in Melrose, Louisiana, was owned by a freed African American woman slave at the turn of the nineteenth century. Marie Therese, whose last name is not known but who was called "Coin-Coin," had 10 children by the original French landowner, Claude Thomas Pierre Metoyer, and four earlier children by other men. Metoyer brought her freedom and left her and her sons 70 acres of the 13,000-acre plantation.

Coin-Coin lived in the 1833 plantation home; raised cattle; grew tobacco, corn, and cotton; and constructed some buildings that still stand today. She then used the profits to obtain the freedom of her children. But she later suffered from poor business and the Civil War, and the property eventually was acquired by Cammie Garret Henry and her husband, John Hamilton Henry. Mrs. Henry was a patron of the arts who had many writers and artists as guests. She converted two slave quarters, added several buildings, and preserved many of the historic structures. The 12-acre site now has eight buildings with furnishings dating from 1796 to the early 1900s.

Melrose Plantation Home Complex, Melrose General Delivery, Melrose, LA 71452 (mailing address: PO Box 2248, Natchitoches, LA 71457). Phone and fax: 318/379-0055. E-mail: *melrose@worldnet.la.net.* Hours: July–Oct.— 2–5 daily; remainder of year — 12–4 daily; closed major holidays. Admission: adults, $7; students 13–17, $4; children 6–12, $3; children under 6, free.

Nicodemus National Historic Site. The Nicodemus National Historic Site in Kansas protects and interprets one of the few surviving black towns founded by African Americans during the Reconstruction period following the Civil War. Nicodemus was established in 1877 when several hundred blacks settled in the area to take advantage of the government's offer of free or inexpensive land in the American West. The population grew to approximately 700, but declined to less than 50 after the railroad bypassed the town and it suffered from drought, dust storms, the Depression, and general lack of work. The National Park Service is working with the remaining residents to preserve five historic structures — First Baptist Church, African Methodist Episcopal Church, St. Francis Hotel, Nicodemus School, and Nicodemus Township Hall.

Nicodemus National Historic Site, 304 Washington Ave., Nicodemus, KS 67625. Phone: 785/839-4233. Fax: 785/839-4325. Web site: *www.nps.gov/nico.* Hours: 8:30–5 daily; closed New Year's Day, Thanksgiving, and Christmas. Admission: free.

The Oaks. The Oaks was the first home of educator Booker T. Washington, who was chosen in 1881 to establish and head Tuskegee Institute in Tuskegee, Alabama, for practical training of Negroes in the trades and professions and made it into one of the leading institutions in the field. He built the house adjacent to the campus in 1899 of bricks made by students and faculty. The house is furnished with original Washington furniture and personal effects and reflects the broad interests of the family. It now is part of the Tuskegee Institute National Historic Site (see separate listing), with guided tours being conducted by National Park Service interpretive staff members.

The Oaks, Tuskegee Institute National Historic Site, PO Drawer 10, Tuskegee, AL 36088. Phone: 334/727-3200. Fax: 334/727-3201. Web site: *http://bama.ua.edu/~g_gwem.htm.* Hours: 9–5 daily; closed New Year's Day, Thanksgiving, and Christmas. Admission: free.

Old Courthouse National Historic Site. The Old Courthouse in St. Louis, Missouri, is where the *Dred Scott* case was held. In 1846, Scott, a slave, filed a lawsuit for his freedom against his owner, John Sanford. He claimed he was a free man because he once lived in Illinois, a free state, and in the Northwest Territory, where the Ordinance of 1787 adopted by the Congress of the Confederation had forbidden slavery. Two of three trials in the case were held in the Old Courthouse, with the final decision being made by the U.S. Supreme Court.

Chief Justice Roger B. Taney wrote the court's 1857 opinion, saying Scott did not have the right to sue because slaves were not considered citizens,

he was a slave when his owner took him to Illinois, the 1787 Northwest Territory legislation was not valid, and the Fugitive Slave Clause of the Constitution and a bill banning the slave trade after 1808 both recognized the right to have slaves as property. The decision caused an uproar among blacks, their supporters, and others, including Abraham Lincoln, a senatorial candidate in Illinois, who said the decision was made improperly and should be reversed. Fortunately, Scott was freed by his owner a few weeks after the decision. But the court decision aroused the ire of abolitionists and influenced the start of the Civil War. Scott died a year later after working as a hotel porter in St. Louis.

The Old Courthouse, which now has exhibits describing the *Dred Scott* case, served as a house of justice, a site for speeches and debates, and a public gathering place for pioneers planning their westward journeys in the nineteenth century. Before the Civil War, slaves also were sold on its steps to settle estates. The original courthouse was built in 1828 and then remodeled and enlarged several times before being officially completed in 1862. The courthouse, with its iron-framed dome rising to more than 190 feet, dominated the St. Louis skyline until the turn of the twentieth century. Thirteen courtrooms were in use from 1845 until 1930, but the courtroom in which the *Dred Scott* trials were held no longer exists. The historic courthouse now is part of the nearby Jefferson National Memorial Park, which features the 630-foot-high Gateway Arch.

Old Courthouse National Historic Site, 11 N. 4th St., St. Louis, MO 63102. Phones: 314/655-1600 and 314/655-1700. Web site: *www.nps.gov/jeff.* Hours: 8–4:30 daily; closed New Year's Day, Thanksgiving, and Christmas. Admission: free.

Olustee Battlefield State Historic Site. One of the bloodiest battles of the Civil War in proportion to the number of troops involved was fought on February 20, 1864, at the Olustee Battlefield State Historic Site in Florida. It also was the largest Civil War battle in Florida. A Union force of 5,500 men — one-third of whom were African Americans — clashed with nearly the same number of Confederate forces.

Battle casualties totaled 1,861 Union and 946 Confederate soldiers as the southern troops defeated the northern army, which sought to disrupt transportation links and food supplies; capture cotton, turpentine, and timber; gain black recruits for the army; and induce northern supporters in east Florida to organize a loyal state government. The retreating Union forces returned to Jacksonville and occupied several other coastal towns and sites along the St. Johns River until the end of the war. The battlefield site now has a monument commemorating the Olustee fight and an interpretive center with exhibits, and the battle is reenacted every February.

The Olustee battle is remembered for another reason. Three African American groups were part of the Union forces — 54th Massachusetts Volunteers, 1st North Carolina Colored, and 8th U.S. Colored Troops of Pennsylvania. One of the soldiers was Corporal James Henry Gooding from Massachusetts. He was one of those wounded, taken prisoner, and later died at Andersonville Prison. In 1863, he had written to President Lincoln to protest the lower pay black soldiers received than that given white troops. A month after Gooding died in 1864, Congress passed legislation providing equal pay.

Olustee Battlefield State Historic Site, off U.S. Rte. 90, PO Box 40, Olustee, FL 32072. Phone: 386/758-0400. Web site: *http://extlabl.entnem.ufl.edu/olustee.* Hours: site — open 24 hours; visitor center — 9–5 Thurs.–Mon.; closed Tues.–Wed. and major holidays. Admission: free.

Philipsburg Manor. See Dutch Historic Sites section.

Shelley House. The modest 1906 two-story home of the J. D. Shelley family in St. Louis, Missouri, played an important role in addressing the issue of restrictive racial covenants in housing. In 1930, Shelley, his wife, and six children moved from Mississippi to St. Louis to escape the racial oppression of the South. But they found many of the homes in St. Louis were covered by racially restrictive covenants that restricted their sale only to Caucasians. The Shelleys challenged the discriminatory practice by buying a home from an owner who agreed not to enforce the racial covenant. Another property owner, Louis D. Kraemer, sued to enforce the covenant and prevent the Shelley family from acquiring title to the building.

The trial court ruled in the Shelleys' favor, but the Missouri Supreme Court reversed the decision when appealed. The Shelleys then went to the U.S. Supreme Court, and the court rendered the landmark decision in 1948 that racially restrictive covenants cannot be enforced by courts since it would constitute state action denying due process of law in violation of the 14th Amendment to the Constitution. The case did not outlaw covenants, but it reinforced the 14th Amendment's guarantee of equal protection under laws, including the right to acquire, enjoy, own, and dispose of property. It also told African Americans that positive social change could be achieved through law and the

courts. The Shelley house now is a private residence and is not open to the public.

Shelley House, 4600 Labadie Ave., St. Louis, MO. Not open to public, but visitors may drive or walk by.

Stono River Slave Rebellion Site. The Stono River Slave Rebellion Site in Rantowles, South Carolina, nearly 20 miles southwest of Charleston, is a national historic landmark. It is where a group of about 20 Carolina slaves led by an Angolan named Jemmy marched in 1739 carrying banners and shouting "Liberty." Other slaves joined them along the way, increasing the number to more than 80. It is not known what caused the rebellion, although it is believed that the runaway slaves were on their way to St. Augustine, Florida, where the Spanish had given freedom and land to other escaping slaves. Another factor was that a Security Act was about to be enacted in response to the colonists' fear of a slave insurrection. It would have required all white men to carry firearms to church on Sundays at a time when they usually did not carry weapons and slaves were allowed to work for themselves.

The fleeing slaves first went to a shop that sold firearms and ammunition, armed themselves, and killed the two shopkeepers. They then began burning houses and killing between 20 and 25 white people as they made their way south of the Stono River. By this time, a colonial militia set out in pursuit and then confronted the armed band. When the blacks opened fire, the whites began firing back, bringing down 14 slaves. By dusk, about 30 slaves were dead and the remainder had escaped. All were later captured and executed. This was followed by the passage of the Negro Act, which prohibited slaves from assembling in groups, growing their own food, earning their own money, and learning to read. Some of these restrictions were in effect before the rebellion, but they were not strictly enforced.

Stono River Slave Rebellion Site Landmark, off U.S. Rte. 17, west bank of Wallace River, Rantowles, SC 29449. Hours: open 24 hours. Admission: free.

Tremé Neighborhood and Villa Meilleur. The Tremé neighborhood, located adjacent to the French Quarter in New Orleans, Louisiana, is said to be the first African American neighborhood in the nation and where jazz originated. In 1729, the Tremé neighborhood was the only place in the United States where slaves were allowed to congregate freely. The Tremé Villa Meilleur complex, which houses the New Orleans African-American Museum of Art, Culture, and History and is the site of visual and performing arts, has anchored renewal of the area.

The Villa Meilleur, built between 1828 and 1829 by Simon Meilleur, is considered to be the finest example of Creole Villa construction in the city, but has deteriorated over the years and was damaged by Hurricane Katrina in 2005. The city of New Orleans purchased the property in 1991 and is rehabilitating the former architectural jewel. More than half of the complex has been converted to housing, the museum, and an arts center. Future plans call for restoring the hurricane-damaged complex and adding a walking museum of the historic site, a museum devoted to the Mardi Gras Indians, and various arts-related activities.

Tremé Neighborhood and Villa Meilleur, 1418 Gov. Nicholls St., New Orleans, LA 70116 (contact: New Orleans Division of Housing and Neighborhood Development). Phone: 504/658-4200. Hours: neighborhood — open 24 hours; Villa Meilleur — varies with events.

Tuskegee Institute National Historic Site. Tuskegee Normal School, which later became Tuskegee Institute, opened in Alabama in 1881 to educate newly freed blacks in the trades and professions. It became one of the most successful historically black universities under the leadership of Booker T. Washington and the work of such faculty members as Dr. George Washington Carver.

The legacy of Washington, Carver, and many others now is preserved in the university's Historic Campus District, which features the original buildings constructed by students with bricks made in the institute's brickyard. They include The Oaks, President Washington's 1899 home; the university's old administration building and library; and the George Washington Carver Museum, devoted to Dr. Carver's life and scientific contributions (see separate listings).

Tuskegee Institute National Historic Site, 1212 W. Montgomery Rd., PO Drawer 10, Tuskegee Institute, AL 36088-0010. Phones: 334/727-3200 and 334/727-6390. Faxes: 334/727-1448 and 334/727-4597. Web site: *www.nps.gov/tuin*. Hours: 9–4:30 daily; closed New Year's Day, Thanksgiving, and Christmas. Admission: free.

Weeksville Heritage Center. The Society for the Preservation of Weeksville and Bedford-Stuyvesant History, which has preserved four historic houses from a vibrant and self-sufficient African American community settled in the 1830s in Brooklyn, New York, is in the midst of a five-year restoration and expansion program. The Hunterfly Road houses, which are on the National Registry of Historic Places in the United States, are part of the society's efforts — with its Weeksville Heritage Center — to further appreciation of the African

American legacy in Brooklyn and to foster community empowerment and lifelong learning through research, interpretation, and presentation of Weeksville history.

The Weeksville neighborhood is named for James Weeks, an African American stevedore and respected member of the early black community, who purchased land there in 1838. It soon became home to teachers, ministers, and other black professionals, including the first female physician in the state and the first African American police officer in New York City. Weeksville had its own schools, churches, an orphanage, an old peoples home, and one of the first African American newspapers. During the violent draft riots of 1863, the community also served as a refuge for hundreds of African Americans who fled Manhattan.

Today, the society has a 12,400-square-foot site that includes the four historic houses, an open grass area which creates an almost rural atmosphere in the middle of Brooklyn's inner city, and the Weeksville Heritage Center, which offers tours of the houses and site. In 2006, plans were announced to completely restore the historic houses, develop the grounds around the site, and build a new multiuse museum education center. In addition to exhibitions, the center will have a library, archives, auditorium-theater, workshop space, and other facilities. In addition, plans call for a re-created kitchen garden, with vegetables and herbs similar to the ones once used by the community; an intergenerational storytelling garden; a re-established Hunterfly Road originally used by Native Americans; and historical signage and markers throughout the houses, site, and new building.

Weeksville Heritage Center, Society for the Preservation of Weeksville and Bedford-Stuyvesant History, 1698 Bergen St., Brooklyn, NY 11213 (mailing address: PO Box 130120, St. John's Station, Brooklyn, NY 11216). Web site: *www.weeksvillesociety.org*. Hours: 10–4:30 Tues.–Fri; Sat.–Sun. by appointment; closed Mon. and major holidays. Admission: center — free; tour — $3 per person for groups up to 15; groups up to 30, $90; seniors, children under 13, and neighborhood residents, free.

ALBANIAN

Museums and Galleries

Archbishop Fan Noli Library and Photo Gallery. The Albanian Orthodox Archdiocese in America has a library with occasional displays and a photo gallery depicting major events in the life and work of the church at St. George Cathedral in Boston, Massachusetts. The library is named for the Rev. Fr.

Fan Stylian Noli (later Metropolitan), who organized St. George Cathedral in 1908 and later became premier of Albania.

Archbishop Fan Noli Library and Photo Gallery, St. George Cathedral, 523 E. Broadway, South Boston, MA 02127. Phone: 617/268–1275. Fax: 617/268–3184. E-mail: *albboschurch@juno.com*. Web site: *www.albanianchurch.org*. Hours: varies. Admission: donation.

ARABIAN

Museums and Galleries

Arab American National Museum. The Arab American National Museum, which opened in 2005 in Dearborn, Michigan, the nation's largest Arab American community, is devoted to the history, life, culture, and contributions of Arab Americans. The 38,500-square-foot facility seeks to further knowledge and understanding of Arab Americans and their presence in the United States.

The museum, which also functions as a community and resource center, has two semi-permanent exhibits and presents changing exhibitions. One long-standing exhibit features Arab civilization and its contributions to science, medicine, mathematics, and astronomy. In addition, it displays Arab architecture and decorative arts. The second exhibit consists of three thematic sections — the history of Arab American immigration from 1500 to the present, life of Arab Americans at different time periods, and contributions of individuals and community organizations.

Arab American National Museum, 13624 Michigan Ave., Dearborn, MI 48126. Phone: 313/582–2266. Fax: 313/582-1086. E-mail: *aanm@accesscommunity.org*. Web site: *www.theaanm.org*. Hours: 10–6 Wed. and Fri.-Sat.; 10–8 Thurs.; 12–5 Sun.; closed Mon.-Tues., New Year's Day, Thanksgiving, and Christmas. Admission: adults, $6; seniors, students, and children 6–12, $3; children under 6, free.

ARCTIC PEOPLES (*also see* Multicultural; Native American)

Museums and Galleries

Alaska Heritage Museum. Alaskan history and cultures are the focus of the Alaska Heritage Museum in the Wells Fargo Bank building in Anchorage. It displays an extensive collection of Alaska native artifacts, fine art by Alaskan artists, and exhibits a stagecoach relating to the bank's role in the Alaskan gold rush. A reference library also has books on Alaskan history and other subjects.

Alaska Heritage Museum, Wells Fargo Bldg., 301 W. Northern Lights Blvd., Anchorage, AK 99503. Phone: 907/265- 2834. Fax: 907/265–2860. Hours: 12–4 Mon.-Fri.; closed Sat.-Sun., bank holidays, New Year's, Thanksgiving, and Christmas. Admission: free.

Alaska Native Heritage Center. The Alaska Native Heritage Center in Anchorage introduces visitors to Alaskan native traditions and customs of the past and present on its 26-acre campus. A 26,000-square-foot Welcome House celebrates contemporary native cultures, while the outdoor facilities feature ancient traditions, tales from the past by storytellers, dance performances, and tours of five outdoor village sites surrounding a small lake.

Alaska Native Heritage Center, 8800 Heritage Center Dr., Anchorage, AK 99505. Phones: 907/330–8000 and 800/315-6608. Fax: 907/330–8030. Web site: *www.alaskanative.net*. Hours: mid–May–mid Sept — 8 A.M.-10 P.M. daily; late Oct.-mid–Apr.—10:30–4:30 Sat. and by appointment. Admission: adults, $9; seniors and military, $8.95; children 7-16, $5.95; children under 7, free.

Alutiiq Museum and Archaeological Repository. The Alutiiq Museum and Archaeological Repository in Kodiak, Alaska, seeks to preserve and interpret the prehistoric and historic cultural traditions and legacy of the indigenous people of the Gulf of Alaska. The museum has more than 100,000 objects in 400 collections, primarily from archaeological assemblages in the Kodiak Archipelago.

The museum and archaeological repository has the largest collection of Eskimo Aleut material culture in the world, largely from the Karluk One collection, a remarkably preserved prehistoric village with wooden objects, basketry, cordage, bateen, fur, feathers, and botanical remains, as well as stone, bone, ivory, and shell materials. The museum also displays archaeological materials from the eighteenth and nineteenth centuries, including objects from the site of a massacre where Russian fur traders attacked a native village, a Russian-era workstation where Alutiiq men hunted sea otters for the fur trade, and a mid-nineteenth-century Alutiiq settlement.

Alutiiq Museum and Archaeological Repository, 215 Mission Rd., Suite 101, Kodiak, AK 99615. Phone: 907/4867004. E-mail: *receptionist@alutiiqmuseum. com*. Web site: *www.alutiiqmuseum.com*. Hours: June-Aug.— 9–5 Mon.-Fri.; Sun. by appointment; closed Sat.; remainder of year — 9–5 Wed.-Fri.; 10:30–4:30 Sat.; closed Sun.-Tues. and major holidays. Admission: adults and children over 11, $3; children under 12, free.

Baranov Museum. The Baranov Museum, located in a 200-year-old national historic landmark building in Kodiak, Alaska, traces the region's history from Alutiiq culture and the Russian colonial period to the early American era. The museum contains items from the Kodiak Historical Society relating to Kodiak's natural and cultural heritage. The building housing the Baranov Museum, also known as Erskine House or the Russian American Magazin, was the ca.1800 fur warehouse and office of the Alexander Baranov Company or Russian American Company. It later became the home of the W. J. Erskine family.

Baranov Museum, Kodiak Historical Society, 101 Marine Way, Kodiak, AK 99615. Phone 907/486–5920. Fax: 907/486–3165. E-mail: *baranov@ak.net.* Hours: June-Aug—10–4 Mon.-Sat.; 12–4 Sun.; remainder of year—10–3 Tues.-Sat.; closed Sun.-Mon. and major holidays. Admission: adults and children over 12, $3; children under 13, free.

Inupiat Heritage Center. Inupiat Heritage Center is located at Ilisagvik College, a community college in Barrow, Alaska, dedicated to perpetuating and strengthening Inupiat (Eskimo) culture, language, values, and traditions. The heritage center interprets the history and culture of the Inupiat. The newly renovated campus is situated at the former site of the United States Naval Arctic Research Laboratory.

Inupiat Heritage Center, Ilisagvik College, PO Box 749, Barrow, AK 99723. Phone: 907/852-5494. Hours: 8:30–5 Mon.-Fri. Admission: free.

Jensen Arctic Museum. See Museums Honoring Individuals section.

Peary-MacMillan Arctic Museum and Arctic Studies Center. See Museums Honoring Individuals section.

Sheldon Jackson Museum. See Museums Honoring Individuals section.

Sheldon Museum and Cultural Center. The history and blending of diverse cultures in the Chilkat Valley region are the focus of the Sheldon Museum and Cultural Center in Haines, Alaska. The exhibits feature artifacts and art of the Tlingit Indians, as well as some materials of the Eskimos and Athabascans, in interpreting the area's history, with emphasis on the period since European contact. Among the displays are a Tlingit tribal house diorama depicting daily life and activities; a dance diorama with native costumes, masks, headdresses, and dance materials; collections of native carvings, potlatches, trade goods, bentwood boxes, spruce root baskets, and Chilkat blankets; two turn-of-

the-twentieth-century period rooms; and a Fresnel lighthouse lens that was operational in the area from 1907 to 1973.

Sheldon Museum and Cultural Center, 11 Main St., PO Box 269, Haines, AK 99827. Phone: 907/766–2366. Fax: 907/766–2368. E-mail museum: *director@aptalaska.net.* Web site: *http://sheldonmuseum.org.* Hours: mid–May-mid–Sept.—10–5 daily; remainder of year—1–4 Mon.-Fri.; closed Sat.-Sun. and major holidays. Admission: adults, $3; children under 12, free.

Simon Paneak Memorial Museum. See Museums Honoring Individuals section.

Southeast Alaska Indian Cultural Center. See Sitka National Historical Park in Historic Sites section.

Totem Heritage Center. See Native American Museums and Galleries section.

Yupiit Piciryarait Cultural Center and Museum. Clothing, household items, and hunting and gathering implements used by the Yupiit-Cup'ik Eskimo and Athabascan people of the Yukon-Kuskokwim Delta in ancient and contemporary times can be seen at the Yupiit Piciryarait Cultural Center and Museum in Bethel, Alaska. The cultural center-museum also presents changing exhibitions related to the region.

Yupiit Piciryarait Cultural Center and Museum, 420 Chief Eddie Hoffman Hwy., PO Box 219, Bethel, AK 99559. Phone: 907/543–1819. Fax: 907/543–1885. E-mail: *joan_hamilton@yahoo.com.* Hours: 12–5 Tues.-Sat.; closed Sun.-Mon. and major holidays Admission: adults, $1 suggested donation; children, free.

Museums Honoring Individuals

Jensen Arctic Museum. The Jensen Arctic Museum at Western Oregon University in Monmouth interprets Arctic culture through collections of historic and contemporary art, tools, apparel, and other materials of the indigenous Arctic peoples. The museum is named for its founder, Paul H. Jensen, an adventurer, educator, collector, and philanthropist whose love of the Arctic people, their art and lifestyle, and the environment earned him the title of Angyalik (Captain of the Ship) from the Eskimo Council of Elders. Among the museum's holdings are a 27-foot walrus-hide whale hunting boat; a re-created Inuit house of stone, bone, and hide; and over 10,000 Arctic photographs from the 1890s to the present.

Jensen Arctic Museum, Western Oregon University, The Cottage, 590 W. Church St., Monmouth, OR 97361. Phone: 503/838–8468. Fax: 503/838-8289. E-mail: *arctic@wou.edu.* Web site: *www.wou.*

edulpresident/advancement/jensen/index/php. Hours: 10–4 Wed.-Sat.; closed Sun.-Tues., New Year's Day, Thanksgiving, and Christmas. Admission: adults and children over 11, $2 suggested donation; children under 12, $1 suggested donation.

Peary-MacMillan Arctic Museum and Arctic Studies Center. The Peary-MacMillan Arctic Museum and Arctic Studies Center at Bowdoin College in Brunswick, Maine, is named for two Arctic explorers and Bowdoin graduates — Robert E. Peary (class of 1877) and Donald B. MacMillan (class of 1898). The museum's collections include Arctic exploration gear, natural history specimens, and art and anthropological materials produced primarily by the Inuit cultures of Labrador and Greenland. It has permanent exhibits on Arctic environments and peoples and Peary's 1908 to 1909 North Pole expedition, and presents changing exhibitions of Arctic photographs and other topics. The studies center focuses on the prehistory, history, anthropology, and environment of northern peoples and Arctic exploration.

Peary-MacMillan Arctic Museum and Arctic Studies Center, Bowdoin College, Hubbard Hall, 9500 College Station, Brunswick, ME 04011–8495. Phones: 207/725–3416 and 207/725–3062. Fax: 207/725–3490. Web site: *http://academic.bowdoin.edu/arctic-museum.* Hours: 10–5 Tues.-Sat.; 2–5 Sun.; closed Mon. and national holidays. Admission: free.

Sheldon Jackson Museum. The core of the collection at Sheldon Jackson Museum, founded in 1887 in Sitka, Alaska, came from the Rev. Dr. Sheldon Jackson, a Presbyterian missionary who served as general agent for education in Alaska in the 1890s. Dr. Jackson collected while traveling extensively in Alaska between 1880 and 1900. He acquired nearly 5,000 items, including Tlingit, Eskimo, Aleut, and Athabaskan baskets; totem poles; Eskimo masks; and traditional clothing noted for its beautiful ornamentation and fine sewing. Among the other objects on display are full-sized kayaks and baidarka, and argillite carvings made of softly glowing black rocks from the Queen Charlotte Islands of the Pacific coast. The museum is located at Sheldon Jackson College and housed in the first concrete building — an unusual octagonal structure — constructed in the territory of Alaska in 1895.

Sheldon Jackson Museum, Sheldon Jackson College, 104 College Dr., Sitka, AK 99835. Phone: 907/747–8981. Fax: 907/747–3004. E-mail: *scott_mcadams@ced.state.ak.us.* Web site:*www.museums.state.ak.us/sheldon%20jackson.* Hours: mid–May–mid–Sept.— 9–5 daily; closed major holidays; remainder of year —10–4 Tues.-Sat.; closed Sun.-Mon. and major holidays. Admission: adults, $4 in summer and $3 in winter; children under 19, free.

Simon Paneak Memorial Museum. The Simon Paneak Memorial Museum in the Alaskan village of Anaktuvuk Pass is named in honor of an early community leader and respected elder. It is devoted to the history, culture, and transitional lifestyle of the Nunamiut Eskimos. The exhibits relate the story of the origin, history, and way of life of the Nunamiut; seasonal pattern of subsistence activities; importance of caribou to their economy, culture, and once nomadic lifestyle; origin and environment of the Brooks Range; and settling of the last group of nomadic Eskimos into the village of Anaktuvuk.

Simon Paneak Memorial Museum, 341 Mekiana Rd., PO Box 21085, Anaktuvuk Pass, AK 99721. Phone: 907/661–3413. Fax 907/661–3414. E-mail: *grant_spearman@north-slope.org.* Web site: *www.-north-slope.org/nsb/55.htm.* Hours: 8:30–5 daily; closed major holidays. Admission: adults, $10; children, free.

Historic Sites

Baranov Museum. See Museums and Galleries section.

Russian Bishop's House. See Russian Historic Sites section.

Sitka National Historical Park. The Sitka National Historical Park in Sitka, Alaska, was the site of the 1804 Battle of Sitka in which Russian fur traders and Aleut natives defeated the Tlingit Indians. It was the last major resistance to European domination of native Alaskans. The 107-acre historical park now is devoted largely to the history and culture of the Tlingits. The visitor center features collections and exhibits of the Tlingits and a slide show on the losing battle, and the Southeast Alaska Indian Cultural Center on the grounds gives demonstrations of traditional wood and silver carving by Tlingit artists. Twenty-eight historic Tlingit and Haida totem poles also line the park trail along Sitka Sound.

The visitor center also has Russian American historical and archaeological collections, historical photographs, archives, and herbarium specimens. The 1842 Russian Bishop's House (see Russian Historic Sites section), a two-story log structure in downtown Sitka which served as a bishop's residence for 130 years and now is under the care of the park, is one of four original Russian structures still remaining in North America. It is a national historic landmark that has been restored to its 1853 appearance with original and period furnishings.

Sitka National Historical Park, 106 Metlakatla St., Sitka, AK 99835 (mailing address: 103 Monastery St., Sitka, AK 99835). Phone: 907/747–0110. Fax: 907/747–5938. E-mail: *sue-thorsen@nps.gov.* Web site: *www.nps.gov/sitk*. Hours: 8–5 daily; closed New Year's Day, Thanksgiving, and Christmas. Admission: park — free; visitor center — mid-May-Sept.: adults, $4; children under 13, free; remainder of year — free.

ARMENIAN

Museums and Galleries

Armenian Cultural Foundation Library and Museum. The Armenian Cultural Foundation in Arlington, Massachusetts, has a library and museum that seek to preserve and enhance Armenian history, culture, and letters. The foundation, housed in a Greek Revival mansion, is dedicated to the memory of Yeghia Demirjibashian, an Armenian poet, philosopher, and mystic. It has collections of Armenian manuscripts, publications, documents, music, and other materials.

Armenian Cultural Foundation Library and Museum, 441 Mystic St., Arlington, MA 02474–1108. Phone 617/545- 3090. Web site: *www.armenianculturalfoundation.org*. Hours: 9–12 Mon.-Thurs. by appointment; closed Fri.-Sun. and major holidays. Admission: free.

Armenian Library and Museum of America. The Armenian Library and Museum of America in Watertown, Massachusetts, has the largest collection of Armenian artifacts and related materials in North America. They include such items as textiles, oriental rugs, rare books, coins, folk and religious art, and oral histories. The exhibits are presented in Bedoukian Hall, a contemporary art gallery, and several side galleries.

Armenian Library and Museum of America, 65 Main St., Watertown, MA 02472. Phone: 617/926–2562. Fax: 617/926–0175. E-mail: *gary@armenianlibraryandmuseum.org*. Web site: *www.almainc.org*. Hours: 6–9 P.M. Thurs.; 1–5 Fri.-Sun.; closed Mon.-Wed., New Year's Day, Easter, Thanksgiving, and Christmas. Admission: adults, $2; children, free.

ASIAN (*also see* Cambodian; Chinese; Indian; Japanese; Korean; Tibetan)

Museums and Galleries

Arthur M. Sackler Gallery. See Freer Gallery of Art and Arthur M. Sackler Gallery.

Asian American Arts Centre. The mission of the Asian American Arts Centre in New York City is to promote the preservation and creative vitality of Asian American cultural growth and its historical and aesthetic linkage to other communities. It presents and interprets American and Asian contemporary art forms through exhibitions, performances, and public education. The center is located in Chinatown, but many of its exhibitions and performances also have traveled to other locations in the city and country.

Among the center's recent exhibitions have been the works of 270 Chinese artists, over 70 years of Asian American artistry, and the reintegration of tradition in contemporary art. The center has over 400 contemporary works and examples of about 200 Chinese folk art in its collections, and has developed the largest historical archive of Asian American artists, containing slides of over 1,500 artists.

Asian American Arts Centre, 26 Bowery, New York, NY 10013. Phone: 212/233–2154. Fax: 212/766–1287. E-mail: *aaartsctr@aol.com*. Web site: *www.artspiral.org*. Hours: 12:30–6-30 Mon.-Wed. and Fri.; 12:30–7:30 Thurs.; closed Sat.-Sun. and major holidays. Admission: free.

Asian American Comparative Collection. The Laboratory of Anthropology at the University of Idaho in Moscow has an Asian American Comparative Collection consisting of artifacts, manuscripts, photographs, oral histories, books, films, and other materials pertaining largely to the Chinese and Japanese, and to a lesser extent the Filipinos and Koreans, in the Pacific Northwest. Representative items are displayed on a changing basis. The collection's curator, Dr. Priscilla Wegars, who has conducted research and archaeological surveys and digs of Chinese historical sites in the region, also offers guided tours of such sites.

Asian American Comparative Collection, University of Idaho, Laboratory of Anthropology, PO Box 441111, Moscow, ID 83844. Phone: 208/885–7905. Fax: 208/885–5878. Hours: varies. Admission: free.

Asian Art and Culture Center. The Asian Art and Culture Center at Towson University in Baltimore, Maryland, has over 1,000 art objects from Cambodia, China, India, Indonesia, Japan, Korea, Nepal, Thailand, and Tibet. In addition to exhibitions, the center presents concerts, lectures, films, workshops, and demonstrations to further understanding and appreciation of the art and culture of Asia.

Asian Art and Culture Center, Towson University, 8000 York Rd., Baltimore, MD 21252–0001. Phone: 410/704–2807. Hours: 11–4 Mon.-Fri.; 1–4 Sat.; closed Sun., major holidays, and when university not in session. Admission: free.

Asian Art Museum of San Francisco, Chong-Moon Lee Center for Asian Art and Culture. The

Asian Art Museum of San Francisco holds one of the most comprehensive collections of Asian art in the world. It has more than 17,000 treasures representing cultures throughout Asia and spanning 6,000 years of history. More than half of the collection was donated by Chicago industrialist Avery Brundage in the 1960s when the museum was founded. Since then another substantial museum addition has been the Chong-Moon Lee Center for Asian Art and Culture, which has become part of the museum's name.

Over 2,500 artworks offer a comprehensive introduction to all the major cultures of Asia in the museum's galleries. They cover three major themes that have influenced Asian art — development of Buddhism, trade and exchange, and local beliefs and practices. Among the works on display in the permanent galleries are monumental South Asian stone sculptures, Chinese jades, Korean paintings, Tibetan thagkas, Cambodian Buddhas, Islamic manuscripts, and Japanese ceramics.

Asian Art Museum of San Francisco, Chong-Moon Lee Center for Asian Art and Culture, 200 Larkin St., San Francisco, CA 94102. Phone: 415/581–3500. Fax: 415/581–4700. E-mail: *info@asianart.org*. Web site: *www.asianart.org*. Hours: 10–5 Tues.-Sun.; closed Mon., New Year's Day, Thanksgiving, and Christmas. Admission: adults, $10; seniors, $7; college students and children 13–17, $6; children under 13, free; after 5 Thurs., $5 for everyone over 12; 1st Tues. every month, free.

Asian Society Museum. The Asian Society operates an art museum at its headquarters in New York City as part of its efforts to strengthen relationships and deepen understanding among the peoples of the United States and Asia. The museum's collection features nearly 300 works of art in their historical and cultural context, including masterworks from South, Southeast, and East Asia, dating from 2000 B.C. to the nineteenth century. The core of the collection was donated by Mr. and Mrs. John D. Rockefeller III. It reflects the great achievements and wide diversity of Asian arts and cultures. The museum also presents changing exhibitions of Asian art from other sources.

Asian Society Museum, 725 Park Ave., New York, NY 10021. Phone: 212/288–6400. Fax: 212/517–8315. Web site: *www.asiansociety.org*. Hours: 11–6 Tues.-Sat. (also until 9 Fri., except July 4-Labor Day); closed Mon. and major holidays. Admission: adults, $10; seniors, $7; students, $5; children under 16, free; also free 6–9 Fri.

Freer Gallery of Art and Arthur M. Sackler Gallery. The Smithsonian Institution in Washington, D.C., has two adjoining museums featuring Asian art connected by an underground exhibition space — the Freer Gallery of Art and the Arthur M. Sackler Gallery. The Freer Gallery has a world-renowned collection of art from China, Japan, Korea, South and Southeast Asia, and the Near East, while the Sackler Gallery features Chinese, Near Eastern, and South and Southeast Asian art, as well as Indian, Japanese, Korean, and Islamic artworks. The two galleries are administered jointly.

The Freer Gallery, which opened in 1923 in an Italian Renaissance-style building on the Mall, was founded by Charles Lang Freer, a Detroit manufacturer who gave his collections and funds for a building to house them. The gallery was the first Smithsonian museum for fine arts. The gallery's collections, which have nearly tripled since the initial gift, include such works as Chinese paintings, Japanese folding screens, Korean ceramics, Buddhist sculpture, and Indian and Persian manuscripts.

The Sackler Gallery opened in 1987 to house a gift of Asian art from Dr. Arthur M. Sackler, a research physician and medical publisher from New York City. He also gave $4 million toward construction of the gallery building. Among the gallery's highlights are early Chinese bronzes and jades, ancient Near Eastern ceramics and metalware, Chinese paintings and lacquerware, South and Southeast Asian sculpture, Japanese prints and contemporary porcelain, ancient Islamic arts, and Indian, Japanese, and Korean paintings.

Freer Gallery of Art, Smithsonian Institution, Jefferson Dr. at 12th St., S.W., Washington, DC 20506 (mailing address: PO Box 37012, MRC 707, Washington, DC 20013–7012). Phone: 202/633–4880. Fax: 202/357–4911. Web site: *www.asia.si.edu*. Hours: 10–5:30 daily; closed Christmas. Admission: free.

Arthur M. Sackler Gallery, Smithsonian Institution, 1050 Independence Ave., S.W., Washington, DC 20560. Phone: 202/633–4880. Fax: 202/357–4911. Web site: *www.asia.si.edu*. Hours: 10–5:30 daily; closed Christmas. Admission: free.

Hammond Museum and Japanese Stroll Garden. The Hammond Museum and Japanese Stroll Garden in North Salem, New York, presents changing Asian art exhibitions and features a Japanese garden. The museum and garden were the creation of Natalie Hays Hammond, daughter of the cofounder and developer of the long-lost King Solomon's Mines in South Africa. The museum and garden, founded in 1957, is located at the site of Ms. Hammond's home and includes her longtime residence. The Stroll Garden incorporates indigenous plantings with popular and rare Japanese and Chinese specimens.

Hammond Museum and Japanese Stroll Garden,

This is one of the Chinese art galleries at the Asian Art Museum of San Francisco, Chong-Moon Lee Center for Asian Art and Culture, which has over 15,000 artworks from throughout Asia that span 6,000 years of history. *Photo by Kaz Tsurura © Asian Art Museum of San Francisco. Used by permission.*

28 Deveau Rd., PO Box 326, North Salem, NY 10560. Phone: 914/669-5033. Fax: 914/669-8221. E-mail: *gardenprogram@yahoo.com*. Web site: *www.hammondmuseum.org*. Hours: early Apr.-early Nov.—12–4 Wed.-Sat.; closed Sun.-Tues. and remainder of year. Admission: adults, $5; seniors and students over 11, $4; children under 12, free.

Honolulu Academy of Art. The holdings of the Honolulu Academy of Arts in Hawaii are almost equally divided between Asian and Western art. The Asian collection is one of the museum's principal strengths and is considered among the most important assemblages of its kind in American museums. The Asian collection consists of over 16,500 works from China, Japan, Korea, India, and Southeast Asia. They include approximately 690 Japanese paintings ranging from twelfth-century hand scrolls to twentieth-century screens and scrolls and about 625 Chinese paintings, of which 115 date from the Ming dynasty or earlier. The museum also has an extensive collection of artworks that incorporates the cross-cultural influences initiated by commerce between the East and West. In addition to paintings and prints, the collection includes such decorative arts as furniture, ceramics, silver, carved ivory, and textiles.

Honolulu Academy of Arts, 900 S. Beretania St., Honolulu, HI 96814–1495. Phone: 808/532–8700. Fax: 808/5328787. E-mail: *webmaster@honoluluacademv.org*. Web site: *www.honoluluacademy.org*. Hours: 10–4:30 Tues.-Sat.; 1–5 Sun.; closed Mon. and major holidays. Admission: adults, $7; seniors, military, and students over 12, $6; children under 13, free.

Lentz Center for Asian Culture. The Lentz Center for Asian Culture at the University of Nebraska in Lincoln is dedicated to the enrichment of knowledge and understanding of Asia. The center, established by Professor and Mrs. Donald Lentz, presents exhibitions of Asian art and artifacts and other cultural activities. Lentz is an authority on Asian music. The center contains many of the Asian musical instruments and other objects collected by the couple.

Lentz Center for Asian Culture, University of Nebraska-Lincoln, Hewit Place., 1155 Q St., Lincoln, NE 68588–0252. Phone: 402/472–5841. Fax: 402/472–0463. E-mail: *bbanks@uni.edu*. Web site: *www.uni.edu/lentz*. Hours: 10–5 Tues.-Fri.; 11–5 Sat.;

1:30–4 Sun.; closed Mon., university holidays, and between exhibitions. Admission: $2 suggested donation.

Mai Wah Museum. The Mai Wah Society in Butte, Montana, conducts research, presents exhibits, and offers public programs about the history, culture, and conditions of Asian people in the Rocky Mountains region. The society also is restoring the adjoining Wah Chong Tai Co. and Mai Wah Noodle Parlor buildings, site of a museum with permanent and temporary exhibits using artifacts and historical photographs that tell the story of Asian immigrants in Butte and the West.

Mai Wah Museum, 17 W. Mercury St., PO Box 404, Butte, MT 59703. Phone: 406/723–3231. E-mail: *info@maiwah.org.* Web site: *www.maiwah.org.* Hours: June-Sept.—11–5 Tues.-Sat.; closed Sun.-Mon., major holidays, and remainder of year. Admission: adults, $3; children, free.

Pacific Asia Museum. The Pacific Asia Museum, housed in a historic 1924 Chinese Imperial Palace-style building in Pasadena, California, has more than 14,000 rare and representative examples of art and artifacts from Asia and the Pacific Islands. They include such works as Japanese and Chinese ceramics, sculpture, scrolls, screens, and woodblock prints; textiles of China, Japan, Philippines, Korea, Indonesia, Thailand, and India; folk art of Asia; Tibetan thankas and bronzes; Southeast Asian ceramics; and ethnographic materials from the Pacific Islands. The objects are featured in permanent and changing exhibitions.

Pacific Asia Museum, 46 N. Los Robles Ave., Pasadena, CA 91101. Phone: 626/449–2742. Fax: 626/449–2754. Email: *info@pacificasiamuseum.org.* Web site: *www.pacificasiamuseum.org.* Hours: 10–5 Wed.-Sun. (also to 8 Fri.); closed Mon.-Tues. and major holidays. Admission: adults, $7; seniors and students over 11, $5; children under 12, free.

Pacific Heritage Museum. Changing exhibitions highlighting the artistic, cultural, and economic history of the Pacific Rim are presented at the Pacific Heritage Museum, founded in San Francisco, California, in 1984 by the Bank of Canton of California, now the United Commercial Bank. The 10,000-square–foot museum is housed in the historic 1875 U.S. Subtreasury Building, which was gutted by the ensuing fire following the 1906 earthquake. The structure subsequently was reconstructed, but retained only the first of the original four stories, which is what survives today. The museum also has a permanent display on the history of the building.

Pacific Heritage Museum, 608 Commercial St., San Francisco, CA 94111. Phone: 415/399–1124. Fax:

415/989–0103. E-mail: *ted.lin@unitedcb.com.* Web site: *www.ibankunited.com/phm.* Hours: 10–4 Tues.-Sat.; closed Sun.-Mon. and major holidays. Admission: free.

Seattle Asian Art Museum. The Seattle Asian Art Museum, a branch of the Seattle Art Museum, located in Volunteer Park, features collections and exhibits of Japanese, Korean, Chinese, Indian, and Southeast Asian art. More than 500,000 visitors come to the museum annually to see the popular permanent exhibits and changing exhibitions in the 1933 art modern building.

The Japanese collection is considered one of the most distinguished outside Japan. The holdings include significant examples of ink painting, calligraphy, Buddhist sculpture, metalwork, and folk textiles. Chinese artworks span the Neolithic period through the nineteenth century, with its large-scale Chinese Buddhist sculpture being particularly noteworthy. Korean art contains folding screens, celadons, and early stoneware ceramics, and the South and Southeast Asian collection has Buddhist and Hindu sculpture in stone and bronze, paintings, decorative arts, and early Thai ceramics.

Seattle Asian Art Museum, Volunteer Park, 1400 E. Prospect St., Seattle, WA 98112–3303 (mailing address: PO Box 22000, Seattle, WA 98122–9700). Phone: 206/654–3137. Fax: 206/654–3191. E-mail: *webmaster@seattleartmuseum.org.* Web site: *www.seattleartmuseum.org.* Hours: 10–5 Tues.-Sun. (also to 9 Thurs.); closed Mon., New Year's Day, Columbus Day, Thanksgiving, and Christmas. Admission: adults, $5; seniors, students, and children 13–17, $3; children under 13, free; 1st Thurs. and Sat. of month, free.

Texas State Museum of Asian Cultures and Educational Center. The Texas State Museum of Asian Cultures and Educational Center, formerly the Asian Cultures Museum and Education Center, in Corpus Christi, Texas, seeks to further greater understanding of Asian cultures through exhibits, educational programming, and special events. Many of the museum's 8,000 objects and documents were provided by Mrs. Billie Tumble Chandler, who lived and taught English in Japan for 17 years before returning to Corpus Christi. The collection later was expanded to include items from other Pacific Rim nations and the Indian subcontinent. In 1974, Mrs. Chandler's arts foundation started the museum, which recently was designated the official state museum of Asian cultures by the Texas Legislature.

Texas State Museum of Asian Cultures and Educational Center, 1809 N. Chaparral St., Corpus Christi, TX 78401. Phone: 361/882-2641. Fax: 361/

882–5718. E-mail: *asianculturesmuseum@sbcglobal.net.*
Web site: *www.asianculturesmuseum.org.* Hours: 9–5
Tues.-Sat.; closed Sun., New Year's Day, Easter,
Thanksgiving, and Christmas. Admission: adults, $5;
students, $3.

**Trammell and Margaret Crow Collection of
Asian Art.** The Trammell and Margaret Crow Collection of Asian Art in Dallas, Texas, is dedicated
to the arts and cultures of China, Japan, India, and
Southeast Asia. The artworks were collected by real
estate developer Trammel Crow and his wife, Margaret, and are displayed in four galleries adjacent
to the Trammel Crow Center in downtown Dallas.

The collection includes Japanese scrolls, screens,
and objects in rock crystal, lacquer, ceramics, and
bronze; carved jades of China's Ming dynasty and
Chinese paintings, sculptures, porcelains, and decorative and ritual items; and the arts of India, Cambodia, Thailand, Myanmar, and Tibet. Many of
the works represent deities from such religions as
Buddhism, Confucianism, Daoism, Hinduism,
and Jainism.

Trammel and Margaret Crow Collection of Asian
Art, 2010 Flora St., Dallas, TX 75201–2335. Phone:
214/979–6430. Fax: 214/979–6439. E-mail: *market-
ing@crowcollection.org.* Web site: *www.crowcollection.
org.* Hours: 10–5 Tues.-Sun. (also to 9 Thurs.); closed
Mon. and major holidays. Admission: free.

Museums Honoring Individuals

Wing Luke Asian Museum. The Wing Luke
Asian Museum in Seattle, Washington, is named
for a Seattle lawyer who was the state's assistant attorney general and then the first Asian American
city councilman in the Pacific Northwest. He was
instrumental in passing the open housing ordinance
in Seattle and fought for civil rights, urban renewal,
and historic preservation before dying in a plane
crash in 1965.

The museum is devoted to the history, culture,
and art of Asian Pacific Americans in the Northwest
region of the United States. The centerpiece exhibit depicts the 200-year story of immigration and
settlement of Asians and Pacific Islanders in the
state of Washington. It is the only exhibit in the
nation that integrates the many different experiences of 10 Asian Pacific American ethnic groups —
the Cambodians, Chinese, Filipinos, Japanese, Koreans, Laotians, Pacific Islanders, South Asians,
Southeast Asian hill tribes, and Vietnamese. The
museum also has such exhibits as the history of
Seattle's Chinatown and Japanese internment
camps during World War II.

Wing Luke Asian Museum, 407 7th St., S., Seattle, WA 98104. Phone: 206/623–5124. Fax: 206/
623–4559. E-mail: *folks@wingluke.org.* Web site:
www.wingluke.org. Hours: 11–4:30 Tues.-Fri.; 12–4
Sat.-Sun.; closed Mon. and major holidays. Admission: adults, $4; seniors and students over 12, $3; children 5–12, $2; children under 5, free; free 1st Thurs.
of month.

AUSTRIAN (*also see* German)
Museums and Galleries

Austrian Cultural Forum. The Austrian Cultural
Forum in New York City seeks to further appreciation of contemporary Austrian cultural achievements in the United States. The forum, an agency
of the Republic of Austria, offers cultural projects
reflecting the most recent artistic and intellectual
trends and relevant perspectives. The theme of its
most recent offerings was "Transforming Modernity" (cultural developments in view of the impact
of digital works on the arts and culture at large). In
addition to discussions and programs on issues pertaining to the theme of transforming modernity,
the facility presented exhibitions on the visual arts
and architecture.

Austrian Cultural Forum, 11 W. 52nd St., New
York, NY 10022. Phone: 212/319–5300. Fax: 212/
644–8660. E-mail: *desk@acfny.org.* Web site: *www.
acfny.org.* Hours: 10–6 Mon.-Sat.; closed Sun. and
major holidays. Admission: free.

Bukovina Society Headquarters Museum. See
German Museums section

Georgia Salzburger Society Museum. The Georgia Salzburger Society in Rincon, Georgia, perpet-
uates the memory of the Salzburger exiles who
came to Georgia from the German principality of
Salzburg (now in Austria) in 1734, 1736, and 1741
seeking religious freedom. They were among the
20,000 exiled by the Catholic archbishop and
prince of Salzburg — most of whom went to East
Prussia and Holland. The society has a museum,
housed in the 1769 Jerusalem Lutheran Church
building, devoted to the history and principles of
the early Salzburger settlers and their descendents
in Georgia. The museum's collections include furniture, tools, letters, deeds, maps, and Bibles of the
settlers and their descendents from just before and
after the Civil War.

Georgia Salzburger Society Museum, 2980 Ebenezer
Rd., Rte. 1, Box 4788, Rincon, GA 31326. Phone:
912/754–7001. Fax: 912/754–7001. E-mail: *info@
georgiasalzburgers.com.* Web site: *www.georgiasalzburg-
ers.com.* Hours: 3–5 Wed. and Sat.-Sun.; closed remainder of week and major holidays. Admission: donation.

BASQUE
Museums and Galleries

Basque Museum and Cultural Center. The Basque Museum and Cultural Center in Boise, Idaho, interprets the history and culture of the Basques and their life in Idaho, surrounding states, and the United States. Boise is the center of one of the largest Basque settlements outside of Spain. Basques began coming to the region in the late nineteenth century when recruited to herd sheep in the high deserts of the intermountain West. The museum and cultural center has exhibits, a library, archives, and educational programs to perpetuate, preserve, and promote awareness of Basque history and culture. The facility opened in 1985 in the 1864 Cyrus Jacobs-Uberuaga House, the oldest surviving brick house in Boise and a former Basque boardinghouse, and later moved to its present expanded site.

Basque Museum and Cultural Center, 611 Grove St., Boise, ID 83702. Phone 208/343–2671. Web site: *www.basquemuseum.com*. Hours: 10–4 Tues.-Fri; 11–3 Sat.; closed Sun.-Mon. and major holidays. Admission: free.

Four Rivers Cultural Center and Museum. See Multicultural Museums and Galleries section.

The largest and most comprehensive collection of British art outside the United Kingdom is at the Yale Center for British Art at Yale University in New Haven, Connecticut. Some of the collection is shown in the fourth floor galleries in this photograph. *Richard Caspole, Yale Center for British Art.*

BRITISH (*also see* Scottish; Welsh)

Museums and Galleries

Yale Center for British Art. The Yale Center for British Art at Yale University in New Haven, Connecticut, has the largest and most comprehensive collection of British art outside the United Kingdom. The collection, presented to the university by financier Paul Mellon, includes paintings, sculpture, drawings, prints, rare books, and manuscripts reflecting the development of British art, life, and thought since the Elizabethan period. The museum opened in 1977 in a four-story concrete, steel, and glass structure with a double courtyard designed by prominent architect Louis I. Kahn.

The museum's collections illustrate British life and culture from the sixteenth century to the present, with the emphasis on the period considered the golden age of British art — between the birth of William Hogarth in 1697 and the death of Joseph Mallord William Turner in 1851. The museum has over 1,900 paintings, 20,000 drawings, 30,000 prints, 100 sculptures, and 30,000 books and manuscripts, as wells as microfiches, photographs, and other materials. In addition to its permanent exhibits, the museum presents temporary exhibitions ranging from some aspects of its collections to international loan shows.

Yale Center for British Art, Yale University, 1080 Chapel St., PO Box 208280, New Haven, CT 06520–8280. Phone: 203/432–2800. Fax: 203/432–4538. E-mail: *ycba.info@yale.edu*. Web site: *www.yale.edu/ycba*. Hours: 10–5 Tues.- Sat.; 12–5 Sun.; closed Mon. and major holidays. Admission: free.

Historic Sites

Philipsburg Manor. See Dutch Historic Sites section.

St. John's Episcopal Church and Museum. St. John's Episcopal Church in Hampton, Virginia, is the oldest continuous English-speaking parish in the United States. The church was the only one founded by English settlers in 1610, with its current site and building dating from 1727. It is the only Hampton building standing today that survived the town's burning during the Civil War. The parish has a museum with early Bibles, prayer books, photographs, audiovisual materials, and artifacts from the original seventeenth century church building, as well as gravestones of early English settlers.

St. John's Episcopal Church and Museum, 100 W. Queens Way, PO Box 313, Hampton, VA 23669. Phone: 757/722-2568. Web site: *www.stjohnshampton.org*. Hours: 9–3 Mon.-Fri.; 9–12 Sat.; 8 and 10:30 Sun. services. Admission: free.

CAMBODIAN (*also see* Asian)
Museums and Galleries

Cambodian American Heritage Museum and Killing Fields Memorial. The Cambodian Association of Illinois operates the Cambodian American Heritage Museum and Killing Fields Memorial in Chicago, Illinois. Located in the Cambodian Community Center, the museum is devoted to the Khmer Rouge's killing fields and atrocities in which 2 million perished in Cambodia in the 1970s and the resettlement and new lives of escaping Cambodians and their children. The association provides bilingual programming to address the interrelated social and economic needs of Cambodian Americans in the Chicago area.

Cambodian American Heritage Museum and Killing Fields Memorial, Cambodian Assistant of Illinois, 2831 W. Lawrence Ave., Chicago, IL 60625. Phone: 773/878-7090. Fax: 773/878-5299. E-mail: *cai@cambodianassociation.org*. Web site: *www.cambodian-association.org*. Hours: 10–4 Mon.-Fri.; 12–4 Sat.; closed Sun. and major holidays. Admission: free.

Cambodian Cultural Museum and Killing Fields Memorial. The Cambodian Cultural Museum and Killing Fields Memorial in the Seattle suburb of White Center, Washington, was opened in 2004 by Cambodian refugee Dara Duong, who wanted local Cambodian youth to know about their heritage and what their elders endured during the 1970s killing fields atrocities by the Khmer Rouge in Cambodia. The museum contains photographs of many of the people tortured and killed during that violent period of history and exhibits of Cambodian art, sculpture, and history.

Cambodian Cultural Museum and Killing Fields Memorial, 9800 16th Ave., S.W., Seattle, WA 98106. Phones: 206/763-8088 and 206/730-7740. Hours: 8–5 Mon.-Fri.; 9–5 Sat.-Sun. Admission: adults, $7; students and children under 15, $3.

Historic Sites

Cambodian Buddhist Shrine. The Cambodian Buddhist Society in Silver Spring, Maryland, seeks to conserve the Cambodian Buddhist religion and Cambodian culture and to provide training and assistance to Cambodians in the area. It also has a Buddha Hall that is a Cambodian shrine with all the characteristics of a typical vihara in Cambodia. The exterior of the shrine is decorated with all the Cambodian artworks reserved for a Buddhist temple. Inside the building is a giant Buddha image sitting on an altar surrounded by smaller images; there are also large paintings depicting the life of the Buddha and two large crystal chandeliers.

Cambodian Buddhist Society Shrine, 13800 New Hampshire Ave., Silver Spring, MD 20904. Phone and fax: 301/622-6544. Web site: *www.cambodian-buddhist.org*. Hours: by appointment. Admission: free.

CHINESE (*also see* Asian)
Museums and Galleries

China Institute Gallery. The China Institute Gallery in New York City is dedicated to the exhibition of traditional Chinese art. Since its founding in 1966, the gallery has presented over 90 focused exhibitions of Chinese paintings, calligraphy, architecture, decorative art, folk art, photography, and textiles curated by internationally recognized scholars.

China Institute Gallery, Chinese Institute in America, 125 E. 65th St., New York, NY 10021. Phone: 212/744-8181. Fax: 212/628-4159. E-mail: *gallery@chinainstitute.org*. Web site: *www.chinainstitute.org/gallery*. Hours: 10–5 Mon.-Sat. (also to 8 Tues. and Thurs.); closed major holidays and between exhibitions. Admission: adults, $5; seniors and students over 11, $3; children under 12, free; free 6–8 Tues. and Thurs.

Chinatown Heritage and Visitors Center. The history of the Chinese in Southern California is presented at the Chinatown Heritage and Visitors Center operated by the Chinese Historical Society of Southern California in Los Angeles. The center, which occupies two adjoining Victorian buildings, also contains artifacts uncovered during excavations for the Metro Red Line at Union Station, which was the location of the city's original Chinatown. Tours of Chinatown also are offered by the society.

Chinatown Heritage and Visitors Center, Chinese Historical Society of Southern California, 411 Bernard St., Los Angeles, CA 90012. Phone: 323/222-0856. E-mail: *chssc@earthlink.net*. Web site: *www.chssc.org*.

Hours: 11–3 Wed.- Fri.; 12–4:30 Sun.; closed Mon.-Tues. and Sat. Admission: free

Chinese American Museum. The Chinese American Museum, located in the El Pueblo de Los Angeles Historical Monument in Los Angeles, California (see separate listing), seeks to foster greater understanding and appreciation of America's diverse heritage by sharing the history, cultural legacy, and continuing contributions of Chinese Americans. The exhibits use historical documents, artifacts, and photographs to illustrate the rich culture and heritage of Chinese Americans, and present their challenges and achievements from the earliest pioneers to the newest immigrants.

Chinese American Museum, 423–425 N. Los Angeles St., Los Angeles, CA 90012 (contact information: Friends of the Chinese American Museum, 125 Paseo de la Plaza, Suite 400, Los Angles, CA 90012). Phones: 213/485–8567 and 213/485–8484. Faxes: 213/485–8238 and 213/473–4224. E-mail: *curator@ camla.org*. Web site: *www.camla.org*. Hours: 10–3 Tues.-Sun.; closed Mon. and major holidays. Admission: adults, $3 suggested donation; seniors and students, $2 suggested donation.

Chinese-American Museum of Chicago. The Chinese-American Museum of Chicago opened in 2005 in Chicago's Chinatown. Housed in a restored 1896 factory building formerly occupied by Ouong Yick Co., it features changing exhibitions relating to Chinese-American culture and history in the Midwest. A recent exhibition dealt with the cultural influence of silk and wood in Chinese life. The museum is now closed because of a fire in 2008.

Chinese-American Museum of Chicago, 238 W. 23rd St., Chicago, IL 60616. Phone: 312/949–1000. Fax: 312/9499100. E-mail: *office@ccamuseum.org*. Web site: *www.ccamuseum.org*. Hours: 9:30–1:30 Fri.; 10–5 Sat.-Sun.; closed Mon.-Thurs. and major holidays. Admission: adults, $2; seniors, students, and children under 12, $1.

Chinese Culture Center of San Francisco. Exhibitions of Chinese art are presented at the Chinese Culture Center of San Francisco. The center also offers docent-conducted walks of San Francisco's Chinatown. The center recently reopened after being closed for renovations.

Chinese Culture Center of San Francisco, 750 Kearny St., 3rd Floor, San Francisco, CA 94108. Phone: 415/986–1822. Fax: 415/986–2825. E-mail: *info@c-c-c.org*. Web site: *www.c-c-c.org*. Hours: 10–4 Tues.-Sat.; closed Sun.-Mon. and major holidays. Admission: free.

Chinese Culture Institute Gallery. The Chinese Culture Institute in Boston, Massachusetts, promotes cultural understanding through educational and cultural activities, including a gallery that displays changing exhibitions. The institute also has a collection of artworks, books, photographs, and archival materials on Chinese culture and history and related subjects.

Chinese Culture Institute Gallery, 276 Tremont St., Boston, MA 02116–5604. Phone: 617/542–4599. Fax: 617/338- 4274. Hours: 9:30–5 Tues.-Sat.; closed Sun.-Mon. and major holidays. Admission: free.

Chinese Historical Society of America Museum. The Chinese Historical Society of America in San Francisco, California, has a museum with a permanent exhibit on the history of the Chinese in the United States, with the emphasis on Chinese immigration and the role of the Chinese in the settlement of San Francisco and the American West. The society also presents changing exhibitions in two other galleries. The society has the largest collection of Chinese American artifacts in the nation.

Chinese Historical Society of America Museum, 965 Clay St., San Francisco, CA 94108. Phone: 415/391–1188. Fax: 415/391–1150. Web site: *www. chsa.org*. Hours: 12-5 Tues.-Fri.; 12–4 Sat.-Sun.; closed Mon. and major holidays. Admission: adults, $3; seniors and college students, $2; children 6–17, $1; children under 6, free.

Dai Loy Museum. The Dai Loy Museum tells the story of Locke, California, the only town built exclusively by the Chinese for the Chinese in the United States. It is housed in a former gambling house that was owned by Lee Bing, founder of the town in 1915. The community was settled by immigrant Chinese agricultural workers in the Sacramento Delta after fire destroyed the Chinese section of nearby Walnut Grove.

Dai Loy Museum, Main St., Locke, CA 95690. Phone: 916/776–1661. Web site: *www.locketown. com/museum*. Hours: 11–5 Sat.-Sun.; closed remainder of week. Admission: adults, $1.25; children and students, 75¢.

Forbidden Gardens. Forbidden Gardens in Katy, Texas, is an unusual outdoor museum that replicates some of China's major historic sites in scaled versions. Guided tours take visitors to see such sights as the terra-cotta army of 6,000 soldiers in formation as they were buried in the third century B.C. reproduced in 1/3 scale; palace buildings and hundreds of figures in the 250-acre Forbidden City, built between 1406 and 1420 and reproduced in 1/20th scale within a 40,000-square-foot pavilion; the 1700s vacation lodge for emperors, scholars, and others who lived and worked in the Forbidden City; and rooms with exhibits on the architecture and weapons of the historic period.

Forbidden Gardens, 235 Franz Rd., Katy, TX 77493. Phones: 281/347–8000 and 281/347–8096. E-mail: *askus@forbidden-gardens.com*. Web site: *www.forbidden-gardens.com*. Hours: 10–5 Fri.-Sun.; closed remainder of week and major holidays. Admission: adults, $10; seniors, teachers, and students 6–18, $5; children under 6, $3, but one child under 6 admitted free with each adult and senior.

Museum of Chinese in the Americas. Artifacts, art, photographs, papers, oral histories, and other objects are used at the Museum of Chinese in the Americas in New York City to document the history, challenges, and contributions of the Chinese in North and South America. Permanent exhibits trace personal stories of Chinese Americans and how they addressed the difficulties of leaving their homeland and settling in a new world, and the history of Chinatown areas in New York City and other cities. Changing exhibitions illustrate various aspects of the Chinese American experience. The museum is housed in an 1893 former school building.

Museum of Chinese in the Americas, 70 Mulberry St., 2nd Floor, New York, NY 10013. Phone: 212/619–4785. Fax: 212/619–4720. E-mail: *info@moca-nyc.org*. Web site: *www.moca-nyc.org*. Hours: 12–6 Tues.-Sun. (also to 7 Fri.); closed Mon. and major holidays. Admission: adults, $3; seniors and students over 11, $1; children under 12, free; free on Fri.

San Diego Chinese Historical Museum. The San Diego Chinese Historical Museum seeks to preserve and share the Chinese American experience and history with the community at large. Since its founding in 1996 by the San Diego Chinese Historical Society, the museum has presented more than 40 exhibits relating to Chinese culture and history in San Diego and the world. The museum also has a tranquil garden with a koi pond.

San Diego Chinese Historical Museum, 404 3rd Ave., San Diego, CA 92101. Phone: 619/338–9888. Fax: 619/338–9889. E-mail: *info@sdchm.org*. E-mail: *www.sdchm.org*. Hours: 10:30–4 Tues.-Sat.; 12–4 Sun.; closed Mon. and major holidays. Admission: adults and children over 11, $2; children under 12, free.

Historic Sites

Bok Kai Temple. The Bok Kai Temple is a historic nineteenth-century Chinese site in Marysville, California, that is being restored by the Chinese community and the Marysville Yuba County Chamber of Commerce. As the work and fund raising continues, the interior of the house of worship can be visited only by appointment.

Bok Kai Temple, City of Marysville Bok Kai Temple, PO Box 18844, Marysville, CA 95901. Phone:

530/743–6501. Web site: *www.bokkaitemple.org*. Hours: by appointment. Admission: free.

Chew Kee Store. The ca. 1855 Chew Kee Store remains intact as one of the few remnants of the once thriving Chinese community in Fiddletown, California. Dr. Yee Fong Cheung established an herb shop in the rammed earth structure during the California Gold Rush to serve Chinese miners and railroad workers. The store later also provided groceries and supplies to the Chinese community. It remains today much the same as during the early days, with shelves and drawers of herbs and living quarters in the rear where Dr. Yee lived and treated patients.

Chew Kee Store, Main St., Fiddletown, CA 05629. Phones: 209/245–3530 and 209/245–6459. Hours: Apr.-Oct.—12–4 Sat. and by appointment; closed remainder of week and year. Admission: donation.

Chinese House/OR. & N. Railroad Museum. The Chinese House Railroad Museum in Echo, Oregon, is located in the building that housed Chinese who worked on the railroad and served as the railroad section headquarters in the late 1800s. The Chinese and white workers had separate houses and privy pits. The museum has a large collection of medicine bottles, alcohol containers, and Chinese artifacts excavated from the privy pit, as well as tools, photographs, and other items used by the early Union Pacific Railroad and Oregon Railway and Navigation Company.

Chinese House/O.R. & N. Museum, 230 W. Bridge St., PO Box 426, Echo, OR 97826. Phone: 541/376–8411. Fax: 541/376–8218. E-mail: *ecpl@centurytel.net*. Web site: *www.echo-oregon.com/chinese.html*. Hours: May-Oct.—10–4 Mon.-Fri.; closed Sat.-Sun.; remainder of year —1–4 Mon.-Thurs. (check city hall for admittance) or by appointment; closed Fri.-Sun. Admission: free.

Joss House State Historic Park. The Temple of the Forest Beneath the Clouds at the Joss House State Historic Park in Weaverville, California, is the oldest continuously used Chinese temple of worship in the state. The current Joss House was built in 1874 after earlier structures were destroyed by a series of fires. The Taoist temple contains religious artifacts brought to the area by the Chinese during California's gold rush, as well as art objects, photographs, mining tools, and wrought iron weapons used in the 1854 Tong War. There is a fee for tours of the Joss House, but admission to the visitor center is free.

Joss House State Historic Park, State Historic Park, PO Box 1217, Weaverville, CA 96093. Phone: 530/623–5284. E-mail: *weavervillejosshouse@calgov.gov*. Web sites: *www.parks.cal.gov/?page_id=457* and *www.trinity-county.com/joss.htm*. Hours: 10–4 Wed.-Sun.; closed

Mon.-Tues. and major holidays. Admission: adults and children over 16, $2; children under 17, free.

Kam Wah Chung & Co. Museum. Two Chinese immigrants, Lung On and Ing Hay, purchased the building on the site of the present-day Kam Wah Chung & Co. Museum in 1887 for their homes, businesses, and the social and religious center of the Chinese community in John Day, Oregon. Lung On started a general store, while Ing Hay operated an herbal medicine and pulse diagnosis business. The site now has been restored and contains thousands of artifacts and other historical materials from the days it served Chinese miners and their families.

Kam Wah Chung & Co. Museum, 450 E. Main St., John Day, OR 07845. Phones: 541/575-0547 and 800/551-6949. Web site: *www.grantcounty.cc/events/kamwahchung.htm.* Hours: May-Oct.— 9–12 and 1–5 Mon.-Sat.; 1–5 Sun.; remainder of year — 9–12 Tues.; 1–5 Thurs.; closed remainder of week. Admission: adults, $3; seniors, $2.50; children over 4, $1.50; children under 5, free.

Ng Shing Gung. Ng Shing Gung was a Chinese religious and community center when built in a Chinatown known as Heinlenville in San Jose, California, in 1888. The center offered Chinese calligraphy and literature classes for children, and had an elaborately carved and gilded altar on the second floor. But the residents of the Chinatown neighborhood gradually were integrated, the Heinlenville estate went bankrupt, and the site became the property of the city of San Jose in the 1930s. The city then razed all the buildings except Ng Shing Gung, which was dismantled in 1949. However, the historic religious and community center was reconstructed in 1991 as part of the Chinese Historical and Cultural Project and relocated to the 12-acre History San Jose outdoor complex at Kelley Park. It features exhibits and a video on Heinlenville Chinatown and the life and contributions of Chinese Americans in Santa Clara Valley.

Ng Shing Gung, History Park, Kelley Park, San Jose, CA 95112 (mailing address: History San Jose, 1650 Senter Rd., San Jose, CA 95112-2599). Phone: 408/287-2290. Fax: 408/287-2291. E-mail: *dcrosson @historysanjose.org.* Web site: *www.historysanjose.org.* Hours: 12–5 Tues.-Sun.; closed Mon., New Year's Day, Independence Day, Thanksgiving, and Christmas. Admission: free.

Oroville Chinese Temple. The 1863 Oroville Chinese Temple in Oroville, California, once served as a place of worship for a community of 10,000 Chinese residents. The restored temple now is a historic site with religious figures, tapestries, writings, screens, altars, and information on Chinese immigrants during the California gold rush. An innovative collaboration with the Bancroft Library also has resulted in online access to the temple's digital archive of approximately 12,500 images documenting Chinese immigration to California and the American West from 1850 to 1920.

Oroville Chinese Temple, 1500 Broderick St., Oroville, CA 95965 (mailing address: 1735 Montgomery St., Oroville, CA 95965). Phones: 530/538-2415 and 888/676-8453. Web site: *www.oroville-city.com.* Hours: Feb.-Oct.—12–4 daily; remainder of year—1–4 Tues.-Wed.; 12–4 Thurs.-Mon.; closed major holidays. Admission: adults and children over 11, $2; children under 12, free.

Botanical Gardens

New York Chinese Scholar's Garden. The New York Chinese Scholar's Garden is located at the Staten Island Botanical Garden on Staten Island, New York. Traditional Chinese gardens originated almost 2,000 years ago during the Han Dynasty, but most scholar's gardens date back only to the more recent Ming and Qing dynasties. A scholar's garden would have been an enclosed private garden built by a scholar or an administrator retiring from the emperor's court for contemplative and sensual purposes. The Staten Island scholar's garden is enclosed by walls and has eight pavilions and covered walkways. These are organized in an irregular manner to create two major courtyards and six smaller ones of varying sizes.

New York Chinese Scholar's Garden, Staten Island Botanical Garden, 1000 Richmond Terrace, Staten Island, NY 10301. Phone: 718/273-8200. Fax: 718/442-3645. Web site: *www.sibg.org.* Hours: 10–5 Tues.-Sun.; closed Mon. and major holidays. Admission: $5.

CROATIAN

Museums and Galleries

Croatian Ethnic Institute Museum. The Croatian Ethnic Institute, founded in 1975 by Croatian Franciscans, operates a museum, archives, library, and research center in Chicago, Illinois. The museum contains historical and artistic items related to Croatian heritage and folklore, including artifacts, musical instruments, currency, and stamps. The archives are the largest repository of personal papers, manuscripts, and correspondence of people of Croatian descent in the United States and Canada, and the library has over 12,000 volumes relating to Croatian culture, history, language, fine arts, literature, and other subjects. The research center conducts studies on the sociological, demographic, religious, and political aspects of Croatian and other migrations and their impact.

Croatian Ethnic Institute Museum, 4851 W. Drexel Blvd., Chicago, IL 60615. Phone: 773/373–4670. Fax: 773/3734746. E-mail: *croetljubo@aol.com*. Web site: *www.croatian-institute.org*. Hours: by appointment. Admission: free.

Croatian Heritage Museum and Library. Exhibits of Croatian folk art, fine art, history, and current events are presented at the Croatian Heritage Museum and Library, located in the Croatian Lodge Complex in Eastlake, Ohio. The museum has collections of Croatian artifacts, textiles, folk costumes, wood carvings, metal work, sculpture, leather work, and paintings, and the library contains a wide variety of books and journals relating to Croatian history and culture.

Croatian Heritage Museum and Library, Our Croatia, Inc., Croatian Lodge Complex, 34900 Lakeshore Blvd., Eastlake, OH 44095. Phone: 440/946–2044. E-mail: *information@croatianmuseum.com*. Web site: *www.croatianmuseum.com*. Hours: 7–10 P.M. Fri.; other times by appointment; closed Christmas. Admission: free.

CUBAN (*also see* Hispanic)

Museums and Galleries

Center for Cuban Studies. The Center for Cuban Studies in New York City provides information and activities relating to contemporary Cuba and seeks to further normalization of relations between Cuba and the United States. It has an Art Space Gallery featuring paintings, sculptures, photographs, and posters by Cuban artists, and operates a Cuban Art Space Web site with pages of Cuban artworks for viewing, rent, or sale.

Center for Cuban Studies, 124 W. 23rd St., New York, NY 10011. Phone: 212/242–0559. Fax: 212/242–1937. E-mail: *cubanctr@igc.org*. Web sites: *www.cubaupdate.org/gallery.htm* and *www.cubanartspace.net*. Hours: 11–7 Tues.-Fri.; 12–5 Sat.; closed Sun.-Mon. and major holidays. Admission: free.

Cuban Museum. The Cuban Museum of Arts and Culture in Coconut Grove, Florida, has become simply the Cuban Museum in nearby Coral Gables. The museum was founded by Cuban exiles to preserve and interpret the cultural heritage of their homeland. The new site, which is expected to open by 2008, will house historical documents, artifacts, artworks, and memorabilia inherent to the Cuban cultural heritage and offer educational and aesthetic programs pertaining to Cuban culture in freedom.

Cuban Museum, 214 Giralda Ave., PO Box 14–

4291, Coral Gables, FL 33134. Phone: 305/529–5400. Web site: *www.cubanmuseum.org*. Hours and admission: still to be determined.

CZECH (*also see* Slovak; German)

Museums and Galleries

Burleson County Czech Heritage Museum. The Burleson County Czech Heritage Museum in Caldwell, Texas, preserves and promotes the heritage and culture of the Czech people in Europe and the Czech settlers in the Burleson County area in Texas. Among the diverse displays are a Czech shepherd's bagpipe and flutes, rare cut-crystal and pottery, Czech dolls, and everyday items used by early Czech settlers in Texas.

Burleson County Czech Heritage Museum, Fawn and Shaw Sts., Caldwell, TX 77836. Phones: 979/567–1555 and 979/535–4895. Web site: *www.rtiscom/reg/caldwell/org/museum.htm*. Hours: by appointment. Admission: free.

Czech and Slovak Sokol Minnesota Museum. Czech and Slovak Sokol Minnesota Museum in St. Paul is a social, cultural, educational, and gymnastic organization that seeks to preserve and transmit the vitality of Czech and Slovak heritage to future generations. It has a museum, library, and archives to further Czechoslovakian history and culture in the region.

Czech and Slovak Sokol Minnesota Museum, 383 Michigan St., Phone: 651/290–0542. E-mail: *sokolmn@aol.com*. Web site: *www.sokolmn.org*. Hours: by appointment. Admission: free.

Czech Center New York. The Czech Center New York is part of a network of 19 Czech cultural centers operated by the Czech Ministry of Foreign Affairs. The New York City center, the only one outside of Europe, is focused primarily on the latest and most innovative works of Czech artists. It also presents concerts, dance performances, films, traveling exhibitions, and a street fair.

Czech Center New York, 1109 Madison Ave., New York NY 10028. Phone: 212/288–0830. Fax: 212/288–0971. E-mail: *info@czechcenter.com*. Web site: *www.czechcenter.com*. Hours: 9–5 Tues.-Fri. (also to 7 Thurs.); closed Sat.- Mon. and Christmas Eve, Day, and day after. Admission: free.

Czech Cultural Center Houston. A museum and art gallery are being developed as part of the new Czech Cultural Center Houston in Houston, Texas. They will have artifacts, paintings, sculpture, and photographs, as well as displays of porcelain and crystal, examples of folk arts, and changing exhibitions. The cultural center also will have a performance hall, library, genealogical resource center, and other facilities.

Czech Cultural Center Houston, 4920 San Jacinto, Houston, TX 77004. Phone: 713/528–2060. Fax: 713/528–2017. Web site: *www.czechcenter.org*. Hours and admission: still to be determined.

Czech Memorial Museum. The Czech Memorial Museum in Jennings, Kansas, has more than 1,000 artifacts and memorabilia pertaining to Czech settlement in the area. Jennings is a small farming community founded by Czechoslovakian settlers in 1888. The museum is housed in the former Methodist Church that was gutted and then restored for use as a museum on Czech history and life in the community.

Czech Memorial Museum, 114 Kansas Ave., Jennings, KS 67643. Phone: 785/578–2470. Hours: by appointment. Admission: free.

Czechoslovak Heritage Museum. The Czechoslovak Heritage Museum, a part of the CSA Fraternal Life insurance company in Oak Brook, Illinois, is devoted to the culture and traditions of Czech, Slovak, and Moravian heritages. It contains folk costumes, dolls, puppets, crystal, ceramics, needlework, artworks, religious statues, prayer books, historical items, and records of CSA and other societies that have merged with it over the years.

Czechoslovak Heritage Museum, CSA Fraternal Life, 122 W. 22nd St., Oak Brook, IL 60523. Phones: 630/472–0500 and 800/543–3272. E-mail: *lifecsa@aol.com*. Web site: *www.csafraterallife.org*. Hours: 10–4 Mon.-Fri.; closed Sat., Sun., and major holidays. Admission: donation.

House of Memories Museum. See Wilson Czech Opera House and House of Memories Museum in Historic Sites section.

Louisiana Czech Museum. The Louisiana Czech Museum being developed in Libuse, Louisiana, will celebrate the contributions of Czech immigrants to Louisiana. It will be devoted primarily to the history and artifacts of Czech families who have settled in the region since the early twentieth century. It will contain folk costumes, glassware, crystal, ceramics, wheat and cornhusk weavings, kraslice eggs, artworks, dolls, stamps, books, and other items.

Louisiana Czech Museum, PO Box 47, Libuse, LA 71348. Phone: 318/483–3134. E-mail: *webmaster@mailczechmuseum.com*. Web site: *www.czechmuseum.com*. Hours and admission: still being determined.

Moravian Historical Society. See German Museums and Galleries section.

Moravian Museum of Bethlehem. See German Museums and Galleries section.

National Czech and Slovak Museum and Library. The National Czech and Slovak Museum and Library in Cedar Rapids, Iowa, is the nation's largest and most comprehensive museum interpreting Czech and Slovak history and culture. Its principal exhibit, "Homelands: the Story of the Czech and Slovak People," tells the story of the Czechs and Slovaks from the days of Slavic tribes entering central Europe through the 1993 action that separated Czechoslovakia into two distinct countries. The exhibit contains fine and folk art, glassware, ceramics, folk costumes, maps, military information, an early printing press, and a restored nineteenth-century immigrant house.

The museum also has two-dimensional exhibits in its north and south halls and presents two to three temporary exhibitions in the Robert J. Petrik Gallery each year. The museum collection and library holdings total more than 30,000 items. In 1995, Presidents Bill Clinton of the United States, Vaclav Havel of the Czech Republic, and Michal Kovac of the Slovak Republic presided over the dedication of the museum and library building.

National Czech and Slovak Museum and Library, 30 16th Ave., S.W., Cedar Rapids, IA 52404–5904. Phone: 319/362-8500. Fax: 319/363–2209. Web site: *www.ncsml.org*. Hours: May-Oct. — 9:30–4 Mon.-Sat.; 12–4 Sun.; remainder of year — 9:30–4 Tues.-Sat.; 12–4 Sun.; closed Mon. and national holidays. Admission: adults, $7; seniors, $6; children 5-16, $2; children under 5, free.

Old Salem. See German Museums and Galleries section.

Sokol Greater Cleveland Museum. Sokol Greater Cleveland in Ohio is one of the largest of 44 Sokol organizations in North America devoted to the physical, mental, and cultural advancement of its members. It also seeks to preserve and further Czech American heritage and culture. Its Czech Cultural Center, which contains a museum, library, and archives devoted to Sokol history and activities, is located in the historic Bohemian National Hall in Cleveland.

Sokol Greater Cleveland Museum, Bohemian National Hall, 4939 Broadway Ave., Cleveland, OH 44127. Phone: 216/883–0675. Web site: *www.sokolgreatercleveland.org*. Hours: 10–3 Sat. and by appointment. Admission: free.

Sokol South Omaha Czechoslovak Museum. The history and culture of Czechs in Omaha, Nebraska, are the focus of the Sokol South Omaha Czechoslovak Museum, which also has displays of hand-cut crystal, folk costumes, memorabilia, and photographs. The Sokol facility in southern Omaha seeks to preserve and promote Czech heritage and culture while providing gymnastic and other services to members and the Czech community.

Sokol South Omaha Czechoslovak Museum, 2021 U St., Omaha, NE 68107. Phones: 402/291–2893 and 402/731- 1065. Web site: *http://home.earthlink.net/~vbenak/contact.htm*. Hours: by appointment. Admission: free.

SPJST Library, Archives, and Museum. Artifacts and memorabilia of early Czech settlers in Texas are featured at the SPJST Library, Archives, and Museum in Temple, Texas. The facility is located at SPJST, the Czech insurance company originally chartered as the Slavonic Benevolent Order of the State of Texas. Among the items on display are early housewares, musical instruments, clocks, folk costumes, quilts, and agricultural implements. The exhibits include a pioneer kitchen, blacksmith shop, and a replica of the first Czech home built in Texas, as well as medical and military displays.

SPJST Library, Archives, and Museum, 520 N. Main St., PO Box 100, Temple, TX 76503. Phones: 254/773–1575 and 800/727–7578. Fax: 254/774–7447. E-mail: *vanicek@spist.com*. Web site: *www.spjst.com*. Hours: 8–12 and 1–5 Mon.- Fri.; closed Sat.-Sun. and major holidays. Admission: free.

Texas Czech Heritage and Cultural Center. The Texas Czech Heritage and Cultural Center now is under development in La Grange, Texas. The complex, adjacent to the Fayette County Fairgrounds, will include a museum, library, archives, and living history village. Several early Texas-Czech buildings already have been donated for the village, including the Kalich farmhouse, which has been restored and serves as a visitor center on the grounds. An amphitheater also has been built and eventually will be joined outdoors by an immigrants' memorial wall, memorial rose garden, and the early twentieth-century living-history village with historic structures, dance hall, covered pavilion, and Czech restaurant. Plans also call for a Texas Polka Music Museum to be included in the complex.

Texas Czech Heritage and Cultural Center, Visitor Center, 250 W. Fairgrounds Rd., La Grange, TX 78945. Phone: 888/785–4500. Web site: *www.czechtexas.org*. Hours: 10–4 Mon.-Fri.; closed Sat.-Sun. and major holidays. Admission: free.

Wilber Czech Museum. The Wilber Czech Museum, located in Wilbur, one of the largest Czech settlements in Nebraska, interprets the history and culture of Czech pioneers who settled in the area beginning in the 1860s. It has exhibits of early tex-

tiles, clothing, quilts, tools, dolls, and other historical materials, and contains period rooms depicting an early home, grocery, meat market, barber shop, dentist's office, schoolroom, and shop.

Wilber Czech Museum, 102 W. 3rd St., PO Box 253, Wilber, NE 68465. Phone: 402/821–2183. Web site: *http://saline.unl.edu/museum.htm*. Hours: 1–4 daily; other times by appointment; closed national holidays. Admission: free.

Museums Honoring Individuals

Albin Polasek Museum and Sculpture Gardens. The Albin Polasek Museum and Sculpture Gardens in Winter Park, Florida, is a tribute to noted Czech American sculptor and artist Albin Polasek. The story of Polasek's art career is shown in the main gallery, residence, and chapel, along with the works of various other artists and private collections. Dozens of his sculptures can be seen throughout the three acres of lakeside gardens at his retirement home. Polasek retired in 1949 after 30 years as head of sculpture at the Art Institute of Chicago. He died in 1965 at the age of 85.

Albin Polasek Museum and Sculpture Gardens, 633 Osceola Ave., PO Box 1691, Winter Park, FL 32789. Phone: 407/647–6292. Fax: 407/647–0410. Web site: *www.polasek.org*. Hours: Sept.-June — 10–4 Tues.-Sat.; 1–4 Sun.; closed Mon. and July-Aug. Admission: adults, $5; seniors, $4; students, $3; children under 12, free.

Bily Clock Museum & Antonin Dvorak Exhibit. The Bily brothers — Joseph C. and Frank L. — were Czech farmers and carpenters in Spillville, Iowa, who enjoyed carving as a hobby. This led them to carving clocks with simple tools, many of them homemade. Their clocks combined artistry with music and mechanical figures such as the apostles, bands, and cuckoos. Despite many offers for the clocks, they refused to part with the clocks and left the entire collection to the town after their deaths. The clocks now are housed in a building occupied by Bohemia-born composer Antonin Dvorak during a visit to Spillville in 1893. In addition to the Bily clocks, the museum has an exhibit honoring Dvorak.

Bily Clock Museum, S. Main St., PO Box 258, Spillville, IA 52168. Phone: 319/562–3569. E-mail: *bilyclocks@mchsi.com*. Web site: *www.bilyclocks.org*. Hours: May-Oct. — 8–5:30 daily; remainder of year — 10–4 daily. Admission: varies from $1 to $3.50, depending on size of group.

Historic Sites

Burnside Plantation. See German Historic Sites section.

Colonial Industrial Quarter. See German Historic Sites section.

Historic Bethabara Park. See German Historic Sites section.

Historic New Ulm. See German Historic Sites section.

Wilson Czech Opera House and House of Memories Museum. The historic Wilson Czech Opera House in Wilson, Kansas, was built in 1901 and once was the scene of Czech and other performances and a social hall for the community. It now is the meeting hall for the Czech Lodge and features the House of Memories Museum, which tells the story of Wilson and the Czechs from the first settlers to the present. In addition to a pictorial history of the area, the museum contains such items as handmade dolls and toys, folk costumes, hand-painted eggs, a side-sod-buster plow, early tools, hand-carved native stone, and Czech glassware.

Wilson Czech Opera House and House of Memories Museum, 415 27th St., Old Hwy. 40, PO Box 271, Wilson, KS 67490–0271. Phones: 785/658–3505 and 785/658–3343. Web site: *www.lasr.net/leasure/kansas/ellsworth/lwilson/attl.htm*. Hours: 10–12 and 1–4 Mon.-Sat., 1–4 Sun. Admission: free.

DANISH (*also see* Scandinavian)
Museums and Galleries

Danish Immigrant Museum. The life, culture, and diversity of Danish American immigrants and their descendants are depicted at the Danish Immigrant Museum in Elk Horn, Iowa. The museum traces the immigration of Danes to America and explores the culture, arts, and other aspects of Danish life. It has collections of clothing, tools, household furnishings, art, photographs, and other items and two historic structures on its 20-acre site — an early chapel and a 1908 house known as Bedstemor's (Grandmother's) House.

Danish Immigrant Museum, 2212 Washington St., PO Box 470, Elk Horn, IA 51531. Phone: 712/764–7001. Fax: 712/764–7002. E-mail: *info@danishmuseum.org*. Web site: *www.danishmuseum.org*. Hours: May 15-Sept. 15 — 9–5 Mon.-Fri.; 10–5 Sat.-Sun.; remainder of year — 9–5 Mon.-Fri.; 10–5 Sat.; 12–5 Sun.; closed New Year's Day, Thanksgiving, and Christmas. Admission: adults, $5; children, $1.50.

Elverhoj Museum of History and Art. The Elverhoj Museum of History and Art in the Danish-oriented Solvang, California, is a community museum devoted to the history of the city, Danish-American pioneers and their heritage, and the arts.

It is housed in the hand-crafted Danish farmhouse-style former home of painter and sculptor Viggo Brandt-Erichsen and his wife, painter and art teacher Martha Mott. The structure is based on the large farmhouses of eighteenth-century Jutland in northern Denmark. Much of the museum is devoted to Danish culture and the Danish-American experience.

Elverhoj Museum of History and Art, 1624 Elverhoy Way, Solvang, CA 93464. Pone: 805/686–1211. Fax: 805/686–1822. E-mail: *info@elverhoj.org*. Web site: *www.elverhoj.org*. Hours: 1–4 Wed.-Thurs.; 12–4 Fri.-Sun.; closed New Year's Day, Easter, Thanksgiving, and Christmas Eve and Day. Admission: adults, $3 suggested donation; children under 13, free.

Museums Honoring Individuals

Hans Christian Andersen Museum. The Hans Christian Andersen Museum in Solvang, California, honors the noted Danish writer of more than 160 fairy tales, including *The Ugly Duckling*, *The Little Mermaid*, and *The Princess and the Pea*. The museum has exhibits on Andersen's life and work, many of his illustrated books, a model of his childhood home, antique tools for making wooden shoes, singer Jenny Lind (Andersen's unrequited love), and actor Jean Hersholt (noted Andersen scholar).

Hans Christian Andersen Museum, Book Loft Bldg., 1680 Mission Dr., Solvang, CA 93463. Phone: 805/688–2052. Web site: *www.solvangca.com/museum/hl.htm*. Hours: 10–5 daily. Admission: free.

Historic Sites

Christiansted National Historic Site. The Christiansted National Historic Site in St. Croix, U.S. Virgin Islands, protects historic structures and interprets the Danish economy and way of life on the islands between 1733 and 1917. Christiansted was the capital of the former Danish West Indies. The islands have been under seven flags since discovery by Christopher Columbus in 1493. Five historic structures are part of the seven-acre historic site — 1738 Fort Christianvaern, 1749 Danish West Indies & Guinea Company warehouse, 1753 Steeple Building, 1844 Danish Custom House, and 1856 Scale House. These structures are used to interpret Danish colonial administration, military and naval establishment, international trade (including slave trade), religious diversity, architecture, trades, and crime and punishment.

Christiansted National Historic Site, Danish Custom House, 2100 Church St., Suite 100, Christiansted, St. Croix, U.S. Virgin Islands 00820. Phone: 340/773–1460. E-mail: *chri_superintendent@nps.gov*. Web site: *www.nps.gov/chri.* Hours: site — 8–5 daily; museum — 8–5 Mon.-Fri.; 9–5 Sat.-Sun. Admission: adults and children over 15, $3; children under 16, free.

Historic Solvang. The city of Solvang, California, is one of the nation's most Danish communities. It began as a Spanish village — the first European settlement in Santa Ynez Valley — built around the Mission Santa Inés in 1804. By the early twentieth century, however, the community became known for its Danish architecture, customs, and lifestyle. In 1911, Danish clergy and educators, while searching for a site for a folk school and possible home for Danish immigrants, found the fertile valley and purchased a portion of a sprawling ranch in the area. They named it Solvang, which means "sunny field."

In the years that followed, many Danish immigrants settled there and the town became known for its Danish-style buildings, windmills, bakeries, organizations, celebrations, and museums (see separate listings for Elverhoj Museum and Hans Christian Andersen Museum). Many of Solvang's shopkeepers wear Danish costumes and fly American and Danish flags, and a replica of a 1915 Copenhagen streetcar is pulled through town by Belgian draft horses.

Historic Solvang (contact: Solvang Conference and Visitors Bureau, 1511 Mission Dr., PO Box 70, Solvang, CA 93464–6144). Phones: 805/688–0701 and 800/468–6765. Fax: 805/688–8620. Web site: *www.solvangusa.com.*

Whim Museum. The Whim Museum is located in the 1751 Whim Great House on one of the most prosperous sugar plantations of the seventeenth, eighteenth, and nineteenth centuries near Frederiksted on St. Croix Island in the U.S. Virgin Islands. The Whim Plantation was started by Patrick Donough in 1751 and inherited by Christopher MacEvoy, Jr., who enlarged the estate and built the superb example of Danish neo-classicism as adapted for use in the West Indies. The old slave quarters site is north of the T-shaped complex.

Whim Museum, Center Line Rd., Frederiksed, St. Croix Island, U.S. Virgin Islands 00840. Phone: 340/772–0598. Hours: 10–3 Mon.-Fri.; closed Sat.-Sun. and major holidays. Admission: adults, $8; seniors and students, $5; children 6–12, $4; children under 6, free.

DUTCH (*also see* German)

Museums and Galleries

Dutch Village. Dutch Village in Holland, Michigan, is a theme park that resembles a living-history museum. It recreates a village in the Netherlands of over 200 years ago and has a Kiederdracht (costume) Museum with Dutch folk costumes, a diorama depicting a Dutch country scene, and exhibits on cheese making and dolls with 150 provincial costumes. Costumed interpreters present the history and culture of the Dutch in a setting of Dutch architecture, formal gardens, canals, and windmills. The park also has such other attractions as a 25-bell carillon, antique carousel, wooden shoe factory, Amsterdam street organs, klompen (wooden shoe) dancers, and Dutch swing ride.

Dutch Village, 12350 James St., Holland, MI 49424. Phone: 800/285–7177. Fax: 616/396–1476. E-mail: *info@dutchvillage.com.* Web site: *www.dutch village.com.* Hours: late Apr.-late May — 9–6 daily; Memorial Day weekend-Labor Day —10–6 daily; day after Labor Day-early Oct. —10–5 daily; closed after first full week in Oct. until third week in Apr. Admission: adults, $10; seniors, $9; children 4–15, $5; children under 4, free.

Holland Museum. The Holland Museum in Holland, Michigan, is a local history and Dutch heritage museum. It traces the history of the city from the arrival of the founding Dutch settlers in 1847, and displays materials relating to the Dutch heritage and traditions. The museum, housed in a 1914 restored former post office building, has exhibits of early Dutch settlers' artifacts and memorabilia, a period room, and collections of Dutch pewter, Delft, cooper furniture, and costumes. The museum also oversees two nearby historic Dutch houses — the 1874 Cappon House and 1867 Settlers House (see listing in Historic Sites section).

Holland Museum, 31 W. 10th St., Holland, MI 49423. Phone: 616/394–1362. Fax: 616/394–4756. E-mail: *hollandmuseum@hollandmuseum.org.* Web site: *www.hollandmuseum.org.* Hours: 10–5 Mon. and Wed.-Sat. (also to 8 Thurs.); 2–5 Sun.; closed Tues. and major holidays. Admission: adults, $3; families, $7.

Huguenot Historical Society and Huguenot Street. See French Museums and Galleries section.

Little Netherlands Museum and Windmill Island Municipal Park. See Windmill Island Municipal Park and Little Netherlands Museum in Historic Sites section.

Pella Historical Village. The Pella Historical Village, an open-air museum with more than 20 buildings grouped around a courtyard, is located in Pella, Iowa, which was founded in 1847 by Dutch emigrants fleeing religious intolerance. The word "pella" stands for "city of refuge." The town, which resembles a village in the Netherlands, has many tulip gardens, an animated musical town clock with figures from the community's history, and an annual tulip festival, in addition to the historical structures at Pella Historical Village.

Among the buildings at the village, operated by the Pella Historical Society, are an 1843 pioneer log cabin, 1851 Wyatt Earp boyhood home, 1853 store, 1874 schoolhouse, a replica of Pella's first church, and such other structures as a gristmill, blacksmith shop, and pottery shop. Two of the newest additions to the village are an interpretive center and the 124-foot-high Vermeer Mill, the nation's tallest working windmill that is a grain mill built in the Netherlands and patterned after an 1850s Dutch windmill.

Pella Historical Village, Pella Historical Society, 507 Franklin St., PO Box 145, Pella, IA 50219-0145. Phone: 515/628-2409. Fax: 515/628-9192. E-mail: *pellatuliptime@iowatelecom.net*. Web site: *www.pellatuliptime.com/historical-village*. Hours: Mar.—10–4 Mon.-Sat.; Apr.-Dec.—9–5 Mon.-Sat.; closed Sun., Jan.- Feb., New Year's Eve, Thanksgiving, and Christmas. Admission: adults, $8; students K-12, $2.

Volendam Windmill Museum. An 80-foot windmill with 68-foot sail arms is featured at the Volendam Windmill Museum at Charlie Brown's Christmas Tree Farm in Milford, New Jersey. The windmill contains ca. 1700 to 1800 milling tools, millstones, and wooden shoes. The windmill was built by the late Paul Jorgenson and his wife, and the tree farm was developed in 1985 to help support the windmill. The windmill now is surrounded by 85,000 Douglas fir trees. The windmill is closed temporarily for repairs.

Volendam Windmill Museum, Charlie Brown's Christmas Tree Farm, 231 Adamic Hill Rd., Holland Twsp., Milford, NJ 08848. Phone: 908/995-4365. Web site: *www.charliebrowns-treefarm.com*. Hours: closed temporarily, but normally 12–4:30 Sat.-Sun. in May-Sept.; closed remainder of week and year. Admission: adults, $2.50; seniors, $1.50; children, $1.

Windmill Island Municipal Park and Little Netherlands Museum. The Windmill Municipal Park in Holland, Michigan, is the site of a ca. 1761 restored Dutch windmill brought to the United States from The Netherlands in 1964. The windmill houses the Little Netherlands Museum, which contains an exhibit on old Holland. The city park also has a Dutch carousel, drawbridge, Amsterdam street organ, floral garden, and tropical greenhouse, and presents exhibitions, films, and wooden shoe dance performances.

Windmill Island Municipal Park and Little Netherlands Museum, 1 Lincoln Ave., Holland, MI 49423. Phone: 616/355-1030. Fax: 616/355-1035. E-mail: *windmill@cityofholland.com*. Web site: *www.windmillisland.org*. Hours: May—9–6 Mon.-Sat.; 11:30–6 Sun.; June—10–5 Mon.-Sat.; 11:30–5 Sun.; July-mid-Sept.—

10–5 Mon.-Sat.; 11:-6 Sun.; mid–Sept.-Oct.—limited hours vary; closed remainder of year. Admission: adults, $7; children 5–12, $4; children under 5, free.

Historic Sites

Cappon House Museum and Settlers House. A lovely 1874 Italianate-style home in Holland, Michigan, is the site of the Cappon House Museum. The house was the family residence of Isaac Cappon, a poor Dutch immigrant who became wealthy and was Holland's first mayor. The interior reflects the Victorian times and features handcrafted woodwork, bronze hardware, and original family furnishings produced in Michigan. The Settlers House, a simple 1867 structure that exemplifies the life of a working class family in the late nineteenth century, is located in the next block. Both houses are operated by the Holland Museum.

Cappon House Museum, 228 W. 9th St., Holland, MI 49423 (mailing address: Holland Museum, 31 W. 10th St., Holland, MI 49423). Phones: 616/392-6740 and 616/394-1362. Fax: 616/394-4756. E-mail: *hollandmuseum@hollandmuseum.org*. Web site: *www.hollandmuseum.org*. Hours: June-Oct.—1–4 Wed.-Sat.; closed Sun.-Tues.; remainder of year—1–4 Fri.-Sat.; closed Sun.-Thurs. and major holidays. Admission (includes Settlers House): adults, $3; families, $7.

Settlers House, 190 W. 9th St., Holland, MI 49423 (mailing address: Holland Museum, 31 W. 10th St., Holland, MI 49423). Phones: 616/392-9084 and 616/394-1362. Fax: 616/394-4756. Hours: June-Oct.—1–4 Wed.-Sat. closed Sun.-Tues.; remainder of year—1–4 Fri.-Sat.; closed Sun.-Thurs. and major holidays. Admission (includes Cappon House Museum): adults, $3; families, $7.

Dekker Huis/Zeeland Historical Museum. The Dekker Huis/Zeeland Historical Museum in Zeeland, Michigan, is housed in the restored 1876 home and grocery store of Dirk Dekker and his wife, Leuntie. The museum, which contains period artifacts and furnishings, tells of the early Dutch settlement and its development since.

Dekker Huis/Zeeland Historical Museum, 37 E. Main St., PO Box 165, Zeeland, MI 49464. Phone: 616/772-4079. E-mail: *dekker@sirus.com*. Web site: *www.ci.zeeland.mi.us/zhs/zeelandmuseum.htm*. Hours: Mar.-Sept.—10–4 Thurs. and 10–2 Sat.; closed remainder of week; Oct.-Feb.—10–2 Sat.; closed remainder of week. Admission: free.

Dutch House. The Dutch House in New Castle, Delaware, traces its origins to the late seventeenth century. It was when New Castle was a bustling port for Dutch, English, Swedish, and Finnish settlers and traders. The historic frame house contains an array of Dutch colonial artifacts, such as a kas cupboard, spoon rack, and 1714 Bible, that reflect the lifestyle and traditions in early America. Dutch House is one of the New Castle Historical Society's three historic structures

Dutch House, 32 E. 3rd St., New Castle, DE 19720. Phone: 302/322–0168. E-mail: *nchistorical@ aol.com*. Web site: *www.newcastlehistory.org/*. Hours: Apr.-Dec.—11–4 Wed.-Sat.; 1–4 Sun.; closed remainder of year. Admission: adults and children over 12, $4; children 2–12, $1.50; children under 2, free

Mabee Farm Historic Site. The Mabee Farm Historic Site, located along the Mohawk River in Rotterdam Junction, New York, preserves an eighteenth-century Dutch farm and interprets colonial farm life. Tours are given of the house, inn, and slave quarters with a brief history of the Mabee family. Six or more hands-on colonial demonstrations, such as weaving, blacksmithing, and broom making, are given to school groups at the historic site by the Schenectady County Historical Society interpreters.

Mabee Farm Historic Site, 1080 Main St., Rotterdam Junction, NY 12150. Phone: 518/887–5073. Fax: 518/887–5746. E-mail: *mabee@nyca.rr.com*. Web site: *www.mabeefarm.org*. Hours: May-Sept.—10–4 Tues.-Sat. and by appointment all year; closed Sun.-Mon. Admission: adults, $3 donation; children, $2 donation.

Old Dutch Parsonage State Historic Site. The Old Dutch Parsonage in Somerville, New Jersey, was constructed in 1751 with funds from three Dutch Reformed Church congregations in Raritan Valley. It was first occupied by the Rev. John Frelinghuysen, a member of George Washington's staff during the Revolutionary War. He was succeeded by the Rev. Jacob Hardenbergh, who later became the first president of Queen's College, now Rutgers University. The parsonage remained a pastor's residence until 1810, when the building was sold and then acquired by the Central Railroad of New Jersey. When the railroad planned to demolish the building as part of a renovation program, interested people were able to relocate the house to its present location. It now is a state historic site and features furnishings as they may have appeared in 1780.

Old Dutch Parsonage State Historic Site, 71 Somerset St., Somerville, NJ 08876–2812. Phone: 908/725–1015. Web site: *www.state.nj.us/dep/parksandforests/historic/olddutch-wallace/odwh-home.htm*. Hours: 10–4 Wed.-Sat.; 1–4 Sun.; closed Mon.-Tues. and major holidays. Admission: donation.

Philipsburg Manor. The Philipsburg Manor in Sleepy Hollow, New York, is a 1750 farming, milling, and trading center that was operated by the Philipses, a family of Anglo-Dutch merchants. The family rented land to tenant farmers of diverse European backgrounds and relied on a community of 23 enslaved Africans to operate the complex. Interpreters in period costumes now invite visitors to tour the farm with its historic breeds of oxen, cows, sheep, and chickens; take part in hands-on activities of the period; and see a theatrical vignette about enslavement in the colonial north. The public also can tour the manor house, gardens, and working grist mill. Philipsburg Manor is part of the Historic Hudson Valley tour program of six historic sites in the area.

Philipsburg Manor, 381 N. Broadway (Rte. 9), Sleepy Hollow, NY 10591 (contact: Historic Hudson Valley, 150 White Plains Rd., Tarrytown, NY 10591). E-mail: *mail@hudsonvalley.org*. Web site: *www.hudsonvalley.org*. Hours: Apr.-Oct.—10–5 Wed.-Mon.; Mar. and Nov.-Dec.—10–4 Wed.-Mon.; closed Tues., Jan.-Feb., New Year's Day, Thanksgiving, and Christmas. Admission: adults, $12; seniors, $10; children 5–17, $6; children under 5, free.

Van Wyck Homestead Museum. The 1732 Dutch colonial home of Isaac Van Wyck in Fishkill, New York, was requisitioned by the Continental Army in 1776 for use as the headquarters for a northern supply depot during the Revolutionary War. It served as the headquarters for Generals Horatio Gates and Israel (or Rufus) Putnam others and a meeting place for Continental leaders during the Revolutionary War. In adjoining fields, barracks were built to accommodate an encampment of over 2,000 soldiers. The old barracks and other facilities later were torn down.

The Van Wyck home now houses the Van Wyck Homestead Museum, operated by the Fishkill Historical Society. The museum tells how the area was settled by early Dutch colonists and the role played by the Van Wyck site in the Revolutionary War. Among the exhibits are a working colonial kitchen and a collection of artifacts from the Continental Army encampment of 1776 to 1783. A library also has many of the original documents of the period..

Van Wyck Homestead Museum, 504 Rte. 9, PO Box 133, Fishkill, NY 12524–0133. Phone: 845/896–9560. E-mail: *vanwyckhomestead@aol.com*. Web site: *www.fishkillridge.org/history/vanwyck.htm*. Hours: June-Oct.—1–4 Sat.-Sun.; other times by appointment. Admission: free.

EGYPTIAN

Museums and Galleries

Rosicrucian Egyptian Museum. Ancient Egyptian history, culture, and art are displayed at the Rosicrucian Egyptian Museum, a part of the Rosicrucian Order's park that includes a contemporary art gallery, planetarium, and science center in San Jose, California. The museum contains Assyrian, Babylonian, and Egyptian artifacts, including such objects as paintings, sculpture, pottery, Coptic textiles, jewelry, utensils, bronze tools, glass and alabaster vessels, amulets, mummies, and funerary boats and models, and a replica of an Egyptian rock tomb and an eighteenth dynasty Egyptian garden.

Rosicrucian Egyptian Museum, Rosicrucian Park, 1342 Naglee Ave., San Jose, CA 95191–0001. Phones: 408/9473600 and 408/947–3635. Fax: 408/947–3638. E-mail: *curator@egyptianmuseum.org.* Web site: *www.egyptianmuseum.org.* Hours: 10–5 Tues.-Fri.; 11–6 Sat.-Sun.; closed Mon. and major holidays. Admission: adults, $9; seniors and students, $7; children 5–10, $5; children under 5, free.

ENGLISH *see* BRITISH

FINNISH (*also see* Scandinavian)

Museums and Galleries

Finnish American Heritage Center. The Finnish American Heritage Center at Finlandia University (formerly Suomi College) in Hancock, Michigan, consists of a museum, art gallery, theater, and archive. The center, located in a remodeled 1885 Catholic church building, presents exhibits, lectures, plays, musical programs, and community events. It contains artifacts, artworks, documents, and other materials about Finnish history and culture.

Finnish American Heritage Center, Finlandia University, 601 Quincy St., Hancock, MI 49930. Phone: 906/487–7302. Fax: 906/487–7557. E-mail: j*ames_kurtti@finlandia.edu.* Web site: *www.finlandia.edu/department/fahc/fahc.html.* Hours: 8–4 Mon.-Sat.; closed Sun. Admission: free.

Finnish-American Historical Society of the West. The Finnish-American Historical Society of the West in Portland, Oregon, is dedicated to preserving the cultural heritage of Finnish settlers in the American West. The society, which maintains the Erik Lindgren Home as a monument to the early settlers, has a museum, library, and archives with artifacts, books, manuscripts, oral histories, and printed materials.

Finnish-American Historical Society of the West, PO Box 5522, Portland, OR 97208. Phone 503/239–2486. Hours: open summer weekends and holidays. Admission: donation.

FRENCH (*also see* Acadian)

Museums and Galleries

Franco-American Collection. The Franco-American Collection at Lewiston-Auburn College of the University of Southern Maine in Lewiston contains artifacts, documents, photographs, and other materials pertaining to Franco-American history and culture in the state and region. It also has materials relating to such areas as politics, religion, language, education, industry, business, theater, music, genealogy, civic leaders, and local history. Americans of French descent have been the largest ethnic group in Maine for generations.

Franco-American Collection, Lewiston-Auburn College, University of Southern Maine, 51 Westminster St., Lewiston, ME 04240. Phone: 207/753–6545. Web site: *www.usm.maine.edu/lac/franco/about.html.* Hours: 8:30–5 Mon. and Wed.; 8–12 Thurs.; closed remainder of week and major holidays. Admission: free.

French Art Colony. The French Art Colony in Gallipolis, Ohio, is a regional multi-arts center that preserves French culture through the fine arts. The gallery, housed in an 1855 Greek Revival former home, has a monthly art show, presents workshops in area schools, hosts meetings, and offers a variety of classes.

French Art Colony, 530 1st Ave., PO Box 472, Gallipolis, OH 45631. Phone: 740/446–3834. Fax: 740/446–3834. Email: *facart@zoomnet.net.* Web site: *www.facart.home.zoomnet.net.* Hours: 10–3 Tues.-Fri.; 1–5 Sun.; closed Mon. and Sat. Admission: free.

Huguenot Historical Society and Huguenot Street. The Huguenot Historical Society in New Paltz, New York, preserves and interprets the history and homes of the Huguenot refugees who fled northern France because of political and religious persecution and founded the community in 1677. The museum has seventeenth- and eighteenth-century French and Dutch documents, manuscripts, and furnishings.

The society also sponsors Huguenot Street, which has such historic stone houses as the 1692 to 1894 Deyo House, 1694 to 1735 Hugo Freer House, 1698 to 1735 Bevier-Elting House, 1705 DuBois Fort, 1721 Jean (Jacob) Hasbrouck House, 1721 Abraham (Daniel) Hasbrouck House, and 1799 LeFevre House. A reconstruction of a 1717 French church also is in the historic neighborhood. Organized house tours are offered. A tour office, exhibition space, and museum shop are located in DuBois Fort.

Huguenot Historical Society, 18 Broadhead Ave., New Paltz, NY 12561–1403. Phone: 845/255–1660. Fax: 845/255–0376. E-mail: *info@huguenotstreet.org.* Web site: *www.huguenotstreet.org.* Hours: May-Oct.—10–4 Tues.-Sun.; closed Mon. and remainder of year. Admission: adults, $10; seniors, $9; students over 11, $5; children 5–11, $3; children under 5, free.

Isle a la Cache Museum. The Isle a la Cache Museum in Romeoville, Illinois, features hands-on exhibits on fur trade between French voyageurs and Potawatomi Indians in the late eighteenth century. It was a period when it was stylish for Europeans to wear fur hats made from beavers from places like the Des Plaines River, where the Will County Forest Preserve District museum is located. Translation of the French phrase "isle a la cache" is "island of the hiding place."

Isle a la Cache Museum, 501 E. 135th St., Romeoville, IL 60446. Phone: 815/886–1467. Web site: *www.fpdwe.org/contactus.cfm.* Hours: 10–4 Tues.-Sat.; 12–4 Sun.; closed Mon. Admission: free.

Museums Honoring Individuals

Father Marquette National Memorial. The Father Marquette National Memorial in St. Ignace, Michigan, honors Father Jacques Marquette, a French Jesuit missionary who established Michigan's earliest European settlements at Sault Ste. Marie and St. Ignace in 1668 and 1671. He helped French explorer Louis Jolliet map the Mississippi River and lived among the Great Lakes Indians from 1665 to his death in 1675. The museum was destroyed by fire in 2000, but the auditorium, an interpretive trail, and panoramic views of the Mackinac Bridge remain. The memorial, located in St. Ignace in Straits State Park, is interpreted in cooperation with the Michigan Department of Natural Resources.

Father Marquette National Monument, 720 Church St., St. Ignace, MI 49781. Phone: 906/643–8620. Fax: 906/643-9320. Hours: Memorial Day-Labor Day — 9:30–5 daily; closed remainder of year. Admission: $4 per vehicle.

Marquette Mission Park and Museum of Ojibwa Culture. See Native American Museums Honoring Individuals section.

Michel Brouillet House and Museum. The life of early French settlers in Vincennes, Indiana, is depicted at the Michel Brouillet House and Museum. The museum, housed in Brouillet's 1806 restored French pioneer home, contains early furnishings and has exhibits on French fur traders, Indians, prehistoric implements, fossils, and other subjects.

Michel Brouillet House and Museum, 509 1st St., PO Box 1979, Vincennes, IN 47591. Phone: 812/882–7422. Fax: 812/882-0928. Hours: Memorial Day-Labor Day —12–5 Wed.-Sat.; other times by appointment. Admission: adults, $1; children 50¢.

Napoleonic Society of America. The life and times of Napoleon Bonaparte, the fabled French emperor at the turn of the eighteenth century, are the focus of the Napoleonic Society of America's historical exhibits in Clearwater, Florida. The society has artifacts, weapons, prints, and books of the era.

Napoleonic Society of America, 1115 Ponce de Leon Blvd., Clearwater, FL 33756. Phone: 610/581–0400. Fax: 610/581–0400. E-mail: *napoleonicl@juno.com.* Web site: *www.napoleonic-societv.com.* Hours: 9–5 Mon.-Fri.; closed Sat.-Sun. Admission: free.

Historic Sites

Felix Vallé House State Historic Site. The Felix Vallé House State Historic Site, located in the National Historic Landmark District in Ste. Genevieve, Missouri, offers visitors a glimpse of the state's French colonial past with three early houses. The village was settled by French Canadians in the late 1740s. It now has some of the nation's finest examples of French colonial architecture. The Felix Vallé House, a Federal-style building constructed in 1818 and used as a residence and mercantile store by one of the community's leading French families, has been restored and furnished to reflect the 1830s. The home also interprets the American influence on the French community following the Louisiana Purchase. Across the street is the 1819 Dr. Benjamin Shaw House, with interpretive exhibits on the site and village. The third historic house is the 1792 Amoureux House, a vertical log structure showing the construction techniques used by early French settlers and displaying a diorama of Ste. Genevieve in 1832.

Felix Vallé House State Historic Site, 198 Merchant St., PO Box 89, Ste. Genevieve, MO 63670. Phone: 573/883–7102. Fax: 573/883–9630. Email: *felix_ valle.state.historic.site@dnr.mo.gov.* Web site: *www. mostateparks.com/felixvalle.htm.* Hours: 10–4 Mon.-Sat.; 12–5 Sun. Admission: adults, $2.50; children 6–12, $1.50; children under 6, free.

Fort Matanzas National Monument. See Spanish Historic Sites section.

Fort St. Jean Baptiste State Historic Site. The Fort St. Jean Baptiste State Historic Site in Natchitoches, Louisiana, marks the site of a 1732 French frontier military outpost and trade center serving the French, Spanish, and Caddo Indians. The fort, which has been reconstructed, continued to be operated by the French until France's defeat in the French and Indian War forced her to cede Louisiana to Spain. The Spanish then ran the fort , but later abandoned it because its strategic importance as a territorial protector had diminished. By the time the United States acquired the territory in 1803, only the ruins remained.

The rebuilt fort, located along the west bank of the Cane River, contains barracks, commandant's house, guardhouse, bastions, powder magazine, trading warehouse, church, slave quarters, and various huts. An interpretive center is nearby. The historic site is a living history museum with costumed soldiers, craftspeople, and other personnel.

Fort St. Jean Baptiste State Historic Site, 130 Moreau, Natchitoches, LA 71458. Phone: 318/357–3101. Fax: 318/357–7055. Web site: *www.crt.state.la.us.* Hours: 9–5 daily; closed New Year's Day, Thanksgiving, and Christmas. Admission: adults and children over 11, $2; seniors and children under 12, free.

French Azilum Historic Site. The French Azilum (Asylum) Historic Site, located on a lovely horseshoe bend of the meandering Susquehanna River near Towanda, Pennsylvania, is where a group of French exiles settled in 1793. Some of the refugees were loyal to the replaced French king and left France to escape imprisonment or death during the French Revolution. Others fled the French colony of Santo Domingo (Haiti) to escape the carnage of mulatto and slave uprisings inspired by the French Assembly's declaration of equality.

The original town consisted of approximately 50 houses on over 20 acres. Although none of the original structures remain, many of their foundations still can be seen. Artifacts from the settlement are displayed in a ca. 1790 reconstructed and relocated log cabin. Tours also are offered of the restored 1836 LaPorte farmhouse, built by a descendant of the colony, that reflects French influence, culture, and art. It has several outbuildings and a number of outdoor exhibits.

French Azilum Historic Site, Rural Rte. 2, Box 266, Towanda, PA 18848. Phone: 570/265–3376. E-mail: *frenchazilwn@epix.net.* Web site: *www.frenchazilum.org.* Hours: May 1–15 — 12–4 Sat.-Sun.; closed remainder of week; May-15-Oct. 20 — 12–4 Thurs.-Mon.; closed Tues.-Wed. Admission: adults, $5; seniors, $4.50; students, $3; preschool children, free.

French Legation Museum. The French Legation in Austin, Texas, was built in 1840 to 1841 for the charge d'affaires who represented the government of France in the Republic of Texas. However, the French representative, Jean Pierre Dubois de Saligny, who ordered the construction of the historic structure, may never have lived in the house. He returned to France in 1841. The house became the home of Dr. and Mrs. Joseph Robertson in 1848 and remained in the family until 1949, when it was purchased by the state of Texas and operated as a historic site by the Daughters of the Republic of Texas. It has been restored and contains furnishings from the original French house and the Robertson family.

French Legation Museum, 802 San Marcos St., Austin, TX 78702. Phone 512/472–8180. Fax: 512/472–9457. E-mail: *dubois@french-legation.mus.tx.us.* Web site: *www.frenchlegationmuseum.org.* Hours: 1–5 Tues.-Sun.; closed Mon. and major holidays. Admission: adults, $4; seniors, $3; students and teachers, $2.

Huguenot Church. The 1845 Huguenot Church in Charleston, South Carolina, is one of the last remaining French Protestant churches in the nation. Services were conducted in French for 150 years before switching to English. However, a French liturgy service is held every spring. The first church on the site was built in 1687. Guided tours are offered.

Huguenot Church, 135 Church St., Charleston, SC 29401. Phone: 843/722–4385. Hours: Mar.-June and Sept.-Nov. — 10–4 Mon.-Thurs.; 10–1 Fri.; closed Sat.-Sun. and remainder of year. Admission: donation.

Kent Plantation House. The ca. 1796 Kent Plantation House in Alexandria, Louisiana, is a classic example of French colonial architecture and one of the oldest standing structures in the state. It preserves the homestead of a successful Creole family of the Louisiana colonial period. The plantation, located on the original land grant from the king of Spain to Pierre Baillio II, also offers insight into the French, Spanish, and American cultures that have influenced Louisiana and the history and culture of central Louisiana between 1795 and 1855. Among the early outbuildings at the plantation are an open hearth kitchen, carriage house, milk house, slave cabin and house, barn, and sugar mill.

Kent Plantation House, 3601 Bayou Rapides Rd., Alexandria, LA 71303. Phone: 318/487–5998. Fax: 318/442–4154. E-mail: *admin@kenthouse.org.* Web site: *www.kenthouse.org.* Hours: 9–5 Mon.-Sat.; closed Sun. Admission: adults, $6; seniors and military, $5; children 6–12, $2; children under 6, free.

Lac qui Parle Mission. The Lac qui Parle Mission, a state historic site northwest of Montevideo, Minnesota, was the site of one of the earliest churches and schools in Minnesota and where the first church bell tolled in the state and the Bible was translated from French into the Dakota language. The site overlooking the Minnesota River is where Joseph Renville, an explorer and fur trader whose father was French and his mother was Dakota, originally established a fur trading post in 1826. The mission was established by missionaries whom he invited to the area. The mission has been reconstructed and has exhibits about life at the pre-territorial trading post and mission, the role of Renville, the missionaries and their work, and the environmental impact of humans on trails along the river. The site is managed by the Chippewa County Historical Society.

Lac qui Parle Mission, County Rd. 13, Montevideo, MN 56265 (mailing address: Chippewa County Historical Society, PO Box 303, Montevideo, MN 56265). Phone: 320/269–7636. E-mail: *lacquiparle@ mnhs.org*.Web site: *www.montevideomn.com*. Hours: late Apr.-Labor Day — 8–8 daily; closed remainder of year. Admission: free.

Longfellow-Evangeline State Historic Site. See Acadian Historic Sites section.

Roque House. The Roque House in Natchitoches, Louisiana, is a restored 1803 French colonial building that has furnishings and artifacts reflecting early French culture in the United States. It also has a visitor center and exhibits on the house and period in American history.

Roque House, 1 Rue Beauport, Natchitoches, LA 71457 (mailing address: 424 Jefferson St., Natchitoches, LA 71457). Phone: 318/352–1714. Hours: 9–6 daily. Admission: free.

Sainte Marie Among the Iroquois. Sainte Marie Among the Iroquois is a re-creation of the 1657 French mission that once stood on the shores of Onondaga Lake in Liverpool, New York. The site is devoted to a history of the early French Americans and their interaction with the Iroquois Indians. The county park has an interpretive center, costumed interpreters, and demonstrations of carpentry, blacksmithing, cooking, and other activities of the period.

Sainte Marie Among the Iroquois, 106 Lake Dr., Liverpool, NY 13088. Phone: 315/453–6768. E-mail: *stemarie1857@yahoo.com*. Web site: *www.onondagacountyparks.com/parks/sainte_marie*. Hours: early May-early Oct.—1 -5 Sat.-Sun.; late Nov.-mid–Dec.— 5–9 Fri.-Sat.; closed remainder of year. Admission: adults, $2; seniors, $1.50; children 6–17, $1; children under 6, free.

GERMAN (*also see* Austrian; Swiss)

Museums and Galleries

Alpine Hills Historical Museum. See Swiss Museums section.

Amana Heritage Museum. See Amana Colonies in Historic Sites section.

American Historical Society of Germans from

Russia Cultural Heritage Research Center. Artifacts, memorabilia, and buildings from the turn of the twentieth century are used at the American Historical Society of Germans from Russia Cultural Heritage Research Center in Lincoln, Nebraska, to tell the story of the emigration of German Russians to the United States. The center's Amen Family Historical Village contains a museum, chapel, general store, blacksmith shop, barn, and railroad caboose. The museum has exhibits on such topics as early German Russian settlements in the West, folklore, farming, and family and bridal traditions.

The Volga Germans, as they are called, largely maintained their German culture, language, traditions, and religions (Evangelical Lutheranism and Roman Catholicism). The Germans originally went to Russia with special rights as a group at the invitation of Catherine the Great in the late 1700s. But when the rights were revoked as the Russians sought to conscript them into the army during the latter part of the nineteenth century, many of the Germans — who had little commitment to the Russian Empire — emigrated to avoid the draft. During World War II, the Volga Germans also were placed in concentration camps and relocated eastward by Joseph Stalin, who feared they would collaborate with the invading Nazis. They never returned to the Volga region as they emigrated to other areas of Russia and later to their ancestral homeland of Germany and to the United States and Canada.

American Historical Society of Germans from Russian Cultural Heritage Research Center, 631 D St., Lincoln, NE 68502–1199. Phone: 402/474–3363. Fax: 402/474–7229. E-mail: *ahsgr@ahsgr.org*. Web site: *www.ahsgr.org*. Hours: 9–4 Mon.-Fri.; Sat. by appointment; closed Sun. and major holidays. Admission: free.

American Historical Society of Germans from Russia Library-Museum. The Central California Chapter of the American Historical Society of Germans from Russia in Fresno has a library-museum devoted to the history and culture of the ethnic Germans living near the Volga River and the Black Sea in Russia who migrated to the United States in the nineteenth and twentieth centuries. The collection consists of artifacts, books, and arrival materials.

American Historical Society of Germans from Russia Library-Museum, 3233 N. West St., Fresno, CA 93705–3402. Phone: 559/229–8287. Web site: *www.ahsgr.org*. Hours: by appointment. Admission: free.

Amish and Mennonite Heritage Center. The Amish and Mennonite Heritage Center near Berlin, Ohio, seeks to further public understanding of the

Amish and Mennonite way of life. Centerpiece of the center is *Behalf,* a 10-foot by 265-foot cycloramic mural by the late German artist Heinz Gaugel that illustrates the history of the Amish, Mennonites, and Hutterites and the progression of the Anabaptist Movement, interwoven with the story of the early Christian church and the Reformation. The viewing is followed by a 15-minute video presentation.

The German-speaking Anabaptists (meaning "Rebaptisers") got their name from their opposition to infant baptism, which they considered to be unscriptural and not true baptism. But they believed in baptism for all adults who were old enough to express their belief in the Christian faith. The movement began in Switzerland in 1525, when the first documented adult baptisms occurred in Zurich. It spread to Germany and elsewhere in Europe, but after being persecuted by the Protestant and Catholic state churches, the followers migrated to Russia and then to North America. The Old Order Amish and Old Order Mennonites often are confused by others because of their many similarities. The largest Amish settlement in world now is located in the Berlin area in Ohio.

Amish and Mennonite Heritage Center, County Rd. 77, Berlin, OH 44610. Phone: 330/893–3192. Hours: Apr.-Nov.— 9–4:30 Mon.-Sat.; closed Sun. and remainder of year. Admission: $2 suggested donation.

Amish Village. The Amish Village near Strasburg, Pennsylvania, offers guided tours that interpret the history and customs of the 24,000 Old Order Amish living in Lancaster County. They are known for their restricted dress and avoidance of such modern devices as automobiles and electricity. The museum features a blacksmith shop with tools of the smithy's trade, furnished one-room schoolhouse, barn with farm animals, Amish buggies and wagons, and operating smokehouse, waterwheel, and windmill.

Amish Village, Rte. 1, PO Box 115, Strasburg, PA 17579. Phone: 717/687–8511. Fax: 717/687–8478. Hours: Mar.Nov.— 9–5 Mon.-Sat.; 1–5 Sun.; closed remainder of year. Admission: adults, $6.75; children 6–12, $2.75; children under 6, free.

Blue Ridge Farm Museum. The Blue Ridge Institute and Museum at Ferrum College in Ferrum, Virginia, has a Blue Ridge Farm Museum that recreates an 1800s Virginia-German farmstead. Interpreters in period costumes prepare meals over an open hearth, drive oxen, do blacksmithing, and perform numerous other household and farm chores of the period. Heirloom vegetables and historic breeds of livestock can be seen in the gardens

and around the log farm buildings. The institute and museum was established in the early 1970s to document, interpret, and present the folk heritage of the Blue Ridge region. One of the highlights each year is the Blue Ridge Folklife Festival in October, featuring old-time crafts, music, foods, customs, and competitions.

Blue Ridge Farm Museum, Blue Ridge Institute and Museum, Ferrum College, 20 Museum Dr., PO Box 1000, Ferrum, VA 24088. Phone: 540/365–4416. Fax: 540/365–4419. E-mail: *bri@ferrum.edu.* Web site: *www.blueridgeinstitute.org/farm.htm.* Hours: mid–May–mid–Aug.—10–5 Sat.; 1–5 Sun.; closed remainder of week and year. Admission: adults, $5; seniors and children 6–15, $4; children under 6, free.

Brethren in Christ Historical Library and Archives. The Brethren in Christ Historical Library and Archives at Messiah College in Grantham, Pennsylvania, contains more than 600 artifacts from church life in addition to paper documents. A small display area contains various items from the collection. The denomination began around 1775 when a group of Mennonites in Lancaster County came in contact with ministers preaching the "new birth" and eventually formed their own church body.

Brethren in Christ Historical Library and Archives, Messiah College, Murray Library, 1 College Ave., PO Box 3002, Grantham, PA 17027. Phone: 717/691–6048. Fax: 717/691–6042. E-mail: *archives@messiah.edu.* Hours: Sept.-May — 9–12 and 1–3 Mon.-Fri.; June-Aug.— 9–5 Mon.-Wed.; 9–3 Thurs.; closed remainder of week. Admission: free.

Bukovina Society Headquarters-Museum. The Bukovina Society of the Americas, consisting of Germans from the Bukovina region of the old Austrian-Hungarian Empire, has its headquarters and museum in Ellis, Kansas. The ruling Hapsburg family headed by Emperor Franz Joseph invited German-speaking people to settle in the empire's sparsely populated forests in the duchy of Buckenland (Bukovina) in the late 1700s and early 1800s. When land later became scarce and railroads in the Western Hemisphere began recruiting the hard-working Germans, many decided to take advantage of the offers of free homestead land and employment in the United States, Canada, and South America in the late nineteenth century.

Starting in 1886, Bukovina Germans began emigrating to Ellis, which now has the largest concentration of such Germans in the nation. Bukovina no longer exists as a political entity, with the land later being absorbed by Romania and the northern part ceded to the Soviet Union in 1947. The Bukovina Society now has its headquarters and museum, featuring artifacts, art, and archival materials from

Bukovina emigrants, in an 1873 former church building in Ellis.

Bukovina Society Headquarters-Museum, 722 Washington St., PO Box 81, Ellis, KS 67637. E-mail: *info@bukovinasociety.org*. Web site: *www.bukovinasociety.org*. Hours: Tues.-Sat. afternoons and by appointment. Admission: free.

DANK Chicago Museum. The German American National Congress in Chicago, Illinois, opened the DANK Chicago Museum on the fourth floor of its historic building in 2006. The museum features German-American history, traditions, artifacts, and profiles on leading German-American figures. It initially is primarily an educational resource for schools, but plans call for the museum to be expanded and to provide more culturally relevant and interactive exhibits for schools and the public.

DANK Chicago Museum, German American National Congress, 4740 N. Western Ave., Chicago, IL 60625. Phone: 773/561-9181. E-mail: *dank@dankhaus.com*. Web site: *www.dankhaus.com*. Hours: 11-1 Sat. and by appointment. Admission: free.

Frankenmuth Historical Museum. The city of Frankenmuth in Michigan's Saginaw Valley was settled by 15 German immigrants in 1845 and later became known as "Michigan's Little Bavaria." The story of Frankenmuth's founding and later development is told at the Frankenmuth Historical Museum, which features artifacts and archival materials from the nineteenth century and describes the German American influence on the community.

Frankenmuth Historical Museum, 613 S. Main St., Frankenmuth, MI 48734. Phone: 989/652-9701. Fax: 989/652-9390. E-mail: *frankenmuthmuseum@yahoo.com*. Web site: *http://frankenmuth.michigan.museum*. Hours: Apr.-Dec.—10:30-5 Mon.-Fri. (also to 7 Fri.); 10-8 Sat.; 11-7 Sun.; remainder of year —12-4 Mon.-Thurs. and Sun.; 10:30-5 Fri.; 10-5 Sat.; closed New Year's Day, Easter, Thanksgiving, and Christmas. Admission: adults, $1; children, 50¢.

Freeman Museum and Archives. The Freeman Museum and Archives in Freeman, South Dakota, is an ethnic-oriented community museum that focuses largely on the history and culture of the German Mennonite residents from Russia. The museum contains exhibits and collections relating to pioneer settlers, German-Russian cultural artifacts, early life in South Dakota, and nineteenth-century Plains Indians. An exhibit on the daily life of German-Russian immigrant settlers has early furniture, household items, tools, general store, and a summer kitchen, and a display on special times in pioneer life includes a formal living room, clothing, glassware, musical instruments, and materials relating to religious observances, weddings, and funerals. The museum also has an 1879 pioneer home, 1902 rural schoolhouse, and two rural churches.

Freeman Museum and Archives, 748 S. Main St., Freeman, SD 57029 (mailing address: 718 E. 6th St., Freeman, SD 57029). Phones: 605/925-4237 and 605/925-4587. Fax: 605/925-4271. E-mail: *archves@freemanmuseum.org*. Web site: *www.freemanmuseum.org*. Hours: June-Aug.—1-4:30 Wed. and Fri.; 1-4:30 Sun.; Sept.-Oct.—1:30 Sun; other times by appointment. Admission: adults, $4; students in grades 5-12, $2.50; children under 6, free.

Georgia Salsburger Society Museum. See Austrian Museums section.

German American Heritage Center. The German American Heritage Center in Davenport, Iowa, has displays, programs, and special events relating to German American history and culture.

German American Heritage Center, 712 W. 2nd St., Davenport, IA 52802-1410. Phone: 563/322-8844. Fax: 563/884-5616. E-mail: *director@gahc.org*. Hours: 1-4 Tues. and Sun. and by appointment. Admission: free.

German Culture Museum. The German Culture Museum, which occupies a mid–nineteenth- century house in Walnut Creek, Ohio, traces the area's German and Anabaptist roots. Among the displays are a portrait of Jonas Stutzman, the county's first Amish settler; a miniature working replica of Tuferversteck, a historic Anabaptist hiding place in Switzerland; and early furniture, tools, and memorabilia.

German Culture Museum, Olde Pump St., PO Box 51, Walnut Creek, OH 44687. Phones: 330/893-2510 and 330/852-4494. Hours: June-Oct.—12:30-4:30 Thurs.-Sat.; closed remainder of year. Admission: donation.

German Heritage Museum (Cincinnati). The German Heritage Museum in Cincinnati, Ohio, presents the history, culture, and contributions of German-Americans in the greater Cincinnati area. It serves as a repository of historical records and artifacts of the contributions of many local German-Americans and the 20 organizations that are part of the German-American Citizens League of Greater Cincinnati. A ca. 1840 log house, which the museum formerly occupied, has been moved and reassembled at the museum's current location in West Fork Park.

German Heritage Museum, 4790 W. Fork Rd., Cincinnati, OH 45247. Phone: 513/598-5732. Web site: *www.gael.org/museum.html*. Hours: Apr.-Dec.—1-5 Sun.; closed remainder of week and year. Admission: free.

German Heritage Museum (Roberts Cove). The history and culture of the German colony in the French Acadian area of southwest Louisiana are depicted at the German Heritage Museum, located in the Roberts Cove area near Rayne, Louisiana. The German settlement in a region known as Cajun Country was founded in 1880 by a small Catholic group led by the Rev. Peter Leonard Thevis, who left New Orleans because of the yellow fever epidemic. They were joined shortly thereafter by about 175 families fleeing religious persecution and military impressments in Germany. In addition to the St. Leo IV Church and the museum, which opened in 2002, the German community has an annual Roberts Cove Germanfest each October.

German Heritage Museum, 716 E. Roberts Cove Rd., Rayne, LA 70678. Phone: 337/334–8354. Hours: 10–2 Tues.-Fri.; closed Sat.-Mon. and major holidays. Admission: $2 per person.

Germans from Russia Heritage Society Library and Archives. The Germans from Russia Heritage Society in Bismarck, North Dakota, has a library and archives that preserves and interprets the history and cultural heritage of the German immigrants from the Volga region of Russia who emigrated to America in the seventeenth and eighteenth centuries. Many of the immigrants settled in North Dakota.

Germans from Russia Heritage Society Library and Archives, 1125 W. Turnpike Ave., Bismarck, ND 58501. Phone: 701/223–6157. E-mail: *rachel@grhs.org.* Web site: *www.grhs.org.* Hours: 8–4:30 Mon.-Fri.; closed Sat.-Sun. and major holidays. Admission: free.

Germantown Historical Society. The Germantown Historical Society in Philadelphia is dedicated to the history of German Township (Germantown and now the neighboring Mt. Airy and Chestnut Hill) in northwest Philadelphia. Its museum and library collections consist of more than 50,000 objects, documents, and photographs from the seventeenth to twentieth centuries — many relating to the German founding and growth of Germantown, the first German settlement in the nation.

The main gallery displays furniture from early German times to colonial highboys, tall case clocks, Victorian chairs, and Colonial Revival secretaries, as well as Peale paintings. Another exhibit features period domestic objects and shows how domestic practices and patterns of living have changed over the years. The extensive textile collection includes Germantown and Quaker samplers from the early 1700s; German quilts, coverlets, and bedspreads from the eighteenth century; and textile tools, quilt patterns, and dye cards from Germantown textile mills. The costume collection is composed of over 8,000 pieces of clothing, ranging from the clothing of German settlers to more contemporary items.

Germantown Historical Society, 5501 Germantown Ave., Philadelphia, PA 19144–2291. Phone: 215/844–1683. Fax: 215/844–2831. E-mail: *info@germantownhistory.org.* Web site: *www.germantownhistory.org.* Hours: 9–5 Tues. and Thurs.; 1–5 Sun.; other times by appointment; closed major holidays. Admission: adults, $5; seniors and students over 11, $4; children under 12, $2.

Goschenhoppen Folklife Library and Museum. The Goschenhoppen Folklife Library and Museum, located in Red Men's Hall in Green Lane, Pennsylvania, depicts the local Pennsylvania Dutch (German) culture prior to 1870, an era of handmade furniture and textiles. The site is operated by Goschenhoppen Historians, Inc., founded in 1964 to preserve the folk culture of Goschenhoppen, one of the nation's oldest continuously existing Pennsylvania German communities.

The trades are portrayed in a weaver's shop, cobbler's shop, and turner's shop. Among the items on display are a paint-decorated corner cupboard, Pennsylvania German rope bed with straw ticking, 1864 Pomplitz and 1820 Ziegler pipe organs, eighteenth-century fireplace for hearth cooking, 1860 cook stove-era kitchen, decorative needlework, and footpedal lathe. Among the other exhibits are a mid-nineteenth-century parlor, flax preparation unit, reconstructed Pennsylvania Dutch attic, and country store with post–1870 manufactured goods.

Goschenhoppen Folklife Library and Museum, Red Men's Hall, Rte. 29, PO Box 476, Green Lane, PA 18054–0476. Phone: 610/367–8286. E-mail: *redmens_hall@goschenhoppen.org.* Web site: *www.goschenhoppen.org.* Hours: Apr.-Oct.—1 :30–4 Sun.; other times by appointment. Admission: free.

Hartzler Library Art Gallery. Contemporary artworks are featured at the Hartzler Library Art Gallery at Eastern Mennonite University in Harrisonburg, Virginia. The gallery is on the third floor of the library. The university also has a student art gallery in the old student center.

Hartzler Library Art Gallery, Eastern Mennonite University, Hartzler Library, 1200 Park Rd., Harrisonburg, VA 22802. Phone: 540/432–4000. Fax: 540/432–4444. Hours: Sept.-May—7:45–11 Mon.-Thurs.; 7:45–6 Fri.; 10–5 Sat.; 2–11 Sun.; June-Aug.—8–5 daily; closed major holiday. Admission: free.

Heimat Museum. The Heimat Museum in Lake Villa, Illinois, contains artifacts and memorabilia pertaining to Danube-Swabian culture. The museum, located in a building that formerly housed the German-Hungarian Old Peoples Home, is operated by the American Aid Society of German Descendants, which has its clubhouse in Chicago.

Heimat Museum, American Aid Society of German Descendants, Rte. 132, Lake Villa, IL 60046. Web site: *www.geocities.com.idsociety/museum.html?20054*. Hours: varies. Admission: free.

Heritage Village. Heritage Village in Mountain Lake, Minnesota, celebrates the Russian-Mennonite and German-Lutheran immigrants who were settlers in the area in the late 1800s and early 1900s. Twenty-one historic buildings, many built in the nineteenth century and restored, have displays depicting pioneer life the area. The structures include a 125-year-old farmhouse built in traditional European style with an attached summer kitchen and granary, chapel, general store, schoolhouse, hospital, post office, bank, railroad depot, and barber shop. Heritage Village also is home to the Minnesota Hall of Fame Telephone Museum. In September, a Heritage Fair is held in which costumed guides conduct tours of the buildings and their exhibits.

Heritage Village, County Rd. 1, PO Box 152, Mountain Lake, MN 56159. Phone: 507/427–2023. E-mail: *conductorron@swwnet.com*. Web site: *www.mountainlakemn.com*. Hours: Memorial Day-Labor Day—1–5 daily; closed remainder of year. Admission: adults and children over 7, $3; children under 8, free.

Historic Hermann Museum. The Historic Hermann Museum in Hermann, Missouri, is housed in the 1871 German School building, which was the only privately owned public schoolhouse in the state when founded and the only one to conduct classes in both German and English. The city was founded by German immigrants and the museum has exhibits and memorabilia related to the city's German past as well as later development. Among the museum's historic objects are furnishings made in Germany around the turn of the twentieth century.

Historic Hermann Museum, 312 Schiller St., Hermann, MO 65041. Phone: 573/486–2017. Fax: 573/486–2017. Web site: *www.historichermann.com*. Hours: Apr.-Oct.—10–4 Tues.-Sat.; 12–4 Sun.; closed Mon. and remainder of year. Admission: adults and children over 12, $2; children 6–12, $1; children under 6, free.

Historic Sauder Village. Historic Sauder Village near Archbold, Ohio, is a living-history museum with historic structures, craft: demonstrations, and collections of artifacts that depict rural life in northwest Ohio in the late 1800s. It was opened in 1976 by Erie J. Sauder, founder of a leading ready-to-assemble furniture company, who want to show how hard it was for early Germans and other Europeans to transform a wilderness into tilled fields and productive farms in the region.

The re-created village has 19 restored structures that are either historic or have parts that are from early buildings, a turn-of-the-twentieth-century farmstead with animals, a historical museum, and various other facilities. It has costumed interpreters and demonstrations given by such craftsmen as a silversmith, gunsmith, tinsmith, woodworker, potter, glass blower, spinner, weaver, cooper, and broom maker. The museum building displays over 10,000 artifacts and other objects, including such items as clothing, household furnishings, textiles, tools, agricultural implements, and water and heating equipment used by early settlers.

Historic Sauder Village, 22611 State Rte. 2, PO Box 235, Archbold, OH 43502. Phones: 419/446–2541 and 800/590–9755. Fax: 419/445–5251. E-mail: *info@saudervillage.org*. Web site: *www.saudervillage.org*. Hours: May-Oct.—10–5 Tues.-Sat.; 12–4 Sun.; closed Mon. (except holidays) and remainder of year. Admission: adults, $12; students 6–16, $6; children under 6, free.

Illinois Amish Interpretive Center. The Illinois Amish Interpretive Center in Arcola tells the story of the Old Order Amish and features artifacts gathered from the local Amish community, including a buggy that is over 100 years old. An introductory video is presented on the central Illinois Amish and exhibits cover such subjects as Amish barns, weddings, and other aspects of Amish history and life. Visitors also can schedule tours of an Amish home, farm, business, or countryside and arrange to have a meal in an Amish home.

Illinois Amish Interpretive Center, Locust St., Arcola, IL 61910. Phones: 217/268–3599 and 888/452–6474. Fax: 217/268/4810. E-mail: *amishcenter@consolidatedd.net*. Web site: *www.amishcenter.com*. Hours: Mar.-Nov.— 9–5 Mon.-Sat.; closed Sun.; remainder of year — by appointment. Admission: adults, $2.75; seniors, $2.50; children 5–11, $2.25; children under 5, free.

Illinois Mennonite Heritage Center. The Illinois Mennonite Heritage Center near Metamora interprets the faith and life of Mennonites in the state. The center complex, operated by the Illinois Mennonite Historical and Genealogical Society, includes a museum, library, and archives. The museum contains items used in households, schools, and congregations; distinctive clothing; medical equipment; and other objects. Also on the site are a restored Sutter barn, farm and woodworking tools and machinery, a restored Grandfather house and windmills; and a prairie arboretum of native Illinois grasses, flowers, and trees.

Illinois Mennonite Heritage Center, 675 State Rte. 116, Metamora, IL 61548–7732. Phone: 309/367–2551. E-mail: *info@imhgs.org*. Web site: *www.imhgs.org*. Hours: Apr.-Oct.—10–4 Fri.-Sat.; 1:30–4:30 Sun.; closed Easter, Mother's Day, Father's Day, Sundays before Memorial and Labor days, and remainder of week and year. Admission: $2 suggested donation.

Iowa Mennonite Museum and Archives. The Iowa Mennonite Museum and Archives, located in the Kalona Historical Village in Kalona, contains records, artifacts, and memorabilia of Mennonite and Amish history, cultures, and lifestyles in Iowa. The historical village features 13 restored historic structures and three specialized museums. Admission to the village includes the Mennonite museum.

Iowa Mennonite Museum and Archives, Kalona Historical Village, 715 D Ave., Kalona, IA 52247–0292. Phone: 319/656–3232. Web site: *www.kalonaiowa.org*. Hours: Apr.-mid–Oct.—10–4 Mon.-Sat.; remainder of year—11–3 Mon.-Sat.; closed Sun. and major holidays. Admission to village: adults and children over 12, $6; children 7–12, $2.50; children under 7, free; families, $20.

Juniata District Mennonite Historical Society. The Juniata District Mennonite Historical Society in Richfield, Pennsylvania, was formed in 1951 to preserve and make available Mennonite historical materials from the area. Since then the society has been instrumental in the founding of the Brick Mennonite Church and has established a historical center with a museum, research library, and archives. The center contains a variety of historical materials donated by families, including a 1540 Froschauer Bible and a deed signed by Benjamin Franklin. The society also has restored the ca. 1774 Fort Pomfret, also known as the Grayhill homestead, that was the home of Richfield's first settler, John Grayhill, who was known as Johannes Krahbiel. It is believed that the stone structure was one of a series of forts constructed as defense against Indians west of the Susquehanna River.

Juniata District Mennonite Historical Society, Historical Center, Rte. 35, HCR 63, Richfield, PA 17086. Phone: 717/694–3543. Hours: 7–9 P.M. Tues., 9–4:30 Sat., and by appointment. Admission: free.

Kauffman Museum. The permanent exhibit at the Kauffman Museum at Bethel College in North Newton, Kansas, tells how the Mennonites came from Europe to America's central plains in the 1870s and their encounters with the prairie environment and its peoples. The museum also presents changing special exhibitions, and has a tallgrass prairie reconstruction with over 15 species of grasses and more than 100 wildflower species and a historic farmstead with heritage flower and vegetable gardens around an 1875 house and 1886 barn.

Kauffman Museum, Bethel College, 2801 N. Main St., North Newton, KS 67117–0531. Phone: 316/283–1612. Fax: 316/283–2107. E-mail: *kauffman@bethelks.edu*. Web site: *www.bethelks.edu/kauffman*. Hours: 9:30–4:30 Tues.-Fri.; 1:30–4:30 Sat.-Sun.; closed Mon. and major holidays. Admission: adults, $3; children 6–16, $1.50; children under 6, free.

Kidron-Sonnenberg Heritage Center. The Kidron-Sonnenberg Heritage Center in Kidron, Ohio, documents the history of Mennonite Anabaptists in the area. The center, maintained by the Kidron Community Historical Society, has an extensive collection of furniture, tools, crafts, and Fraktur — an old world style of calligraphy embellished with decorative motifs. It also has a restored 1820s log structure and various items brought from Europe by the first Mennonite settlers.

Kidron-Sonnenberg Heritage Center, 13153 Emerson Rd., PO Box 234, Kidron, OH 44636. Phone: 330/857–9111. Hours: June-Sept.—11–3 Thurs.-Sat.; closed Sun.-Wed.; Oct.-Dec. and Mar.-May—11–3 Thurs. and Sat.; closed remainder of week and Jan.-Feb. Admission: donation.

Lancaster Mennonite Historical Society. The Lancaster Mennonite Historical Society in Lancaster, Pennsylvania, has artifacts, photographs, manuscripts, oral histories, records, and other materials pertaining to Mennonite and Amish historical, religious, and cultural experiences in the southeastern and south central regions of the state. The society offers a program of changing exhibitions.

Lancaster Mennonite Historical Society, 2215 Millstream Rd., Lancaster, PA 17602–1499. Phone 717/393–9745. Fax: 717/393–8751. E-mail: *limhs@lmhs.org*. Web site: *www.lmhs.org*. Hours: 8:30–4:30 Tues.-Sat.; closed Sun.-Mon. and major holidays. Admission: adults. $5; seniors, $4.50; children 7–12, $3; children under 7, free.

Landis Valley Museum. Landis Valley Museum, a living-history village in Lancaster, Pennsylvania, preserves, displays, and interprets Pennsylvania German material, culture, and heritage from 1740 through 1940. The museum features a diverse collection of artifacts, exhibits, and buildings that reflect early German rural life in Pennsylvania and Lancaster County. Founded in 1925, the museum has grown from a handful of historic structures to a complex of exhibit buildings, a crossroads village, craft and skill demonstrations, and adjoining farmsteads with historical breeds of animals and heirloom plants.

Among the historic attractions are a 1700 log farm, 1830s to 1840s Brick farmstead, 1857 Landis Valley Hotel, 1870s Isaac Landis farm and Pierce Landis complex, 1890 schoolhouse, and such other early 1800s structures as a harness shop, tavern, gun shop, implement shed, print shop, and craft building. The museum's collections include Pennsylvania German decorative arts, textiles, agricultural implements, vehicles, and folk culture. A visitor center, which resembles an eighteenth-century market building, features a film that introduces visitors to the historical complex and provides a perspective on the history of early rural Pennsylvania. It also contains changing exhibits on aspects of the museum's collections.

Landis Valley Museum, 2451 Kissel Hill Rd., Lancaster, PA 17601. Phone: 717/569–0401. Fax: 717/580–2147. Web site: *www.landisvalleymuseum.org.* Hours: 9–5 Mon.-Sat.; 12–5 Sun.; closed New Year's Day and Christmas. Admission: adults, $9; seniors, $7; children 6–17, $6; children under 6, free.

Leo Baeck Institute Gallery. See Jewish Museums and Galleries section.

Menno-Hof Mennonite-Amish Visitors Center. The Menno-Hof Mennonite-Amish Visitors Center in Shipshewana, Indiana, informs visitors about the faith and life of Mennonites and Amish, as well as Anabaptist history and lifestyle, through multimedia presentations, historical environments, and colorful displays.

Menno-Hof Mennonite-Amish Visitors Center, 510 S. Van Buren St., PO Box 701, Shipshewana, IN 46565. Phone: 219/768–4117. E-mail: *director@shipshewana.com.* Web site: *www.shipshewana.com.* Hours: Jan.-Mar.—12–4 Tues.-Fri.; 10–5 Sat.; closed Mon.-Sun. and New Year's Day; Apr.-May and Sept.-Dec.—10–5 Mon.-Sat.; closed Sun., Thanksgiving, and Christmas; June-Aug.—10–5 Mon.-Sat. (also to 7 Tues.); closed Sun. Admission: donation.

Mennonite Heritage Center (Harleysville). The story of Mennonite faith and life in southeastern Pennsylvania is told at the Mennonite Heritage Center in Harleysville, Pennsylvania. An interpretive video about local Mennonites and their neighbors is presented in a room designed to resemble an early meeting house. The center has two permanent exhibits: *Work and Hope*, which traces the early European history of the Anabaptist Movement and continues through the settlement of the Mennonites in Penn Woods and through the Revolutionary War, and the Fraktur Exhibit, which features a collection of the colorful art form brought to America by the Pennsylvania Germans. Changing exhibitions also are presented.

Mennonite Heritage Center, 565 Yoder Rd., PO Box 82, Harleysville, PA 19438. Phone: 215/256–3020. Fax: 215/256–3023. E-mail: *info@mhep.org.* Web site: *www.mhep.org.* Hours: 10–5 Tues.-Fri.; 10–2 Sat.; 2–5 Sun.; closed Mon. and major holidays. Admission: $5 donation.

Mennonite Heritage Museum (Goessel). The Mennonite Heritage Museum in Goessel, Kansas, is a living tribute to the German Mennonite families that left Russia for religious freedom in 1874 and settled on the Kansas plains in Goessel. The museum complex consists of eight buildings. They include the Immigrant House and Turkey Red Wheat Palace with exhibits and six historic buildings that have been moved to the site. The historic structures include the 1875 Krause House and one-room schoolhouse, 1902 Schroeder barn, 1906 Preparatory School, 1910 Goessel State Bank, and 1911 Friesen House.

Mennonite Heritage Museum, 200 N. Popular St., PO Box 231, Goessel, KS 67053. Phone: 620/367–8200. E-mail:*mhmuseum@futureks.net.* Web site: *www.skyways.lib.ks.us/museums/goessel.* Hours: Mar.-Apr. and Oct.-Dec.—12–4 Tues.-Fri.; 1–4 Sat.-Sun.; May-Sept—10–4:30 Tues.-Fri.; 1–4:30 Sat.-Sun.; Jan.-Feb.— by appointment; closed Mon. and major holidays. Admission: adults and children over 11, $3; seniors, $2; children under 12, $1.50.

Mennonite Information Center and Biblical Tabernacle Reproduction. The Mennonite Information Center in Lancaster, Pennsylvania, interprets the faith and practices of the Amish and Mennonite peoples and explains the meaning of the original Old Testament Tabernacle. Visitors can tour a life-size reproduction of the intricately designed tabernacle located on the site.

Mennonite Information Center and Biblical Tabernacle Reproduction, 2209 Millstream Rd., Lancaster, PA 17602- 1494. Phone: 717/299–0954. Fax: 717/290–1585. E-mail: *menninfctr@desupernet.net.* Web site: *http://mennoniteinfoctr.tripod.com.* Hours: Apr.-Oct.— 8–5 Mon.-Sat.; Nov.-Mar.— 8:30–4:30 Mon.-Sat.; closed Sun. Admission: center — free; tabernacle — adults, $6; seniors, $5.50; children 7–12, $3.50; children under 7, free.

Mennonite Library and Archives. The Mennonite Library and Archives, operated by Bethel College with the Mennonite Church USA in North Newton, Kansas, collects, preserves, and makes available personal papers, manuscripts, documents, prints, paintings, lithographs, photographs, periodicals, books, and other archival materials related to Mennonite and Anabaptist studies. It has about 35,000 books, 5,600 volumes of bound periodicals, and approximately 4,300 cubic feet of archival records. The Mennonite Church USA also has a second archives at Goshen College in Indiana.

Mennonite Library and Archives, Bethel College, 300 E. 27th St., North Newton, KS 67117–0531. Phone: 316/264- 5304. Fax: 316/284–5843. Web site: *www.bethelks.edu/services/mla/information*. Hours: 10–12 and 1–5 Mon.-Fri.; closed Sat.-Sun. and major holidays. Admission: free.

Mennonite Settlement Museum. The Mennonite Settlement Museum in Hillsboro, Kansas, is devoted to early Mennonite immigrant village life in Kansas and features a number of historic structures. The restored 1876 Peter Paul Loewen House is the only traditional Russian clay brick house in North America. Other structures include the 1876 Pioneer Adobe House, 1886 one-room Kreutziger School, 1909 William Schaeffler House, and a replica of the 1876 Jacob Friesen Flouring Mill that once stood in the Mennonite settlement of Gnadenau.

Mennonite Settlement Museum, 501 S. Ash St., Hillsboro, KS 67063. Phone: 620/947–3775. E-mail: *hillsboro_museums@yahoo.com*. Web site: *http://adobehouse.mennonite.net*. Hours: Mar.-Dec.—10–12 and 1:30–4 Tues.-Fri.; 2–4 Sat.-Sun.; closed Mon., major holidays, and remainder of year. Admission: adults, $3; students, $1.

Moravian Historical Society. The Moravian Historical Society in Nazareth, Pennsylvania, presents the story of the Moravian Church and its contributions to American history and culture. It has numerous artifacts, artworks, photographs, manuscripts, records, books, and other materials that document the history of German Moravian settlers and customs since the eighteenth century. It offers a program of permanent, changing, and traveling exhibits on Moravian and local history and culture.

Moravian Historical Society, 214 E. Center St., Nazareth, PA 18064. Phone: 610/759–5070. Fax: 610/759–2461. Web site: *www.moravianhistoricalsociety.org*. Hours: 1–4 Sun.-Fri.; 10–4 Sat.; closed major holidays. Admission: adults, $5; seniors and students 6–18, $3; children under 6, free; families, $12.

Moravian Museum of Bethlehem. The Moravian Museum of Bethlehem preserves and interprets the history, culture, and religious traditions of the German Moravian immigrants who settled in the Bethlehem, Pennsylvania, area. It has collections of religious items, domestic objects, textiles, tools, furniture, musical instruments, clothing, and archival materials relating to the Moravian community, and maintains a number of historic sites.

The historic structures include the 1741 Gemeinhaus (community house), the oldest building in Bethlehem; 1752 Apothecary and Herb Garden, and 1758 Nain House, a building constructed and lived in by Native Americans that was part of a Moravian mission village. The museum is housed in Gemeinhaus, which originally was an enormous five-story log structure that served as the sect's all-purpose building.

Moravian Museum of Bethlehem, 66 W. Church St., Bethlehem, PA 18018 (mailing address: 459 Old York Rd., Bethlehem, PA 10818). Phone: 610/867–0173. Fax: 610/694–9960. Web site: *www.historicbethlehem.org*. Hours: Mar.-Thanksgiving—10–5 Thurs.-Sat.; 12–5 Sun.; closed Mon.-Wed.; Christmas season—10–5 Mon.-Sat.; 12–5 Sun.; closed remainder of year and national holidays. Admission: adults and children over 12, $7; children 6–12, $4; children under 6, free.

Old Salem Museums and Gardens. Old Salem—now called the Old Salem Museums and Gardens—in Winston-Salem, North Carolina, is a living-history re–creation of the eighteenth-century Moravian Church town of Salem, founded in 1766. The German-speaking Moravians came to the area in 1753 and built four communities, with Salem being the major commercial and religious center. The Moravians, a Protestant faith that began in the 1400s in the province of Moravia, now part of the Czech Republic, established a community in Herrnhut, Germany, from where they went out as missionaries and to found settlements. Salem remained a church-governed town until the mid–1800s.

The village, called the Historic Town of Salem, is located adjacent to downtown Winston-Salem, and has about 100 restored or reconstructed buildings from the1760 to 1850 period. Several of the buildings remain as private properties, including the 1778 Fourth House, a half-timbered communal house that is one of the oldest original houses in Salem. Fifteen of the houses at the outdoor museum can be visited. Costumed interpreters are located in most buildings to provide historical background and to demonstrate historic trades and domestic activities.

Old Salem has a visitor center with historical exhibits. The 1794 Boys School building also contains displays on various aspects of Moravian life. Three other museums are located in the village—Museum of Early Southern Decorative Arts, Old Salem Children's Museum, and Old Salem Toy Museum. Visitors can purchase a one- or two-day ticket, with the one-day including two museums and the two-day being good for admission to all the museums.

Old Salem Museums and Gardens, 600 S. Main St., Winston-Salem, NC 27101 (mailing address: PO Box F, Salem Station, Winston-Salem, NC 27108). Phones: 336/721–7300, 336/727–7350 (weekends), and 800/653–7253. Fax: 336/721–7335. E-mail: *webmaster@oldsalem.org.* Web site: *www.oldsalem.org.* Hours: Apr.-Dec.— 9:30–4:30 Mon.-Sat.; 1-5 Sun.; closed Easter, Thanksgiving, and Christmas Eve and Day; Jan.-Mar.— 9:30–4:30 Tues.-Sat.; 1–5 Sun.; closed Mon. Admission: 1 day — adults, $21; children 6–16, $10; 2 day — adults, $24; children 6–16, $10; children under 6, free.

Pennsylvania Colony of Nebraska Historical Society Museum. The Pennsylvania Colony of Nebraska Historical Society has purchased the Henry Heim House in Dawson, Nebraska, for a museum on the history and culture of the colony's settlers in the state. The house is being remodeled while collecting artifacts and raising funds for the project continues.

Pennsylvania Colony of Nebraska Historical Society Museum, Henry Heim House, Dawson, NE 68337 (contact: Robert Williamson, Rural Rte. 1, Box 127, Dawson, NE 68337). Phone: 402/877–2485. E-mail: *bobw@penncolonynebraska.org.* Web site: *http://penncolonynebraska.org.* Hours/admission: still to be determined.

Pennsylvania German Cultural Heritage Center at Kutztown University. The Pennsylvania German Cultural Heritage Center at Kutztown University in Kutztown, Pennsylvania, is dedicated to the preservation of Pennsylvania German (also known as Pennsylvania Dutch) history, folklore, and traditions. The center is located on a 30-acre nineteenth-century farmstead with a stone farmhouse, barn, small restored buildings, 1870 one-room schoolhouse, library, and two reconstructed log houses that will be part of a proposed log village. It has over 10,000 artifacts, numerous historical documents, and Pennsylvania German family genealogical records. Pennsylvania German Cultural Heritage Center at Kutztown University, 22 Luckenbill Rd., PO Box 306 Kutztown, PA 19530. Phones: 610/683–1589 and 610/683–1330. E-mail: *heritage@kutztown.edu.* Web site: *www.kutztown.edu/community/pgchc.* Hours: 10–12 and 1–4 Mon.-Fri.; other times by appointment; closed major holidays. Admission: adults, $5; students and children,$3.

People's Place Quilt Museum. Exhibits of antique Amish and Mennonite quilts and other decorative arts are featured at the People's Place Quilt Museum in Intercourse, Pennsylvania. A new show is presented each year. The museum is located on the second floor of the historic Old Country Store, known for its locally handcrafted items. A Story Walk on the west side of the building contains historical information about the building, village, and area.

People's Place Quilt Museum, Old Country Store, 3510 Old Philadelphia Pike, PO Box 419, Intercourse, PA 17634. Phone: 800/828–8218. Fax: 888/768–3433. E-mail: *custserv@ppquiltmuseum. com.* Web site: *www.ppquiltmuseum.com.* Hours: 9–5 Mon.-Sat.; closed Sun. Admission: free.

Society of the Danube Swabians Museum. The Society of the Danube Swabians of Chicago is a German ethnic and cultural organization whose original members were immigrants who came to the United States after World War II. The society, formed to keep the culture, traditions and German language alive, operates a cultural center with a museum in suburban Des Plaines. It contains household items, tools, furniture, and dolls in traditional costumes of the different Danube Swabian regions.

Society of the Danube Swabians Museum, 625 E. Seegers Rd., Des Plaines, IL 60016. Phone: 847/296–6172. Web site: *http://dpkhome.northstarnet.org/danubes.* Hours: varies. Admission: free.

Sophienburg Museum and Archives. The Sophienburg Museum and Archives in New Braunfels, Texas, is housed in a fieldstone veneer building on the site of the headquarters of the original German colony founded in 1845 in the Republic of Texas. The city has become the largest settlement of Germans in the state. The museum relates the history of Germans in the city with artifacts and exhibits of early life in New Braunfels. Among its features are displays of an early German general store, bakery, pharmacy, shoemaker's shop, saloon, barber shop, cabinet maker's shop, and doctor's office. The archives have documentary information about the founding and growth of New Braunfels and the German emigration into Texas. Sophienburg Museum and Archives, 401 Coll St., New Braunfels, TX 78130. Phone: 830/629–1572. Fax: 830/629–3906. E-mail: *sophienburg@nbtx.com.* Web site: *www.nbtx.com/sophienburg.* Hours: 10–4 Tues.-Sat.; closed Sun.-Mon. and major holidays. Admission: adults, $5; students under 18, free.

Texas Wendish Heritage Museum. The Texas Wendish Heritage Museum in Giddings, Texas, preserves and interprets the artifacts and documents of the Wendish culture. In 1854, about 500 Wends (now called Sorbs) came to Texas as Slavic Lutheran immigrants from Lusatia in eastern Germany in search of religious freedom and the right to speak their native language. The museum tells this story and the role of the Rev. Jan Kilian in organizing the exodus. Texas Wendish Heritage Museum, 1011 County Rd. 212, Giddings, TX 78942. Phone: 979/366–244. Fax: 979/366-2805. E-mail: *windish@bluebon.net.* Web site: *http://wendish.concor*

dia.edu. Hours: 1–5 Tues.-Sun.; closed Mon. and major holidays. Admission: adults, $2; students and children, free.

Vereins Kirche Museum. Founded in 1935, the Vereins Kirche Museum was the first museum in Fredericksburg, Texas. The museum building, a replica of the original built in Germany in 1847, has exhibits on the city and the history, culture, and role of German settlers in the area. The museum is one of two operated by the Gillespie County Historical Society. The other is the Pioneer Museum, which began with the purchase of Henry Kammlah's ca. 1849 to 1887 home, smokehouse, and barn in 1956 and has been expanded with six major structures since its founding.

Vereins Kirche Museum, Center of Markeplaza in 100 block of W. Main St., Fredericksburg, TX 78624 (mailing address: Gillespie County Historical Society, 312 W. San Antonio St., Fredericksburg, TX 78624). Phone: 830/997-7832. Fax: 830/997-3891. E-mail: *sbuford@pioneermuseum.com.* Web site: *www.pioneermuseum.com.* Hours: 10-4 Mon.-Sat.; 1-4 Sun.; closed major holidays. Admission: adults and children over 11, $1; children under 12, free.

Museums Honoring Individuals

Conrad Weiser State Park. Conrad Weiser, who was born in the German principality of Wurttemberg in 1696, emigrated to America with his family in 1709 when his father decided to heed Britain's Queen Anne's invitation to inhabitants of the Rhine Valley to migrate to England and the British colonies in America. The Weiser family settled on the New York frontier where Conrad learned the language, customs, and statesmanship of the Iroquois Confederacy (Six Nations). In 1729, he moved with his wife and children (and other Germans) to the Tulpehocken Valley near the present town of Womelsdorf, Pennsylvania, where he was a major landholder, farmer, tanner, and businessman. He also became a prominent colonial leader as a diplomat, judge, community planner, soldier, and Pennsylvania's foremost Indian treaty maker.

In 1928, the Conrad Weiser Memorial Park was established in his honor at his homestead near Womelsdorf. The 24-acre park, designed by the

The building of the Vereins Kirche Museum in Fredericksburg, Texas, is a replica of the original built in Germany in 1847. The museum, operated by the Gillespie County Historical Society, contains exhibits on the city and the history, culture, and role of German settlers in the area. *Vereins Kirche, Fredericksburg, Texas, courtesy Gillespie County Historical Society, Fredericksburg, Texas, Photograph by Larry Miller.*

Olmsted brothers, later became a state park. It features Weiser's eighteenth-century home, springhouse, and gravesite. The park also contains a statue of Iroquois Chief Shekilammy, with whom Weiser worked to improve relations and bring peace between the settlers and Indians in Pennsylvania in the first half of the 1700s. A visitor center interprets Weiser's life and contributions.

Conrad Weiser State Park, 28 Weiser Rd., Womelsdorf, PA 19567. Phone: 610/589-2934. Web site: *www.berksweb.com/conrad.html.* Hours: 9-5 Wed.-Sat.; 12-5 Sun.; closed Mon.-Tues. and major holidays. Admission: free.

Peter Wentz Farmstead. The Peter Wentz Farmstead, established in 1744 by Peter and Rosanna Wentz in Worcester, Pennsylvania, features a large 1758 Georgian-style stone house with architectural aspects and distinctive interior paint decoration that reflect their German heritage. The farm served as the headquarters for General George Washington in 1777 during the Revolutionary War. It is where Washington planned his attempt to keep British forces from occupying Philadelphia that resulted in the Battle of Germantown later that year.

The farm was purchased by Melchior Schultz, a minister of the Schwenkfelder faith, in 1794. He and his descendants continued to live and farm there until 1969. The site then was purchased by Montgomery County and restored, with the house being furnished to reflect its appearance at the time of the American Revolution. Pennsylvania German culture and early American farm life now are featured in exhibits and special events.

Peter Wentz Farmstead, Skippack Pike and Shearer Rd., PO Box 240, Worcester, PA 19490. Phone: 610/584–5104. Fax: 610/584–6860. E-mail: *peterwentzfarmstead@mail.montcopa.org*. Web site: *www.montcopa.org*. Hours: 10–4 Tues.-Sat.; 1–4 Sun.; closed Mon. and county holidays. Admission: free.

Schwenkfelder Library and Heritage Center. The Schwenkfelder Library and Heritage Center in Pennsburg, Pennsylvania, preserves, exhibits, and interprets the artifacts, manuscripts, and books related to the Schwenkfelders. The Schwenkfelders are followers of Casper Schwenkfeld von Ossig, a theologian who lived in Germany from 1489 to 1561. He had questions about the meaning and practice of the Lord's Supper and sought inner spiritual truth that would lead Christians to real understanding of the Lord's Supper. When Schwenkfeld and his supporters suspended the celebration of the Lord's Supper until everyone could come together in Christian unity, they were called heretics and harassed, imprisoned, and forced to flee. In the 1730s, many emigrated to southeastern Pennsylvania, where the library and heritage center tells the story of the Schwenkfelders.

Schwenkfelder Library and Heritage Center, 105 Seminary St., Pennsburg, PA 18073. Phone: 215/679–3103. Web site: *www.schwenkfelder.com*. Hours: 9–4 Tues.-Fri. (also to 8 Thurs.); 10–3 Sat.; 1–4 Sun.; closed Mon. and most national holidays. Admission: donation.

1719 Hans Herr House and Museum. The 1719 Hans Herr House and Museum in Willow Creek, Pennsylvania, was created in the late 1960s when the historic house was restored to its colonial-era appearance and the Lancaster Conference Mennonite Historical Society acquired the land around the house. It now is devoted to collecting, preserving, and interpreting artifacts relating to the history, life, and faith of the Mennonites of Lancaster County.

The grounds include about 11 acres of the original 530 acres granted to Christian Herr in 1710. He built the house in 1719 and relatives constructed two other farmhouses still on the property — the Georgian-style 1852 Shaub House and the Victorian-style 1890s Huber House, which serves as a visitor center and tells about the Hans Herr House, named for the elderly patriarch of the family. The museum has three exhibit buildings and a working blacksmith shop, smokehouse, and outdoor bake oven.

1719 Hans Herr House and Museum, 1849 Hans Herr Dr., Willow Street, PA 17584. Phone: 717/464–4438. E-mail: *info@hansherr.org*. Web site: *www.hansherr.org*. Hours: Apr.-Nov.— 9–4 Mon.-Sat.; closed Sun., Thanksgiving, and remainder of year. Admission: free.

Sutter's Fort State Historic Park. See Swiss Museums Honoring Individuals section.

Warkentin House. The Warkentin House in Newton, Kansas, is an 18-room Victorian house museum completed in 1887 by Mennonite immigrant Bernhard Warkentin, who became known for promoting German-Russian Mennonite settlement in the central plains region and for improving central European wheat varieties that revolutionized American grain production. The historic house, which still has much of its original furniture and features craftsmanship from throughout the world, provides a look at how Warkentin and his wife, Wilhelmina, lived at the turn of the twentieth century. The Warkentins also owned a historic homestead near Halstead, Kansas, that was used for wheat hybridization experiments.

Warketin House, 211 E. 1st St., Newton, KS 67114. Phone: 316/283–3113. Hours: Jan.-Mar.— by appointment; Apr.-May —1–4:30 Sat.-Sun.; June-Aug.—1–4:30 Tues.-Sun.; Sept.-Dec.—1–4:30 Sat.-Sun.; closed remainder of week and major holidays. Admission: adults, $3; children 5–12, $1.50; children under 5, free.

Historic Sites

Amana Colonies. The Amana Colonies in Amana, Iowa, were founded in 1855 by members of the Community of True Inspiration, who emerged in the early 1700s as part of the Pietist and Spiritualist Movement within the Lutheran Church in Germany. The Inspirationists placed emphasis on the development and nurture of inner life via direct mystical contact with God, with a strong commitment to church discipline and close community relationships. About 800 German Inspirationists immigrated to Buffalo, New York, in 1842, and later bought 18,000 acres in Iowa for a new communal

A quilter is shown working in one of the early period galleries at the Amana Heritage Museum in Amana, Iowa. The museum, housed in three nineteenth-century buildings, depicts the history of the Amana Colonies, originally founded as a communal community in 1855 by German Inspirationists. The communal way of life was discontinued in 1932. *Courtesy Amana Heritage Society.*

settlement, called Amana, a word taken from the Old Testament Song of Solomon, meaning "to remain faithful." In 1932, the communal way of life was discontinued and strict regulations on dress and lifestyle were gradually eliminated. However, church life continues with its spiritualistic pattern and simple worship in unadorned meeting houses.

The Amana Colonies, as the community is called, consists of seven closely-knit villages. The Amana Society, Inc., corporate heir to the land and economic assets of communal Amana, owns and manages some 26,000 acres of farm, pasture, and forest land. More than 400 buildings from the communal era still stand as reminders of the past. The community has numerous small craft shops and industries, with the best known and largest business being Amana Refrigeration, maker of Amana refrigerators.

The story of the Amana Colonies is told at the Amana Heritage Museum, composed of three nineteenth-century buildings. The 1864 Noé House, which originally was a communal kitchen and then a doctor's residence, traces the history and development of Amana. An 1870 schoolhouse contains an audiovisual presentation on Amana's history, a communal school display, and collections of toys, dolls, handwork, and carpet weaving. The

third building, a washhouse and woodshed during the communal period, houses wine-making and gardening exhibits.

The Amana Colonies have four other specialized museums and various historic structures, such as the 1857 High Amana General Store that has remained virtually unchanged. The museums are the historic 1865 Amana Community Church, one of seven Community of True Inspiration churches in the community; Communal Kitchen and Cooper Shop Museum, an 1863 structure that is the only intact communal era kitchen remaining in the Americas; Communal Agriculture Museum, located in an 1860 barn that formerly housed oxen and horses and now features agricultural implements used on Amana's communal farms; and Homestead Store Museum, a former general store that now interprets the role of industry, commerce, and Amana's relationship to the outside world and has exhibits on carpet weaving, printing, bookbinding, tinsmithing, and the woolen mill industry.

Amana Colonies Visitors Center, 622 46th Ave., PO Box 310, Amana, IA 52203. Phones: 319/622–7622 and 800/579-2294. E-mail: *info@amana-colonies.com*. Web site: *www.amanacolonies.com*. Hours: 9–5 Mon.-Sat.; 10–5 Sun. Admission: free.

Amana Heritage Museum, 4310 220th Trail,

Amana, IA 52203. Phone: 319/622–3567. Fax: 319/622–6481. E-mail: *amherit@juno.com.* Web site: *www.amanaheritage.org.* Hours: Apr.-Oct —10–5 Mon.-Sat.; 12–5 Sun.; remainder of year —10–5 Sat.; closed Sun.-Fri. Admission: adults, $5; children under 18, free.

Bethel German Colony. The historic Bethel German Colony in Bethel, Missouri, began in 1844 when Wilhelm Keil, a charismatic religious leader, led a small group of German settlers from Pennsylvania to 2,560 acres in Shelby County to form a communal religious community. By 1855, the community had grown to 650 residents and 4,700 acres. But Keil grew increasingly restless and took a group of about 75 Bethel settlers to form a new colony in the Willamette Valley of the Oregon Territory (see Old Aurora Colony). However, both communities were disbanded in 1879 after Keil's death. Much of Bethel remains as it did over 150 years ago. More than 30 original colony structures are still standing, and it is possible to visit several houses with furnishings from the 1840s period. The site also has a visitor center with displays and artifacts relating to the colony's history.

Bethel German Colony, 127 N. Main St., Bethel, MO 63434–1033. Phone: 660/284–6493. Hours: 10–5 daily; closed New Year's Day, Thanksgiving, and Christmas. Admission: free.

Burnside Plantation. The 1748 Burnside Plantation in Bethlehem, Pennsylvania, was established by James Burnside, the first representative from Northampton County elected to the state's Provincial Assembly. It later became part of the Moravians' agricultural system in Bethlehem and the neighboring community of Nazareth. The historic farm contains the restored 1748 to 1818 farmhouse, two 1840s barns, high horsepower wheel, corn crib, wagon shed, large kitchen garden, and orchard. It now is part of the Historic Bethlehem Partnership.

Burnside Plantation, 1461 Shoenersville Rd., Bethlehem, PA 18018 (mailing address: Historic Bethlehem Partnership, 459 Old York Rd., Bethlehem, PA 18018–5830). Phones: 610/868–5044. Web site: *www.historicbethlehem.org.* Hours: mid–June-early Sept. —12–4 Sat.; closed remainder of week and year. Admission site — adults, $7; children 6–12, $4; children under 6, free; Historic Bethlehem Partnership pass to 7 historic sites — adults, $10; children 6–12, $7; children under 6, free.

Colonial Industrial Quarter. The Moravians' Colonial Industrial Quarter in Bethlehem, Pennsylvania, was America's first industrial park over 260 years ago. Among the restored structures still located at the historic site are the 1761 tannery, 1762 waterworks (a national landmark), and 1869 Luck-enback Mill (which now houses the Historic Bethlehem Partnership), as well as the reconstructed 1750–61 smithy with its anvils, forges, and bellows. Among the colonial visitors to the site were George Washington and John Adams.

Colonial Industrial Quarter, 459 Old York Rd., Bethlehem, PA 459 Old York Rd., Bethlehem, PA 18018. Phone: 610/882–0450. Fax: 610/882–0460. Web site: *www.historicbethlehem.org.* Hours: mid-–June-early Sept. —12–4 Thurs.-Sun.; closed remainder of week and year. Admission: site — adults, $7; children 6–12, $4; children under 6, free; Historic Bethlehem Partnership pass to 7 historic sites — adults, $10; children 6–12, $7; children under 6, free.

Deutschheim State Historic Site. The Deutschheim State Historic Site in Hermann, Missouri, was created in 1979 to preserve, protect, and share the state's German and German-American culture, heritage, crafts, folkways, foodways, lifestyles, and traditions. By 1860, more than half of Missouri's foreign-born residents were Germans, and today about half of the state's residence claim at least one grandparent of German ancestry. Hermann was founded by German settlers and was the most systematic and best organized of Missouri's seven German settlement societies. The Deutschheim State Historic Site includes four historic structures — 1840 Pommer-Gentner House, 1842 to 1869 Strehly House, 1857 winery, and 1883 barn — as well as gardens and a museum with exhibits on the history and culture of the German settlement. The houses contain furnishings and decorative arts of the period.

Deutschheim State Historic Site, 107 W. 2nd St., Hermann, MO 65041. Phone: 573/486–2200. Fax: 573/486–2249. E- mail: *deutschheim.state.historic.site@dnr.mo.gov.* Web site: *www.mostateparks.com/deutschheim.htm.* Hours: tours begin 9:30, 11:15, 1, and 2:30 daily; closed New Year's Day, Easter, Thanksgiving, and Christmas. Admission: adults, $2, children over 5, $1.25; children under 6, free.

Fort Klock Historic Restoration. Fort Klock, a fortified stone farmstead built in 1750 in St. Johnsville, New York, by Palatine German immigrant Johannes Klock, has been restored as a national historic landmark. It is part of a 30-acre complex of original colonial farm structures that also contain a working blacksmith shop, a new world Dutch barn, carriage house, cheese house, and an early nineteenth-century schoolhouse.

Fort Klock Historic Restoration, 7214 State Hwy., PO Box 42, St. Johnsville, NY 13452. Phone: 518/568–7779. Web site: *www.bluekabuto.com/fortklock.* Hours: Memorial Day-Columbus Day — 9–5 Tues.-Sun.; closed Mon. and remainder of year. Admission: small fee.

Gemeinhaus. See Moravian Museum of Bethlehem in Museums section.

German Village. The historic German Village section of Columbus, Ohio, resulted from the passage of the Refugee Lands bill by the Congress of the United States in 1796. The legislation enabled individuals from Canada and Nova Scotia who supported the American cause in the Revolutionary War to obtain frontier land for settlement. A tract of unsurveyed and uninhabited land 4.5 miles wide and 48 miles long was set aside in central Ohio for such settlement. In 1802, John McGowan, a Revolutionary War veteran who had immigrated to Nova Scotia, claimed 328 acres and then sold lots to early German settlers. This was the beginning of German Village, a 233-acre historic neighborhood district in downtown Columbus known for its historic houses and German restaurants and activities. The German Village Society spearheads the activities and preservation of the historic neighborhood and operates a visitor center in the German Village Meeting Haus that serves as town hall. A video about German Village can be seen at the visitor center.

German Village Visitor Center, 588 S. 3rd St., Columbus, OR 43215. Phone: 614/221–8888. Web site: *www.germanvillage.org*. Hours: 9–4 Mon.-Fri.; 10–2 Sat.; closed Sun. Admission: free.

Historic Bethabara Park. Historic Bethabara Park in Winston-Salem, North Carolina, is the site of the 1753 Moravian settlement in North Carolina. It contains the reconstructed 1754 village and 1756 to 1763 palisade fort, 1757 graveyard, reconstructed 1759 community garden and 1761 medical garden, restored 1782 Potter's House, restored 1788 Gemeinhaus (church, meeting place, school, and minister's house for the settlement), 1803 Herman Buttner House, 175-acre wildlife preserve, and archaeological foundations.

The site has the longest unbroken record of early pottery manufacturing in the United States, spanning the 1750s to the 1850s, and the community and medical gardens are the earliest known such gardens in the country. The written records, journals, inventories, and maps of the early Moravian settlers also have become an important body of research materials for the study of the nation's colonial history.

Historic Bethabara Park, 2147 Bethabara Rd., Winston-Salem, NC 27106. Phone: 336/924–8191. Fax: 336/924–0535. Web site: *www.bethabara park.org*. Hours: Apr.-Nov.—10:30–4:30 Tues.-Fri.; 1:30–4:30 Sat.-Sun.; closed Mon., Thanksgiving, and remainder of year. Admission: grounds — free; exhibit buildings — adults, $2; children, $1.

Historic New Harmony. New Harmony, Indiana, is the site of two of America's earliest utopian communities. The first was Harmonie on the Wabash (1814 to 1824), which was founded by the Harmony Society, a group of Separatists from the German Lutheran Church. The founding group, led by Johann George Rapp, left their first American communal home in Harmonie, Pennsylvania, to acquire a much larger tract of land. They built a well-planned 2,000-acre German religious community that was largely self-sufficient. It had 126 family houses, four large brick dwellings, two large granaries, wool and cotton factories, 35-acre orchard, 15-acre vineyard, 5-acre vegetable garden, and such equipment as a steam engine and a threshing machine. It was largely self-sufficient. However, in 1824 the group moved back to Pennsylvania (see Old Economy Village) and sold the property to Robert Owen, a Welsh-born industrialist and social philosopher, for a second utopian community — a communitarian experiment. He wanted to create a more perfect society with free education and the abolition of social classes and personal wealth. But it proved to be unsuccessful.

The present town of New Harmony consists largely of many Harmonist and late nineteenth-century buildings, gardens, and a reconstructed Harmonist Labyrinth. Eight Harmonist sites and 25 buildings from the pioneering German period can be seen in central New Harmony, which is still a small community of less than 1,000 residents. But it has a museum, library, gallery, theater, conference center, and visitor center with guided tours of 15 historic sites that include period rooms and exhibits relating to specific subjects.

Historic New Harmony, 5061/2 Main St., PO Box 579, New Harmony, IN 47631. Phone: 812/682–4488. Fax: 812/682–4313. E-mail: *harmony@ usi.edu*. Web site: *www.newharmony.org*. Hours: mid–Mar.-Dec.— 9:30–5 daily; remainder of year — by appointment. Admission: adults, $10; seniors, $9; children 7–17, $5; children under 17, free; families, $25.

New Harmony State Historic Site, North and Arthur Sts.., PO Box 607, New Harmony, IN 47631. Phone: 812/682–4488. Fax: 812/682–4313. E-mail: *newharmonyshs@dynasty.net*. Web site: *www.ai.org /ism*. Hours: Mar.-Dec.—10–4 daily; closed remainder of year. Admission: adults, $10; seniors, $9; children 7–17, $5; children under 7, free.

Historic New Ulm. New Ulm, Minnesota, founded in 1854 by German immigrants, is one of America's most Germanic communities. It still has a distinctly German appearance and atmosphere, with German-style monuments, carillon clock, shrine, brewery, architecture, and festivals. The story of New Ulm is told at the Brown County Historical Society, housed in a 1910 German-style building, which contains exhibits and artifacts relating to early settlers, American Indians, and the Dakota Conflict of 1862, when New Ulm was nearly destroyed by raiding Indians. The settlers were driven from the city during the Dakota Conflict, but returned to rebuild the town.

Among New Ulm's features are such monuments as the German Bohemian Immigrant Monument, which honors early settlers who came from the German-speaking western rim of Bohemia; a bronze monument at the courthouse square commemorating the heroism of the Dakota Conflict defenders; and the Hermann Monument, a 102-foot statue honoring the ancient Teutonic hero who defeated the Romans in A.D. 9 and is considered the father of Germany. Other highlights include the Glockenspiel, a freestanding carillon clock tower with 37 bells and animated figurines that depict the history of New Ulm; Way of the Cross Shrine, with 14 Bavarian-made stations portraying the life of Christ; August Schell Brewery, an 1860 German brewery with tours and exhibits; Concord Singers, internationally known for their festive German music; and such events as Fasching, a German version of the Mardi Gras; Heritagefest, an old world celebration of history and culture; and Oktoberfest, a German fall festival.

Brown County Historical Society, 2 N. Broadway, New Ulm, MN 56073–1714. Phone: 507/233–2616. Fax: 507/354–1068. E-mail: *bchs@browncountyhistorymuseum.org.* Web site: *www.browncountyhistorymuseum.org.* Hours: Memorial Day-Labor Day — 9–4 Mon.-Fri.; 1–5 Sat.-Sun.; remainder of year — 9–4 Mon.-Fri.; 1–5 Sat.; closed Sun. and national holidays. Admission: adults, $3; students and children, free.

Old Aurora Colony. The Old Aurora Colony in Oregon was a utopian communal settlement established by Wilhelm Keil, a charismatic Prussian tailor and self-styled physician who attracted a following with his fundamental Christian preaching centered on the golden rule and sharing effort and possessions. It was the second colony he founded. He bought land along the Pudding River in 1856 and moved 75 followers from his first colony in Bethel, Kansas (see Bethel German Colony). The colony grew to 600 residents by 1867, but both colonies were dissolved after Keil's death in 1877. Today, about 20 colony and post-colony structures — many owned by descendants of the colonists — are part of Aurora's historic district. The Old Aurora Colony Museum contains artifacts, traces the history of the community, and sometimes presents demonstrations of early crafts.

Old Aurora Colony Museum, 15018 2nd St., PO Box 202, Aurora, OR 97002. Phone: 503/678–5754. E-mail: *info@auroracolonymuseum.com.* Web site: *www.auroracolonymuseum.com.* Hours: Feb.-Dec.,— 11–4 Tues.-Sat.; 12–4 Sun.; closed Mon., Jan., and major holidays. Admission: adults, $6; seniors, $5; students, $2; children under 5, free.

Old Economy Village. Old Economy Village, a historic site in Ambridge, Pennsylvania, interprets the history and preserves the material culture of the Harmony Society, a nineteenth- century German Christian communal group. It was the third home of the Harmonists, a group of initially 800 farmers and craftsmen led by Separatist Johann George Rapp, who emigrated from Iptingen in southwest Germany in 1804 seeking religious and economic freedom. They first established a communal settlement in Harmonie, Pennsylvania, and then moved to Indiana (see Historic New Harmony) before returning to western Pennsylvania in 1824 to found Oekonomie, now better known as Old Economy Village, along the Ohio River in Beaver County.

The Harmonists developed a simple, pietistic lifestyle based upon the early Christian Church that gained worldwide recognition for its religious devotion and economic prosperity. Despite their agricultural and industrial success, one-third of the followers left in 1832, Father Rapp died in 1847, and only a few Harmonists remained by the end of the nineteenth century. In 1905, the Harmonist Society was dissolved and its holdings were sold.

Old Economy Village resulted from the purchase of six acres, along with 17 buildings, in 1916 by the Commonwealth of Pennsylvania. The historic site, with its six acres and 17 restored structures built between 1824 and 1830, now is a national historic landmark administered by the Pennsylvania Historical and Museum Commission. It is surrounded by Ambridge's National Register Historic District. In addition to the buildings and grounds, Old Economy Village has a library, archives, and 16,000 artifacts that provide insight into one of the nation's earliest and longest surviving communal utopias.

Old Economy Village, 270 16th St., Ambridge, PA 15003. Phone: 724/266–4500. Fax: 724/266–3010. E-mail: *mlandis@state.pa.us.* Web site: *www.oldeconomyvillage.org.* Hours: 9–5 Tues.-Sat.; 12–5 Sun.; closed Mon. and major holidays. Admission: adults, $7; seniors, $6; children 6–17, $5; children under 6, free.

Peter Wentz Farmstead. See Museums Honoring Individuals section.

Pioneer Adobe House Museum. See Mennonite Settlement Museum in German Museums and Galleries section.

Schoenbrunn Village State Memorial. Schoenbrunn Village State Memorial near New Philadelphia, Ohio, is the site of the first town in Ohio. It began as a Moravian mission to the Delaware Indians in 1772 by missionary David Zeisberger of the German Protestant sect whose beliefs included pacifism. The Moravians were invited to establish the mission by Delaware Chief Netawatwes. The Moravians and their Native American converts drew up Ohio's first civil code and built its first schoolhouse and Christian church.

During the Revolutionary War, the town tried to remain neutral, but met with continual harassment from two directions. In 1777, it became necessary to abandon the site after being pressured by hostile Indians under British influence on one side and American frontiersmen pushing further into the territory on the other. The missionaries and the Christian Indians moved to Lichtenau, but were forced to leave in 1781 by the British, who believed the missionaries were informing the Americans of troop movements. Some of the Christian Indians were permitted to return to the mission site, but were captured by American militia and accused of assisting British Indians in a series of raids. In a bloody massacre, 96 of the Indians were executed. The Moravian Delaware village was burned by Indians during this frontier fighting.

The missionaries' diaries and annual reports detailing their activities were preserved by the Moravian Church and used to relocate the town of Schoenbrunn. The Ohio Historical Society acquired the site in 1923 and has been reconstructing the town ever since. Seventeen log structures have been rebuilt, including the meetinghouse, schoolhouse, and various log cabins. The site also has gardens, the original mission cemetery, and a visitor center. A museum traces the history of the town and costumed volunteers help bring the village and its customs to life.

Schoenbrunn Village State Memorial, State Rte. 259, PO Box 129, New Philadelphia, OH 44663 (also PO Box 508, Zoar, OH 44697). Phones: 330/339-3636 and 800/762-2711. E-mail: *shawkins@ohiohistorv.org*. Web site: *www.ohiohistorv.org*. Hours: Memorial Day-Labor Day — 9:30-5 Wed.-Sat.; 12-5 Sun.; closed Mon.-Tues. and remainder of year. Admission: adults, $7; children 6-12, $3; children under 6, free.

1743 Palatine House Museum. The 1743 Palatine House Museum, housed in an old Lutheran parsonage in Schoharie, New York, is devoted to the colonial life of settlers who came from the Palatinate region of present-day Germany. It contains eighteenth- and nineteenth-century artifacts and displays. The Schohaire Colonial Heritage Association, which operates the museum, also presents early weaving demonstrations; offers spinning, weaving, dyeing, and herb workshops; and has another museum in an 1891 railroad depot.

1743 Palatine House Museum, Schohaire Colonial Heritage Assn., 1743 Palatine House, Spring St., PO Box 554, Schoharie, NY 12157. Phones: 518/295-7585 and 518/295-7505. Fax: 518/295-6001. E-mail: *scha@midtel.net*. Web site: *www.midtel.net/-scha*. Hours: May-Oct.—12-4 Sat.-Mon.; closed remainder of week and year. Admission: adults, $2.50; students, $1.

Sutter's Fort State Historic Park. See Swiss Historic Sites section.

Volkening Heritage Farm at Spring Hill. The Volkening Heritage Farm in Schaumburg, Illinois, depicts daily life in a German American farming community in the area during the 1880s. The Schaumburg Park District site at Spring Hill includes the Boeger family's mid-nineteenth-century Greek Revival vernacular farmhouse home and a summer kitchen, kitchen gardens, woodhouse, outhouse, smokehouse, wagon shed, com crib, sheep shed, hog house, and barn. Costumed interpreters tell visitors about the activities, possessions, and lives of German Americans in area farming communities in the late 1800s.

Volkening Heritage Farm at Spring Hill, 201 S. Plum Grove Rd., Schaumburg, IL 60194 (mailing address: Schaumburg Park District, 235 E. Beech Dr., Schaumburg, IL 60193). Phone: 847/490-7020. Fax: 847/985-2114. E-mail: *info@parkfun.com*. Web site: *www.parkfun.com/dir/spv/farm.html*. Hours: Apr.-Oct.— 9-2 Mon.-Fri.; 10-4 Sat.- Sun.; Feb.-Mar.— 12-4 Sun.; closed New Year's Day, Thanksgiving, Christmas, and remainder of week and year (but grounds and trails open daily: 8-8 in Apr.-Oct. and 8-5 Nov.-Mar.). Admission: free.

Zoar Village State Memorial. The Zoar Village State Memorial in Zoar, Ohio, marks the site of a communal community founded in 1817 by a group of German religious dissenters called the Society of Separatists of Zoar who sought refuge from religious persecution. The historic site, which continues to have old world charm, features 10 restored buildings where visitors can get a better understanding of the life of the agrarian Separatists.

The buildings include the Number One House, kitchen-magazine complex, garden house, bakery, tin shop, dairy, wagon shop, blacksmith shop, store, and Bimeler Museum. Some structures are staffed by costumed interpreters and contain such items made or used by the Separatists as German American folk arts and crafts, furniture, textiles, and tools. The village, which is administered by the Ohio Historical Society, also has such special events as harvest festivals, garden tours, and holiday celebrations.

Zoar Village State Memorial, 198 Main St., PO Box 404, Zoar, OH 44697. Phones: 330/874–4336 and 800/874–4336. Fax: 330/874–2936. E-mail: *zoar@cannet.com*. Web site: *www.ohiohistory.org/places/zoar*. Hours: Apr.-May and Sept.-Oct.— 9:30–5 Sat.; 12–5 Sun.; closed Mon.-Fri.; Memorial Day-Labor Day — 9:30–5 Wed.-Sat.; 12–5 Sun. and holidays; closed Mon.-Tues. and remainder of year. Admission: adults and children over 12, $7; children 6–12, $3; children under 6, free.

GREEK
Museums and Galleries

Hellenic Cultural Museum. The struggles, achievements, social life, and tragedies of Greek immigrants and their descendants are presented at the Hellenic Cultural Museum in Salt Lake City, Utah. The museum, located on the lower level of the Holy Trinity Cathedrals, has exhibits on Greek history and culture, Greek immigrants, mining and railroad workers, military service, and other aspects of Greek life in Utah and America. It displays early clothing, folk costumes, mining tools, dolls, manuscripts, letters, photographs, and other artifacts and memorabilia in interpreting the story of Greek immigrants and Greek Americans. The first Greek settlers came to Utah in 1870.

Hellenic Cultural Museum, 279 South 300 West, Salt Lake City, UT 84101–1797. Phone: 801/359–4163. Fax: 801/328–9688. Hours: 9–12 Wed.; 12–1 Sun.; closed remainder of week. Admission: free.

Hellenic Museum and Cultural Center. The Hellenic Museum and Cultural Center in Chicago's Greektown traces the history of Greek immigration to America, celebrates the Hellenic heritage and culture, and displays the artistic work of the Greeks and Greek Americans in the visual, literary, and performing arts. The museum, which has more than 6,000 objects in its collections, is located at a temporary site while a new, larger home is being constructed.

Hellenic Museum and Cultural Center, 801 W. Adams St., 4th Floor, Chicago, IL 60607. Phone: 312/655–1234. Fax: 312/655–1221. E-mail: *info@hellenicmuseum.org*. Web site: *www.hellenicmuseum.org*. Hours: 10–4 Tues.-Fri.; 11–4 Sat.; closed Sun.-Mon. and major holidays. Admission: $5 suggested donation.

Historic Sites

St. Photios Greek Orthodox National Shrine. The St. Photios Greek Orthodox National Shrine

in St. Augustine, Florida, is dedicated to the first colony of Greek people who came to America in 1768. Five hundred Greek colonists were brought to Florida by Dr. Andrew Turnbull. The shrine is located in the 1749 Avero House, where some members of the initial Greek colony later lived. The historic house was purchased by the Greek Orthodox Archdiocese in 1965. It now contains a memorial chapel, exhibits, and a video on the first Greek immigrants.

St. Photios Greek Orthodox National Shrine, 41 St. George St., PO Box 1960, St. Augustine, FL 32085. Phone: 904/829–8205. Fax: 904/829–8707. E-mail: *info@stphotios.com*. Web site: *www.stphotios.com*. Hours: 9–5 daily; closed New Year's Day, Greek Orthodox Easter, Thanksgiving, and Christmas. Admission: free.

HAWAIIAN (*also see* Oceanic Peoples)
Museums and Galleries

Bailey House Museum. The Bailey House Museum, operated by the Maui Historical Society in Wailuku, Hawaii, is devoted to the history and culture of nineteenth-century Maui. It features artifacts, paintings, and furnishings from the historic period. The museum is located on the site of the royal compound of Kahekili, the last ruling chief of Maui. The building served as the mission station for the Wailuku Female Seminary for Girls until 1847 and then was occupied by artist Edward Bailey and his family until 1888. Some of Bailey's paintings are among the displays.

Bailey House Museum, Maui Historical Society, 2375-A Main St., Wailuku, Maui, 96793. Phone: 808/244–3326. Fax: 808/244–3920. E-mail: *info@mauimuseum.org*. Web site: *www.mauimuseum.org*. Hours: 10–4 Mon.-Sat.; closed Sun. and major holidays. Admission: adults and children over 12, $5; seniors, $4; children 7–12, $1; children under 7, free.

Bishop Museum. The Bishop Museum in Honolulu, Hawaii, is the premier cultural and natural history museum in the Pacific. It was founded in 1889 by Charles Reed Bishop as a memorial to his late wife, Princess Bernice Pauahi Bishop, the last direct descendant of the royal Kamehameha family. She was the heir apparent to the kingdom of Hawaii, but declined to take the throne so she could devote herself to the cause of educating Hawaiian children. The museum originally was created to house royal family heirlooms of the princess and a large collection of Hawaiian artifacts, but later was expanded to cover Hawaiian and Pacific island culture and natural history.

The museum has over 1 million artifacts and 2 million plant and animal specimens, including the finest collections of feather caps, helmets, kahilis (royal standards), and other Hawaiian cultural and artistic works. Its Hawaiian and Polynesian halls contain exhibits and artifacts on the history and culture of the Hawaiian and Pacific island peoples, as well as royal treasures and the region's natural history. The museum's newest addition is the Science Adventure Center, which features Hawaii's natural environment. It has a 26-foot walk through volcano, an exhibit where visitors can descend to the ocean floor, and a 160-foot Hawaiian origins tunnel with artworks, natural sounds, rare native species, interactive exhibits, and a children's tree house. The museum also has a planetarium and operates a maritime center and ethnobotanical gardens at other locations.

Bishop Museum, 1523 Bernice St., Honolulu, HI 96817-2704. Phone: 808/847-3511. Fax: 808/841-8968. E-mail: *museum@bishopmuseum.org.* Web site: *www.bishopmuseum.org.* Hours: 9–5 daily; closed major holidays. Admission: non-resident adults, $14.95; resident adults, $7.95; seniors, $11.95; children 4–12, $6.95; children under 4, free.

Hana Cultural Center and Museum. The Hana Cultural Center and Museum in Hana on the island of Maui in Hawaii is dedicated to the preservation and interpretation of the history of Hana. It has historic structures, artifacts, photographs, documents, and other materials. Among the historic buildings are the old courthouse, historic jail house, and Kauhale complex of four early structures — house, meetinghouse, cooking house, and canoe-storage building. A museum also has historical displays.

Hana Cultural Center and Museum, 4974 Uakea Rd., PO Box 27, Hana, Maui, HI 06713. Phone: 808/248-8622. Fax: 808/248-8620. E-mail: *hccm@aloha.net.* Web site: *http://planet-hawaii.com/hana.* Hours: 10–4 daily; closed New Year's Day and Christmas. Admission: free.

Hawaii's Plantation Village. Hawaiian plantation life in the early 1900s is depicted at Hawaii's Plantation Village, an outdoor historical museum and botanical garden at Waipahu Cultural Garden Park in Waipahu, Hawaii. Visitors are taken on a guided tour of the 50-acre plantation grounds, gardens, and buildings just below the Oahu Sugar Mill. It includes 30 restored and replicated ethnically oriented houses once occupied by Hawaiian, Chinese, Portuguese, Puerto Rican, Japanese, Filipino, Korean, and Okinawan plantation workers, as well as the community bath, camp offices, and plantation store. The houses contain personal artifacts and ethnic and cultural materials of the eight major ethnic groups that worked on the plantations. The lifestyles and experiences of the workers are interpreted during the tour.

Hawaii's Plantation Village, 94–695 Waipahu St., Waipahu, HI 06797. Phone: 808/677-0110. Fax: 808/676-6727. E-mail: *hpv.wapahu@verizon.net.* Web site: *www.hawaiiplantationvillage.org.* Hours: 10–2 Mon.-Sat.; closed Sun. and major holidays. Admission: adults and children over 11, $13; seniors, $10; military and Kama'aina, $7; children 4–11, $5; children under 5, free.

Kauai Museum. The Kauai Museum in Lihue, Hawaii, is a history and art museum that emphasizes the history, artifacts, and art relating to the island of Kauai. The museum occupies two buildings and features collections of such artifacts as poi pounders, pohaku, calabashes, and tapa. Exhibits cover such topics as the history of Kauai from a geological and archaeological standpoint, pre-contact and post-contact Hawaii, Captain Cook's arrival, life in early Kauai villages, early sugar plantation life, and the missionary era.

Kauai Museum, 4428 Rice St., PO Box 248, Lihue, Kauai, HI 96766. Phone: 808/245-6931. Fax: 808/245-6864. Email: *museum@kauaimuseum.org.* Web site: *www.kauaimuseum.org.* Hours: 9–4 Mon.-Fri.; 10–4 Sat.; closed Sun. and major holidays. Admission: adults, $7; seniors, $4; youth 13–17, $3; children, 6–12; children under 6, free.

Lyman Museum and Mission House. The natural and cultural history of Hawaii and an 1839 historic missionary home are featured at the Lyman Museum and Mission House in Hilo on the island of Hawaii. The mission house was built by David and Sarah Lyman, who were members of the fifth company of Protestant missionaries from New England to arrive in Hawaii. They lived in the New England-style house until their deaths in the early 1880s. The house, which has been restored and contains many of the Lyman furnishings, reflects life in Hawaii in the 1860s. A museum with five galleries has been added, with the principal exhibit dealing with the social and cultural history of the many peoples of Hawaii.

Lyman House and Mission House, 276 Haili St., Hilo, HI 96720. Phone: 808/935-5021. Fax: 808/969-7685. E-mail: *info@lymanmuseum.org.* Web site: *www.lymanmuseum.org.* Hours: 9:30–4:30 Mon.-Sat.; closed Sun. and major holidays. Admission: adults, $10; seniors, $8; children 6–17, $3; children under 6, free.

Museums Honoring Individuals

Bailey House Museum. See Museums section.

Bishop Museum. See Museums section.

Lyman House and Mission Museum. See Museums section.

Queen Emma Summer Palace. See Historic Sites section.

Historic Sites

Ali'iolani Hale-King Kamehameha V Judiciary History Center of Hawaii. Ali'iolani Hale, historic home of Hawaii's Supreme Court in Honolulu since 1874, also is the site of the King Kamehameha V Judiciary History Center of Hawaii. In addition to conducting and encouraging research and disseminating information, the center collects, preserves, and displays materials interpreting more than 200 years of legal and judiciary history in Hawaii. It has a restored 1913 courtroom and artifacts, manuscripts, documents, and videos relating to the history.

Ali'iolani Hale-King Kamehameha V Judiciary History Center of Hawaii, 417 S. King St., Honolulu, HI 96813. Phone: 808/539–4999. Fax: 808/539–4996. E-mail: *jihchawaii@yahoo.com*. Web site: *http://ljhchawaii.topcities.com/exhibits.html*. Hours: 9–4 Mon.-Fri.; closed Sat.-Sun. and state and national holidays. Admission: free.

Hulihe'e Palace. The ca. 1838 Hulihe'e Palace along the coast in Kailua-Kona, Hawaii, was the vacation residence of Hawaiian royalty. It now is a historical museum, restored to the Kalakaua dynasty period, operated by the Daughters of Hawaii. The palace, which has six rooms, two oceanfront lanai, and lovely grounds, contains artifacts, furnishings, portraits, quilts, tapa, and featherwork from the Kalakaua period.

Hulihe'e Palace, 75–5718 Alii Dr., Kailua-Kona, HI 96740. Phones: 808/329–1877 and 808/329–9555. Fax: 808/329–1321. E-mail: *hilihee@ilhawaii.net*. Web: *www.huliheepalace.org*. Hours: 9–4 Mon.-Sat.; 10–4 Sun.; closed major holidays. Admission: adults. $6; seniors, $4; students and children, $1.

'Iolani Palace. 'Iolani Palace in downtown Honolulu was the office residence of the kingdom's last two monarchs — King Kalakaua, who built the palace in 1882, and his sister and successor, Queen Lili'uokalani. The palace was the center of social and political activities during the monarchy period. It also was the site of the trial of Queen Lili'uokalani in 1895 after Hawaii became a republic in 1894. She was found guilty of knowing about a rebellion by her supporters to restore the monarchy and imprisoned for eight months in an upstairs room. Hawaii became a territory of the United States in 1900 and a state in 1959.

At the end of the monarchy, the palace was converted into legislative halls and executive offices. After the state capitol was built adjacent to the palace grounds in 1968, the building was restored to its former grandeur and opened as a museum in 1978. It now features portraits of King Kalakaua, Queen Lili'uokalani, and various French, German, Russian, and British rulers and leaders.

'Iolani Palace, King and Richards Sts., Honolulu, HI 96813 (mailing address: PO Box 2259, Honolulu, HI 96804-9983). Phone: 808/522–0822. Fax: 808/532–1051. E-mail: *info@iolanipalace.org*. Web site: *www.iolanipalace.org*. Hours: 9–4 Tues.-Sat.; closed Sun.-Mon. and major holidays. Admission: adults, $6; children under 17, $3; children under 5 not admitted; free 1st Sun. of month.

Mission Houses Museum. The Mission Houses Museum in Honolulu provides a look into nineteenth-century Hawaii. The museum, founded in 1920 by the Hawaiian Mission Children's Society, includes three restored structures — 1821 Hale La'au mission house, 1831 Chamberlain House that was a home and storehouse, and 1841 printing house where the Hawaiian language was first printed. Guided tours interpret the cultural interaction of Hawaiians, missionaries, and foreigners in the 1820 to 1863 missionary period, and include much of Hawaii's history before and after the period.

Mission Houses Museum, 553 S. King St., Honolulu, HI 96813-3002. Phone: 808/531–0481. Fax: 808/545–2280. Hours: 10–4 Tues.-Sat.; closed Sun.-Mon., New Year's Day, Thanksgiving, and Christmas. Admission: adults, $10; seniors, military, and Ka-ma'aina, $8; students and children over 5, $6; children under 6, free.

Pu'uhonua o Hōnaunau National Historical Park. The Pu'uhonau o Hōnaunau National Historical Park in Honaunau, Hawaii, preserves the site where — from the fifteenth to the early nineteenth century — Hawaiians who broke a kapu or ancient law could avoid death by fleeing to this place of refuge. It also was a place where defeated warriors and non-combatants could find refuge during times of battle.

In addition to the refuge site, the 182-acre park includes a massive 1550 stone wall that separates the royal grounds from the refuge and such archaeological sites as temple platforms, royal fish ponds, sledding tracks, and coastal village sites. The Hale o Keawe Temple and several thatched structures also have been reconstructed. The park has a visitor center, orientation talks, and costumed interpreters who give demonstrations of carving, weaving, making of tapa cloth from mulberry bark, and the playing of traditional games.

The 'Iolani Palace in Honolulu was the residence of the Hawaiian kingdom's last two monarchs — King Kalakaua, who built the palace in 1882, and his sister and successor, Queen Lili'uokalani. After Hawaii became part of the United States, the place was used by the islands' legislature and as executive offices and later restored to its former grandeur and opened as a museum featuring historical photographs of past rulers and leaders. *Courtesy The Friends of 'Iolani Palace.*

Pu'uhonua o Hōnaunau National Historical Park, off State Hwy. 160, PO Box 129, Honaunau, HI 96726. Phones: 808/328–2326 and 808/328–2288. Fax: 808/328–9485. Hours: 6-8 Mon.-Thurs.; 6-11 Fri.-Sun. Admission: adults, $2; children under 17, free.

Pu'ukohola Heiau National Historic Site. The temple at the Pu'ukohola Heiau National Historic Site near Kawaihae, Hawaii, was directly associated with the founding of the Hawaiian kingdom. It was constructed in 1790 to 1791 by Kamehameha the Great and his followers to incur the favor of the war god Kuka'ilimoku. Kamehameha had conquered the islands of Maui, Lanai, and Molokai by 1790, but was not able to lay full claim to the home island of Hawaii because of opposition from Keōua Kūahu'ula, his chief rival and cousin.

When Kamehameha asked his prophet for guidance, he was told to build a large heiau (temple)

dedicated to his family war god. When the temple was completed, he invited his cousin for the dedication ceremonies. After Keōua Kūahu'ula arrived, a fight broke out and he and most of his party were killed. The body then was carried up to the heiau and offered as a sacrifice to the war god. The death of Keōua Kūahu'ula ended all the opposition on the island of Hawaii, and subsequent conquests and treaties resulted in Kamehameha becoming king of all the Hawaiian islands by 1810. The monarchy continued to rule until it was overthrown in 1893.

The stone framework of the Pu'ukohola Heiau still can be seen at the site. On a nearby hillside are the ruins of Mailekini Heiau, believed to have been the older war or agricultural temple used by Kamehameha's ancestors. He had converted it into a fort. The site also has a visitor center.

Pu'ukohola Heiau National Historic Site, 62–3601 Kawaihae Rd., PO Box 44340, Kamuela,

HI 96743–9720. Phone: 808/882–7218. Fax: 808/882–1215. E-mail: *emest-young@nos.gov.* Web site: *www.nps.gov/puhe.* Hours: 7:30–4 daily. Admission: free.

Queen Emma Summer Palace. Queen Emma, wife of King Kamehameha IV, was one of the earliest symbols of the Hawaiian Islands' cosmopolitan culture. Born in 1836, she was descended from Hawaiian chieftains and John Young, the Englishman who became the friend and advisor of Kamehameha the Great, the first monarch. The Queen Emma Summer Palace, located in a Hawaiian-Victorian setting on the outskirts of Honolulu, was her summer mountain retreat that she shared with her family. It was willed to her by the son of John Young. The palace, now operated by the Daughters of Hawaii, features rare artifacts and personal memorabilia of Hawaii's royalty and other Hawaiian and Victorian treasures.

Queen Emma Summer Palace, 2913 Pali Hwy., Honolulu, HI 96817. Phone: 808/595–6291. Fax: 808/595–4395. E- mail: *doh1903@hawaii.rr.com.* Web site: *www.daughtersofhawaii.org.* Hours: 9–4 daily; closed major holidays. Admission: adults, $6; seniors, $4; children under 16, $1.

Botanical Gardens

Hawaii Tropical Botanical Garden. More than 2,000 species of tropical plants from throughout the world are displayed at the Hawaii Tropical Botanical Garden in Papaikou on the large island of Hawaii. The garden, located in a beautiful valley on the ocean, contains collections of palms, heliconias, gingers, bromeliads, and hundreds of other rare and exotic plants. The valley garden has nature trails that take visitors through a tropical rainforest, across bubbling streams, and past views of waterfalls and ocean vistas along the rugged Pacific coast.

Hawaii Tropical Botanical Garden, 27–717 Old Mamalahoa Hwy., PO Box 80, Papaikou, HI 96781. Phone: 808/964–5233. Fax: 808/964/1338. E-mail: *htbg@ilhawaii.net.* Web site: *www.htbg.com.* Hours: 9–5 daily; closed New Year's Day, Thanksgiving, and Christmas. Admission: adults, $15; children 6–16, $5; children under 6, free.

Honolulu Botanical Gardens. The Honolulu Botanical Gardens operated by the city and county of Honolulu, Hawaii, consists of five distinct tropical gardens in different ecological settings around the island of Oahu. The gardens are the Foster Botanical Garden, founded in the 1850s and the oldest garden, which features mature tropical plants, downtown Honolulu; Ho'omaluhia Botanical Garden, plantings from major tropical regions around the world, Kaneohe; Koko Crater Botanical Garden, xeriscape garden, slopes and basin of Koko Crater; Lili'uokalani Botanical Garden, native Hawaiian plants, just north of Foster Garden; and Wahiawa Botanical Garden, plants that thrive in a tropical rain forest, between the Waianae and Koolau mountain ranges.

Honolulu Botanical Gardens, Dept. of Parks and Recreation, 50 N. Vineyard Blvd., Honolulu, HI 96817. Phone: 808/522–7060. Fax: 808/522–7050. E-mail: *hbg@honolulu.gov.* Web site: *www.co.honolulu.hi.us/parks/hbg.* Hours: Foster, Ho'omaluhia, and Wahiawa — 9–4 daily; Lili'uokalani and Koko Crater — dawn-dusk daily. Admission: all free but Foster, which is: adults, $5; students 6–12, $3; children under 6, free.

National Tropical Botanical Garden. Plants of Hawaii and Polynesia are featured at the National Tropical Botanical Garden in Kalaheo, Hawaii. In addition to having tropical gardens of extraordinary beauty and historical significance, the botanical garden advances scientific research, public education, and plant conservation. The facility includes four gardens and three preserves in Hawaii and one in south Florida, totaling over 1,600 acres.

The National Tropical Botanical Garden headquarters is located at the McBryde Garden on the south shore of Kauai. It is home to the largest collection of native Hawaiian flora. The Allerton Garden — known as Lawai-kai in Hawaiian — is adjacent to the McBryde. It is the garden paradise first imagined by Hawaii's Queen Emma in the late nineteenth century and then by Alexander McBryde at the turn of the twentieth century, and later created by Robert and John Gregg Allerton. The Limahuli Garden on the north shore of Haena is the largest of the gardens, having more than 1,000 acres in a verdant topical valley covering three distinct ecological zones. The Kabanu Garden amid black lava flows along the Hana coast is devoted largely to plants of value to the people of Polynesia, Micronesia, and Melanesia. The Kampong Garden on Biscayne Bay in Coconut Grove, Florida, features flowering trees and tropical fruit cultivars.

National Tropical Botanical Garden, 3530 Papalina Rd., Kalaheo, HI 96741. Phone: 808/332–7324. Fax: 808/332- 9765. E-mail: *members@nthg.org.* Web site: *www.nthg.org.* Hours and admission: varies with the gardens.

HISPANIC (*also see* Cuban; Mexican; Puerto Rican; Spanish)

Museums and Galleries

Arte Américas. Art Américas in Fresno, California, features the arts of Mexico, Latin America, California, and the Southwest. It presents from 12 to 18 changing exhibitions during the year and outdoor concerts from May through September.

Arte Américas, 1630 Van Ness Ave., Fresno, CA 93721. Phone: 559/266–2623. Fax: 559/268–6130. E-mail: *director@arteamericas.org*. Web site: *www.arteamericas.org*. Hours: 11–5 Tues.-Sun. (also to 8 on Thurs.); closed Mon. Admission: adults, $3; seniors and students, $2; children under 5, free.

Caribbean Cultural Center. The Caribbean Cultural Center in New York City presents exhibitions, and programs on the arts, crafts, and cultural history of Caribbean and African peoples.

Caribbean Cultural Center, 408 W. 58th St., New York, NY 10019. Phone: 212/307–7420. Fax: 212/315–1086. Hours: 10–6 Mon.-Fri.; closed Sat.-Sun. and major holidays. Admission: donation.

Casa de Unidad Cultural Arts and Media Center. The Casa de Unidad Cultural Arts and Media Center in Detroit, Michigan, seeks to discover, develop, celebrate, and advance Hispanic-Latino arts, their humanistic and spiritual values, and their traditions in southwest Detroit and elsewhere. In addition to presenting art exhibitions in its gallery, the center provides technical assistance to artists holding workshops, concerts, and performances.

Casa de Unidad Cultural Arts and Media Center, 1920 Scotten St., Detroit, MI 38209. Phone: 313/843–9598. Fax: 313/643–7307. Web site: *www.casadeunidad.com*. Hours: 10–4:30 Mon.-Fri.; closed Sat.-Sun. and major holidays. Admission: free.

Center for Cuban Studies. See Cuban Museums and Galleries section.

Center for Latino Arts and Culture. The Center for Latino Arts and Culture at Rutgers University in New Brunswick, New Jersey, researches, documents, interprets, and promotes Latino, Hispanic, Caribbean, and Latin American arts and culture. The center, housed in a ca. 1910 American Foursquare-style house on the main campus, offers exhibitions, programs, and publications to advance Latino artistic production, scholarship, and traditions.

Center for Latino Arts and Culture, Rutgers University, 122 College Ave., New Brunswick, NJ 08901–1165. Phone: 732/932–1263. Fax: 732/932–1589. Web site: *http://latinocenter.rutgers.edu*. Hours: 9–5 Mon.-Fri. and by appointment. Admission: free.

Chicano Humanities and Arts Council. See Mexican Museums and Galleries section.

Cuban Museum. See Cuban Museums and Galleries section.

El Museo Cultural de Santa Fe. El Museo Cultural de Santa Fe celebrates Santa Fe's and New Mexico's Hispanic heritage. It presents exhibits, arts events, educational classes and workshops, and community events devoted to the state's Hispanic culture, art, and traditions. The museum, which occupies a 31,000-square-foot former warehouse, also sponsors an annual Contemporary Hispanic Market and Contemporary Hispanic Artists Winter Market.

El Museo Cultural de Santa Fe, 1615 Paseo de Peralta, Santa Fe, NM 87501. Phone: 505/992–0591. E-mail: *info@elmuseocultural.org*. Web site: *www.elmuseocultural.org*. Hours: 1–5 Tues.-Fri.; 10–5 Sat.; closed Sun.-Mon. Admission: free.

El Museo del Barrio. See Puerto Rican Museums and Galleries section.

El Museo Latino. Founded in 1993, the El Museo Latino in Omaha, Nebraska, was the first Latino art and history museum and cultural center in the Midwest. The focus of the museum is the art and history of Latino people in the region and the Americas. It presents exhibits, films, performances, educational programs, and special events.

El Museo Latino, 4701 S. 25th St., Omaha, NE 68107. Phone: 402/731–1137. Fax: 402/731–7012. E-mail: *webmaster@elmuseolatino.org*. Web site: *www.elmuseolatino.org*. Hours: 10–5 Mon.-Fri. (also to 7 Tues.); closed Sat.-Sun. and major holidays. Admission: adults, $5; college students, $4; seniors and children K-12, $3.50.

Fonda del Sol Visual Arts Center. The Fonda del Sol Visual Arts Center in Washington, D.C., is a bilingual community museum dedicated to presenting, promoting, and preserving the cultural heritage and arts of the Americas. It offers changing exhibitions of the works of contemporary artists and craftsmen and selections from its permanent collection of pre–Colombian art, santos, folk, and contemporary art. It also sponsors concerts, lectures, poetry readings, performance art programs, exhibit tours, educational programs, and the annual Caribbeana Festival, which features Caribbean art and culture.

Fonda del Sol Visual Arts Center, 2112 R St., N.W., Washington, DC 20008. Phone: 202/483–2777. Web site: *www.dkmuseums.com/fondo.html*. Hours: 12:30–5:30 Tues.-Sat.; closed Sun.-Mon. and major holidays. Admission: donation.

Four Rivers Cultural Center and Museum. See Multicultural Museums and Galleries section.

Hispanic Society of America. The Hispanic Society of America in New York City is a free museum and reference library for the study of the arts and cultures of Spain, Portugal, and Latin America. Its collections and exhibits relate to the culture of the Iberian Peninsula from prehistoric times to the present, and include paintings, sculptures, ceramics, textiles, costumes, and other materials from Spain, Portugal, Latin America, and the Philippines.

Hispanic Society of America, on Broadway between 155th and 156th Sts., New York, NY 10023 (mailing address: 613 W. 155th St., New York, NY 10032). Phone: 212/926-2234. Fax: 212/690-0743. E-mail: *info@hispanicsocietv.org.* Web site: *www.hispanicsocietv.org.* Hours: 10–4:30 Tues.-Sat.; 1–4 Sun.; closed Mon. and major holidays. Admission: free.

La Casa de la Raza. La Casa de la Raza in Santa Barbara, California, is a Hispanic cultural and social services agency that presents art exhibitions, poetry readings, and folklore, dance, and theater programs.

La Casa de la Raza, 601 E. Montecito St., Santa Barbara, CA 93103. Phone: 805/965-8581. Fax: 805/965-6451. Hours: 9–9 Mon.-Fri.; closed Sat.-Sun. and major holidays. Admission: free.

La Raza Galeria Posada. La Raza Galeria Posada in Sacramento, California, seeks to advance, celebrate, and preserve the art and culture of the Chicano, Latino, and Native populations for present and future generations. The art center and museum, housed in the Heilbron Mansion, a Victorian landmark, presents a year-round series of folk, traditional, and contemporary art exhibitions, as well as literary events, musical programs, and community cultural activities.

La Raza Galeria Posada, 1421 R St., Sacramento, CA 95814. Phone: 910/446-5133. Fax: 916/446-5801. Hours: 11–3 Tues.-Thurs., 11–8 Fri.-Sat.; closed Sun.-Mon., Easter, Thanksgiving, and Christmas. Admission: free.

Latin American Art Museum. The Latin American Art Museum in Coral Gables, Florida, has collections and presents exhibitions of contemporary Hispanic and Latin American art, including Spain and non–Spanish speaking countries like Brazil and Haiti. The museum recently changed its name from the Florida Museum of Hispanic and Latin American Art.

Latin American Art Museum, 2206 S.W. 8th St., Miami, FL 33135-4914. Phone: 305/644-1127. Fax: 305/261-6996. E-mail: *hispmuseum@aol.com.* We site: *www.latinartmuseum.org.* Hours: 11–5 Tues.-Fri.; 11–4 Sat.; closed Sun.-Mon. Admission: free.

Latino Heritage Museum. The Latino Heritage Museum is a touring multimedia presentation that is a tribute to Latino scientists, inventors, and pioneers in the fields of science, aerospace, communications, medicine, business, sports, politics, arts,

and entertainment. It includes exhibits of over 100 artifacts, videos, and a collection of memorabilia, photographs, letters, and autographs of Hispanic pioneers in many fields. The show is designed to inspire and motivate young people.

Latino Heritage Museum, 271 Cadman Plaza East, Suite 21158, Brooklyn, NY 11202. E-mail: *latinoheritage101@hotmail.* Web site: *www.latinoheritage101.com.* Hours and admission: varies with location.

Latino Museum of History, Art, and Culture. The Latino Museum of History, Art, and Culture in Los Angeles, California, is devoted primarily to Latino art. The museum was closed in 2000, but recently reopened at a new location.

Latino Museum of History, Art, and Culture, 201 N. Los Angeles St., Los Angeles, CA 90012. Phone 213/626-7600. Fax: 213/626-3830. E-mail: *latinomuseum@earthlink.net.* Hours: 10–4 Mon.-Sat.; closed Sun. and major holidays. Admission: free.

Los Colores. See Mexican Museums and Galleries section.

Mexican Museum. See Mexican Museums and Galleries section.

Mexic-Arte Museum. See Mexican Museums and Galleries section.

Millicent Rogers Museum of Northern New Mexico. The Millicent Rogers Museum of Northern New Mexico in Taos features jewelry, textiles, pottery, basketry, paintings, weavings, dolls, ceramics, and religious materials relating to Native American and Hispanic history, art, and culture. The Hispanic collections are largely religious and decorative arts, and include such items as artworks, weavings, furniture, tinwork, embroideries, sculptures, tools, utensils, agricultural implements, and historic and contemporary santos (religious images).

Among the Native American offerings are Navajo and Pueblo jewelry, Hopi and Zuni kachina dolls, Navajo textiles, Pueblo pottery, and baskets from a number of southwestern tribes. Two of the four permanent exhibits are the Millicent Rogers collection of jewelry and Maria Martinez family collection of ceramics.

Millicent Rogers Museum of Northern New Mexico, 1504 Museum Rd., PO Box A, Taos, NM 87571. Phone: 505/758-2462. Fax: 505/758-5751. E-mail: *mrm@newmex.com.* Web site: *www.millicentrogers.org.* Hours: Apr.- Oct.—10–5 daily; remainder of year—10–5 Tues.-Sun.; closed Mon. and major holidays. Admission: adults, $7; New Mexico residents, $5; seniors and students, $6; children under 16, $2; families, $12; free for Taos County residents every Sun.

Mission Cultural Center for Latino Arts. The Mission Cultural Center for Latino Arts in San Francisco, California, consists of a group of activists with a shared vision to develop, preserve, and promote Latino cultural arts that reflect the living tradition and experiences of Chicano, Central and South American, and Caribbean peoples. The center displays changing art exhibitions and offers performing events, lectures, films, and classes.

Mission Cultural Center for Latino Arts, 2868 Mission St., San Francisco, CA 94110. Phone: 415/821-1155. Fax: 415/648-0933. Web site: *www.missionculturalcenter.org.* Hours: 10–5 Tues.-Sat.; closed Sun.-Mon. and major holidays. Admission: $2 per person.

Museo Alameda. The story of Latino experiences in America is told through art, history, and culture at the Museo Alameda, which opened in 2007 in Market Square, a three-block-square area that features Mexican shops, galleries, and restaurants in San Antonio, Texas. The museum, located in a 39,000-square-foot former food market with 20,000 square feet of exhibition space, is part of the Alameda National Center for Latino Arts and Culture. Now one of the nation's largest Hispanic museums, it formerly operated as a museum without walls, circulating exhibitions and presenting educational programs.

Two of the museum's 12 galleries are devoted to the historic Alameda Theater and the cultural area. The other nine galleries feature changing exhibitions of Hispanic-related objects on loan from the Smithsonian Institution. The museum is one of the affiliated institutions of the Smithsonian. It also has a sculpture garden and a project space for emerging and established artists to create new works.

Museo Alameda, 101 S. Santa Rosa, San Antonio, TX 78207. Phone: 210/299–4300. Web site: *www.thealameda.org.* Hours:10–6 Tues.-Sat.; 12–6 Sun.; closed Mon. Admission: adults, $8; seniors and students, $5; children under 6, free.

Musee Chicano. See Mexican Museums and Galleries section.

Museo de Arte de Ponce. See Puerto Rican Museums and Galleries section.

Museo de Arte Religioso de Porta Coeli. See Puerto Rican Museums and Galleries section.

Museo de las Americas (Denver). The Museo de las Americas in Denver, Colorado, fosters understanding and appreciation for the achievements of Latino people of the Americas by exhibiting and interpreting their diverse art, history, and cultures from ancient times to the present.

Museo de las Americas, 861 Santa Fe Dr., Denver, CO 80204. Phone: 303/571–4401. Fax: 303/607–

9761. E-mail: *gloria@museo.org.* Web site: *www.museo.org.* Hours: 10–5 Tues.-Sat.; closed Sun.-Mon. and major holidays. Admission: adults, $5; seniors and students, $4; children under 13, free

Museo de las Américas (San Juan). The Museo de las Américas in San Juan, Puerto Rico, is dedicated to the folk art in the Americas. The museum, housed in the nineteenth-century Bailaja Barracks at the entrance to El Morro, also has a collection of Puerto Rican santos and presents changing exhibitions of paintings by artists from throughout the Spanish-speaking world .

Museo de las Américas, Cuartel de Bailaja, 2nd Floor, San Juan, Puerto Rico 00901 (mailing address: PO Box 902- 3634 Old San Juan, PR 00902–3634). Phone: 787/724–5052. Fax: 787/722–2848. E-mail: *musame@prtc.net.* Web site: *www.prtc.net/~musame.* Hours: 10–4 Tues.-Sun.; closed Mon. and major holidays. Admission: free.

Museo Fuerte Conde de Mirasol. See Puerto Rican Museums and Galleries section.

Museum and Center for Humanistic Studies. See Puerto Rican Museums and Galleries section.

Museum of Anthropology, History, and Art (University of Puerto Rico). See Puerto Rican Museums and Galleries section.

Museum of Art of Puerto Rico. See Puerto Rican Museums and Galleries section.

Museum of Contemporary Art of Puerto Rico. See Puerto Rican Museums and Galleries section.

Museum of History, Anthropology, and Art. See Puerto Rican Museums and Galleries section.

Museum of Latin American Art. Artworks from all of Latin America's Spanish-speaking regions can be seen at the Museum of Latin American Art in Long Beach, California. They include paintings, sculptures, works on paper, and mixed media. Changing exhibitions of traditional and contemporary Latin art also are presented.

Museum of Latin American Art, 628 Alamitos Ave., Long Beach, CA 90802. Phone: 562/437-1689. Fax: 562/437-7043. E-mail: *info@molaa.com.* Web site: *www.molaa.com.* Hours: 11:30–7:30 Tues.-Sat.; 12–6 Sun.; closed Mon. Admission: adults, $5; seniors and students, $3; children under 12, free.

National Hispanic Cultural Center. The National Hispanic Cultural Center in Albuquerque, New Mexico, is devoted to the study, advancement, and presentation of Hispanic culture, arts, and humanities. The $50 million state center occupies over 50

acres in the traditionally Hispanic neighborhood of Barelas along the Rio Grande River.

National Hispanic Cultural Center, 1701 4th St., S.W., Albuquerque, NM 87102. Phone: 505/248-2261. Fax: 505/246-2613. E-mail: *webmaster@hcc.state.nm.us*. Web site: *www.nhccnm.org*. Hours: 10–5 Tues.-Sun.; closed Mon., New Year's Day, Easter, Thanksgiving, and Christmas. Admission: adults, $3; seniors, $2; children under 17, free.

National Museum of Mexican Art. See Mexican Museums and Galleries section.

Plaza de la Raza Cultural Center for the Arts and Education. Plaza de la Raza Cultural Center for the Arts and Education is a multidisciplinary cultural arts center in the Los Angeles, California area.

The plaza features four collections — Vincent Price Collection, ceramic, wood, and stone artifacts; Plaza Hispanic Collection, prints and works on paper; Plaza Folk Art Collection, artworks produced in Mexico; and Jose Galvez Collection, photographs.

Plaza de la Raza Cultural Center for the Arts and Education, 3540 N. Mission Rd., Los Angeles, CA 90031. Phone: 323/223-2475. Fax: 323/223-1804. E-mail: *admin@plazaraza.org*. Web site: *www.plaza raza.org*. Hours: 9–8 Mon.-Fri., 11–2 Sat.; closed major holidays. Admission: free.

Popular Arts Museum. See Puerto Rican Museums and Galleries section.

Spanish Institute. See Spanish Museums and Galleries section.

Museums Honoring Individuals

Dr. Jose Celso Barbose Museum and Library. See Puerto Rican Museums Honoring Individuals section.

Luis Muñoz Rivera Library and Museum. See Puerto Rican Museums Honoring Individuals section.

Pablo Casals Museum. See Puerto Rican Museums Honoring Individuals section.

Pancho Villa State Park. See Mexican Museums Honoring Individuals section.

Puerto Rican Cultural Center Juan Antonio Corretjer. See Puerto Rican Museums Honoring Individuals section.

Historic Sites

The Alamo. See Mexican Historic Sites section.

Baca House. The Baca House, an 1869 two-story territorial-style adobe house that is part of the Trinidad History Museum in Trinidad, Colorado, was the home of Felipe Baca, a Hispanic businessman, rancher, and community leader. The adobe dwelling reflects the eclectic mixture of Hispanic and Anglo furnishings typical of prosperous Spanish-American families in the region at the time. It has whitewashed walls, ornately carved and upholstered furniture, colorful Spanish textiles, religious objects, and a garden with a traditional outdoor oven and vegetables and herbs typically grown for use in a nineteenth-century Hispanic home.

Baca House, Trinidad History Museum, 300 E. Main St., Trinidad, CO 81082. Phone: 719/846-7217. Fax: 719/8450117. Web site: *www.coloradohistory.org/hist_sites/trinidad/bacahouse.htm*. Hours: May-Sept.—10–4 daily; remainder of year — by appointment. Admission: adults, $5; seniors, $4.50; children 6–16, $2.50; children under 6, free.

Caparra Ruins Historical Museum and Park Museum. See Puerto Rican Historic Sites section.

Caquana Indian Ceremonial Park and Museum. See Native American Prehistoric Sites and Museums section.

Casa Blanca Museum. See Puerto Rican Historic Sites section.

El Morro National Monument. See Native American Prehistoric Sites and Museums section.

El Paso Museum of Archaeology at Wilderness Park. See Native American Prehistoric Sites and Museums section.

El Pueblo de Los Angeles Historic Monument. See Mexican Historic Sites section.

El Pueblo History Museum. See Spanish Historic Sites section.

Hacienda Buena Vista. See Puerto Rican Historic Sites section.

La Encinos State Historic Park. See Spanish Historic Sites section.

La Hacienda de los Martinez. See Spanish Historic Sites section.

Mission Santa Barbara. See Spanish Historic Sites section.

Olivas Adobe Historic Park. See Spanish Historic Sites section.

Petaluma Adobe State Historic Park. See Mexican Historic Sites sectional.

Rancho los Alamitos Historic Ranch and Gardens. See Spanish Historic Sites section.

Rancho los Cerritos Historic Site. See Spanish Historic Sites section.

Salinas Pueblo Missions National Monument. See Spanish Historic Sites section.

San Agustin de Isleta Mission. See Spanish Historic Sites section.

San Juan National Historic Site. See Puerto Rican Historic Sites section.

Santuario de Nuestra Señora de Guadalupe. See Spanish Historic Sites section.

Tubac Presidio State Historic Park. See Spanish Historic Sites section.

HUNGARIAN

Museums and Galleries

American Hungarian Museum. The American Hungarian Museum in Passaic, New Jersey, collects and exhibits Hungarian memorabilia, art, and folk art and crafts, and other related materials. The museum, located on the second floor of Reid Memorial Library, has a permanent exhibit of Hungarian historical materials, folk art, and photographs; presents changing exhibitions; and offers lectures, performances, film showings, and workshops.

American Hungarian Museum, Reid Memorial Library, 80 3rd St., PO Box 2049, Passaic, NJ 07055. Phones: 973/473–0013 and 973/836–4860. Web site: *http://hungaria.org/ahm/muzeum*. Hours: Oct.-May — varies with library hours, special programs 1–5 Sun.; rest of year — by appointment. Admission: free.

Bukovina Society Headquarters Museum. See German Museums and Galleries section.

Hungarian Folk-Art Museum. The Hungarian Folk-Art Museum in Port Orange, Florida, collects and displays Hungarian folklore and folk art objects, clothing, ceramics, photographs, and related materials. It is operated by the Cardinal Mindszenty Society of Florida.

Hungarian Folk-Art Museum, 546 Ruth St., Port Orange, FL 32127. Phone: 904/767–4292. Fax: 904/788–6785. E- mail: *mhorvath386@aol.com*. Hours: 9–9 Mon.-Fri.; 9–12 Sat.; closed Sun. and major holidays. Admission: donation.

Hungarian Heritage Museum. The Hungarian Heritage Museum in Cleveland, Ohio, seeks to interpret Hungarian culture and the experiences of Hungarians in northwestern Ohio to educate, inspire, and enrich others. The newly reopened museum in downtown Cleveland has exhibits on Hun-

garian folk costumes and art, formal attire, embroidery, ecclesiastical art, magyars of eastern Transylvania, and Hungarian-American life.

Hungarian Heritage Museum, Galleria at Erieview, 1309 E. 9th St., Cleveland, OH 44114 (mailing address: Cleveland Hungarian Heritage Society, PO Box 24134, Cleveland, OH 44124). Phones: 216/523–3900 and 440/442–3466 (phone/fax). Hours: 11–3 Wed.-Sat. (also to 5 Fri.); closed Sun.-Tues. and major holidays. Admission: free.

Museum of the American Hungarian Foundation. The Museum of the American Hungarian Foundation, formerly the Hungarian Heritage Center, in New Brunswick, New Jersey, depicts the cultural and historical heritage of American Hungarians. The foundation, which moved to New Brunswick from Elmhurst College in Illinois in 1959 when it funded the Hungarian studies program at Rutgers University, seeks to further understanding and appreciation of the Hungarian cultural and historical heritage in the United States. The museum features exhibits of Hungarian naïve art, works of American and Hungarian artists and photographers, and aspects of Hungarian-American history, art, culture, and traditions.

Museum of the American Hungarian Foundation, 300 Somerset St., PO Box 1084, New Brunswick, NJ 08903. Phone: 732/846–5777. Fax: 732/249–7033. E-mail: *info@ahfoundation.org*. Web site: *www.ahfoundation.org*. Hours: 11–4 Tues.-Sat.; 1–4 Sun.; closed Mon. and major holidays. Admission: donation.

New York Hungarian House. The New York Hungarian House in New York City helps members and others to learn about Hungarian history, literature, geography, language, and current developments. Its sponsoring organizations present exhibits, lectures, concerts, performances, and social events. The house has a Hungarian reference and lending library and a historical collection.

New York Hungarian House, 213 E. 82nd St., New York, NY 10028. Phone: 212/249–9360. Web site: *www.magyarhaz.org*. Hours and admission: varies.

ICELANDIC (*also see* Arctic Peoples; Scandinavian)

Museums and Galleries

Icelandic State Park and Pioneer Heritage Center. The influence of Icelandic settlers in North Dakota's pioneer days is shown at the Pioneer Heritage Center at Icelandic State Park near Cavalier. The center is a tribute to the Icelandic and other pioneers in North Dakota during the 1870 to 1920 period. Exhibits, living history demonstrations, and historic buildings illustrate the culture, values, and beliefs the Icelandic settlers brought to the frontier during the homestead era. Among the park's features are the Gunlogson Homestead and four historic structures — a church, school, community hall, and log cabin — which have been relocated and restored at the site.

Icelandic State Park and Pioneer Heritage Center, 13571 Hwy. 5, Cavalier, ND 58220. Phone: 701/265-4561. Fax: 701/265-4443. E-mail: *isp@ state.nd.us.* Web site: *www.ndparks.com.* Hours: mid–May–Labor Day — 9–8 Mon.-Thurs.; 9–6 Fri.-Sun.; remainder of year — 9–5 Mon.-Fri.; 1–5 Sun.; closed Sat. Admission: $5 per vehicle.

INDIAN, AMERICAN *see* NATIVE AMERICAN

IRISH

Museums and Galleries

American Irish Historical Society. The American Irish Historical Society in New York City has a research library and sometimes presents art and other Irish-related exhibitions. The historical society, housed in a ca. 1900 townhouse, has the most complete private collection of Irish and Irish-American history and literature in the United States. The library also contains historic Irish letters, papers, music, and theater, as well as works of art by noted Irish artists. American Irish Historical Society, 991 5th Ave., New York, NY 19928. Phone: 212/288-2263. Fax: 212/628-7927. E-mail: *info@aihs.org.* Web site: *www.aihs.org.* Hours: 10:30–5 Mon.-Fri.; closed Sat.-Sun. and national holidays. Admission: free.

Irish American Heritage Center. Artifacts and other materials reflecting Irish history and culture can be seen at the Irish American Heritage Center in Chicago. Among the historic objects on display are Irish china, tapestry, a piano, lace, an organ, and maps. Traveling art exhibitions also are presented in the art gallery across the hall. The museum was opened officially by Ireland's president, Mary Robinson, in 1991 and she now is honorary president of the museum.

Irish American Heritage Center, 4626 N. Knox Ave., Chicago, IL 60630. Phone: 773/282-7035. Fax: 773/282-0380. E-mail: *info@irishamhc.com.* Web site: *www.irishamhc.com.* Hours: by appointment and during cultural programs and traveling art exhibitions in the gallery. Admission: free.

Irish American Heritage Museum. The Irish American Heritage Museum in Albany, New York, interprets Irish America history and culture through its exhibits, collections, and programs. The museum, which is housed in a ca. 1850 Italianate building, has numerous objects representing the history of the Irish in America in its collections and has presented exhibits on such subjects as the Irish immigration experience, 69th New York Regiment, Ancient Order of Hibernians, Irish women, and Irish in religion, labor, and business.

Irish American Heritage Museum, 991 Broadway, Suite 101, Albany, NY 12204. Phone: 518/432-6598. Fax: 518/449-2540. E-mail: *irishamermuseum@ cs.com.* Web site: *www.irishamericanheritagemuseum. org.* Hours: Memorial Day-Labor Day —12–4 Wed.-Sun.; closed Mon.-Tues.; remainder of year — by appointment. Admission: free.

Irish Village East Durham. The Irish Village East Durham, a living history museum, is under development at the Michael J. Quill Irish Cultural and Sports Centre in East Durham, New York. Plans call for a nineteenth-century Irish village modeled after rural towns located in three counties — Limerick, Tipperary, and northern Cork — in the province of Munster in southern Ireland. The first historic cottage from Ireland already has arrived and been installed at the site. The 108-acre Quill Cultural and Sports Centre, named for a Transport Workers' Union leader, contains festival pavilions, Gaelic football and baseball fields, and other facilities.

Irish Village East Durham, Michael J. Quill Irish Cultural and Sports Centre, Rte. 145, PO Box 320, East Durham, NY 12423. Phones: 518/634-2286 and 800/434-3378. Fax: 518/634-2058. E-mail: *irishcenter@hughes.net.* Web site: *www.east-durham.org.* Hours and admission: still to be determined.

ITALIAN

Museums and Galleries

American Italian Museum. The American Italian Museum in New Orleans traces the history of Italians in the Southeast and their contributions to Louisiana and the United States. The museum has exhibits about such topics as Italian immigration and family life, role of Italians in the Mardi Gras, Italian musicians who pioneered jazz music in the early 1900s and other famous musicians, and St. Joseph's Day Altar and Sicilian immigrants in New Orleans. The museum is operated by the American Italian Renaissance Foundation, which also has a Hall of Honor, Louisiana American Italian Sports Hall of Fame, Giovanni Schiavo Collection on Italian American history, and Dr. John Adriani Collection on anesthesiology.

American Italian Museum, American Italian Renaissance Foundation, 537 S. Peters St., New Orleans,

LA 70130. Phone: 504/522–7294. Web site: *www. airf.org.* Hours: 10–3 Wed.-Thurs.; closed Fri.-Tues. and major holidays. Admission: free.

Italian American Museum. The Italian American Museum in New York City is located at the John D. Calandra Italian American Institute on the Queens College campus of City University of New York. It is dedicated to exploring the heritage of Italy and Italian Americans by presenting individual and collective struggles and achievements of Italians and their heirs to the American way of life. By interpreting objects and reminiscences, the museum tells of notable contributions by Italians and Italian Americans to American culture.

Italian American Museum, John D. Calandra Italian American Institute, Queens College, City University of New York, 28 W. 44th St., 17th Floor, New York, NY 10036. Phone: 212/642–2020. Fax: 212/642–2069. E-mail: *info@italianamericanmuseum.org.* Web site: *www.italianamericanmuseum.org.* Hours: 10–4 Mon.-Thurs. and by appointment; closed major holidays. Admission: free.

Italian Cultural Center. Italian paintings, sculpture, and models of famous buildings are featured at the Italian Cultural Center in Stone Park, Illinois. The center, operated by the Missionaries of St. Charles-Scalabrinians and located in the original seminary building, consists of a museum, art gallery, and library. Its primary mission is to further the enhancement and appreciation of cultural and artistic endeavors among Americans of Italian heritage, recent immigrants, and the American public.

Italian Cultural Center, 1621 N. 39th Ave., Stone Park, IL 60165. Phone: 708/345–3842. Web site: *www.italianculturalcenter.net.* Hours: 10–4 Mon.-Fri.; closed Sat.-Sun. and major holidays. Admission: free.

Museo ItaloAmericano. The Museo ItaloAmericano, located at the Fort Mason Center in San Francisco, California, is devoted to Italian and Italian American art and culture. It displays works by Italian and Italian American artists and offers educational programs furthering appreciation of Italian art and culture.

Museo ItaloAmericano, Fort Mason Center, Bldg. C, San Francisco, CA 94123. Phone: 415/673–2200. Fax: 415/673–2292. E-mail: *sfmuseo@sbcglobal.net.* Web site: *www.museoitaloamericano.org.* Hours: 12–4 Wed.-Sun.; closed Mon.-Tues. Admission: adults, $3; seniors and students, $2; children under 12, free; free 1st Wed. of month.

National Italian American Sports Hall of Fame. The National Italian American Sports Hall of Fame in Chicago, Illinois, preserves and promotes the history and heritage of Italian Americans in sports. It honors Italian American athletes who have made lasting contributions to sports and society, featuring artifacts and memorabilia from its collections. Among the more than 200 inductees are Joe DiMaggio and Phil Rizzuto in baseball; Hank Luisetti, basketball; Rocky Marciano, boxing; Phil and Tom Esposito, hockey; Brian Boitano, figure skating; Vince Lombardi and Alan Ameche, football; Jennifer Capriati, tennis; and Eddie Arcaro, horse racing.

National Italian American Sports Hall of Fame, 1431 W. Taylor St., Chicago, IL 60607. Phone: 312/226–5566. Fax: 312/226–5678. Web site: *www.niashf.org.* Hours: 9–5 Mon.-Fri.; 11–4 Sat.-Sun.; closed major holidays. Admission: adults, $5; seniors and children over 15, $3; children under 16, free.

Museums Honoring Individuals

Garibaldi-Meucci Museum. The Garibaldi-Meucci Museum on Staten Island, New York, honors pioneer inventor Antonio Meucci and legendary Italian hero Giuseppe Garibaldi. It is located in the 1845 Gothic Revival house where Meucci and his wife lived and invited Garibaldi to join them after he arrived in New York City seeking refuge in 1850. They worked together in Meucci's candle factory from 1850 to 1854, when Garibaldi returned to Italy and provided the leadership that unified Italy.

When Garibaldi died in 1884, a plaque in his honor was placed on door of the Meucci house. The house later was moved to its present location, turned over to the Order Sons of Italy in America, restored, and then opened as the Garibaldi-Meucci Museum in 1956. It has collections and displays of artifacts and other materials pertaining to the life and work of Meucci and Garibaldi, Italian history and culture, and contemporary Italian and Italian American heritage and culture.

Garibaldi-Meucci Museum, 420 Tompkins Ave, Staten Island, NY 10305. Phone: 718/442–1608. Fax: 718/442–8635. E-mail: *info@garibaldimeuccimuseum. org.* Web site: *www.garibaldimeuccimuseum.org.* Hours: 1–5 Tues.-Fri.; closed Sat.-Mon. and major holidays. Admission: $3 suggested donation.

JAPANESE (*also see* Asian)
Museums and Galleries

Four Rivers Cultural Center and Museum. See Multicultural Museums and Galleries section.

Japanese American Cultural and Community Center. The Japanese American Cultural and Community Center in Los Angeles, California, seeks to further understanding of Japanese culture by offering visual and performing arts programs and serving as a center to enhance community activities. It also provides office space to a wide variety of nonprofit cultural, educational, and community-based organizations in Los Angeles.

Japanese American Cultural and Community Center, 244 S. San Pedro St., Suite 505, Los Angeles, CA 90012. Phone: 213/628–2725. Fax: 213/617–8576. Web site: *www.jacce.org*. Hours: varies with events, but office open 9–6 Mon.-Fri. Admission: varies with events.

Japanese American National Museum. The Japanese American National Museum in Los Angeles, California, is dedicated to the history, culture, and experiences of Americans of Japanese ancestry. The museum founders were motivated by the desire for Japanese Americans to preserve their rich heritage and cultural identity. The museum first opened in the historic Nishi Hongwanji Buddist Temple in the Little Tokyo neighborhood in 1992 and later expanded to an 85,000-square-foot new pavilion across the street, making it the largest Japanese American museum in the nation. It has presented exhibitions on such topics as early immigration and settlement, World War II incarceration and military service, resettlement, history and culture of Japan, traditional Japanese art, and Japanese American art and design.

Japanese American National Museum, 369 E. 1st St., Los Angeles, CA 09912. Phone: 213/625–0414. Fax:213/625-1770. Web site: *www.janm.org*. Hours: 10–5 Tues.-Sun. (also to 8 Thurs.); closed Mon., New Year's Day, Thanksgiving, and Christmas. Admission: adults, $8; seniors, $5; students and children 6–17, $4; children under 6, free.

Japanese Cultural Center of Hawaii. The Japanese Cultural Center of Hawaii in Honolulu was founded to preserve and promote knowledge of Japanese American culture and history from 1885 to contemporary times. In addition to changing exhibitions on Japanese and Japanese American history, culture, and art, the center offers performing arts programs, arts and crafts classes, school presentations, and other educational programming.

Japanese Cultural Center of Hawaii, 2454 S. Beretania St., Honolulu, HI 96826. Phone: 808/945–7633. Fax: 808/944-1123. E-mail: *info@jcch.com*. Web site: *www.jcch.com*. Hours: 10–4 Tues.-Sat.; closed Sun.-Mon. Admission: non–Hawaiians, $5; Hawaiian residents, $3; children under 6, free.

Japan Society Gallery. Founded in 1907 in New York City, the Japan Society is a major resource on Japan. It offers programs in the arts, business, education, and public affairs. Its gallery presents changing exhibitions of Japanese art. Among the society's other activities are performing arts programs, films, and lectures.

Japan Society Gallery, 333 E. 47th St., New York, NY 10017. Phones: 212/715–1233 and 212/832–1155. Fax: 212/715–1262. E-mail: *amunroe@japansociety.org*. Web site: *www.japansociety.org*. Hours: during exhibitions —11–6 Tues.-Fri. (also to 9 Fri.); 11–5 Sat.-Sun.; closed Mon. and between exhibitions. Admissions: adults, $5; seniors and students, $3.

Morikami Museum and Japanese Gardens. The Morikami Museum and Japanese Gardens in Delray Beach, Florida, has become a center for Japanese arts and culture in south Florida since its founding in 1977. The 200-acre complex has two museum buildings with a permanent exhibit on Yamato Colony, a Japanese farming community in south Florida 100 years ago, and changing exhibitions; a teahouse with viewing gallery; and expansive Japanese gardens with a tropical bonsai collection, pine forests, small lakes, strolling paths, nature trails, and park and picnic areas.

The museum's collections contain over 5,000 Japanese art objects and artifacts and more than 200 textile pieces and fine art works. It also has a lakeside terrace with a Japanese courtyard garden, library, tea ceremonies, educational programs, and traditional Japanese festival celebrations.

Morikami Museum and Japanese Gardens, 4000 Morikami Park Rd., Delray, FL 33446. Phone: 561/495–0233. Fax: 561/499–2557. E-mail: *morikami@co.palm-beach.fl.us*. Web site: *www.morikami.org*. Hours: 10–5 Tues.-Sun.; closed Mon. and major holidays. Admission: adults, $10; seniors, $9; children 6–18, $7; children under 6, free.

Museums Honoring Individuals

Noguchi Museum. The Noguchi Museum in Long Island City, New York, features the sculptures of Isamu Noguchi. It contains a comprehensive collection of his works in stone, metal, wood, and clay, as well as models for public projects and gardens, dance sets, and Akari Light Sculptures. The museum consists of 13 galleries in a converted factory building — Noguchi's former studio — that encircles a garden with major granite and basalt sculptures. Exhibits cover Noguchi's life and works.

Noguchi Museum, 9–01 33rd Rd., Long Island City, NY 11106 (mailing address: 32–37 Vernon Blvd., Long Island City, NY 11106). Phone: 718/204–7088. Fax: 718/278–1248. E-mail: *museum@noguchi.org*. Web site: *www.noguchi.org*. Hours: 10–5 Wed.-Fri.; 11–6 Sat.-Sun.; closed Mon.-Tues., New Year's Day, Thanksgiving, and Christmas. Admission: adults, $10; seniors and students, $5; children under 12, free.

Botanical Gardens

Brooklyn Botanic Garden Japanese Hill-and-

The history, culture, and experiences of Americans of Japanese ancestry are presented to the public and school groups at the Japanese American National Museum in Los Angeles, California. The 85,000-square-foot museum is the largest Japanese American museum in the United States. *Courtesy Japan American National Museum and photographer Don Farber.*

Pond Garden. The Japanese Hill-and-Pond Garden at the Brooklyn Botanic Garden in Brooklyn, New York, was the first Japanese garden to be created in an American public garden. Opened in 1915, it was considered to be the masterpiece of Japanese landscape designer Takeo Shiota. The garden is a blend of the ancient hill-and-pond style and the more recent stroll-garden style in which various landscape features are gradually revealed along winding paths. The Brooklyn garden features hills, a waterfall, a pond, and an island, and such architectural elements as wooden bridges, stone lanterns, a viewing pavilion, the torii or gateway, and a Shinto shrine.

Japanese Hill-and-Pond Garden, Brooklyn Botanic Garden, 1000 Washington Ave., Brooklyn, NY 11225–1099. Phone: 718/623–7200. Fax: 718/857–2430. E-mail: *info@bbg.org.* Web site: *www.bbg.org.* Hours: Apr.-Sept.— 8-6 Tues.-Sun. and holidays; closed Mon.; remainder of year — 8–4:30 Tues.-Sun. and holidays; closed Mon., New Year's Day, Thanksgiving, and Christmas. Admission: adults, $5; seniors and students, $3; children under 16, free; free on Tues. and 10–12 Sat.; free for seniors on Fri.; free weekdays mid–Nov.-Feb.

Chicago Botanic Garden Elizabeth Hubert Malott Japanese Garden. The Elizabeth Hubert Malott Japanese Garden at the Chicago Botanic Garden in Glencoe, Illinois, is known as Sansho-En, a garden of three islands. The tranquil garden features styled plants and judiciously placed stones, with 30,000 recently installed new plants along the shoreline. The year-round Japanese Garden is one of 26 gardens at the botanical garden founded in 1965. The many walks are supplemented by tram tours.

Elizabeth Hubert Malott Japanese Garden, Chicago Botanic Garden, 1000 Lake Cook Rd., Glencoe, IL 60022. Phone: 847/835–5440. Fax: 847/835–4484. E-mail: *cbglib@nslsilus.org.* Web site: *www.chicagobotanic.org.* Hours: 8-sunset daily; closed Christmas. Admission: free, but $16 parking.

Hakone Gardens. Hakone Gardens in Saratoga, California, are the oldest Japanese-style residential gardens in the Western Hemisphere. The gardens with their peaceful settings, statues, ponds, and waterfalls cover 18 acres in the verdant hills of Saratoga. Classes are offered in traditional Japanese art forms such as ikebana and tea ceremony, and the annual Matsuri Festival with Japanese foods and Asian cultural entertainment is held in the spring and the Tea Ceremony Festival featuring different Japanese tea schools is in the fall.

Hakone Gardens, 21000 Big Basin Way, PO Box 2324, Saratoga, CA 95070. Phone: 408/741–4994. Fax: 408/741- 4993. E-mail: *hakone@hakone.com.* Web site: *www.hakone.com.* Hours: 10–5 Mon.-Fri.; 11–5 Sat.-Sun.; closed New Year's Day and Christmas. Admission: adults, $4; seniors and students, $3.50; children under 5, free.

Hammond Museum and Japanese Stroll Garden. The Hammond Museum and Japanese Stroll Garden in North Salem, New York, is a cross-cultural center with exhibits, programs, events, music, arts, and garden to provide links between the East and West. Its changing art exhibitions, sensual Japanese garden, and other activities seek to promote global awareness and understanding. The stroll garden also informs visitors about the environment, design, and Japanese gardening.

Hammond Museum and Japanese Stroll Garden, 28 Deveau Rd., PO Box 326, North Salem, NY 10560. Phone: 914/669–5033. Fax: 914/669–8221. E-mail: *gardenprogram@yahoo.com.* Web site: *www.hammondmuseum.org.* Hours: 12–4 Wed.-Sat.; closed Sun.-Tues. Admission: adults, $5; seniors and students, $4; children under 12, free.

Japanese Friendship Garden. The popularity of the Japanese Tea Pavilion at the 1915 Panama-California Exposition in San Diego, California, led to the formation of the Japanese Friendship Garden in the city's Balboa Park. It was followed in 1950 by the San Diego-Yokohama Sister City relationship and succeeding exchanges that further increased interest and support in the garden with the original tea house, a sukiya-style Japanese exhibit house, gardens, and other attractions. Plans are under way to add an herb and tea garden, waterfall and lily pond, cherry tree grove, walking trails, viewing pavilion, outdoor amphitheater, and traditional and contemporary tea houses.

Japanese Friendship Garden, Balboa Park, 2125 Park Blvd., San Diego, CA 92101–4792 (contact: Japanese Friendship Garden Society of San Francisco, Balboa Park Administration Bldg., San Diego, CA 92101–4792). Phone: 619/232–2721. Fax: 619/232–0917. E-mail: *jfgsd@niwa.org.* Hours: 10–4 Tues.-Sun.; closed Mon. Admission: adults, $3; seniors, $2.50; military and students, $2; children under 6, free.

Japanese Garden. The Japanese Garden in Van Nuys, California, features collections of Japanese plants, flowers, and trees. Tours are given of the 6.5-acre garden.

Japanese Garden, 6100 Woodley Ave., Van Nuys, CA 91406. Phone: 818/756–8166. Fax: 818/756–9648. E-mail: *bse@san.lacity.org.* Web site: *www.thejapanesegarden.com.* Hours: 12–3:15 Mon.-Thurs.; 10–3:15 Sun.; closed Fri.-Sat. Admission: adults, $3; seniors and children under 10, $2.

Japanese Garden on Mirror Lake. The Japanese Garden on Mirror Lake is located at the west end of Delaware Park, the main park in the Buffalo, New York, Olmsted Parks System. Completed in 1974, the garden represented a horticultural gesture of friendship between the sister cities of Buffalo and Kanazawa, Japan. The garden covers six acres along Mirror Lake and includes three islands connected to the mainland by bridges. It currently is undergoing redevelopment.

Japanese Garden on Mirror Lake, Delaware Park, E. Meadow Dr., Buffalo, NY 14216 (mailing address: Delaware Park, 84 Parkside Ave., Buffalo, NY 14216). Phones: 716/851–5806 and 716/884–9660. Web site: *http://members.localnet.com/shujir/garden.* Hours: 8-10 daily. Admission: free.

Morikami Museum and Japanese Gardens. See Museums and Galleries section.

UCLA Hannah Carter Japanese Garden. The UCLA Hannah Carter Japanese Garden in the Bel Air section of Los Angeles, California, resembles similar gardens in Kyoto, Japan. Nearly all the trees and plants belong to species grown in Japan and the garden's major structures — main gate, teahouse, bridges, and shrine — were built in Japan and reassembled here by Japanese artisans. The major symbolic rocks, antique stone carvings, and water basins also came from Japan. The garden was donated in 1965 by a former chairman of the university's Board of Regents and named for his wife.

UCLA Hannah Carter Japanese Garden, University of California at Los Angeles, 10619 Bellagio Rd., Los Angeles, CA 90024 (mailing address: Garden Administrative Office, UCLA Hannah Carter Japanese Garden, 10920 Wilshire Blvd., Suite 1520, Los Angeles, CA 90024–65180). Phone: 310/794–0320. Fax: 310/794–9208. E-mail: *gardens@support.ucla.edu.* Web site: *www.japanesegarden.ucla.edu.* Hours: 10–3 Tues.-Wed. and Fri. by reservation only; closed remainder of week. Admission: free.

JEWISH

Museums and Galleries

American Jewish Historical Society. See Center for Jewish History.

American Jewish Museum. The American Jewish

Museum, located at the Jewish Community Center of Greater Pittsburgh in Pennsylvania, explores Jewish art, history, and culture. It operates as a forum to support, celebrate, and develop living Jewish arts and artists and as a learning place. The museum seeks to create programming that enables viewers to examine the relevance of historical subjects, Judaic concepts, art, and creativity in their own lives. Its exhibits are presented in the gallery spaces of the center's Irene Kaufmann Building and the Alex and Leona Robinson Building.

American Jewish Museum, Jewish Community Center of Greater Pittsburgh, 5738 Forbes Ave., PO Box 81980, Pittsburgh, PA 15217. Phone: 412/521–8911. Fax: 412/521–7044. Web site: *www.jccpgh.org/museum.asp*. Hours: 9-9:30 Mon.-Thurs.; 9–6 Fri.; 1–6 Sat.; 6–6 Sun.; closed Jewish and national holidays. Admission: free.

Ann Randall Gallery. See Chase/Freedman Gallery and Ann Randall Gallery.

Arizona Jewish Historical Society. The Arizona Jewish Historical Society in Phoenix is devoted to the Arizona and Southwest experience of Jews and their contributions to the state's political, economic, social, and cultural development. The society makes use of the documents, artifacts, maps, photographs, and oral histories in its collections in its changing exhibitions on such subjects as early Jewish experiences, pioneer clans, and Jewish merchants, lawyers, entertainers, and athletes. Most of the exhibitions are available to other organizations as traveling exhibits.

Arizona Jewish Historical Society, 4710 N. 16th St., Suite 201, Phoenix, AZ 85016. Phone: 602/241–7870. Fax: 602/264–9773. E-mail: *azjhs@aol.com*. Web site: *www.azjhs.org*. Hours: Aug.-June — 9:30–3:30 Mon.-Fri.; closed Sat.-Sun., July, and Jewish and major holidays. Admission: free.

Benjamin and Dr. Edgar R. Cofeld Judaic Museum of Temple Beth Zion. The Benjamin and Dr. Edgar R. Cofeld Judaic Museum of Temple Beth Zion in Buffalo, New York, seeks to preserve Jewish history and culture, with the emphasis on religious traditions. Its collections include Judaic artifacts from the tenth century to the present, including Jewish ceremonial items, folk art and textiles, Holocaust remembrances, coins and medallions, books, and historical memorabilia.

Benjamin and Dr. Edgar R. Cofeld Judaic Museum of Temple Beth Zion, 805 Delaware Ave., Buffalo, NY 14209 (mailing address: 183 High Park Blvd., Buffalo, NY 14226). Phone: 716/836–6565. Fax: 716/831–1126. E-mail: *tbz@webt.com*. Web site: *www.tbz.org*. Hours: 9–4 Mon.-Fri.; 11–12 Sat.; closed Sun. and Jewish holidays. Admission: free.

Beth Ahabah Museum and Archives. The Congregation Beth Ahabah Museum and Archives in Richmond, Virginia, is devoted to the history and culture of the city's Jewish community. It preserves and displays the records and artifacts of the Kahal Kadosh Beth Shalome and Congregation Beth Ahabah and documents relating to the Richmond and Southern Jewish experiences. The museum and archives, housed in an early twentieth-century house adjacent to the congregation's sanctuary, has three galleries of changing exhibitions featuring objects from the archives.

Beth Ahabah Museum and Archives, Congregation Beth Ahabah, 1109 W. Franklin St., Richmond, VA 23220. Phone: 804/353–2668. Fax: 804/358–3451. E-mail: *bama@bethahabah.org*. Web site: *www.bethahabah.org*. Hours: 10–3 Sun.-Thurs.; closed Fri.-Sat. and Jewish holidays. Admission: $3 suggested donation.

B'nai B'rith Klutznick National Jewish Museum. The B'nai B'rith Klutznick National Jewish Museum in Washington, D.C., is dedicated to preserving and promoting the heritage and contributions of the Jewish people. Its exhibits trace Jewish history from antiquity to the present and focus on the Jewish experience in America. The collections range from Jewish contemporary art to ethnographic and archaeological holdings from biblical through modem times. The museum also houses the National Jewish American Sports Hall of Fame and administers the Philip and Mildred Lax Archive, containing papers and documents relating to the unique status of Jews throughout the world's tumultuous times of change.

B'nai B'rith Klutznick National Jewish Museum, 1640 Rhode Island Ave., N.W., Washington, DC 20036. Phones: 202/857–6583 and 202/857–6513. Fax: 202/857–2700. E-mail: *museum@bnaibrith.org*. Web site: *www.bnaibrith.org*. Hours: 12–3 Mon.-Thurs. and by appointment; closed Jewish and national holidays. Admission: free.

Boston Center for Jewish Heritage. The Boston Center for Jewish Heritage was founded in Boston, Massachusetts, in 1995 to restore the historic 1919 Vilna Shul synagogue and to explore the traditions of the American Jewish experience through exhibits and programs. The Vilna Shul, which has been restored and serves as the home for the museum, was built by Jews from Vilna, Lithuania, and is the last intact example of over 50 synagogues that once flourished in Boston. The museum presents exhibits on Jewish immigration, history, and culture, as well as the historic synagogue.

Boston Center for Jewish Heritage, 18 Phillips St., Boston, MA 02004. Phone: 617/523–2324. Fax: 781/459–2660. Web site: *www.bcjh.org*. Hours: Mar.-

Nov.—11–5 Wed.-Fri. and Sun.; closed Jewish holidays and remainder of week and year. Admission: free.

Center for Jewish History. The Center for Jewish History in New York City is a part of the American Jewish Historical Society, the oldest national ethnic historical organization in the United States. Founded in 1892, the society seeks to foster awareness and appreciation of the American Jewish heritage and to serve as a scholarly resource for research. Its Center for Jewish History presents changing exhibitions relating to the American Jewish experience.

Center for Jewish History, American Jewish Historical Society, 15 W. 16th St., New York, NY 10011. Phone: 212/294–6160. Fax: 212/294–6161. E-mail: *ajhs@ajhs.org.* Web site: *www.ajhs.org.* Hours: 9–5 Mon.-Thurs.; 9–2 Fri.; 11–5 Sun.; closed Sat. and national and major Jewish holidays. Admission: free.

Chase/Freedman Gallery and Ann Randall Gallery. The Greater Hartford Jewish Community Center in West Hartford, Connecticut, has two art galleries — the Chase/Freedman Gallery and the smaller Ann Randall Gallery. The galleries, located in the lobby of the center's Herbert Gilman Theater, present from six to eight exhibitions each year of contemporary, classical, and avant-garde art.

Chase/Freedman Gallery and Ann Randall Gallery, Greater Hartford Jewish Community Center, 335 Bloomfield Ave., West Hartford, CT 06117. Phone: 860/236–4521. Fax: 860/233–0802. Web site: *www.ghicc.org./aandc/chasefreedman.html.* Hours: 9 A.M.-9 P.M. Mon.-Thurs.; 9–5 Fri. and Sun.; closed Sat. and Jewish holidays. Admission: free.

Children's Galleries for Jewish Culture. The Children's Galleries for Jewish Culture, operated by the Jewish Children's Learning Lab in New York City, helps school-age children explore Jewish culture and history through interactive exhibitions and related educational programs. The Learning Lab seeks to foster in children of all backgrounds a positive and relevant attitude to Jewish heritage and to further learning through hands-on problem solving.

Children's Galleries for Jewish Culture, Jewish Children's Learning Lab, 515 W. 20th St., Suite 4E, New York, NY 10011. Phone: 212/924–4500. Fax: 212/924–9908. E-mail: *jcllcm@aol.com.* Web site: *www.jcllcm.com.* Hours: 2–5 Sun. and by appointment; closed Sat. and Jewish holidays. Admission: free.

Contemporary Jewish Museum. The Contemporary Jewish Museum in San Francisco, California, is building a $43 million new home designed by noted architect David Liberkind. The construc-

tion transforms the shell of a 1907 power substation in the city's Yerba Buena cultural district into a 60,000-square-foot museum. It is scheduled to open in June 2008. Meanwhile, the museum continues to present exhibitions of Jewish art and culture at its long-time Steuart Street location.

Contemporary Jewish Museum, 121 Steuart St., San Francisco, CA 94105 (mailing address: 282 2nd Sl., 2nd Floor, San Francisco, CA 94105). Phone: 415/344–8800. Fax: 415/344–8815. E-mail: *info@thecjm.org.* Web site: *www.thecjm.org.* Hours: 12–6 Sun.-Thurs.; closed Fri.-Sat. and Jewish and national holidays. Admission: adults, $5; seniors and students, $4; children under 12, free; free 3rd Mon. of month.

Dallas Holocaust Museum and Center for Education and Tolerance. The Dallas Holocaust Museum and Center for Education and Tolerance in Dallas, Texas, contains artifacts and photographs from the Holocaust and Jewish life in Europe before the Holocaust, with special attention to one day (April 19, 1943) during the Holocaust. It also has a library on the Holocaust and anti–Semitism.

Dallas Holocaust Museum and Center for Education and Tolerance, 211 N. Record St., Suite 100, Dallas, TX 75202–3361. Phone 214/741–7500. Fax: 214/747–2270. E-mail: *info@dallasholocaustmuseum.org.* Web site: *www.dallasholocaustmuseum.org.* Hours: 9 A.M.-9:30 P.M. Mon.-Thurs.; 9–6 Fri.; 1–6 Sat.; 8–6 Sun.; closed Rosh Hashanah, Yom Kippur, and Christmas. Admission: adults, $6; seniors, military, students, and children under 18, $4 (not recommended for children under 6th grade level).

Dennis and Phillip Ratner Museum. The Dennis and Phillip Ratner Museum in Bethesda, Maryland, was founded by two cousins who wanted to foster love of the Bible through the graphic arts. The museum takes visitors through the Hebrew Bible via visual arts. It has exhibits of reproductions of the art of masters on biblical themes, works of professional and student artists, children's art on biblical themes, and sculptures, drawings, paintings, and graphics by Phillip Rainer. The museum also presents seasonal exhibits illustrating the holidays, customs, and Halacha (Jewish law), as well as traveling exhibitions.

Dennis and Phillip Ratner Museum, 10001 Old Georgetown Rd., Bethesda, MD 20814. Phone: 301/897-1518. Web site: *www.ratnermuseum.com.* Hours: 10–4:30 Sun. (also Sun.-Thurs. for groups); closed remainder of week. Admission: free.

Elizabeth S. and Alvin I. Fine Museum of the Congregation Emanu-El. The Elizabeth S. and Alvin I. Fine Museum of the Congregation Emanu-El in San Francisco, California, is named for the late rabbi and his wife, who initiated having displays at the temple. Rabbi Fine viewed the arts as a fundamental expression of Jewish spirituality and the temple museum as a place in which congregants could "worship the Lord in the beauty of holiness." Display cases first were installed in the foyer of the main sanctuary, then in the chapel corridor, and more recently in the Martin A. Meyer Reception Room. The museum, which began in 1957, has grown from a small collection of archival documents and ritual objects to changing exhibitions of works by Jewish artists in the Bay Area and such themes as Jewish American identity, contemporary experience of Jewish holidays and rituals, and the variety of religious practices in Israel.

Elizabeth S. and Alvin I. Fine Museum of the Congregation Emanu-El, 2 Lake St., San Francisco, CA 94118. Phone: 415/751–2535. Fax: 415/751–2511. E-mail: *mail@emanuelsf.org*. Web site: *www.emanuelsf.org*. Hours: 1–3 Tues.-Thurs. and by appointment; open on weekends only to attendees after religious services or classes. Admission: free.

El Paso Holocaust Museum and Study Center. The El Paso Holocaust Museum and Study Center now occupies a temporary facility in downtown El Paso, Texas, after a 2004 fire destroyed its building adjacent to the Jewish Community Center. The museum was founded in memory of those who died and survived the Holocaust, with respect for those who lost family and friends. The museum seeks to combat prejudice and bigotry through education and by instilling mankind with the value and dignity of human life.

El Paso Holocaust Museum and Study Center, 101 S. Kansas St., El Paso, TX 79901. Phone and fax: 915/351–0048. E-mail: *info@elpasoholocaustmuseum.org*. Web site: *www.elpasoholocaustmuseum.org*. Hours: 1–4 Tues.-Thurs.; closed remainder of week and Jewish and national holidays. Admission: free.

Florida Holocaust Museum. The Florida Holocaust Museum in St. Petersburg honors the memory of millions of innocent men, women, and children who suffered or died in the Holocaust. The museum's permanent exhibit, "History, Heritage, and Hope," depicts the history of the individuals who confronted the extremes of hatred and persecution in their homes and communities. Changing exhibitions pertaining to Jewish history, culture, and art also are presented.

Florida Holocaust Museum, 55 5th St. S., St. Petersburg, FL 33701. Phones: 727/820–0100 and 800/960–7448. Fax: 727/821–8435. E-mail: *nbrand@flholocaustmuseum.org*. Web site: *www.flholocaustmuseum.org*. Hours:10–5 Mon.- Fri.; 12–5 Sat.-Sun.; closed Rosh Hashana, Yom Kippur, New Year's Day, Thanksgiving, and Christmas. Admission: adults, $8; seniors and college students, $7; students under 18,

$4; children under 16 must be accompanied by an adult.

Fred Wolf, Jr., Gallery. The Fred Wolf, Jr., Gallery displays arts and crafts by Jewish local, national, and international artists at the Raymond and Miriam Klein Branch Jewish Community Center in Philadelphia, Pennsylvania. The gallery also draws upon its collections of Judaic artifacts dating to the eighteenth century and paintings, prints, sculptures, and photographs from the early 1900s to the present and paintings, prints, sculptures, and photographs from the early 1900s to the present.

Fred Wolf, Jr., Gallery, Raymond and Miriam Klein Branch Jewish Community Center, 10100 Jamison Ave., Philadelphia, PA 19116. Phone: 215/698–7300. Fax: 215/673–7447. E-mail: *pactman@phillyjcc.com*. Web site: *www.phillyjcc.com/branches/klein.html*. Hours: 9 A.M.-9 P.M. Mon.-Thurs.; 9–4 Fri. and Sun.; closed Sat. and Jewish holidays. Admission: free.

Gladys and Murray Goldstein Cultural Center of Temple Israel. The Gladys and Murray Goldstein Cultural Center of Temple Israel in New Rochelle, New York, presents changing Judaica and other exhibits at the temple.

Gladys and Murray Goldstein Cultural Center of Temple Israel, 1000 Pinebrook Blvd., New Rochelle, NY 10804. Phone: 914/235–1800. Fax: 914/235–1854. Web site: *www.tinr.org*. Hours: 10–4 Mon.-Fri.; 9–12 Sun.; closed Sat. Admission: free.

Goldman Art Gallery. See Weiner Judaic Museum and Goldman Art Gallery.

Goldsmith Gallery. See Library of the Jewish Theological Seminary Exhibits.

Goodwin Holocaust Museum and Education Center of the Delaware Valley. The Goodwin Holocaust Museum and Education Center of the Delaware Valley in Cherry Hill, New Jersey, resulted from the merger of the Holocaust Awareness Museum at Gratz College in Melrose Park, Pennsylvania, and the Holocaust Resource Center of the Jewish Community Relations Council of Southern New Jersey, assisted by a grant from the Goodwin Foundation. Americans.

The Goodwin Holocaust Museum, located at the new Jewish Community Campus in Cherry Hill, New Jersey, contains Holocaust artifacts and memorabilia, although some of the collection formerly at Gratz College has been returned to the newly reopened Holocaust Awareness Museum and Education Center in Philadelphia (see separate listing). The center also operates a speakers bureau of Holocaust survivors and liberators; an education center offering teacher and student training programs; a Holocaust library and media center; and a program of Holocaust awareness presentations and special events.

Goodwin Holocaust Museum and Education Center of the Delaware Valley, Jewish County Campus, 1301 Springdale Rd., Cherry Creek, NJ 08003. Phone: 856/751–9500. Fax: 856/751–1697. Web site: *http://mpdn.org/goodwinhalocaust_museum.htm*. Hours: 9 A.M.–9 P.M. Mon.-Thurs.; 9–3 Fri.; 10–5 Sun.; closed Sat. and Jewish and major holidays. Admission: free.

Gotthelf Art Gallery. The Gotthelf Art Gallery is part of a multi-disciplinary artistic program at the San Diego Center for Jewish Culture in La Jolla, California. The center seeks to expand and enrich cultural life by presenting Jewish artistic expressions, encouraging the preservation of Jewish culture and heritage, and nurturing new creativity in the arts. Changing exhibitions of works by Jewish artists are featured in the art gallery.

Gotthelf Art Gallery, San Diego Center for Jewish Culture, Lawrence Community Center, Family Campus, 4126 Executive Dr., La Jolla, CA 92037. Phone: 858/457–3030. Web site: *www.sdcjc.lfjce.org*. Hours: 10–5 Mon.-Fri.; 12–5 Sun.; closed Sat. Admission: free.

Harold and Vivian Beck Museum of Judaica. The Harold and Vivian Beck Museum of Judaica, housed in the lobby of the main sanctuary and the gallery above at the Beth David Congregation in Miami, Florida, displays selections from a Judaica fine arts collection and presents special art exhibitions. Its exhibits of artifacts and paintings depict the life cycle, Jewish festivals, and the Sabbath and include general Jewish memorabilia and visual arts.

Harold and Vivian Beck Museum of Judaica, Beth David Congregation, 2625 S.W. 3rd Ave., Miami, FL 33129. Phone: 305/854–3911. Fax: 305/285–5841. E-mail: *info@beth-david.com*. Web site: *www.beth david.com*. Hours: 8:30–4:30 daily; closed Jewish and major holidays. Admission: free.

Hebrew Union College-Jewish Institute of Religion Museum. The Hebrew Union College-Jewish Institute of Religion Museum in New York City is the visual extension of the spiritual, cultural, and educational life of the seminary for Reform Judaism — the nation's oldest institution of Jewish higher education. Many of the college and seminary museum's exhibitions illuminate the 4,000 years of Jewish experience; show the creativity of contemporary artists exploring Jewish identity, history, culture, and experience; interpret core Jewish values, texts, and beliefs; or highlight the creativity of contemporary Israeli artists and strengthen cultural ties between North America and Israel.

The museum also presents exhibitions on Jewish history, culture, and contemporary creativity at the Joseph and Backman galleries, Petrie Great Hall, Klingenstein Rare Book Room, and Chaim and Rivka Heller Archives Gallery at the New York City site. The Hebrew Union College-Jewish Institute of Religion also operates museums at its three other locations in Cincinnati, Los Angeles, and Jerusalem.

Hebrew Union College-Jewish Institute of Religion Museum, 1 W. 4th St., New York, NY 10012. Phone: 212/824- 2205. Web site: *www.huc.edu/museum/ny*. Hours: 9–5 Mon.-Thurs.; 9–3 Fri.; closed Sat. and most Sun. Admission: free.

Herbert and Eileen Bernard Museum of Judaica. The Herbert and Eileen Bernard Museum of Judaica, located within the Temple Emanu-El in New York City, has three galleries of Jewish Art, religious ornaments, and Temple memorabilia of beauty and rarity. The museum also sponsors an annual gallery lecture series and presents changing exhibitions that explore the intersections of Jewish identity, history, and material culture.

Herbert and Eileen Bernard Museum of Judaica, Congregation Emanu-El of the City of New York, 1 E. 65th St., New York, NY 10021–6596. Phone: 212/744–1400. Fax: 212/570–0826. Hours: 10–4:30 Sun.-Thurs.; 10–4 Fri.; 1–4:30 Sat. Admission: free.

Hillel Jewish Student Center Gallery. The Hillel Jewish Student Center at the University of Cincinnati in Cincinnati, Ohio, has a gallery which displays Jewish ritual objects and art exhibits.

Hillel Jewish Student Center Gallery, Rose Warner House, 2615 Clifton Ave., Cincinnati, OH 45220. Phone: 513/221–6728. Fax: 513/221–7134. E-mail: *email@hillelcincinnati.org*. Hours: 9–5 Mon.-Thurs.; 9–3 Fri.; closed Sat.-Sun. and Jewish and national holidays. Admission: free.

Hineni Heritage Center. The Hineni Heritage Center in New York City preserves and interprets Jewish history, culture, heritage, and identity. It has exhibits on such subjects as the Jewish way of life, country and people of Israel, and the Holocaust.

Hineni Heritage Center, 232 West End Ave., New York, NY 10023. Phone: 212/496–1660. Fax: 212/496–1908. E-mail: *hineni@hineni.org*. Web site: *www.hineni.org*. Hours: by appointment. Admission: free.

Holocaust Awareness Museum and Education Center. The Holocaust Awareness Museum and Education Center, the nation's first Holocaust museum, began in 1959 in Philadelphia, Pennsylvania, in the basement of the late Yaakov Riz, a Soviet labor camp survivor, who had assembled a large collection of Holocaust-related artifacts and memorabilia. The museum moved to Gratz College in Melrose, Pennsylvania, and then merged with a similar organization (which became the Goodwin Holocaust Museum and Education Center of the Delaware Valley) in Cherry Hill, New Jersey, before returning in 2001 to southeast Philadelphia, where it is housed at the Klein Branch of the Jewish Community Center.

Holocaust Awareness Museum and Education Center, Klein Branch, Jewish Community Center, Room 210, 10100 Jamison Ave., Philadelphia, PA 19116. Phone: 215/464–4701. E-mail: *information@holocausteducationcenter.org*. Web site: *www.holocausteducationcenter.org*. Hours: 10–4 Mon.-Thurs.; closed Fri.-Sun. and Jewish and national holidays. Admission: free.

Holocaust Documentation and Education Center. The Holocaust Documentation and Education Center, now located in North Miami Beach, Florida, is developing a new museum in Hollywood, Florida. The museum, which will tell the story of the Holocaust, plans to open within two years. The center has been recording interviews with Holocaust survivors, liberators, and rescuers since its founding in 1979.

Holocaust Documentation and Education Center, 13899 Biscayne Blvd., Suite 404, North Miami Beach, FL 33181 (new site will be: 20301 Harrison St., Hollywood, FL 33020). Phone: 305/919–5690. Fax: 305/919–5691. E-mail: *info@hdec.org*. Web site: *www.hdec.org*. Hours and admission: still to be determined.

Holocaust Memorial Center. The Holocaust Memorial Center, which recently moved from West Bloomfield, Michigan, to an expanded facility in Farmington Hills, Michigan, has a memorial flame in the lobby with one wall listing the number of Jews killed by country during the Holocaust and another wall giving the names of the concentration camps and massacre sites where so many of the deaths occurred.

The center's exhibits track the history of the Jewish people paralleling major events in world history over 4,000 years; Jewish culture and religious beliefs and Jewish presence in Europe in the 1930s; the rise of the Nazis and the story of World War II; the concentration camps and efforts to annihilate the Jews of Europe; the post-war world and the establishment of Israel; and honoring the thousands of non–Jews who saved or tried to save Jews during the Holocaust. Holocaust Memorial Center, 28123 Orchard Lake Rd., Farmington Hills, MI 48334. Phone: 248/553–2400. Fax: 248/553–2433. E-mail: *info@holocaustcenter.org*. Web site: *www.holocaustcenter.org*. Hours: June-Aug. —

10–4 Sun.-Thurs.; closed Fri.-Sat.; remainder of year —10–4 Sun.-Thurs.; 9–1 Fri.; closed Sat. and Jewish and national holidays. Admission: free.

Holocaust Memorial Resource and Education Center of Central Florida. The Holocaust Memorial Resource and Education Center of Central Florida in Maitland, Florida, examines the past to learn from the lessons of the Holocaust. The permanent exhibit presents an overview of the Holocaust and serves as a memorial to the victims. It consists of 12 segments, each introducing a major theme of the Holocaust. Artifacts of the Holocaust are exhibited throughout the museum.

Six memorial lamps are on the front wall of the museum, representing the 6 million victims of the Holocaust. Also on display are statues honoring the survivors and liberators of the Holocaust, drawings of the concentration camps as remembered by a survivor, and plaques from members of the community honoring family members and friends who were victims of the Holocaust.

Holocaust Memorial Resource and Education Center of Central Florida, 851 N. Maitland Ave., PO Box 941508, Maitland, FL 32794. Phone: 407/628–0555. Fax: 407/628–1079. E-mail: *info@holocaustedu.org*. Web site: *www.holocaustedu.org*. Hours: 9–4 Mon.-Thurs.; 9–1 Fri.; 1–4 Sun.; closed Sat. and Jewish and national holidays. Admission: free.

Holocaust Museum Houston. The stories of Holocaust survivors living in the Houston, Texas, metropolitan area are featured in the permanent exhibit at the Holocaust Museum Houston. The exhibit also looks at life before the Holocaust, rise of Adolph Hitler and Nazism, disruption of normal life and segregation, imprisonment and extermination in concentration camps, and the roles of collaborators, bystanders, rescuers, and liberators. The museum also has two galleries for changing art and photography exhibitions, education center, and library and archives.

Holocaust Museum Houston, 5401 Caroline St., Houston, TX 77004. Phone: 713/942–8000. Fax: 713/942–7953. E- mail: *museum@hmh.org*. Web site: *www.hmh.org*. Hours: 9–5 Mon.-Fri.; 12–5 Sat.-Sun.; closed 1st day of Rosh Hashana, Yom Kippur, New Year's Day, Thanksgiving, and Christmas. Admission: free.

Holocaust Museum of Southwest Florida. The Holocaust Museum of Southwest Florida in Naples, Florida, grew out of an idea from 19 seventh grade students who were studying the Holocaust at Golden Gate Middle School in 1973. The interest resulted in an exhibit on the Holocaust with artifacts, assistance, and funding from others, and later to the founding of the museum devoted to the Holocaust.

Holocaust Museum of Southwest Florida, 4760 Tamiami Trail North, Suite 7, Sandalwood Sq., Naples, FL 34103. Phone: 239/263–9200. Fax: 239/263–9500. E-mail: *webmaster@hmswfl.org*. Web site: *www.hmswfl.org*. Hours: 1–4 Tues.-Fri.; 1–4 Sun.; closed Mon. and Sat. Admission: $5.

Illinois Holocaust Museum and Education Center. The Illinois Holocaust Museum and Education Center in Skokie, Illinois, is expanding to improve its efforts to help Holocaust survivors heal, preserve their personal belongings, and educate people on the events that led to the killing of 6 million Jews during the Holocaust. A new 64,000-square-foot center, which will tell the Holocaust story largely through eyewitness accounts and artifacts, will replace the museum's current location in 2009. Among the additions to the museum will be a railroad boxcar similar to the ones that took Jews to concentration camps during the Holocaust. The museum is operated by the Holocaust Memorial Foundation of Illinois.

Illinois Holocaust Museum and Education Center, Holocaust Memorial Foundation of Illinois, 4255 Main St., Skokie, IL 60076–2063 (new site will be: 9603 Woods Dr., Skokie, IL). Phone: 847/677–4684. Fax: 847/677–4684. E-mail: *info@hmfi.org*. Web site: *www.hmfi.org*. Hours: 9–4:30 Mon.-Thurs.; 9–3 Fri.; 12–4 Sun.; closed Sat. and Jewish and national holidays. Admission: free.

Isaacs Gallery. The Isaacs Gallery at the Osher Marin Jewish Community Center in San Rafael, California, presents a series of visual art exhibitions that illustrate the complexity and rich diversity of worldwide Jewish culture. Three or four exhibitions of paintings, sculpture, photography, and other creative media are scheduled each year, often in collaboration with live performances and events that explore similar themes.

Isaacs Gallery, Osher Marin Jewish Community Center, 200 N. San Pedro Rd., San Rafael, CA 94903. Phone: 415/444–8000. Fax: 415/491–1235. E-mail: *info@marinicc.org*. Web site: *www.marinicc.org*. Hours: 6–9:30 Mon.-Thurs.; 6–6 Fri.; 8–6 Sat.-Sun.; closed Jewish and national holidays. Admission: free.

Janice Charach Epstein Gallery. The Janice Charach Epstein Gallery, located in the Jewish Community Center of Metropolitan Detroit in West Bloomfield, Michigan, presents changing exhibitions of art created by Jewish artists and art with Jewish themes. Exhibitions have included such diverse arts as paintings, glass, ceramics, fiber arts, photography, and multimedia works.

Janice Charach Epstein Gallery, Jewish Community Center of Metropolitan Detroit, 6600 W. Maple Rd., West Bloomfield, MI 48322. Phone: 248/432–5448. Web site: *www.jccdet.org/about/gallery.html*.

Hours: 10–5 Mon.- Thurs. (also to 7 Thurs.); 11–4 Sun.; closed Fri.-Sat. and Jewish holidays. Admission: free.

Jewish Children's Museum. The Jewish Children's Museum in the Crown Heights section of Brooklyn, New York, enables children — and their parents — to explore Jewish history and heritage in a stimulating and interactive environment. The seven-story museum has hands-on exhibits that focus on Jewish holidays, biblical history, the land of Israel, contemporary Jewish life, and other areas. It seeks to educate both Jewish and non–Jewish children about Judaism and tolerance. The museum features multimedia techniques, an art gallery, two computer laboratories, a game show studio, a craft workshop, a miniature golf course, and an audiovisual theater.

Jewish Children's Museum, 792 Eastern Pkwy., Brooklyn, NY 11213. Phone: 718/467–0600. Fax: 718/467–1300. Email: *info@jcm.museum*. Web site: *www.jcmonline.org*. Hours: 10–4 Mon.-Thurs.; 10–6 Sun.; closed Fri.-Sat. (but open 8–11 Sat. night in Jan.-Mar.) and Jewish holidays. Admission: $10 per person; children under 2, free.

Jewish Heritage Collection. The Addlestone Library at the College of Charleston in Charleston, South Carolina, has a Jewish Heritage Collection among its special collections. It documents the Jewish experience in the state from colonial times to the present. The collection emphasizes individuals over institutions, encompassing recorded interviews, manuscripts, photographs, genealogies, memoirs, home movies, and other primary sources.

Jewish Heritage Collection, College of Charleston, Addlestone Library, College of Charleston, Charleston, SC 29424. Phone: 843/953–8028. Fax: 843/953–8019. E-mail: *rosengartend@cofc.edu*. Web site: *www.cofc.edu/?-pages/atc.html*. Hours: 9–5 Mon.-Fri.; closed Sat.-Sun. and major holidays. Admission: free.

Jewish local, state, and regional sports halls of fame. More than 15 local, state, and regional Jewish sports halls of fame — in addition to several national Jewish sports halls of fame (listed separately — honor athletes, coaches, and others who have made contributions to sports in the United States. Nearly all are located at Jewish community centers and have annual hall of fame inductions and plaque or photo displays. The hours vary, but virtually all are closed on Jewish and national holidays, with the admission generally being free.

Among these halls of fame are the Canton Jewish Community Center Hall of Fame, Canton, Ohio; Chicago's Jewish Hall of Fame, Northbrook, Illinois; Columbus Jewish Community Center Hall of Fame, Columbus, Ohio; Greater Washington

Jewish Sports Hall of Fame, Rockville, Maryland; JCC Sports Hall of Fame, Cleveland Heights, Ohio; Michigan Jewish Sports Hall of Fame, West Bloomfield; Milwaukee Jewish Community Center Sports Hall of Fame, Milwaukee; Philadelphia Jewish Sports Hall of Fame, Philadelphia; Rhode Island Jewish Athletes Hall of Fame, Providence; St. Louis Jewish Sports Hall of Fame, St. Louis; Southern California Jewish Sports Hall of Fame, Los Angeles; Western Pennsylvania Jewish Sports Hall of Fame, Pittsburgh; and YM/YWCA of Northern Jersey Sports Hall of Fame, Wayne, New Jersey.

The Jewish Museum. The Jewish Museum in New York City is major art museum exploring Jewish culture. It began in 1904 with the gift of 26 Jewish ceremonial art objects to the Jewish Theological Seminary, under whose auspices it still operates. The museum now has over 28,000 objects of different media, including fine arts, Judaica, and broadcast media, that reflect Jewish culture. It is located in the 1908 Felix Warburg Mansion, an elegant six-floor French Gothic structure on Fifth Avenue along New York's Museum Mile.

The museum's permanent exhibit, "Culture and Continuity: the Jewish Journey," explores Jewish culture and history through art. The two-floor exhibit features 800 works from the museum's diverse collection of art, archaeology, ceremonial objects, photographs, interactive media, and television excerpts. It examines the Jewish experience over 4,000 years and asks two questions — how has Judaism been able to thrive for thousands of years around the world under difficult and sometimes tragic circumstances, and what constitutes the essence of Jewish identity? The museum also presents temporary exhibitions, lectures, workshops, films, concerts, walking tours, and community outreach programs, as well as operating a library of Judaica references.

The Jewish Museum, 1109 5th Ave., New York, NY 10128. Phone: 212/423–3200. Fax: 212/423–3232. E-mail: *jinfo@thejm.org.* Web site: *www.thejewishmuseum.org.* Hours: 11–5:45 Sun.-Thurs. (also to 8 Thurs.); 11–3 Fri.; closed Sat., major Jewish holidays, New Year's Day, Martin Luther King, Jr., Day, and Thanksgiving. Admission: adults, $10; seniors and students, $7.50; children under 12, free.

Jewish Museum of Florida. The Jewish Museum of Florida, located in the 1936 former synagogue that housed Miami Beach's first congregation, traces Jewish history in Florida since 1763 and communicates Jewish history, values, and issues. The museum was founded in 1995 after a traveling exhibition depicting the Jewish experience in the state traveled to 13 cities in 1990 to 1994 and generated great interest. The museum's core exhibit is devoted to the same subject with stories of immigration, life cycles and rituals, building community, discrimination, making a living, acculturation, and identity. A timeline wall of Jewish history and three films augment the exhibit. The exhibit is supplemented with changing exhibitions.

Jewish Museum of Florida, 301 Washington Ave., Miami Beach, FL 33139. Phone: 305/672–5044. Fax: 305/6725933. E-mail: *mzerivitz@jewishmuseum.com.* Web site: *www.jewishmuseum.com.* Hours: 10–5 Tues.-Sun.; closed Mon. and Jewish and major holidays. Admission: adults, $6; seniors and students, $5; children under 6, free; families, $12; free on Sat.

Jewish Museum of Maryland. The Jewish Museum of Maryland in Baltimore interprets the Jewish experience in America with emphasis on Jewish life in the state. The museum, which was founded in 1960 to rescue and restore the historic Lloyd Street Synagogue, has become a cultural center for those interested in Jewish history and traditions. The museum site now consists of three structures — a museum building with a library and archives and two restored synagogues, the 1876 B'nai Israel Synagogue and the 1845 Lloyd Street Synagogue. The museum's exhibits draw upon a collection of over 6,000 objects, including manuscripts, documents, records, photographs, ceremonial art, costumes, textiles, paintings, folk art, and furniture.

Jewish Museum of Maryland, 15 Lloyd St., Baltimore, MD 21202. Phone: 410/732–6400. Fax: 410/732–6451. E-mail: *jinfo@jewishmuseummd.org.* Web site: *www.jewishmuseummd.org.* Hours: 12–4 Tues.-Thurs. and Sun.; closed Mon., Fri.-Sat., and major Jewish and national holidays. Admission: adults, $8; students, $4; children under 13, $3.

Jewish Sports Hall of Fame. The Jewish Sports Hall of Fame at the Suffolk Y Jewish Community Center in Commack, New York, evolved from a local hall and later state hall of fame. It honors Jewish sports figures who have distinguished themselves in sports. The objective is to foster Jewish identity through athletics. Among those honored with plaques in the community center are Hank Greenburg in baseball; Sid Luckman, football; Red Auerbach, basketball coach; Benny Leonard, boxing; Sarah Hughes, ice skating; Henry Wittenberg, wrestling; Shep Messing, soccer; Marilyn Ramenofsky, swimming; and Mel Allen, sports announcer.

Jewish Sports Hall of Fame, Suffolk Y Jewish Community Center, 74 Hauppauge Rd., Commack, NY 11725. Phone: 531/462–9800. Fax: 631/462–9462. Web site: *www.jewishsports.org.* Hours: 6-10 Mon.-Thurs.; 6–5:15 Fri.; 8:30-9 Sun.; closed Sat. and Jewish and national holidays. Admission: free.

Jewish Women's Archive. The Jewish Women's Archive in Brookline, Massachusetts, gathers and transmits information about the rich legacy of Jewish women and their contributions to Jewish families, communities, people, and the world. It offers exhibits on the Web about outstanding Jewish women in such fields as civil rights, athletics, politics, religion, motherhood, and the feminist movement.

Jewish Women's Archive, 138 Harvard St., Brookline, MA 02446. Phone: 617/232-2258. Fax: 617/975-0109. E-mail: *webmaster@jwa.org*. Web site: *www.jwa.org*. Hours: open 24 hours. Fee: free.

Judah L. Magnes Museum. The Judah L. Magnes Museum in Berkeley, California, explores Jewish life and culture with exhibitions that draw upon its rich collections of fine arts and ceremonial objects, the archives of the Western Jewish History Center, and the Blumenthal Rare Book and Manuscript Library. It uses special exhibitions, educational programming, and publications in covering significant issues of contemporary life, promoting public dialogue and scholarship, and furthering understanding of the Jewish past.

The museum has more than 30,000 objects in its collections, including paintings, posters, prints, sculptures, films and photographs illustrating various aspects of the Jewish experience throughout history. The Western Jewish History Center has the world's largest archive on the historical and cultural experiences of Jews in the 13 western states, while the Blumenthal Rare Book and Manuscript Library contains more than 12,000 rare and illustrated books, manuscripts, maps, sheet music, and recordings.

Judah L. Magnes Museum, 2911 Russell St., Berkeley, CA 94705. Phone: 510/549-6950. Fax: 510/849-3673. E-mail: *info@magnes.org*. Web site: *www.magnes.org*. Hours: 10–4 Sun.-Thurs.; closed Fri.-Sat. and Jewish and major holidays . Admission: $4 suggested donation.

Judaica Collection. The Jean Byers Sampson Center for Diversity in Maine in the Glickman Family Library at the University of Southern Maine in Portland includes a Judaica Collection containing the Rosalyne E. and Sumner T. Bernstein papers and other materials. The Bernsteins were community leaders in Maine. The Special Collections branch of the library also has a small exhibition area.

Judaica Collection, Jean Byers Sampson Center for Diversity in Maine, University of Southern Maine, Special Collections, Glickman Family Library, 314 Forest Ave., Portland, ME 04104–9301. Phone: 207/780–4275. Hours: 1–5 Mon., Wed., and Fri.; closed remainder of week. Admission: free.

Judaica Museum of Central Synagogue. Artifacts and other objects of Jewish life and ritual are displayed at the Judaica Museum of Central Synagogue in New York City. The exhibits, presented in the 1872 Moorish Revival building that houses the synagogue and in the Community House lobby across the street, concentrate on the Jewish way of life throughout the world and Jewish cultural and moral values as seen through artifacts and objects. The roots of the synagogue go back to 1839 and its 1872 sanctuary is the oldest Jewish house of worship in continuous use in New York City.

Judaica Museum of Central Synagogue, 123 E. 55th St., New York, NY 10022. Phone: 212/838-5122. Fax: 212/644- 2168. E-mail: *membership@censyn.org*. Web site: *www.censyn.org*. Hours: 9–4:30 Mon.-Fri.; closed Sat.-Sun. and Jewish holidays. Admission: free.

Judaica Museum of the Hebrew Home for the Aged at Riverdale. Artifacts reflecting the customs and ceremonies of European and Asian Jewry over the last three centuries are featured at the Judaica Museum in the Norman and Adele Morris Wing of River House West at the Hebrew Home for the Aged in Riverdale, New York. The museum has more than 800 Jewish ceremonial objects. In addition to permanent exhibits, it presents temporary exhibitions of works of local artists and from collections.

Judaica Museum of the Hebrew Home for the Aged at Riverdale, 5961 Palisade Ave., Riverdale, NY 10471. Phones: 718/549-8700. Hours: 1–4:30 Mon.-Thurs.; 1–5 Sun.; closed Fri.-Sat. and Jewish and national holidays. Admission: free.

Kahal Kadosh Beth Elohim Museum. The Kahal Kadosh Beth Elohim Synagogue in Charleston, South Carolina, has a small museum with artifacts relating to the history of the Reform congregation. The congregation is one of the oldest in the nation, being established in 1749 and located at the site since 1824. Among the museum's holdings is a letter written to the congregation by George Washington.

Kabal Kadosh Beth Elohim Museum, 86 Hasell St., Charleston, SC 29401. Phone: 803/723-1090. Hours: 10–12 Mon.-Fri.; closed Sat.-Sun. Admission: free.

Kansas City Jewish Museum and Epsten Gallery at Village Shalom. The Kansas City Jewish Museum is a museum without walls that operates the Epsten Gallery at the Village Shalom in Overland Park, Kansas. The gallery at the Shalom facility for the aged seeks to enrich the lives of residents and further humanity and tolerance through art.

Kansas City Jewish Museum and Epsten Gallery at Village Shalom, 5500 W. 123rd St., Overland Park, KS 66209. Phone: 913/266–8413. E-mail: *ksmith@villageshalom.org*. Web site: *www.epstengallery.org*. Hours: 11–4 Tues.-Fri., 1–4 Sat.-Sun.; closed Mon. and Jewish and major holidays. Admission: free.

Kehila Kedosha Janina Synagogue Museum. The Kehila Kedosha Janina Synagogue, a small Jewish congregation of Romaniotes on New York City's historic Lower East Side, seeks to make people aware of its heritage through a museum that will familiarize them with its history and customs. The synagogue is the only one in the Western Hemisphere of the obscure Jewish community. It has remained virtually unchanged since being built in 1927 by Romaniote Jews from Janina, Greece.

Kehila Kedosha Janina Synagogue Museum, 280 Broome St., New York, NY 10002. Phone: 212/431–1619. Web site: *www.kkism.org*. Hours: 11–4 Sun. and by appointment. Admission: free.

Koret Gallery. The Koret Gallery at the Albert L. Schultz Jewish Community Center in Palo Alto, California, features changing exhibitions of works by Jewish artists.

Koret Gallery, Albert L. Schultz Jewish Community Center, 4000 Middlefield Rd., Bldg. R, Palo Alto, CA 94303. Phone: 650/493–9400. E-mail: *info@paloaltojcc.org*. Web site: *www.paloaltojcc.org*. Hours: 9–5 Mon.-Fri.; closed Sat.-Sun. and Jewish holidays. Admission: free.

Leo Baeck Institute Gallery. The Leo Baeck Institute in New York City is devoted to the study of the history of German-speaking Jewry from its origins to the Holocaust and to preserving its culture. Founded in 1955, the institute is named for the rabbi who was the leader of German Jewry during its darkest years, survived the concentration camp, and became its first international president. The institute, part of three centers (Jerusalem, London, and New York), has an archives, library, gallery, and art, photography, and artifact collections. It also conducts research, offers lectures, and holds conferences.

Exhibitions are mounted in the gallery on a variety of themes illustrated with items from its collections. Among the recent exhibitions have been "Perils of Prominence," on the decisive role Jewish artists, journalists, composers, and architects played in defining modernity in the Weimar years; "Destination Shanghai: Refuge for Stateless Jews," a display of art by Shanghai Jews that also included etchings, rare photos, and documents; and "Credit Due: Eight German-Jewish Artists Persecuted by the Nazis," featuring works by artists who could never regain their pre-war prominence.

Leo Baeck Institute Gallery, 15 W. 16th St., New York, NY 10011. Phone: 212/744–6400. Fax: 212/988–1305. E-mail: *lbaeck@lbi.cih.org*. Web site: *www.lbi.org*. Hours: 9:30–4:30 Mon.-Thurs.; closed Fri.-Sun. and Jewish and national holidays. Admission: free.

Library of the Jewish Theological Seminary Exhibits. The Library of the Jewish Theological Seminary in New York City has exhibits that enable the public to become better acquainted with the treasures of Jewish heritage collected by the library. The exhibits are mounted three times a year from the collections of manuscripts, incunabula, rare printed Hebrew books, broadsides, and prints, as well as ketubbot, megillot, and Genizah fragments. The showings are presented in the Goldsmith Gallery and on the first and fifth floors of the library building.

Library of the Jewish Theological Seminary Exhibits, 3080 Broadway, New York, NY 10027. Phone: 212/678–8082. Web site: *www.jitsa.edu/library*. Hours: 8–9 Mon.-Thurs.; 8–5 Fri.; 9:30–9 Sun.; closed Sat. and Jewish and national holidays. Admission: free.

Lillian and Albert Small Jewish Museum. The Jewish Historical Society of Greater Washington tells the story of the local Jewish community from the mid-nineteenth century to the present at its Lillian and Albert Small Jewish Museum, housed in the restored 1876 Adas Israel Synagogue, the oldest synagogue in the Washington, D.C., area. In addition to exhibits, it has archival collections, educational programs, publications, and a library.

Lillian and Albert Small Jewish Museum, Jewish Historical Society of Greater Washington, 600 I St., N.W., Washington, DC 20001. Phone: 202/789–0900. Fax: 202/789–0485. E-mail: *info@jhsgw.org*. Web site: *www.jhsgw.org*. Hours: Sun.-Thurs. by appointment; closed Fri.-Sat. and major Jewish holidays. Admission: free.

Los Angeles Museum of the Holocaust. The Los Angeles Museum of the Holocaust, founded in 1961 by survivors of the Nazi Holocaust, commemorates the martyrs of the Holocaust and relates the experience of Jews in pre-war Europe. Among the museum's collections are Holocaust artifacts, a scale model of the Sobibor Concentration Camp, and a collection of Leksley satiric watercolors from the Terezin Concentration Camp in Czechoslovakia. A new facility is being developed for the museum.

Los Angeles Museum of the Holocaust, 5435 Wilshire Blvd., Suite 303, Los Angeles, CA 90048 (mailing address: 6435 Wilshire Blvd., Los Angeles, CA 90048–4907). Phone: 323/651–3704. Fax: 323/651–3706. E-mail: *museumgroup@jewishla.org*. Web site: *www.lamuseumoftheholocaust.org*. Hours:

10–4 Mon.-Thurs.; 10–2 Fri.; 12–4 Sun.; closed Sat. and Jewish and national holidays. Admission: free.

Maltz Museum of Jewish Heritage. The history, traditions, and achievements of the Jewish community are featured at the Maltz Museum of Jewish Heritage, which opened in 2005 in Beechwood, Ohio. The stories of individuals and families in the Cleveland area are presented in interactive exhibits, films, oral histories, artifacts, and photographs. The permanent exhibit has sections on Jewish immigration, the Holocaust, the founding of Israel, Jewish entertainers, and American patriotism. Other highlights include the Temple-Tifereth Israel Gallery, containing Judaica, artworks, and other treasures from the Holocaust, and Wall of Remembrance, with a memorial garden honoring Holocaust survivors and Jewish war veterans.

Martz Museum of Jewish Heritage, 2929 Richmond Rd., Beechwood, OH 44122. Phone: 216/593-0575. Fax: 216/593-0576. E-mail: *info@mmjh.org*. Web site: *www.maltzjewishmuseum.org*. Hours: 10–5 Sun.-Fri. (also to 8 Fri.); 12–5 Sat.; closed Jewish holidays and Thanksgiving. Admission: adults, $12; seniors and students over 11, $10; children 5–11, $5; children under 5, free.

Mania Nudel Holocaust Learning Center. The Mania Nudel Holocaust Learning Center at the David Posnack Jewish Community Center in Davie, Florida, is dedicated to furthering remembrance and understanding of the Holocaust. Through the coordinated efforts of the community center and the Rose and Jack Orloff Central Agency for Jewish Education, the learning center provides continuous exhibitions of Holocaust artifacts and photographs and an extensive Holocaust library, lectures, films, multimedia programs, teacher workshops, and a speaker's bureau.

Mania Nudel Holocaust Learning Center, David Posnack Jewish Community Center, 5850 S. Pine Island Rd., Davie, FL 33328. Phone: 954/434–0499. Fax: 954/434–1741. E-mail: *info@dpjcc.org*. Web site: *www.dpjcc.org*. Hours: 5:30-10:30 Mon.-Thurs.; 5:30–5 Fri.; 1–6 Sat.; 7–8 Sun.; closed Jewish and national holidays. Admission: free.

May Museum of Temple Israel. The May Museum of Temple Israel at Long Island's oldest Reform congregation in Lawrence, New York, presents changing exhibitions.

May Museum of Temple Israel, Temple Israel of Lawrence, 140 Central Ave., Lawrence, NY 11559. Phone: 516/239-1140. E-mail: *info@templeisrael-lawrence.org*. Web site: *www.templeisrael-lawrence.org*. Hours: by appointment Admission: free.

Mizel Center for Arts and Culture and Singer Gallery. The Mizel Center for Arts and Culture in Denver, Colorado, offers programs and events spanning the cultural spectrum to the Jewish community and area. In addition to exhibitions of modern and contemporary art with an emphasis on works by Jewish artists in the Singer Gallery, the center has concerts, films, theatrical performances, author appearances, literary and film festivals, and multidisciplinary programs.

Mizel Center for Arts and Culture, 350 S. Dahlia St., Denver, CO 80246. Phone: 303/316–6360. Fax: 303/320–0042. Email: *contact@jccdenver.org*. Web site: *www.mizelcenter.org*. Hours: 9–4 Mon.-Fri.; 1–4 Sun.; closed Sat. and Jewish and major holidays. Admission: free.

Mizel Museum. The Mizel Museum, which occupies an annex building at the Congregation Rodef Shalom in Denver, Colorado, has opened an exhibition space near the new Daniel Libeskind-designed addition to the Denver Art Museum. The space is in a courtyard and outdoor spaces with the art museum in downtown Denver. The museum's prize-winning "Bridges of Understanding" exhibit, which promotes intercultural respect and awareness through themes and rituals common to diverse peoples, has been redesigned and at least 10 changing exhibitions of art, history, and culture are scheduled each year at the museum.

Mizel Museum, 4000 S. Kearney St., Denver, CO 80224. Phone: 303/394-9993. Fax: 303/394-1119. E-mail: *ellen@mizelmuseum.org*. Web site:*www.mizelmuseum.org*. Hours: 8:30–5 Mon.-Fri.; closed Sun. and Jewish and national holidays. Admission: free.

Mollie and Louis Kaplan Judaica Museum. The Mollie and Luis Kaplan Judaica Museum at the Congregation Beth Yeshurun in Houston, Texas, has displays of Judaica, fine arts, illustrated manuscripts, coins, medals, and books. It also offers slide-lecture programs on synagogues of ancient Israel and northern Italy in the fourteenth through the twentieth centuries.

Mollie and Louis Kaplan Judaica Museum, Congregation Beth Yeshurun, 4525 Beachnut Blvd., Houston, TX 77096–1881. Web site: *www.bethyeshurun.org/museuml.htm*. Hours: 10–4 daily. Admission: free.

Morton B. Weiss Museum of Judaica. The Morton B. Weiss Museum of Judaica at the Kam Isaiah Israel Congregation in Chicago, Illinois, preserves local Jewish religious history and contains religious, ceremonial, and other objects and archival materials related to Jews in America and Europe. It has unusual illuminated marriage contracts and rare manuscripts in Judeo-Persian and Jetall.

Morton B. Weiss Museum of Judaica, Kam Isaiah

The Museum of Jewish Heritage — A Living Memorial to the Holocaust, in New York City, is housed in this six-sided, six-tiered building that is a symbol of the 6 million Jews who died in the Holocaust. The museum tells the stories of survivors and preserves the memory of those who perished in the Holocaust. *Courtesy Museum of Jewish Heritage — A Living Memorial to the Holocaust and photographer Thomas Hinton.*

Israel Congregation, 1100 Hyde Park Blvd., Chicago, IL 60615. Phone: 312/924–1234. Fax: 312/924–1238. Hours: 9–4 Mon.-Fri.; 10–12 Sun.; closed Sat. Admission: free.

Museum of Jewish Heritage — A Living Memorial to the Holocaust. The Museum of Jewish Heritage-A Living Memorial to the Holocaust in New York City honors those who died in the Holocaust by celebrating their lives. The six-sided, six-tiered museum —a symbol of the 6 million Jews who died in the Holocaust — tells the stories of survivors and preserves the memory of those who perished. The museum's core exhibit contains personal objects, photographs, and films that illustrate the history of Jewish heritage and events in the twentieth century. The museum also presents changing exhibitions, performances, educational programs, and special events in its Robert M. Morgenthau Wing.

Museum of Jewish Heritage-A Living Memorial to the Holocaust, 36 Battery Pl., New York, NY 10280. Phone: 646/437–4200. Fax: 646/437–4311. E-mail: *aspilka@mjhnyc.org. Web site: www.mjhnyc.org.* Hours: 10–5:45 Sun.- Thurs. (also to 8 Wed.); 10–3 Fri. (10–5 DST); closed Sat., Jewish holidays, and Thanksgiving.

Admission: adults, $10; seniors, $7; students, $5; children under 13; free; free 4–8 on Wed.

Museum of the Southern Jewish Experience. The Museum of the Southern Jewish Experience in Jackson, Mississippi, preserves, interprets, and documents Jewish life in the South through exhibits, public programs, publications, historical preservation, and community outreach. The museum uses two historically significant sites in Utica and Natchez to tell the story. The Utica facility with exhibit galleries and a program center is on the 300-acre site of the Henry S. Jacobs Camp. It features numerous objects from disbanded congregations across the region. In Natchez, the 1843 Temple B'nai Israel serves as the site for tours and the showing of the award-winning documentary, *The Natchez Jewish Experience.*

Museum of the Southern Jewish Experience, 4915 Interstate 55 North, Suite 204B, Jackson, MS 39206 (mailing address: PO Box 16528, Jackson, MS 39236–0528). Phone: 601/362–6357. Fax: 601/366–6293. E-mail: *information@msje.org.* Web site: *www.msje.org.* Hours: by appointment. Admission: adults, $5; children, free.

Museum of Tolerance. The Museum of Tolerance, educational arm of the Simon Wiesenthal Center in Los Angeles, California, challenges visitors to confront bigotry and racism and to understand the Holocaust in historic and contemporary contexts. Using interactive techniques, the exhibits focus on two themes — the dynamics of racism and prejudice in America and the history of the Holocaust that killed 6 million Jews. The museum, housed in a 165,000-square-foot, eight-floor building, has collections of Holocaust artifacts and extensive materials pertaining to World War II, Nazi Holocaust, concentration camps, twentieth-century genocide, racism, and human rights, as well as a library, archives, and art and photography collections.

Museum of Tolerance, Simon Wiesenthal Center, 9786 W. Pico Blvd., Los Angeles, CA 90035. Phones: 310/553-8403 and 310/553-9036. Fax: 310/553-4521. E-mail: *webmaster@wiesenthal.net*. Web site: *www.museumoftolerance*. Hours: Apr.-Oct.—10-4 Mon.-Thurs.; 10-3 Fri.; 10:30-5 Sun.; remainder of year —11:30-4 Mon.-Thurs.; 10-1 Fri.; 11-5 Sun.; closed Jewish and major holidays. Admission: adults, $10; seniors, $8; students over 11, $7; children 3-11, $6; children under 3, free.

My Jewish Discovery Place Children's Museum. My Jewish Discovery Place Children's Museum at the Soref Jewish Community Center in Fort Lauderdale, Florida, is a hands-on museum of Jewish history and values dedicated to providing an environment where creativity, learning, and play become a bridge to understanding in a multicultural world. It has exhibits on such subjects as archaeological digs, immigration, Kibbutz, traditions, holiday meals, peace, and Jerusalem's Western Wall.

My Jewish Discovery Place Children's Museum, Soref Jewish Community Center, 6501 W. Sunrise Blvd., Fort Lauderdale, FL 33313. Phone: 954/792-6700. Fax: 945/792-4839. E-mail: *smckenna. org*. Web site: *www.sorefjcc.org*. Hours: 10-5 Tues.-Fri.; 12-4 Sun.; closed Mon., Sat., and Jewish and major holidays. Admission: adults and children over 6, $4; children 2-6, $3; children under 2, free; families, $12.

National Jewish Children's Museum. The National Jewish Medical and Research Center in Denver, Colorado, has a National Jewish Children's Museum with changing exhibitions of art works and personal comments by child and adolescent patients about living with a chronic illness. The works are produced in various therapy group and individual sessions at the center, the only facility in the world dedicated exclusively to the treatment of respiratory, immune, and allergic disorders.

National Jewish Children's Museum, National Jewish Medical and Research Center, 1400 Jackson St.,

Denver, CO 80206. Web site: *http://nationaljewish.org*. Phone: 303/388-4461. Hours: varies. Admission: free.

National Museum of American Jewish History. The National Museum of American Jewish History, located on Independence Mall in Philadelphia, Pennsylvania, is the only museum in the nation dedicated exclusively to collecting, preserving, and interpreting artifacts pertaining to the American Jewish experience. The museum has more than 10,000 artifacts relating to the history of more than 300 years of American Jewish life. It currently shares its location with the historic Congregation Mikvek Israel, but has announced plans to construct a new home on the mall.

National Museum of American Jewish History, Independence Mall East, 55 N. 5th St., Philadelphia, PA 19106-2197. Phone: 215/823-3811. Fax: 215/923-0763. E-mail: *nmajh@nmaih.org*. Web site: *www. nmajh.org*. Hours: 10-5 Thurs.; 10-3 Fri.; 12-5 Sun.; closed Sat., New Year's Day, Thanksgiving, and major Jewish holidays and festivals. Admission: free.

National Museum of American Jewish Military History. The National Museum of American Jewish Military History in Washington, D.C., documents, preserves, and interprets the contributions of Jewish Americans in the armed forces of the United States and works to combat anti–Semitism. The museum has a Hall of Heroes that honors Jewish American recipients of the Medal of Honor, a permanent exhibit on the life and work of Major General Julius Klein, and changing exhibitions on such topics as Jewish women in the military, liberating concentration camps, and Jewish military chaplains. Its collections include uniforms, firearms, medals, personal papers, documents, and photographs.

National Museum of American Jewish Military History, 1811 R St., N.W., Washington, DC 20009. Phone: 202/2656280. Fax: 202/482-3192. E-mail: *nmajmh@nmajmh.org*. Web site: *www.nmajmh.org*. Hours: 9-5 Mon.-Fri.; 1-5 Sun.; closed Sat. and Jewish and national holidays. Admission: free.

National Yiddish Book Center Visitors Center. The National Yiddish Book Center on the campus of Hampshire College in Amherst, Massachusetts, has a Visitors Center with a gallery, exhibitions, gardens, library, and bookstore. The book center, founded in 1980 to rescue endangered Yiddish and modem Jewish books, occupies a 37,000-square-foot building that serves as a resource for those who want to explore the meaning and relevance of Yiddish culture and modem Jewish literature. Since its opening, the book center has recovered more than 1.5 million Yiddish books, many of which were scarce and deteriorating and have been restored or reprinted.

National Yiddish Book Center Visitors Center, Hampshire College, Harry and Jeanette Weinberg Bldg., 1021 West St., Amherst, MA 01002. Phone: 413/256–4900. Fax: 413/256–4700. E-mail: *visit@ bikher.org*. Web site: *http://yiddishbookcenter.org*. Hours: 10–3:30 Mon.-Fri.; 11–4 Sun.; closed Sat. and Jewish and major holidays. Admission: free.

Nebraska Jewish Historical Society and Riekes Museum. The Nebraska Jewish Historical Society and Riekes Museum, housed in the Jewish Community Center in Omaha, Nebraska, features a recreation of the 90-year-old B'nai Jacob Adas Yeshuron Synagogue that closed two decades ago. The museum also has a "Wall of Synagogue History" tracing the history of synagogues in Nebraska and Iowa and a Hall of Memories with artifacts and photographs depicting Jewish life and culture in the region since the 1860s.

Nebraska Jewish Historical Society and Riekes Museum, 333 S. 132nd St., Omaha, NE 68154. Phone: 402/334–6442. E-mail: *njhs@jewishomaha.org*. Hours: 10–4 Mon.-Thurs.; closed Fri.-Sun. and Jewish and national holidays. Admission: free.

Ohef Sholom Temple Archives. The Ohef Sholom Temple, founded in 1844 in Norfolk, Virginia, has an archival room with over 2,500 objects relating to the history of the temple and Jews in the area. Changing exhibitions, such as the recent one on World War II and the Jewish community of Tidewater, also are presented by the archives.

Ohef Sholom Temple Archives, 530 Raleigh Ave., Norfolk, VA 23507. Phone: 757/625–4295. Fax: 757/625–3762. E-mail: *archives@ohefsholom.org*. Web site: *www.ohefsholom.org*. Hours: 9–5 Mon.-Fri.; closed Sat.-Sun. and Jewish and national holidays. Admission: free.

Oregon Jewish Museum. After operating as a museum without walls for more than a decade, the Oregon Jewish Museum moved into park office space and then into a storefront location in Portland's Old Town. The museum, which is devoted to Jewish art and history, has an extensive collection documenting Jewish life in Oregon for 150 years, resulting from a merger with the Jewish Historical Society of Oregon. Among its recent exhibitions have been "Faces and Places of Old South Portland" and "Jews@Work: 150 Years of Commerce and Industry in Oregon."

Oregon Jewish Museum, 310 N.W. Davis St., Portland, OR 97209. Phone: 503/226–3600. Fax: 503/226–1800. E-mail: museum@ojm.org. Web site: *www.ojm.org*. Hours: 11–2 Tues.-Fri.; 1–4 Sun.; closed

Mon., Sat., and Jewish and national holidays. Admission: $3 per person.

Philadelphia Museum of Jewish Art and Congregation Rodeph Shalom Collection. The Philadelphia Museum of Jewish Art, which presents contemporary art that illuminates the Jewish experience, is located in the Congregation Rodeph Shalom, the oldest German synagogue in the Western Hemisphere. The museum has a permanent exhibit of important works by such accomplished artists as William Anatasi, Chaim Gross, Tobi Kahn, Jean Snyder, Shelley Spector, Boaz Vaadia, and Roman Vishniac. It also organizes changing solo and group exhibitions of works in various mediums by artists of diverse backgrounds.

In addition, the synagogue displays ceremonial objects from its Leon J. and Julia S. Obermayer Collection of Ritual Jewish Art in the entrance foyer. These rare pieces of ceremonial art dating from the eighteenth through twentieth centuries were created for the observance of the Sabbath and holidays and the celebration of life-cycle events.

Philadelphia Museum of Jewish Art, Congregation Rodeph Shalom, 615 N. Broad St., Philadelphia, PA 19123. Phone: 215/627–6747. Fax: 215/627–1313. E-mail: *info@rodephshalom.org*. Web site: *www.rode phshalom.org*. Hours: 10–4 Mon.-Thurs.; 10–2 Fri.; 10–12 Sun.; closed Sat. and Jewish and major holidays. Admission: free.

Rosenzweig Gallery. The Rosenzweig Gallery at the Judea Reform Congregation in Durham, North Carolina, is operated by the Jewish Heritage Foundation of North Carolina. It presents three to four exhibitions each year featuring contemporary work with Jewish themes, including an annual exhibition and sale of art on Jewish themes.

Rosenzweig Gallery, Judea Reform Congregation, 1933 W. Cornwallis Rd., Durham, NC 27795. Phone and fax: 919/932–1844. Web Site: *www.jhfnc.org*. Hours: 8:30–5 Mon.-Thurs.; 8:30–3:30 Fri.; Sun. during religious school hours; closed Sat. and Jewish and major holidays. Admission: free.

Sherwin Miller Museum of Jewish Art. See Museums Honoring Individuals section.

Skirball Cultural Center. The Skirball Cultural Center, a part of Hebrew Union College-Jewish Institute of Religion on top of Sepulveda Pass in the Santa Monica Mountains of Los Angeles, California, explores the connections between 4,000 years of Jewish heritage and the vitality of American democratic ideals. It has a museum and offers music, theater, comedy, film, and literary programs. The museum was founded in 1913 by the National Foundation of Temple Sisterhood at Hebrew Union College in Cincinnati. It moved to Los

Angles in 1972, although branch museums on the Cincinnati and Jerusalem college campuses share the collections.

Jewish cultural history, biblical archaeology, and art are the focus of the museum. The museum's core exhibit, "Visions and Values: Jewish Life from Antiquity to America," traces the experiences and accomplishments of Jewish people over the centuries. Exhibits cover such topics as Jewish practices, history, ethnographic culture, and arts, and include items such as religious objects, statuary, mosaics, pottery, clothing, and photographs.

Skirball Cultural Center Museum, Hebrew Union College-Jewish Institute of Religion, 2701 N. Sepulveda Blvd., Los Angeles, CA 90049. Phone: 310/440–4500. Fax: 310/440–4595. E-mail: *kradcliffe@skirball.org*. Web site: *www.skirball.org*. Hours: 12–5 Tues.-Sat. (also to 9 Thurs.); 11–5 Sun.; closed Mon. and Jewish and national holidays. Admission: adults, $8; seniors and students, $6; children under 12, free; free on Thurs.

Skirball Museum. The Cincinnati, Ohio, branch of the Skirball Museum is one of four museums operated by the Hebrew Union College-Jewish Institute of Religion. The others are in New York City, Los Angeles, and Jerusalem, Israel. The museum, located in Mayerson Hall, houses a collection of Jewish ceremonial and ritual objects, as well as Jewish archaeological artifacts from the Nelson Glueck School of Biblical Archeology in Jerusalem. Other exhibits depict Torah study, aspects of the Holocaust, modern Israel, and American Judaism with an emphasis on Cincinnati and the college and institute.

The museum's permanent exhibit, "An Eternal People: The Jewish Experience," focuses on the cultural heritage of the Jewish people as conveyed through seven thematic galleries-immigration, Cincinnati Jewry, archaeology, Torah, Jewish festivals and life-cycles, Holocaust, and Israel. The museum also has a hands-on learning and research facility, featuring artifacts discovered by the institution's excavations in Israel, for furthering the study of archaeology and integrating it with biblical and ancient Near Eastern history and culture. In addition, the museum presents changing exhibitions.

Skirball Museum (Cincinnati), Hebrew Union College-Jewish Institute of Religion, Mayerson Hall, 3101 Clifton Ave., Cincinnati, OH 45220. Phone: 513/221–1875. Fax: 513/221–0316. Web site: *www.huc.edu/museums/cn*. Hours: 11–4 Mon.-Thurs.; 2–5 Sun.; closed Sat. and Jewish and national holidays. Admission: free.

Spertus Museum. The Spertus Museum, part of the Spertus Institute of Jewish Studies in Chicago,

Illinois, moved into the institute's new $55 million building facing Grant Park and Lake Michigan in late 2007. It presents exhibitions, programs, and children's activities to celebrate, challenge, and advance modern Jewish identity. It uses objects from its own collection and elsewhere to demonstrate the powerful and reciprocal effect between Jewish and broader culture. The museum has a collection of over 18,000 artifacts and artworks spanning 3,500 years of Jewish history, religious tradition, art, and ethnography.

The Spertus collection focuses on and reflects aspects of Jewish history and culture, including Jewish artistic movements, artists, and others who have contributed significantly to Jewish heritage. The collection includes paintings, drawings, prints, graphics, photographs, and sculptures from before the eighteenth century to the twentieth century; ethnographic and decorative arts; archaeological artifacts from the Middle East; architectural elements and decorations; coins, medals, seals, weights, and stamps; historical documents and ephemera; manuscripts and books; and audiovisual materials.

Spertus Museum, Spertus Institute of Jewish Studies, 610 S. Michigan Ave., Chicago, IL 60605. Phones: 312/322-1700 and 312/322-1747. Fax: 312/922–3934. E-mail: *museum@spertus.edu*. Web site: *www.spertus.edu/museum*. Hours: 10–5 Sun.-Thurs. (also to 7 Thurs.); 10–3 Fri.; closed Sat. and Jewish and national holidays. Admission: adults, $5; senior, students, and children, $3; families, $10; free on Fri.

Star Gallery. The Star Gallery at the Leventhal Sidman Jewish Community Center in Newton Centre, Massachusetts, presents exhibitions that address issues of Jewish culture and identity, as well as Jewish art and traveling exhibitions.

Star Gallery, Leventhal Sidman Jewish Community Center, 333 Nahanton St., Newton Centre, MA 02159. Phone: 617/985–7410. Web site: *www.lsjcc.org*. Hours: 8-9 Mon.-Thurs.; 8–4 Fri.; 9–5 Sun.; closed Sat. and holidays. Admission: free.

Sylvia Plotkin Judaica Museum. The Sylvia Plotkin Judaica Museum at the Temple Beth Israel in Scottsdale, Arizona, contains Jewish religious, ceremonial, archaeological, and arts objects from 1600 to the present. It also tells the story of Jewish pioneers in Arizona from 1850 to 1920. The museum is named for the wife of a rabbi who was instrumental in the museum's founding in 1966.

Sylvia Plotkin Judaica Museum, Temple Beth Israel, 10460 N. 56th St., Scottsdale, AZ 85253–1133. Phone: 480/951–0323. Fax: 480/951–7150. E-mail: *museum@temkebethisrael.org*. Web site: *www.spjm.org*. Hours: June-Aug.—10–3 Tues.-Thurs.; closed Fri.-Mon.; remainder of year—10–3 Tues.-Fri.; 12–3 Sun.;

closed Mon., Fri., and Jewish and national holidays. Admission: adults, $3 suggested donation; children, free.

Temple Beth Shalom Judaica Museum. Permanent exhibits and changing exhibitions of ritual objects, paintings, and photographs depict the heritage of Jewish people around the world at the Temple Beth Shalom Judaica Museum on Long Island in Roslyn Heights, New York.

Temple Beth Shalom Judaica Museum, 401 Roslyn Rd., Roslyn Heights, NY 11577. Phone: 516/621–2288. Hours: 9–5 Mon.-Thurs.; 9–3 Fri.; closed Sat.-Sun. and Jewish and national holidays. Admission: free.

Temple B'rith Kodesh Museum. The Temple B'rith Kodesh Museum in Rochester, New York, preserves and displays objects and records relating to Jewish and temple history.

Temple B'rith Kodesh Museum, 2131 Elmwood Ave. Rochester, NY 14618–1021. Phone: 716/244–7060. Hours: by appointment and during Temple services and events. Admission: free.

Temple Judea Museum of Keneseth Israel. The Temple Judea Museum of Keneseth Israel in Elkins Park, Pennsylvania, resulted from the 1984 merger of the Judaica collections of two Philadelphia-area synagogues — Temple Judea and Reform Congregation Keneseth Israel. The museum has Judaica artifacts from throughout the world that signify the observances of Judaism and other historical objects. Among the highlights are a major collection of silver ceremonial objects, the second oldest American ketubah (marriage contract), an embroidered Torah wimpel (binder) that survived the Holocaust, a 1574 religious commentary printed in Venice, and a unique contemporary Elijah's Chair used in covenant ceremonies.

Temple Judea Museum of Keneseth Israel, Reform Congregation Keneseth Israel, 8339 Old York Rd., Elkins Park, PA 19027. Phones: 215/887–2027 and 215/887–8700. Fax: 215/887–1070. E-mail: *tjmuseum@aol.com.* Web site: *www.kenesethisrael.org/mus. htm.* Hours: 9–5 Mon.-Fri. and by appointment; closed Sat.-Sun. and Jewish and national holidays. Admission: free.

Temple Mickve Israel Archival Museum. The Temple Mickve Israel in Savannah, Georgia, is one of the oldest Jewish congregations in the South. It was founded in 1733 by 42 Jewish settlers. The temple has an archival museum that preserves and displays artifacts and other historical materials related to local Jewish religious and cultural heritage. Among the exhibited materials are the fifteenth-century Torah scroll brought to Savannah by the first settlers and letters from 10 presidents, including George Washington, Thomas Jefferson, and James Madison.

Temple Mickve Israel Archival Museum, Monterey Sq., 20 E. Gordon St., Savannah, GA 31401. Phone: 912/233–1547. Fax: 912/233–3086. *Email: mickveisr@aol.com.* Web site: *www.mickveisrael.org.* Hours: 10–12 and 2–4 Mon.-Fri.; closed Sat.-Sun. and Jewish and national holidays. Admission: free; tours — $3 per person.

Temple Museum of Religious Art. The Temple Museum of Religious Art, housed in the Temple-Tifereth Israel in Cleveland, Ohio, features a comprehensive collection of religious and Judaic art. The exhibits include Torah hangings dating to the seventeenth century; antiques and household pottery from the Holy Land region from 2000 B.C. to Roman times; fold art objects made and used by Jews in many countries; historic documents, manuscripts, and Bibles; and sculptures, paintings, and lithographs by noted Jewish artists.

Temple Museum of Religious Art, Temple-Tifereth Israel, 1855 Ansel Rd., University Circle at Silver Park, Cleveland, OH 44106. Phone: 216/831–3233 and 216/791–7755. Faxes: 216/791–7043 and 216/831–4216. Web site: *www.ttti.org./museum.asp.* Hours: by appointment; closed Jewish and national holidays.

Union for Reform Judaism Library and Museum. The Union for Reform Judaism, which serves Reform congregations in North America, has a library-museum with ceremonial objects, works by Jewish artists, and books on synagogue architecture, art, and other areas.

Union for Reform Judaism Library and Museum, 633 3rd Ave., New York, NY 10017. Phone: 212/650–4040. Fax: 212/650–4239. E-mail: *urj@ urj.org.* Web site: *www.urj.org.* Hours: 9:30–5 Mon.-Fri.; closed Sat.-Sun. and Jewish holidays and festivals. Admission: free.

United States Holocaust Memorial Museum. The United States Holocaust Memorial Museum in Washington, D.C., is America's memorial to the millions of people murdered by the Nazis during the Holocaust between 1933 and 1945. Chartered by Congress and located adjacent to the Mall, it has become the largest and most popular museum devoted to the documentation, study, and interpretation of Holocaust history, with an annual attendance of nearly 1.4 million.

Founded in 1993, the museum's seeks to advance and disseminate knowledge about the Holocaust, preserve memory of those who suffered, and encourage visitors to reflect upon the moral and spiritual questions raised by the events of the Holocaust. It strives to broaden public understanding of the Holocaust through exhibits, research, and publications; collecting and preserving material evidence; art and artifacts relating to the Holocaust; distribution of educational materials; and public programming.

The museum's permanent exhibit, "The Holocaust," spans three floors with more than 900 artifacts, 70 video monitors, and theaters that include historic footage and eyewitness testimonials. It has three sections — "Nazi Assault," "Final Solution," and "Last Chapter." It is supplemented by changing special exhibitions and a children's exhibit. The museum's Wexner Learning Center also presents exhibitions on such topics as the American liberators, Nuremberg trials, anti–Semitism, and genocide emergency in Darfur, Sudan. It also has a registry of nearly 200,000 survivors and their families in the United States and 59 countries.

United States Holocaust Memorial Museum, 100 Raoul Wallenberg Pl., S.W., Washington, DC 20024–2126. Phone: 202/488–0400. E-mail: *visitor-swmail@ushmm.org*. Web site: *www.ushmm.org*. Hours: 10–5:30 daily; closed Yom Kippur and Christmas. Admission: free.

Weiner Judaic Museum and Goldman Art Gallery. The Weiner Judaic Museum and the Goldman Art Gallery are located at the Jewish Community Center of Greater Washington in Washington, D.C. The Weiner Museum is devoted to the history, ethnology, archaeology, and art of Judaica, while the Goldman Gallery presents changing exhibitions of art by Jewish artists.

Weiner Judaic Museum and Goldman Art Gallery, Jewish Community Center of Greater Washington, 6125 Montrose Rd., Rockville, MD 20852. Phone: 301/881–0100. Fax: 301/881–5512. Web site: *www. iccgw.org*. Hours: 5:30-10:30 Mon.-Thurs.; 5:30–5 Fri. (also to 5:30 Memorial Day-Labor Day); 12:30–5:30 Sat.; 7-9 P.M. Sun.; closed Jewish and national holidays. Admission free.

William Breman Jewish Heritage Museum. The William Breman Jewish Heritage Museum in downtown Atlanta, Georgia, interprets the Holocaust and the history of Jews in Atlanta from 1845 to the present and offers changing exhibitions. The museum, housed in the Selig Center, is operated by the Jewish Federation of Greater Atlanta and named for the donor, a retired steel company owner.

William Breman Jewish Heritage Museum, Selig Center, 1440 Spring St., N.W., Atlanta, GA 30309. Phones: 404/873–1661 and 678/222–3700. E-mail: *jjleavev@atljf.org*. Web site: *www.atlantajewishfederation.org*. Hours: 10–5 Mon.-Thurs.; 10–3 Fri.; 1–5 Sun.; closed Sat., major Jewish holidays, and some federal holidays. Admission: adults, $10; seniors, $6; students, $4; children 3–6, $2; children under 3, free.

Yeshiva University Museum. The Yeshiva University Museum, located in the Center for Jewish History in New York City, presents changing exhibitions that celebrate the culturally diverse intellectual and artistic achievements of the Jewish experience. The primary focus is on the interpretation of Jewish history from a multi-disciplinary perspective. The exhibitions are of two types — examinations of the Jewish community or historic events, and displays by emerging or established contemporary artists working on Jewish themes. The museum has four galleries and an outdoor sculpture garden.

Yeshiva University Museum, 15 W. 16th St., New York, NY 10011. Phone: 212/294–8330. Fax: 212/294–8335. E-mail: *sherskowitz@yum.cih.org*. Web site: *www.yumuseum.org*. Hours:11–5 Sun., Mon.-Thurs. (also to 8 Mon.); 11–2 Fri.; closed Sat. and Jewish holidays. Admission: adults, $8; seniors and students, $6; children under 5, free.

Zimmer Children's Museum. The Zimmer Children's Museum in Los Angeles, California, incorporates Jewish and community values and ethics in teaching children and their families about big ideas and making a difference in their homes and the world. The museum, located on the lobby level of the Goldsmith Jewish Federation Center, uses interactive learning, creative self-expression, and art experiences to promote values that help make a better society. Its innovative statewide youTHink outreach education program, jointly developed with the Center for American Studies and Culture, engages students in the fourth through twelfth grades in contemporary issues and civic action through art, and motivates them to think, form their own opinions, express their views, and make a difference in their communities.

Zimmer Children's Museum, 6505 Wilshire Blvd., Suite 100, Los Angeles, CA 90048. Phone: 323/761–8989. Fax: 323/761–8990. E-mail: *info@zimmermuseum.org*. Web site: *www.zimmermuseum.org*. Hours: 10–5 Tues.; 12:30–5 Wed.-Thurs. and Sun.; 10–12:30 Fri.; closed Mon., Sat., and most Jewish and national holidays. Admission: adults, $5; children 3–12, $3; children under 3, free.

Museums Honoring Individuals

Frank Rosenthal Memorial Collection. The Frank Rosenthal Memorial Collection at the Temple Anshe Sholom in Olympia Fields, Illinois, has nearly 900 objects collected by Rabbi Frank F. Rosenthal. The collection in display cases includes tools and arrowheads from 15,000 B.C., religious objects from the Byzantine and Roman periods, and jewelry and ceremonial objects from the Holocaust.

Frank Rosenthal Memorial Collection, Temple Anshe Sholom, 20820 Western Ave., Olympia Fields, IL 60461. Phone: 708/748–6010. E-mail: *rburrows@templeanshesholom.org.* Hours: 9–5 Mon.-Thurs.; 9–4 Fri.; closed Sat.-Sun. and Jewish and national holidays. Admission: free.

Sherwin Miller Museum of Jewish Art. The Sherwin Miller Museum of Jewish Art in Tulsa, Oklahoma, is named for the museum's first curator. It was founded in 1966 with the acquisition of a collection of Judaica by Miller. Originally named the Gershon and Rebecca Fenster Museum of Jewish Art, it was renamed in 2000 in recognition of Miller's seminal vision. The museum, which now has the largest collection of Judaica in the Southwest, utilizes both art and history to preserve and interpret Jewish culture. Its exhibits are organized into five groupings — archaeology, ritual objects, life cycle, ethnology, and history.

Sherwin Miller Museum of Jewish Art, 2021 E. 71st St., Tulsa, OK 74136. Phone: 918/492–1818. Fax: 918/492–1888. E-mail: *info@iewishmuseurn.net.* Web site: *www.iewishmuseurn.nel.* Hours: 10–5 Mon.-Fri.; 1–5 Sun.; closed Sun. and major Jewish and national holidays. Admission: adults, $5.50; seniors, $4.50; students, $3; children under 6, free.

Historic Sites

Eldridge Street Project. The purpose of the Eldridge Street Project in New York City is to restore and preserve the 1887 Eldridge Street Synagogue and to interpret it with cultural and educational programs for a diverse audience. The lower East Side landmark, the first great house of worship built in America by Eastern European Jews, was rescued from near collapse by the project. The building now serves as a learning center for exploring architecture and historic preservation, synagogue life and customs, inter-group experience, and art and cultural experiences based on Jewish and humanistic themes. The project has a pictorial display and tours of the synagogue and neighborhood.

Eldridge Street Project, Eldridge Street Synagogue, 12 Eldridge St., New York, NY 10002. Phone: 212/219–0888. E- mail: *contact@eldridgestreet.org.* Web site: *www.eldridgestreet.org.* Tour hours: 11–4 Sun. and Tues.-Thurs. Tour fees: adults, $5; seniors and students, $3.

Gomez Mill House. The Gomez Mill House in Marlboro, New York, is the oldest surviving Jewish residence in North America. The fieldstone block house with 3-feet-thick walls was built by Luis Moses Gomez, who had fled from the Spanish Inquisition, after he purchased 6,000 acres along the Hudson Highlands in 1714. Located on the site of an ancient Indian ceremonial campground, the fortress-like structure has served as a frontier trading post, center of patriot activity in the Revolutionary War, and home of writers, artists, and men of affairs. While serving as a fur trader, Gomez became the first president of the synagogue of New York's Spanish and Portuguese congregation. The historic house has been inhabited continuously for nearly three centuries.

Gomez Mill House, 11 Mill House Rd., Marlboro, NY 12542. Phone: 845/236–3126. E-mail: *gomezmillhouse@juno.com.* Web site: *www.gomez.org.* Hours: late Apr.-Oct.—10–4 Wed-Sun.; closed Mon.-Tues. and remainder of year. Admission: adults, $7.50; seniors, $5; students, $2; children under 6, free.

JCRS Isaac Solomon Synagogue. The JCRS Isaac Solomon Synagogue, a modest 1926 brick and stucco structure in Moorish style in Lakewood, Colorado, was part of a non-sectarian tuberculosis sanatorium operated by the Jewish Consumptives' Relief Society since 1904. Thousands came to the Denver area in search for a cure for tuberculosis. Many got better in the clear air and high altitude while others did not. The relief society became the American Medical Center for Cancer Research in 1954, and now has a foundation which is restoring the synagogue as a living testament to the movement and in memory of those who created, supported, and were treated at the TB facility. Plans call for it to be a living history museum and life-cycle events center. The long unused synagogue is located in a quiet comer of the center's former site, now occupied by the Rocky Mountain College of Art + Design.

JCRS Isaac Solomon Historic Synagogue, 1600 Pierce St., Lakewood, CO 80214. Phone: 303/987–1316. E-mail: *info@isaacsolomonsynagogue.org.* Hours and admission: still to be determined.

Touro Synagogue Historic Site. The 1763 Touro Synagogue in Newport, Rhode Island, is the oldest synagogue in the United States and one of the most architecturally distinguished buildings of eighteenth-century America. The classical Georgian building, designed by Peter Harrison, one of the nation's first and finest architects, was built in the colony founded by Roger Williams on the principle of religious tolerance. The synagogue also has a link to George Washington's visit to Newport in 1790, after which he wrote "To the Hebrew Congregation in Newport Rhode Island," proclaiming that the United States "gives to bigotry no sanction, to persecution no assistance."

Tours are given of the Touro Synagogue, a national historic site which continues as a living house of worship and the destination of tens of thousands of visitors who come every year to see the synagogue's ageless beauty and be inspired with an appreciation of religious freedom. Efforts now are under way to restore the Touro Synagogue, build a visitor education center, and redesign the park in which it is located.

Touro Synagogue, 85 Touro St., Newport, RI 02840. Phone: 401/847–4794. Web site: *www.touro synagogue.org.* Tour hours: July-Labor Day—10–5 Mon.-Fri. and Sun.; May-June and day after Labor Day-Oct.—1–3 Mon.-Fri.; 11–3 Sun.; Nov.-Feb.—1–3:30 Mon.-Fri.; 11–3 Sun.; closed Sat. Tour fees: adults and children over 12, $5; children under 13, free.

Botanical Gardens

Rodef Shalom Biblical Botanical Garden. The Rodef Shalom Biblical Botanical Garden, operated by the Rodef Shalom Congregation in Pittsburgh, Pennsylvania, features the agriculture, horticulture, and archaeology of the ancient Holy Land in the Near East. It has more than 100 temperate and tropical plants in a desert setting with a waterfall, stream, and simulated Jordan River that flows through the garden from Lake Kineret to the Dead Sea. A biblical verse accompanies each plant. Each season, a special theme of ancient Near Eastern horticulture is presented with plants from neighboring Egypt, Mesopotamia, and sometimes the Holy Land that became Israel.

Rodef Shalom Biblical Botanical Garden, 4905 5th Ave., Pittsburgh, PA 15213. Phone: 412/621–6566. Fax: 412/6215475. E-mail: *jacob@rodefshalom.org.* Web site: *www.biblicalgardenpittsburgh.org.* Hours: June-mid–Sept.—10–2 Sun.-Thurs. (also 7–9 Wed.); closed Fri.-Sat. (but open 12–1 Sat. in June-Aug.) and remainder of year. Admission: free.

KOREAN (*also see* Asian)

Museums and Galleries

Korean American Museum. The Korean American Museum in Los Angeles, California, preserves and interprets the history, culture, and achievements of Korean Americans. It also discusses issues facing the Korean community and honors the legacy of Korean immigrants and their families. Changing exhibitions have been presented on such subjects as Korean American contemporary art, small businesses, adoptions, continuity and change, and spiritual practices, rituals, icons, and faith.

Korean American Museum, 3727 W. 6th St., Suite 400, Los Angeles, CA 90020. Phone: 213/388–4229. Fax: 213/381- 1288. E-mail: *info@kamuseum.org.* Web

site: *www.kamuseum.org.* Hours: 11–6 Wed.-Fri.; 11–3 Sat.; closed Sun.-Tues. and national holidays. Admission: free.

Korean Cultural Center, Los Angeles. The Korean Cultural Center in Los Angles, California, provides insights into the cultural heritage of Korea. Operated by the Korean Ministry of Culture and Tourism, the center presents exhibits, lectures, films, and other activities to further public understanding and appreciation of Korea. The center's museum features artifacts relating to Korean history and aesthetics. The center also has a first floor gallery that displays full-scale replicas of several wall friezes in the Seokguram Buddhist Grotto Temple and a second-floor gallery contains changing exhibitions of works by Korean artists.

Korean Cultural Center, Los Angeles, 5505 Wilshire Blvd., Los Angeles, CA 90036. Phone: 323/936–7141. Fax 323/936–5712. E-mail *info@kccla.org.* Web site: *www.kccla.org.* Hours: 9–5 Mon.-Fri.; closed Sat.-Sun. and Korean and American national holidays. Admission: free.

KURDISH

Museums and Galleries

Kurdish Library and Museum. The Kurdish Library and Museum in Brooklyn, New York, is the only institution of its kind in the Western Hemisphere. The library, which operates under a charter from the University of the State of New York, contains books and other publications on Kurdish history, culture, and contemporary affairs, while the museum displays kilims and other weavings, mannequins in traditional costumes, and artifacts from Turkey, Iraq, and Iran.

Kurdish Library and Museum, 144 Underhill Ave., Brooklyn, NY 11238. Phone: 718/783–7930. Fax: 718/398–4365. E-mail: *kurdishlib@aol.com.* Web site: *www.thekurdishlibrarv.com.* Hours: 10–3 Mon.-Thurs. and by appointment; closed major holidays. Admission: free.

LATINO *see* Hispanic

LATVIAN

Museums and Galleries

American Latvian Association's Ethnographic and Cultural Collection. The American Latvian Association's Ethnographic and Cultural Collection currently is located at the Daugavas Vanagi House in the Bronx, New York, but is moving to the Latvian Center Preidaine in Howell Township near Freehold, New Jersey. Started in 1977, the collection features Latvian ethnographic and other articles of historic and cultural value. They include folk costumes, weavings, embroideries, forgings, wicker works, leather crafts, woodworks, documents, drawings, photographs, and books relating to Latvia from earlier times to the recent past. Among the materials are a 1680 large brooch, a pair of 1825 mittens, and late 1899s textiles and clothing. American Latvian Association Ethnographic and Cultural Collection, Daugavas Vanagi House, 115 W. 183rd St., Bronx, NY 10453. Phones: 212/367–8099 and 718/933–8167. Web sites: *http://alausa.org.* and *www.nylatvian.org.* Hours: varies. Admission: free.

Latvian Center Garezers. The Latvian Center Garezers, a human services organization in Three Rivers, Michigan, preserves and interprets Latvian history and culture and provides educational opportunities for Latvian Americans. It has a collection of artifacts, works of art, and books and operates a museum, art gallery, and library.

Latvian Center Garezers, Inc., 57732 Lone Tree Rd., Three Rivers, MI 49093. Phone: 269/244–5441. Fax: 269/244–8380. E-mail: *garezers@garezers.org.* Web site: *www.garezersorg.* Hours: July-mid–Aug.— 2–4 Sat.-Sun.; closed remainder of week and year. Admission: donation.

Latvian Folk Art Museum. The Latvian Folk Art Museum in Chicago, Illinois, is devoted to the textiles and folk and ceremonial costumes of Latvia.

Latvian Folk Art Museum, 4146 N. Elston Ave., Chicago, IL 60618. Phone: 773/588–2085. Fax: 773/588–3405. Hours: 10–1 daily and by appointment; closed major holidays. Admission: free.

Latvian Museum. The Latvian Museum, located on the lower level of the Latvian Lutheran Church in Rockville, Maryland, has exhibits on Latvian history, folk culture, immigration, and life in America and collections of traditional Latvian costumes, textiles, and crafts; farm tools; documents; and photographs. Among the rarest items are an early Latvian Bible, a large coopered storage barrel, a flax break, and a spinning wheel — all from the late 1800s.

Latvian Museum, 400 Hurley Ave., PO Box 432, Rockville, MD 20850–3121. Phone: 301/340–1914. Fax: 301/762-5438. E-mail: *alainfo@alasua.org.* Web site: *http://alausa.org.* Hours: by appointment. Admission: free.

LITHUANIAN

Museums and Galleries

American Lithuanian Cultural Archives. The Lithuanian Catholic Academy of Science operates the American Lithuanian Cultural Archives (usually known as ALKA for its Lithuanian name) in Putnam, Connecticut. Founded in the early 1920s, the archives collected artifacts, folk art, paintings, documents, periodicals, books, and other Lithuanian-oriented materials. In more recent years, it has added a museum and a library. The museum displays art and artifacts from the archives and most of the books are in the library.

American Lithuanian Cultural Archives, 37 Marycrest, PO Box 608, Putnam, CT 06260. Phone: 203/928–5197. Hours: by appointment. Admission: donation.

Balzekas Museum of Lithuanian Culture. Cultural artifacts, art, publications, and other materials of Lithuanians and Lithuanian Americans are featured at the Balzekas Museum of Lithuanian Culture in Chicago, Illinois. The museum was started in 1966 by Stanley Balzekas, Jr., in a two-flat building next to his auto dealership with his personal collection of art, armor, and rare maps. It moved to expanded facilities in 1986 and now has even more comprehensive collections, exhibits, and programs. The museum's principal exhibit, "Lithuania Through the Ages," depicts Lithuanian history and culture from prehistory to the present. It also presents changing art and other exhibitions. The museum has become the largest Lithuanian resource center outside of Lithuania.

Balzekas Museum of Lithuanian Culture, 6500 S. Pulaski Rd., Chicago, IL 60629. Phone: 773/582–6500. Fax: 773/582–5133. E-mail: *editor@balzekas lithuanianmuseum.org.* Web site: *www.lithaz.org/museums/balzekas.* Hours: 10–4 daily; closed New Year's Day, Easter, and Christmas. Admission: adults, $4; seniors and students, $3; children under 13, $1.

Lithuanian Museum. The Lithuanian Museum, part of the Lithuanian Research and Studies Center in Chicago, Illinois, has exhibits on the history, art, folk costumes, textiles, posters, industry, commerce, military, religion, music, coins, medicine, and other aspects of Lithuania. Some of its offerings are presented through two subsidiary museums — Lithuanian Museum of Medicine and Archives and Ramovenal Military Museum — located on the premises. The medical museum and archives is the only museum outside Lithuania that traces the lives and careers of physicians from Lithuania, while the military museum is devoted to the Lithuanian resistance movement and struggle for independence.

Lithuanian Museum, Lithuanian Research and Studies Center, 5620 S. Claremont Ave., Chicago, IL 60636. Phone: 312/434–4545. Fax: 312/434–9363. E-mail: *lithuanianresearch@ameritech.net.* Hours:

9:15–3:30 Tues.-Fri.; 9:15–2 Fri.; closed Sun.-Mon. and major holidays. Admission: free.

Lithuanian Museum and Cultural Center. The Lithuanian Museum and Cultural Center in Frackville, Pennsylvania, is operated in the anthracite coal region of the state by the local council of the Knights of Lithuania. It contains artifacts, memorabilia, and books from early Lithuanian immigrants who came to work in the coal mines, as well as original, straw, marguciai, and mushroom art.

Lithuanian Museum and Cultural Center, 37 S. Broad Mountain Ave., Frackville, PA 17931. Phone: 570/874–4092. Hours: by appointment. Admission: free.

Lithuanian Museum of Art. The Lithuanian Museum of Art at the Lithuanian World Center in Lemont, Illinois, presents exhibitions by native and immigrant Lithuanian artists. It was created in 1989 by the federation of four arts organizations — Lithuanian Art Gallery _iurlionis, Art Society Dailé, Lithuanian Institute of Fine Arts, and Lithuanian Folk Art Institute. Each has its own collections and staff, and collectively have staged nearly all of the museum's exhibitions. They range from paintings, graphic arts, and wood sculptures to fiber art, three-dimensional works, and decorated Easter eggs.

Lithuanian Museum of Art, Lithuanian World Center, 14911 12th St., Lemont, IL 60439. Phones: 630/257–2034 and 630/257–8787. Hours: 11–2 Sat.-Sun.; weekdays by appointment; closed major holidays. Admission: adults, $5; seniors, $3; children, $2.

Lithuanian Museum of Medicine and Archives. See Lithuanian Museum.

Ramovenal Military Museum. See Lithuanian Museum.

Sisters of St. Casimir Museum of Lithuanian Culture. A collection of Lithuanian cultural and religious artifacts is displayed in the Sisters of St. Casimir Museum of Lithuanian Culture in Chicago, Illinois. The museum, developed by Sister m. Perepetua Gudavičius (Gudas), occupies several rooms in the Motherhouse of the Sisters of St. Casimir.

Sisters of St. Casimir Museum of Lithuanian Culture, 2601 W. Marquette Rd., Chicago, IL 60629. Phone: 773/7761324. Hours: by appointment. Admission: free.

MACEDONIAN

Museums and Galleries

Bulgarian-Macedonian National Educational

and Cultural Center. See Bulgarian Museums section.

Macedonian Patriotic Organization Museum. The Macedonian Patriotic Organization was started in 1922 to work for the independence of Macedonia and strengthen loyalty and patriotism among immigrants and their descendants in the United States and Canada. After the establishment of Macedonia as an independent state, the organization's mission was broadened to work for human, civil, and economic rights for all Macedonians of the world and to promote and preserve their ethnic traditions, customs, and history. In 1928, the organization began publishing its *Macedonian Tribune* newspaper, which now has an archives that also functions as a museum with artifacts, art, manuscripts, photographs, oral histories, and other materials about Macedonian history and culture.

Macedonian Patriotic Organization Museum, Macedonian Tribune, 124 W. Wayne St., Fort Wayne, IN 46802. Phone: 219/422–5900. Fax: 219/422–4379. Web site: *www.macedonian.org.* Hours: by appointment. Admission: free.

MEXICAN (*also see* Hispanic)

Museums and Galleries

Chicano Humanities and Arts Council Gallery. The art and culture of the Chicano-Latino community in the Denver, Colorado, metropolitan area is featured at the Chicano Humanities and Arts Council Gallery. The nonprofit organization is dedicated to the preservation and promotion of Chicano-Latino art, culture, and humanities in the region. Changing exhibitions of works by Chicano-Latino artists are presented in the CHAC Gallery.

Chicano Humanities and Arts Council Gallery, 772 Santa Fe Dr., Denver, CO 80204. Phone: 303/571–0440. E-mail: *info@chacweb.org.* Web site: *www.chacweb.org.* Hours: 10–4 Wed.-Thurs.; 12–10 Fri.; 12–4 Sat.-Sun.; closed Mon.-Tues. and major holidays. Admission: free.

The Mexican Museum. The Mexican Museum in San Francisco, California, currently is located at the Fort Mason Center, but is building a new home in the heart of the city's Yerba Buena arts district at Mission and Third streets. The new seven-story facility will increase the museum's space from 10,000 to 63,000 square feet. The museum has over 12,000 objects of Mexican, Latino, and Chicano art and culture in its collections, and presents changing historical and contemporary exhibitions.

The Mexican Museum, Fort Mason Center, Bldg. D, Marina Blvd. and Buchanan St., San Francisco,

Adults and children enjoy the changing exhibitions of works by Mexican and Mexican American artists at the National Museum of Mexican Art in Chicago, Illinois. The museum, which has 48,000 square feet of exhibit space, seeks to stimulate, preserve, and further appreciation of Mexican art and culture. *Courtesy National Museum of Mexican Art and photographer Arturo González de Alba.*

CA 94123. Phone: 415/202–9700. Fax: 415/441–7683. E-mail: *info@mexicanmuseum.org*. Web site: *www.mexicanmuseum.org*. Hours: 11–5 Wed.-Sat.; closed Sun.-Tues. and major holidays. Admission: adults, $3; seniors and students, $2; children under 12, free.

Mexic-Arte Museum. The Mexic-Arte Museum in Austin, Texas, seeks to further cultural enrichment and education through the presentation and promotion of traditional and contemporary Mexican, Latino, and Latin American art and culture. Its main gallery houses exhibitions of art from Mexico and other Latin American countries and works by Chicano and Latino artists. The museum also supports and presents new and experimental artworks in its back gallery.

Mexic-Arte Museum, 419 Congress St., PO Box 2273, Austin, TX 78768. Phone: 512/480-9373. Fax: 512/480-8626. E-mail: *director@mexic-artemuseum.*

org. Web site: *www.mexic-artemuseum.org*. Hours: 10–6 Mon.-Thurs.; 10–5 Fri.-Sat.; 12–5 Sun. closed major holidays. Admission: adults, $5; seniors and students, $4; children under 12, $1.

Musee Chicano. The Musee Chicano in downtown Phoenix, Arizona, is a Chicano-Latino museum and cultural center that presents changing local, national, and international exhibitions on the art, history, and culture of Mexicans and Latinos. It showcases both emerging and established talent in the visual, performing, and literary arts and offers related workshops, classes, and seminars.

Musee Chicano, 147 E. Adams St., Phoenix, AZ 85004-2331. Phone: 602/441-0003. E-mail: *lizguna@cox.net*. Web site: *www.museochicano.com*. Hours: 10–4 Tues.-Sat.; closed Sun.-Mon. and major holidays. Admission: adults, $2; seniors and children, $1.

Museo Alameda. See Hispanic Museums and Galleries section.

National Museum of Mexican Art. The National Museum of Mexican Art, formerly the Mexican Fine Arts Center Museum in Chicago, Illinois, is the nation's largest Latino arts institution. It seeks to stimulate, preserve, and further appreciation of the richness and beauty of Mexican art and culture. The museum, which has 48,000 square feet of exhibit space, features a permanent exhibit, "Mexicanidad: Our Past Is Present," and changing exhibitions of works by Mexican and Mexican American artists.

The permanent exhibit traces elements of the Mexican culture historically in five sections — Mexican Pre-Cuauhtémoc, Colonial Mexico, Independence to Revolution, Post-Mexican Revolution to Present-day Mexico, and Mexican Experience in the U.S. The museum also has a youth-oriented exhibit section and youth-run radio station, and offers numerous educational programs and performing arts events.

National Museum of Mexican Art, 1852 W. 19th St., Chicago, IL 60608. Phone: 312/738-1503. Fax: 312/738-9740. E-mail: *carlost@mfacmchicago.org*. Web site: *www.mfacmchicago.org*. Hours: 10-5 Tues.-Sun.; closed Mon. and major holidays. Admission: free.

Plaza de la Raza Museum and Boathouse Gallery The Plaza de la Raza and Boathouse Gallery in Los Angeles, California, is a cultural center that offers programs in arts education and serves as an arts center and school of performing and visual arts. It also has an art museum, housed in a historic boathouse gallery, that presents changing exhibitions and has collections of Mexican American folk life of southern California, works by Latino artists, and photographs by Jose Galvez.

Plaza de la Raza Museum and Boathouse Gallery, 3450 N. Mission Rd., Los Angeles, CA 90031. Phone: 323/223-2475. Fax: 323/223-1804. E-mail: *olivia. chumacero@plazadelaraza.org*. Web site: *www.plaza delaraza.org*. Hours: 10-6 Mon.-Fri.; 10-5. Sat.; closed Sun. and major holidays. Admission: most exhibitions free.

Museums Honoring Individuals

Mexico-Cárdenas Museum. The Mexico-Cárdenas Museum near Waxhaw, North Carolina, honors General Lazaro Cárdenas, president of Mexico from 1934 to 1940, and his commitment to the indigenous peoples of Mexico. The museum resulted from his friendship with William Cameron Townsend, founder of the Wycliffe Bible Translators and Summer Institute of Linguistics. Cárdenas made possible Townsend's efforts to bring written language, education, and health services to the more remote areas of Mexico and for the indigenous languages to be studied and recorded by the institute. The museum contains artifacts, folk art, costumes, and photographs of Mexico's indigenous peoples, as well as translations of the Bible in various dialects discovered by the institute. The museum is part of JAARS Inc., which provides technical support services to Wycliffe and SIL International.

Mexico-Cárdenas Museum, 6409 Davis Rd., PO Box 248, Waxhaw, NC 28173. Phone: 704/843-6066. Fax: 704/8436200. E-mail: *webmaster@laars. org*. Web site: *www.laars.org/museums.shtml*. Hours: 9-12 and 1-3:30 Mon.-Sat.; closed Sun. and major holidays. Admission: free.

Olivas Adobe Historic Park. See Historic Sites section.

Pancho Villa State Park. In 1916, Mexican soldiers led by General Francisco "Pancho" Villa attacked a small American border town and military camp in Columbus, New Mexico. Columbus was left a smoking ruin. General John Pershing and a punitive expeditionary force were sent into Mexico to pursue Villa and his raiders, but they vanished into the Mexican backcountry and never were found. The site of the armed incursion in Columbus now is a 60-acre state park named for Villa. It contains four historic structures from the military outpost (Camp Furlong) — headquarters, customs, recreation, and judge advocate's buildings. The 1902 customs house now is a visitor center for Pancho Villa State Park. It has historical exhibits on Villa, the 1916 raid, and the Pershing expedition.

Pancho Villa State Park, State Hwys. 9 and 11, PO Box 224, Columbus, NM 88029. Phone: 505/531-2711. Fax: 505/531-2115. Web site: *www. emnrd.state.nm.us/nmparks/pages/parks/pancho/pancho.htm*. Hours: open 24 hours. Admission: $4 per private vehicle.

Historic Sites

The Alamo. The Alamo in San Antonio, Texas, is where 189 Texans held out for 13 days in 1836 before losing their lives to a Mexican army of nearly 4,000 under the command of General Antonio López de Santa Anna. Among the defenders who lost their lives were frontiersmen James Bowie and Davy Crockett. The battle inspired the rallying cry "Remember the Alamo" in the Texas fight for independence from Mexico. The heroic stand gave General Sam Houston time to organize his troops and defeat Santa Anna's forces in the Battle of San Jacinto to give birth to the Republic of Texas.

The site that later became San Antonio originally was a Coaluiltecan Indian village. It is where the Franciscan Mission San Antonio de Valero and its protecting fort were built in 1718. The name of the mission was changed to Mission del Alamo del Parras when the Spanish cavalry occupied it in 1803. The mission was established to serve Spanish and Mexican colonists and to Christianize and educate Indians. But the Alamo became a military post when the mission era ended as a result of increased hostility by the Apache and Comanche tribes and inadequate military support.

Americans began to settle in the San Antonio area in the early 1800s, and soon outnumbered Mexicans and became resistant to Mexican rule. In 1835, a provisional government was established in the region by disgruntled American and Mexican colonists, with Houston as the head of the Texan army. A struggle for control of San Antonio followed, resulting in the Battle of the Alamo. The mission site was abandoned by the Mexicans in 1836 and later served as a quartermaster's depot for the U.S. Army. The historic state site has been under the care of the Daughters of the Republic of Texas since 1905.

Each year more than 2.5 million people visit the Alamo complex that still has two of its buildings dating from the mission period and the 1836 battle — the Alamo Church and the Long Barrack. The church has become a shrine to the Alamo battle and the barrack is a museum with a film on the history of the Alamo. Also on the site are the Alamo Gift Museum, with exhibits on Alamo archaeology and Texas history, and a Wall of History, an outdoor exhibit on the Alamo's history.

The Alamo, 300 Alamo Plaza, San Antonio, TX 78205 (mailing address: PO Box 2599, San Antonio, TX 78299). Phone: 210/225–1391. Fax: 210/354–3602. E-mail: *dstewart@thealamo.org.* Web site: *www.thealamo.org.* Hours: 95:30 Mon.-Sat.; 10–5:30 Sun. (open to 7 Fri.-Sat. in June-Aug.); closed Christmas Eve and Day. Admission: free.

Alvarado Adobe. The Alvarado Adobe in San Pablo, California, is the reconstructed early Castro family adobe home which originally was on the site. It later was occupied by California governor Juan Bautiste Alvarado from 1848 to 1882. The house, operated by the city, has a rancho-era bedroom and a Victorian parlor and displays on local history and artifacts of the Ohlone Indians who once lived in the area.

Alvarado Adobe, 13831 San Pablo Ave., San Pablo, CA 94806. Phones: 510/215–3092 and 510/215–7518. Web site: *www.ci.san-pablo.ca.us/main/museums.htm.* Hours: 12–4 Sun.; closed remainder of week. Admission: free.

Casa Adobe de San Rafael. The Casa Adobe San Rafael in Glendale, California, is representative of many early homes of Mexican Americans in California. It now is a museum of early California furniture and artifacts. Guided tours are offered of the house operated by the Glendale Parks and Recreation Division.

Casa Adobe de San Rafael, 1330 Dorothy Dr., Glendale, CA 91202. Phone: 818/548–2000. Fax: 818/548–3789. Hours: June-Aug.—1–4 Sun.; closed Mon.-Sat.; remainder of year—1–4 1st Sun. of month; closed remainder of month. Admission: free.

El Morro National Monument. See Native American Prehistoric Sites and Museums section.

El Paso Museum of Archaeology at Wilderness Park. See Native American Prehistoric Sites and Museums section.

El Pueblo de Los Angeles Historical Monument. The El Pueblo de Los Angeles Historical Monument commemorates the oldest section of Los Angeles, California, near where Spanish and Mexican settlers first established a farming community in 1781 that later became Los Angeles. It consists of 27 historic buildings, ranging from an 1818 adobe dwelling to a 1926 Spanish-style church clustered around a ca. 1825 plaza. Eleven of the structures are open to the public — four of which have been restored as museums.

Museums in the historic neighborhood include the 1818 Avita Adobe, which reflects the Hispanic lifestyle of California in the 1840s; 1858 Masonic Hall, a museum of the Order of Free Masons and Lodge 42; 1884 Old Plaza Firehouse, which displays firefighting equipment and memorabilia from the nineteenth century; and 1887 Sepulveda House (where the visitor's center is located), representing the architectural and social transportation of Los Angeles from purely Mexican traditions to a combination of Mexican and Anglo cultures. Another highlight is the Olvera Street marketplace, where the street is closed to vehicular traffic and features handcrafted Mexican and other products.

El Pueblo de Los Angeles Historical Monument, 125 Paseo de la Plaza, Suite 400, Los Angeles, CA 90012. Phones: 213/628–1274 and 213/680–2525. Fax: 213/485–8238. E-mail: *scheng@mailbox.lacitv. org.* Web site: *www.cityofla.org/elp.* Hours: open 24 hours, with various hours for museums. Admission: free.

Olivas Adobe Historic Park. The restored 1847 two-story adobe hacienda of Raymundo Olivas built in the Monterey style is a monument to the rancho period of California's history at the Olivas Adobe Historic Park in Ventura. Olivas was a cavalryman in the Mexican army who received with Felipe Lorenzana a grant of 4,670 acres for military service. He built the house on their shared ranch, which eventually was purchased and restored by yeast entrepreneur Max Fleischmann.

Upon Fleischmann's death, the building was given to the city of Ventura and opened as a museum in 1972. It contains furnishings of the rancho period, as well as 100-year-old fuchsias and grapevines that can be traced to the days of Father Junípero Serra and the founding of the initial Spanish missions in California in the late eighteenth and early nineteenth centuries. Artifacts from the adobe and rancho eras in Ventura County also are housed in an adjacent building.

Olivas Adobe Historic Park, 4200 Olivas Park Dr., PO Box 99, Ventura, CA 93001. Phone: 805/658–4728. Fax: 805/648–1030. Hours: grounds —10–4 daily; house —10–4 Sat.-Sun; closed Mon.-Fri., New Year's Day, Easter, Thanksgiving, and Christmas. Admission: free.

Pancho Villa State Park. See Museums Honoring Individuals section.

Petaluma Adobe State Historic Park. The 1836 to 1846 adobe house of Mariano Guadalupe Vallejo, the Mexican general who became one of the wealthiest and most influential men in early California, is preserved at the Petaluma Adobe State Historic Park near Petaluma. The huge house, which formed a quadrangle around a central courtyard, was the centerpiece of the cattle ranch which once covered 175,000 acres. The initial grant of land to Vallejo, who was commandant of the presidio in San Francisco, was made by the Mexican government in 1822 to reward him and encourage his leadership in settling the area north of San Francisco Bay. The adobe house has authentic period furniture and interpretive displays and a visitor center describes the ranch activities that took place there.

Petaluma Adobe State Historic Park, 3325 Old Adobe Rd., Sonoma, CA 94952. Phone: 707/762–4871. Web site: *www.parks.sonoma.net.* Hours: 10–5 daily; closed New Year's Day, Thanksgiving, and Christmas. Admission: adults, $3; children 6–12, $2; children under 6, free.

Sanchez Adobe Historic Site. A historic rancho in Pacifica, California — now the Sanchez Adobe Historic Site — was built by Don Francisco Sanchez in 1842 through 1846 and occupied by him from 1839 to 1862. Sanchez was granted two leagues of land (approximately the size of the present-day city of Pacifica) by the governor of Alta California. The living history site, which had been mission land before being confiscated by the Mexican government in 1834, was occupied from prehistoric Indian times until it became a historic landmark in 1953.

Sanchez Adobe Historic Site, 1000 Linda Mar Blvd., Pacifica, CA 94044. Phone and fax: 650/359–1462. Web site: *www.ci.pacifica.ca.us/sanchez.html.* Hour: 10–4 Tues.-Thurs.; 1–5 Sat.-Sun.; closed major holidays. Admission: free.

Santuario de Nuestra Señora de Guadalupe. See Spanish Historic Sites section.

MULTICULTURAL (*also see* Arctic Peoples; Asian; Hispanic; Oceanic Peoples)

Museums and Galleries

Alaska Heritage Museum. See Arctic Peoples Museums and Galleries section.

Alaska Native Heritage Center. See Arctic Peoples Museums and Galleries section.

Bowers Museum. The Bowers Museum in Santa Ana, California, features the traditional arts and historic and cultural objects of North and South American Indian cultures and the peoples of the Pacific Rim, Oceania, Africa, Asia, and Southeast Asia. Since expanding in 1992, the Bowers Museum — formerly the Bowers Museum of Cultural Art — has opened six permanent galleries and presented more than 45 special exhibitions about cultures around the world. It occupies a mission-style building with a bell tower and open courtyard.

Bowers Museum, 2002 N. Main St., Santa Ana, CA 92706. Phone: 714/567–3600. Fax: 714/567–3603. E-mail: *pkeller@bowers.org.* Web site: *www.bowers.org.* Hours: 11–4 Tues.-Sun.; closed Mon., New Year's Day, Independence Day, Thanksgiving, and Christmas. Admission: adults, $17 weekdays, $19 weekends; seniors and students, $12 weekdays, $14 weekends; children under 5, free.

Center for Western Studies. The Center for Western Studies at Augustana College in Sioux Falls, South Dakota, is devoted largely to the history and cultures of the Scandinavians and Northern Plains Indians in the region. It has artifacts, artworks, manuscripts, periodicals, and other materials related especially to the Norwegians, Germans from Russian, and Sioux Indians. The center seeks to preserve, study, and interpret the history and cultures of the northern prairie plains.

Center for Western Studies, Augustana College, Fantle Bldg., 2201 S. Summit Ave., Box 727, Sioux Falls, SD 57197. Phone: 605/274–4007. Fax: 605/274–4999. E-mail: *cws@augie.edu.* Web site: *www.augie.edu/cws.* Hours: 8–12 and 1–5 Mon.-Fri.; 10–2 Sat.; closed Sun. and major holidays. Admission: free.

Craft and Folk Art Museum. Folk, traditional, and contemporary arts, crafts, and design of different cultures are presented at the Craft and Folk Art Museum in Los Angeles, California. The museum tries to expand visitor awareness of the extraordinary range of human experiences embodied in objects made by hand in cultures around the world.

Craft and Folk Art Museum, 5814 Wilshire Blvd., Los Angeles, CA 90036. Phone: 323/937–0708. Fax: 323/937–5576. E-mail: *craftfolkart@yahoo.com.* Web site: *www.cafam.org.* Hours: 11–5 Wed.-Sun.; closed Mon.-Tues. and major holidays. Admission: adults, $3.50; seniors and students, $2.50; children under 13, free; free 1st Wed. of month.

Ellis Island Immigration Museum. See Historic Sites section.

Ethnic Heritage Center. The Ethnic Heritage Center at Southern Connecticut State University in New Haven has special library collections of five different cultures, organized with the assistance of ethnic historic societies. The center collects, preserves, and disseminates historical and cultural materials to celebrate the cultural differences and similarities of the African, Irish, Italian, Jewish, and Ukrainian American ethnic groups. The participating historical societies include the Greater New Haven African-American Historical Society, Connecticut Irish-American Historical Society, Italian-American Historical Society of Connecticut, Jewish Historical Society of Greater New Haven, and Connecticut Ukrainian-American Historical Society.

Ethnic Heritage Center at Southern Connecticut State University, Wintergreen Bldg., Room 117, 501 Crescent St., New Haven, CT 06515. Phone: 203/392–6126. Web site: *www.southernct.edu/departments/ehc/heading.htm.* Hours: 9:30–12:30 Mon. and Wed.; 9:30–2:30 Tues. and Thurs.-Fri.; closed Sat.-Sun. and national holidays. Admission: free.

Ethnic Heritage Museum. The Ethnic Heritage Museum in Rockford, Illinois, is a small facility that presents changing exhibitions related to ethnic cultures and participates in various ethnic festivals and other observances. Its collections include materials related to the first settlers in the area — representing African, Irish, Italian, Latino, Lithuanian, and Polish American cultures.

Ethnic Heritage Museum, 1129 S. Main St., Rockford, IL 61101 (mailing address: PO Box 382, Rockford, IL 61105). Phones: 815/962–7402 and 815/877–2888. Fax: 815/962–7402. E-mail: *efedeli@aol.com.* Hours: Feb.-Dec.— 2–4 Sun and by appointment; closed Jan. and major holidays. Admission: adults, $2; students and children, $1.

Four Rivers Cultural Center and Museum. In tracing the history of eastern Oregon and southwestern Idaho, the Four Rivers Cultural Center and Museum in Ontario, Oregon, emphasizes the role of the Japanese, Basques, Europeans, Hispanics, and Native Americans who settled in the area. The center — named for the four rivers (Snake, Payette, Malheur, and Owyhee) that converge near Ontario — originally was planned as a tribute to the Japanese Americans who were interned during World War II, some of whom settled in the area after the war. But the Japanese Americans convinced museum planners to celebrate all the cultures that flourished in the area. The exhibits now cover the history and cultures of all five ethnic groups.

Four Rivers Cultural Center and Museum, 676 S.W. 5th Ave., Ontario, OR 97914. Phone: 541/889–8191. Fax: 541/889–7628. E-mail: *cfugate@fmtc.com.* Web site: *www.4rcc.com.* Hours: 10–5 Mon.-Sat.; closed Sun. and major holidays. Admission: adults, $4; seniors and children 6–14, $3; children under 6, free.

Frontier Culture Museum of Virginia. The Frontier Culture Museum of Virginia in Staunton is a state-operated outdoor living-history museum that features six exhibits comprising historic farm buildings from Germany, Ireland, Great Britain, and Virginia. The restored structures serve as the setting for interpretation and educational programs designed to show the diverse Old World origins of early immigrants to America, how they lived in their homelands, how they came to this country, and how they created the life together on the American frontier that helped shape the United States.

The buildings include an 1600s farm building from Hördt, Germany; a 1700s farm structure from County Tyrone in Ulster (Northern Ireland), as well as a 1700s Ulster forge; a 1600s farmhouse from the parish of Hartlebury in Worcestershire, England; and an 1800s American farm from Botetourt County in Virginia. The outdoor museum also has the Bowman House, which was built starting in 1773 by or for a naturalized German immigrant in what was then Augusta County. Living-history demonstrations are given of the social and economic lives of the different immigrant groups.

Frontier Culture Museum of Virginia, 1290 Richmond Rd., Staunton, VA 24401. Phone: 540/332–7850. Fax: 540/332–9989. E-mail: *info@fcmv.virginia.gov.* Web site: *www.frontier.virginia.gov.* Hours: mid–Mar.-Nov.— 9–5 daily; remainder of year — 10–4 daily; closed New Year's Day, Thanksgiving, and Christmas. Admission: adults, $10; seniors, $9.50; students over 12, $9; children 6–12, $8; children under 6, free.

Hawaii's Plantation Village. See Hawaiian Museums and Galleries section.

Heritage of the Americas Museum. The historic art and culture of native peoples of the United States are among the displays at the Heritage of the Americas Museum at Cuyamaca College in El Cajon, California. The exhibits, located in the anthropology wing, include the paleo and archaic points of early humans, art of peoples of the past, and beadwork, dance regalia, and other artifacts of the Hopi, Cheyenne, Eskimo, and other cultures. The museum's four wings are devoted to natural history, archaeology, art, and education.

Heritage of the Americas Museum, Cuyamaca College, 1211 Cuyamaca College Dr. West, El Cajon, CA 92019. Phone: 619/670–5194. Fax: 619/670–5198. E-mail: *bud.lueck@gcced.net*. Web site: *www.cuyamaca. net/museum*. Hours: 10–4 Tues.-Fri.; 12–4 Sat.; closed Sun. and major holidays. Admission: adults, $3; seniors, $2; students, $1; children under 12, free.

Historical Society of Pennsylvania (Balch Institute for Ethnic Studies). In 2002, the extensive ethnic and immigrant collections of the Balch Institute for Ethnic Studies in Philadelphia, Pennsylvania, were merged with those of the Historical Society of Pennsylvania, founded in 1824 in Philadelphia. With the Balch addition, the historical society became a major center for the documentation and study of ethnic communities and immigrant experiences from the late nineteenth century to the present.

The Balch collections include numerous artifacts from ethnic groups, such as costumes and accessories, decorative arts and crafts, votive items, manuscripts, photographs, and printed materials. They now are part of the historical society's nearly 20 millions of manuscripts, books, prints, drawings, maps, photographs, and other historical materials.

Historical Society of Pennsylvania, 1300 Locust St., Philadelphia, PA 19107–5699. Phone: 215/732–6200. Fax: 215/732–2680. E-mail: *hsp_lan@hsp.org*. Web site: *www.hsp.org*. Hours: 12:30–5:30 Tues.-Thurs. (also to 8:30 Wed.); 10–5:30 Fri.; closed Sat.-Sun. and national holidays. Admission: adults, $6; students, $3.

Lawrence History Center. The Lawrence History Center, formerly known as the Immigrant City Archives and Museum, in Lawrence, Massachusetts, seeks to preserve the immigrant heritage of the city. It has historic photographs, records, oral histories, and family and individual immigrant items in four 1883 Essex Company buildings where Lawrence was founded. In addition to the city's ethnic heritage, the center has collections pertaining to nineteenth-century engineering, industrialization, labor, health, and social change and economic patterns.

Lawrence History Center, 6 Essex St., Lawrence, MA 01840. Phone: 978/686–9230. Fax: 978/975–2154. E-mail: *pjaysane@lawrencehistorycenter.org*. Web site: *www.lawrencehistorycenter.org*. Hours: 9–4 Tues.-Sat.; closed Sun.-Mon. and major holidays. Admission: adults, $25; seniors, students, and children, $10.

Lower East Side Tenement Museum. The mission of the Lower East Side Tenement Museum, located in one of the nation's most renowned immigrant neighborhoods in New York City, is to further tolerance and historical perspective through the interpretation of immigrant and migrant experiences on Manhattan's Lower East Side. The museum's programs are centered in an 1863 tenement, the first structure of urban, working class, poor, and immigrant peoples preserved in the United States.

Guided tours of the restored apartments at the site interpret the lives of actual residents from different historical periods. The tours of the 1870s Gumpertz family apartment and 1830s Baldizzis flat show the impact of economic depressions; visits to the 1890s Levine and 1910s Rogarshevsky apartments illustrate the neighborhood's connection to the garment industry; and an unrestored apartment demonstrates the impact of the nineteenth-century Reform Movement's campaign to improve housing. Walking tours of the neighborhood also are offered. In addition, the museum has the nation's first archive and collections documenting these immigrant and migrant tenement experiences in an urban environment.

Lower East Side Tenement Museum, 90 Orchard St., New York, NY 10002 (mailing address: 91 Orchard St., New York, NY 10002). Phone: 212/431–0233. Fax: 212/431–0402. E-mail: *lestm@tenement. org*. Web site: *www.tenement.org*. Hours: walking and tenement tours —11–5 Tues.-Sun.; closed Mon. and major holidays. Admission: adults, $12; seniors and students, $10; children under 5, free.

LSU Rural Life Museum. The lifestyles and cultures of pre-industrial Louisiana are featured at the LSU Rural Life Museum, located at Louisiana State University's Burden Research Plantation, an agricultural research experiment station in Baton Rouge. The museum uses its extensive collection of tools, utensils, furniture, farming equipment, and other materials to interpret the rural heritage of Indians, Acadians, French, Spanish, English, German, and African Americans under the 10 flags that have flown over Louisiana.

The museum, which was founded in 1970 by the Burden family, has seven buildings illustrating Louisiana folk architecture (most moved from other locations), a barn with artifacts dealing with everyday life dating from prehistoric times to the early twentieth century, and a working plantation that shows life on a typical nineteenth-century plantation. Among the numerous original structures on the plantation grounds are slave cabins, sick house, blacksmith shop, church, and schoolhouse. Windrush Gardens, with 25 acres of semiformal gardens, also is located at the site.

LSU Rural Life Museum, 4500 Essen Lane, Baton Rouge, LA 70801 (mailing address: PO Box 80498, Baton Rogue, LA 70898). Phone: 225/765–2437. Fax: 225/765–2637. E-mail: *rulife@lsu.edu*. Web site: *www.rurallife.lsu.edu*. Hours: 8:30–5 daily; closed New Year's Day, Easter, Thanksgiving, and Christmas Eve and Day. Admission: adults and children over 11, $5; seniors, $4; children 5–11, $3; children under 5, free.

Mathers Museum of World Cultures. The Mathers Museum of World Cultures at Indiana University in Bloomington has ethnological, historical, and archaeological collections from North America, Latin America, Europe, Africa, Asia, and Oceania. The museum, formerly known as the William Hammond Mathers Museum, has over 20,000 objects and 10,000 photographs in its collections, with the strengths being traditional musical instruments and Native American and Eskimo materials. In addition to using many of these materials in its permanent exhibits, the museum presents changing cultural exhibitions that focus largely on subsistence, ceremonial, and ethnological overviews.

Mathers Museum of World Cultures, Indiana University, 416 N. Indiana Ave., Bloomington, IN 47408 (mailing address: 601 E. 8th St., Bloomington, IN 47408–3812). Phone: 812/855–6873. Fax: 812/855–0205. E-mail: *mathers@indiana.edu*. Web site: *www.indiana.edu/~mathers*. Hours 9–4:30 Tues.-Fri.; 1–4:30 Sat.-Sun.; closed Mon. and national holidays. Admission: free.

Mingei International Museum. The Mingei International Museum in Balboa Park in San Diego, California, seeks to further understanding of the art of all cultures of the world. It has collections of art, dolls, toys, beads, and theater, music, and dance materials, and features changing exhibitions of traditional and contemporary folk art, crafts, and design. The museum also operates a North County satellite museum in Escondido, California. The word "mingei," originally coined by a Japanese scholar, is used in many arts of the world for "arts of the people."

Mingei International Museum, Balboa Park, 1439 El Prado, San Diego, CA 92101 (mailing address: PO Box 553, La Jolla, CA 92038). Phone 619/239–0003. Fax: 619/239–0605. E-mail: *mingei@mingei.org*. Web site: *www.mingei.org*. Hours: 10–4 Tues.-Sun.; closed Mon. and national holidays. Admission: adults, $6; seniors, military, students, and children, 6–17, $3; children under 6, free.

North County branch, 155 W. Grand Ave., Escondido, CA 92025. Phone: 760/735–3355. Fax: 760/735–3306. Hours: 1–4 Tues.-Sat.; closed Sun.-Mon. and national holidays. Admission: adults, $6; seniors, military, students, and children 6–17, $3 children under 6, free.

Museum of Craft and Folk Art. Exhibitions of local and international craft and folk art are presented at the Museum of Craft and Folk Art in San Francisco, California. The museum, which recently moved from the historic Fort Mason Center to the downtown Yerba Buena museum district, features exhibitions of traditional and contemporary folk art and crafts from different cultures around the world that are designed to connect with and inspire diverse communities.

Museum of Craft and Folk Art, 51 Yerba Buena Lane, San Francisco, CA 94103. Phone: 415/227–4888. Fax: 415/227–4351. E-mail: *info@mocfa.org*. Web site: *www.mocfa.org*. Hours: 11–7 Tues.-Fri.; 11–5 Sat.-Sun.; closed Mon. and major holidays. Admission: adults, $5; seniors, $4; children to 18, free.

Museum of International Folk Art. The largest collection of textiles, costumes, ceramics, dolls, toys, and other folk art from around the world can be seen at the Museum of International Folk Art in Santa Fe, New Mexico. The museum, which is part of the Museum of New Mexico system, seeks to promote international goodwill and global understanding through folk arts.

The museum, which has over 130,000 objects from more than 100 countries, features two permanent exhibits — "Multiple Visions: A Common Bond" in the Girard Wing and "Familia y Fe/Family and Faith" in the Hispanic Heritage Wing. The Girard exhibit presents hide paintings, tinwork furniture, jewelry, straw appliqué, horse gear, weavings, and santos, three-dimensional bultos, and painted retablos that span four centuries from the Spanish colonial period to the twentieth century. Changing exhibitions also are offered in the Hispanic gallery of artists representing living artistic traditions from varied Hispanic-Latino cultures.

Rotating exhibitions are presented in two other wings. Materials from the museum's collections and field studies of specific cultures or art forms — such as those from Turkish, Tibetan, and Swedish traditions — are shown in the Bartlett Wing, while textiles, garments, and objects from the museum's exceptional collection are featured in the Neutrogena Wing.

Museum of International Folk Art, Museum Hill at Camino Lejo, Santa Fe, NM 87505 (mailing address: PO Box 2087, Santa Fe, NM 87504–2087). Phones: 505/476–1200 and 505/476–1204. Fax 505/476–1300. E-mail: *info@moifa.org*. Web site: *www.moifa. org*. Hours: 10–5 Tues.-Sun.; closed Mon., New Year's Day, Easter, Thanksgiving, and Christmas. Admission: out-of-state visitors, $7; New Mexico residents, $5; four-day pass to five Santa Fe state museums, $15 per person; seniors and children under 17, free on Wed.; New Mexico residents, free on Sun.

Museum of the Migrating People. The Museum of the Migrating People in the Bronx, New York, contains artifacts, documents, photographs, and memorabilia depicting the immigration experiences of Americans. The museum, which is affiliated with the New York City Board of Education, is housed in the Harry S. Truman High School.

Museum of the Migrating People, Harry S. Truman High School, 750 Baychester Ave., Bronx, NY 10475. Phones: 718/904–5400 and 718/904–6300. Hours: school year — by appointment; closed school holidays and remainder of year. Admission: free.

Museum of Peoples and Cultures. The Museum of Peoples and Cultures at Brigham Young University in Provo, Utah, is a museum of archaeology and ethnology specializing in the native cultures and artifacts of the Great Basin, American Southwest, Mesoamerica, Peru, and Polynesia. It presents changing exhibitions, largely from the more than 40,000 artifacts and 50,000 photographs and slides from the Mormon university's collections of archaeological research materials and artifacts.

Museum of Peoples and Cultures, Brigham Young University, 105 Allen Hall, 700 North 100 East, Provo, UT 84602. Phone: 801/422–0020. Fax: 801/422–0026. E-mail: *mpc_programs@byu.edu*. Web site: *www.fhss.byu/anthro/mpoc/main.htm*. Hours: Jan. 3-June and Aug.-Dec. 22 — 9–5 Mon.-Fri.; closed Sat.-Sun. and major holidays. Admission: free.

Nationality Rooms. The Nationality Rooms at the University of Pittsburgh in Pittsburgh, Pennsylvania, depict the heritages of 28 cultures — and at least four other rooms are under development. The rooms in the 42-story Cathedral of Learning were completed between 1938 and 2000. They serve as expressions of ancestral traditions with varying themes and contents, but usually representing the highly creative periods or aspects of the various heritages. In addition to serving as classrooms, the rooms are used for ethnically oriented exhibitions, tours, lectures, concerts, and social events.

Nationality Rooms, University of Pittsburgh, 1209 Cathedral of Learning, Pittsburgh, PA 15260. Phone: 412/624–6000. E-mail: *natrooms@pitt.edu*. Web site: *www.pitt.edu/~natrooms*. Tour hours: 9–2:30 Mon.-Sat.; 11–2:30 Sun. and holidays; closed New Year's Day, Thanksgiving, and Dec. 24–26. Tour fee: adults, $3; children 8–18, $1; children under 8, free.

Old World Wisconsin. Old World Wisconsin, operated by the State Historical Society of Wisconsin in Eagle, is the largest outdoor museum of rural life in America. It portrays the history of immigration and resettlement in the late nineteenth and early twentieth centuries in the state. The museum, which covers nearly 600 acres, has 67 historic structures built by nineteenth-century immigrants that have been restored and grouped in 10 ethnic farmsteads and an 1870s crossroads village. Among the cultures with farmsteads are Danish, Finnish, German, Norwegian, Polish, and Yankee, as well as an African American area. The museum also has a visitor center and 11 historic gardens with heirloom vegetables and flowers.

The historic structures range from an 1840 Fossebrekke cabin from southern Wisconsin to the 1915 Ketola farmstead from the northern section of the state. Exhibits tell the stories of early settlers from different cultures in pursuit of the American Dream. Interpreters in period costumes are located throughout the open-air museum. Visitors also can participate in such activities as a temperance rally, shake hands with a Progressive-era politician, milk a cow, card and sin wool, make a shingle or milking stool, and play games of the era. The museum has 100 breeds of cattle, sheep, hogs, horses, and chickens on the farmsteads.

Old World Wisconsin, S103 W37890 State Hwy. 67, Eagle, WI 53119. Phone: 262/594–6300. Fax: 262/594–6342. E-mail: *oww@wisconsinhistory.org*. Web site: *www.wisconsinhistory.org/oww*. Hours: July-Labor Day —10–5 Mon.-Sat.; 12–5 Sun.; May-early June and day after Labor Day-Oct.—10–3 Mon.-Fri.; 10–5 Sat.; 12–5 Sun.; early June-remainder of month —10–4 Mon.-Fri.; 10–5 Sat.; 12–5 Sun.; closed remainder of year. Admission: adults, $14; seniors, $12.80; children 5–12, $8.50; children under 5, free; families, $39.

Petterson Museum of Intercultural Art. Exhibits of textiles, costumes, masks, ceramics, bronzes, sculptures, and other folk and fine arts from cultures throughout the world are presented at the Petterson Museum of Intercultural Art at Pilgrim Place, a cultural and religious community for retired church workers founded in Claremont, California, in 1915. The extensive collections of international arts and crafts, grouped into 11 regions of the world, were donated by retiring missionaries, pastors, and others from their services and travels in other coun-

Schottler Farm is one of the nineteenth-century ethnic farms re-created at Old World Wisconsin in Eagle. The multicultural museum, which covers nearly 600 acres, features 10 ethnic farmsteads and 67 historic structures built by Wisconsin immigrants in the 1800s. It is the largest outdoor museum of rural life in America. *Courtesy Old World Wisconsin, State Historical Society of Wisconsin, and photographer Lloyd C. Heath.*

tries. The museum, founded in 1968, is named for Alice Petterson, who initially served as artistic coordinator, and her husband, Richard, noted ceramist and professor of art at Scripps College, for their work and contributions to the museum.

Petterson Museum of International Art, Pilgrim Place, 730 Plymouth Rd., Claremont, CA 91711 (mailing address: 600 Avery Rd., Claremont, CA 91711). Phones: 909/399–5544 and 909/621–9581. Fax: 909/399–5508. E-mail: *cgil@pilgrimplace.org.* Web site: *www.pilgrimplace.org.* Hours: 2–4 Sun. and by appointment; closed Easter, Thanksgiving, and Christmas. Admission: free.

Polynesian Cultural Center. See Hawaiian Museums and Galleries section.

San Diego Museum of Man. The San Diego Museum of Man, housed in the 1915 California Building in San Diego's Balboa Park, focuses on human bio-cultural development, with ethnological and archaeological collections and exhibits on the diverse cultures of the world. It has artifacts and other materials pertaining to peoples of the western Americas; physical anthropology primarily from California, the Southwest, and Peru; and antiquities from Egypt and elsewhere.

San Diego Museum of Man, 1350 El Prado, Balboa Park, San Diego, CA 92101. Phone: 619/239–2001. Fax: 619/239–2749. E-mail: *sphillips@museumofman.org.* Hours: 10–4:30 daily; closed New Year's Day, Thanksgiving, and Christmas. Admission: adults, $6; seniors, $5; children 6–17, $3; children under 6, free.

School of Nations Museum. The School of Nations Museum, founded in 1930 at Principia College in Elsah, Illinois, has Native American and pre–Columbian artifacts, Asian art objects, and collections of decorative arts, textiles, costumes, pottery, and dolls from other regions of the world. The museum features permanent and temporary exhibits and a children's hands-on program.

School of Nations Museum, Principia College, Elsah, IL 62028 (mailing address: 13201 Clayton Rd., St. Louis, MO 63131–1099). Phones: 618/374–5236 and 618/314–2100, Ext. 3073. Faxes: 314/275–3519 and 314/275–3504. Hours: 8–5 Tues.-Wed. and by appointment; closed college holidays. Admission free.

Spurlock Museum. The Spurlock Museum on the Urbana-Champaign campus of the University of Illinois is an ethnically oriented museum of world history and culture (formerly named the World

Heritage Museum). It has six galleries devoted to various cultures — African, American Indian, Asian, Eastern, European, and Mediterranean. They celebrate the diversity of cultures through time and around the world, highlighting such collections as Plains Indian cultural artifacts, cuneiform tablets, Meroviginian jewelry, ancient pottery, and Canelos Quechua ceramics.

Spurlock Museum, University of Illinois at Urbana-Champaign, Lincoln Hall 600 S. Gregory St., Urbana, IL 61801. hone: 217/333–2360. Fax: 217/244–9419. E-mail: *cudiamat@uiuc.edu.* Web site: *www.spurlock.uiuc.edu.* Hours: 12–5 Tues.; 9–5 Wed.-Fri.; 10–4 Sat.; 12–4 Sun.; closed Mon. and university holidays.

UCLA Fowler Museum of Cultural History. The UCLA Fowler Museum of Cultural History at the University of California at Los Angeles explores the art and material culture primarily from Africa, Asia, the Pacific, and the Americas. The museum, established in 1963 to consolidate the various collections of non–Western artifacts on the campus, has more than 150,000 art and ethnographic objects and 600,000 archaeological objects representing prehistoric, historic, and contemporary cultures. They include such items as pre–Columbian ceramic vessels of Peru, Yoruba beaded arts from Nigeria, batik textiles of Indonesia, and papier-mâché sculptures from Mexico.

UCLA Fowler Museum of Cultural History, University of California at Los Angeles, Los Angeles, CA 90024 (mailing address: PO Box 951549, Los Angeles, CA 90095–1549). Phone: 310/825–9672. Fax: 310/206–7007. E-mail: *fowlerws@arts.ucla.edu.* Web site: *www.fowler.ucla.edu.* Hours: 12–5 Wed.-Sun. (also to 8 Thurs.); closed Mon.-Tues. and university holidays. Admission: free.

University of Texas Institute of Texan Cultures. The University of Texas Institute of Texan Cultures in San Antonio is dedicated to furthering understanding of cultural history, science, and technology and their influence upon the people of Texas. The institute first opened at the Texas Pavilion at the 1969 HemisFair and has continued to function as a museum. It now features exhibits on 26 ethnic and cultural groups and has a Back 40 living-history area where visitors can experience the life of early Texans in several buildings that recreate life in historical settings.

The Institute of Texan Cultures seeks to encourage acceptance and appreciation of cultural differences as well as common humanity. It provides a form for diversity and the dynamics between cultural history and scientific discovery. The institute features a multimedia dome show, *Faces and Places of Texas,* and exhibits on topics relating to the mul-ticultural heritage of the state. Interpreters also interact with visitors at such areas as the puppet theater, chuck wagon, textile, and various ethnic areas. The institute also has an oral history program to document Texas history, and presents an annual Texas Folklife Festival in celebration of the state's cultural diversity.

University of Texas Institute of Texan Cultures, 801 S. Bowie St., San Antonio, TX 78205–3296. Phone: 210/458–2300. Fax: 210/458–2205. Email: *jfavor@utsa.edu.* Web site: *www.texancultures.utsa.edu.* Hours: 9–6 Tues.-Sat.; 12–5 Sun.; closed Mon., New Year's Day, Easter, Thanksgiving, and Christmas. Admission: adults, $7; seniors, military, and children 3–12, $4; children under 3, free.

Museums Honoring Individuals

Petterson Museum of Intercultural Art. See Museums and Galleries section.

Historic Sites

Ellis Island Immigration Museum. Between 1892 and 1954, 12 million immigrants were processed through Ellis Island in New York City's lower harbor. Today, exhibits at the Ellis Island Immigration Museum in the old processing center tell the story. The museum is part of the Statue of Liberty National Monument and Ellis Island Immigration Museum complex administered by the National Park Service on two adjacent islands reached by ferry. In addition to exhibits, the museum has collections of historic photographs, art, artifacts, films, and oral histories from the processing period. The Statue of Liberty, a 151-foot copper statue bearing the torch of freedom that was a friendship gift of the people of France in 1886, also has two exhibits on the history of the historic statue.

Ellis Island Immigration Museum, Statue of Liberty National Monument and Ellis Island Immigration Museum, Liberty Island/Ellis Island, NY 10004. Phones: 212/363–3200 and 866/782–8834. Fax: 212/363–6302. E-mail: *stli_info@nps.gov.* Web sites: *www.ellisisland.com* and *www.nps.gov/stli.* Hours: Memorial Day-Labor Day — 8:30–6 daily; remainder of year — 9:30–5 daily; closed Christmas. Admission: free (but time pass required).

Representative Other Museums with Extensive Multicultural Collections and/or Exhibits

American Museum of Natural History. The American Museum of Natural History in New York City has seven cultural halls with artifacts amassed over more than a century. The exhibit halls include the Eastern Woodlands and Plains Indians, Northwest Coast Indians, and halls about African, Asian, Mexican and Central American, Pacific, and South American peoples. The museum, which has an annual attendance of around 4 million, occupies 21 interconnected buildings with more than 40 exhibition halls and over 32 million specimens and cultural artifacts.

American Museum of Natural History, Central Park West at 79th St., New York, NY 10024. Phone: 212/769-5100. Fax: 212/769-5018. E-mail: *communications@amnh.org.* Web site: *www.amnh.org.* Hours: 10–5:45 daily; closed Thanksgiving and Christmas. Admission: adults, $13 suggested donation; seniors and students, $10 suggested donation; children 2–12, $7.50; children under 2, free.

Burke Museum of Natural History and Culture. See Representative Other Museums with Extensive Native American Collections or Exhibits in Native American section.

Haffenreffer Museum of Anthropology. See Representative Other Museums with Extensive Native American Collections or Exhibits in Native American section.

Iron Country Museum. The Heritage Hall at Iron County Museum, an outdoor historical museum in Caspian, Michigan, is devoted to the ethnic heritage of miners, loggers, farmers, and others who immigrated to the area. Ethnic art on the hall's beams reflects some of the 39 pioneer ethnic groups that settled in the county, with the major cultures being Scandinavian, Polish, Italian, and English.

Iron County Museum, 101–02 Museum Rd. (off State Hwy. 189), PO Box 272, Caspian, MI 49915 (mailing address: 233 Bernhardt Rd., Iron River, MI 49915). Phones: 906/265-2617 and 906/265-3942. E-mail: *icmuseum@up.net.* Web site: *www.ironcountymuseum.com.* Hours: June-Aug.–9–5 Mon.-Sat.; 1–5 Sun.; May and Sept.–10–4 Mon.-Sat.; 1–4 Sun.; other times by appointment. Admission: adults, $7; students and children, $2.50.

Maxwell Museum of Anthropology. See Representative Other Museums with Extensive Native American Collections or Exhibits in Native American section.

Milwaukee Public Museum. The European Village, a re-creation of houses and shops in 33 European cultures as they may have appeared in 1875 through 1925, is one of the highlights of the Milwaukee Public Museum in Milwaukee, Wisconsin. The structures in the simulated village are built to scale and furnished with a folk culture theme. They provide a look at the daily life, skills, and traditions of many Europeans who came to the United States at that time. The museum also has collections and exhibits pertaining to other cultures around the world.

Milwaukee Public Museum, 800 W. Wells St., Milwaukee, WI 53233. Phone: 414/278-2700. Fax: 414/278-6100. E-mail: *smedley@mpm.edu.* Web site: *www.mpm.edu.* Hours: 9–5 Mon.-Sat.; 12–5 Sun.; closed Independence Day, Thanksgiving, and Christmas Eve and Day. Admission: adults, $11; seniors, $8; children 3–15, $6; children under 3, free; Milwaukee County residents free on Mon.

National Museum of Natural History. The National Museum of Natural History, a part of the Smithsonian Institution complex of museums on the Mall in Washington, District of Columbia, has more than 2 million cultural artifacts among its collection of over 125 natural science specimens and cultural artifacts.

The National Museum of Natural History is one of the world's leading museums of research, collections, education, and exhibits in the natural history field. The Smithsonian began its extensive collections after being founded in 1846, with many of the specimens and artifacts being part of the natural history museum when it opened in 1910. The museum building now covers 1.5 million square feet — with 325,000 square feet devoted to exhibits and public space. The annual attendance is more than 5.5 million.

National Museum of Natural History, 10th St. and Connecticut Ave., N.W., Washington, DC 20560 (mailing address: PO Box 37012, Smithsonian Institution, Washington, DC 20013-7012. Phone: 202/357-1300. Fax: 202/357-4779. Web site: *www.mnh.si.edu.* Hours: 10–5:30 daily; closed Christmas. Admission: free.

Peabody Museum of Archaeology and Ethnology. See Representative Other Museums with Extensive Native American Collections or Exhibits in Native American section.

Phoebe A. Hearst Museum of Anthropology. See Representative Other Museums with Extensive Native American Collections or Exhibits in Native American section.

University of Pennsylvania Museum of Archaeology and Anthropology. The University of Pennsylvania Museum of Archaeology and Anthropology in Philadelphia has 1.5 million objects in its archaeological and ethnological collections from such regions as the Near East, Egypt, Mediterranean, Americas, Africa, Oceania, Asia, and Europe. It presents 23 major long-term exhibits and has four galleries for changing exhibitions. Some exhibits are devoted to the cultural heritage of ancient Egypt,

A display of a Blackfeet family inside a tepee is among the cultural exhibits at the American Museum of Natural History in New York City. A considerable number of natural history and anthropology museums have exhibits relating to the history and culture of Native Americans. © *American Museum of Natural History.*

Greece, Rome, Mesopotamia, Canaan, Israel, and the Etruscan world. Others are concerned with such cultures as African, Chinese, Southwestern Native American, Alaskan Native Peoples, Polynesian, and Buddhists in India and Southeast Asia.

The Southwest gallery focuses on the culture of four American Indian tribes—Apache, Hopi, Navajo, and Zuñi, while the Alaskan exhibit interprets the traditions of three groups of people—Tlingit, Athapaskan, and Eskimo. The African and Polynesian exhibits look at the history and culture of the cradle of mankind continent and central Pacific region respectively. The China gallery features monumental art.

University of Pennsylvania Museum of Archaeology and Anthropology, 3260 South St., Philadelphia, PA 19104–6324. Phone: 215/898–4000. Fax 215/898–0657. E-mail: *websiters@museum.upenn.edu.* Web site: *www.museum.upenn.edu.* Hours: Memorial Day–Labor Day—10–4:30 Tues.-Sat.; closed Sun.-Mon.; remainder of year—10–4:30 Tues.-Sat.; 1–5 Sun.; closed Mon. and national holidays. Admission: adults, $8; seniors and students, $5; children under 6, free.

NATIVE AMERICAN (*also see* Multicultural)

Museums and Galleries

Abbe Museum in Acadia National Park. The history and culture of Native Americans in Maine are the focus of Abbe Museum in Acadia National Park and its downtown branch in Bar Harbor, Maine. The museum, opened in 1928 by Dr. Robert Abbe as a trailside museum, is one of only two remaining private museums in the national park system.

The museum displays many of its Indian artifacts and other objects from a collection of more than 50,000 objects spanning 10,000 years to the present. The collection includes such stone-based tools as knives, axes, projectile points, and fishing weights; objects shaped from bone, including combs, needles, fish hooks, and harpoons; some of the earliest known styles of pottery in Maine; and more recent beads, copper tools, pipes, jewelry, baskets, and woodcarving. The museum in the park is open only during the summer season, but the newly opened branch in Bar Harbor with a circular gallery called Circle of the Four Directions is operated year-round.

Abbe Museum, Acadia National Park, Sieur de Monts Spring, PO Box 286, Bar Harbor, ME 04609. Phone: 207/288–3519. Fax: 207/288–8979. E-mail: *info@abbemuseum.org*. Web site: *www.abbemuseum. org*. Hours: Memorial Day weekend-mid–Oct.— 9–4 daily; closed remainder of year. Admission: adults, $2; children 6–15, $1; children under 6 and Native Americans, free.

Abbe Museum Downtown, 26 Mount Desert St., PO Box 286, Bar Harbor, ME 04609. Phone: 207/288–3519. Fax: 207/288–8979. E-mail: *info @abbemuseum.org*. Web site: *www.abbemuseum.org*. Hours: Mar.-June and Sept.-Dec.— 9–5 Thurs.; July-Aug.— 9–5 daily; closed Jan.-Feb., New Year's Day, Thanksgiving, and Christmas. Admission: adults, $6; children 6–15, $2; children under 6 and Native Americans, free.

Agua Caliente Cultural Museum. The Agua Caliente Cultural Museum in Palm Springs, California, interprets the history and culture of the Agua Caliente band of Cahuilla Indians and other Cahuilla peoples. It uses artifacts, stories, and photographs to trace the history from prehistoric times to the present. The Agua Caliente and other related bands are believed to have lived in the area for approximately 3,000 years. They were deeded 32,000 acres for a reservation in 1876, of which about 6,700 acres are now within the city limits of Palm Springs. Funds are being raised to build a new, larger museum.

Agua Caliente Cultural Museum, 219 S. Palm Canyon Dr., Palm Springs, CA 92262 (mailing address: 471 E. Tahquitz Canyon Way, Palm Springs, CA 92262). Phone: 760/778–1079. Fax: 760/322–7724. E-mail: *mail@accmuseum.org*. Web site: *www.accmuseum.org*. Hours: Memorial Day-Labor Day—10–5 Fri.-Sat.; 12–5 Sun.; closed Mon.-Thurs.; Sept.-May—10–5 Wed.-Sat.; 12–5 Sun.; closed Mon.-Tues., New Year's Day, Thanksgiving, and Christmas. Admission: free.

Akta Lakota Museum and Cultural Center. The Akta Lakota Museum and Cultural Center at St. Joseph's Indian School in Chamberlain, South Dakota, features artifacts, art, quillwork, beadwork, and other objects related to Lakota culture and heritage in permanent and temporary exhibits. It also has a gallery in which local artists can display and sell their work. Visitors also can see the Our Lady of the Sioux Chapel, which has stained-glass windows depicting the sacred rites of the Lakota and activities of the local Catholic church, which is on the school grounds.

Akta Lakota Museum and Cultural Center, St. Joseph's Indian School, 1301 N. Main St., Chamberlain, SD 57325. Phones: 605/734–3452 and 800/798–3452. Fax: 605/734–3388. E-mail *akta-lakota@stjo.org*. Web site: *www.aktalakota.org*. Hours: Memorial Day-Sept.— 8–6 Mon.-Sat.; 9–5 Sun.; Oct.-May — 8–5 Mon.-Fri.; closed Sat.-Sun. and national holidays. Admission: free.

Akwesasne Museum. The Akwesasne Museum on the St. Regis Mohawk Indian Reservation in Hogansburg, New York has over 3,000 artifacts on display relating to the history and culture of the Mohawks. They include arrowheads, stone implements, pottery fragments, and baskets. The largest collection in the museum is black ash splint basketry, which is representative of the many kinds of decorative and functional baskets made by the Akwesasne. The museum, which is part of the Akwesasne Cultural Center, plays an active role in the continuation of Mohawk culture in the community by offering classes to enable Akwesasne basket makers and other artisans to pass on traditional art forms to the next generation. The cultural center also has a library with more than 28,000 books, including one of the largest Native American collections in the region.

Akwesasne Museum, St. Regis Mohawk Indian Reservation, 321 State Rte. 37, Hogansburg, NY 13655–3114. Phones: 518/358–2240 and 518/358–2461. Fax: 518/358–2649. E-mail: *akwmuse@north-net.org*. Web site: *www.akwesasneculture.org*. Hours: July-Aug.— 8:30–4:30 Mon.-Fri.; closed Sat.-Sun.; Sept.-June — 8:30–4:30 Mon.-Fri.; 11–3 Sat.; closed Sun. and major holidays. Admission: adults, $2; children 5–16, $1; children under 5 and Native Americans, free.

Alaska Heritage Museum. See Arctic Peoples Museums and Galleries section.

Alaska Indian Arts. Totems, dance masks, and other native items are created by Indian carvers using traditional methods at Alaska Indian Arts, a living-history Tlingit village and museum at the site of the former Fort William H. Seward in Haines, Alaska. The carvers work in the former hospital building of the old military fort. Other structures, located at the former parade grounds, include a replica of a tribal house, a trapper's cabin, several caches, and a number of totem poles. Tlingit dance performances also are given at the Chilkat Center for the Arts during the summer in a building that predates the fort.

Alaska Indian Arts, Historic Bldg. 13, Fort William H. Seward, PO Box 271, Haines, AK 99827. Phone: 998/766–2160. Fax: 907/766–2105. E-mail: *mail@ alaskaindianarts.com*. Web site: *www.alaskaindian*

arts.com. Hours: museum — 9–12 and 1–5 Mon.-Fri.; closed Sat.-Sun. and national holidays; dance performances — mid–May–mid–Sept.: 7:30 P.M. Mon.-Thurs. Admission: museum — free; dance performances — adults, $10; students, $5; children under 5, free.

Alaska Native Heritage Center. See Arctic Peoples Museums and Galleries section.

Alutiiq Museum and Archaeological Repository. See Arctic Peoples Museums and Galleries section.

American Indian Heritage Museum. The Powhatan Renape Nation presents a multifaceted look at Native American culture at its American Indian Heritage Museum in Rancocas, New Jersey. The museum is devoted to American Indian history, culture, and traditions with exhibits on the village life of many tribes and a wide variety of artifacts, including tools, clothing, weapons, musical instruments, and decorative arts. It also has a gallery featuring paintings, photography, sculpture, drawings, and woodcarvings of contemporary American Indian artists.

American Indian Heritage Museum, 730 Rancocas Rd., PO Box 225, Rancocas, NJ 08073. Phone: 609/261–4747. E-mail: *powhatan@powhatan.org.* Web site: *www.powhatan.org/museum.html.* Hours: Sept.-June — 10–3 1st and 3rd Sat. and Tues. and Thurs. by appointment; closed remainder of week; July.-Aug. — 10–3 1st and 3rd Sat.; closed remainder of week. Admission: adults, $5; seniors, $4; children under 13, $3.

Amerind Foundation Museum. The Amerind Foundation Museum in Dragoon, Arizona, contains archaeological, ethnographic, historic, and contemporary exhibits of American Indians. It is operated by a nonprofit research institution devoted to the study, preservation, and interpretation of prehistoric and historic Native American cultures. In addition to archaeological objects excavated in the Southwest and Mexico, the museum features examples of beadwork, clothing, ritual masks, weavings, shields, weapons, and other items from Hopi, Navajo, Apache, Plains, Northwest Coast, and other tribes, as well as art on western themes by such artists as William Leigh, Carl Oscar Borg, and Frederic Remington.

Amerind Foundation Museum, 2100 N. Amerind Rd., PO Box 400, Dragoon, AZ 85609. Phone: 520/586–3666. Fax: 520/586–4679. E-mail: *amerind@amerind.org.* Web site: *www.amerind.org.* Hours: 10–4 Tues.-Sun.; closed Mon. and major holidays. Admission: adults, $5; seniors, $4; children 12–18, $3; children under 12, free.

Anishinaubag Intercultural Center. A Plains Indian tepee village, Mandan earth lodge, Ojibwa log roundhouse, and exhibits on the culture of various tribes are part of the Anishinaubag Intercultural Center, located at a Lutheran camp near Belcourt, North Dakota.

Anishinaubag Intercultural Center, BIA Hwy. 7, Belcourt, ND 58316. Phone: 701/477–5519. Hours: varies. Admission: free.

Antelope Valley Indian Museum. The Antelope Valley Indian Museum, which stands against towering rock formations in the Mojave Desert near Lancaster, California, has collections and exhibits relating largely to American Indian cultures of the Great Basin (east and southeast of the Sierra Nevada Mountains). It is housed in an unusual Swiss chalet-style house that contains large granite boulders inside and outside the building.

The structure originally was built by artist Howard Arden Edwards in 1928. He used the upper level as an exhibit area for his collection of prehistoric and historic Indian artifacts. The house later was purchased by anthropology buff Grace Wilcox Oliver, who remodeled and expanded the building and added her own Indian artifacts, opening the house as the Antelope Valley Indian Museum in the early 1940s. The state of California acquired the property and Oliver's collection in 1979 and it became one of the state's regional Indian museums.

Antelope Valley Indian Museum, 15701 E Ave., Lancaster, CA 93535 (mailing address: Mojave Desert Sector, California State Dept. of Parks and Recreation, 43779 15th St. West, Lancaster, CA 93534).- E-mail: *emoore@parks.ca.gov.* Web site: *www.avim. parks.ca.gov.* Hours: Sept.-June–11–4 Sat.-Sun.; other times by appointment. Admission: adults, $4; children under 17, free.

A:shiwi A:wan Museum and Heritage Center. A:shiwi A:wan Museum and Heritage Center at the Zuñi Pueblo in New Mexico features the art, artifacts, photographs, and archives of the tribe. The Zuñi (A:shiwi) are one of the largest pueblos and the only surviving settlement of the Seven Cities of Cibola sought by Spanish explorer Francisco Vásquez de Coronado in his search for gold in 1540 to 1541. The museum and heritage center is considered an eco-museum in harmony with the cultural and environmental values of the Zuñi people. The historic Our Lady of Guadalupe Mission, originally built by Spanish missionaries in 1629 and later destroyed twice before being rebuilt in 1969, also is located at the pueblo.

A:shiwi A:wan Museum and Heritage Center, Zuñi Pueblo, 1222 State Hwy. 53, PO Box 1009, Zuñi, NM 87327–1009. Phone: 505/782–4403. Fax: 505/782–4503. E-mail: *aamhc-museum@yahoo.com.* Web site: *www.ashiwimuseum.org.* Hours: May-early Sept.— 9–5:30 Mon.-Sat.; closed Sun.; Oct.-Apr.—

9–5:30 Mon.-Fri.; closed Sat.-Sun., tribal holidays, New Year's Day, Thanksgiving, and Christmas. Admission: free.

Ataloa Lodge Museum. See Museums Honoring Individuals section.

Barona Cultural Center and Museum. The Barona Cultural Center and Museum in Lakeside, California, is devoted to the preservation and interpretation of San Diego County's Native American culture and history. The cultural center and museum of the Barona band of Mission Indians have more than 2,000 artifacts, some dating back 10,000 years; maps and treaties of ancient tribal territories; and dioramas illustrating such activities as pottery making and stone tool flaking. Among the artifacts on display are coiled baskets, grinding stones, beads, and ceramic objects used in ceremonies.

Barona Cultural Center and Museum, 1095 Barona Rd., Lakeside, CA 92040. Phone: 619/443–6612. Web site: *www.baronamuseum.org*. Hours: 12–5 Tues.-Sun.; closed Mon. and major holidays. Admission: free.

Bishop Paiute-Shoshone Cultural Center. The Bishop Paiute-Shoshone Cultural Center in Bishop, California, has exhibits on Paiute and Shoshone Indian history and culture. The center, which is closed temporarily for renovation, features a reconstructed Paiute camp and displays of native clothing, baskets, tools, shelter, and food sources.

Bishop Paiute-Shoshone Cultural Center, 2301 W. Line St., Bishop, CA 93514. Phones: 760/873–3584 and 760/873–5107. Hours: 9–5 Mon.-Fri.; 10–4 Sat.-Sun.; closed temporarily and major holidays. Admission: free.

Buechel Memorial Lakota Museum. See Museums Honoring Individuals section.

California Indian Museum and Cultural Center. The California Indian Museum and Cultural Center, which has moved from San Francisco's Presidio to Santa Rosa, seeks to portray California Indian history and cultural from an Indian perspective. The museum and cultural center, which now shares a building with the National Indian Justice Center and Intertribal Court of California, tells the story of natural abundance, human conflict, pain and suffering, and rebirth of Native Americans in the state.

California Indian Museum and Cultural Center, 5250 Aero Dr., Santa Rosa, CA 95403.Phone: 707/579–3004. Fax: 707/579–9019. E-mail: *cim andcc@aol.com*. Web site: *www.cimcc.org*. Hours: 9–5 Mon.-Fri.; closed Sat.-Sun. and major holidays. Admission: free.

California State Indian Museum. The California State Indian Museum in Sacramento presents the history, culture, and arts and crafts of Native Americans in the state. The museum, the first state-operated museum devoted to California's first inhabitants, contains artifacts, crafts, and contemporary artwork of the state's American Indians. It also has examples of Indian objects from elsewhere in North America and an Indian demonstration village. Among the items on display are intricately woven baskets, ceremonial dance regalia, sacred objects, headdresses, and native instruments. The museum is part of the California State Department of Parks and Recreation, which also operates a network of regional Indian museums in the state.

California State Indian Museum, 2618 K St., Sacramento, CA 95816. Phone: 916/324–0971. Fax: 916/322–5231. Web site: *www.parks.ca.gov*. Hours: 10–5 daily; closed New Year's Day, Thanksgiving, and Christmas. Admission: adults, $2; children under 17, free.

Center of Southwest Studies. The Center of Southwest Studies at Fort Lewis College in Durango, Colorado, consists of a museum, archive, and research and teaching facility with an emphasis on Native American history and culture in the Four Corners area. It has an interdisciplinary academic program in Southwest history, art, anthropology, archaeology, geology, and other fields. The museum contains Anasazi pottery, Navajo textiles, Zuñi fetishes, kachinas, paintings, and other artifacts and artworks. Its Durango Collection features textiles and weavings representing 800 years of weaving in the Southwest. The center's archive has over 100 special collections of American Indians and other fields in the Southwest.

Center of Southwest Studies, Fort Lewis College, 1000 Rim Dr., Durango, CO 81301. Phone: 970/247–7456. Fax: 970/247–7422. E-mail: *broko_j@fortlewis.edu*. Web site: *http://swcenter.fortlewis.edu*. Hours: museum —1–4 Mon.-Fri. and by appointment; closed Sat.-Sun and state and federal holidays. Admission: free.

Chaw'se Regional Indian Museum and Indian Grinding Rock State Historic Park. See Indian Grinding Rock State Historic Park and Chaw'se Regional Indian Museum in Historic Sites section.

Chehalis Tribal Center. The Chehalis Tribal Center on the Chehalis Indian Reservation along the Chehalis River in Oakville, Washington, contains information about the tribe that refused to sign a treaty or move when assigned to the Quinault Indian Reservation in the 1850s. The tribe got its own 4,224-acre reservation in 1864 with the assistance of an Oakville teacher who helped the Chehalis to homestead land that now is part of the reservation.

Chehalis Tribal Center, Chehalis Indian Reservation, 420 Howanut Rd., Oakville, WA 98568. Phone: 360/273–5911. Hours: 8–4:30 Mon.-Fri.; closed Sat.-Sun. and major holidays. Admission: free.

Cherokee Heritage Center and Cherokee National Museum. The Cherokee Heritage Center in Tahlequah, Oklahoma, consists of the Cherokee National Museum and two historic village reconstructions — Tsa La Gi Ancient Village and Adams Corner Rural Village. The museum is on the site of the 1851 Cherokee Female Seminary that burned in 1887. It is housed in a building that symbolizes a traditional Cherokee dwelling, built low to the ground and illuminated at both ends by natural lighting. It features a permanent exhibit on the Trail of Tears and presents changing exhibitions and two major art shows annually.

The Tsa La Gi Ancient Village shows how a Cherokee community would have looked prior to European contact. It has replicas of 42 traditional homes and meeting houses like those used long before the forced removal of the Cherokees from the Southeast to Indian Territory (now Oklahoma) in 1838 to 1839. Nine restored 1875 to 1890 structures from before Indian Territory became the state of Oklahoma can be seen at Adams Corner Rural Village. A small farm is adjacent to the village, containing cattle, horses, and chickens from breeds originally brought to Indian Territory by the Cherokees. Visits to the villages are included in the museum admission.

Cherokee Heritage Center and Cherokee National Museum, Wills Rd., PO Box 515, Tahlequah, OK 74465. Phone: 918/456–6007. Fax: 918/456–6165. E-mail: *info@cherokeeheritage.org*. Web site: *www.cherokeeheritage.org*. Hours: 10–5 Mon.-Sat.; 1–5 Sun.; closed Christmas. Admission: adults, $8.50; seniors and college students, $7.50; children K-12, $5; children under 5, free.

Chickasaw Council House Museum. The Chickasaw Council House Museum in Tishomingo, Oklahoma, contains the Indian tribe's first council house and a large collection of art, artifacts, and archival materials. The original 1855 to 1858 log Chickasaw Council House, where the tribal constitution was drafted and ratified, now is protected in the museum's first gallery. A second gallery has exhibits on notable Chickasaw individuals, and an art gallery features contemporary Chickasaw painting, sculpture, pottery, and other native arts.

The 1898 granite Chickasaw National Capitol Building, which the tribe was forced to leave to be used as the Johnson County Court House in 1907 when Oklahoma became a state, also is located near the museum. The historic building later was purchased and restored by the Chickasaw. It now has displays on the tribe's history and the building's construction.

Chickasaw Council House Museum, Court House Sq., 102 N. Fisher St., Tishomingo, OK 73460. Phone: 580/371–3351. E-mail: *museum@chickasaw. net*. Web site: *www.chickasaw.net*. Hours: 8–4:30 Tues.-Fri., 10–4:30 Sat.; closed Sun.-Mon. and legal holidays. Admission: free.

Chieftains Museum and Major Ridge Home. See Museums Honoring Individuals section.

Chief Timothy State Park and Alpowai Interpretive Center. See Museums Honoring Individuals section.

Chumash Interpretive Center and Oakbrook Regional Park. The Chumash Interpretive Center, located in a wilderness area of Oakbrook Regional Park in Thousand Oaks, California, features exhibits on Chumash Indian history and culture and interpretations of cave pictographs (painted pictures on rocks) found at the site. A re-created Chumash village, called Little S'pwi, also is outdoors. The exhibits contain artifacts; rock art; replicas of clothing, tools, a tomol canoe; and paintings that depict Chumash Indians in Ventura County prior to European contact. A nature walk to the Chumash village and a cave containing pictographs is offered on Saturdays.

Chumash Interpretive Center, Oakbrook Regional Park, 3290 Lang Ranch Pkwy., Thousand Oaks, CA 91362. Phone: 805/492–8076. Fax: 805/492–7996. E-mail: *chumashcenter@verizon.net*. Web sites: *www.chumashinterpretivecenter.org*. and *www.chumashcenter.org*. Hours: 12–3 Tues.-Fri.; 10–3 Sat. (also 11–3 Sun. in summer); closed Mon. Admission: center — $5 donation; children under 6, free; nature walk — $10 donation; children under 6, free.

Citizen Potawatomi National Tribal Museum. The Citizen Potawatomi National Tribal Museum in Shawnee, Oklahoma, preserves and interprets artifacts relevant to the indigenous cultures of the Great Lakes region, with the emphasis on the Anishinabe Potawatomi. The museum seeks to further understanding of the tribe's history, heritage, values, art, philosophy, crafts, medicines, language, and societal structure. It recently moved into a new facility in the Cultural Heritage Center, with permanent exhibits on the tribe's history and culture and changing exhibitions on thematic subjects, such as everyday textiles and how they have changed over the years.

Citizen Potawatomi Nation Tribal Museum, Cultural Heritage Center, 1601 S. Gordon Cooper Dr., Shawnee, OK 74801. Phones: 405/275–3121 and 800/880–9880. E-mail: *estewart@potawatomi. org*. Web site: *www.potawatomi.org*. Hours: 8–5 Mon.-Sat.; closed Sun. and major holidays. Admission: free.

Colorado River Indian Tribes Museum. The Colorado River Indian Tribes Museum, located at the tribal government complex on the reservation near Parker, Arizona, traces the history and culture of American Indian tribes along the lower Colorado River. It is devoted largely to the Mohave and Chemehuivi tribes, but also has exhibits pertaining to other past and present cultures — Navajo, Hopi, Anasazi, Hohokam, and Patayan. Nearby sights include the 1917 Mohave Presbyterian Mission, 1860 La Paz territorial mining town, and Memorial Monument marking the site of the 1942 through 1945 Japanese War Relocation Center.

Colorado River Indian Tribes Museum, Rte 1, Box 23-B, Parker, AZ 85344. Fax: 928/660–5675. Web site: *www.crittourism.rraz.net*. Hours: 8–5 Mon.-Fri.; closed Sat.-Sun. and major holidays. Admission: free.

Colter Bay Indian Arts Museum. The Colter Bay Indian Arts Museum, which also serves as a visitor center for Grand Teton National Park in Colter Bay Village, Wyoming, displays 1875 through 1900 American Indian artifacts from the David T. Vernon Collection.

Colter Bay Indian Arts Museum, Grand Teton National Park, Colter Bay Village, WY 83012 (mailing address: PO Drawer 170, Moose, WY 83012). Phones: 307/739–3594 and 307/739–3399. Fax: 307/739–3504. E-mail: *alice_hart@nps.gov/grte*. Web site: *www.nps.gov*. Hours: mid–May-early June and Sept. after Labor Day — 8–5 daily; early June-Labor Day — 8–8 daily; closed remainder of year. Admission: free.

Colville Confederated Tribes Museum. The Colville Confederated Tribes Museum on the Colville Indian Reservation at Coulee Dam, Washington, tells of the history and arts of the confederated tribes — Moses-Columbia, Wenatchee, Okanogan, Entiat-Chelan, Methow, Nez Percé, Palus, Nespelem, Colville, San Poil, and Lake. The museum has displays of historic photographs, basketry, beadwork, clothing, and tools from the area, as well as a diorama showing traditional salmon fishing, a mounted buffalo, artworks by tribal artists, and two murals depicting the Nez Percé Trail and Kettle Falls before it was submerged by Coulee Dam.

Colville Confederated Tribes Museum, Colville Indian Reservation, 512 Mead Way, Coulee Dam, WA 99116. Phone: 509/633–0751. Fax: 509/633–2320. Hours: Apr.-Dec.—10–6 Mon.-Sat.; closed Sun. and Dec. 31-Mar. Admission: donation.

Coos Tribal Hall. The Confederated Tribes of Coos, Lower Umpqua, and Siuslaw have a small exhibit on their history in the Coos Tribal Hall in Coos Bay, Oregon.

Coos Tribal Hall, Confederated Tribes of Coos, Lower Umpqua, and Siuslaw, 338 Wallace St., Coos Bay, OR 97420. Phones: 541/888–3536 and 541/888–9577. Web site: *www.ctclusi.org*. Hours: 8–5 Mon.-Fri.; closed Sat.-Sun. and national holidays. Admission: free.

Cortez Cultural Center. The Cortez Cultural Center, housed in a historic 1909 adobe building in Cortez, Colorado, contains interpretive exhibits on the archaeology and culture of American Indians, with the emphasis on the Basketmaker and Pueblo periods of the Ancestral Puebloan peoples (Anasazi). The center, which was created in 1987 to promote intercultural understanding, also has displays on the nearby Ute Mountain Ute, Pueblo, and Navajo tribes and early Southwest pioneers. In addition, traveling exhibitions and showings of local artists are presented.

A mural on the back of the building depicts a traditional pueblo, and American Indian dances are performed on the adjoining plaza Monday through Saturday evenings during the summer. Following the dances, talks are given by storytellers, historians, and artists about Indian cultures. A farmer's market also is held at the center every Saturday morning during the summer and fall, and weekly lectures, slide shows, and music programs are offered from September through May.

Cortez Cultural Center, 25 N. Market St., Cortez, CO 81321. Phone: 970/565–1151. Fax: 970/565–4075. E-mail: *cultural@fone.net*. Web site: *www. cortezculturalcenter.org*. Hours: Memorial Day-Labor Day —10–10 Mon.-Sat.; closed Sun.; remainder of year —10–5 Mon.-Sat.; closed Sun., New Year's Day, Thanksgiving, and Christmas. Admission: free.

Creek Council House Museum. The Creek Council House Museum in Okmulgee, Oklahoma, contains artifacts and other materials that trace the history of the Creek people (also known as Muscogee) from Georgia and Alabama to Oklahoma. The museum is located in the 1878 Creek Council House that originally served as the capitol of the Muscogee Nation and housed the executive and judicial branches of government.

Creek Council House Museum, 106 S. 6th St., Okmulgee, OK 74119. Phone: 918/756–2324. Fax: 918/756–3671. E-mail: *creekmuseum@scglobal.net*. Web site: *http://creekcouncilhouse.com*. Hours: 10–4:30 Tues-Sat.; closed Sun.-Mon. and legal holidays. Admission: free, but charges for special exhibitions.

Crow's Shadow Institute of the Arts Gallery. The Crow's Shadow Institute of the Arts, housed in the historic St. Andrew's Mission schoolhouse in Pendleton, Oregon, has a gallery that presents changing art exhibitions from the institute's collections and the works of local, visiting, and other artists. One of the American Indian arts center's recent highlights was "Dog Head Stew Portfolio," an international portfolio exchange which celebrates Native American traditions and cultural persistence with works that honor or criticize past and present representations of American Indian culture. The Crow's Shadow Institute was founded by prominent Umatilla landscape painter James Lavadour; his wife, JoAnn; and other Umatilla tribal members to assist Native American artists in rural eastern Washington and Oregon.

Crow's Shadow Institute of the Arts Gallery, St. Andrew's Church schoolhouse, 48004 St. Andrew's Rd., Pendleton, OR 97801. Phone: 541/276–3954. Fax: 541/276–3397. E-mail: *crow@crowsshadow.org*. Web site: *www.crowsshadow.org*. Hours: 8–5 Mon.-Fri., but may vary with events; closed Sat.-Sun. and major holidays. Admission: free.

Cupa Cultural Center Museum. The history, culture, and traditions of the Cupeño and Luiseño Indians are presented at the Cupa Cultural Center on the Pala Indian Reservation in Pala, California. The center has artifacts and historical photographs relating to the food, clothing, religion, and other aspects of tribal life, as well as historical information on the removal of the Cupeños from Cupa (now Warner's Hot Springs) and Wilakalpa to the Luiseño town of Pala in 1903. The Pala Reservation now is the only California Indian reservation with an active mission, Mission San Antonio de Pala.

Cupa Cultural Center Museum, Pala Indian Reservation, Pala Temecula Rd., PO Box 445, Pala CA 92059. Phone: 760/742–1590. Fax: 760/742–4543. E-mail: *lmir635565@aol.com*. Hours: 8–4:30 Mon.-Fri.; Sat.-Sun. by appointment; closed major holidays. Admission: free.

Curtis Hill Indian Museum. More than 20,000 arrowheads, 500 axes, and a wide assortment of Indian pipes, pottery, beadwork, and weapons are featured at the Curtis Hill Indian Museum in Swisher, Iowa. It represents the collection of George Zalesky, who has been collecting Native American artifacts and other materials for more than 50 years.

Curtis Hill Indian Museum, 1612 N.E. Curtis Bridge Rd., Swisher, IA 57338. Phone: 319/848–4323. Hours: by appointment. Admission: donation.

Daybreak Star Arts Center and Sacred Circle Gallery of American Indian Art. The Sacred Circle Gallery of American Indian Art at the Day-break Star Arts Center in Discovery Park in Seattle, Washington, presents changing exhibitions of Native American art from its collections and individual and group showings of contemporary art by artists in residence and others. The arts center, operated by the United Indians of All Tribes Foundation, provides educational, human, social, and cultural programs to Native Americans in the area.

The center resulted from the 1970 occupation of nearby Fort Lawton, an active military post that was declared surplus, by protesting Native Americans who wanted the site to become a facility to serve Indians in the area. The United Indians of All Tribes Foundation, which was formed in the process, was granted 20 acres in Discovery Park for a cultural center and its efforts to improve the spiritual, social, economic, educational, and cultural needs of Native Americans in the community.

Among the cultural center's many activities are the Daybreak Star Arts Center and its Sacred Circle Gallery; an annual July powwow with over 400 dancers, 25 drum groups, and more than 60 arts and crafts booths in connection with Seattle's annual Seafair celebration; and a seasonal Indian Art Market for the sale of arts and crafts every second Saturday of the month from October through March and every Saturday in December.

Sacred Circle Gallery of American Indian Art, Daybreak Star Arts Center, Discovery Park, 3801 W. Government Way, PO 99100, Seattle, WA 98199–1014. Phone: 206/285–4425. Fax: 206/282–3640. E-mail: *info@unitedindians.com*. Web site: *www.unitedindians.com*. Hours: 10–5 Tues.-Sat.; 12–5 Sun; closed Mon. and major holidays. Admission: free.

Eiteljorg Museum of American Indians and Western Art. The Eiteljorg Museum of American Indians and Western Art in Indianapolis, Indiana, seeks to further appreciation and understanding of the art, history, and cultures of the indigenous peoples of North America and the American West. It has comprehensive collections of Native American and western art, featuring traditional and contemporary works by such artists as T. C. Cannon, Allan Houser, Georgia O'Keeffe, Frederic Remington, Charles Russell, N. C. Wyeth, and Kay Walkingstick.

The museum's Mihtohseenionki (The People's Place) Gallery features rare objects, art, historical photographs, and interactive displays and audiovisuals about Indiana's three indigenous peoples (Delaware, Miami, and Potawatomi). Other galleries contain art and artifacts of other Indian tribes from across the nation, including pottery, basketry, woodcarvings, beadwork, and clothing. An education center enables visitors to explore Native American and western culture through demonstrations, workshops, and other hands-on activities.

Eiteljorg Museum of American Indians and Western Art, 500 W. Washington St., Indianapolis, IN 46204. Phone: 317/636–9378. Fax: 317/264–1724. E-mail: *museum@eiteljorg.org.* Web site: *www.eiteljorg.org.* Hours: Memorial Day-Labor Day —10–5 Mon.-Sat.; 12–5 Sun.; remainder of year—10–5 Tues.-Sat.; 12–5 Sun.; closed Mon., New Year's Day, Thanksgiving, and Christmas. Admission: adults, $7; seniors, $6; students and children 5–17, $4; children under 5, free.

Five Civilized Tribes Museum. The Five Civilized Tribes Museum, housed in the 1875 Union Indian Agency Building in Muskogee, Oklahoma, features the history, arts, and crafts of five tribes — Cherokee, Chickasaw, Choctaw, Creek, and Seminole. Traditional American Indian paintings and sculptures on tribal subjects are among the exhibits.

Five Civilized Tribes Museum, 1101 Honor Heights Dr., Muskogee, OK 74401. Phones: 918/683–1701 and 877/587–4237. Fax: 918/683–3070. E-mail: *the5tribes@azalea.net.* Web site: *www.fivetribes.org.* Hours 10–5 Mon.-Sat.; 1–5 Sun.; closed New Year's Day, Thanksgiving, and Christmas. Admission: adults, $3; seniors, $2; students, $1.50; children under 6, free.

Flathead Indian Museum. Arts, crafts, and artifacts, primarily from the Flathead and Kootenai tribes, are shown at the Flathead Indian Museum on the Flathead Indian Reservation in St. Ignatius, Montana. Representative materials from major tribes across the nation also are displayed. Among the exhibits are jewelry, rugs, clothing, pottery, and tools from the 1800s; historic photographs, and such mounted animals as a white buffalo, coyotes, and bears. A trading post also is located at the site.

Flathead Indian Museum, 1 Museum Lane, 32621 U.S. Hwy. 93, PO Box 460, St. Ignatius, MT 59865. Phone: 406/745–2951. Fax: 406/745–2961. E-mail: *jeanine@allardauctions.com.* Hours: Apr.-Sept.— 9–8 daily; remainder of year—9–5 daily. Admission: free.

Fort Yuma Quechan Indian Museum. The Quechan tribe operates the Fort Yuma Quechan Indian Museum on the former site of a military post on its reservation along the Colorado River near Winterhaven, California. It is housed in an 1855 building dating from Camp Yuma, which became Fort Yuma in 1861. The museum, devoted to the history and culture of the tribe and the early Spanish and military eras, contains clay figures, flutes, gourd rattles, headdresses, bows and arrows, war clubs, pottery, clothing, cradles, and historic photographs. Also nearby is the 1922 St. Thomas Mission, which occupies the former site of the Concepcion Mission, where Father Francisco Gares was killed in the 1781 Quechan Revolt against Spanish rule.

Fort Yuma Quechan Museum, 350 Picacho Rd., Winterhaven, CA 92283–9769 (mailing address: PO Box 1899, Yuma, AZ 85366–9352). Phone: 760/ 572–0661. Fax: 760/572–2102. Hours: 8–5 Mon.-Fri.; 1–4 Sat.; closed Sun., New Year's Day, Easter, and Christmas. Admission: adults and children over 11, $1; children under 12, free.

Frisco Native American Museum and Natural History Center. The Frisco Native American Museum and Natural History Center in Frisco, North Carolina — on Hatteras Island on the Outer Banks of the state — contains exhibits of American Indian artifacts, art, and culture, and natural history materials from the area. The museum, founded in 1986 to preserve and interpret the island's Indian history, features the artifacts and arts of the Algonquians, the first inhabitants of Hatteras Island, but also contains materials from other tribes throughout North America. The collection includes a dug-out canoe found on the museum's property and artifacts discovered at the site of East Carolina University's archaeological dig at Buxton Village.

Frisco Native American Museum and Natural History Center, 53536 Hwy. 12, PO Box 399, Frisco, NC 27936. Phone: 252/995–4440. Fax: 252/995–4030. E-mail: *admin@nativeamericanmuseum.org.* Web site: *www.nativeamericanmuseum.org.* Hours: 11–5 Tues.-Sun.; Mon. by appointment; closed Thanksgiving and Christmas. Admission: $5 per person; seniors, $3; families, $15.

Gallup Cultural Center. Twenty-five historical dioramas, Native American artifacts, and historic and contemporary artworks can be seen at the Gallup Cultural Center in Gallup, New Mexico. The center, a project of the Southwest Indian Foundation, is housed in the historic Santa Fe Railway depot in Gallup, main trading center for the Navajo, Zuñi, and other tribes in the region. During the summer, the city of Gallup presents nightly Indian dances adjacent to the center.

Gallup Cultural Center, 201 E. U.S. Hwy. 66, Gallup, NM 87301. Phone: 505/863–4131. Fax: 505/863–6698. Hours: Memorial Day-Labor Day — 9–4 Mon.-Sat.; closed Sun.; remainder of year — 9–4 Mon.-Fri.; closed Sat.-Sun. and major holidays. Admission: free.

George W. Brown, Jr., Ojibwe Museum and Cultural Center. See Museums Honoring Individuals section.

Grand Ronde Tribal Center. Traditional baskets, trade beads, a mortar and pestle for grinding camas lily bulbs, and historical photographs are among the artifacts and arts and crafts displayed at the Grand Ronde Tribal Center in Grand Ronde, Oregon. The Confederated Tribes of Grand Ronde also have a Veterans Memorial honoring tribal members who served in the armed services. The Grand Ronde Indian Reservation is home to the Umpqua, Molalla, Rouge River, Kalpuya, and Chasta tribes.

Grand Ronde Tribal Center, Confederated Tribes of Grand Ronde, 9615 Grand Ronde Rd., Grand Ronde, OR 97347. Phones: 503/879–5211 and 800/422–0232. Fax: 503/879–2117. E-mail *info@grandronde.org*. Web site: *www.grandronde.org*. Hours: 8–5 Mon.-Fri.; closed Sat.-Sun. and major holidays. Admission: free.

Haskell Indian Nations University Cultural Center and Museum. The Haskell Indian Nations University in Lawrence, Kansas, has a cultural center and museum with interpretive exhibits on the history and museum collections of Haskell — the only government boarding school that evolved into a four-year university for Native Americans. Haskell began as an Indian industrial training school in 1884 and became an inter-tribal university in 1993. It now enrolls about 1,000 students from 150 tribes.

In addition to tracing Haskell's history, the museum displays collections of traditional clothing, jewelry, basketry, pottery, beadwork, and other artifacts, as well as artworks from such artists as Don Secondine, Alan Houser, Franklin Gritts, and Dick West. They are supplemented with historical materials from the university's archives, which include the Frank R. Rinehart Historical Photograph Collection.

Haskell Indian Nations University Cultural Center and Museum, 155 Indian Ave., PO Box 5013, Lawrence, KS 66046. Phone: 785/832–6686. Fax: 785/832–6687. E-mail: *csatpauhoodle@haskell.edu*. Web site: *www.haskell.edu*. Hours: 9:30–5 Mon.-Fri.; closed Sat.-Sun. and national holidays. Admission: free.

Hauberg Indian Museum and Black Hawk State Historic Site. See Black Hawk State Historic Site and Hauberg Indian Museum in Museums Honoring Individuals section.

Heard Museum. One of the nation's richest collections of artifacts and arts of Native Americans in the southwest can be found at the Heard Museum in Phoenix, Arizona. It has more than 35,000 traditional and contemporary objects in its newly expanded 130,000-square-foot facility, which is eight times the size of the original 1929 building. The artifacts and arts, which range from prehistoric days to the present, are largely displayed in 10 galleries and outdoor courtyards. Others are shown at two branch museums — Heard Museum North in Scottsdale and Heard Museum West in Surprise, Arizona.

The museum was founded by Dwight and Maie Heard, who wanted to share their extensive Southwest collections with the public. The holdings were enhanced with such acquisitions as Senator Barry Goldwater's Kachina Doll Collection, Read Mullan Collection of Contemporary Navajo Rugs, C. G. Wallace Jewelry Collection, Fred Harvey Indian Art Collection, and artifacts and arts and crafts from Indian tribes. The museum also has been a leader in encouraging and collecting the paintings, sculpture, and graphics of contemporary Native American artists.

Among the museum's galleries are Native Peoples of the Southwest, with baskets, jewelry, pottery, textiles, and a Navajo hogan, Apache wickiup, and Hopi corn-grinding room; Katsina Doll Gallery, with hundreds of hand-carved Hopi katsina dolls; and two galleries devoted to traditional and contemporary art. The Heard Museum also resents three major festivals annually — Guild Indian Fair and Market, featuring nearly 500 Native American artists; World Championship Hoop Dance Contest, a competition of American and Canadian native dancers; and Festival for Children and Spanish Market, which includes children's crafts, Spanish-oriented items, and other activities.

Heard Museum, 2301 N. Central Ave., Phoenix, AZ 85004–1323. Phones: 602/252–8848 and 602/252–8840. Fax: 602/252–9757. E-mail: *jmeyers@heard.org*. Web site: *www.heard.org*. Hours: 9:30–5 daily closed major holidays. Admission: adults, $10; seniors, $9; students, $5; children 6–12, $3; children under 6, free.

Heard Museum North, 34505 N. Scottsdale Rd., Box 22, Scottsdale, AZ 85262. Phone: 480/488–9817. Hours: 10–5:30 Mon.-Sat.; 12–5 Sun.; closed major holidays. Admission: adults, $3; children under 13, free.

Heard Museum West, 16126 N. Civic Center Plaza, Surprise, AZ 85374. Phone: 623/344–2200. Hours: 9:30–5 Tues.-Sun.; closed Mon. and major holidays. Admission: adults, $5; seniors, $4; children 6–12, $2; children under 6, free.

The Heritage Center. Collections of Lakota tribal arts and Native American fine art are displayed at the Heritage Center of Red Cloud Indian School on the Pine Ridge Indian Reservation in Pine Ridge, South Dakota. Among the works are paintings, star quilts, beadwork, quills, pottery, and prints. The museum is housed in the ca. 1888 Holy Rosary Mission, scene of a battle the day after the Wounded Knee Massacre (see separate listing in Historic Sites section). The school was founded in 1888 by the Jesuits and Franciscan Sisters.

The Heritage Center, Red Cloud Indian School, 100 Mission Dr., Pine Ridge, SD 57770. Phone: 605/867–5491. Fax: 605/867–1209. E-mail: *csi mon@redcloudschool.org.* Web site: *www.redcloudin-dianschool.org.* Hours: 8–6 Mon.-Fri.; 9–5 Sat.-Sun.; closed major holidays. Admission: free.

Hoopa Tribal Museum. The Hoopa Tribal Museum on the Hoopa Valley Indian Reservation in Hoopa, California, was created to preserve and share the history and culture of the native people of northern California. It displays the local Indian basketry, ceremonial regalia, redwood dug-out canoes, tools, implements, and other artifacts and objects of the Hupa, Yurok, and Karuk tribes. Guided tours are offered of the museum and historical sites in the valley.

Hoopa Tribal Museum, Hoopa Valley Indian Reservation, Hwy. 96, PO Box 1348, Hoopa, CA 95546–1348. Phone: 530/625–4110. Fax: 530/625–1693. E-mail: *hvtmus@pcweb.net.* Web site: *www.-hoopa-nsn.gov.* Hours: 8–5 Tues.-Fri. (also 10–4 Sat. only during summer); closed Sun. and major holidays. Admission: donation.

Hopi Cultural Center. The Hopi Cultural Center on the Hopi Indian Reservation in Second Mesa, Arizona, interprets the traditions, life, and arts and crafts of the Hopi people. Murals, jewelry, basketry, pottery, weaving, and kachina dolls of the Hopi are displayed in permanent exhibits at the center. Other aspects of Hopi culture are presented in changing exhibitions. Second Mesa is one of 12 traditional villages originally built on three major mesas as protection from other marauding tribes.

Hopi Cultural Center, Hopi Indian Reservation, State Hwy. 264, PO Box 67, Second Mesa, AZ 86043. Phone: 928/734–2401. Fax: 928/734–6651. E-mail: *info@hopiculturalcenter.com.* Web site: *www.hopicul-turalcenter.com.* Hours: May-late Oct.— 8–5 Mon.-Fri.; 9–3 Sat.-Sun.; remainder of year — 8–5 Mon.-Fri.; closed Sat.-Sun. and major holidays. Admission: adults, $3; children under 14, $1.

Indian Arts and Crafts Board. The Indian Arts and Crafts Board, a federal agency in the U.S. Department of the Interior, operates three regional Native American museums in its efforts to promote the economic development of American Indians and Alaska Natives under the Indian Arts and Crafts Act. The board provides promotional opportunities and general business advice to Native American artists, craftspeople, businesses, museums, and cultural centers of federally recognized tribes, and has collections of American Indian and Alaska Native arts and crafts. The three agency museums are the Sioux Indian Museum, Rapid City, South Dakota; Museum of the Plains Indians, Browning, Montana; and Southern Plains Indian Museum, Anadarko, Oklahoma (see separate listings), where Indian arts and crafts are sold.

Indian Arts and Crafts Board. U.S. Dept. of Interior, 1849 C St., N.W., MS 20058-MIB, Washington, DC 20240. Phones: 202/208–3773 and 888/278–1253. Fax: 202/208–5196. E-mail: *iacb@ios.doi.giv.* Web site: *www.doi.gov/iacb.* Hours: 7:45–4:15 Mon.-Fri.; closed Sat.-Sun. and national holidays. Admission: free.

Indian Arts Research Center and School of American Research. More than 10,000 Southwest Indian paintings, textiles, baskets, pottery, jewelry, and other ethnographic and artistic materials are in the collections of the School of American Research's Indian Arts Research Center, a center for advanced study in Santa Fe, New Mexico. The arts and artifacts are stored in two climate-controlled vaults, but the center displays some of the historic and contemporary Pueblo, Navajo, and other Native American objects in an open storage area for study by scholars, artists, and students. A public tour by reservation is offered every Friday.

Indian Arts Research Center, School of American Research, 660 Garcia St., Santa Fe, NM 87505 (mailing address: PO Box 2188, Santa Fe, NM 87504). Phones: 505/945–7205 and 505/954–7200. Fax: 505/954–7207. E-mail: *iarc@sarsf.org.* Web site: *www.sarweb.org.* Hours: 8–5 Mon.-Fri. by appointment (with public tours by reservation at 2 Fri.); closed Sat.-Sun. and major holidays. Admission: adults, $15.

Indian City U.S.A. The daily lives, cultures, and religions of seven American Indian tribes are depicted in partial replicas of Indian villages at Indian City U.S.A. in Anadarko, Oklahoma. Tours conducted by tribal members take visitors through the reconstructed villages of the Caddo, Chiricahua Apache, Kiowa (winter camp), Navajo, Pawnee, Pueblo, and Wichita. The outdoor museum is located at the site of the 1862 massacre of the Tonkawa Indians by a band of Shawnees and other mercenaries during the Civil War.

The tools, cradles, cook utensils, weapons, musical instruments, toys, and games of different tribes are displayed in the villages. During the summer, Indian dances often are performed as part of the tours. Such animals as buffalo, fallow deer, wild turkey, black buck antelope, emus, and llamas also can be seen in an adjoining 140-acre game pasture.

Indian City U.S.A., State Hwy. 8, PO Box 695, Anadarko, OK 73005. Phones: 405/247–5661 and 800/433–5661. Fax: 405/247–5661. E-mail: info@*indiancityusa.com.* Web site: *www.indiancityusa.com.* Hours: 9–5 daily; closed New Year's Day, Thanksgiving, and Christmas. Guided tours: adults, $8.50; children 6–11, $4; children under 6, free.

Indian Museum of Lake County, Ohio. The Indian Museum of Lake County, Ohio, which has operated since 1980 on the Lake Erie College campus in Painesville, moved to the Technical Center in Willoughby, Ohio, in 2006. The museum, operated by the Lake County Chapter of the Archaeological Society of Ohio, contains artifacts and other materials pertaining to American Indians in northeastern Ohio and arts and crafts of Native Americans throughout the nation. The museum has over 26,000 prehistoric artifacts from 10,000 B.C. to A.D. 1650 and Indian arts and crafts from 1800 to 2005.

Indian Museum of Lake County, Ohio, Technical Center, Bldg. B, Door 3, 25 Public Sq., PO Box 883, Willoughby, OH 44096–0883. Phone: 440/951–3813. Web site: *www.indianmuseumoflakecounty.org.* Hours: Sept.-Apr.— 9–4 Mon.-Fri.; 1–4 Sat.-Sun.; remainder of year—10–4 Mon.-Fri.; 1–4 Sat.-Sun.; closed major holidays and holiday weekends. Admission: adults, $2; seniors, $1.50; children K-12, $1; children under 5, free.

Indian Museum of North America and Native American Educational and Cultural Center at Crazy Horse Memorial. The Indian Museum of North America at Crazy Horse Memorial in South Dakota contains an expanding collection of Native American artifacts and arts. The Crazy Horse Memorial (see separate listing) also is home to the Native American Educational and Cultural Center, where many Native American arts and crafts people create their artworks and visit with guests in the nearby cultural center building during the summer season.

Among the museum's features are a collection of ceremonial dress and related items; an exhibit of paintings by Andrew Standing Soldier and Hobart Keith of American Indian life in the late nineteenth and early twentieth centuries; a collection of photographs taken during the same period by J. H. Grabill and other photographers; and an exhibit of 63 tribal flags. In addition, the educational and cultural center displays historical photographs of Native Americans taken by Edward S. Curtis at the end of the nineteenth century and the wheel-turned pottery of Robert Big Elk. The memorial's Orientation and Communication Center also exhibits the paintings of Paul War Cloud and has other Indian displays.

Indian Museum of North America and Native American Educational and Cultural Center, Crazy Horse Memorial, Ave. of the Chiefs, Crazy Horse, SD 57730–9506. Phone 605/573–4681. Fax: 605/673–2185. E-mail: *memorial@crazyhorse.org.* Web site *www.crazyhorse.org.* Hours: Memorial Day weekend-mid–Oct.— 7–9 daily (closes after nightly laser light multimedia show); remainder of year — 8–4:30 daily;

closed Christmas. Admission (to memorial, museum, and other facilities): adults, $10; seniors, $9; Native Americans, military, Custer County residents, Boy and Girl Scouts in uniform, and children under 6, free; or $25 per car ($22 for seniors).

Indian Museum of the Carolinas. The Indian Museum of the Carolinas in Laurinburg, North Carolina, seeks to increase public awareness of past and present native cultures and to further archaeological research in North and South Carolina. The museum has a collection of over 200,000 artifacts, with the emphasis on such southeastern tribes as the Catawba, Cherokee, Coharie, Lumbee, Tuscarora, and Waccamaw-Siouan. The exhibits feature such areas as pottery, tools, weapons, jewelry, costumes, and contemporary art.

Indian Museum of the Carolinas, 607 Turnpike Rd., Laurinburg, NC 28352 (mailing address: PO Box 666, Laurinburg,, NC 28353). Phone: 910/276–5880. Fax: 910/277–5880. Hours: 10–12 and 1–4 Wed.-Thurs.; 1–4 Sun.; closed remainder of week and national holidays. Admission: free.

Indian Pueblo Cultural Center. The history and accomplishments of the Pueblo people from pre–Columbian times to the present are highlighted at the Indian Pueblo Cultural Center, operated in Albuquerque by the 19 Indian pueblos of New Mexico. The center features the history and artifacts of traditional Pueblo cultures and their traditional and contemporary arts and crafts. It has a permanent exhibit on the survival, diversity, and achievements of the 19 pueblos, and a gallery for changing exhibitions of works by living Native American artists and craftspeople — who usually give demonstrations at the center. The center also has a Pueblo House Children's Museum, which offers an introduction to Pueblo history and culture primarily for K-5 children (open by appointment). It also sponsors an Arts and Crafts Fair, American Indian Week, Indian Children's Art Contest, and Indian Traditional Dance.

Indian Pueblo Cultural Center, 2401 12th St., N.W., Albuquerque, NM 87104. Phones: 505/843–7270 and 800/766–4405. Fax: 505/842–6959. E-mail: *preck@indianpueblo.org.* Web site: *www.indianpueblo.org.* Hours: 9–5:30 daily; closed New Year's Day, Thanksgiving, and Christmas. Admission: adults, $6; seniors, $5; students, $3; children under 5, free.

Institute for American Indian Studies. The Institute for American Indian Studies in Washington Green, Connecticut, is an American Indian culture and anthropology museum and an education and research center for the study of indigenous peoples throughout the Western Hemisphere, with emphasis on the Eastern Woodland region. The institute's primary exhibit, "As We Tell Our Stories," consists of seven sections detailing important parts of indigenous culture — land, exchange, clay, corn, living spaces, deer, and Manitou (a spiritual force).

The main exhibit and some changing exhibitions feature items from the institute's collections of 250,000 prehistoric and historic artifacts, primarily from Connecticut and the Northeast. The institute also has a reconstructed Indian village, American Indian Habitats Trail, and arboretum of plants used by Native Americans in the region over the last 10,000 years. Among the special programs are an American Indian studies program, summer field schools, training sessions in archaeology, summer camps, and year-round workshops.

Institute for American Indian Studies, 38 Curtis Rd., PO Box 1260. Washington Green, CT 06793–0260. Phone: 860/868–0518. Fax: 860/868–1649. E-mail: *instituteamer.indian@snet.net.* Web site: *www.birdstone.org.* Hours: 10–5 Mon.-Sat.; 12–5 Sun.; closed major holidays. Admission: adults, $4; seniors, $3.50; children 6–16, $2; children under 6, free.

Iroquois Indian Museum. The Iroquois Indian Museum, housed in a longhouse in Howes Cave, New York, conveys the history, traditions, and arts of the Iroquois Confederacy of six nations — Mohawk, Oneida, Onondaga, Cayuga, Seneca, and Tuscarora — with special attention to the Mohawks in Schoharie County. The Iroquois were considered the most powerful and influential American Indians in eastern North America in the nation's early history.

The exhibits and programs focus on the male-dominated areas of politics, hunting, warfare, games, and chieftainship and the women's realm of the longhouse, clan, crops, and role in politics. In addition to collections of artifacts, arts, and crafts, the museum has a large collection of copies of original papers and records from the 1600s and 1700s.

Iroquois Indian Museum, 324 Caverns Rd., PO Box 7, Howes Cave, NY 12092. Phone: 518/296–8949. Fax: 518/296–8955. E-mail: *info@iroquoismuseum.org.* Web site: *www.iroquoismuseum.org.* Hours: Apr.-June and day after Labor Day-Dec.—10–5 Tues.-Sat.; 12–5 Sun.; closed Mon., Thanksgiving, and Christmas Eve and Day; July-Labor Day—10–5 Mon.-Sat.; 12–5 Sun; Jan.-Mar.— closed. Admission: adults, $7; seniors and students 12–17, $5.50; children 5–11, $4; children under 5, free.

Jicarilla Apache Arts and Crafts Museum. The Jicarilla Apache Arts and Crafts Museum on the Jicarilla Apache Indian Reservation in Dulce, New Mexico, features exhibits of basketry, beadwork, paintings, leatherwork, and other arts and crafts

for which the tribe has become known. The name Jicarilla means little basket. The museum also has exhibits of pictographs and other artifacts relating to the tribe's history. The La Jara Archaeological Site, where cliff dwellings and ruins can be seen, also is located on the reservation.

Jicarilla Apache Arts and Crafts Museum, Jicarilla Apache Indian Reservation, U.S. Hwy. 64, PO Box 507, Dulce, NM 87528. Phone: 505/759–3242. Web site: *www.jicarillaonline.com.* Hours: 8–5 Mon.-Fri.; closed Sat.-Sun. and major holidays. Admission: donation.

Kake Tribal Heritage Museum: The Kake Tribal Heritage Foundation operates a village museum with exhibits on tribal history, life, culture, and arts and crafts in Kake, Alaska.

Kake Tribal Heritage Museum, 422 Totem Way, Kake, AK 99830 (mailing address: 2211 N. Jordan Ave., Juneau, AK 99801). Phones: 907/785–3165, 907/586–1432, and 800/344–1432. Fax: 907/790–3258. Hours: 8–4 Mon.-Fri.; closed Sat.-Sun. and national and state holidays. Admission: free.

Kanza Museum. Bronze busts of five of the most popular Kaw tribal chiefs and five of the last full-blooded Kaw Indians are displayed at the Kaw Nation's Kanza Museum in Kaw City, Oklahoma. The museum also contains tribal artifacts and changing exhibitions on the history and culture of the Kaw. The chiefs honored with busts in a tribal vote include Washunga, Allegawaho, No-pah-wiah, Lucy Eads, and Ish-tah-lesh-yeh. The last living full-blooded Kaw is William A. Mehojah, Sr.

Kanza Museum, 698 Grandview Dr., PO Box 50, Kaw City, OK 74641. Phone: 580/269–2552. Hours: 8–5 Mon.-Fri. and by appointment; closed Sat.-Sun. and major holidays. Admission: free.

Kiowa Tribal Museum. Ten murals by Kiowa artists that interpret the heritage of the Kiowa people dominate the offerings of the Kiowa Tribal Museum in Carnegie, Oklahoma. The museum also displays a large Kiowa Sundance tepee and such native crafts as earrings and brooches, as well as beaded lighters, key chains, and combs. A Warrior Walk outside the museum honors tribal members killed in action and those who served in the U.S. armed forces.

Kiowa Tribal Museum, 9 W. Carnegie, Carnegie, OK 73015. Phone: 580/654–2300. Fax: 580/654–2188. E-mail: *kiowatribalshop@yahoo.com.* Hours: 8–4:30 Tues.-Fri.; 12–4 Mon. and Sat.; closed Sun. and major holidays. Admission: free.

Koshare Indian Museum. The Koshare Indian Museum, home of the Koshare Indian Dancers in La Junta, Colorado, has exhibits on the art and artifacts of the Southwest and Plains Indians under the world's largest self-supporting log roof (containing more than 620 logs). The Koshare dancers are Boy Scouts who interpret Plains and Pueblo Indian dances in the museum's Kiva, a 60-foot-diameter ceremonial round room, in the summer and late December and travel to present school shows in the spring. The museum's collections and exhibits include pottery, beadwork, instruments, quillwork, jewelry, and other materials from many tribes.

Koshare Indian Museum, 115 W. 18th St., PO Box 580, La Junta, CO 81050. Phones: 719/384–4411 and 800/693–5482. Fax: 719/384–8836. E-mail: *tina.wilcox@ojc.edu*. Web site: *www.koshare.org*. Hours: museum — 10–5 daily (also 9 Mon. and Wed.); closed major holidays; dance performances — mid–June-early Aug.: 8 P.M. Fri.-Sat.; Dec. 27–31: 7 P.M. Admission: museum — adults, $4; seniors and students, 7–17, $3; children under 7, free; dance performances — adults, $5; children, $3.

Lake Perris Regional Indian Museum. See Ya'i Heki' Regional Indian Museum.

Lummi Nation Museum. Tribal cultural objects are displayed at the Lummi Nation Museum in Bellingham, Washington. The historical museum is part of the records-archives center at the site.

Lummi Nation Museum, 2616 Kwina Rd., Bellingham, WA 98226. Phone: 360/384–2246. Fax: 360/312–8742. E-mail: *lummiarc@lummi-nation.bia.edu*. Web site: *http://lummi-nsn.gov*. Hours: 8–4:30 Mon.-Fri.; closed Sat.-Sun. and major holidays. Admission: free.

Makah Cultural and Research Center. The largest collection of pre-contact Northwest Coast Indian artifacts is housed at the Makah Cultural and Research Center on the Makah Indian Reservation in Neah Bay, Washington, on Olympia Peninsula. The center has more than 55,000 artifacts that were recovered from archaeological digs at Ozette, one of the tribe's ancestral villages that was buried by a huge mudslide over 500 years ago (see Ozette Archaeological Site in Prehistoric Sites and Museums section).

The center also contains exhibits on Makah tribal history and culture, as well as flora, fauna, wilderness habitat, and sport fishing. Among its displays are a full-size replica of a longhouse, four cedar dug-out canoes, basketry, and whaling and fishing gear. It also offers guided tours of the Ozette Archaeological Site, an ethnobotanical garden, and other sites on the reservation.

Makah Cultural and Research Center, Makah Indian Reservation, Bayview Ave. (State Hwy. 12), Neah Bay, WA 98357. Phone: 360/645–2711. Fax: 360/645–2656. E-mail: *mcrc@olypen.com*. Web site:

www.makah.com/museum.htm. Hours: Memorial Day-mid–Sept.—10–5 daily; remainder of year — 10–5 Wed.-Sun.; closed Mon.-Tues., New Year's Day, Thanksgiving, and Christmas. Admission: adults, $4; seniors and students, $3; children under 6, free.

Malki Museum. The Malki Museum on the Morongo Indian Reservation near Banning, California, has exhibits on the history and culture of the Cahuilla Indians and such other southern California tribes as the Serrano, Chemehuevi, and Chumash.

Malki Museum, Morongo Indian Reservation, 11–795 Fields Rd., Banning, CA 92220. Phones: 908/849–7289 and 908/849–8304. Web site: *www.malkimuseum.org*. Hours: 10–4 Tues.-Fri.; closed Sat.-Mon. and major holidays. Admission: free.

Marin Museum of the American Indian. The Marin Museum of the American Indian, located at a prehistoric site once occupied by Coast Miwok Indians in Novato, California, has collections and exhibits on Native American history, culture, and art, as well as Marin County's prehistoric period and archaeological, ethnographic, and archival materials ranging from Alaska to Peru. Among its holdings are the original photogravures of Indians taken by early western photographer Edward S. Curtis.

Marin Museum of the American Indian, 2200 Novato Blvd., PO Box 864, Novato, CA 94947. Phone: 415/897–4064. Fax: 415/892–7804. E-mail: *office@marinindian.com*. Web site: *www.marinindian.com*. Hours: 10–3 Tues.-Fri., 12–4 Sat.-Sun.; closed Mon. and major holidays. Admission: adults, $5; children, $3.

Mashantucket Pequot Museum and Research Center. The 308,000-square-foot Mashantucket Pequot Museum and Research Center complex in Mashantucket, Connecticut, is the world's largest and one of the most comprehensive Native American museum and research centers. Opened in 1998, the $193.4 million complex has 85,000 square feet of permanent exhibits depicting 18,000 years of Indian and natural history. The focus is on the history and culture of the Mashantucket Pequot Tribal Nation, with other displays on the history and customs of other tribes and the region's natural history.

The museum uses artifacts, archival materials, artworks, text panels, dioramas, re-creations, mannequins, films, videos, and interactive techniques to convey the stories in permanent exhibits and changing exhibitions. Among the many exhibits are a Mashantucket Pequot tribal portrait; a replica glacial crevasse that visitors descend into by elevator; impact of the Wisconsin glacier on land forms; the arrival of Native Americans; life in a cold climate, with life-size replicas of a mastodon and giant beaver; adapting to the changing social and natural environment 6,000 years ago, with four seasonal dioramas; a walk-through re-created sixteenth-century Pequot village; a diorama and four main exhibits on the arrival of the Europeans; tensions with colonists and other tribes preceding the Pequot War of 1637, featuring a large model of the Pequot fort at Mystic and displays of weapons and other military objects from the period; the Pequot War, which started when Connecticut and Massachusetts colonists attacked the Mystic fort; and life on the reservation in 1675–1970s before the tribe received federal recognition in 1983 and began to rebuild the nation, containing a re-created outdoor ca. 1780 farmstead house on two acres with orchards and gardens.

The museum also has changing exhibitions, symposia, craft workshops, concerts, dance performances, children's programs, and other programming activities. In addition, two libraries at the complex — a research library and one for children — have over 45,000 volumes on the histories and cultures of native peoples.

Mashantucket Pequot Museum and Research Center, 110 Pequot Trail, PO Box 3180, Mashantucket, CT 06338–3180. Phones: 860/396-7073 and 800/411-9671. E-mail *dholahan@mptn.org*. Web site: *www.pequotmuseum.org*. Hours: 10–4 daily; closed New Year's Eve and Day, Thanksgiving Eve and Day, and Christmas Eve and Day. Admission: adults, $15; seniors, $13; children 6–15, $10; children under 6, free.

Menominee Logging Camp Museum. The world's largest collection of artifacts from Wisconsin's logging era can be seen at the Menominee Logging Camp Museum just below historic Keshena Falls on Wolf River near Keshena, Wisconsin. The outdoor museum, operated by the Menominee tribe on its reservation, re-creates a mid–1800s logging camp with seven reconstructed log buildings and an extensive collection of logging artifacts. It includes structures like a logging camp office, bunkhouse, carpenter shop, and horse barn, and has such early logging equipment as saws, grinders, and wagons.

Menominee Logging Camp Museum, Menominee Indian Reservation, State Hwy. 47 and Country Rd. VV, PO Box 910, Keshena, WI 54135. Phone: 715/799-3757. Fax: 715/799-5295. E-mail: *mah2@frontiernet.net*. Web site: *www.menominee.nsn.us*. Hours: May-mid–Oct. — 9–3 Tues.-Sun.; closed Mon. and remainder of year. Admission: adults, $5; seniors, $3; children 10–15, $2; children under 10, free; families, $10.

Mid-America All-Indian Center. The Mid-

America All-Indian Center features museum exhibits and a re-created 1850s Indian village at the site of an old Indian council grounds in Wichita, Kansas. The museum contains tribal flags and traditional artifacts and contemporary art depicting American Indian cultures of the past and present, while an outdoor Heritage Village re-creates what life was like for the Kiowa, Cheyenne, Wichita, and Sioux who first lived in the area.

Mid-America All-Indian Center, 650 S. Seneca St., Wichita, KS 67203. Phone: 316/262-5221. Fax: 316/262-4216. Web site: *www.theindiancenter.org*. Hours: museum and village — 10–4 Tues.-Sat.; closed Sun.-Mon., New Year's Eve and Day, Easter, Thanksgiving, and Christmas. Admission: adults, $7; seniors, $5; children 6–12, $3; children under 6, free.

Mille Lacs Indian Museum. The Mille Lacs Indian Museum near Onamia, Minnesota, traces the history of the Mille Lacs band of Ojibwa who came from the East and settled in northern Wisconsin. The museum, operated by the Minnesota Historical Society, tells how the band suffered from broken treaties and struggled to retain its culture, traditions, and homes. Among the exhibits are life-size dioramas showing traditional Ojibwa activities in different seasons. A restored 1930s trading post adjacent to the museum building has exhibits on the area's early tourist trade.

Mille Lacs Indian Museum, Minnesota Historical Society, 43411 Oodena Dr. (U.S. Hwy. 169), Onamia, MN 56359. Phone: 320/532-3632. Fax: 320/532-1625. E-mail: *millelacs@mnhs.org*. Web site: *www.mnhs.org/places/sites/mlim*. Hours: Memorial Day weekend-Labor Day — 10–6 daily; May and Sept. after Labor Day — 11–4 Fri.-Mon.; closed Tues.-Thurs.; Oct.-Apr.— by appointment. Admission: adults, $7; seniors, $6; children 6–17, $4; children under 6, free.

Mitchell Museum of the American Indian. The Mitchell Museum of the American Indian in Evanston, Illinois, depicts the Native American history, culture, and arts of the Woodlands, Plains, Southwest, Northwest, and Arctic. The initial collections that range from the Paleo-Indian period through the present were accumulated by John and Betty Mitchell, who gave them to Kendall College in 1977. Since then, the collections have been expanded by purchases and other donations, and the museum has become an independent nonprofit entity.

Mitchell Museum of the American Indian, 2600 Central Park Ave., Evanston, IL 60201. Phone: 847/475-1030. Fax: 847/475-0911. E-mail: *mitchellmuseum@mindspring.com*. Web site: *www.mitchellmuseum.org*. Hours: 10–5 Tues.-Sat. (also to 8 Thurs.); 12–4 Sun.; closed Mon., New Year's Day, Independence Day, Thanksgiving, Christmas, and last two weeks of Aug. Admission: $5 suggested donation.

Mt. Kearsarge Indian Museum Education and Cultural Center. The Mt. Kearsarge Indian Museum Education and Cultural Center, located on 100 acres at the foot of Mt. Kearsarge in Warner, New Hampshire, is dedicated to increasing public awareness of Native American traditions, philosophy, and art. In addition to exhibits on the Indian way of life, the museum has replicas of Native American dwellings, such as a Southwest pit house, Plains tepee, and Lakota sweat lodge, and woods with plants used by Indians for medicine, food, dyes, and building materials. Eighty-eight acres of wetlands and forest also are being developed as an outdoor classroom for the study of the environment.

Mt. Kearsarge Indian Museum Education and Cultural Center, Kearsarge Mountain Rd., PO Box 142, Warner, NH 03278–0142. Phone: 603/456–3244. E-mail: *mkim@conknet.com*. Web site: *www.indian-museum.org*. Hours: May–Oct.—10–5 Mon.-Sat.; 12–5 Sun.; Nov.—10–5 Sat.; 12–5 Sun.; closed remainder of week and year. Admission: adults, $8.50; seniors and students, $7.50; children 6–13, $6.50; children under 6, free; families, $26.

The Museum at Warm Springs. The histories, traditions, and arts of the Warm Springs, Wasco, and Paiute Indian tribes that comprise the Confederated Tribes of the Warm Springs Reservation are told in exhibits and programs using artifacts, photographs, models, songs, languages, videos, and arts and crafts at the award-winning Museum at Warm Springs in Oregon. A creek flows around volcanic boulders at the entrance to the building, which has walls of traditional basket-weave design, columns of thick fir, and roof lines in the form of a tule mat dwelling, a plank house, and a travois.

Among the exhibits are a replica of a Wasco wedding; models of such native dwellings as a Warm Springs tepee, Wasco plank house, and Paiute wickiup; historical photographs accompanied by recordings of elders discussing their childhoods in the early days on the reservation; displays of corn-husk bags, Klickitat baskets, and Paiute willow baskets; and a videotape of tribal drumming, singing, and dancing. Elders and artists give presentations on weekends during the summer. Programs also are offered on such topics as traditional knot tying, cedar-root basketry, sally bags, artifacts, tribal landmark history, poetry, singing, and dancing.

The Museum at Warm Springs, Confederated Tribes of the Warm Springs Reservation, 2189 Hwy. 26, PO Box 753, Warm Springs, OR 97761. Phone: 541/553–3331. Fax: 541/533–3338. E-mail: *carol@redmond.net.com*. Web site: *www.warmsprings.com/*

museum. Hours: Memorial Day-Labor Day — 9–5 daily; remainder of year — 9–5 Wed.-Sun.; closed Mon.-Tues., New Year's Day, Thanksgiving, and Christmas. Admission: adults, $6; seniors, $5; students 13–18 and other tribal members, $4.50; children 5–12, $3; children under 5, free.

Museum of Indian Arts and Culture and Laboratory of Anthropology. The Museum of Indian Arts and Culture and Laboratory of Anthropology in Santa Fe, New Mexico, is a museum with exhibits of Southwest native art and material culture from prehistoric to contemporary times and a research and study center with one of the world's finest collections of Southwest Indian artifacts. The museum, one of four in the Museum of New Mexico system, occupies a new building adjacent to the laboratory's 1931 Spanish Pueblo Revival-style structure on Museum Hill, also the site of three other museums.

The museum features pottery, basketry, woven fabrics, jewelry, crafts, and other materials largely from the laboratory's more than 50,000 objects representing the Pueblo, Navajo, Apache, and other indigenous cultures of the Southwest. Among the recent exhibitions have been nearly 100 pre-contact and historic objects from the collections, the ceramic history of pottery making in Pueblo communities, and the use of Native American icons in popular culture. The museum also offers online exhibitions on such topics as the life and pottery of Maria Martinez, Navajo men as weavers, and Native American art and artifacts of the Route 66 era.

Museum of Indian Art and Culture and Laboratory of Anthropology, 710 Camino Lejo, Santa Fe, NM 87505 (mailing address: PO Box 2087, Santa Fe, NM 87504–2087). Phones: 505/476–1250 and 505/476–1247. Fax: 505/476–1330. E-mail: *info@miaclab.org*. Web site: *www.miaclab.org*. Hours: 10–5 Tues.-Sun.; closed Mon., New Year's Day, Easter, Thanksgiving, and Christmas. Admission: New Mexico residents, $6; non-residents, $8; 4-day pass to four museums in Museum of New Mexico system and Museum of Spanish Colonial Art, $18.

Museum of Indian Culture. The Lenni Lenape Historical Society in Allentown, Pennsylvania, is devoted to preserving and furthering public understanding and appreciation of the local Lenape (Delaware Indian) and other Native American cultures. The museum is located in Bieber House, an eighteenth-century farmhouse on the site of a historical Lenape village in Little Lehigh Parkway, which is part of the Delaware Lehigh Heritage Corridor and State Heritage Park. The founders of the society and museum are descendants of the American Indians who had settlements throughout Lehigh Valley before the arrival of the Europeans.

The Museum at Warm Springs in Warm Springs, Oregon, presents the histories, traditions, and arts of the three tribes — Warm Springs, Wasco, and Paiute — that comprise the Confederated Tribes of the Warm Springs Reservation. This is the entrance to the award-winning complex that has a creek flowing around volcanic boulders at the entrance. The building has walls of traditional basket-weave design, thick fir columns, and roof lines in the form of a tule mat dwelling, a plank house, and a travois. *Courtesy the Museum at Warm Springs.*

The museum contains artifacts, cultural items, agricultural tools, and related materials and has a replica of a traditional Lenape village on the grounds.

Museum of Indian Culture, Lenni Lenape Historical Society, 2825 Fish Hatchery Rd., Allentown, PA 18103–9801. Phone: 610/797–2121. Fax: 610/797–2801. E-mail: *lenape@lenape.org*. Web site: *www.lenape.org*. Hours: 12–4 Fri.-Sun.; closed Mon.-Thurs. and national holidays. Admission: adults, $4; seniors and children under 13, $3.

Museum of Ojibwa Culture and Marquette Mission Park. See Marquette Mission Park and Museum of Ojibwa Culture in Museums Honoring Individuals section.

Museum of the Cherokee Indian. The story of the Cherokees from prehistoric times to the present is told at the Museum of the Cherokee Indian in Cherokee, North Carolina, in a new $3.5 mil-

lion exhibit with computer-generated imagery, special effects, audio, and an extensive display of artifacts. The museum is operated by the Eastern band of the Cherokee, which also has a living-history museum, the Oconaluftee Indian Village (see separate listing), at another site.

The Museum of the Cherokee Indian's exhibit begins with animation of early Cherokee myths; continues through the Paleo-Indian period when mastodons were killed with simple spears; and follows with people adapting the environment to their needs in the Archaic and Woodland periods, creating agriculture, trade, and villages; engaging in elaborate ceremonial activities of the Mississippian period; and experiencing contact that brought trade, disease, war, hardships, resettlement, and many cultural changes.

Museum of the Cherokee Indian, 589 Tsali Blvd., PO Box 1599, Cherokee, NC 28719. Phone: 828/497–3481. Fax: 828/497–4985. E-mail: *little-*

john@cherokeemuseum.org. Web site: *www.chero-keemuseum.org.* Hours: mid–June-Aug.— 9–7 Mon.-Sat.; 9–5 Sun.; remainder of year — 9–5 daily; closed New Year's Day, Thanksgiving, and Christmas. Admission: adults, $9; children 6–13, $6; children under 6, free.

Museum of the Native American Resource Center. The Native American Resource Center is a multi-faceted museum and research institute of the University of North Carolina at Pembroke. The museum, housed in historic Old Main, features exhibits of American Indian artifacts, arts, and crafts from tribes throughout the nation, with the emphasis on Native Americans in Robeson County who are largely descendants of three language families — Eastern Siouan, Iroquoian, and Algonkian. The resource center is involved in such research as the archaeology of southeastern North Carolina, American Indian health issues, and Native American history and contemporary issues.

Museum of the Native American Resource Center, University of North Carolina at Pembroke, PO Box 1510, Pembroke, NC 28372-1510. Phone: 910/521–6282. E-mail: *nativemuseum@uncp.edu.* Web site: *www.uncp.edu/nativemuseum.* Hours: 8–5 Mon.-Fri.; closed Sat.-Sun. and major holidays. Admission: free.

Museum of the Plains Indian. The Museum of the Plains Indian near Browning, Montana, features the historic, social, ceremonial, and contemporary arts and crafts of the Northern Plains tribal peoples, including the Blackfeet, Crow, Northern Cheyenne, Sioux, Assiniboine, Arapaho, Shoshone, Nez Percé, Flathead, Chippewa, and Cree. Among the items exhibited are historic clothing, horse gear, weapons, household implements, baby carriers, and toys. The museum also presents promotional sales exhibitions featuring works of contemporary arts and crafts by emerging American Indian artists and craftspeople. On the museum grounds, visitors can see painted tepees and a monument to sign language used in trading by the diverse tribes of the region.

The museum is one of three operated by the U.S. Department of the Interior's Indian Arts and Crafts Board that provides promotional assistance to Native American artists, craftspeople, and cultural organizations. The other regional museums are the Sioux Indian Museum in Rapid City, South Dakota, and Southern Plains Indian Museum in Anadarko, Oklahoma (see separate listings).

Museum of the Plains Indian, U.S. Hwys. 2 and 89 West, PO Box 410, Browning, MT 59417. Phone: 406/338-2230. Fax: 406/338-7404. E-mail: *mpi@ 3rivers.net.* Web site: *www.iach.doi.gov.* Hours: June-Sept.— 9–4:45 daily; remainder of year —10–4:30 Mon.-Fri.; closed Sat.-Sun., New Year's Day, Thanks-giving, and Christmas. Admission: June-Sept.—adults, $4; children 6–12, $1; children under 6, free; remainder of year — free.

Nanticoke Indian Museum. The history and artifacts of the Nanticoke tribe are the main attraction at the Nanticoke Indian Museum in Millsboro, Delaware. The museum, housed in a former schoolhouse, displays such artifacts as pottery, spears, jewelry, arrowpoints, stones, clothing, baskets, and tools. It also has displays of traditional Indian dress and artifacts from other tribes.

Nanticoke Indian Museum, 27073 John J. Williams Hwy., Millsboro, DE 19966. Phone: 302/945-7022. E-mail: *nanticoke@verizon.net.* Web site: *www.nanticokeindians.org/museum.* Hours: Apr.—10–4 Fri-Sat.; closed Sun.-Thurs.; May-Dec.—10–4 Tues.-Sat.; closed Sun.-Mon. and major holidays; Jan.-Mar.— closed. Admission: adults, $2; children, $1.

National Hall of Fame for Famous American Indians. Forty-one outstanding Native American are honored with sculptured busts in the National Hall of Fame for Famous American Indians in Anadarko, Oklahoma. Thirty-eight of the busts are in an outdoor sculpture garden and three that are fragile are in the adjoining city visitor center. The hall was founded in 1952 by Logan Billingsley while employed by the U.S. Indian Service in Anadarko before Indian Territory became the state of Oklahoma. His bust is at the west entrance outside the hall of fame area.

Among the American Indians in the hall of fame are such noted chiefs and warriors as Pontiac (Ottawa), Osceola (Seminole), Black Hawk (Sac and Fox), Tecumseh (Shawnee), Sitting Bull (Sioux), Joseph (Nez Percé). Cochise (Chiricahua Apache), and Geronimo (Apache). Others include Pocahontas, a chieftain's daughter who saved Virginia leader John Smith's life; Sequoyah, inventor of the Cherokee alphabet and contributor to the science of written language Sacajawea, Shoshone guide and interpreter for the 1804 to 1806 Lewis and Clark Expedition; John Ross and Stand Waite, Cherokee leaders on different sides of the Civil War; Charles Curtis, the Kaw who is the only person of Indian descent to serve as the nation's vice president; Jim Thorpe, the great Sac and Fox football player and all-around athlete; and Will Rogers, popular Cherokee entertainer and humorist.

National Hall of Fame for Famous American Indians, U.S. Hwy. 62 East, PO Box 695, Anadarko, OK 73005. Phones: 405/247-5555 and 405/247-3331. Fax: 405/247-5571. E-mail: *dailynews@tanet.net.* Hours: 9–5 Mon.-Sat.; 1–5 Sun.; closed New Year's Day, Thanksgiving, and Christmas. Admission: free.

National Museum of the American Indian. The National Museum of the American Indian, one of the Smithsonian Institution museums on The Mall in Washington, D.C., is dedicated to the preservation, study, and exhibition of the history, life, languages, literature, and arts of Native Americans. The 258,000-square-foot museum, which cost $110 million and opened in 2004, has the world's largest collection of Indian cultural materials — nearly 1 million objects of aesthetic, religious, and historical significance, as well as everyday articles for utilitarian use. It also has two branches — the George Gustav Heye Center, and exhibition and education facility in New York City, and the Cultural Resources Center, which houses the museum's collections, library, and archives in Suitland, Maryland (see separate listings).

The museum's collections, which scan all major American Indian culture areas of the Americas, include virtually every tribe in the United States and Canada and some cultures in Central and South American and the Caribbean region. The holdings range from the Paleo-Indian period to contemporary arts and crafts. Approximately 800,000 of the items in the collections were obtained when the Smithsonian acquired the collections of the closed Museum of the American Indian, founded in New York City in 1916 by banker George Gustav Heye, who amassed the artifacts and other objects at the turn of the twentieth century.

The National Museum of the American Indian has permanent galleries and temporary exhibitions. The three permanent exhibits are "Our Universe: Traditional Knowledge Shapes Our World," which focuses on the spiritual relationship between mankind and the natural world and ancestral native teachings; "Our People: Giving Voice to Our Histories," an exploration of events that shaped the lives and outlook of native peoples from 1492 to the present; and "Our Lives: Contemporary Life and Identities," which examines the identities of native peoples in the twenty-first century and how those identities are affected by deliberate choices made in challenging circumstances. The temporary exhibitions display changing selections from the collections, contemporary arts, and thematic topics.

National Museum of the American Indian, Smithsonian Institution, 4th St. and Independence Ave., S.W., Washington, DC 20024. Phone: 633-1000. Fax: 202/393-3235. Web site: *www.nmai.si.edu.* Hours: 10-5 daily (also to 8 Thurs.); closed Christmas. Admission: free.

Native American Heritage Center and Woolaroc Museum. See Woolaroc Museum and Native American Heritage Center in Representative Other Museums with Extensive Native American Collections or Exhibits section.

Native American Heritage Museum. The Native American Heritage Museum at a state historic site near Highland, Kansas, tells of the emigrant Indian tribes that relocated in the 1830s and 1840s to an area that later became northern Kansas and southern Nebraska. The museum is housed in an 1845 three-story Presbyterian mission on the Oregon-California Trail that also served as a dormitory and school for Iowa, Sac, and Fox Indians. It traces the history of the tribes beginning with their resettlement resulting from the Indian Removal Act of 1836 and treaties. The museum also has interactive exhibits in which Native Americans tell their stories, and displays of quillwork, baskets, and other works by present-day descendants of the emigrant tribes.

Native American Heritage Museum, 1737 Elgin Rd., Highland, KS 66035. Phone: 785/442-3304. E-mail: *nahm@kshs.org.* Web site: *www.kshs.org/ places/nativeamerican/index.htm.* Hours: 10-5 Wed.-Sat.; 1-5 Sun; closed Mon.-Tues. and major holidays. Admission: adults, $3; seniors, students, and K-12 children, $2; children under 5, free.

Native American Museum. The Native American Museum in Terre Haute, Indiana, concentrates on Indian history from prehistoric to modern times, with special emphasis on the history of native tribes of the western Great Lakes, Wabash River Valley, and Ohio's Lower River Valley. The city-operated museum has a wigwam, longhouse, and such artifacts as Indian cooking utensils, clothing, baskets, weapons, and dolls.

Native American Museum, 5170 E. Poplar St., Terre Haute, IN 47803. Phone: 812/877-6007. Fax: 812/232-7313. Hours: 9-5 Mon.-Sat.; 12-5 Sun.; closed major holidays. Admission: free.

Navajo Nation Museum. The initial segments of a new comprehensive core exhibit, "The Culture and History of the Navajo," has opened at the Navajo Nation Museum in Window Rock, Arizona. It makes use of the museum's focused collections of historic, ethnographic, and arts objects. In addition, the museum presents changing thematic exhibitions on diverse aspects of the Navajo people and culture. Its contemporary building also houses the Navajo Nation's library and research collection.

Navajo Nation Museum, Hwy. 264 and Post Office Loop Rd., PO Box 1840, Window Rock, AZ 86515. Phone: 928/871-7941. Fax: 928/871-7942. E-mail: *gibrown@navajomuseum.org.* Hours: 8-5 Mon.-Fri. (also to 8 Wed.); 9-5 Sat.; closed Sun. and tribal and national holidays. Admission: free.

Nokomis Learning Center. The Nokomis Learn-

This wall display of artifacts was part of an inaugural historical exhibition at the National Museum of the American Indian in Washington, D.C. The $110 million Native American museum, which is part of the Smithsonian Institution, is one of the nation's largest ethnic museums with 258,000 square feet and a collection of nearly 1 million American Indian cultural materials. *Courtesy National Museum of the American Indian, Smithsonian Institution, and photographer R.A. Whiteside.*

ing Center in Okemos, Michigan, is a Native American cultural center that preserves and interprets the history, culture, and arts of the Anishinaabe people (Ojibwa, Odawa, and Potawatomi nations). The center presents exhibitions, programs, and special events. Among the changing exhibitions have been such subjects as historic Great Lakes textiles, Native American technologies of Michigan, and Native American treaty signers in the Great Lakes region. The programs and special events include the woodland Indian Art Market, Native Youth Art Competition, and Wiikongewin Fall Feast.

Nokomis Learning Center, 5153 Marsh Rd., Okemos, MI 48864–1198. Phone: 517/349–5777. Fax: 517/349–8560. E-mail: *info@nokomis.org.* Web site: *www.nokomis.org.* Hours: 10–4 Tues.-Fri.; 12–5 Sat.; closed Sun. and major holidays. Admission: adults, $2 suggested donation; children, $1 suggested donation.

Notah Dineh Museum. The Notah Dineh Museum, part of the Notah Trading Company in Cortez, Colorado, has displays of a wide array of historic American Indian art and artifacts. Among the objects exhibited are cradleboards, beaded toys, ceremonial gloves and moccasins, tomahawks, breastplates, pottery, weavings, fetishes, woven baskets, jewelry, sand paintings, sculpture, kachinas, and Navajo rugs, including the largest known Two Grey Hills rug, which measures 12 by 18 feet.

Notah Dineh Museum, Notah Dineh Trading Co., 345 W. Main St., Cortez, CO 81321. Phones: 970/565–9607 and 800/444–2024. E-mail: *notah@ fone.net.* Web site: *www.notahdineh.com.* Hours: 9–6:30 Mon.-Sat.; closed Sun. and major holidays. Admission: free.

Nowetah's American Indian Museum. Nowetah's American Indian Museum near New Portland, Maine, contains Indian artworks from throughout the United States, Canada, and South America. Among objects on display are 400-year-old Maine Indian sweetgrass-brown ash splint baskets, porcupine quill birch bark containers, bark cradle boards, bark moose calls, moosehair-embroidered moccasins, pipe bags, and a 10-foot bark hunter canoe.

Nowetah's American Indian Museum, Rte. 27, Box 40, New Portland, ME 04961–3821. Phone: 207/ 628–4981. E-mail: *nowetah@sofcom.com*. Hours: 10–5 daily; closed Thanksgiving and Christmas. Admission: free.

Nuui Cunni Cultural Center. The Nuui Cunni Cultural Center in Lake Isabella, California, is a gathering place, museum, and library for Paiute and Shoshone Indians in the Kern River Valley. The museum, housed in a round house that overlooks Lake Isabella, contains reed-coiled, reed-woven, and pine-needle baskets; arrowheads; a mudhead kachina doll; and other tribal materials. Outside the center is a dance arbor made of lodge pole pine where local Native Americans practice traditional Paiute dances performed at the center.

Nuui Cunni Cultural Center, 2600 State Hwy. 55, Lake Isabella, CA 93240. Phone: 760/549–0800. Hours: June-Oct.— 9–4 Tues.-Sat.; remainder of year — 9–3 Tues.-Sat.; closed Sun.-Mon. and major holidays. Admission: free.

Oconaluftee Indian Village. The Oconaluftee Indian Village in Cherokee, North Carolina, is a living-history re-creation of a 1750 Cherokee village in a forest setting. Guided tours take visitors to see a preserved seven-sided council house, early huts and cabins, and such live demonstrations as the hollowing out of a 10-person canoe and the making of beads, baskets, arrowheads, masks, pipe bowls, and blow guns. Nature trails and the Cherokee Botanical Garden also are located on the grounds operated by the Eastern Band of the Cherokee Indians, which also operates the Museum of the Cherokee Indian (see separate listing).

Oconaluftee Indian Village, Drama Rd., PO Box 398, Cherokee, NC 28719. Phones: 818/497–2315 and 828/497–2111. E-mail: *travel@nc-cherokee.com*. Web site: *www.cherokee-nc.com*. Hours: mid-May– late Oct.— 9–5:30 daily; closed remainder of year. Admission: adults, $15; children 6–13, $6; children under 6, free.

Oneida Nation Museum. Exhibits at the Oneida Nation Museum in Oneida, Wisconsin, focus on the history, culture, social change, and worldview of the Oneida people. The museum, located on the site of the original Wisconsin reservation land, also traces the movement of the Oneida Indians from the state of New York to Wisconsin and describes the history, culture, and arts of the Iroquois Confederacy. The museum's collections include early clothing, tools, lace, quillwork, moose-hair work, dolls, toys, medicines, weapons, photographs, and Civil War artifacts. A replica of an early longhouse and two nature trails also are on the grounds.

Oneida Nation Museum, W892 County Trunk EE (off State Hwy. 54), De Pere, WI 54115 (mailing address: PO Box 365, Oneida, WI 54155). Phones: 920/869–2768 and 800/236–2214. Fax: 920/869–2959. E-mail: *museum@oneidanation.org*. Web site: *www.museum.oneidanation.org*. Hours: June-Aug.— 9–5 Tues.-Sat.; closed Sun.-Mon.; remainder of year — 9–5 Tues.-Fri.; closed Sat.-Mon. and most holidays. Admission: adults, $2; seniors and children over 16, $1; children under 17 and tribal members, free.

Osage Nation Tribal Museum. When the Osage Nation Tribal Museum opened in 1938 on the Osage Indian Reservation in Pawhuska, Oklahoma, it was the only museum owned by an American Indian tribe. Today, it is the oldest continually operated tribal museum in North America. The museum, housed in an 1847 building that was a chapel, schoolhouse, and dormitory, has a collection of over 6,000 objects and two galleries that interpret much of the material culture of the Osage. The exhibits feature historical documents, maps, photographs, paintings of tribal chiefs and dignitaries, and videos on such arts and crafts as Osage ribbon work, shawl making, and beadwork.

Osage Nation Tribal Museum, 819 Grandview, PO Box 779, Pawhuska, OK 74056. Phone: 918/ 267–5441. Fax: 918/287–1060. E-mail: *kreckorn@osagetribe.org*. Web site: *www.osagetribe.com/museum. html*. Hours: 8:30–5 Tues.-Sat.; closed Sun.-Mon. and major holidays. Admission: free.

Pamunkey Indian Museum. The Pamunkey Indian Museum near King William, Virginia, is devoted to the life and culture of the Pamunkey Indians. It has artifacts dating back 11,000 years and collections of crafts by tribal people. Powhatan's burial mound also is located at the site.

Pamunkey Indian Museum, State Rte. 633, Rte 1, Box 2220, King William, VA 23086. Phone: 804/843–4792. Hours: 10–4 Tues.-Sat.; 1–4 Sun.; closed Mon. Admission: adults, $2.50; children 6–12, $1.25; children under 6, free.

Penobscot Nation Museum. The Penobscot Nation Museum on Indian Island, Maine, is devoted to the tribal and artistry of the four tribes of the Wabanaki Confederacy (Penobscot, Passamaquoddy, Maliseet, and Mik Mag). Among the items on display are prehistoric stone tools, ceremonial root clubs, clothing, beadwork, basketry, and a birch bark canoe. Artisans often demonstrate their crafts, such as weaving baskets, doing beadwork, and carving walking sticks and root clubs.

Penobscot Nation Museum, 12 Downstreet St., Indian Island, ME 04468. Phone: 207/827–4153. E-mail: *firekpr@hotmail.com*. Hours: 9–2 Mon.-Thurs.;

10–3 Sat.; closed Fri., Sun., and major holidays. Admission: free.

The People's Center. The traditional lifestyles and histories of the Salish, Kootenai, and Pend d'Oreille people are presented at the People's Center, just north of the tribal complex in Pablo, Montana. The permanent exhibit, "The First Sun: The Beginning," depicts tribal life from before European contact to the Treaty of Hellgate in 1855 when the Flathead Indian Reservation was formed. Changing exhibitions also are presented on varied subjects ranging from Salish faces to beaded bags.

The People's Center, 53235 Hwy. 93, Pablo, MT 59855. Phones: 406/675–0160 and 800/883–5344. Fax: 406/675–0260. E-mail: *tours@peoplescenter.org*. Web site: *www.peoplescenter.org*. Hours: 9–5 daily; closed major holidays. Admission: adults, $3; seniors and children, $2.

Picuris Pueblo Museum. The Picuris Pueblo Museum near Peñasco, New Mexico, normally has historical exhibits, artifacts, and contemporary arts and crafts — such as weaving, beadwork, and the tribe's distinctive reddish-brown clay pottery — on display. But the museum currently is undergoing renovation at the mountain pueblo, which was established in 1250 to 1300. The museum is the starting point for self-guided tours of the old village ruins and a number of early kivas on a hill overlooking the pueblo. The historic San Lorenzo de Picuris Mission, founded in 1621, also is located in the pueblo. It was destroyed in the 1680 Pueblo Revolt, rebuilt after the 1692 Spanish re-conquest, and recently restored over eight years by tribal members.

Picuris Pueblo Museum, Picuris Pueblo, State Hwy. 205 at Indian Rte. 201, PO Box 127, Peñasco, NM 87553. Phone: 505/587–2519. Hours: 9–6 Mon.-Sun.; closed major holidays. Admission: free.

Plains Indian Museum and Buffalo Bill Historical Center. The histories, cultures, traditions, values, and arts of Plains Indians are presented at the Plains Indian Museum, one of five museums at the Buffalo Hill Historical Center (also separate listing in Museums with Extensive Native American Collections or Exhibits section) in Cody, Wyoming. In addition to displaying historical and contemporary arts and crafts, the museum tells the stories of people behind the objects and the context in which the objects were made and used in daily and ceremonial life.

The majority of the collection is from the ca. 1880 to 1930 early reservation period and relates largely to such tribes as the Lakota, Crow, Arapaho, Shoshone, and Cheyenne. The museum sponsors the annual Plains Indian Museum Powwow and

has a Robbie Powwow Garden at the historical center. The admission covers all five museums at the center. The other museums are the Buffalo Bill Museum, Whitney Gallery of Western Art, Cody Firearms Museum, and Draper Museum of Natural History.

Plains Indian Museum, Buffalo Bill Historical Center, 720 Sheridan Ave., Cody, WY 82414. Phone: 307/587–4771. Fax: 307/578–4066. E-mail: *thomh@bbhc.org*. Web site: *www.bbhc.org*. Hours: June-Sept. 15—7–8 daily; Sept. 16-Oct.—8–5 daily; Nov.-Mar.—10–3 Tues.-Sun.; closed Mon., Thanksgiving, Christmas, and New Year's Day; Apr.—10–5 daily. Center admission: adults, $15; seniors, $13; students over 17, $6; children 6–17, $4; children under 6, free.

Pocono Indian Museum. The Pocono Indian Museum in Bushkill, Pennsylvania, traces the history of the Delaware tribe and displays many of its artifacts, tools, and weapons.

Pocono Indian Museum, Rte. 209, Bushkill, PA 18324. Phone: 570/588–9338. E-mail: *dream348@ptd.net*. Web site: *www.poconoindianmuseum.com*. Hours: Memorial Day-Labor Day — 9:30–7 daily; remainder of year—10–5:30 daily; closed Easter, Thanksgiving, and Christmas. Admission: adults, $6; seniors, $3.50; children 6–16, $2.50; children under 6, free.

Poeh Museum. The Poeh Museum operated by the Pueblo of Pojoaque near Santa Fe, New Mexico, is a Native American art and culture museum with emphasis on the art and artists from six Tewa-speaking tribes of northern New Mexico. It seeks to preserve, display, and interpret the traditional and contemporary art and culture of the pueblos.

Poeh Museum, Pueblo of Pojoaque, 78 Cities of Gold Rd., Santa Fe, NM 87501. Phone: 505/455–3334. Fax: 505/455–0174. E-mail: *poehmuseum@poehcenter.com*. Web site: *www.poehmuseum.com*. Hours: 9–4 Mon.-Fri.; closed Sat.-Sun., Thanksgiving, Feast Day, and Christmas. Admission: free.

Puyallup Tribal Museum. Exhibits of baskets, carved masks, drums, paintings, and historical photographs of tribal members are presented at the small Puyallup Tribal Museum in Tacoma, Washington. A new, larger museum is being planned by the tribe.

Puyallup Tribal Museum, 2002 E. 28th St., Tacoma, WA 98404. Phone: 253/573–7901. Hours: 9–5 Mon.-Fri.; closed Sat.-Sun. and major holidays. Admission: free.

Red Earth Indian Center. Permanent and temporary displays of Native American artifacts and art are offered by the Red Earth Indian Center in Oklahoma City, Oklahoma. The center is located at the Omniplex, a cultural and educational complex that houses a number of museums, galleries, a planetarium, gardens, and a greenhouse. Admission to the Omniplex includes all the attractions. Among the objects exhibited at the Indian center are cradleboards, totem poles, and artworks from the museum's collections, which date from the prehistoric period to the present.

Red Earth Indian Center, Omniplex, 2100 N.E. 52nd St., Oklahoma City, OK 73111. Phone: 405/427–5228. Fax: 405/427–8079. E-mail: *redearth@redearth.org*. Web site: *www.redearth.org*. Hours: 9–5 Mon.-Fri.; 9–6 Sat.; 11–6 Sun.; closed major holidays. Omniplex admission: adults, $9.50; seniors and children 3–16, $8.25; children under 3, free.

Sainte Marie Among the Iroquois. See French Museums and Galleries section.

San Ildefonso Pueblo Museum. The San Ildefonso Pueblo Museum at the tribe's pueblo near San Fe, New Mexico, exhibits traditional and contemporary pottery, paintings, and other artifacts and arts, with emphasis on San Ildefonso history and pottery making. The museum, housed in the Pueblo Governor's Office Building, is dedicated to Maria Martinez, who is known for matte black-on-black style pottery, which she perfected with her husband, Julian, in 1919. She taught her family and other members of the tribe the unique style of pottery making. She was assisted by her four sisters, who did much of the pottery work as a team.

San Ildefonso Pueblo Museum, San Ildefonso Pueblo, U.S. Hwy, 84/285 and State Hwy. 502, Rte. 5, Box 315-A, Santa Fe, NM 87501. Phones: 505/455–2273 and 505/455–3549. Hours: 8–5 Mon.-Fri.; closed Sat.-Sun., during ceremonial dances, and major holidays. Admission: $5 per car for pueblo and museum.

Satwiwa Native American Indian Culture Center and Santa Monica Mountains National Recreation Area. The Satwiwa Native American Indian Culture Center is located along a former Chumash Indian trade route in the 153,075-acre Santa Monica Mountains National Recreation Area — the world's largest urban national park — near Newbury, California. Satwiwa, which means "the bluffs," was the name of a nearby Chumash village. The center, established by the National Park Service in partnership with the Friends of Satwiwa, has historical exhibits on the Chumash and Tongva-Garielino cultures.

Satwiwa Native American Indian Culture Center, Santa Monica Mountains National Recreation Area, 4926 W. Portrero Rd., Newbury Park, CA 91320. Phones: 805/499–2837 and 805/370–2301. Fax: 805/370–1850. Web site: *www.nps.gov/samo*. Hours: 9–5 Sat.-Sun; closed Mon.-Fri. and most national holidays. Admission: free.

Schingoethe Center for Native American Cultures. The Schingoethe Center for Native American Cultures at Aurora University in Aurora, Illinois, resulted from a 1989 gift of more than 6,000 artifacts, arts, and related materials from Herbert and Martha Schingoethe. Since then, the largely Southwestern collection has been expanded by other gifts to include other American Indian cultural areas. The center has three exhibit galleries and a research library in Dunham Hall, also funded by the Schingoethes. The museum holds an annual powwow on Memorial Day weekend with dancers from throughout the nation.

Schingoethe Center for Native American Cultures, Aurora University, Dunham Hall, 1400 Marseillaise Pl., Aurora, IL 60506 (mailing address: 347 S. Gladstone Ave., Aurora, IL 60506–4892). Phones: 630/844–5402 and 630/844–7843. Fax: 630/844–8884. E-mail: *museum@aurora.edu*. Web site: *www.aurora.edu/museum*. Hours: 10–4 Tues.-Fri.; 1–4 Sun.; closed Mon. Sat., and university holidays. Admission: free.

Seeds of Our Ancestors Museum. The Skokomish Indian tribe operates the Seeds of Our Ancestors Museum on its reservation in Shelton, Washington. Historical and contemporary baskets, masks, art, and other materials are displayed in the museum, which is housed in the tribal center.

Seeds of Our Ancestors Museum, Skokomish Indian Reservation, Tribal Center Rd., Shelton, WA 98584. Phone: 360/426–4232. Fax: 360/877–5943. Hours: 9–4 Mon.-Fri.; closed Sat.-Sun. and major holidays. Admission: donation.

Seminole Nation Museum. The Seminole Nation Museum in Wewonka, Oklahoma, traces the history of the Seminole Indians from the time of their removal from Florida on the Trail of Tears to the establishment of their nation's capital in what was then Indian Territory. It also tells of the Freemen, the African-American men and women who became citizens of the Seminole Nation after the Civil War.

Among the museum's exhibits are a re-creation of the pioneer town of Wewoka, containing replicas of an early house, schoolhouse, and business and professional offices; a display area devoted to the Oklahoma oil boom, which once was the lifeblood of the Wewoka area; an art gallery featuring the works of Native American artists and craftspeople; and a room dedicated to the tribe's service men and women with memorabilia and artifacts, some dating from the Civil War.

Seminole Nation Museum, 524 S. Wewoka Ave., PO Box 1532, Wewoka, OK 74884–1532. Phone: 405/257–5580. E-mail: *semuseum@okplus.com*. Web site: *www.wewoka.com/museum.htm*. Hours: Feb.-Dec.—1–5 Tues.-Sun.; closed Mon., Jan., and major holidays. Admission: free.

Seneca-Iroquois National Museum. The Seneca-Iroquois National Museum on the Allegany Indian Reservation in Salamanca, New York, contains historic and contemporary materials reflecting the history and culture of the Seneca Indians and other Iroquois nations of the Northeast. The permanent exhibits include a partially reconstructed longhouse; a rebuilt log cabin; a clan animal display; modern Iroquois art; and exhibits of such traditional Iroquois workmanship as baskets, beadwork, and silverwork. Changing exhibitions also are presented.

Seneca-Iroquois National Museum, Allegany Indian Reservation, 814 Broad St., Salamanca, NY 14779. Phone: 716/945–1760. Fax: 716/945–1383. E-mail: *seniroqm@localnet.com.* Web site: *www.seneca-museum.org.* Hours: May-Oct.— 9–5 Mon.-Sat.; 12–5 Sun.; remainder of year — 9–5 Mon.-Fri.; closed Sat.-Sun. and major holidays. Admission: adults, $5; seniors and college students, $3.50; children, 7–16, $3; children under 7, free.

Shako:wi Cultural Center. See Museums Honoring Individuals section.

Sheldon Jackson Museum. See Arctic Peoples Honoring Individuals section.

Sherman Indian Museum. The Sherman Indian Museum, housed in the federally-operated Sherman Indian High School in Riverside, California, has exhibits of baskets, clothing, beadwork, pottery, tools, and other Native American artifacts, as well as a display on Indian boarding schools. The artifacts and other materials from tribes throughout the nation and changing exhibitions are shown in four galleries. The high school began as an Indian boarding school in nearby Perris in 1892 and moved to Riverside, changed its name, and started serving only high school students in 1970.

Sherman Indian Museum, Sherman Indian High School, 9010 Magnolia Ave., Riverside, CA 92503. Phone: 909/276–6719. Fax 909/276–6332. E-mail: *isisquoc@sihs.bia.edu.* Hours: 1–4 Mon.-Fri.; other times by appointment; closed major holidays. Admission: $1 suggested donation.

Shoshone-Bannock Tribal Museum. The Shoshone-Bannock Tribal Museum on the Fort Hall Indian Reservation near Pocatello, Idaho, gives the history and culture of the two tribes who were dominant in the southeastern region of the state. The museum, located on the site of the original Fort Hall on the Oregon Trail on the 544,000-acre reservation, features artifacts from the site of the old fort, historic photographs dating from 1895, and beaded articles and buckskin crafts made on the reservation. The principal annual event is the Shoshone-Bannock Indian Festival and All-Indian Rodeo held in August.

Shoshone-Bannock Tribal Museum, Fort Hall Indian Reservation, Simplot Rd., PO Box 793, Fort Hall, ID 83203. Phone: 208/237–9791. Hours: May-Aug.—10–6 daily; remainder of year —10–5 Mon.-Fri.; closed Sat.-Sun., New Year's Day, Thanksgiving, and Christmas. Admission: adults, $2 seniors, $1; children 6–18, 50¢; children under 6, free.

Shoshone Tribal Cultural Center. Exhibits of tribal arts and crafts and such historical materials as treaty documents, agreements, maps, and photographs are displayed at the Shoshone Tribal Cultural Center on the Wind River Indian Reservation in Fort Washakie, Wyoming. One of the claimed burial sites for Sacajawea, the Shoshone guide-interpreter for the Lewis and Clark Expedition, is west of Fort Washakie, and the grave of Chief Washakie, the popular chief who died in 1900 at the age of 102, is in the old military cemetery on the reservation. Washakie was buried with military honors — the first given to an Indian chief.

Shoshone Tribal Cultural Center, Wind River Indian Reservation, 30 Ethete Rd., PO Box 1008, Fort Washakie, WY 82514–1008. Phone: 307/332–9106. Fax: 307/332–3055. Hours 8–4:45 Mon.-Fri.; closed Sat.-Sun., American Indian Day, annual tribal ceremonies in Aug., and tribal and national holidays. Admission: free.

Sicangu Heritage Center Museum. The Sicangu Heritage Center on the Antelope Lake campus of Sinte Gleska University in Mission, South Dakota, houses a museum that interprets the historical, cultural, and aesthetic objects that tell the story of the Rosebud Sioux tribe from the earliest times to the present. The heritage center also contains Lakota archives, a historical research center, and historic preservation office that feature a collection of papers, objects, and sites which document the history and culture of the Sicangu (Brule) people.

Sicangu Heritage Center Museum, Sinte Gleska University, Antelope Lake Campus, PO Box 675, Mission, SD 57555. Phone: 605/856–8211. Fax: 605/856–5027. E-mail: *heritagecenter@sinte.edu.* Web site: *www.sinte.edu/heritage_cntr/index.htm.* Hours: 9–5 Mon.-Fri. and by appointment; closed Sat.-Sun. and major holidays. Admission: free.

Sierra Mono Indian Museum. The history and way of life of the two clans of the North Fork Mono tribe — the Golden Eagle and the Coyote — are featured at the Sierra Mono Indian Museum in North Fork, California. The museum contains tribal artifacts, baskets, beadwork, and exhibits on fishing, hunting, acorn gathering, cooking, healing, games, ceremonies, and wildlife.

Sierra Mono Indian Museum, 57839 Rd. 225, PO Box 426, North Fork, CA 93643. Phone: 559/877–2115. Web site: *www.north-fork-chamber. com.* Hours: 9–4 Tues.-Sat.; closed Sun.-Mon. and major holidays. Admission: adults, $3; seniors, $2; students, $1; children under 6, free.

Siletz Tribal Cultural Center. The Siletz Tribal Cultural Center on Government Hill on the Siletz Indian Reservation in Siletz, Oregon, has artifacts and historical documents about the 27 tribal bands that comprise the Confederated Tribes of Siletz. The bands originally ranged from northern California to southern Washington. The center also has a display on the history of Yaquina Bay. The confederacy currently is developing an expanded cultural center and museum.

Siletz Tribal Cultural Center, Silez Indian Reservation, 402 Parkway, PO Box 549, Siletz, OR 97380. Phones: 541/444–8208 and 800/922–1399. E-mail: *hawkeye@ctsi.nsn.us.* Web site: *http://ctsi.nsn/us.* Hours: 8–4:30 Mon.-Fri.; closed Sat.-Sun. and tribal and national holidays. Admission: free.

Sioux Indian Museum. The Sioux Indian Museum in Rapid City, South Dakota, is one of three regional Native American museums administered by the Indian Arts and Crafts Board of the U.S. Department of the Interior to promote contemporary Indian arts and crafts (see separate listings for the agency and other two museums — Museum of the Plains Indian in Browning, Montana, and Southern Plains Indian Museum in Anadarko, Oklahoma).

The museum presents changing exhibitions of contemporary Sioux arts and crafts by emerging artists and craftspeople and displays an array of historic clothing, horse gear, weapons, cradleboards, toys, and household implements. The museum is located in the Journey Museum complex, which also includes a geology and pioneer museums and an archaeological research center. The Journey Museum tells the 2-million-year story of the Northern Plains from the perspective of Lakota Indians, pioneers, and today's scientists. It also contains Sioux art and artifacts from the city's Duhamel Collection.

Sioux Indian Museum, Journey Museum Complex, 222 New York St., Rapid City, SD 57701 (mailing address: PO Box 1504, Rapid City, SD 57709). Phones: 605/394–2381 and 605/394–2382 (also fax). E-mail: *montileau@journeymuseum.org.* Web sites: *www.journeymuseum.org* and *www.doi.gov/museum/ museum_sioux.html.* Hours: Memorial Day-Labor Day — 9–5 daily; remainder of year — 10–5 Mon.-Sat.; 1–5 Sun.; closed New Year's Day, Thanksgiving, and Christmas. Complex admission: adults, $7; seniors, $6; children 11–17, $5; children under 11, free.

Sitka National Historical Park. See Historic Sites section.

Six Nations Indian Museum. The Six Nations Indian Museum near Onchiota, New York, houses pre-contact and post-contact artifacts, contemporary arts and crafts, diagrammatic charts, posters, and other cultural items of the Haudenosaunee (Six Iroquois Nations Confederacy). It also has objects representative of other American Indian cultures. The museum was founded in 1954 by Ray, Christine, and John Fadden in a replica of a Haudenosaunee bark house they built.

Six Nations Indian Museum, 1462 County Rd. 60, HCR 1, Box 1, Onchiota, NY 12989. Phone: 518/891–2299. E-mail: *redmaple@northnet.org.* Web site: *http://tuscaroras.com/graydeer/pages/sixnations.htm.* Hours: July-Labor Day — 10–6 Tues.-Sun.; closed Mon.; May-June and Sept. day after Labor Day-Oct. — by appointment; closed remainder of year. Admission: adults, $2; children, $1; Native Americans, free.

Sky City Cultural Center and Haak'u Museum. The 40,000-square-foot Sky City Cultural Center and Haak'u Museum opened in 2006 at the base of the mesa of the Pueblo of Ácoma, believed to be the oldest continuously inhabited city in the United States. The facility, which replaced the pueblo's visitor center that burned in 2000, features exhibits of Ácoma culture, pottery, and early textiles. To visit the pueblo itself, however, visitors must be accompanied by a tour guide.

When Francisco Vásquez de Coronado and his Spanish forces reached New Mexico in 1540, the Ácoma people lived on the steep 370-foot mesa, worked in the plains below, and returned to the village at night. The pueblo, however, was nearly destroyed in 1598 when Juan de Oñate and 70 of his men retaliated for the killing of 13 Spanish soldiers who were thrown off a cliff after they tried to take grain from pueblo storehouses. The San Estéban del Rey Mission, built in 1629 to 1841 during Spanish rule (see Spanish Historic Sites section), still can be seen in the pueblo as part of tours.

Sky City Cultural Center and Haak'u Museum, Ácoma Pueblo, Interstate 40 West, Exit 102, PO Box 310, Pueblo of Ácoma, NM 87034. Phones: 505/469–1052 and 800/747–0181. Fax: 505/552–7204. E-mail: *bvallo@acomaenterprises.com.* Web site: *www.skycity.com.* Hours: May-Oct.–8–6 daily; remainder of year — 8–5 daily; closed during tribal ceremonials. Admission: center — free; guided tour of pueblo — adults, $10; seniors, $9; children 6–17, $7; children under 6, free.

Smoki Museum. The Smoki Museum, patterned after early pueblo structures both in architecture and interior design in Prescott, Arizona, is primarily an anthropological museum of American Indian art and culture. It has collections and exhibits of prehistoric Southwest Indian artifacts and contemporary basketry and ceramics.

Opened in 1935, the museum contains collections of pre–Columbian and contemporary pottery; pre–Columbian jewelry; Southwest basketry, textiles, kachinas, and stone artifacts; and Plains Indian war bonnets, clothing, beadwork, and tools. The museum building, constructed of native stone and wood, uses thousands of pine logs for the columns, vigas, and latillas of the ceiling, as well as slab doors and window enclosures. It also has a Hopi-style kiva and a Zuñi-style fireplace.

Smoki Museum, 147 N. Arizona St., PO Box 10224, Prescott, AZ 86304. Phone: 520/445-1230. Fax: 520/777-0573. E-mail: *smoki@futureone.com*. Web site: *www.smoki.com*. Hours: May–Sept.—10–4 Mon.-Sat.; 1–4 Sun.; Oct.—10–4 Sat.; 1–4 Sun.; closed remainder of year. Admission: adults, $4; students and children under 12, free.

Southeast Alaska Indian Cultural Center. See Sitka National Historical Park in Arctic Peoples Historic Sites section.

Southern Plains Indian Museum. The Southern Plains Indian Museum in Anadarko, Oklahoma, features the artifacts and arts of western Oklahoma tribal peoples and the works of emerging Native American contemporary artists and craftspeople. The museum is one of three operated by the Indian Arts and Crafts Board of the U.S. Department of the Interior to promote American Indian arts and crafts — the others being the Museum of the Plains Indians in Browning, Montana, and the Sioux Indian Museum in Rapid City, South Dakota (see separate listings).

The exhibits contain such varied historic materials as clothing, shields, weapons, baby carriers, and toys from the Kiowa, Comanche, Kiowa-Apache, Southern Cheyenne, Southern Arapaho, Wichita, Caddo, Delaware, and Fort Still Apache tribes. A series of changing exhibitions display the arts and crafts of contemporary arts and craftspeople.

Southern Plains Indian Museum, 715 E. Central Blvd., PO Box 749, Anadarko, OK 73005. Phone: 405/247-6221. Fax: 405/247-7593. Web site: *www. doi.gov/iacb/museums/museum_s_plains2.html*. Hours: 9–5 Tues.-Sat.; closed Sun.-Mon., New Year's Day, Thanksgiving, and Christmas. Admission: free.

Southern Ute Cultural Center and Museum. The Southern Ute Cultural Center and Museum on the tribe's reservation in Ignacio, Colorado, has exhibits on the history, culture, and arts of the Southern Ute Indians. The core exhibit is "The Ute Circle of Life," which depicts the life of the tribe and contains clothing, tools, and other objects; a multimedia slide show on Ute history; and a video on the Bear Dance. The museum also displays historic photographs featuring the traditional dress and adornments of the Utes; beadwork and leather materials dating from the early 1800s to the present; and Anasazi artifacts from excavations in the area. In addition, it presents changing exhibitions and sponsors the annual Southern Ute Fair and Powwow, art festivals, and other events.

Southern Ute Cultural Center and Museum, Southern Ute Indian Reservation, State Hwy. 172 North, PO Box 737, Ignacio, CO 81137. Phone: 970/563-9583. Fax: 970/563-4641. E-mail: *sum@frontier.net*. Web site: *www.southernutemuseum. org*. Hours: May 15-Oct. 15 —10–6 Mon.-Fri.; 10–3 Sat.-Sun.; remainder of year —10–5:30 Mon.-Fri.; closed Sat.-Sun. Admission: adults, $1; children under 13, 50¢; Southern Ute tribal members, free.

Southold Indian Museum. The Southold Indian Museum in Southold, New York, has one of the largest collections of Algonquin ceramic pottery and an impressive collection of early pots and bowls carved out of soapstone. The museum also displays projectile points, knife and hoe blades, hammers, gouges, drills, mortars, pestles, clothing, fishing tackle, food, children's games and toys, and other items relating primarily to the Long Island Algonquin Indians. The museum, founded in 1925, is operated by the Long Island chapter of the New York State Archeological Association.

Southold Indian Museum, 1080 Main Bayview Rd., PO Box 268, Southold, NY 11971-3431. Phone and fax: 631/765-5577. E-mail: *indianmuseum@ aol.com*. Web site: *http://southoldindianmuseum.org*. Hours: July-Aug.—1:30–4:30 Sat.-Sun. and by appointment; remainder of year —1:30–4:30 Sun. and by appointment; closed New Year's Day, Easter, Thanksgiving, and Christmas. Admission: adults, $2 suggested donation; children, free.

Southwest Museum of the American Indian. The highly regarded Southwest Museum of the American Indian in Los Angles, California, is undergoing major changes. Founded in 1907, it is one of the nation's oldest Native American museums. But the museum has suffered from building deterioration and water damage and now has only limited offerings and access on weekends as it undergoes rehabilitation of the building; conservation of its collection of over 250,000 objects, and change in operations. The museum, which is part of the Autry National Center, eventually will move from its Arroyo site to a new facility at the Griffith Park campus, where the center's Museum of the American West is located. The current building then will be used for a sampling of the collection, public programs, and educational uses.

Visitors now can see a portion of the collections in open storage in the exhibit halls, color photos over dioramas to show what has been removed due to water damage, and displays on the history and rehabilitation of the museum. The renovations are expected to be completed by 2010. when the museum will open in its new cultural format. No date has been set for the construction or opening at the new site in Griffith Park.

Meanwhile, the museum is working on the conservation of many of its archaeological and ethnographic objects representing the indigenous cultures of America, as well as its extensive holdings of California, Spanish, and Mexican colonial art and artifacts and western Americana paintings. Among the collections are over 11,000 baskets, 7,000 pottery vessels from the Southwest, and 6,600 Latin American colonial paintings, textiles, religious icons, and other works of decorative and folk art from southwestern United States, Mexico, and Central and South America.

Southwest Museum of the American Indian, 234 Museum Dr., Los Angeles, CA 90065. Phone: 323/221–2164. Fax: 323/224–8223. E-mail: *info@ southwestmuseum.org*. Web site: *www.southwestmuseum.org*. Hours: 12–5 Sat.-Sun.; closed Mon.-Fri. and major holidays. Admission: free.

Steilacoom Tribal Cultural Center and Museum. The history, art, and artifacts of the Steilacoom tribe and other Salish peoples are displayed at the Steilacoom Tribal Cultural Center and Museum in Steilacoom, Washington. The cultural center and museum, housed in a 1903 former church building, has exhibits ranging from the pre–Columbian era to the present, including a replica of an archaeological dig at the Chamber Creek village site; collections of traditional clothing, baskets, tools, photographs, and other historical materials; and changing six-month exhibitions of Native American art and artifacts.

Steilacoom Tribal Cultural Center and Museum, 1515 Lafayette St., PO Box 88419, Steilacoom, WA 98388–1323. Phone: 253/584–6308. Hours: 10–4 Tues.-Sat.; closed Sun.-Mon. and major holidays. Admission: adults, $3; seniors and students 6–18, $1; children under 6, free.

Sumeg Village at Patrick's Point State Park. Sumeg Village is a re-created Yurok Indian village at Patrick's Point State Park near Trinidad, California. The village includes traditional family dwellings, a sweat house, a dance house, changing houses, and a redwood dug-out canoe. The build-ings are made of split redwood planks, are partially sunken below ground level, and have circular openings as entrances. A garden with native plants that were used for food, medicine, and baskets is next to the village. The Yurok, who originally inhabited the site, reconstructed the village and now use it for educational programs and ceremonial dances, which are open to the public.

Sumeg Village, Patrick's Point State Park, 4150 Patrick's Point Dr., Trinidad, CA 95570. Phone 707/677–3570. Web site: *www.parks.ca.gov*. Hours: dawn-dusk daily. Admission: village — free; park — $6 per car, but $5 for seniors.

Suquamish Museum. The history and culture of the Suquamish Indians are presented at the Suquamish Museum on the Fort Madison Indian Reservation in Suquamish, Washington. The museum features two permanent exhibits — "The People and Way of Life at D'suq'wuh" and "The Eyes of Chief Seattle" — which include the tribe's traditional ways of living as seen by Chief Seattle (for whom the city of Seattle is named). Among the areas covered are food gathering, summer dwellings, fishing, and boarding schools. The exhibits also make use of legends and songs to document history. Outside the museum, visitors sometimes can see a cedar canoe being carved.

Suquamish Museum, Fort Madison Indian Reservation, 15838 Front St., PO Box 498, Suquamish, WA 98392–0498. Phone: 360/394–8496. Fax: 360/598–6295. E-mail: *mjones@suquamish.nsn,us*. Web site: *www.suquamish.nsn.us*. Hours: May-Sept.—10–5 daily; remainder of year—11–4 Fri.-Sun.; closed Mon.-Thurs., New Year's Day, Easter, Thanksgiving and day after, and Christmas. Admission: adults, $4; seniors, $3; children under 12, $2.

Tahlonteeskee Cherokee Courthouse Museum. See Museums Honoring Individuals section.

Tamástslikt Cultural Center. The Tamástslikt Cultural Institute at the foot of the Blue Mountains on the Umatilla Indian Reservation near Pendleton, Oregon, serves as the interpretive center for the Confederated Tribes of Cayuse, Umatilla, and Walla Walla. It has over 10,000 square feet of exhibits on the history and culture of the tribes, which go back over 10,000 years. The displays tell of tribal life on the Columbia Plateau before the nineteenth century, the impact of white settlement on the tribes, and tribal life on the reservation today. The institute is located on the grounds of the Whitehorse Resort and Casino.

Tamástslikt Cultural Institute, Umatilla Indian Reservation, 72789 Hwy. 331, Pendleton, OR 97801–3379. Phone: 541/966–9748. Fax: 541/966–9927. E-mail: *tci.visitors@tamastslikt.org*. Hours: 9–5

Mon.-Sat.; closed Sun., New Year's Day, Thanksgiving, and Christmas. Admission: adults, $6; seniors and students, $4; children under 5, free; families, $12.

Tantaquidgeon Indian Museum. The Tantaquidgeon Indian Museum in Uncasville, Connecticut, displays artifacts and crafts of the Mohegans and other New England tribes, as well as some Southeast, Southwest, and Northern Plains cultures. The museum was started by two Mohegan Indians — John Tantaquidgeon and his son, Harold — in 1930. The following year Gladys Tantaquidgeon joined her father and brother in operating the modest one-room museum. It has been operated ever since by family and friends.

Tantaquidgeon Indian Museum, 1819 Norwich-New London Turnpike, Uncasville, CT 06382-1320. Phone: 860/862-6144. Fax: 860/862-6025. Hours: June-Oct.—10-3 Tues.-Fri.; closed Sat.-Mon. and remainder of year. Admission free.

Three Tribes Museum. The history, culture, and arts of the Mandan, Hidatsa, and Arikara tribes of the Fort Berthold Indian Reservation are featured at the Three Tribes Museum, a heritage center in Four Bears Memorial Park near New Town, North Dakota. History is traced through documents and photographs and the cultures and arts are interpreted largely through artifacts. Other displays contain clothing, foods, and historical photographs depicting Indian frontier scouts, military service, ranching, rodeo performers, and other subjects. The Fort Berthold Veterans Monument also is located on the museum grounds.

Three Tribes Museum, Fort Berthold Indian Reservation, State Hwy. 23, PO Box 147, New Town, ND 58763. Phones: 701/627-4477 and 701/862-3301. Fax: 701/627-3805. E-mail: *tatmuseum@restel.net*. Web site: *www.mhanation.com*. Hours: mid-Apr.-Oct.—10-6 daily; closed remainder of year. Admission: adults, $3; seniors and students, $2; children under 13, free.

Tillicum Village. Tillicum Village at historic Blake Island State Park across the bay from Seattle, Washington, is a combination Northwest Coast Indian arts center and a restaurant in a large cedar longhouse styled like an ancient communal dwelling. In addition to seeing cultural exhibits and carving demonstrations, visitors have a native-style baked salmon lunch or dinner and see Northwest Coast Indian dance performances.

The longhouse combines the architectural elements of northern and southern Northwest Coast tribes, featuring huge log beams and supports, hand-split cedar planks, massive doors with carved and painted panels, muraled walls, and the aroma of alder smoke and cedar. The village and park can be reached only by boat trips from Pier 55 on Seattle's central waterfront. The Tillicum Village entry fee includes the boat trip. The 475-acre state park contains 16 miles of hiking trails and 5 miles of beaches.

Tillicum Village, Blake Island State Park, Blake Island, WA (mailing address: 2992 S.W. Avalon Way, Seattle, WA 98126). Phones: 206/933-8600 and 800/426-1205. Web site: *www.tillicumvillage.com*. Hours: ticket office — 9-5 Mon.-Fri.; closed Sat.-Sun.; boat trips from Seattle — usually 11:30-3:30; 4:30-8:30, and 6:30-10:30; but hours and dates vary sometimes and should be checked; closed mid-Dec.-Dec. 31. Rates (including boat trip, meal, and taxes): adults, $69; seniors, $62; children 5-12, $25; children under 5, free.

Totem Heritage Center. The Totem Heritage Center in Ketchikan, Alaska, was founded in 1976 to preserve endangered nineteenth-century totem poles from endangered Tlingit and Haida village sites near the community. The poles now are displayed at the city-operated center with other totems — a total of 17 — and other Native American artifacts. The traditional arts and crafts of the Tlingit, Haida, and Tsimshian cultures also are preserved and promoted through a program of native arts and crafts demonstrations, classes, and other activities. The city also operates the Tongass Historical Museum, a general museum which has exhibits and artifacts relating to the three tribes among its offerings.

Totem Heritage Center, 601 Deermount St., Ketchikan, AK 99901 (mailing address: 629 Dock St., Ketchikan, AK 99901). Phone: 907/225-5900. Fax: 907/225-5901. E-mail: *museumdir@city.ketchikan.ak.us*. Web site: *www.city.ketchikan.ak.us/departments/museums/contact.html*. Hours: mid-May-Sept. — 8-5 daily; remainder of year —1-5 Tues.-Fri.; closed Sat.-Mon. and major holidays. Admission: adults and children over 12, $5; children under 13, free.

Tunica-Biloxi Native American Museum. The Tunica-Biloxi Native American Museum on the Tunica-Biloxi Indian Reservation in Marksville, Louisiana, contains exhibits and artifacts on the history and culture of the tribe. However, it is closed temporarily while undergoing renovation. The museum is near the Marksville State Historic Site, which preserves a prehistoric American Indian ceremonial center with numerous earthworks (see separate listing in Prehistoric Sites and Museums section).

Tunica-Biloxi Native American Museum, Tunica-Biloxi Indian Reservation, 150 Melacon Dr., PO Box 1589, Marksville, LA 71351. Phones: 318/253-8174 and 800/488-6674. Fax: 318/253-7711. E-mail:

musum@tunica.org. Web site: *www.tunica.org/museum.htm.* Hours: 8:30–4 Mon.-Sat., but temporarily closed; closed Sun., tribal holidays, Thanksgiving, and Christmas. Admission: adults, $2; seniors, students, and children, $1.

Turtle Mountain Chippewa Indian Heritage Center. The history and culture of the Turtle Mountain Band of Chippewa Indians — based partly on the traditions of the Ojibway and Metis peoples — is the focus of the Turtle Mountain Chippewa Indian Heritage Center on the tribe's reservation in Belcourt, North Dakota. The exhibits feature artifacts, sculptures, paintings, crafts, and three dioramas showing the Chippewa Band's transition from the woodlands to the plains. The heritage center is operated by the Turtle Creek Chippewa Historical Society.

Turtle Mountain Chippewa Indian Heritage Center, Turtle Creek Chippewa Historical Society, Turtle Creek Chippewa Indian Reservation, BIA Hwy. 5, PO Box 257, Belcourt, ND 58316. Phone: 701/477–2640. Fax: 701/477–0065. E-mail: *tmche@utma.com.* Web site: *www.chippewa.etma.com.* Hours: 10–5 Mon.-Fri.; closed Sat.-Sun. and major holidays. Admission: free.

Turtle Mountain Interpretive Center. The Turtle Mountain Interpretive Center at Turtle Mountain Community College near Belcourt, North Dakota, features exhibits on the Chippewa Indians. It also serves as a site for classes, workshops, and other training programs.

Turtle Mountain Interpretive Center, Turtle Mountain Community College, BIA Hwy. 7, PO Box 340. Belcourt, ND 58316. Phones: 701/477–0501 and 701/477–7862. Hours: varies. Admission: free.

Ute Indian Museum. The Ute Indian Museum in Montrose, Colorado, serves as a visitor center and a museum on the history and culture of the Ute tribes and the lives of Chief Ouray of the Southern Ute tribe and his wife, Chipeta, who is buried on the grounds. The museum, operated by the Colorado Historical Society, is located on the site where the Ourays' government-built adobe home burned in 1945.

The exhibits include a Ute historical timeline; a Ute wickiup; dioramas depicting Ute life and beliefs; a computerized kiosk interpreting the Utes' ceremonial Bear Dance; and numerous historical photographs and artifacts, including dance skins, beadwork, feather bonnets, and leather garments. Many of the artifacts belonged to the peace-loving Chief Ouray, Chipeta, and other Ute historical figures, such as Ignacio, Colorow, and Buckskin Charlie. A marker honoring the 1776 Dominquez-Escalante Expedition also is located at the site.

Ute Indian Museum — Montrose Visitor Center, 17253 Chipeta Dr., Montrose, CO 821401 (mailing address: PO Box 1736, Montrose, CO 81402). Phone: 970/249–3098. Fax: 970/252–8741. E-mail: *cj.brafford@state.co.us.* Web site: *www.coloradohistory.org.* Hours: Memorial Day-Oct.—9–4:30 Mon.-Sat.; 11–4:30 Sun.; remainder of year — 9–4:30 Mon.-Sat.; closed Sun., New Year's Day, Thanksgiving, and Christmas. Admission: adults, $3.50; seniors, $3; students 6–16, $1.50; children under 6, free.

Ute Mountain Tribal Park. The Ute Mountain Tribal Park in Towaoc, Colorado, was established by the Ute Mountain Ute tribe on its reservation to preserve and interpret the culture of the Anasazi (Ancestral Puebloans) and the tribe. The 125,000-acre park, just south of Mesa Verde National Park in the Four Corners area, has a visitor centermuseum from which full-day and half-day guided tours are conducted of the preserve and the historic cliff dwellings, kivas, storage rooms, and rock art of its early inhabitants. All tours must be arranged in advance. The visitor center-museum has exhibits about Anasazi and Ute Mountain Ute tribal history and culture.

Ute Mountain Tribal Park, Visitor Center and Museum, Hwys. 160 and 666, PO Box 109, Towaoc, CO 81334. Phones: 970/749–1452 and 800/847–5485. Fax: 970/564–5317. E-mail: *utepark@fone.net.* Web site: *www.utemountainute.com/tribalpark.htm.* Hours: Mar.-Oct.— 8–4:30 Mon.-Sat. by appointment; closed Sun.; remainder of year — 8–3 Wed.-Sat. by appointment (subject to weather); closed Sun.-Tues. Admission: visitor center-museum — free; tours — full day: $42 per person; half day: $22 per person; special rates for children and school groups.

Walatowa Visitor Center. The history, culture, arts, and crafts of the Jémez tribe are presented at the Walatowa Visitor Center at the Jémez Pueblo northwest of Bernalillo, New Mexico.

Walatowa Visitor Center, Jémez Pueblo, 7413 State Hwy. 4, Jémez Pueblo, NM 87024. Phone: 505/834–7235. Fax: 505/834–2221. E-mail: *tourism@jemezpueblo.org.* Web site: *www.jemezpueblo.org.* Hours: 8–5 daily; closed major holidays. Admission: free.

Waponahki Museum and Resource Center. Tribal tools, baskets, beaded artifacts, moccasins, fishing nets, old photographs, and the works of noted Passamaquoddy artist Tomah Joseph can be seen at the Waponahki Museum and Resource Center near Perry, Maine. Joseph, who developed a close relationship with President Franklin D. Roosevelt, was known for his distinctive etchings on birch bark

Waponahki Museum and Resource Center, Rte. 190, Pleasant Point, Perry, ME 04667. Phone: 207/853–4001. Web site: *www.wabanaki.com*. Hours: 8–11 and 1–3 Mon.-Fri.; closed Sat.-Sun. Admission: free.

Wa-Swa-Goning. Wa-Swa-Goning is a re-created 1700s Ojibwe village along the shore of Moving Cloud Lake on the Lac du Flambeau Indian Reservation near Lac du Flambeau, Wisconsin. Wa-Swa-Goning was the name the Ojibwe used for the whole area, while the French fur traders called it Lac du Flambeau (Lake of Fire) when they saw the torches the Ojibwe used on the lake while spearing fish at night. Tours are given of the village, which has traditional Ojibwe lodges, as well as seasonal villages, a maple sugar camp, and displays of baskets, traps, birch bark canoes, and other native materials.

Wa-Swa-Goning, Lac du Flambeau Indian Reservation, PO Box 1059, Lac du Flambeau, WI 54538. Phones: 715/588–2615 and 715/588–3560 (also fax). E-mail: *nick@wasswagoning.com*. Web site: *www.was wagoning.org*. Hours: mid–May–Sept.—10–4 Tues.-Sat.; closed Sun.-Mon. and remainder of year. Admission: adults, $7; seniors and children 5–12, $5; children under 5, free.

Wheelwright Museum of the American Indian. The Wheelwright Museum of the American Indian in Santa Fe, New Mexico, presents changing exhibitions of historic and contemporary Native American art, primarily from the Southwest. Two major exhibitions are displayed in the main gallery each year and the smaller galleries usually feature one-person shows by Native American artists and photographers. The museum, which also has a large trading post, is designed to resemble a Navajo hogan (like a cribbed log home).

The museum was founded in 1937 by Mary Cabot Wheelwright, a Bostonian who had a lifelong interest in religions of the world, in collaboration with Hastlin Klah, a Navajo medicine man. They were concerned that the ceremonial heritage of the Navajo people was being lost and sought to save the sacred material. First called the House of Navajo Religion, the name soon was changed to Museum of Navajo Ceremonial Art. But the vitality of the Navajo ceremonial system continued and the museum returned much of the material to the Navajo Nation in the 1970s. The museum's scope then was broadened to include traditional and contemporary American Indian art and the name was changed to the Wheelwright Museum of the American Indian in 1977.

Wheelwright Museum of the American Indian, Museum Hill, 704 Camino Lejo, Old Santa Fe Trail, Santa Fe, NM 87505 (mailing address: PO Box 5153, Santa Fe, NM 87502). Phones: 505/982–4636 and 800/607–4636. Fax: 505/989–7386. E-mail: *wheel-wright@wheelwright.org*. Web site: *www.wheelwright. org*. Hours: 10–5 Mon.-Sat.; 1–5 Sun.; closed New Year's Day, Thanksgiving, and Christmas. Admission: free.

White Mountain Apache Cultural Center and Museum. The White Mountain Apache Cultural Center and Museum — also known to the tribe as *Nohwike Basgowa* (House of Our Footprints) — in Fort Apache, Arizona, serves as a repository for the tribe's cultural heritage. It preserves and interprets oral histories, archival materials, and objects of cultural, historical, and artistic significance to the White Mountain Apache people. The museum, located at the 288-acre Fort Apache Historic Park, features exhibits of historic and contemporary baskets, bowls, water jugs, and other Apache-made objects. A reconstructed Apache village and the Theodore Roosevelt Indian School also are at the site.

White Mountain Apache Cultural Center and Museum, Log Cabin Rd., PO Box 507, Fort Apache, AZ 85926. Phone: 928/338–4625. Fax: 928/338–1716. Web site: *www.wmat.nsn.us*. Hours: Memorial Day–Labor Day — 8–5 Mon.-Sat.; closed Sun.; remainder of year — 9–5 Mon.-Fri.; closed Sat.-Sun. Admission: adults, $5; seniors and children 6–17, $3; tribal members and children under 6, free.

Wichita Tribal Museum. The Wichita tribe's administration building in Anadarko, Oklahoma, is the home of the small Wichita Tribal Museum. It consists largely of display cases with artifacts, photographs, and information on the history and culture of the tribe.

Wichita Tribal Museum, Administration Bldg., PO Box 729, Anadarko, OK 73005. Phone: 425/247–2425. Hours: 8–5 Mon.-Fri.; closed Sat.-Sun. and major holidays. Admission: free.

Woodruff Museum of Indian Artifacts. The Woodruff Museum of Indian Artifacts, located in the Bridgeton Free Public Library in Bridgeton, New Jersey, contains over 20,000 artifacts relating to the history and life of the Minsi, Unalachtigo, and Lenni-Lenape, the original American Indians in area.

Woodruff Museum of Indian Artifacts, Bridgeton Free Public Library, 150 E. Commerce St., Bridgeton, NJ 08302. Phone: 856/451–2620. Fax: 856/455–1049. Hours: 1–4 Mon.-Fri.; 11–2 Sat.; closed Sun. and major holidays. Admission: free.

Ya'i Heki' Regional Indian Museum. The Ya'i Heki' Regional Indian Museum at the Lake Perris State Recreation Area in Perris, California, interprets the history and culture of American Indian tribes in the southern California desert region. The museum is one of a series of state regional Native American museums administered by the California State Department of Parks and Recreation.

Ya'i Heki' Regional Indian Museum, Lake Perris State Recreation Area, 17801 Lake Perris Dr., Perris, CA 92571. Phones: 951/940–5656 and 951/940–5600. Fax: 951/940–5669. Web site: *www.parks.ca.gov/?page_id=651.* Hours: 10–2 Wed.; 10–4 Sat.-Sun.; closed remainder of week and major holidays. Admission: museum — free; park — $3 per car.

Yakama Nation Cultural Heritage Center. The Yakama Nation Cultural Heritage Center near Toppenish, Washington, has exhibits pertaining to the history and culture of the 14 Confederated Tribes and Bands of the Yakama Indian Nation. The center, housed in a building based on the Yakama's traditional mat-covered longhouse, contains an earthen lodge made of willow branches, reeds, grasses, and mud; a string diary made of hemp twine; and collections of fishing gear, baskets, tools, and other artifacts and materials from the Northwestern Plateau Indian nation. Six changing exhibitions also are mounted each year. In addition, demonstrations are given of Klickitat basketry, beadwork, woodcarving, and buckskin work.

Yakama Nation Cultural Heritage Center, Confederated Tribes and Bands of the Yakama Indian Nation, 100 Speelyi Loop, PO Box 151, Toppenish, WA 98948. Phone: 509/865-2800. Fax: 509/865-5749. Web site: *www.wolfenet.com/~yingis/hert.html.* Hours: 9–5 daily. Admission: adults, $4; seniors and students, $2; children 7–10, $1; children under 7, free.

Ysleta del Sur Cultural Art Center. Exhibits on the history, artifacts, arts, and crafts of the Tigua Indians and weekend presentations of traditional dances and bread baking are offered at the Ysleta del Sur Cultural Art Center on the Tigua Indian Reservation, now part of El Paso, Texas. The 1681 Ysleta Mission, the oldest mission in Texas, also is located nearby. The Tigua community was established in 1681 by refugees from a bloody Indian uprising that expelled the Spanish and Christian Indians from present-day New Mexico. The historic Ysleta Mission was founded in the same year (see separate listing in Spanish Historic Sites section).

Ysleta del Sur Cultural Art Center, Tigua Indian Reservation, 305 Yaya Lane, El Paso, TX 79907–5621. Phone: 915/859-5287. Fax: 915/860-8972. Hours: 9–4 Tues.-Fri.; 9–5 Sat.-Sun.; closed Mon. and major holidays. Admission: free.

Zia Cultural C enter. The Zia Cultural Center at the Zia Pueblo near Bernalillo, New Mexico, features exhibits of pottery, sculpture, weavings, and paintings produced by the tribe. Also located

nearby is the Our Lady of Assumption Church, an early seventeenth-century mission that is open during Sunday services every other week. A Corn Dance is one of the highlights of the pueblo's annual Feast Day celebration on August 15.

Zia Cultural Center, Zia Pueblo, 135 Capitol Square Dr., Zia Pueblo, NM 87053. Phones: 505/867-3304 and 505/864-3308 (also fax). Hours: 8–5 Mon.-Fri.; closed Sat.-Sun. and some tribal religious and ceremonial days. Admission: donation.

Ziibiwing Center of Anishinable Culture and Lifeways. The history and culture of the Saginaw Chippewa Indian tribe and other Great Lakes Anishinabek are depicted at the Ziibiwing Center of Anishinable Culture and Lifeways in Mt. Pleasant, Michigan. Among the displays are historical documents, paintings, and tribal artifacts.

Ziibiwing Center of Anishinable Culture and Lifeways, 6650 E. Broadway, Mt. Pleasant, MI 48858. Phones: 989/775-4750 and 800/225-8172. Fax: 989/775-4770. Web site: *www.sagchip.org/ziibiwing/index.htm.* Hours: 10–6 Mon.-Sat.; closed Sun. and major holidays. Admission: adults, $5.50; college students, $4.50; seniors, military, and children 5–17, $3.75; children under 5, free.

Museums Honoring Individuals

Ataloa Lodge Museum. The Ataloa Lodge Museum at Bacone College in Muskogee, Oklahoma, is named for Mary Stone McLendon, a Chickasaw whose Indian name was Ataloa (Little Song). She taught at the college from 1927 to 1935, when Bacone was the only Indian college in the nation. She also served as field secretary for the college and collected many of the items for her dream — an Indian museum at the college. The museum became a reality in 1932 and was named in her honor after her death in 1967.

The museum has more than 20,000 objects, including such American Indian artifacts and materials as pottery, projectile points, paintings, baskets, clothing, blankets, rugs, kachinas, quillwork, moose-hair embroidery, ceremonial items, decorative materials, weapons, canoes, and contemporary art. Some of the collection came from the families of such Indian leaders as Geronimo, Chief Joseph, and Pleasant Porter. The museum also has prehistoric fossils and other historic materials, including documents by President Abraham Lincoln, Chief John Ross, and others. The stone-and-log museum building has a fireplace made of rocks and stones provided by Indian tribes from the lands where they lived.

Ataloa Lodge Museum, Bacone College, 2299 Old Bacone Rd., Muskogee, OK 74403. Phones:

918/683–4581 and 888/682–5514. Fax: 9818/687–5913. Hours: 10–12 and 1–4 Mon.-Fri. and by appointment; closed national holidays. Admission: adults, $2; children, free.

Black Hawk State Historic Site and Hauberg Indian Museum. The Black Hawk State Historic Site near Rock Island, Illinois, honors the Sauk warrior who led pro-British Indians against American forces in the War of 1812 and later initiated the Black Hawk War in 1832. Prehistoric Indians and nineteenth-century tribes, including the Sauk (Sac) and Mesquakie (Fox), once lived on the 208-acre site along the Rock River. Saukenuk, the Sauk capital located adjacent to the historic site, was destroyed by Americans during the Revolutionary War because some members of the tribe had given military support to the British.

When several Sauk chiefs ceded the village land to the United States in 1804, Black Hawk refused to recognize the cession as legal and his followers defended the site and defeated the Americans in two Mississippi River battles. But the Sauk and Mesquakie were forced to move across the river into Iowa in the 1820s when white settlers came into the area. In 1832, Black Hawk led more than 1,000 members of the tribe back into Illinois in an attempt to regain the land. But they were chased into southern Wisconsin and later defeated in the Battle of Bad Axe by Illinois militia and U.S. troops.

The Black Hawk State Historic site now is primarily a recreational and nature park, but it does contain the Hauberg Indian Museum, the only museum devoted exclusively to the Sauk and Mesquakie tribes. The museum has replicas of Sauk winter and summer dwellings, dioramas depicting 1750–1830 lifestyles and activities of the Sauk and Fox tribes, and such artifacts as trade goods, jewelry, and domestic items.

Black Hawk State Historic Site and Hauberg Indian Museum, State Rte. 54 and Black Hawk Rd., Rock Island, IL 61201 (mailing address: 1510 46th Ave., Rock Island, IL 6l201). Phone: 309/788–9536. Fax: 309/788–9865. E-mail: *haubermuseum@aol.com*. Hours: Mar.-Oct.— 9–12 and 1–5 Wed.-Sun.; closed Mon.-Tues.; remainder of year — 9–12 and 1–4 Wed.-Sun.; closed Mon.-Tues., New Year's Day, Thanksgiving, and Christmas. Admission: free.

Black Kettle Museum. The Black Kettle Museum, close to the Washita Battlefield National Historic Site near Cheyenne, Oklahoma, is devoted to the respected leader of the Southern Cheyenne, the Cheyenne people, and the attack led by Lieutenant Colonel George Armstrong Custer on Black Kettle's peaceful village in 1868. The museum, operated by the Oklahoma Historical Society, also served as the

interpretive center for the historic site while the recently completed Cultural Heritage Center was constructed at the battlefield. It has exhibits on the Battle of the Washita, Black Kettle and the Cheyenne, 1860 to 1880 U.S. Cavalry, and 1860 to 1880 arts and crafts of Plains Indians.

Black Kettle, who survived the 1864 Sand Creek Massacre in Colorado, sought peace for his people and signed the Little Arkansas treaties in 1865 and Medicine Lodge Treaty in 1867. But he and his wife, Medicine Woman, were among the many Cheyenne killed when Custer's troops attacked Black Kettle's camp along the Washita River while searching for Cheyenne and Arapaho warriors responsible for raids along the Saline and Solomon rivers in Kansas (see separate listing for Washita Battlefield National Historic Site in Historic Sites section).

Black Kettle Museum, 101 S. L.L. Males St., PO Box 252, Cheyenne, OK 73628–0252. Phone: 580/497–3929. E-mail: *bkmus@dobsonteleco.com*. Web site: *www.ok-history.mus.ok.us/mus-sites/masnum03.htm*. Hours: 10–11:45 and 1–4 Tues.-Fri.; 9–5 Sat.-Sun.; closed Mon. and legal holidays. Admission: adults, $1 suggested donation; children, free.

Buechel Memorial Lakota Museum. The Buechel Memorial Lakota Museum at the St. Francis Indian Mission in St. Francis, South Dakota, features many of the artifacts and other historical materials collected by Father Eugene Buechel, former superior of the mission for whom the museum is named. Buechel, who spent 49 years among the Sioux, was the author of a Lakota Bible history, a prayer book and hymnal, and a Lakota grammar book. The museum depicts Lakota Sioux lifeways and transition into the twentieth century.

Buechel Memorial Lakota Museum, St. Francis Indian Mission, 350 S. Oak St., PO Box 499, St. Francis, SD 57572. Phone: 605/747–2745. Fax: 605/747–5057. E-mail: *museum@gwtc.net*. Web site: *www.sfmission.org*. Hours: May-Oct.— 8–5 daily; remainder of year — by appointment. Admission: free.

Chief John Ross House. The 1797 home of Cherokee Chief John Ross has been preserved in his honor in Rossville, Georgia. The two-story log house was built by John McDonald, a Scottish trader who was his grandfather. Ross moved into the house after his mother, Mollie Ross, the daughter of McDonald and his Cherokee wife, died in 1808. The house served as a post office, country store, schoolhouse, and council room during the period Ross lived in it. When he started spending more time at the confluence of the Etowah and Oostanaula rivers, where he operated a ferry and had additional property, he sold the house to a relative in 1827. The town of Rossville is named for Ross, who also founded Ross's Landing, which later became Chattanooga. The house now contains historical furniture and exhibits and is the focus of special events.

Chief John Ross House, 200 E. Lake Ave., Rossville, GA 30741 (mailing address: 826 Chickamauga Ave., Rossville, GA 30741). Phone: 706/861–3954. Fax: 706/861–3967. Hours: May-Sept.—10–2 Mon.-Sat.; closed Sun., major holidays, and remainder of year. Admission: free.

Chieftains Museum and Major Ridge Home. The Chieftains Museum and Major Ridge Home in Rome, Georgia, is housed in a 1790 log cabin that was expanded in 1828 to a larger plantation house—called the Chieftains—belonging to Cherokee leader Major Ridge. In addition to honoring Ridge and preserving and interpreting the heritage represented by the National Historic Landmark house, the museum includes the history and traditions of the Cherokee Indians and the clash of cultures in the Southeast that culminated in the Trail of Tears forced march to Indian Territory (Oklahoma) in 1838 and 1839.

During the War of 1812, Ridge led a contingent of Cherokees who fought along with American forces against the British and the Creek Red Sticks. In 1814, the Cherokees were a decisive factor in defeating the Creeks at the Battle of Horseshoe Bend. Because of his role in recruiting and leading the Cherokees, Ridge was made a major by General Andrew Jackson. Thereafter, Ridge used the rank as his first name.

Ridge and his family moved into the two-story dog-trot cabin on the east bank of the Oostanaula River in the early 1800s and then expanded it into a stately while plantation house, from which they operated a ferry, trading post, and plantation with numerous crops, orchards, and slaves. The Cherokees, however, were still viewed by many as uneducated savages and some wanted their fertile land and gold deposits. Faced with increasing pressure, Ridge and others signed the Treaty of New Echota in 1835 that sold the Cherokee land to the United States. The Ridge family moved to Indian Territory in 1837, and shortly afterwards other Cherokee were being rounded up and forced to leave for Indian Territory during one of the worst winters on record. During the 800-mile trip, as many as 4,000 (about one-quarter of the people) died. The embittered survivors blamed the treaty party and the Ridge family for their suffering. In 1839, Major Ridge and a nephew, Elias Boudinot, were killed by representatives of a small Cherokee group who met in secret, held a trial, and declared that the treaty signers were guilty of treason.

Chieftains Museum and Major Ridge Home, 501 Riverside Pkwy., Rome, GA 30161 (mailing address: PO Box 373, Rome, GA 30152). Phone: 706/291–9494. Fax: 706/291–2410. E-mail: *chmuseum@ bellsouth.net.* Web site: *www.chieftainsmuseum.org.* Hours: 9–3 Tues.-Fri.; 10–4 Sat.; closed Sun.-Mon. and major holidays. Admission: adults, $3; seniors, $2; children, $1.50.

Chief Oshkosh Native American Arts. Chief Oshkosh Native American Arts is an art gallery in Egg Harbor, Wisconsin, named for the 1827 to 1858 chief of the Menominee Indian tribe. The Menominee leader moved the tribe from the upper Wisconsin River to the tribal reservation on the west side of Keshena Falls in 1852. The gallery displays artworks by Native American artists.

Chief Oshkosh Native American Arts, 7631 Egg Harbor Rd., Egg Harbor, WI 54209. Phone: 920/868–3240. Hours: May-Labor Day—10–6 Tues.-Sun.; closed Mon.; Sept.-Christmas—10–6 Fri.-Sun.; closed Mon.-Thurs., most holidays, and remainder of year. Admission: free.

Chief Plenty Coups Museum State Park. Chief Plenty Coups Museum State Park near Pryor, Montana, is named for the last traditional chief of the Crow tribe. The chief's house, store, burial site, and springs are located at the 195-acre park. Chief Plenty Coups, who lived from 1848 to 1932 and presided over the tribe's transition from a nomadic life to living on a reservation, donated his property to "the people" for a peace park and requested that the park and museum be dedicated to the Crow tribe, not just to him. The chief's ca. 1909 log house contains personal items and interpretive exhibits on his life and Crow culture.

Chief Plenty Coups Museum State Park, Edgar Rd., PO Box 100, Pryor, MT 59066. Phone: 406/252–1289. Fax: 406/252–6668. E-mail: *plentycoups@ plentycoups.org.* Web site: *www.plentycoups.org.* Hours: May-Sept.—park: 8–8 daily; museum: 10–5 daily; closed remainder of year. Admission: non-residents, $2; state residents, free.

Chief Timothy State Park and Alpowai Interpretive Center. Chief Timothy State Park, located on the site of the mid–1800s Alpowai encampment of the Nez Percé tribe near Clarkston, Washington, honors the chief who was a trusted friend of the early settlers in the area. The park's Alpowai Interpretive Center tells about the Nez Percé history, culture, and village, including the Lewis and Clark Expedition meeting with the tribe.

Chief Timothy State Park and Alpowai Interpretive Center, 13766 U.S. Hwy. 12, Clarkston, WA 99403. Phone: 509/758–9580. Web site: *www.state parks.com/chief_timothy.html.* Hours: May-Sept.—

park: 8–10 daily; interpretive center: 12–8 Fri.-Sun.; closed Mon.-Thurs. and remainder of year. Admission: park — $5.36 per car; interpretive center: free.

Coronado State Monument. See Prehistoric Sites and Museums section.

Crazy Horse Memorial. The world's largest sculpture — the Crazy Horse Memorial in the Black Hills near Custer, South Dakota — is a tribute to the great Oglala Sioux Indian leader. When completed, it will be 563 feet high and 641 feet long and show Crazy Horse sitting atop his stallion with his left arm outstretched, pointing to the nearby Sioux burial grounds. The face of Crazy Horse has been completed and work is progressing on the remainder of the memorial. The Indian Museum of North America at the foot of the sculpture already is open (see separate listing in Museums and Galleries section).

The project was initiated in 1939 by Sioux chief Henry Standing Bear (speaking on behalf of tribal leaders) when he asked New England sculptor Korczak Ziolkowski, who won first prize for sculpture at the 1939 New York World's Fair and assisted Gutzon Borglum in carving the Mt. Rushmore Memorial, to carve a mountain memorial to Crazy Horse. World War II intervened, but in 1946 Ziolkowski accepted the invitation and began work on the memorial. He bought a 600-foot monolith in the Black Hills and made a marble scale model of the sculpture.

The following year Ziolkowski moved to the site, built a log studio-home and workshop (which still exists and can be visited), and decided to carve the memorial in the round, rather than just the top 100 feet as originally planned. He worked on the huge sculpture with his wife, Ruth, and their 10 children until his death in 1982. Since then, Ruth and the family have spearheaded the project. Approximately 1 million people now visit the site each year to see the work on the memorial and visit the adjacent Indian Museum of North America, founded in 1972, and other facilities. In the summer, an outdoor laser light multimedia show also is presented each evening.

Crazy Horse Memorial, Ave. of the Chiefs, Crazy Horse, SD 57730–9506. Phone: 605/673–4681. Fax: 605/673–2185. E-mail *memorial@crazyhorse.org*. Web site: *www.crazyhorse.org*. Hours: Memorial Day weekend-mid-Oct. — 7–9 daily (closes after a nightly laser light multimedia show); remainder of year — 8–4:30 daily; closed Christmas. Admission: adults, $10; seniors, $9; Native Americans, military, Custer County residents, Boy and Girl Scouts in uniform, and children under 6, free; or carload, $24; senior carload, $21.

Father Marquette National Memorial. See French Museums Honoring Individuals section.

George W. Brown, Jr., Ojibwe Museum and Cultural Center. The George W. Brown, Jr., Ojibwe Museum and Cultural Center, named for a prominent tribal elder, has artifacts dating from the mid-eighteenth century; dioramas of the four seasons of Ojibwe life; exhibits of tribal clothing, birch bark canoes, arts, and crafts; and a French trading post. One of the highlights at the museum and cultural center, located on the Lac du Flambeau Chippewa Indian Reservation in Lac du Flambeau, Wisconsin, is a 24-foot dug-out canoe believed to be from the mid–1700s that was recovered from a nearby lake.

George W. Brown, Jr., Ojibwe Museum and Cultural Center, Peace Pipe Rd., PO Box 804, Lac du Flambeau, WI 54538. Phone: 715/588–3333. Hours: May-Oct. — 10–4 Mon.-Sat.; closed Sun.; remainder of year — 10–2 Tues.-Thurs.; closed Fri.-Mon. and major holidays. Admission: adults, $2; children 5–15, $1; children under 5, free.

Jesse Peter Museum. The Jesse Peter Museum at Santa Rosa Junior College in Santa Rosa, California, is named for the faculty member and initial director who was a naturalist and explorer who made expeditions to the American Southwest in the 1930s to collect Native American art and geological specimens. Among the ceramic treasures found by Peter were works by the highly regarded Lucy Lewis (Acoma) and Nampeyo (Hopi).

The museum, which opened as a natural history museum with a small collection of American Indian art in 1940, later was converted to an art museum featuring ethnographic arts, with the emphasis on Native Americans. The museum also has some works from other parts of the Americas, Africa, Asia, and the Pacific. It contains permanent exhibits on American Indian basketry, pottery, kachinas, jewelry, and models of a Pomo roundhouse and a Hopi pueblo. They are supplemented by changing ethnographic exhibitions.

Jesse Peter Museum, Santa Rosa Junior College, Bussman Hall, 1501 Mendocino Ave., Santa Rosa, CA 95401. Phone: 707/527–4479. Fax: 707/524–1861. E-mail: *bbenson@santarosa.edu*. Web site: *www.santarosa.edu/museum*. Hours: mid-Aug.-mid-May — 9–5 Mon.-Fri.; closed Sat.-Sun., summer, and college and major holidays. Admission: free.

Jim Thorpe Home. The 1917 to 1923 home of Jim Thorpe, the Sauk and Fox Olympian and All-American football star, became a historic house museum featuring his track and field awards and family items in Yale, Oklahoma. Thorpe won the decathlon and pentathlon at the 1912 Olympics,

CRAZY HORSE MEMORIAL FOUNDATION
1/34™ SCALE MODEL
MOUNTAIN 3/4™ MILE IN DISTANCE
KORCZAK, SCULPTOR

The Crazy Horse Memorial in the Black Hills near Custer, South Dakota, honors the great Oglala Sioux Indian leader. A sculpture showing Crazy Horse sitting atop his stallion with an outstretched left arm is the world's largest sculpture. It will be 563 feet high and 641 feet long when completed. This photograph shows the scale model in front of the actual sculpture where it is being carved. *Courtesy Crazy Horse Memorial.* © Crazy Horse Memorial Foundation.

but later was disqualified for losing his amateur status. However, his medals were restored in 1982. Thorpe also was named to the All-American football team while playing for the Carlisle Indian School in 1911 and 1912, and he later played professional baseball (1913 to 1919) and football (1919 to 1926) and served as the first president of the National Football League in 1920 and 1921. The town of Jim Thorpe, Pennsylvania, also is named in his honor

Jim Thorpe Home, 706 E. Boston Ave., Yale, OK 74085. Phone: 918/387-2815. Hours: 10–5 Tues.-Sat.; 1–5 Sun.; closed Mon. and major holidays. Admission: free.

Junaluska Memorial and Museum. The Junaluska Memorial and Museum, which honors the Cherokee leader and warrior, is located at his burial site in the Great Smoky Mountains near the Nantahala River in Robbinsville, North Carolina.

Junaluska reportedly saved General Andrew Jackson's life from Creek Indians in the 1814 Battle of Horseshoe Bend. But after Jackson became president, he demanded the removal of the Cherokees to Indian Territory (later Oklahoma). It also was in Robbinsville that the infamous 1838 to 1839 Trail of Tears had its beginning. Junaluska appealed without success to keep his people in their North Carolina homeland. When he returned to Robbinsville many years later, the state of North Carolina granted him 337 acres on which he built his farm and on which he lived until his death in 1855.

Junaluska's burial site has a seven-sided monument around the grave. Seven granite markers — one for each of the seven Cherokee clans — tell of his life and achievements. The museum contains exhibits on Junaluska and Cherokee history in the area; a collection of early projectile points, pottery, stone tools, and other artifacts; and arts and crafts from Choeah Valley (now Snowbird Indian community).

Junaluska Memorial and Museum, 1 Junaluska Dr., PO Box 1209, Robbinsville, NC 28771. Phone: 828/470–4727. Fax: 828/479–4636. E-mail: *friendsofjuno@dnet.net*. Web site: *www.junaluska.com*. Hours: 8–4:30 Mon.-Fri. and by appointment Sat.-Sun.; closed major holidays. Admission: free.

Marquette Mission Park and Museum of Ojibwa Culture. The Marquette Mission Park in St. Ignace, Michigan, memorializes Father Jacques Marquette, the French Jesuit priest who established a mission there in 1671, explored the Mississippi to the Arkansas River with Louis Jolliet in 1673, and spent 1674 and 1675 on a mission with the Illinois Indians. He is buried next to the chapel in the park.

The Museum of Ojibwa Culture, also located in the park, depicts Straits of Mackinac life over 300 years ago when Ojibwa, Huron, Odawa, and French lifestyles met at the protected bay. The exhibits show Ojibwa culture and traditions, the French contact period, and results of the site's archaeology. Outdoor exhibits and a Huron longhouse also are on the grounds, the site of an annual Native American art festival and powwow around Labor Day.

Marquette Mission Park and Museum of Ojibwa Culture, 500 N. State St., St. Ignace, MI 49781–1429. Phone: 906/643–9161. Web site: *www.stignace.com/attractions/ojibwa*. Hours: park — dawn-dusk daily; museum — Memorial Day weekend-early Oct.: 1:30–5:30 daily; closed remainder of year. Admission: park — free; museum — adults, $2; elementary students, $1; preschool children, free; families, $5.

National Shrine of Blessed Kateri Tekakwitha and Native American Exhibit. The National Shrine of Blessed Kateri Takakwitha near Fonda, New York, honors the young woman who became the first Native American saint in the United States. She was born in Auriesville in 1656 of an Algonquin mother and Mohawk chief. They and a son died of smallpox when Kateri was four years old. She survived, but her face was badly scarred and her eyesight was impaired. As a result, she was named Tekakwitha, which means "she who bumps into things."

Tekakwitha was taken in by her uncle and when she was eight she said she wanted to devote her life to God, despite the opposition of her foster parents. She was baptized in 1676 in a little chapel in the village of Caughnawaga, and when she became 18 she began taking instructions in the Catholic faith. But when she was subjected to ridicule and scorn by Indian villagers, she fled by canoe to the Mission of St. Francis Xavier, a settlement of Christian Indians near Montreal, in Canada, where she made her first Holy Communion and a vow of perpetual virginity.

While in Canada, she taught prayers to children, worked with the elderly and sick, and was known for her great devotion to the Blessed Sacrament and the Cross of Christ. She was called "Lily of the Mohawks." However, she suffered from a serious illness and died shortly before her 24th birthday. Several persons, including the priest who attended to her during the last illness, reported that she appeared to them and that many healing miracles were attributed to her. In recognition of her faith and contributions, Kateri was declared blessed by Pope John Paul II in 1980.

Caughnawaga, the place near Fonda where Kateri lived for much of her short life, is the site of her shrine and a Native American exhibit. The Indian village site was discovered in 1950 and excavated by 1957, displaying the outlines of 12 longhouses and a stockade. It is the nation's only completely excavated Iroquois village. A Mohawk-style chapel and an exhibit also are located in a nearby 1782 renovated barn. The chapel, which commemorates the one in which Kateri was baptized, is on the upper floor, and the exhibit on the lower floor. The exhibit contains artifacts from many American Indian tribes and a model of how the Mohawk village of Caughnawaga looked 300 years ago. The site also has a Kateri rosary circle and statue and a replica longhouse used for guests.

National Shrine of Blessed Kateri Tekakwitha and Native American Exhibit, Rte. 5, Box 627, RD1. Fonda. NY 12068. Phone: 518/853–3646. Fax: 518/853–3371. E-mail: *kkenny@nycap.rr.com*. Web site: *www.katerishrine.com*. Hours: May-Oct.— 9–6 daily; other times by appointment. Admission: free.

Oscar Howe Art Center. The Oscar Howe Art Center in Mitchell, South Dakota, has a collection of more than 20 paintings by Yantonai Sioux artist Oscar Howe and changing exhibitions of work by regional artists. The art center is housed in the restored 1902 Carnegie Library building, where Howe painted the dome mural *Sun and Rain Clouds Over Hills* as part of a Works Progress Administration project in the 1940s.

Oscar Howe Art Center, 119 W. 3rd Ave., PO Box 1161, Mitchell, SD 57301. Phone: 605/996–4111. Fax: 605/996–4667. Hours: 10–5 Tues.-Sat.; closed Sun.-Mon. and major holidays. Admission: free.

Sacajawea State Park and Interpretive Center. The Sacajawea State Park and its Sacajawea Interpretive Center near Pasco, Washington, honor the young Shoshone woman who served as guide and interpreter for the Lewis and Clark Expedition. The park is located at the confluence of the Snake and Columbia rivers where the exhibition camped, hunted, repaired equipment, and met with some 200 Sahaptin-speaking Indians in 1805. The interpretive center tells the story of the Lewis and Clark Expedition, the role of Sacajawea, and their activities at the site. It also contains stone and bone tools dating from 200 to 12,000 years ago of the Sahaptin- and Cayuse-speaking tribes along the Columbia, Snake, Palouse, and Walla Walla rivers.

Sacajawea State Park and Interpretive Center, 2503 Sacajawea Park Rd., Pasco, WA 99301. Phone: 509/545–2361. Web site: *www.parks.wa.gov/lewisandclark/lcsacainterctr.* Hours: park — 8-dusk daily; interpretive center — mid–May-Labor Day —12–5 Fri.-Tues.; closed Wed.-Thurs. and remainder of year. Admission: free.

San Ildefonso Pueblo Museum (dedicated to Maria Martinez). See Museums and Galleries section.

Shako:wi Cultural Center. The Shako:wi Cultural Center at the Oneida Indian Nation in Oneida, New York, is named for the late Richard Chrisjohn (whose Shako:wi name means "he gives"), a member of the Wolf clan who was the tribe's long-time representative. The center, which occupies an impressive white pine log building, is devoted to the history and culture of the Oneida, including the role it played as the first ally of the colonists during the Revolutionary War. The building is filled with objects and stories of the past and present of the Oneida people. Among the arts and crafts on display are baskets, carvings, beadwork, rattles, dolls, and wampum belts and pouches made by tribal members.

Shako:wi Cultural Center, Oneida Indian Nation, 5 Territory Rd., Oneida, NY 13421–9304. Phone 315/829–8801. Fax: 315/363–1843. Web site: *www.oneida-nation.net.* Hours: 9–5 daily; closed American Indian Day (the Fri. before Labor Day) and major holidays. Admission: free.

Sheldon Jackson Museum. See Arctic Peoples Museums Honoring Individuals section.

Sitting Bull Burial State Historic Site. See Historic Sites section.

Tahlonteeskee Cherokee Courthouse Museum. The Tahlonteeskee Cherokee Courthouse Museum, which tells the story of the Cherokees who came to Indian Territory (Oklahoma) to form the first settlement, is named for Chief Tahlonteeskee, who founded the nation. It is located in the tribe's reconstructed 1829 council house and courthouse, with the original cabin being adjacent, near Gore, Oklahoma.

The council house initially was the capitol and courthouse of the western portion of the Cherokee Nation. It became the seat of the entire Cherokee Nation when eastern Cherokees were forced to take the Trail of Tears forced march in 1838 and 1839 to join their western counterparts. But the capitol was moved to Tahlequah in 1843 when the eastern Cherokees regained control of the tribal government. The reconstructed council house now serves as a visitor center and museum with exhibits and artifacts relating to the tribe's history.

Tahlonteeskee Cherokee Courthouse Museum, U.S. Hwy. 64, Rte. 2, Box 37–1, Gore, OK 74435. Phone: 918/489–5663. Fax 918/489–2217. E-mail: *fgilliam@twinterritories.com.* Web site: *www.twinterritories.com.* Hours: 9–5 Mon.-Fri.; 1–5 Sun., and by appointment; closed major holidays. Admission: free.

Historic Sites

Baranov Museum. See Arctic Peoples Museums and Galleries section.

Bear Paw Battlefield. The Bear Paw Battlefield near Chinook, Montana, was the site of the last battle of the Nez Percé War of 1877. It is where Chief Joseph and his followers surrendered to Colonel Nelson A. Miles after attempting to escape to Canada rather than move to a smaller Indian reservation. On behalf of the 432 survivors, Chief Joseph gave his rifle to Miles, saying, "From where the sun now stands, I will fight no more, forever."

Five bands of Nez Percé— consisting of approximately 800 people, including 125 warriors — began a 1,300-mile journey from northeastern Oregon and central Idaho over the Bitterroot Mountains and through the Montana Territory in the summer of 1877. They were pursued by the U.S. Army for nearly four months and fought two major battles — the Battle of the Big Hole (see separate listing) near Wisdom, Montana, and the Battle of Bear Paw — before surrendering 40 miles south of the Canadian border after five days of fighting. Both battlefields now are part of the Nez Percé National Historical Park (see separate listing). Bear Paw has a walking trail and picnic facilities. Its visitor center with exhibits on the Nez Percé flight, Bear Paw Battlefield, and national historical park is located at Blaine County Museum in Chinook.

Bear Paw Battlefield, Nez Perce National Historical Park, U.S. Hwy. 2, PO Box 26, Chinook, MT 59523. Phone: 406/357–3130. Web site: *www.nps.gov/nepe.* Hours: May-Sept.— dawn-dusk daily; closed remainder of year. Admission: free.

Bear Paw Battlefield Visitor Center, Blaine County Museum, 501 Indiana St., PO Box 927, Chinook, MT 59523. Phone: 406/357–2590. Fax: 406/357–

2199. Hours: June-Aug.— 8–5 Mon.-Sat.; 12–5 Sun.; May and Sept.— 8–5 Mon.-Fri.; closed Sat.-Sun.; remainder of year —1–5 Mon.-Fri.; closed Sat.-Sun. and major holidays. Admission: free.

Big Hole National Battlefield. The Battle of the Big Hole west of Wisdom, Montana, was a significant juncture in the Nez Percé War of 1877 because of the number of lives lost. It also led to the climactic Battle of Bear Paw near Chinook, Montana (see separate listing). The fleeing band of Nez Percé, led by Chief Joseph, refused to moved to a smaller reservation and sought to escape to Canada. When confronted at Big Hole, the Nez Percé repulsed the U.S. Army troops and civilian volunteers, but suffered 60 to 90 casualties and were forced to leave behind many of their belongings, while the military lost 29 dead and 40 wounded.

The Big Hole National Battlefield is a memorial to the people who fought and died there on August 9 and 10 in 1877. It memorializes Chief Joseph's Nez Percé men, women, and children; the 7th U.S. Infantry soldiers; and the Bitterroot volunteers who were involved in the battle. A visitor center has a video presentation and exhibits of historical photographs, quotations, and personal belongings of some of the battle participants and noncombatants. The Big Hole and Bear Paw battlefields now are part of the Nez Percé National Historical Park (see separate listing), headquartered in Spalding, Idaho, which extends over 1,500 miles in five states. It includes 38 sites that reflect the history and culture of the Nez Percé and their relationships with early explorers, missionaries, miners, settlers, and soldiers.

Big Hole National Battlefield, State Hwy. 237, PO Box 237, Wisdom, MT 59761. Phone: 406/689–3155. Fax: 406/689-3151. Web site: *www.nps.gov/biho.* Hours: Memorial Day-Sept.— 9–6 daily; remainder of year — 9-5 daily; closed New Year's Day, Thanksgiving, and Christmas. Admission: $5 per car or $3 per person.

Black Hawk State Historic Site. See Museums Honoring Individuals section.

Chickasaw Council House Museum. See Museums and Galleries section.

Chickasaw Village Site. The Chickasaw Village Site in the Natchez Trace Parkway northwest of Tupelo, Mississippi, was the location of a fortified Chickasaw community from 1500 to 1600. It now has foundation markers, interpretive panels about the historic site, an exhibit shelter with information about the Chickasaw, and a nature trail along some of the plants the tribe used for food and medicine.

Chickasaw Village Site, Natchez Trace Pkwy., Mile-post 261.8, Tupelo, MS 38804 (mailing address: Visitor Center, Natchez Trace Pkwy, 2680 Natchez Trace, Tupelo, MS 38804). Phones: 662/680–4027 and 800/305–7417. Hours: dawn-dusk daily; closed Christmas. Admission: free.

Chickasaw White House. The Chickasaw White House — once considered a mansion on the frontier — was the home of Chickasaw governor Douglas Henry Johnson and his family from 1898 to 1971 on the north edge of Emet, Oklahoma. It was the scene of many important political and social events during Johnson's long 36-year tenure as tribal governor. He was instrumental in keeping white adventurers off tribal rolls, maintaining tribal control over Indian schools, and saving tribal government by insisting that Washington live up to its treaty obligations in regard to taxes. The historic house is undergoing restoration by the Chickasaw Nation, with plans for exhibits, guided tours, and the return of much of the original furniture.

Chickasaw White House, Emet, OK 73450 (mailing address: PO Box 1548, Ada, OK 74821). Phone: 580/436–2603. Web site: *www.chickasaw.net/site06/heritage/250_953.htm.* Hours and admission: still to be determined.

Creek Council House Museum. See Museums and Galleries section.

Double Ditch Indian Village State Historic Site. The site of a large earth lodge village inhabited by Mandan Indians from about 1675 to 1780 is preserved at the Double Ditch State Historic Site north of Bismarck, North Dakota. It contains the remains of dome-shaped dwellings of logs and earth, refuge mounds, and fortification ditches of the agricultural tribe. Only circular depressions remain of the approximately 150 earth lodges that ranged from 20 to 65 feet in diameter at the site — one of seven to nine such Mandan villages at the time near the mouth of the Heart River. It is believed all the villages in the area were abandoned when a massive smallpox epidemic swept the region about 1780. The site, administered by the State Historical Society of North Dakota, has signage and a small fieldhouse shelter at the entrance.

Double Ditch State Historic Site, off State Hwy. 1804, Bismarck, ND 58505 (mailing address: State Historical Society of North Dakota, 612 E. Boulevard Ave., Bismarck, ND 58505–0830). Phone: 701/328–2666. Fax: 701/328-3710. Web site: *www.state.nd.us/hist/doubleditch/doubleditch.htm.* Hours: dawn-dusk daily. Admission: free.

Fort William H. Seward. See Alaska Indian Arts in Arctic Peoples Museums and Galleries section.

Ganondagan State Historic Site. The Native

American community of Ganondagan in Victor, New York (just south of Rochester), once was a flourishing, vibrant center for the Seneca people. The village, known as the Town of Peace, was destroyed in 1687 by French Canadian forces led by the Marquis de Denonville, governor general of New France, who sought to annihilate the Seneca and eliminate them as competitors in the international fur trade. The Seneca survived as one of the six American Indian nations that comprised the Iroquois Confederacy, but Ganondagan was only a site for looting, excavation, and desecration for nearly 300 years before becoming a national historic landmark in 1964.

The site now is protected and has a full-size replica of a seventeenth-century Seneca bark longhouse; a visitor center and illustrated interpretive signs about Seneca history, customs, and beliefs; and three self-guided trails, including one leading to a mesa where visitors can see where a huge palisaded granary once stored hundreds of thousands of bushels of corn.

Ganondagan State Historic Site, 1488 Victor Bloomfield Rd. at State Rte. 444, PO Box 113, Victor, NY 14564. Phones: 585/924–5848 and 585/924–5414. Fax: 585/742–1732. E-mail: *friends@frontiernet.net*. Web site: *www.ganondagan.org*. Hours: site and trails — 8-sunset daily (weather permitting); visitor center — mid–May-late Oct.: 9–5 Tues.-Sun.; closed Mon. and remainder of year. Admission: site — free; guided tour of visitor center, bark longhouse, and trails: adults, $3; children, $2.

Grand Village of the Natchez Indians. The Grand Village of the Natchez Indians is located at a 128-acre state site that was the tribe's 1682 to 1729 main ceremonial center in Natchez, Mississippi. The Natchez Indians inhabited what is now southwestern Mississippi from 700 to 1773, reaching their zenith in the mid–1500s. The ceremonial site now has three ceremonial mounds, a reconstructed Natchez house, and a museum with artifacts from the site and exhibits about the history and culture of the tribe. Two of the mounds — Great Sun's Mound and Temple Mound — have been excavated and rebuilt to their original sizes and shapes. A religious structure once stood on Temple Mound and housed the remains of chiefs.

Grand Village of the Natchez Indians, 400 Jefferson Davis Blvd., Natchez, MS 39120. Phone: 601/446–6501. Fax: 601/446–6503. E-mail: *gvni@bkbank.com*. Web site: *www.mdah.state.ms.us*. Hours: 9–5 Mon.-Sat.; 1:30–5 Sun.; closed New Year's Day, Labor Day, Thanksgiving, and Christmas. Admission: free.

Historic Taos Pueblo. The oldest continuously inhabited community in the nation is the historic Taos Pueblo, a UNESCO world heritage cultural site constructed between 1000 and 1450 adjacent to the city of Taos, New Mexico. The most northern of the 19 pueblos in the state is best known for its two five-story adobe terraced communal dwellings still used by some members of the tribe. The pueblo remains much as it did before being conquered by the Spaniards in the seventeenth century. Approximately 150 people still live in the adobe dwellings, while many others now have homes in the surrounding areas.

The pueblo also contains the ruins of the San Gerónimo Mission, originally built by Spanish missionaries in 1619. It was destroyed in the Pueblo Revolt of 1680, rebuilt in 1706, and demolished again in 1847 by the U.S. Army during the Indian-Mexican uprising in New Mexico. It has been replaced by the St. Jerome Chapel, named for the patron saint of the pueblo. Visitors are welcome to tour the pueblo, but there is an entrance fee, as well as a fee for taking pictures.

Taos Pueblo, Tourism Office, PO Box 1846, Taos, NM 87571. Phone: 505/758–1028. E-mail: *tourism@taospueblo.com*. Web site: *www.taospueblo.com*. Hours: 8–4:30 daily; closed 10 weeks in late winter–early spring (and sometimes last week in Aug.) for religious activities. Admission: adults, $10; students, $5; children under 13, free; still, movie, or video camera fees, $5 each.

Hubbell Trading Post National Historic Site: The Hubbell Trading Post National Historic Site in Ganado, Arizona, is where John Lorenzo Hubbell opened the first trading post on the Navajo Indian Reservation in 1876. Hubbell became a trusted friend of the Navajo and he and his family operated the trading post for over 60 years. During that period, Hubbell and his two sons owned 30 trading posts, two wholesale houses, several ranches and farms, business properties, and stage and freight lines. Hubbell died in 1930 and was buried with his wife and a Navajo friend on a hill overlooking the trading post.

The Hubbell Trading Post in Ganado became a national historic site operated by the National Park Service in 1967. The trading post is still operating and looks much as it did under Hubbell. It is the oldest continuously operating trading post in the Navajo Nation. In addition to visiting the trading post, visitors can see the adjacent Hubbell home and explore the visitor center, which has exhibits and demonstrations of rug weaving and other native arts and crafts.

Hubbell Trading Post National Historic Site, Hwy. 264, PO Box 150, Ganado, AZ 86505-0150. Phone: 928/755–3475. Fax: 928/755–3405. E-mail: *e_chamberlin@nps.gov*. Web site: *www.nps.gov/hutr*. Hours:

May-Sept.— 8–6 daily; remainder of year — 8–5 daily; closed New Year's Day, Thanksgiving, and Christmas. Admission: adults, $2; children under 17, free.

Iliniwek Village State Historic Site. The largest and best preserved site of any known Illinois Indian village is the Iliniwek Village State Historic Site southeast of St. Francisville, Missouri. It existed from 1640 to 1683 when Europeans were just contacting Native Americans in the region. The Illinois Indians were the first American Indians that Louis Jolliet and Father Jacques Marquette encountered in Missouri in 1673 during their expedition down the Mississippi River. At the time, the village had about 300 lodges and around 8,000 people. Among the artifacts found at the site are ceramics and stone tools of the tribe, as well as such European contact objects as glass beads, metal objects, and Jesuit trade rings. Outdoor signage interprets the history and daily life of the Illinois Indians and the Jolliet and Marquette expedition.

Iliniwek Village State Historic Site, County Rd. B, St. Francisville, MO 63430 (mailing address: _ Battle of Athens State Historic Site, County Hwy. CC, Rte. 1, Box 26, Revere, MO 63465). Phones: 660/877–3871 and 800/334–6946. E-mail: *moparks@dnr.mo.gov*. E-mail: *www.moparks.com/iliniwek.htm*. Hours: dawn-dusk daily. Admission: free.

Indian Grinding Rock State Historic Park and Chaw'se Regional Indian Museum. Bedrock mortars and examples of the crafts and technology of the Miwok and other American Indian groups in the Sierra Nevada foothills can be seen at the Indian Grinding Rock State Historic Park and its Chaw'se Regional Indian Museum near Pine Grove, California. The 136-acre park preserves a great outcropping of marbleized limestone with some 1,185 mortar holes — the largest collection of bedrock mortars in North America. The Miwok ground acorns and other seeds in meal in the cup-shaped depressions in the stone. The grinding rock also contains a number of decorative carvings, circles, spoked wheels, animal and human tracks, and other patterns, some said to be 2,000 to 3,000 years old.

The park also has a museum and a nearby reconstructed Miwok village. The Chaw'se Regional Indian Museum (Chaw'se is the Miwok word for grinding rock) is housed in a two-story building resembling a traditional native roundhouse. It tells about the Miwok and grinding rock and displays collections of basketry, feather regalia, jewelry, arrowpoints, and other tools of the Northern, Central, and Southern Miwok; Maidu; Konkow; Monache; Nisenan; Tubalulabal; Washo; and Foohilol Yokuts.

Indian Grinding Rock State Historic Park and Chaw'se Regional Indian Museum, 14881 Pine Grove-Volcano Rd., Pine Grove, CA 95665. Phone: 209/296–7488. Fax: 209/296–7528. Web site: *www.parks.ca.gov/?page_id+553*. Hours: 11–5 Wed.-Fri.; 10–4 Sat.-Sun; closed Mon.-Tues., New Year's Day, Thanksgiving, and Christmas. Admission: park —$5 per car; $4 for senior car; museum — free.

Jémez State Memorial. The ruins of the 1280 to 1680 Guiswea Towa Indian pueblo and a ca. 1621 Spanish mission are located at the Jémez State Monument near Jémez Springs, New Mexico. Guiswea, named for the many hot springs in the area, was one of several villages the Tewa-speaking Jémez people built in the narrow mountain valley and the adjoining steep, sculptured mesas.

In the seventeenth century, the San José de los Jémez Mission was constructed during the Spanish colonization of New Mexico. However, the Jémez people later abandoned the site and moved a few miles south to what is now the Jémez Pueblo, which became the center of the religious activities. The massive ruins of the mission are considered among the most impressive in the Southwest. A visitor center operated by the New Mexico Department of Cultural Affairs now interprets the historic events from the perspective of the Jémez people.

Jémez State Monument, State Hwy. 4, PO Box 143, Jémez Springs, NM 87025. Phones: 505/829–3530 and 800/495–1279. Fax: 505/829–3530. E-mail: *giusewa@sulphurcanyon.com*. Web site: *www.nmmonuments.org*. Hours: 8:30–5 daily Wed.-Mon.; closed Tues., New Year's Day, Easter, Thanksgiving, and Christmas. Admission: adults, $3; children under 17, free; state residents, $1 on Wed.; seniors, free on Wed.

Kaw Mission State Historic Site. The Kaw Mission State Historic Site in Council Grove, Kansas, is where 30 Kaw (or Kansas) Indian boys lived and studied from 1851 to 1854. It was an Indian boarding school that was operated by the Methodists on the Kansas Indian Reservation. The two-story stone building preserved by the Kansas State Historical Society now contains artifacts and exhibits on Kaw history and culture, the mission school, and the nearby Santa Fe Trail.

Kaw Mission State Historic Site, 500 N. Mission St., Council Grove, KS 66846. Phone: 620/767–5410. Fax: 620/767–5816. E-mail: *kawmission@kshs.org*. Web site: *www.kawmission.org*. Hours: 10–5 Wed.-Sat.; 1–5 Sun.; closed Mon.-Tues. and state holidays. Admission adults, $2; seniors and students, $1; children under 5, free.

Knife River Indian Villages National Historic Site. The remains of five American Indian villages are preserved at the Knife River Indian Villages Historic Site near Stanton, North Dakota. The site is one of the oldest continuously occupied sites in North America. The Hidatsa, Mandan, and Arikara Indians were living along the Missouri River when the first European Americans arrived in the eighteenth century.

Three villages were the center of the Hidatsa people when the Lewis and Clark Expedition stopped at the site in 1804. It also was where Shoshone interpreter-guide Sacajawea and her trader husband, Toussaint Charbonneau, joined the exploratory party. Earth lodge depressions, cache pits, and fortification ditches — some that go back as far as 3,500 years — still can be seen at the site. The visitor center has an orientation film, historical exhibits, interpretive programs, and cultural demonstrations.

Knife River Indian Villages National Historic Site, 564 County Rd. 37, PO Box 9, Stanton, ND 58571. Phone: 701/745-3300. Fax: 701/745-3708. E-mail: *knri_information@nps.gov.* Web site: *www.nps.gov/ knri.* Hours: Memorial Day-Labor Day — 7:30-6 daily; remainder of year — 8-4:30 daily; closed New Year's Day, Thanksgiving, and Christmas. Admission: free.

Little Bighorn Battlefield National Monument. The Little Bighorn Battlefield National Monument near Crow Agency, Montana, is where the Northern Plains Indians fought their last major battle to preserve their ancestral way of life. They won the battle, but lost the war against the U.S. government's campaign to end their nomadic way of life and have them settle on reservations. It was in the valley of the Little Bighorn River in the summer of 1876 that several thousand Lakota Sioux and Cheyenne warriors killed 263 U.S. Army soldiers and attached personnel, including Lieutenant Colonel George Armstrong Custer and every member of his immediate 7th Cavalry command. The attacking Indians scattered after the battle, but were pursued and most later returned to the reservation or surrendered. Others were killed in such climactic confrontations as the Wounded Knee Massacre (see separate listing).

The Battle of the Little Bighorn was one of a series of encounters after the Civil War as settlers, miners, speculators, and others moved into Indian territories, frequently ignoring treaties and the sanctity of Indian hunting grounds. After gold was discovered in 1874 in the Black Hills, near an Indian reservation, thousands of gold-seekers moved into the region in violation of the 1868 Fort Laramie Treaty. Sioux and Cheyenne then began raiding settlements and travelers outside their reservation, and the commissioner of Indian affairs ordered the tribes to stop their attacks and return to the reservation. When the Indians did not comply, the U.S. Army was sent to enforce the edict. This resulted in a number of frontier battles, including the Battle of the Little Bighorn. Custer originally had 600 men, but divided his regiment into three battalions, with the three companies each being assigned to Major Marcus A. Reno and Captain Frederick W. Benteen. Custer and Reno moved to attack a large Indian encampment, but were intercepted by a large force of Indians. Reno was able to retreat to the Little Bighorn River bluffs, where he was joined by Benteen, and to fight off the surrounding Indians. But Custer and his men were caught on a hillside and died in a fierce battle. The Reno and Benteen companies suffered 53 killed and 52 wounded before being rescued by other columns. Altogether, the Indians lost about 100 dead in the Little Bighorn fighting.

The national monument now has a visitor center with exhibits, military and Indian artifacts, and a video explaining the battle. Nearby are Battle Ridge, where Custer's forces fought a losing battle and were killed, and the Custer National Cemetery. Markers indicating where Custer's men died can be seen along Battlefield Road, which traces Custer's final moments.

Little Bighorn Battlefield National Monument, Interstate 90 and U.S. Hwy. 212, PO Box 39, Crow Agency, MT 59022-9939. Phone: 406/638-2621. Fax: 406/638-2623. E-mail: *darrell_cook@nps.gov.* Web site: *www.nps.gov/libi.* Hours: Memorial Day-Labor Day — 8-6 daily; remainder of year — 8-4:30 daily; closed New Year's Day, Thanksgiving, and Christmas. Admission: $10 per car or $5 per person.

Los Encinos State Historic Park. See Spanish Historic Sites section.

Marquette Mission Park and Museum of Ojibwa Culture. See Museums Honoring Individuals section.

Mission San Antonio de Pala. See Spanish Historic Sites section.

Molander Indian Village State Historic Site. The Molander Indian Village State Historic Site north of Price, North Dakota, is where Awaxawi Hidatsa Indians lived from the early 1700s until 1781, when more than half of the inhabitants died in a smallpox epidemic. Faint depressions still show the location of nearly 40 earth lodges, which were protected by a large fortification ditch with bastions. The site also has the remains of an 1882 log cabin and stable built by an early settler, but are not related to the Indian village. The site has interpretive signage, but no facilities.

Molander Indian Village State Historic Site, State Hwy. 1806, Price, ND 58530 (contact: State Historical Society of North Dakota, 612 E. Boulevard Ave., Bismarck, ND 58505). Phone: 701/328-2666. Fax: 701/328-3710. Web site: *www.state.nd. us/hist/sitelist.html*. Hours: dawn-dusk daily. Admission: free.

Monument Valley Navajo Tribal Park. The Monument Valley Navajo Tribal Park, which straddles the Arizona and Utah state line in the Four Corners area, is best known for its isolated monoliths of red sandstone that rise 400 to 1,000 feet and serve as the backdrop in western movies. The fragile rock pinnacles are located in Mystery Valley at the 91,696-acre desert park at the western edge of the Navajo Indian Reservation between Kayenta, Arizona, and Mexican Hat, Utah. The towering Mitten Buttes and Merrick Butte can be seen from the visitor center, which contains information about the tribal park and has other facilities. Self-guided and guided tours also are available, as well as horseback and four-wheel-drive trips among the sandstone monoliths. Navajo vendors also sell arts, crafts, native food, and souvenirs at roadside stands near the visitor center.

Monument Valley Navajo Tribal Park, PO Box 360289, Monument Valley, UT 84536 (also contract: Navajo Parks and Recreation Department, PO Box 2520, Window Rock, AZ 86515). Phones: 435/727-5874, 435/727-5875, and 928/871-6647 (Window Rock). Web site: *www.navajonationparks.org/htm/ monumentvalley.htm*. Hours: May-Sept. — 6-8 daily; remainder of year — 8-5 daily; closed Christmas and at noon on Thanksgiving. Admission: adults, $5; children under 10, free.

Native American Heritage Museum State Historic Site. The Native American Heritage Museum is located at an 1845 former Presbyterian mission on the old Oregon-California Trail near Highland, Kansas, that was used to educate Iowa, Sac, and Fox Indian children. The museum tells the story of the Indian tribes that were forced to emigrate to Kansas in the 1800s and adapt their traditional woodlands cultures to the rolling prairie landscape. It also contains quillwork, baskets, beadwork, and other works of descendants of the tribes.

Native American Heritage Museum State Historic Site, 1737 Elgin Rd., Highland, KS 60035. Phones: 785/442-3304 and 785/442-3374. E-mail: *nahm@ kshs.org*. Web site: *www.schs.org*. Hours: 10-5 Wed.-Sat.; 1-5 Sun.; closed Mon.-Tues. and major holidays. Admission: adults, $3; seniors and students, $2; children under 5, free.

Nez Percé National Historical Park. The Nez Percé National Historical Park, which has its head-quarters and a museum-like visitor center in Spalding, Idaho, includes 38 sites scattered over 1,500 miles in five states (Idaho, Montana, Oregon, Washington, and Wyoming). It commemorates the history and stories of the Nez Percé and their interaction with explorers, fur traders, missionaries, soldiers, settlers, gold miners, and farmers who moved through and into the region.

The historical park is based at the site of an early Indian village and the 1838 mission established by the Reverend Henry H. Spaulding and his wife, Eliza, who came to central Idaho to convert the Nez Percé and other Indian tribes in the area. They built their first mission in 1836 about two miles up Lapwai Creek from Clearwater River, where they located their second mission two years later. While converting some natives, the Spaldings built a house, planted Idaho's first orchard, introduced crop irrigation, published New Testament verses in Nez Percé translations, and developed the first lumber mill, gristmill, and school in the territory. Only the fireplace of the house and a nearby Nez Percé cemetery still remain. In 1862, the U.S. Army constructed Fort Lapwai near the mission site to prevent clashes between pioneers and the Nez Percé. A few of the surviving buildings are still in use. Other historic buildings at the site are the 1862 Nez Percé Indian Agency building and the 1911 Watson's Store that served both settlers and Indians.

The Nez Percé have lived in the valleys of the Clearwater and Snake rivers and their tributaries for thousands of years. They met and helped the Lewis and Carl Expedition with supplies and other assistance in 1805. Fifty years later, after pressure from the U.S. government, the tribe agreed to set aside their ancestral home as a reservation. But when gold was found on the reservation, some bands of the Nez Percé were pressured into signing a treaty that reduced their reservation to one-tenth its original size. Chief Joseph and his band refused to move to the smaller reservation, and when the U.S. Army sought to force them, he and his followers fought back, which started the Nez Percé War of 1877. For nearly four months, the Army followed and fought Chief Joseph and his band as they sought to flee through five states to Canada. They engaged in two major battles — Bear Paw and Big Hole (see separate listings) — before surrendering at the Big Hole Battle. The Nez Percé were relocated to Oklahoma for eight years before the survivors returned to the Pacific Northwest.

The Nez Percé National Historic Trail now marks much of the escape path used by the tribe in 1877, and the Nez Percé National Historical Park encompasses nearly all the land involved in the war. The park's visitor center in Spalding tells the story of the site, the tribe's history and culture, the meeting with the Lewis and Clark Expedition, the Nez Percé War of 1877, and the national historical park.

Nez Percé National Historical Park, 39063 U.S. Hwy. 95, Spalding, ID 83540. Phone: 208/843–2261. Fax 208/843–2001. E-mail *bob_chenoweth@ nps.gov*. Web site: *www.nps.gov/nepe*. Hours: Memorial Day-Labor Day — 8–5:30 daily; remainder of year — 8–4:30 daily; closed New Year's Day, Thanksgiving, and Christmas. Admission: free.

Oconaluftee Indian Village. See Museums and Galleries section.

Okeechobee Battlefield National Historic Landmark. The 1837 Battle of Okeechobee north of Lake Okeechobee in central Florida changed the course of the six-year Second Seminole War in which the tribe refused to relocate to the trans-Mississippi West along with other tribes of the Southeast. On Christmas Day, Colonel Zachary Taylor's troops attacked Seminole and Miccosukee warriors (and allied runaway slaves from Georgia and the Carolinas) who refused to move to Indian Territory (Oklahoma). Taylor's forces overwhelmed the opposition, hastened the end of the war and development of the Southeast, earned Taylor a promotion to general, and helped him win the presidency in 1848. Many artifacts are said to be buried in the sawgrass and pineland forest of the battlefield, but few outward signs of the battle remain. The state of Florida purchased 145 acres of the privately owned and endangered 640-acre site in 2006 for development as a state park with an interpretive center and museum and reenactments of the battle. The state also is considering buying more of the site, which is faced with possible development as a subdivision or shopping center.

Okeechobee Battlefield, U.S. Hwy. 441/95 (4 miles southwest of Okeechobee), Okeechobee, FL. Phones: 863/634–2126 and 863/467–0105. E-mail: *information@okeeinfo.com*. Web site: *www.okeechobeebattlefield.com*. Hours and admission: still to be determined.

Old Mission State Park. The Old Mission State Park near Cataldo, Idaho, features the oldest standing building in the state. The Mission of the Sacred Heart was built with one-foot-thick walls and without nails between 1848 and 1853 by members of the Coeur d'Alene tribe and Catholic missionaries. The mission building and its adjacent parish house have been restored and the nearby historic cemetery has been preserved. A visitor center has interpretive exhibits on the mission, the area, and the Coeur d'Alene Indians. The tribe holds an annual pilgrimage and traditional food serving at the park as part of the Coming of the Black Robes Pageant on August 15.

Old Mission State Park, Interstate 90, Exit 39, PO Box 30, Cataldo, ID 83810. Phone: 208/682–3814. Fax: 208/682–4032. E-mail: *old@idpr.state.id.us*. Web site: *www.idahoparks.org/parks/oldmission. html*. Hours: June-Aug.— 8–6 daily; remainder of year — 9–5 daily; closed New Year's Day, Thanksgiving, and Christmas. Admission: $4 per car.

Osage Village State Historic Site. The earliest known site of an Osage Indian village is located at the Osage Village State Historic Site near Walker, Missouri. The archaeological site, dating from 1700 to 1775, was where the tribe first encountered Europeans. Visitors can walk through the site and read about Osage history and life on an outdoor exhibit kiosk.

Osage Village State Historic Site, County Rd. C, Walker, MO 64790 (mailing address: Harry S. Truman Birthplace State Historic Site, 1009 Truman Ave., Lamar, MO 64759). Phone 417/682–2279. Fax: 417/682–6304. Hours: dawn-dusk daily. Admission: free.

Palace of the Governors. See Spanish Historic Sites section.

Pawnee Indian Village Museum State Historic Site. The Pawnee Indian Village Museum State Historic Site north of Republic, Kansas, is where as many as 2,000 Kitkehahki (Republican) Pawnees lived in more than 40 lodges in the 1820s. The museum displays numerous artifacts and the excavated floor of one of the largest lodges (covering almost 2,000 square feet) in telling the story of the history of the Pawnee Nation. The remains of 22 lodge sites, storage pits, and a fortification wall also can be seen at the historic site.

Pawnee Indian Village Museum State Historic Site, 480 Pawnee Trail (State Rte. 2166), Republic, KS 66964. Phone: 785/361–2255. Fax: 785/361–2255. E-mail: *piv@kshs.org*. Web site: *www.kshs.org/places/ pawneeindian/index.htm*. Hours: 10–5 Wed.-Sat.; 1–5 Sun.; closed Mon.-Tues. and major holidays. Admission: adults, $3; seniors and students, $2; children under 5, free.

Pecos National Historical Park. The Pecos National Historical Park near Pecos, New Mexico, preserves 12,000 years of history. It includes an ancient and later pueblo of the Pecos and two Spanish colonial missions, as well as sites of the Santa Fe Trail, Battle of Glorieta Pass in the Civil War, and an early twentieth-century ranch.

The Pecos Pueblo was a regional power that commanded the trade path between pueblo farmers of the Rio Grande and hunting tribes of the buffalo plains between 1300 and 1838. The initial pueblo, located at a strategic passage through the southern end of the Sangre de Cristo Mountains, was centered in a five-story-high frontier fortress with a population of 2,000. But only the ruins remain today. When Conquistador Francisco Vásquez de Coronado and his army arrived in 1540, the Spaniards were welcomed with music and gifts. It also was where Coronado heard of Quivira from a Plains Indian captive. After being told it was a city of gold, he set out to find it in 1541. But he never did. When Coronado learned the Indian confessed to luring the army into the plains to die, he had him strangled and returned to Mexico.

The Spaniards returned to New Mexico nearly 60 years later when silver was found in the region. The land across the Rio Grande River was claimed for Spain by Don Juan de Oñate and efforts were made to colonize and convert the Pueblo Indians. An imposing adobe mission was built south of the Pecos Pueblo, but when the Pueblo Revolt of 1680 broke out because of increasing Spanish demands and Indian resentments, the church was destroyed, the priest was killed, and the Indians built a kiva at the site. Twelve years later, a Spanish force led by Diego de Vargas returned to the village and was welcomed back. A smaller church with a convent then was built in the more relaxed Spanish-Pecos pueblo. By the 1780s, however, the pueblo suffered from Comanche raids, migration, and loss of its position as a trade center. By the time the Santa Fe Trail passed by in 1821, Pecos had become nearly a ghost village. The last survivors left the site in 1838 to join Towa-speaking relatives at the Jémez Pueblo. Only some of the walls and foundations of the pueblo and mission remain from that period.

The historical park now has a visitor center with exhibits that tell the Pecos Pueblo story, featuring historical photographs and such artifacts as stone tools, pottery, and bone implements. Other exhibits are devoted, with artifacts, to the early Spanish presence, the Santa Fe Trail, and the nearby Battle of Glorieta Pass during the Civil War (tours are offered to the restricted site). Among the other sights are several Puebloan ruins, two reconstructed kivas, a nineteenth-century Spanish frontier settlement, a late 1800s Santa Fe Trail stage stop, and the 1926 Forked Lightning Ranch house.

Pecos National Historical Park, State Rd. 63, PO Box 418, Pecos, NM 87552–0418. Phone: 505/757–6414. Fax: 505/757–8460. E-mail: *peco_visitor_in formation@nps.gov*. Web site: *www.nps.gov/peco*. Hours: Memorial Day-Labor Day — 8–6 daily; remainder of year — 8–4:30 daily; closed New Year's Day and Christmas. Admission: adults, $3; children under 17, free.

Pipestone National Monument. Since the seventeenth century, Plains Indians have been coming to a quarry near Pipestone, Minnesota, to obtain the red stone used to make ceremonial pipes. The site now is the known as the Pipestone National Monument. Although stone pipes were first used by prehistoric peoples of North America some 2,000 years ago, it is believed that it was not until the acquisition of metal tools from European traders that the Sioux, Pawnee, and other Plains Indians began coming to the quarry to dig for the durable but relatively soft stone for their pipes.

The stone, which ranges in color from mottled pink to brick red, still can be quarried today by anyone of Indian ancestry. The grounds also are used for cultural and religious activities by Native Americans. The pipestone carvings, however, now are appreciated as artworks as well as ceremonial objects. The 282-acre site has a visitor center and the Upper Midwest Cultural Center that have collections of pipestone pipes. The visitor center also contains exhibits and slide presentations on the history and significance of the area and the cultural center presents demonstrations of pipe making in April-October by native craftspeople using stone from the quarry.

Pipestone National Monument, 36 Reservation Ave., Pipestone, MN 56164. Phone: 507/825–5464. Fax: 507/825–5466. E-mail: *pipe_superintendent@ nps.gov*. Web site: *www.nps.gov/pipe*. Hours: Memorial Day-Labor Day — 8–6 Mon.-Thurs., 8–8 Fri.-Sun.; remainder of year — 8–5 daily; closed New Year's Day, Thanksgiving, and Christmas. Admission: adults, $3; children under 17 and Native Americans, free; families, $5.

Rosebud Battlefield State Park. The Rosebud Battlefield State Park along the Rosebud River north of Decker, Montana, is where Sioux, Cheyenne, and other Indian warriors defeated General George Crook's troops from Fort Fetterman in an important military engagement in 1876. The battle preceded and led to the Battle of the Little Bighorn (see separate listing) in which Lieutenant Colonel George Armstrong Custer and his 7th Cavalry soldiers and attached personnel were killed eight days later 25 miles to the northwest. The 3,052-acre park contains interpretive signage and a self-guided auto tour through the battlefield area, but lacks other facilities.

Rosebud Battlefield State Park, 3 miles west of County Rd. 314, Decker, MT 59025 (contact: Region 7 Headquarters, Montana Fish, Wildlife, and Parks Dept., PO Box 1630, Miles City, MT 59301–1630). Phone: 406/232–0900. Fax: 406/323–4368. Web site: *www.fwp.state.mt.net*. Hours: dawn-dusk daily. Admission: free.

Salinas Pueblo Missions National Monument. See Spanish Historic Sites section.

Shawnee Indian Mission State Historic Site. The Shawnee Indian Mission State Historic Site near Fairway, Kansas, is located at one of the earliest pre-territorial Indian missions and schools in the state. The Shawnee Methodist Mission was established in 1830, followed by a manual labor school at the site in 1839. At its height, the school on the Shawnee Indian Reservation had 16 buildings and nearly 200 boys and girls from many different tribes. Three of the mission-school buildings still remain, and one of the structures is open for touring. It contains a typical classroom and exhibits on the site's history and types of trades taught at the school.

Shawnee Indian Mission State Historic Site, 3403 W. 53rd St., Fairway, KS 66205-2654. Phone 913/262-0867. E-mail: *shawneemission@ksks.org*. Web site: *www.kshs.org/places/shawnee/index.htm*. Hours: 9-5 Tues.-Sat.; 1-5 Sun.; closed Mon. and major holidays. Admission: adults, $3; students, $2; seniors, $1; children under 5, free.

Sitka National Historical Park. See Arctic Peoples Historic Sites section.

Sitting Bull Burial State Historic Site. The Sitting Bull Burial State Historic Site in Fort Yates, North Dakota, is where Hunkpapa Sioux leader Sitting Bull originally was buried in the military cemetery adjacent to the fort after being killed while being arrested . He was a war chief and medicine man who died in a skirmish with Indian police during the Ghost Dance unrest of 1890. Sitting Bull, who had fought against U.S. Army forces at the Battle of the Little Bighorn and elsewhere, had sponsored Ghost Dance ceremonies at the Standing Rock and Pine Ridge Indian reservations which centered around the doctrine of a Paiute holy man named Wavoka. It called for a special dance by which Indians could enter a land free of white men, and furthered the belief that a special garment (a Ghost Dance shirt) would protect the wearer from bullets. Government authorities felt the doctrine would result in a recurrence of hostilities and sought to crush the movement and arrest its leaders.

When Sitting Bull refused to sign the Great Sioux Agreement of 1889, Indian police were sent to arrest him at his cabin. Some of his supporters resisted and a fight ensued in which Sitting Bull, seven of his followers, and six Indian policemen died. Sitting Bull initially was buried at the military post, but years later Clarence Gray Eagle, son of Sitting Bull's brother-in-law, requested that the remains be moved to Grand River, South Dakota. The request was denied by the state of North Dakota. But a group led by Gray Eagle dug up the body at night in 1953 and reburied it near Mobridge, South Dakota, where it remains today. Monuments honoring Sitting Bull now are located at both sites.

Sitting Bull Burial State Historic Site, Fort Yates Cemetery, Fort Yates, ND 58538 (contact: State Historical Society of North Dakota, 612 E. Boulevard Ave., Bismarck, ND 58505). Phone: 701/328-2666. Fax: 701/328-3710. Web site: *www.state.nd.us/hist/sitelist.html*. Hours: dawn-dusk daily. Admission: free.

Tahlonteeskee Cherokee Courthouse Museum. See Museums Honoring Individuals section.

Tomo-Kahni State Historic Park and Kawaiisu Native American Village. The Tomo-Kahni State Historic Park in Tehachapi, California, protects the site of the Kawaiisu tribal village, called Nooah Village, nestled atop a ridge in the Tehachapi Mountains, overlooking Sand Canyon to the east and Tehachapi Valley to the west. The Kawaiisu, who migrated from the Great Basin, made the site their winter home for 2,000 to 3,000 years, probably because of its moderate temperature and plentiful resources. They are best known for their finely woven baskets of intricate and colorful design.

The remains of the village, located at 4,000 feet and requiring two to three hours of strenuous walking, can be seen only as part of organized tours. Tours begin with an orientation at the Tomo-Kahni Resource Center in Tehachapi. It then is necessary to drive about 12 miles over a rough road to reach where the tour begins.

Tomo-Kahni State Historic Park, Sand Canyon Rd., Tehachaki, CA 93561 (contacts: park office — 43779 15th St. West, Lancaster, CA 93534; resource center — 112 F St., Suite A, Tehachapi , CA 93561). Phone: 661/822-3720. Web site: *www.parks.ca.gov/default.asp?page_id=610*. Hours: Mar.-early June and Sept-.Oct — tour orientation begins at 9 Sat. Admission: adults, $4; children, $2.

Washita Battlefield National Historic Site and Cultural Heritage Center. The Washita Battlefield National Historic Site near Cheyenne, Oklahoma, is where the camp of Chief Black Kettle and his sleeping Cheyenne band were attacked and many killed in 1868 by U.S. troops commanded by Lieutenant Colonel George Armstrong Custer. The attack was the beginning of a campaign to stop raids by Cheyenne and Arapaho warriors in the region. The Indians felt the federal government broke promises made at the signing of the 1867 peace treaty at Medicine Lodge, Kansas, in which the Cheyenne and Arapaho agreed to settle on reservations in western Indian Territory (now Oklahoma). As the Indians surrendered and came to the reservations, the troops disarmed the warriors, took their horses, and arrested their leaders and imprisoned 72 chiefs at Fort Marion in Florida. In the Battle of Washita, however, Chief Black Kettle was a peaceful chief and his village apparently was not involved in the Indian attacks. Black Kettle, his wife, and many children, women, and elderly were killed in the attack.

The historic site has a newly completed Cultural Heritage Center, with exhibits and a film on the battle and the Cheyenne. It also has an overlook, two self-guided trails, and ranger-led tours. The nearby Black Kettle Museum (see separate listing), operated by the Oklahoma Historical Society and which temporarily served as the site's interpretive center until the Cultural Heritage Center was built, has exhibits about the Cheyenne chief, tribe, and battle.

Washita Battlefield National Historic Site, State Hwy. 47A, PO Box 890, Cheyenne, OK 73628. Phone: 580/497-2742. Fax: 580/497-2712. Web site: *www.nps.gpv/waba.* Hours: site — dawn-dusk daily; cultural center — 9–5 daily; closed New Year's Day and Christmas. Admission: free.

Wounded Knee National Historic Landmark.
The Wounded Knee National Historic Landmark near the Pine Ridge Indian Reservation in southwestern South Dakota marks the site of what has become known as the Wounded Knee Massacre. It was an encounter in which a large number of Lakota men, women, and children were killed in the last conflict of the Indian wars in the United States in 1890. A monument now marks the graves of the Indians who died at the site at Wounded Knee Creek.

The incident occurred shortly after Sitting Bull, the charismatic Hunkpapa Sioux leader, was slain by Indian police while being arrested for advocating the Ghost Dance, an outlawed practice in which Indians believed they could have a land without white men by doing the Ghost Dance and they would be protected from bullets by wearing a special Ghost Dance shirt (see separate listing in Historic Sites section). Followers of Sitting Bull tried to escape arrest by fleeing the reservation, traveling through the Badlands, and joining members of the Miniconjou Sioux led by Chief Big Foot. The group was confronted on the snowy banks of Wounded Knee Creek and ordered to surrender their weapons. Some old guns were produced, but a number of warriors, including Black Coyote, objected and medicine man Yellow Bird began chanting the Ghost Dance myth. In the melee, Black Coyote's gun went off and other warriors raised their weapons. The soldiers then were ordered to fire, setting off the one-sided battle. As the Indian warriors fled, the soldiers used their

rapid-firing Hotchkiss machine guns, with some of the bullets hitting the tepees and the frightened women and children as they sought safety in a nearby ravine.

The exact number of dead is not known because some Indians fled into the hills to die or escape. But it is believed that 200 to 300 of the approximately 333 Indians in the camp died in the confusion. The bodies of 84 Indian men, 44 women, and 18 children — many of them frozen in the winter weather — later were found at the site. The Army suffered 25 dead and 39 wounded, some of whom were shot by their own men in the machine gun crossfire. Only 4 men and 47 women and children survivors were returned to the Pine Ridge Reservation by the military.

Wounded Knee National Historical Landmark, unmarked road off U.S. Hwy. 18, 15 miles northeast of Pine Ridge, SD (contact: The Heritage Center, Red Cloud Indian School, Box 100, Pine Ridge, SD 57770). Phone: 605/867-5491. Fax: 605/867-1209. E-mail: *csimon@redcloudschool.org.* Web site: *www.red cloudschool.org.* Hours: dawn-dusk daily. Admission: free.

Prehistoric Sites and Museums

Albinger Archeological Museum. Artifacts of an early Indian culture from 1500 b.c. and later Chumash Indians found at the site can be seen at the Albinger Archaeological Museum in Ventura, California. Early Spanish, Mexican, and Chinese artifacts also have been found at the site. Among the objects discovered have been milling stones, shell beads, arrowheads, bone whistles, crucifixes, medallions, buttons, pottery, and bottles. Outside the museum are such items as a 300 B.C. earthen oven, foundations of a 1787 to 1790 mission church and 1804 to 1834 Indian barracks, and a mission water filtration building.

Albinger Archaeological Museum, 113 E. Main St., PO Box 99, Ventura, CA 93001. Phone: 805/648-5823. Hours: Memorial Day weekend-Labor Day — 10-2 Mon.-Tues.; 10-4 Wed.-Sun.; remainder of year — 10-2 Mon.-Fri.; 10-4 Sat.-Sun.; closed New Year's Day, Easter, Thanksgiving, and Christmas. Admission: free.

Alibates Flint Quarries National Monument.
High Plains Indians came to the site of the Alibates Flint Quarries National Monument north of Fritch, Texas, for thousands of years for the rainbow-hued flint in the red bluffs above the Canadian River. The flint was used to make tools and weapons. The site now can be seen only as part of ranger-led tours.

Alibates Flint Quarries National Monument, Cas Johnson Rd. (off State Hwy. 136), PO Box 1460,

Fritch, TX 79036. Phone: 806/857–3151. Fax: 806/857–2319. Web site: *www.nps.gov/alfl*. Hours: tours by reservation only. Admission: free.

Amerind Foundation Museum. See Museums and Galleries section.

Anasazi Heritage Center. The Anasazi Heritage Center near Dolores, Colorado, is a U.S. Bureau of Land Management is an archaeological research and interpretive center devoted to the preservation, study, and exhibit of prehistoric cultures in the Four Corners area. It also serves as the headquarters for the nearby Canyons of the Ancients National Monument. The Four Corners area is one of the richest archaeological sites in the nation.

The center has more than 2.5 million artifacts, samples, and documents relating to the Anasazi (also known as the Ancestral Puebloan people). Most of the collection is from the Dolores Archaeological Program, the largest single archaeological project in the nation's history conducted during the construction of the McPhee Dam and Reservoir. Between 1978 and 1984, researchers mapped about 1,600 archaeological sites (villages, households, shrines, granaries, and hunting camps) and excavated 120 sites to obtain many of the artifacts studied and displayed at the center. The center also presents changing exhibitions on regional history and Native American cultures.

The remains of two twelfth-century settlements — the Dominquez and Escalante pueblos — are located on the grounds of the Anasazi Heritage Center. The pueblos are named after Spanish friars who explored the area in 1776 and became the first to record archaeological sites in Colorado. The pueblos were excavated and stabilized 200 years later.

Anasazi Heritage Center, Bureau of Land Management, 27501 Hwy. 184, Dolores, CO 81323. Phone: 970/882–5600. Fax: 970/882–7035. E-mail: *marilynn_eastin@co.blm.gov*. Web site: *www.co.blm.gov/ahc*. Hours: Mar.-Oct.— 9–5 daily; remainder of year — 9–4 daily; closed New Year's Day, Thanksgiving, and Christmas. Admission: adults, $3 during Mar.-Oct and free Nov.-Feb.; children under 18, free.

Anasazi Museum and Manitou Cliff Dwellings. See Manitou Cliff Dwellings and Anasazi Museum.

Anasazi State Park. The Anasazi State Park near Boulder, Utah, is located at the site of an Anasazi (Ancestral Puebloan) village believed to have been occupied by an estimated 200 Kayenta Indians from 1050 to 1200, making it one of the largest Anasazi communities west of the Colorado River. Visitors can walk through the partially excavated village and stop at the museum to see Kayenta artifacts from the site and a life-size, six-room diorama of the village.

Anasazi State Park, 460 State Hwy. 12 North, PO Box 1429, Boulder, UT 84716. Phone: 435/335–7308. Fax: 435/335–7352. E-mail: *nrdpr.ansp@state.ut.us*. Web site: *www.stateparks.utah.gov/park_pages/anasazi.htm*. Hours: Memorial Day-Labor Day — 8–6 daily; remainder of year — 9–5 daily; closed New Year's Day, Thanksgiving, and Christmas. Admission: $3 per person or $5 per car; children under 6 and Utah seniors, free.

Angel Mounds State Historic Site. The Angel Mounds State Historic Site in Evansville, Indiana, is one of the best preserved prehistoric American Indian sites in the United States. It was the site of a village of several thousand people of Middle Mississippian culture from 1100 to 1450 and the largest community of its time in the state. Its inhabitants engaged in hunting and farming on the rich bottom lands of the Ohio River, but eventually deserted the site for unknown reasons. The site, operated by the Division of Indiana State Museums and Historic Sites, consists of some of the largest Indian mounds in the nation, as well as a reconstructed village with dwellings, a temple, and a stockade. It also has a museum featuring artifacts from excavations.

Angel Mounds State Historic Site, 8215 Pollack Ave., Evansville, IN 47715. Phone: 812/853–3056. Fax: 812/858–7686. E-mail: *curator@angelmounds.com*. Web site: *www.angelmounds.org*. Hours: Mar.-Dec.— 9–5 Tues.-Sat.; 1–5 Sun.; closed Mon. and Jan.-Feb. Admission: adults, $4; seniors, $3.50; children, $2.

Aztec Ruins National Monument. The Aztec Ruins National Monument in Aztec, New Mexico, preserves one of the finest examples of an Anasazi (Ancestral Puebloan) village. It was around 1100 that a group of ancient people built a monumental three-story-high pueblo, longer than a football field, with as many as 500 rooms and a large kiva over 41 feet in diameter. The Anasazi farmed at the site for half a century and then moved away. A second group moved to the site in approximately 1225, remodeled the old pueblo, and built other structures nearby before abandoning the site by 1300.

Only the ruins of the original multistory pueblo remain today, but visitors can walk through some of the rooms and the restored kiva. Other buildings, kivas, and roads also are located along the nearby Animas River. However, only the Hubbard Site, with the remains of three concentric walls, which are divided into 22 rooms encircling a kiva, is open to the public. A trail leads to the pueblo ruins from the visitor center, which has a film and exhibits on the history of the site. The Aztec ruins got their name from early European American settlers who mistakenly thought the Anasazi inhabitants were related to the Aztecs of central Mexico.

Aztec Ruins National Monument, 84 County Rd. 2900 (Ruins Rd.), Aztec, NM 87410. Phone: 505/334–6174. Fax: 505/334–6372. E-mail: *azru_front_desk@nps.gov*. Web site: *www.nps.gov/azru*. Hours: Memorial Day-Labor Day — 8–6 daily; remainder of year — 8–5 daily; closed New Year's Day, Thanksgiving, and Christmas. Admission: adults, $4; children under 17, free.

Bandelier National Monument. The 32,727-acre Bandelier National Monument near Los Alamos, New Mexico, has more than 2,500 Anasazi (Ancestral Puebloan) living sites among the sheer-walled canyons and mesas in the rugged Pajarito Plateau country. It is best known for its unusual cave-like rooms carved out of rocky slopes and the remains of the circular Tyuonyi Pueblo in Frijoles Canyon a short walk from the visitor center. Another popular site is Tsankawi, north of the main entrance, which has unexcavated ruins, cave dwellings, and petroglyphs.

The Anasazi lived and farmed in the area from approximately the early 1100s to the late 1500s. They initially lived in small scattered settlements, then came together in larger groups (1150 to 1325), and eventually had fewer and bigger villages with as many as 600 rooms and giant kivas three times the prior size. But the people left the area after the Spanish colonized New Mexico in the late 1500s.

Bandelier National Monument, 15 Entrance Rd., State Hwy. 4, Los Alamos, NM 87544 (mailing address: HCR 1, Box 1, Suite 15, Los Alamos, NM 875–9701). Phones: 505/672–3861 and 505/672–0343. Fax: 505/672–9607. E-mail: *band-visitor-center@nps.gov*. Web site: *www.nps.gov/band*. Hours: Memorial Day-Labor Day — 8–6 daily; Mar.-May and Sept.-Nov. — 9–5:30 daily; Dec.-Feb. — 8–4:30 daily; closed New Year's Day and Christmas. Admission: $5 per person or $10 per car.

Bear Creek Mound and Village Site. The Bear Creek Mound and Village Site along the Natchez Trace Parkway northeast of Tupelo, Mississippi, contains a flat-topped square mound about 8 feet high and 85 feet across the base that was built between 1100 and 1300 during the Mississippian period. It was constructed in several stages for ceremonial or elite residential use. Archaeological excavation indicates that a temple or chief's house was located on the mound, with a small village to the south and east of the mound.

Bear Creek Mound and Village Site, Milepost 308.8, Natchez Trace Pkwy., Natchez, MS (contact: Nachez Trace Pkwy., 2680 Natchez Trace Pkwy., Tu-

pelo, MS 38804). Phone: 662/680–4004. Fax: 662/680–4036. E-mail: *gretchen_ward@nps.gov*. Web site: *www.nps.gov/natr*. Hours: dawn-dusk daily. Admission: free.

Besh-Ba-Gowah Archaeological Park. The ruins of a 700-year-old Salado Indian pueblo are featured at the Besh-Be-Gowah Archaeological Park south of Globe, Arizona. Visitors can walk through many of the 300 pueblo rooms, climb ladders to the second floor, and see typical furnishings of the period. They also can see artifacts of the remarkably advanced culture, including colorful cotton garments, tools, and the world's largest collection of Salado pottery, at the municipal park's museum. The Salado culture period was from 1150 to 1450 in the Tonto Basin.

It is believed that the earliest inhabitants of the site were the Hohokam, who established a pit-house settlement about 900 and then abandoned it around 1100. They were followed by the Salado Indians, who began constructing the pueblo in approximately 1225. Archaeologists believe the pueblo became a ceremonial, food storage, and redistribution center. But the Salado mysteriously disappeared from the site after 1400. The pueblo remained uninhabited until the Apache temporarily occupied it after 1600. It was the Apache who named the site Besh-Ba-Gowah, which means "place of metal" or "metal camp."

Besh-Ba-Gowah Archaeological Park, Jesse Hayes Rd., Globe, AZ 85501 (mailing address. 150 N. Pine St., Globe, AZ 85501). Phone: 928/425–0320. Fax: 928/402–1071. E-mail: *beshbagowah@theriver.com*. Hours: 9–5 daily; closed New Year's Day, Thanksgiving, and Christmas. Admission: adults, $3; seniors and students, $2; children under 12, free.

Blackwater Draw Site and Museum. Blackwater Draw near Portales, New Mexico, was the nation's first multicultural Paleo-Indian archaeological site. It was occupied by humans approximately 11,000 years ago. In 1932, evidence of human occupation was found in association with such Late Pleistocene period fauna as the wooly mammoth, camel, horse, bison, saber-toothed tiger, and dire wolf. The site has become one of the most significant and best known archaeological sites in North American archaeology. The site and a museum are located about seven miles north of Eastern New Mexico University, which administers the site. The museum displays and interprets artifacts and related faunal materials excavated from the site.

Blackwater Draw Site and Museum, Eastern New Mexico University, Station 9, U.S. Hwy. 70, Portales, NM 88130 (mailing address: Eastern New Mexico University, Station 3, Portales, NM 88130). Phones: 505/562–2202 and 505/562–1011. Fax: 505/562–

2291. E-mail: *matthew.hillsman@enmu.edu*. Web site: *www.enmu.edu*. Hours: site — Memorial Day-Labor Day: 1–7 daily; Apr.-May and Sept.-Oct.: 1–5 Sat.-Sun.; closed remainder of week and year; museum — Memorial Day-Labor Day: 10–5 Mon.-Sat.; 12–5 Sun.; remainder of year: 10–5 Tues.-Sat.; 12–5 Sun.; closed Mon. and major holidays. Admission: adults, $3; seniors, $2; students, $1; children under 6, free.

Bynum Mound and Village Site. Six burial mounds and an associated habitation area built during the Middle Woodland period between 100 B.C. and A.D. 100 are located at the Bynum Mound and Village Site along the Natchez Trace Parkway southwest of Tupelo, Mississippi. The mounds range from 5 to 14 feet in height. Two of the largest mounds have been restored for public viewing. The remains of four individuals have been found at the base of southernmost mound, and the other large mound covers a log-lined crematory pit with the cremated and unburned remains of several persons. Among the artifacts found are greenstone celts (polished axe heads), cooper spools, and a piece of galena (a shiny lead ore).

Bynum Mound and Village Site, Milestone 232.4, Natchez Trace Pkwy., Tupelo, MS (contact: Natchez Trace Pkwy., 2680 Natchez Trace Pkwy., Tupelo, MS 38804). Phone: 662/680–4004. Fax: 662/680–4036. E-mail: *gretchen_ward@nps.gov*. Web site: *www.nps.gov/natr*. Hours: dawn-dusk daily. Admission: free.

Caddoan Mounds State Historic Site. The Caddoan Mounds State Historic Site in Cherokee County southwest of Alto, Texas, was the southwestern ceremonial center of the Caddoan peoples who flourished on the western edge of the woodlands of eastern American between 1000 B.C. and A.D. 1550. The historic site contains three large earthen mounds from 750 to 1300 — two representing communal precincts and a third that was a burial site for elite members of the community — and a visitor center with interpretive exhibits about the Caddoans and the site.

Caddoan Mounds State Historic Site, State Hwy. 21 West, Cherokee County, TX 75925 (mailing address: Rte. 2, Box 85C, Alto, TX 75925). Phone: 936/858–3218. Fax: 409/858–3227. Web site: *www.tpwd.state.tx.us/park/caddoan*. Hours: 9–4 Fri.-St.; closed Mon.-Thurs. and Christmas Eve and Day. Admission: adults, $2; seniors and students, $1; children under 6, free.

Caguana Indian Ceremonial Park and Museum. The Caguana Indian Ceremonial Park in Utuado, Puerto Rico, is an important 1100 archaeological site displaying primitive engineering by the Taino Indians. The site, which is believed to have religious significance to the Tainos, contains 10 Indian courts with monoliths and petroglyphs among limestone hills. The park also has a museum with artifacts and exhibits on Taino culture. The site is affiliated with the Institute of Puerto Rican Culture.

Caguana Indian Ceremonial Park and Museum, Rd. 11, 12.4 km, Utuado, Puerto Rico (mailing address: PO Box 533, Angeles, Puerto Rico 00611-0533). Phone: 787/894–7325. Fax: 787/894–7310. Hours: 9–4:30 Wed.-Sun.; closed Mon.-Tues. Admission: adults, $2; children 6–12, $1; seniors and children under 6, free.

Cahokia Mounds State Historic Site. The remains of the largest and one of most sophisticated prehistoric native cities in North America is located at the Cahokia Mounds State Historic Site west of Collinsville, Illinois. The 2,200-acre historic site, which has been designated as a UNESCO world heritage site, contains the remnants of the central section of the ancient settlement known today as Cahokia. It was inhabited from about 700 to 1400 and at its peak from 1050 to 1200, the city covered nearly six square miles and may have had as many as 20,000 people. The site, named for a subtribe of the Illiniwek (Illinois) tribe that moved into the area in the 1600s and lived nearby when the French arrived about 1699, had over 120 earthen mounds (of which 109 have been recorded and 68 have been preserved) with dwellings arranged in rows and around open plazas, with the main agricultural fields outside the settlement. The center of the city was surrounded by a two-mile-long stockade, of which several sections have been reconstructed. The fate of the prehistoric residents and city is unknown. The decline seemed to be gradual, beginning in the 1200s and ending with abandonment by 1400, possibly because of a climate change after 1200 that affected crop production. War, disease, social unrest, and declining political and economic power also may have been factors. The Cahokians built three types of mounds. The most common was the platform mound, with its flat top serving as a base for ceremonial buildings or residences for the elite. The other two types — conical and ridgetop — are believed to have been used for burials of important people or to mark important locations. The great platform mound at Cahokia is Monks Mound, the largest Indian mound north of Mexico and the largest prehistoric earthen construction in the New World. It has a base of 14 acres and rises to a height of 100 feet. A massive building that was 105 feet long, 48 feet wide, and 50 feet high once stood on the summit. It is where the principal ruler lived, conducted ceremonies, and governed the city. Excavation of a small ridgetop mound, called Mound 72, has revealed nearly 300 ceremonial and sacrificial burials, mostly of young women in mass graves. Archaeological excavations also at the site have partially uncovered the remains of four and possibly five circular sun calendars, called woodhenges because of their functional similarity to Stonehenge in England. The site also has a large interpretive center with exhibits and artifacts relating to the site.

Cahokia Mounds State Historic Site, 30 Ramey St., Collinsville, IL 62234. Phone: 618/346–5160. Fax: 618/346–5162. E-mail: *cahokiamounds@ezl.com*. Web site: *www.cahokiamounds.com*. Hours: site — 8-dusk daily; interpretive center — mid–Apr.-Sept.: 9–5 daily; remainder of year: 9–5 Wed.-Sun.; closed Mon.-Tues. and most holidays. Admission: adults, $3 suggested donation; children, $1 suggested donation.

Calico Early Man Site. One of the oldest prehistoric tool sites in the Western Hemisphere is located at the Calico Early Man Site near Yermo and Barstow, California. Nearly 12,000 stone tools — some dating back almost 200,000 years — have been discovered at the site, which may contain the oldest evidence of human occupation in the Americas. The first fragments of primitive tools were found along the shoreline of an ancient Pleistocene-era lake by amateur archaeologists in 1942. In 1963, Dr. Louis S. B. Leaky, the renowned archaeologist-paleontologist, came to examine artifacts discovered by county archaeologist Ruth Dee Simpson, and then became the project director until his death in 1972.

The site, which is believed to have been a possible quarry, stone tool workshop, and campsite where nomadic hunters and gatherers stopped to fashion such tools as stone knives, scrapers, punches, picks, chopping tools, and saw-like tools called denticulates. It still is an active dig area with three master pits and numerous test pits. Such early tools as flakes, blades, and bradelets can be seen in the walls and floors of the excavated pits. A visitor center also displays various early tools and has exhibits about the site, located on land administered by the U.S. Bureau of Land Management. Guided tours of the site are available.

Calico Early Man Site, off Interstate 15 (15 miles northwest of Barstow), Yermo, CA 92398 (contact: Friends of Calico Early Man Site, PO Box 535, Yermo, CA 92398). Phone: 760/252–6000). Web site: *www.ca.blm.gov/barstow/calico.html*. Hours: 12:30–4:30 Wed.; 9–4:30 Thurs.-Sun.; closed Mon.-Tues. and major holidays. Admission: adults, $5; seniors, $2; children under 13, $1.

Canyon de Chelly National Monument. The Canyon de Chelly National Monument on the Navajo Indian Reservation east of Chinle, Arizona, is the site of one of the longest continuously in-

habited landscapes of North America. The area has been occupied since 2500 B.C. by five Native American cultures — Archaic, Basketmakers, Anasazi, Hopi, and Navajo — during different periods. The Archaic, Basketmakers, and Anasazi lived in the 26-mile long Canyon de Chelly Canyon and the adjoining Canyon del Muerto until approximately 1350. They were followed by the Hopi in the fourteenth and fifteenth centuries and the Navajo from the seventeenth century to the present. The 83,849-acre national monument is unique in that it still has a living community of Navajo people and the National Park Service works in partnership with the Navajo Nation in managing the site's resources and sustaining the Navajo community.

The site's spectacular canyons have sheer sandstone walls that rise from 30 to 1,000 feet and contain numerous cliff dwellings and pictographs. The principal ruins are the Mummy Cave, White House, and Antelope House. A three-story tower and one of the largest cliff dwellings in the nation are at Mummy Cave. However, it is considered spiritual by American Indians and visitors are not permitted to enter. The architecture of the White House resembles the structures at Chaco Canyon (see separate listing) and the Antelope House got its name from its large pictograph of a running antelope. Visitors must be accompanied by a park ranger or an authorized guide, except for a self–guided trail from the White House overlook to the ruin. Navajo guides also are available for canyon trips, horseback tours, and four-wheel-drive trips through the canyons. A visitor center also has exhibits on the history and occupancy of the canyons and the cliff dwellings, pictographs, and other aspects of the monument.

Canyon de Chelly National Monument, Rte. 7 off Hwy. 191, PO Box 588, Chinle, AZ 86503. Phone: 528/674–5500 Fax: 928/674–5507. Web site: *www.nps.gov/cach*. Hours: May-Sept. — 8–6 daily; remainder of year — 8–5 daily; closed Christmas. Admission: free.

Canyons of the Ancients National Monument. The 164,00-acre Canyons of the Ancients National Monument on the high desert of southwest Colorado has the highest density of archaeological sites in the nation. It has recorded more than 6,000 (out of an estimated 20,000–30,000) archaeological sites — including marks of cultures and traditions spanning 10,000 years. The monument is located near Dolores, Colorado, where the U.S. Bureau of Land Management operates the Anasazi Heritage Center, which serves as the visitor center (see separate listing in Prehistoric Sites and Museums section).

The first people in the region were the Paleo-

Indians who crossed the area while hunting and gathering until about 7500 B.C. They were followed by the more sedentary Basketmakers in 1500 B.C. and then the Anasazi (Ancestral Puebloans) in 750 B.C. The Anasazi farmed through 1300 B.C. before deserting the Four Corners area, probably because of a growing population and widespread drought. Since then, the Navajo and other Indian tribes and European American explorers, settlers, and hunters have lived or passed through the region.

The early homes of the Anasazi consisted of pit-dwellings. They later evolved into cliff dwellings. In addition to the ruins of cliff dwellings, the monument has the remains of villages, field houses, kivas, shrines, sweat lodges, petroglyphs, reservoirs, check dams, and agricultural fields. One of the largest prehistoric settlements in the region is the Sand Canyon Pueblo, which has 420 rooms, 100 kivas, and 14 towers. Among the other archaeological sites are the Lowry Pueblo, with 40 rooms, eight kivas, and a Great Kiva, which is the only developed recreation site within the monument; Painted Hand Pueblo, village ruins with a beautiful standing tower; a 1,000-year-old granary in Cross Canyon; and two McLean Basin towers, featuring 1,000-year-old stone towers with unusual bands of glazed stones.

Canyons of the Ancients National Monument, County Rd. 10 (and other county roads), Dolores, CO (contact: Anasazi Heritage Center, Bureau of Land Management, 237501 Hwy. 184, Dolores, CO 81323). Phone: 970/882–5600. Fax: 970/882–7035. E-mail: *marilynn_castin@co.blm.gov*. Web site: *www.co.blm.gov/canm*. Hours: open 24 hours. Admission: free.

Casa Grande Ruins National Monument. In 1892, the Casa Grande Ruins National Monument near Coolidge, Arizona, became the nation's first archaeological preserve. It honors the prehistoric Hohokam, who built an advanced culture in much of present-day Arizona over 1,000 years ago. They were innovative farmers who lived along the Gila and Salt rivers and their tributaries and developed a distinct culture by A.D. 300 that lasted through the early 1400s. Only the ruins of their villages, irrigation canals, and artifacts remained by the time the Spanish arrived.

The national monument is located at the site of a Hohokam village dating to 500 to 1450. Among the ruins is the ca. 1300 to 1350 Casa Grande (Great House), a four-story-high clay building that is 60 feet long. It is the largest structure known to exist in Hohokam times and one of the biggest and most mysterious prehistoric structures ever built in North America. The site also has a visitor center with exhibits on the Hohokam, Casa Grande, and village life of the period.

Case Grande Ruins National Monument, 1100 Ruins Dr., Coolidge, AZ 85228. Phone: 520/723–3172. Fax: 520/723–7209. E-mail: *peggy_carter@nps.gov*. Web site: *www.nps.gov/cagr*. Hours: 8–5 daily; closed Christmas. Admission: adults, $3; children under 17, free.

Casa Malpais Archaeological Park and Museum. The ruins of a 1250 to 1400 Mogollon pueblo with a unique system of underground catacomb-like rooms are preserved and interpreted at the Casa Malpais Archaeological Park in Springfield, Arizona. Casa Malpais (House of the Badlands) was built by the mountain people on the rim of volcanic rock overlooking the Little Colorado River's Round Valley to take advantage of existing caves, many of which became part of the underground system.

The prehistoric pueblo has over 100 rooms, a large kiva, an enclosing wall, sacred chambers, rock art panels, grinding areas, catacomb burials, trash middens, and an astronomical observatory. The only way to visit the ruins is on guided tours that leave from the Casa Malpais Museum in downtown Springfield. The museum, located two miles south of the archaeological park, contains exhibits on Casa Malpais, Native Americans, and regional history.

Casa Malpais Archaeological Park and Museum, U.S. Hwy. 60, PO Box 390, Springfield, AZ 85938 (museum located at 318 Main St., Springfield, AZ 85938). Phone: 520/333–5375. Fax: 520/333–5690. Web site: *www.wmonline.com/attract/casam./htm*. Hours: museum — 8–4 daily; park tours — 9, 11, and 4 (weather permitting); closed Thanksgiving and Christmas. Admission: museum — free; park tour — adults, $7; seniors, students, and children, $5.

Chaco Culture National Historical Park. Chaco Culture National Historical Park in northwestern New Mexico was the site of a major center of Anasazi (Ancestral Puebloan) culture from 850 to 1250. The site, south of Nageezi, served as the center of ceremony, trade, and administration for the prehistoric Four Corners region. It is known for its distinctive architecture, monumental public and ceremonial buildings, more than 40 miles of prehistoric roads, far-reaching trade network, and surprising astronomical alignments.

The Chacoans built massive stone buildings of multiple stories and hundreds of rooms. The historical park contains the ruins of 13 large structures and several thousand smaller sites. The largest complex is Pueblo Bonito, built in stages from the mid–800s to the 1200s. It had four stories and over 600 rooms and 40 kivas. Among the other building ruins are the 1075 to 1105 Pueblo del Arroyo, with about 280 rooms and more than 20 kivas; the mid–800s to the mid–1100s Una Vida, which had approximately 150 rooms and five ceremonial kivas; and 1125 to 1130 Kin Klestso, a three-story structure containing around 100 rooms and five enclosed kivas. These monumental buildings are believed to have been public buildings used periodically at times of ceremony, commerce, and trading, rather than for traditional housing.

The great houses often were oriented to solar, lunar, and cardinal directions, with the lines of sight allowing communication between the houses. The buildings had sophisticated astronomical markers, communication features, water control devices, and formal earthen mounds around them. The Chacoans also had a solstice marker on the isolated Fajada Butte, where noontime sunlight shines between stone slabs onto two spiral petroglyphs to time equinoxes and solstices. The site, now closed to the public, was used to determine when to plant crops and to measure the years. Despite such innovations, drought and other factors apparently caused Chaco inhabitants to abandon the area by 1200. It is believed that they moved to other Anasazi settlements and later were assimilated into Zuñi, Hopi, Ácoma, and other pueblos. The historical park has a visitor center that tells the Chaco story and displays pueblo and Navajo artifacts and pottery.

Chaco Culture National Historical Park, 1808 Road 7950 (off State Hwy. 44), PO Box 220, Nageezi, NM 87037–0220. Phones: 505/786–7014 and 505/345–2871. Fax: 505/786–7061. E-mail: *chcu@nps.gov.* Web site: *www.nps.gov/chcu.* Hours: park — open 24 hours; visitor center — 8–5 daily; closed New Year's Day, Thanksgiving, and Christmas. Admission: $4 per person or $8 per carload.

Chattahoochee River National Recreation Area. The Paleo, Archaic, Woodland, and Mississippian prehistoric Indians — as well as the later Cherokee and Creek tribes — once lived and traveled through the Chattahoochee River region in the southern Appalachian Mountains. The ancient river area now is a national recreation area, but does have the remains of a number of prehistoric and historic Indian village sites. The first humans were attracted to the river wilderness some 8,000 years ago. A visitor center with exhibits is located in Atlanta, Georgia.

Chattahoochee River National Recreation Area, 1978 Island Ford Pkwy., Atlanta, GA 30350–3400. Phones: 678/538–1200 and 678/538–1280. Fax: 770/399–8087. Web site: *www.nps.gov/chat.* Hours: park — dawn-dusk daily; visitor center — 9–5 daily. Admission: free, but parking fee of $3.

Chimney Rock Archaeological Area. As many as 2,000 Anasazi (Ancestral Puebloans) lived 1,000 years ago on San Juan National Forest lands surrounded by the Southern Ute Indian Reservation west of Pagosa Springs, Colorado. The 4,100-acre site now is the Chimney Rock Archaeological Area, named for two towering chimney-like rock spires that still remain. The site is believed to have been the northernmost, highest, and most remote outpost of the Anasazi. More than 200 homes and ceremonial buildings once occupied the site, where researchers have found the remains of 91 permanent structures, including the 35-room Great House, Ridge House, and Great Kiva, and 27 work camps near farming areas. The grounds now are restricted, but can be seen as part of U.S. Forest Service guided tours during the summer. A visitor center near the entrance has interpretive exhibits with artifacts and models.

Chimney Rock Archaeological Area, U.S. Forest Service, 3179 State Hwy. 151, Pagosa Springs, CO 81147 (mailing address: Chimney Rock Interpretive Program, PO Box 1662, Pagosa Springs, CO 81147). Phones: 970/883–5359 and 970/264–2287. Fax: 970/264–1538. E-mail: *chimneyrock@chimneyrockco.org.* Web site: *www.chimneyrockco.org.* Hours: mid-May-Sept.— 9–4:30 daily; guided tours at 9:30, 10:30, 1, and 2 daily; closed remainder of year. Admission: site — free; tours — adults, $8; children 5–11, $2; children under 5, free.

Chucalissa Archaeological Site and C. H. Nash Museum. The Chucalissa Archaeological Site in Memphis, Tennessee, features a reconstructed fifteenth-century Native American village and the C. H. Nash Museum on the actual site of the prehistoric village. The 187-acre site, which was discovered in 1939 during construction of a state park, has been excavated and preserved, with the re-created village and museum being added in 1955. It now is operated by the Department of Anthropology at the University of Memphis.

The reconstructed village contains Indian mounds, a plaza, a chief's temple, a shaman's house, and a family dwelling from the Mississippian period. The museum, which is named for the first director, has exhibits on the prehistory of the mid–South, southeastern Indian culture, a preserved archaeological excavation trench, and such artifacts as stone tools, pottery, ceramics, and projective points. Among the site's special events are displays of Choctaw crafts and an annual Native American Festival. Chucalissa is a Choctaw word meaning "abandoned house."

Chucalissa Archaeological Site and C. H. Nash Museum, University of Memphis, 1987 Indian Village Dr., Memphis, TN 38109. Phone: 901/785–

3160. Fax: 901/785–0519. E-mail: *dewan@memphis.edu*. Web site: *www.chucalissa.org*. Hours: 9–5 Tues.-Sat.; 1–5 Sun.; closed Mon., major holidays, and when university not in session. Admission: adults, $5; seniors and children, $3.

Coronado State Monument. The Coronado State Monument near Bernalillo, New Mexico, features the partially reconstructed ruins of the Tiwa pueblo of Kuaua, which was occupied from 1300 until abandoned near the end of the sixteenth century. The monument is named for Francisco Vásquez de Coronado, the Spanish explorer who is thought to have camped near the site while searching for gold at the fabled Seven Cities of Cibola in 1540.

An excavated and restored kiva at the site is where many examples of pre–contact mural art were found (the kiva now has mural reproductions of pueblo life with human images and animal figures). Also at the site are the Kuaua Mural Hall, which has 15 panels of excavated original murals, and a visitor center with Indian and Spanish colonial artifacts and a video that presents the past and present lifestyles of the two cultures.

Coranado State Monument, State Hwy. 44, Bernalillo, NM 87004 (mailing address: 485 Kuaua Rd., Bernalillo, NM 87004). Phone 505/867-5351. Fax: 505/867-1733. E-mail: *kjuaua@lobo.net*. Web site: *www.nmculture.org*. Hours: 8:30–5 Wed.-Mon.; closed Tues., New Year's Day, Easter, Thanksgiving, and Christmas. Admission: adults, $3; children under 17, free; state residents, $1 on Sun.; New Mexico seniors, free on Wed.

Crow Canyon Archaeological Center. The Crow Canyon Archaeological Center, a research and education facility near Cortez, Colorado, displays artifacts discovered in the area on the tenth- through thirteenth-centuries occupation of the Mesa Verde region by the Anasazi (Ancestral Puebloans). Participants in the center's educational programs take part in the excavations and research.

Crow Canyon Archaeological Center, 23390 County Rd. K, Cortez, Co 81321. Phone: 970/565-8975. Fax: 970/565-4859. E-mail: *gprior@crow canyon.org*. Web site: *www.crowcanyon.org*. Hours: Mar.-Oct.— 8:30–5 Mon.-Fri.; closed Sat.-Sun. and remainder of year. Admission: free.

Deer Valley Rock Art Center. The Deer Valley Rock Art Center in Glendale, Arizona, has a collection of approximately 1,500 petroglyphs made by early inhabitants from 700 to 10,000 years ago. The rock art, mostly of humans, animals, and designs, are on more than 500 boulders found by the U.S. Army Corps of Engineers when the Adobe Dam was being built to control flooding along Skunk Creek in 1980. The boulders now are on a hillside

outside the center, operated by the Department of Anthropology at Arizona State University.

Deer Valley Rock Art Center, Arizona State University, 3711 W. Deer Valley Rd., Glendale, AZ 85308 (mailing address: PO Box 41998, Phoenix, AZ 85080-1998). Phone: 623/582-8007. Fax: 623/582-8831. E-mail: *dvrac@asu.edu*. Web site: *www.asu.edu/clas/anthropology/dvrac*. Hours: May-Sept.— 8–2 Tues.-Fri.; 9–5 Sat.; 12–5 Sun.; closed Mon. and remainder of year. Admission: adults, $5; seniors and students, $3; children 6–12, $2; children under 6, free.

Dickson Mounds Museum. The Dickson Mounds Museum near Lewistown, Illinois, enables visitors to explore the world of American Indians through 12,000 years of human experience in the Illinois River Valley. The museum, a branch of the Illinois State Museum, has archaeological sites, interpretive exhibits, hands-on activities, and special events in a rural setting. Its permanent exhibits trace the interaction between the early inhabitants and the Illinois River, the various cultures from the Ice Age to the tribal groups, and the life and culture of the Mississippian people whose 800-year-old sites surround the museum. They are supplemented by changing thematic exhibitions. Three historic buildings — an 1839 school, 1850 toll house, and 1907 school — also are located on the grounds.

Dickson Mounds Museum, 10956 N. Dickson Mounds Rd., Lewistown, IL 61542. Phone: 309/547-3721. Fax: 309/547-3189. E-mail: *wiant@museum.state.il.us*. Web site: *www.museum.state.it.us/ismsite/dickson*. Hours: 8:30–5:00 daily; closed New Year's Day, Easter, Thanksgiving, and Christmas. Admission: free.

Edge of the Cedars State Park. The Edge of the Cedars State Park near Blanding, Utah, is located at an Anasazi (Ancestral Puebloan) pueblo occupied from 700 to 1220. The ruins of six residential and ceremonial complexes are on a ridge overlooking Westwater Canyon. The park museum, which has a collection of over 250,000 Paleo-Indian, Archaic, Anasazi, Navajo, and Ute artifacts that have been excavated from public lands in southeast Utah, features exhibits of Anasazi pottery, baskets, and other prehistoric materials.

Edge of the Cedars State Park, 660 West 400 North (off U.S. Hwy. 191), PO Box 788, Blanding, UT 84511. Phone: 435/678-2238. Fax: 435/678-3348. E-mail: *edgeofthecedars@utah.gov*. Web site: *www.parks.state.ut.us/parks/wwwl/edge.htm*. Hours: mid--May-mid-Sept.— 8–8 daily; remainder of year — 9–5 daily; closed New Year's Day and Christmas. Admission: adults, $1; children, free.

Effigy Mounds National Monument. The 2,526-

acre Effigy Mounds National Monument at Harpers Ferry, Iowa, contains 195 earthen mounds — of which 31 are effigies in the shape of mammals, birds, and reptiles. The others are conical, linear, and compound. The mounds were built by eastern Woodland Indians from about 500 B.C. to the early European contact period. Natural features at the site include forests, tallgrass prairies, wetlands, and rivers. The visitor center has exhibits highlighting archaeological and natural specimens and rangers give guided hikes and prehistoric tool demonstrations during the summer.

Effigy Mounds National Monument, 151 State Hwy. 76, Harpers Ferry, IA 52146-7519. Phone: 563/873-3491. Fax: 563/873-3743. E-mail: *efmo_superintendent@nps.gov*. Web site: *www.nps.gov/efmo*. Hours: 8–5 daily, with extended hours Memorial Day weekend-Labor Day and weekends in Oct.; closed New Year's Day, Thanksgiving, and Christmas. Admission: $3 per adult or $5 per car, but free Nov.-Mar.; children under 16, free.

El Malpais National Monument and El Malpais National Conservation Area. The El Malpais National Monument and the adjoining El Malpais National Conservation Area near Grants, New Mexico, contain the excavated ruins of prehistoric Anasazi (Ancestral Puebloan) pueblos. The combined 377,277-acre site also has lava tube caves, spatter cones, and an ancient Zuñi-Acoma trail at the National Park Service's national monument and sculptured sandstone formations and wilderness areas in the surrounding U.S. Bureau of Land Management conservation area.

The site has three visitor centers with exhibits. The monument operates the El Malpais Information Center on the west side, featuring lava displays; the conversation area's El Malpais Ranger Station on the east side contains exhibits about the history of the area; and the jointly operated Northwest New Mexico Visitor Center in Grants has largely natural history displays.

El Malpais National Monument and El Malpais National Conservation Area, State Hwys. 53 and 117 (south of Interstate 40 and Grants), PO Box 846, Grants, NM 87020 (mailing addresses: El Malpais National Monument, 123 E. Roosevelt Ave., Grants, NM 87020 and National Conservation Area, PO Box 846, Grants, NM 87020-0846). Phones: monument — 505/783-4774 and 505/876-2783; conservation area — 505/287-7911. Fax: 505/285-5661. Web site: *www.nps.gov/elma*. Hours: monument and conservation area — open 24 hours; visitor centers — varies, but generally 8–5 daily; closed New Year's Day, Thanksgiving, and Christmas. Admission: free.

El Morro National Monument. The remains of two Anasazi villages and hundreds of petroglyphs are located on top of El Morro National Monument near Ramah, New Mexico. The massive 200-foot-high sandstone bluff known as El Morro (or Inscription Rock) also was a reliable waterhole and camp site for early weary travelers and where approximately 2,000 Spaniards, Mexicans, and Americans inscribed their names between 1605 and 1906.

The Anasazi were the first to find the waterhole hidden at the base of El Morro ("the bluff" or "the heartland" in Spanish). Members of the Anasazi culture moved into the valley after the Colorado Plateau was abandoned and began construction of the two villages about 1275. The larger of the two villages consisted of multiple stories with approximately 875 interconnected rooms around an open courtyard and a number of kivas. The site housed from 1,000 to 1,500 inhabitants, who abandoned the bluff for unknown reasons by 1400. In addition to the pueblo ruins, they left petroglyphs of figures, animals, birds, and various designs.

The first of many Spanish expeditions stopped and rested at El Morro in 1583, with the initial. inscription being carved in the rocky bluff in 1605 by Don Juan de Oñate, who established the first Spanish colony in New Mexico. It was followed by other Spanish messages as late as 1774, and then by inscriptions by Mexicans and later by American expeditions, pioneers, railroad survey crews, and others. The monument now has a visitor center with exhibits on the history of the site and trails to the inscriptions and Anasazi ruins and petroglyphs.

El Morro National Monument, State Hwy. 53, HC 61, Box 43, Ramah, NM 87321-9603. Phone: 505/783-4226. Fax: 505/783-4689. Web site: *www.nps.gov/elmo*. Hours: Memorial Day-Labor Day — 8–7 daily; Apr.-May and Sept.-Oct. — 9–6 daily; Nov.-Mar. — 9–5 daily; closed New Year's Day and Christmas. Admission: adults, $3; children under 17, free.

El Paso Museum of Archaeology at Wilderness Park. The El Paso Museum of Archaeology in El Paso, Texas, traces the history and culture of the area's first inhabitants, the Southwest, and northern Mexico. It features exhibits and dioramas that depict American Indian lives and material culture from the Paleo-Indian hunters of the Ice Age to present-day Indian descendants. The museum, formerly called Wilderness Park Museum, exhibits such artifacts as baskets, ceramics, woodcarvings, textiles, stone tools, and ornaments from many different tribes in the Southwest and Mexico.

El Paso Museum of Archaeology at Wilderness Park, 4301 Transmountain Rd., El Paso, TX 79924. Phone: 915/755-4332. Fax: 915/759-6824. E-mail: *www.elpasotexas.gov*. Hours: 9–5 Tues.-Sat.; closed Sun.-Mon. and major holidays. Admission: free.

Etowah Indian Mounds State Historic Site. Prehistoric earthen mounds from 1000 to 1500 and the remains of a fortified American Indian political and religious center that was the home of several thousand people 400 years ago are located at the Etowah Indian Mounds State Historic Site near Cartersville, Georgia. The 54-acre Moundbuilders site has seven mounds, portions of the original village, borrow pits, a plaza, and a museum.

The largest mound covers three acres and is 63 feet high. The home of a priest-chief, temples, and mortuary houses once were located on the flat-topped mounds in a Mississippian-period society rich in ritual. In some mounds, leaders were buried in elaborate costumes with items they would need in their afterlives. Exhibits at the museum interpret the daily life in the community, with many artifacts showing how inhabitants decorated themselves with shell beads, feathers, copper ear ornaments, tattoos, paint, and complicated hairdos. The museum also displays stone effigies and objects made of wood, sea shells, stone, and copper.

Etowah Indian Mounds State Historic Site, 813 Indian Mounds Rd., S.E., Cartersville, GA 30120. Phone: 770/387–3747. Fax: 770/387–3972. E-mail: *etowah-mounds@bellsouth.net*. Web site: *www.ngeorgia.com/parks/etowah.html*. Hours: 9–5 Tues.-Sat.; 2–5:30 Sun.; closed Mon., New Year's Day, Thanksgiving, and Christmas. Admission: adults, $3; children 6–18, $2; children under 6, free.

Flint Ridge State Memorial. The Flint Ridge State Memorial near Glenford, Ohio, preserves and interprets one of America's mostly widely used prehistoric flint quarries. Prehistoric tools and points made of the high-quality flint have been found from the Atlantic seaboard to Louisiana. In addition to the site of the early quarry, the memorial operated by the Ohio Historical Society has a museum with exhibits about the quarry, geology, flint artifacts, and prehistoric cultures.

Flint Ridge State Memorial, 7091 Brownsville Rd., S.E., Glenford, OH 43739–9609. Phones: 740/787–2476 and 800/283–8707. Fax: 740/373–3680. E-mail: *webmaster@ohiohistory.org*. Web site: *www.ohiohistory.org/places.flint*. Hours: Memorial Day-Labor Day — 9:30–5 Wed.-Sat.; 12–5 Sun.; closed Mon.-Tues.; Sept. after Labor Day-Oct.— 9:30–5 Sat.; 12–5 Sun.; closed remainder of week and year. Admission: adults, $3; seniors, $2.40; children 6–12, $1.25; children under 6, free.

Fort Ancient State Memorial. The Fort Ancient State Memorial near Oregonia, Ohio, is a prehistoric site with 18,000 feet of earthen walls built 2,000 years ago by American Indians who used the shoulder blades of deer, split elk antlers, clam shell hoes, and digging sticks to obtain the dirt. In addition to exhibits about the site, the Fort Ancient Museum interprets the 15,000 years of American Indian history and culture in the Ohio Valley. The site and museum are operated by the Ohio Historical Society.

Fort Ancient State Memorial, 6123 State Rte. 350 (off Interstate 71), Oregonia, OH 45054. Phones: 513/912–4421 and 800/283–8904. Fax: 513/932–4843. E-mail: *jblosser@ohiohistory.org*. Web site: *www.ohiohistory.org/places.ftancien*. Hours: Memorial Day weekend-Labor Day — 10–5 Wed.-Sat.; 12–5 Sun. and holidays; closed Mon.-Tues.; Apr.-late May and Sept. after Labor Day-Oct.— 10–5 Sat.; 12–5 Sun.; closed remainder of week and year. Admission: adults, $7; children 6–12, $3; children under 6, free.

Frémont Indian State Park. One of the nation's largest collections of Frémont Indian (Anasazi) rock art and archaeological sites from 500 to 1300 is located at the Frémont Indian State Park west of Sevier, Utah. The site has nearly 800 panels with approximately 5,000 pictographs and petroglyphs and many Anasazi (Ancestral Puebloan) artifacts from the Clear Creek Canyon area.

Frémont Indian structures and artifacts differ from those at Anasazi sites to the south. They include previously unseen pottery types, dew claw moccasins, unfired clay figurines, and trapezoidal-shaped petroglyphs. The 1,100-acre site has a museum that traces the history of the site and Frémont Indians and displays excavated artifacts. Twelve interpretive trails also take visitors to the rock art and archaeological sites.

Frémont Indian State Park, 11550 Clear Creek Canyon Rd., Sevier, UT 84766–9999. Phone: 435/527–4631. Fax: 435/527–4735. Hours: mid--May-mid–Sept.— 9–6 daily; remainder of year — 9–5 daily; closed New Year's Day, Thanksgiving, and Christmas. Admission: $6 per car or $3 per person.

Gila Cliff Dwellings National Monument. The Gila Cliff Dwellings National Monument north of Silver City, New Mexico, offers a look at the homes and lives of the people of the Mogollon culture who lived in the Gila Wilderness area — the nation's first designated wilderness area — in the Gila National Forest from the 1280s to the early 1300s. The multi–agency Gila Visitor Center has exhibits on the history and people of the prehistoric area. A one-mile trail leads to the ruins of thirteenth-century cliff dwellings with 42 rooms about 175 feet from the floor of the canyon.

Gila Cliff Dwellings National Monument, State Hwy. 15, HC 68, Box 100, Silver City, NM 88061. Phone: 505/536–9461. Fax: 505/536–9344. Web site: *www.nps.gov/giel*. Hours: monument — Memorial Day weekend-Labor Day: 8–6 daily; remainder of year: 9–4 daily; visitor center — Memorial Day weekend-Labor Day: 8–5 daily; remainder of year: 8–4:30 daily; closed New Year's Day, Thanksgiving, and Christmas. Admission: adults, $3; children under 12, free; families, $10.

Grand Mound Historic Site. The Grand Mound Historic Site, located at the confluence of the Rainey and Big Fork rivers on the Canadian border near International Falls, Minnesota, contains the largest Indian burial mound in the upper Midwest. However, it recently was closed to the public. The mound, a Minnesota Historical Society historic site, is one of a group of burial mounds, some of which date to prehistoric Woodland cultures 2,000 years ago.

Grand Mound Historic Site, 6749 State Hwy. 11, International Falls, MN 56649. Phones: 218/327–4482 and 218/285–3332 (also fax). Web site: *www. mnhs.org.* Hours: site is closed.

Grimes Point–Hidden Cave Archaeological Site. The Grimes Point–Hidden Cave Archaeological Site near Fallon, Nevada, consists of two prehistoric sites — Grimes Point, with self-guided tours of stone carvings, and nearby Hidden Cave, where the U.S. Bureau of Land Management gives interpretive tours about Great Basin prehistory twice a month, with tours leaving Churchill County Museum and Archives in Fallon. Prehistoric Indians were in the area at least 8,000 years ago and left numerous petroglyphs and a storage cave.

Grimes Point–Hidden Cave Archaeological Site, U.S. Hwy. 50, Fallon, NV 89406 (contact: Carson City Field Office, Bureau of Land Management, 5665 Morgan Mill Rd., Carson City, NV 89701). Phone: 702/885–6000. E-mail: *r3brown@nv.blm.gov.* Hours: Grimes Point — dawn-dusk daily; Hidden Cave — guided tours 9:30 2nd and 4th Sat. of month; closed major holidays. Admission: free.

Hampson Archeological Museum State Park. The Hampson Archeological Museum State Park in Wilson, Arkansas, has exhibits and artifacts from the Nodena archaeological site, a 15-acre prehistoric Indian farming-based village that thrived nearby along the Mississippi River from 1400 to 1650. Exhibits tell the story of this early aboriginal culture that farmed and hunted while developing an artistic, religious, and political structure and an active trading network.

Hampson Archeological Museum State Park, 2 Lake Dr., PO Box 156, Wilson, AR 72395. Phone: 870/655–8622. E-mail: *hampsonarcheologicalmuseum@arkansas.com.* Web site: *www.arkansasstateparks.com/hampsonmuseum.* Hours: 8–5 Tues.-Sat.; 1–5 Sun.; closed Mon., New Year's Day, Thanksgiv-

ing, and Christmas Eve and Day. Admission: adults, $2.50; children 6–12, $1.50; families, $8.

Hickson Petroglyph Recreation Area. The Hickson Petroglyph Recreation Area east of Austin, Nevada, features American Indian stone carvings from 1000 B.C. to A.D.1500. The Hickson site is near an old Overland and Pony Express Trail off U.S. Highway 50 between Austin and Eureka.

Hickson Petroglyph Recreation Area, U.S. Hwy. 50, Austin, NV 89310 (contact: Bureau of Land Management, PO Box 911, Tonopah, NV 89409. Phone: 775/482–7800. Fax: 775/482–7810. Hours: open 24 hours. Admission: free.

Homolovi Ruins State Park. The 4,000-acre Homolovi Ruins State Park near Winslow, Arizona, is where the Hisatsinom (Anasazi) found a home along the Little Colorado River in the fourteenth century before continuing north to join people (today known as the Hopi) already living on the mesas. The park has more than 300 archaeological sites ranging from small sites to four large pueblo ruins with rock carvings, as well as the site of an 1876 to 1888 Mormon settlement. The visitor center contains exhibits on the Homolovi park site, the ancestral Hopi, and prehistoric artifacts from Homolovi and associated sites. The park also serves as a center of research for the late migration period of the Hopi from the 1200s to the late 1300s.

Homolovi Ruins State Park, State Hwy. 87 North, Exit 257, HCR 63, Box 5, Winslow, AZ 86047–9803. Phone: 520/289–4106. Fax: 520/289–2021. E-mail: *homolovi@pr.statg.az.us.* Web site: *www.pr.state.az. us/parkhtml/homolovi.html.* Hours: park — dawn-dusk daily; visitor center — 8–5 daily; closed Christmas. Admission: $5 per car.

Hopewell Culture National Historical Park. The Hopewell Culture Historical Park near Chillicothe, Ohio, was the focal point of the prehistoric Hopewell culture that built earthen enclosures and mounds in the Ohio River valley from about 200 B.C. to A.D. 500. The enclosures were characterized by earthen walls, often in geometric patterns, and mounds that took the form of squares, circles, and other geometric shapes. Many of these earthworks were built to monumental scale. Some walls were up to 12 feet high and more than 1,000 feet across, while conical and loaf-shaped mounds often found with geometric earthworks sometimes were as high as 30 feet.

The historical park, formerly known as the Mound City Group National Monument, is composed of five separate sites in Ross County — Mound City Group, Hopeton Earthworks, High Bank Works, and Seip Earthworks in addition to the Hopewell site. Hopewell has five earthworks, but many more are found at the other sites in the Scioto River valley near present-day Chillicothe. The Mound City Group has the largest number with 23 earthen mounds. It also is the location of the park's visitor center, which has artifacts, exhibits, an orientation film, and guided tours that provide insight into the social, ceremonial, political, and economic life of the Hopewell people.

Hopewell Culture National Historical Park, 16062 State Rte. 104, Chillicothe, OH 45601–8694. Phone: 740/774–1125. Fax: 740/774–1140. E-mail: *hocu_superintendent@nps.gov*. Web site: *www.nps.gov/hocu*. Hours: park — dawn-dusk daily; visitor center — Memorial Day-Labor Day — 8:30–6 daily; remainder of year: 8:30–5 daily; closed New Year's Day, Thanksgiving, and Christmas. Admission: $3 per person or $5 per car; children under 17, free; admission fee waived in Dec.-Feb.

Horsethief Lake State Park in Columbia Hills State Park. The Horsethief Lake State Park, now part of the Columbia Hills State Park near Goldendale, Washington, has some of the oldest pictographs and petroglyphs in the Northwest. The park site formerly was the largest burial ground of Indians in the area and where Wishram, Cloud, and Lishkam Indians camped while fishing in the Columbia River with nets and spears and Indian trade fairs were held.

The most famous petroglyph in the Columbia Gorge is the large-eyed Tsagaglalal (She Who Watches), carved into stone high on a cliff overlooking the site between 1700 and 1840. The Horsethief site now is located along a lake created by The Dalles Dam near the Celilo Falls, with the Horsethief Butte overlooking the lake like an ancient castle. The public can see the rock art only as part of park tours.

Horsethief Lake State Park, Columbia Hills State Park, State Hwy. 14, Goldendale, WA 98620 (mailing address: PO Box 426, Dallesport, WA 98617). Phone: 509/767–1159. Fax: 509/767–4304. Hours: Apr.-Oct. — 6:30-dusk daily (with park tours at 10 A.M. Fri.-Sat.); closed remainder of year. Admission: free.

Hovenweep National Monument. Six prehistoric Anasazi-era villages spread over a 20-mile expanse of mesa tops and canyons along the Utah-Colorado state line are featured at Hovenweep National Monument. The monument, which is noted for its solitude and undeveloped natural character, has the ruins of many-roomed pueblos, small cliff dwellings, and multi–stored towers scattered in the remote area north of the San Juan River near Cortez, Colorado.

Nomadic Paleo-Indians first visited the area some 10,000 years ago to gather food and hunt. By

around A.D. 900, people similar to the Anasazi (Ancestral Puebloans) settled in the area as farmers, hunters, and gathers. But they are believed to have abandoned the difficult landscape before 1300 because of extended drought, failed crops, water shortage, and perhaps warfare. The village ruins they left behind are now known as Cajon, Cutthroat, Castle, Goodman Point, Hackberry, Holly, and Horseshoe. A visitor center in the Square Tower Group has exhibits with artifacts, photographs, and other materials related to the history and geology of the area.

Hovenweep National Monument, McElmo Canyon Rte., Cortez, CO 81321. Phone: 970/562–4282. Web site: *www.nps.gov/hove*. Hours: monument — open 24 hours; visitor center — Memorial Day-Labor Day: 8–6 daily; remainder of year — 8–5 daily; closed New Year's Day, Thanksgiving, and Christmas. Admission: $3 per person or $6 per car; children under 17, free.

Huff Indian Village State Historic Site. The site of a large prehistoric village occupied about 1450 by approximately 1,000 people ancestral to the Mandan Indians is preserved at the Huff Indian Village State Historic Site south of Huff, North Dakota. An unusual fortification system featuring 10 bastions, a dry moat 15 feet wide, and outward pointing stakes once protected an eight-acre site with at least 103 rectangular earth lodges. The Mandans later changed from long rectangular houses to smaller more compact circular earthlodges. Only depressions and interpretive signs can be seen at the site, but archaeologists have recovered thousands of artifacts from 11 houses and two bastions that have been excavated.

Huff Indian Village State Historic Site, State Hwy. 1806, Huff, ND 58554 (contact: State Historical Society of North Dakota, 612 E. Boulevard Ave., Bismarck, ND 58505). Phone: 701/328–2666. Fax: 701/328–3710. E-mail: *histsoc@state.nd.us*. Web site: *www.nd.us/hist*. Hours: dawn-dusk daily. Admission: free.

Indian Grinding Rock State Historic Park and Chaw'se Regional Indian Museum. See Chaw'se Regional Indian Museum and Indian Grinding Rock State Historic Park in Museums and Galleries section.

Indian Temple Mound Museum and Park. A large ceremonial mound dating from 1200 is the focus of the Indian Temple Mound Museum and Park in Fort Walton Beach, Florida. The mound served as a religious and civic center for American Indians in the area. The site now is a park with a museum which has historical exhibits on the four tribes that lived in the Choctawatchee Bay region for 12,000 years and a collection of 6,000 ceramic artifacts from southeastern tribes — the largest such collection in the nation.

Indian Temple Mound Museum and Park, 139 Miracle Strip Pkwy., S.E., Fort Walton Beach, FL 32548 (mailing address: PO Box 4009, Fort Walton Beach, FL 32549). Phone: 850/833–9595. Fax: 850/833–9675. Web site: *www.fwb.org*. Hours: park — dawn-dusk daily; museum — June-Aug.: 9–4:30 Mon.-Sat.; 12:30–4:30 Sun.; remainder of year: 10–4 Mon.-Fri.; 9–4 Sat.; closed Sun. and major holidays. Admission: adults, $3; seniors and military, $2; children 4–17, $1; children under 4, free.

Jara Archaeological Site. See Jicarilla Apache Arts and Crafts Museum in Museums and Galleries section.

Jeffers Petroglyphs Historic Site. Rock carvings spanning 5,000 years are located at a holy site for the Iowa, Oto, Arapaho, Cheyenne, Lakota, Dakota, Nakota, and Ojibwe Indians at the Jeffers Petroglyphs Historic Site near Comfrey, Minnesota. The petroglyphs, which range from 3000 B.C. to A.D. 1750, depict humans, deer, elk, buffalo, turtles, thunderbirds, atlatis, and arrows. The historic site is a holy place for Native Americans who still come to visit and pray. A visitor center has exhibits and a multimedia presentation about the site.

Jeffers Petroglyphs Historic Site, 27160 County Rd. 2, Comfrey, MN 56019. Phone: 507/628–5591. Fax: 507/628–5593. Web site: *www.jefferspetroglyphs.com*. Hours: Memorial Day-Labor Day —10–5 Mon. and Wed.-Fri.; 10–8 Sat., 12–8 Sun.; closed Tues.; May and Sept.—10–5 Fri.; 12–5 Sun.; closed remainder of week; remainder of year — open only by reservation. Admission: adults, $5; seniors, $4; children 6–17, $3; children under 6, free.

Jefferson County Indian Mounds and Trail Park. The Jefferson County Indian Mounds and Trail Park near Fort Atkinson, Wisconsin, features 11 effigy mounds built by semi-nomadic tribes between 300 and 1642 and the only remaining prehistoric Indian trail that runs through a mounds group. The animal, bird, and conical mounds are at the southern end of the large General Atkinson Group, which originally consisted of 72 mounds within a distance of a mile. The largest mound in the park is the 222-foot Turtle Mound. Also near the park is the Panther Intaglio Mound, the only complete negative mound formed by scooping out the earth to leave and indented impression of an animal.

Jefferson County Indian Mounds and Tribal Park, Koshkonong Mounds Rd. (off old Hwy. 26), Fort Atkinson, WI 53538 (contact: Hoard Historical Museum, 407 Merchants Ave., Fort Atkinson, WI 53538).

Phone: 920/563–7769. Fax: 920/568–3203. E-mail: *hartwick@hoardmuseum.org*. Web site: *www.hoard museum.org*. Hours: dawn-dusk daily. Admission: free.

Ka-Do-Ha Indian Village. The reconstructed Ka-Do-Ha Indian Village near Murfreesboro, Arkansas, is located at a prehistoric site inhabited by Moundbuilders approximately 1,000 years ago. The privately operated village has replica mud and straw houses and a museum with exhibits about the site and mounds and displays of such artifacts as ancient pottery, pipes, and chipped flint.

Ka-Do-Ha Indian Village, 1010 Caddo Dr., PO Box 669, Murfreesboro, AR 71958. Phone: 870/285–3736. Fax: 870/285–4118. E-mail: *caddotc@all tel.net*. Web site: *www.caddotc.com*. Hours: Memorial Day-Labor Day — 9–6 daily; remainder of year — 9–5 daily; closed Thanksgiving and Christmas. Admission: adults, $4; children 6–13, $2; children under 6, free.

Knife River Indian Village National Historic Site. See Historic Sites section.

Kolomoki Mounds Historic Park. The Kolomoki Mounds Historic Park north of Blakely, Georgia, contains seven earthen mounds built between 250 and 950 by the Swift Creek and Weeden Island Indians. They include Georgia's oldest great temple mound, four ceremonial mounds, and two burial mounds. The park's museum, which is partially located inside an excavated mound, has exhibits and a film on the mounds and site.

Kolomoki Mounds Historic Park, 205 Indian Mounds Rd. (off U.S. Hwy. 27), Blakely, GA 39823–9702. Phone: 229/724–2150. Fax: 229/724–2152. E-mail: *kolomoki@alltel.net*. Web site: *www.gastateparks.org/info/kolomoki*. Hours: 8–5 daily; closed New Year's Day, Thanksgiving, and Christmas. Admission: adults, $3; children 6–18, $1.75; children under 6, free.

Makah Cultural and Research Center. See Museums and Galleries section.

Manitou Cliff Dwellings and Anasazi Museum. Visitors can see and walk through transplanted. 1100–1300 Anasazi (Ancestral Puebloan) cliff dwellings at the Manitou Cliff Dwellings in Manitou Springs, Colorado. The prehistoric cliff dwellings and artifacts were moved from southwestern Colorado at the turn of the twentieth century and first opened to the public in 1906. A three-story pueblo-style adobe building was added later to house the Anasazi Museum, which contains Anasazi pottery, tools, weapons, burial urns, and other aspects of prehistoric life in the Four Corners area. Indian dances are performed several times daily on the museum's plaza during the summer months.

Manitou Cliff Dwellings and Anasazi Museum, U.S. Hwy. 24, PO Box 272, Manitou Springs, CO 80829. Phones: 719/685–5242 and 800/354–9971. Web site: *www.cliffdwellingsmuseum.com.* Hours: May–Sept.—9–6 daily; Mar.-Apr. and Oct.-Nov.— 9–5 daily; Dec.-Feb.—10–4 daily; closed Thanksgiving and Christmas. Admission: adults, $8.50; seniors, $7.50; children 7–11, $6.50; children under 7, free.

Marksville State Historic Site. The Marksville State Historic Site, located on a bluff overlooking the Old River adjacent to Marksville, Louisiana, was the site of an A.D.1 to 400 prehistoric village that was a variant of the Hopewell culture centered in the Ohio River Valley.

Six earthen mounds of various sizes and shapes are located inside the main enclosure and others are built outside of it. The site is surrounded by a semi-circular earthwork which is 3,300 feet long and ranges from three to seven feet in height. The three openings in the wall suggest that the purpose of the site was ceremonial rather than defensive. Some of the mounds also are burial sites. The site has a museum with exhibits and artifacts. The Tunica-Biloxi Native American Museum also is located nearby (see separate listing in Museums and Galleries section).

Marksville State Historic Site, 837 Martin Luther King Dr., Marksville, AR 71351. Phones: 318/ 253–8954 and 888/253–8954. E-mail: *marksville@ crt.state.la.us.* Web site: *www.lastateparks.com/marks vil/marksvle.htm.* Hours: 9–5 daily; closed New Year's Day, Thanksgiving, and Christmas. Admission: adults, $4; seniors and children under 13, free.

Menoken Indian Village State Historic Site. The Menoken Indian Village State Historic Site near Menoken, North Dakota, preserves the site of one of the first earth lodge villages in the state. The village originally was believed to have been a 1700s Mandan Indian village, but archaeological excavations later revealed that it was of prehistoric Menoken origin and occupied as early as 1100. The 2.5-acre site had about 20 lodges enclosed by a fortification ditch with four bastions. None of the structures have survived, but depressions indicate where the lodges and the fortification ditch were located. A fieldstone kiosk contains a map and information about the site.

Menoken Indian Village State Historic Site, County Rd. (3 miles northeast of Menoken), Menoken, ND 58558 (contact: State Historical Society of North Dakota, 612 E. Boulevard Ave., Bismarck, ND 58505). Phone: 701/328–2666. Fax: 701/328–3710. E-mail: *histsoc@state.nd.us.* Web site: *www.state. nd.us/hist.* Hours: dawn-dusk daily. Admission: free.

Mesa Verde National Park. The site of Mesa Verde National Park in southwestern Colorado was the home of the Anasazi (Ancient Puebloans) from about 600 to 1300. The Anasazi originally flourished at their mesa home located 2,000 feet above the valley floor and eventually built elaborate stone villages in sheltered alcoves that became known as cliff dwellings. It is believed that the cliff dwellings were built in the last 75 to 100 years before the Anasazi abandoned the site for unknown reasons and possibly merged with pueblo tribes in the region.

Mesa Verde became the nation's first cultural park in 1906 and a UNICEF world heritage center in 1978. It has some of the most notable and best preserved archaeological sites in the United States. The park contains over 600 cliff dwellings and nearly 4,000 surface archaeological sites, most of which are unexcavated and closed to the public. Five large cliff dwellings and a number of smaller ones are open for touring by visitors, three of which can be seen only as part of ranger-guided tours in the spring, summer, and fall. Spruce Tree House and Step House are open for individual visits, while Cliff Palace, Balcony House, and Long House must be toured with guides. In the winter, only Spruce Tree House and some of the smaller sites are open.

Many Mesa Verde artifacts from the 600 to 1300 period are displayed at the Chapin Mesa Archeological Museum, located near Spruce Tree House. The museum has more than 40 exhibits depicting the daily lives and nature of the Anasazi culture. A visitor center — Far View Center near the park entrance — has approximately 30 exhibits about the site and its historic jewelry, pottery, and baskets.

Mesa Verde National Park, PO Box 8, Mesa Verde, CO 81330–0008. Phones: 970/529–4465 and 970/529–5073 (museum). Faxes: 970/529–4637 and 970/529–1117 (museum). Web site: *www.nps.gov/meve.* Hours: park — open 24 hours daily; museum — mid–Apr.-mid–Oct.: 8–6:30 daily; remainder of year: 8–5 daily; visitor center: 8–5 daily; closed remainder of year. Admission: park —$10 per car; museum and visitor center — free; guided tours —$3 per person.

Mitchell Prehistoric Indian Village/Boehnen Museum. The Mitchell Prehistoric Indian Village is located at the site of an eleventh-century pre–Mandan Indian village along Lake Mitchell north of Mitchell, South Dakota. As many as 800 semi-nomadic farmers and hunters once occupied the site. It now is home to the Boehnen Museum, which has a large-scale diorama of how the village may have looked and a prehistoric earth lodge reconstruction. Also located at the site is the Thomsen Center Archeodome, where visitors can see and

The Cliff Palace is one of the highlights of Mesa Verde National Park, home of the Anasazi (Ancient Puebloans) from 600 to 1300 in southwestern Colorado. The cliff dwelling, which can be seen as part of ranger-led tours, is one of over 600 cliff dwellings and nearly 4,000 archaeological sites in the national park. *Courtesy Mesa Verde National Park and National Park Service.*

interact with archaeologists conducting investigations in an enclosed archaeological dig.

Mitchell Prehistoric Indian Village, Indian Village Rd., PO Box 621, Mitchell, SD 57301. Phone: 605/996-5473. Web site: *www.mitchellindianvillage.org.* Hours: Memorial Day weekend-Labor Day — 8-6 daily; May and Sept.— 9-4 daily; remainder of year — 9-4 Mon.-Fri.; closed Sat.-Sun. and major holidays. Admission: adults, $4; seniors, $3.50; children 6-18, $2; children under 6, free.

Montezuma Castle National Monument. The Montezuma Castle National Monument near Camp Verde, Arizona, is the site of one of the nation's best preserved cliff dwellings — a five-story, 20-room cliff dwelling built by the Sinagua Indian farmers over 600 years ago. The cliff dwelling, called Montezuma Castle, is located in a limestone recess high above Beaver Creek in Verde Valley. At the base of the cliff are the ruins of another structure that once was a six-story dwelling with 45 rooms. The Sinagua were dry farmers who moved into the valley about 1125 and disappeared from the

area in the early 1400s. A visitor center has displays on the Sinagua and the site. The monument is near Tuzigoot National Monument, another Sinaguan site with pueblo ruins (see separate listing).

Montezuma Castle National Monument, 2800 Montezuma Castle Rd., Camp Verde, AZ 86322 (mailing address: 527 S. Main St., PO Box 219, Camp Verde, AZ 86322). Phones: 928/567-3322 and 928/567-5276. Fax: 928/567-3597. Hours: Memorial Day-Labor Day — 8-6 daily; remainder of year — 8-5 daily; closed Christmas. Admission: $5 per person or $8 for both Montezuma and Tuzigoot national monuments; children under 17, free.

Moundbuilders State Memorial and Ohio Indian Art Museum. A large complex of geometric earthworks built by the Hopewell culture near 2,000 years ago is preserved at the Moundbuilders State Memorial in Newark, Ohio. It is the site of the most extensive prehistoric earthworks in the nation. The memorial consists of three sites known as the Newark Earthworks — the Great Circle Earthworks, which enclose 26 acres, and two other units,

Octagon Earthworks and Wright Earthworks. It also is the site of the Ohio Indian Art Museum, the nation's first museum devoted exclusively to prehistoric American Indian art. The museum contains prehistoric knives, pottery, pipes, jewelry, and art objects of the Adena and Hopewell cultures from 1000 B.C. to A.D. 700.

The Great Circle Earthworks is the site of prehistoric ceremonial grounds with an embankment 1,200 feet in diameter encircled by earthen walls 8 to 14 feet in height. Octagon Earthworks is located on a golf course of the Moundbuilders Country Club, where greens and fairways have been built inside the best circle-and-octagon earthworks in Ohio. Visitors can get an overview of the mounds from a viewing platform at the edge of the parking lot. The Wright Earthworks has only two low earthen ridges that meet. The sites are operated by the Ohio Historical Society.

Moundbuilders State Memorial and Ohio Indian Art Museum, 99 Cooper Ave., Newark, OH 43055. Phones: 740/344–1920 and 800/600–7174. E-mail: *webmaster@ohiohistory.org*. Web site: *www.ohiohistory.org*. Hours: site — Apr.-Oct.: dawn-dusk daily; closed remainder of year; museum — Memorial Day weekend-Labor Day: 9:30–5 Wed.-Sat.; 12–5 Sun.; closed Mon.-Tues.; Sept.-Oct.: 9:30–5 Sat.; 12–5 Sun.; closed Mon.-Fri. and remainder of year. Admission: sites — free; museum — adults, $3; students, $2; children under 6, free.

Museum of Indian Arts and Culture and Laboratory of Anthropology. See Museums and Galleries section.

Nanih Waiya Mound and Village. The Nanih Waiya Mound and Village, a state prehistoric site northeast of Philadelphia, Mississippi, preserves a large rectangular platform mound possibly made during the Middle Woodland period of 100 B.C. to A.D. 100. Pottery sherds from the period have been found at the adjacent habitation area. However, the mound, which measures 25 feet high, 218 feet long, and 140 feet wide, is typical of rectangular mounds built during the later Mississippian period. The site, which has a Choctaw Indian name meaning "leaning hill," is venerated by the Choctaw tribe. One of the tribe's legends says the mound gave birth to the tribe when people emerged from the underworld here and rested on the mound's slopes to dry before settling in the surrounding region.

Nanih Waiya Mound and Village, State Hwy. 393 (15 miles northeast), Philadelphia, MS 39350. Phones: 662/724–2770 and 800/467–2757. Hours: dawn-dusk daily. Admission: free.

Navajo National Monument. The Navajo National Monument on the Navajo Indian Reservation near Tonalea, Arizona, consists of three of the most intact cliff dwellings of the Anasazi (Ancestral Puebloans). The cliff dwellings — Betatakin, Keet Seel, and Inscription — were occupied for only about 50 years by the Keyenta Anasazi from 1250 to 1300. The well-preserved Betatakin and Keet Seel can be visited only as part of ranger-led tours in the summer. A visitor center has exhibits about the site, Anasazi, and modern Navajo culture and films about prehistoric pueblo people and Betatakin — one of nation's largest cliff dwellings. Navajo craftspeople also demonstrate their rug and basket weaving, silversmithing, and painting.

Navajo National Monument, Navajo Indian Reservation, State Hwy. 564, HC 71, Box 3, Tonalea, AZ 86044–9704. Phone: 928/672–2700. Fax: 928/672–2703. Web site: *www.nps.gov/nava*. Hours: site — open 24 hours daily; visitor center — mid–May-Labor Day: 8–6 daily; remainder of year — 8–5 daily. Admission: free.

Newark Earthworks State Memorial. See Moundbuilders State Memorial.

Ocmulgee National Monument. The Ocmulgee National Monument east of Macon, Georgia, preserves a record of 12,000 years of human life from the Ice Age to the Muscogee Creek people of historic times in the Southeast. The emphasis is on the Mississippians, who farmed the region between 900 and 1200. They brought a more complex way of life to the region and left behind eight earthen mounds and the remains of a 900 to 1100 ceremonial earth lodge. The monument consists of two sections separated by riverine wetlands along the Ocmulgee River. The main unit adjacent to Macon is open to the public and has a visitor center with exhibits about the monument, but the isolated Lamar Mounds and Village unit can be visited only by special permit.

Ocmulgee National Monument, 1207 Emery Hwy., Macon, GA 31217–4399. Phone: 478/752–8257. Fax: 478/752–8259. Web site: *www.nps.gov/ocmu*. Hours: 9–5 daily; closed New Year's Day and Christmas. Admission: free.

Octagon Earthworks. See Moundbuilders State Memorial.

Old Stone Fort State Archaeological Park. The Old Stone Fort State Archaeological Park near Manchester, Tennessee, is located at a 2,000-year-old American Indian ceremonial site on a promontory formed by cliffs and the waterfalls of two rivers. The 50-acre enclosure, which served as a central ceremonial gathering place for approximately 500 years, had a 1.25-mile perimeter and was surrounded by wall-like earthen mounds. The visitor center has exhibits on the history, archaeology, and legends pertaining to the Old Stone Fort and its builders.

Old Stone Fort State Archaeological Park, 732 Stone Fort Dr., Manchester, TN 37355. Phone: 931/723–5073. Web site: *www.state.tn.us/environment/parks/oldstonefort/index.shtml*. Hours: park — 8–dusk daily; visitor center — 8–4:30 daily; closed Christmas. Admission: free.

Ozette Archaeological Site. The Ozette Archaeological Site on the Olympic Peninsula of Washington is the site of a Makah Indian historical whaling village dating to 400 B.C. that was partially buried by a huge mudslide over 500 years a go. The tribe continued to occupy other parts of the village until 1920 when the Makah were relocated north to Neah Bay for government schooling. Storms and tidal erosion since 1966 exposed older parts of the village and attracted pothunters. As a result, tribal members and students from Washington State University embarked on a partial excavation of the site. They recovered over 55,000 artifacts that now are at the Mahah Cultural and Research Center (see separate listing in Museums and Galleries section) in Neah Bay. About 1 percent of the collection is on display, as well as historical exhibits and full-scale replicas of a cedar longhouse and whaling, sealing, and fishing canoes used by the Makah. Access to the Ozette site now is restricted.

Ozette Archaeological Site, near Neah Bay, WA. Access restricted. See Mahah Cultural and Research Center for further information.

Pecos National Historical Park. See Historic Sites section.

Petroglyph National Monument. The 7,236-acre Petroglyph National Monument, located on a volcanic basalt escarpment adjacent to Albuquerque, New Mexico, contains more than 25,000 rock carvings created largely by native peoples and early Spanish settlers to a lesser degree. The carved images of people, animals, brands, and crosses and the associated sites in the area provide insight into a 12,000-year history of human life in the region. A visitor center has exhibits on petroglyphs and the site.

Petroglyph National Monument, 6001 Unser Blvd., N.W. (off Interstate 40), Albuquerque, NM 87120. Phone: 505/899–0205. Fax: 505/899–0207. Web site: *www.nps.gov/petr*. Hours: 8–5 daily; closed New Year's Day, Thanksgiving, and Christmas. Admission: free, except for Boca Negra Canyon entrance, which has a $1 city fee on weekdays and $2 on weekends.

Petroglyphs of the Cosos. The largest concentration of petroglyphs in the Western Hemisphere is said to be in the desert canyons of China Lake Naval Weapons Center, a restricted Navy research and development facility in southwestern California. The northern half of the base, which is used for missile weapons testing, is believed to have more than 100,000 rock carvings spanning 10,000 years on the Coso Range canyon walls. The greatest concentration is in two canyons — Black Canyon and Renegade Canyon (known as Big and Little Petroglyph canyons). After the sites were designated as a national historic landmark in 1964, the Navy agreed to allow limited visitation. An arrangement was made with the Maturango Museum of the Indian Wells Valley in Ridgecrest, California, to conduct limited tours of the three-mile-long Little Petroglyph Canyon. It now is possible to see such images of aboriginal rock art at the site as human forms, naturalistic and stylized animals, prehistoric weapons, and abstract forms and patterns, with the most prevalent image being the desert bighorn sheep.

Petroglyphs of the Cosos, China Lake Naval Weapons Center, CA 93555 (contact for tours: Maturango Museum of the Indian Wells Valley, 100 E. Las Flores Ave., Ridgecrest, CA 93555). Phone: 760/375–6900. Fax: 760/375–0479. E-mail: *matmus@ridgecrest.ca.us*. Hours: 10–5 daily; closed New Year's Day, Thanksgiving, and Christmas. Admission: adults, $3; children over 5, $2; children under 6 free. Petroglyph tours are Sat.-Sun in Mar.-mid–June and Sept.-mid–Dec. Fee is $35.

Pinson Mounds State Archaeological Park. The 1,200-acre Pinson Mounds State Archaeological Park in Pinson, Tennessee, consists of 15 earthen mounds, a geometric enclosure, habitation areas, and related earthworks dating to about A.D. 1 to 500. The mounds are the largest Middle Woodland period mound group in the United States. The biggest mounds were used for ceremonial purposes, and some of the smaller ones held burials. A number of cremation and activity areas also are nearby. A museum, designed like a mound, contains exhibits about the mounds, a Discovery Room for exploration, theater, and archaeological library. An Archaeofest is held each September to celebrate Native American culture and archaeology, featuring storytelling and such craft demonstrations as pottery, basketry, leather work, and jewelry making.

Pinson Mounds State Archaeological Park, 460 Ozier Rd., Pinson, TN 38366. Phone: 731/988–5614. Fax: 731/424–3909. Web site: *www.tnstateparks.com/pinson*. Hours: Mar.-Nov. — 8–5:30 Mon.-Sat., 1–5 Sun.; Dec.-Feb. — 8–4:30 Mon.-Fri.; closed Sat.-Sun. and state winter holidays. Admission: $3 per car.

Pipestone National Monument. See Historic Sites section.

Pueblo Grande de Nevada and Lost City Museum. The ruins of several hundred ancient pithouses, campsites, rock shelters, salt mines, and caves of the Anasazi (Ancestral Puebloan) people make up the Pueblo Grande de Nevada, commonly known as Lost City, south of Overton, Nevada. It was a 30-mile-long settlement thought to have been occupied from about 300 to 1150. Although five miles of the prehistoric community was inundated when Lake Mead was developed, ruins of much of the site still remain — and many of the artifacts can be seen at the Lost City Museum, operated by the Nevada Department of Cultural Affairs.

The site along the Muddy and Virgin river valleys originally was occupied by the Anasazi Basketmakers, who lived in circular pithouses. They were followed by Anasazi who built multi–room pueblos in the valleys. Then came the Paiute Indians, Mormons, and other settlers. Remnants of these cultures and farming, hunting, and mining were found during archaeological excavations. The Lost City Museum, formerly the Boulder Dam Park Museum, contains Anasazi baskets, pottery, weapons, and food found at the site. It also displays Paiute artifacts and baskets, southwestern Indian crafts, pioneer historical materials, early mining and farming equipment, fossils, and minerals.

Pueblo Grande de Nevada and Lost City Museum, 721 S. Hwy. 169, PO Box 807, Overton, NV 89040. Phone: 702/397-2193. Fax: 702/397-8987. E-mail: *lostcity@comment.net*. Web site: *www.nevadaculture. org*. Hours: site — open 24 hours daily; museum — 8:30–4:30 daily; closed New Year's Day, Thanksgiving, and Christmas. Admission: site — free; museum — adults, $3; seniors, $2; children under 18, free.

Pueblo Grande Museum and Archaeological Park. The Pueblo Grande Museum and Archaeological Park is located at the ruins of a 1,500-year-old Hohokam village in Phoenix, Arizona. The prehistoric Hohokam lived and farmed in central and southwestern Arizona about A.D. 1 to 1450. They built adobe villages, often centered around platform mounds and ball courts, and constructed hundreds of miles of canals to irrigate their fields.

The 102-acre park has the ruins of an 800-year-old platform possibly used for ceremonies or as an administrative center, an excavated ball court, some intact irrigation canals, and full-scale reproductions of Hohokam homes. The museum contains exhibits that describe the life of the Hohokam people, feature replicas of Hohokam dwellings, and explore how archaeologists excavate and study clues from ancient and historic sites.

Pueblo Grande Museum and Archaeological Park, 4619 E. Washington St., Phoenix, AZ 85034-1919. Phones: 602/495–0901 and 877/706–4408. Fax: 602/495–5645. E-mail: *pueblo.grande.museum.pks@ phoenix.gov*. Web site: *www.pueblogrande.com*. Hours: 9–4:45 Mon.-Sat.; 1–4:45 Sun.; closed major holidays. Admission: adults, $2; seniors, $1.50; children, $1.

Puye Cliff Dwellings and Communal House Ruins. The Puye Cliff Dwellings and Communal House Ruins at the Santa Clara Pueblo west of Española, New Mexico, contain the remains of cliff dwellings that were occupied by as many as 1,500 people from the 1100s to about 1580. Caves were hollowed for the dwellings in the soft stone along the south mesa wall for nearly a mile. The ruins include a three-story pueblo with 740 rooms and a ceremonial chamber on top of the mesa. It is believed that the prehistoric pueblo was abandoned because of drought. The site now has a visitor center and two trails that lead to the cliff dwellings and the top of the mesa.

Puye Cliff Dwellings and Communal House Ruins, Santa Clara Pueblo, State Hwy. 501, PO Box 580, Española, NM 87532. Phone: 505/753-7326. Fax: 505/753-8988. Web site: *www.hanksville.org/voyage/ misc/puye.html*. Hours: 9–6 daily. Admission: adults, $5; seniors and children 7–14, $4; children under 7, free.

Red Clay State Historic Park. The last Cherokee encampment before the Trail of Tears forced march to Indian Territory (later Oklahoma) in 1838 to 1839 is preserved at the Red Clay State Historic Park in Cleveland, Tennessee, located in the foothills of the Smoky Mountains. A visitor center with nineteenth-century Cherokee artifacts and replicas of a Cherokee council house, farmhouse, corn crib, and barn are on the grounds.

Red Clay State Historic Park, 1140 Red Clay Park Rd., S.W., Cleveland, TN 37311. Phone: 423/ 478-0339. Hours: park — Mar.-Nov.: 8-dusk daily; remainder of year: 8–4:15 daily; visitor center — Mar.-Nov.: 8–4:30 daily; remainder of year: 8–4:15 daily; park and visitor center closed Dec. 22 through New Year's Day. Admission: park — $3 per car; visitor center — free.

San Juan County Archaeological Research Center and Library at the Salmon Ruins. The San Juan County Archaeological Research Center and Library at the Salmon Ruins near Bloomfield, New Mexico, is located at the prehistoric site of large Anasazi (Ancestral Puebloan) pueblo. The massive stone masonry construction of the Salmon Ruins represents one of the classic examples of pre–Columbian Puebloan architecture. The complex is characterized by core and veneer masonry walls, cobble wall foundations, T-shaped doorways, stylized patterns on wall facings, and large symmetrically arranged rooms.

A two-story Chacoan Anasazi complex with over 217 rooms and a Great Kiva, a circular ceremonial structure, dominate the site's plaza. The pueblo was built in 1088 to 1090, but abandoned in approximately 1130. It was reoccupied 50 years later by another Anasazi group with close ties with the Mesa Verde cliff dwellers. These Anasazi made moderate changes in the complex, such as subdividing some rooms and adding numerous small kivas, before leaving by 1285. It is believed that both groups left because of drought conditions.

More than 1.5 million artifacts and scientific samples have been recovered from the site since the ruins were discovered by homesteader George Salmon on his property in the late 1800s. The Salmon Ruins Museum displays some of the artifacts in exhibits about the site. Also located at the site is Heritage Park, which features a historic trading post and displays of such traditional habitations of prehistoric and historic groups of the Four Corners area as a Pleistocene playa, a Basketmakers pithouse, Navajo hogans, and Jicarilla Apache and Ute wickiups and tepees. Other facilities at the ruins include a research center and library.

San Juan County Archaeological Research Center and Library at the Salmon Ruins, 6131 U.S. Hwy. 64, PO Box 125, Bloomfield, NM 87413. Phone: 505/632–2013. Fax: 505/632–8633. E-mail: *sreducation@sisna.com*. Web site: *www.salmonruins.com*. Hours: 8–5 daily; closed New Year's Day, Easter, Thanksgiving, and Christmas. Admission: adults, $3; seniors, $2; children 6–15, $1; children under 6, free.

Seminole Canyon State Park and Historic Site. The Seminole Canyon State Park and Historic Site west of Comstock, Texas, contains 400-year-old pictographs and some of the oldest cave dwellings in North America. The 2,173-acre park has more than 200 sites from 6000 to 2000 B.C. where the painted rocks of prehistoric people are located. They range from single rock paintings to caves with panels of art hundreds of feet long. The paintings are found in the Fate Bell Shelter and other rock cave sites in the Lower Pecos River area, which can be seen only as part of guided tours. The park has an interpretive center, with exhibits on the history of the canyon, pictographs, and caves.

Seminole Canyon State Park and Historic Site, U.S. Hwy. 90 West, PO Box 820, Comstock, TX 78837. Phone: 432/292–4464. Fax: 432/292–4596. Web site: *www.tpwd.state.tx.us/spdest/findadest/parks/seminole_canyon*. Hours: 8–5 daily; closed Christmas. Admission: adults, $5; children 6–12, $2; children under 6, free.

Serpent Mound. Serpent Mound near Peebles, Ohio, is the largest and finest serpent effigy in the United States. The uncoiling serpent originally was thought to be part of the Adena culture of 800 B.C. to A.D. 100, but more recent evidence indicates that the effigy mound was created during the Fort Ancient period of A.D. 1000 to 1550. The head of the serpent is aligned to the summer solstice sunset and the coils appear to be pointed to the winter solstice and equinox sunrises. The site also has three burial mounds and the remains of village from the Adena and Fort Ancient cultures. The Serpent Mound Museum contains exhibits on the effigy mound and the geology of the area. The site is operated by the Ohio Historical Society.

Serpent Mound, 3850 State Rte. 73, Peebles, OH 45660. Phone: 937/587–2796. Fax: 937/587–1116. E-mail *serpent@bright.net*. Web site: *www.ohiohistory. org/places/serpent*. Hours: park — 10–5 Tues.-Sun.; closed Mon., New Year's Day, Thanksgiving, and Christmas; museum — Memorial Day weekend-Labor Day: 10–5 Wed.-Sun.; closed Mon.-Tues.; Oct.-Nov. and Apr.-late May: 10–5 Sat.-Sun.; closed remainder of week and year. Admission: park — $7 per car; museum — free.

Sheboygan Indian Mounds Park. The Sheboyan Indian Mound Park in Sheboygan, Wisconsin, consists of 18 mounds created 1,000 years ago by prehistoric Indian nomadic hunters and gatherers known as the Effigy Mound Builders. More than half of the mounds are of deer, panthers, and fawns, while others are unclassified effigies, linear, oval, and conical. The mounds, which range from one to three feet in height, are believed to have been burial grounds. They were part of 34 mounds recorded in 1927, but some were lost to the plow and the bulldozer before the creation of the park in 1966. The park also has a nature trail.

Sheboygan Indian Mounds Park, 5018 S. 9th St., Sheboygan, WI 53081 (contact: Sheboygan Park Department, 2926 New Jersey Ave., Sheboygan, WI 53081). Phone: 920/459–3440. Hours: dawn-dusk daily. Admission: free.

Spiro Mounds Archaeological Center. The Spiro Mounds Archaeological Center north of Spiro, Oklahoma, has the remains of a prehistoric village and 12 earthen mounds built by an American Indian culture that occupied the site from 850 to 1450. The site, Oklahoma's only archaeological park, has been linked to the Southern Cult, a regional group of mound sites constructed during the Mississippian period, because of the great variety of artifacts recovered and the variety and vitality of its art forms.

Spiro was a major political, religious, and trade center. Its chiefs controlled trade between the plains and the southeastern woodlands. The mounds were used for ceremonial and burial purposes, with many exotic religious rituals being conducted in connection with the death and burial of elite members. The largest mound, called Craig Mound, is 33 feet high and 400 feet long and contains the graves of the culture's most important leaders. An interpretation center has site artifacts and exhibits about the history, mounds, and lifestyle of the prehistoric Spiro Indians. The site is operated by the Oklahoma Historical Society.

Spiro Mounds Archaeological Park, 18154 1st St., Spiro, OK 74959. Phone: 918/962–2062. Fax: 918/962–2062. E-mail: *spiromounds@ipa.net*. Web site: *www.ok-history.mus.ok.us/mus-site/museum28. htm*. Hours: May-Oct.— 9–5 Tues.-Sat.; 12–5 Sun.; closed Mon.; remainder of year — 9–5 Wed-Sat.; 12–5 Sun.; closed Mon.-Tues., New Year's Eve and Day, Thanksgiving, and Christmas. Admission: free.

Sun Watch Indian Village and Archaeological Park. The Sun Watch Indian Village and Archaeological Park in Dayton, Ohio, is a partially reconstructed 800-year-old village from the Fort Ancient period along the Great Miami River. The Fort Ancient people, who were farmers and the last prehistoric culture to occupy the region before the arrival of European settlers, lived in the Middle Ohio River Valley from present-day West Virginia to southeastern Indiana from about 1000 to 1650.

The SunWatch site was discovered by amateur archaeologists in the 1960s as the city of Dayton planned to expand its nearby sewage plant site to the location. After excavations of the Dayton Museum of Natural History (now the Boonshoft Museum of Discovery) uncovered more artifacts, the expanded sewage plant plans were changed and the museum's Dayton Society of Natural History began years of excavations and research. The society then built replicas of five Fort Ancient structures (lath and daub huts with grass thatch roofs) in their original thirteenth-century locations and opened an interpretation center with exhibits and many of the artifacts recovered from the site in 1988. The site also has reconstructed portions of a stockade and a native garden and prairie with plants typical of the period.

Sun Watch Indian Village and Archaeological Site, 2301 W. River Rd., Dayton, OH 45418. Phone: 937/268–8199. Fax: 937/268–1760. E-mail: *asawyer@ sunwatch.org*. Web site: *www.sunwatch.org*. Hours: 9–5 Tues.-Sat.; 12–5 Sun; closed Mon., New Year's Eve and Day, Easter, Thanksgiving, and Christmas Eve and Day. Admission: adults, $5; seniors and students 6–17, $3; children under 6, free.

Three Rivers Petroglyph Site. More than 21,000 rock drawings are scattered over 50 acres of the Three Rivers Petroglyph Site in the northern Chihuahuan Desert near Tularosa, New Mexico. The petroglyphs are of humans, birds, animals, fish, insects, and plants, as well as geometric and abstract designs. They were created by the Jornada Mogollon people who lived in the area between 900 and 1400. Remains of the village still can be seen at the site. The Mogollons lived in pithouses and adobe structures similar to those of the Anasazi.

Three Rivers Petroglyph Site, 3 River Rd. (off U.S. Hwy. 54 and County Rd. B30, 17 miles north of Tularosa), Tularosa, NM 88352 (contact: Bureau of Land Management Field Office, 1800 Marquess St., Las Cruces, NM 88805). Phone: 575/525–4300. Web site: *www.nm.blm.gov*. Hours: open 24 hours daily. Admission: $2 per car.

Toltec Mound Archaeological State Park. The 100-acre Toltec Mounds Archaeological State Park near Scott, Arkansas, is one of the largest and most complex archaeological sites in the Lower Mississippi River Valley. It once had the tallest American Indian prehistoric mounds in the state. The site along Mound Pond is believed to have been a Plum Bayou culture ceremonial and governmental complex built between 600 and 950 and abandoned by 1400.

The prehistoric village originally had an 8- to 10-foot earthen embankment on three sides that extended for 5,298 feet with a ditch on the outside. Sixteen mounds — mostly square and rectangular — were located inside the embankment, with temples and other buildings located on most of the flat tops. Two of the largest mounds were 38 and 50 feet high. Today, only remnants of the embankment and several mounds are visible, but the locations of other mounds have been identified. The site, managed jointly by the Arkansas Department of Parks and Tourism and the Arkansas Archeological Survey, also has a visitor center with exhibits of artifacts, the history of the site, and how archaeologists work.

Toltec Mounds Archaeological State Park, 490 Toltec Mounds Rd., Scott, AR 72142–9212. Phone: 501/961–9442. Fax: 501/961–9221. E-mail: *toltecmounds@arkansas.com*. Web site: *www.arkansasstateparks.com*. Hours: 8–5 Tues.-Sat.; 12–5 Sun.; closed Mon., New Year's Day, Thanksgiving, and Christmas Eve and Day. Admission: adults, $2.68; children 6–12, $1.61; children under 6, free.

Tomo-Kahni Site Historic Park. See Historic Sites section.

Tonto National Monument. The cliff dwellings of the Salado who lived in the Tonto Basin from about 1200 to 1450 are located in the Tonto National Monument near Roosevelt Dam and Roosevelt, Arizona. The Salado, who originally got their name while farming along the Rio Salado (Salt River), were fine craftsmen who produced exquisite polychrome pottery and intricately woven textiles. Many of their works are displayed with exhibits on the Salado history and culture in the visitor center. The site features the ruins of several hillside cliff dwellings. One has 32 ground-floor rooms and a second story, and other consists of 16 ground-floor rooms, a second story, and a 12-room annex.

Tonto National Monument, State Hwy. 188, HC02, Box 4602, Roosevelt, AZ 85545. Phone: 928/467–2341. Fax: 928/467–2225. E-mail: *tont_superintendent@nps.gov*. Web site: *www.nps.gov/tont*. Hours: 8–5 daily; closed Christmas. Admission: adults, $3; children under 16, free.

Town Creek Indian Mound State Historic Site. The Town Creek Indian Mound State Historic Site near Mount Gilead, North Carolina, is believed to have been an important cultural, religious, and political center of Creek-related Indians — known as the Pee Dee culture — during the fourteenth century. The 53-acre site, which evolved from a new cultural tradition in the Pee Dee River Valley about the eleventh century, has a ceremonial center with a number of reconstructed Mississippian-period structures, including a temple surrounded by a mud-plastered palisade on an earthen mound, a priest's dwelling, and a burial house. A visitor center contains a video presentation and interpretive exhibits about the site.

Town Creek Indian Mound State Historic Site, 509 Town Creek Mound Rd., Mount Gilead, NC 27306. Phone: 910/439–6802. Fax: 910/439–6441. E-mail: *towncreek@carolina.net*. Web site: *www.towncreek.nchistoricsites.org*. Hours: 10–4 Tues.-Sat., 1–4 Sun.; closed Mon. and major holidays. Admission: free.

Tusayan Museum. The Tusayan Museum near the ruins of an 800-year-old Anasazi (Ancestral Puebloan) pueblo in Grand Canyon National Park in Arizona traces the history of the site and American Indian tribes in the canyon region. The Anasasi lived in the partially intact rock dwellings for about 20 years around 1200 before abandoning the site, probably because of drought and depletion of natural resources. Free ranger-guided tours of the prehistoric site now are given daily.

The museum contains artifacts, models of the historic dwellings, and exhibits on the Anasazi and Indian tribes in the region. The Tusayan Museum name comes from the Hopi phrase meaning "country of isolated buttes." The park also has two other exhibit areas — a visitor center, with displays and an audiovisual presentation on the natural and human history of the Grand Canyon, and the Yavapai Museum, with exhibits on the geologic history of the region (it also offers panoramic views of the canyon). The Grand Canyon, a UNICEF world heritage site, is the nation's most popular national park with nearly 5 million visitors annually. An estimated 1 to 2 million visit the Tusayan Museum each year.

Tusayan Museum Grand Canyon National Park, Desert View Dr., PO Box 129, Grand Canyon, AZ 86023–0129. Phones: 928/638–2305, 928/638–7769, and 520/638–7888. Fax: 520/638–7797. E-mail: *deanna_prather@nps.gov*. Web site: *www.nps.gov/grca*. Hours: park — open 24 hours daily; museum — 9–5 daily. Admission: park — $10 per person or $20 per car; children under 16, free; museum — free.

Tuzigoot National Monument. The Tuzigoot National Monument near Clarksdale, Arizona, is located on a long desert ridge that rises 120 feet above Verde Valley. It contains the remnants of a Sinaguan pueblo built about 1000. The Sinagua Indians were primarily farmers with trade connections who lived in the village until around 1400. The pueblo consisted of 110 rooms, with some structures having two or three stories. It is located near the Montezuma Castle National Monument, which features a five-story, 20-room cliff dwelling occupied by the Sinagua over 600 years ago (see separate listing).

Tuzigoot National Monument, Tuzigoot Rd., Clarksdale, AZ 86324 (mailing address: 527 S. Main St., PO Box 219, Camp Verde, AZ 86322). Phone: 928/634–5564. Fax: 928/567–3597. E-mail: *moca_adminstrator@nps.gov*. Web site: *www.nps.gov/tuzi*. Hours: Memorial Day-Labor Day — 8–6; remainder of year — 8–5 daily; closed Christmas. Admission: site — $5 per person or $8 for Tuzigoot and Montezuma national monuments; children under 17, free; visitor center — free.

Ute Mountain Tribal Park. See Historic Sites section.

Walnut Canyon National Monument. The ruins of single-story cliff dwellings occupied by the Sinagua Indians from about 1100 to 1250 are located at Walnut Canyon National Monument southeast of Flagstaff, Arizona. The site, which is reached by trails, has a visitor center with exhibits about Sinagua culture and the cliff dwellings.

Walnut Canyon National Monument, Walnut Canyon Rd., Flagstaff, AZ 86004 (mailing address: 6400 N. U.S. Hwy. 89, Flagstaff, AZ 86004). Phone: 928/526–1167. Fax: 928/526–4259. Web site: *www.nps.gov/waca*. Hours: May-Oct.— 8–6 daily; remainder of year — 9–5 daily; closed Christmas. Admission: adults, $5; children under 16, free.

Wickliffe Mounds State Historic Site. The Wickliffe Mounds State Historic Site, located on a bluff overlooking the Mississippi River in Wickliffe, Kentucky, was the site of a village of Mississippian

Moundbuilders from about 1100 to 1350. The site contains the remains of a number of mounds that have been excavated and a visitor center with such artifacts as pottery, stone tools, and bone and shell implements from the site. The center also contains exhibits about the Mississippians and the site, the architecture of the mounds and dwellings, and burial practices of the Mississippian culture. The site, formerly operated by the Murray State University, now is part of the Kentucky Department of Parks.

Wickliffe Mounds State Historic Site, 94 Green St., PO Box 155, Wickliffe, KY 42087. Phone: 270/335-3681. E-mail: *wickliffemounds@ky.gov*. Web site: *http://parks.ky.gov/statehistoricsites/wm*. Hours: Apr.-Oct.— 9-4:30 daily; Dec.-Feb.—10-4 Mon.-Fri.; closed Sat.-Sun.; Mar.— 9-4:30 Tues.-Sat.; closed Sun.-Mon. and all state holidays. Admission: adults, $5; children 6-11, $4; children under 6, free.

Wright Earthworks. See Moundbuilders State Memorial.

Wupatki National Memorial. The agricultural and trading pueblo of Wupatki was the largest, tallest, and perhaps most influential village in the Flagstaff, Arizona, area 800 years ago. The site, 33 miles north of Flagstaff, now is a national monument with ruins of multi-storied masonry structures surrounded by smaller pueblos and pithouses. Nearly 100 people lived in the pueblo and several thousand on the outskirts when Wupatki flourished as a trading center and meeting place of different cultures from 1100 to about 1250, bringing such exotic items as turquoise, shell jewelry, cooper bells, and parrots to the village. The pueblo is located near the Sunset Crater volcano (now also a national monument), which covered the area with lava and ash a century earlier. A visitor center has exhibits about the site and artifacts that relate to the Sinagua-Anasazi culture of the period.

Wupatki National Monument, Sunset Crater Volcano/Wupaki Loop Rd. (Park Rd. 545), Flagstaff, AZ 86004 (mailing address: 6400 N. U.S. Hwy. 89, Flagstaff, AZ 86004). Phone: 928/679-2365. Fax: 928/526-4259. Web site: *www.nps.gov/wupa*. Hours: May-Oct.— 8-5 daily; remainder of year — 9-5 daily; closed Christmas. Admission: adults, $5; children under 16, free.

Representative Other Museums with Extensive Native American Collections or Exhibits

American Museum of Natural History. See Representative Other Museums with Extensive Ethnic Collections or Exhibits in Multicultural section.

Arizona State Museum. The Arizona State Museum, located on the University of Arizona campus in Tucson, is an anthropological museum with collections spanning 12,000 years of human occupation and activity in the greater Southwest. The museum has approximately 175,000 archaeological specimens from excavations pertaining to prehistoric Hohokam, Mogollon, and Anasazi cultures; more than 28,000 ethnographic objects relating to the lifeways of historic and living American Indians; and over 350,000 images and 1,200 linear feet of documents concerning cultural traditions of the Southwest. It possesses the largest whole vessel collection of Southwest Indian pottery in the world. The museum's principal permanent exhibit, "Paths of Life: American Indians of the Southwest," features the origins, history, and contemporary lives of 10 Indian cultures of Arizona and northwest Mexico — the Seri, Tarahumara, Yaqui, O'odham, Colorado River Yumans, Southern Paiute, Pai, Apache, Hopi, and Navajo.

Arizona State Museum, University of Arizona, 1013 E. University Blvd., PO Box 210026, Tucson, AZ 85721-0026. Phones: 520/621-6302 and 520/621-6281. Fax: 520/621-2976. E-mail: *webmaster@email.arizona.edu*. Web site: *www.statemuseum.arizona.edu*. Hours: 10-5 Mon.-Sat.; 12-5 Sun.; closed state and national holidays. Admission: $3 suggested donation.

ASU Museum of Anthropology. Changing exhibitions of archaeology, human origins, society, and culture — with the emphasis on Arizona and the Southwest — are presented by the ASU Museum of Anthropology at Arizona State University in Tempe. It has more than 200,000 archaeological specimens in its collections, including prehistoric ceramic vessels, textiles, figurines, and metal objects; over 1,000 ethnological specimens, such as costumes, musical instruments, and everyday items; and numerous early human skeletal remains and dental casts. The museum also has responsibility for the Deer Valley Rock Art Center in Glendale (see separate listing in Museums and Galleries section).

ASU Museum of Anthropology, Arizona State University, Anthropology Bldg., Cady and Tyler Malls, PO Box, 872402, Tempe, AZ 85287-2402. Phones: 480/965-6224 and 480/965-6213. Fax: 480/965-7671. E-mail: *anthweb@asu.edu*. Web: *www.asu.edu/anthropology/museum*. Hours: Sept.-May —11-3 Mon.-Fri.; closed Sat.-Sun. and most holidays, including Christmas through New Year's Day; June-Aug.— by appointment. Admission: free.

Buffalo Bill Historical Center. See Plains Indian Museum in Museums and Galleries section.

Burke Museum of Natural History and Culture. The Burke Museum of Natural History and Culture at the University of Washington in Seattle has 5 million specimens in its collections — 1 million of which are largely artifacts of past human history from the Pacific Northwest and Pacific Rim. Among its best known artifacts are extensive native archaeological and ethnological collections from the lower Columbia River and Puget Sound regions of the state. It also has artifacts from Oceania, Japan, Europe, and the Middle East. One of its long-term exhibits is "Pacific Voices," devoted to the arts, ceremonies, and personal stories of over 17 different cultures around the Pacific. In addition, the museum has the Erna Gunther Ethnobotanical Garden, which features plants important to American Indians of the Northwest, and the Bill Holm Center, devoted to research and fostering appreciation and understanding of the native arts of the Pacific.

Burke Museum of Natural History and Culture, University of Washington, 17th Ave, N.E., and N.E. 45th St., Box 353010, Seattle, WA 98195–3010. Phones: 206/543–5590 and 206/543–7907. Fax: 206/685–3039. E-mail: *recept@u.washington.edu.* Web site: *www.burkemuseum.org.* Hours: 10–5 daily (also to 8 1st Thurs. of month); closed New Year's Day, Independence Day, Thanksgiving Day, and Christmas Day. Admission: adults, $8; seniors, $6.50; students and children over 4, $5; children under 4, free; free on 1st Thurs. of month.

Carnegie Museum of Natural History. The past and present culture of Native Americans is the focus of the Hall of American Indians at the Carnegie Museum of Natural History in Pittsburgh, Pennsylvania. The Alcoa Foundation-funded hall depicts the daily work, special occasions, and traditions of American Indians, with exhibits interpreting the history and life of four tribes — Iroquois, Hopi, Lakota, and Tlingit. The hall contains Sitting Bull's headdress, more than 100 katsina dolls, and nearly 1,000 other artifacts. It also has lifelike dioramas, interactive exhibits, storytellers, and a theater.

Carnegie Museum of Natural History, 4400 Forbes Ave., Pittsburgh, PA 15213–4080. Phone: 412/622–3131. Fax: 412/622–8837. Web site: *www.carnegiemuseums.org/cmnh.* Hours: July 5-Aug.—10–5 Mon.-Sat.; 12–5 Sun.; remainder of year —10–5 Tues.-Sat.; 12–5 Sun.; closed Mon. and national holidays. Admission: adults, $10; seniors, $7; students and children 3–18, $6; children under 3, free.

Center for Western Studies. See Multicultural Museums and Galleries section.

Denver Art Museum. The Denver Art Museum, which recently opened a $90.5 million spectacular expansion designed by Daniel Libeskind in the Civic Center Cultural Complex in Denver, Col-

orado, has a major American Indian art collection and exhibit. The collection includes more than 18,000 art objects of all cultures and tribes across the United States and Canada. It spans over 2,000 years of artistic creativity from prehistoric times to the present. Among the works in the collection — examples of which are displayed in American Indian Art Gallery — are Pueblo ceramics, Navajo textiles, Northwest Coast sculpture, Plains beadwork, basketry, and oil paintings representing the full range of American Indian art styles.

Denver Art Museum, 100 W. 14th Ave. Pkwy., Denver, CO 80204. Phone: 720/865–5000. Fax: 720/913–0001. E-mail: *web-mail@denverartmuseum. org.* Web site: *www.denverartmuseum.org.* Hours: 10–5 Tues. and Thurs.; 10–10 Wed. and Fri.; 9–5 Sat.-Sun.; closed Mon., Thanksgiving, and Christmas. Admission: Colorado residents — adults, $10; seniors and students, $8; children 6–18, $3; children under 6, free; out-of-state visitors — adults, $13; seniors and students, $10; children 6–18, $5; children under 6, free.

Denver Museum of Nature and Science. The Denver Museum of Nature and Science in Denver, Colorado, has collections and exhibits interpreting the culture of Native Americans, with emphasis on the western interior of the nation. It has 35,000 North and South American Indian archaeological and ethnographic objects in its collections, and exhibits that feature reconstructed native scenes and dwellings, including a Cheyenne tepee, a Navajo hogan, a Northwest Coast clan house, and an Eskimo snow house.

Denver Museum of Nature and Science, 2001 Colorado Blvd., Denver, CO 80205. Phone: 303/370–6357. Fax: 303/331–6492. E-mail: *ngire@dmns. org.* Web site: *www.dmns.org.* Hours: 9–5 daily; closed Christmas. Admission: adults, $10; seniors, students, and children 3–18, $6; children under 3, free.

Eiteljorg Museum of American Indians and Western Art. See Museums and Galleries section.

Field Museum. The Field Museum, formerly the Field Museum of Natural History, in Chicago, Illinois, is a museum of natural and cultural history with more than 20 million objects in its collections, including more than 250,000 artifacts and other items pertaining to native peoples of North America. The largest American Indian exhibit is the "Pawnee Earth Lodge," one of the few full-size reconstructions of an earth lodge in the world. The lodge, partially made of cottonwood, willow, and prairie grass, is a fully furnished dwelling that reflects the traditional ways of the Great Plains tribe. The museum also has exhibits on Eskimos and Northwest Coast Indians, the ancient Americas, and contemporary Native American cultures.

Field Museum, 1400 S. Lake Shore Dr., Chicago, IL 60605–2496. Phone: 312/922–9410. Fax: 312/922–0741. Web site: *www.fieldmuseum.org.* Hours: 9–5 daily; closed Christmas. Admission: Chicago residents — adults, $10; seniors, students, and children 4–11, $6; children under 4, free; other visitors — adults, $12; seniors, students, and children 4–11, $7; children under 4, free.

Four Rivers Cultural Center and Museum. See Multicultural Museums and Galleries section.

Gilcrease Museum. The Gilcrease Museum in Tulsa, Oklahoma, has one of the world's largest and most comprehensive collections of art and artifacts of the American West. Many works relating to American Indians are among its more than 10,000 paintings, drawings, prints, and sculptures by 400 artists from colonial times to the present. The museum also has historical manuscripts, documents, and maps relating to the West. The collection includes artworks by such early western artists as George Catlin, Alfred Jacob Miller, Frederic Remington, Charles M. Russell, and Joseph H. Sharp, as well as such Native Americans as Acee Blue Eagle, Fred Beaver, and Alan Houser.

Gilcrease Museum, 1400 N. Gilcrease Museum Rd., Tulsa, OK 74127–2100. Phones: 918/596–2700 and 888/655–2278. E-mail: *gilcrease@ionet.net.* Web site: *www.gilcrease.org.* Hours: 10–5 daily; closed Christmas. Admission: adults, $7; seniors, $6; college students and children 13–18, $5; children under 13, free with adult.

Haffenreffer Museum of Anthropology. The Haffenreffer Museum of Anthropology, a part of Brown University located on a 400-acre estate in Bristol, Rhode Island, has extensive collections and exhibits on American Indians. Of the more than 110,000 items in its collections, over 15,000 objects are ethnographic, with the strongest area of material culture being Native Americans, largely from New England and the Plains. The museum has four galleries with cultural interpretations, principally of the native peoples of North, Central, and South America. Other exhibits are devoted to Africa, Asia, Middle East, and Oceania.

Haffenreffer Museum of Anthropology, Brown University, 1401 Hope St., Bristol, RI 02809 (mailing address: 12 Sanderson Rd., Smithfield, RI 02917). Phone: 401/245–7500. Fax: 401/245–9339. E-mail: *eec@asri.org.* Web site: *www.asri.org.* Hours: May–Sept. — 9–5 daily; remainder of year — 9–5 Mon.–Sat.; 12–5 Sun.; closed national holidays. Admission: adults, $5; children, $3.

Heritage of the Americas Museum. See Multicultural Museums and Galleries section.

Houston Museum of Natural History. The John P. McGovern Hall of the Americas at the Houston Museum of Natural History in Houston, Texas, celebrates the diversity, cultural traditions, and accomplishments of the indigenous peoples of the Americas, including American Indians. The 12,000-square-foot hall has eight exhibits with artifacts and reconstructed environments of more than 50 diverse cultures from Alaska to Peru. Among the objects displayed are native rugs, pottery, beadwork, kachina dolls, and pre–Columbian gold.

Houston Museum of Natural Science, 1 Hermann Circle Dr., Houston, TX 77030–1799. Phone: 713/639–4602. Fax: 713/523–4125. Web site: *www.nmns.org.* Hours: 9–5 Mon.–Sat.; 11–5 Sun.; closed Thanksgiving and Christmas. Admission: adults, $8; seniors, college students, and children 3–11, $4; children under 3, free.

LSU Rural Life Museum. See Multicultural Museums and Galleries section.

Mathers Museum of World Culture. See Multicultural Museums and Galleries section.

Maxwell Museum of Anthropology. The primary emphasis of the Maxwell Museum of Anthropology at the University of New Mexico in Albuquerque is on the native cultures of the Southwest. It contains extensive collections and two permanent exhibits on indigenous peoples of the region — "People of the Southwest" and "Ancestors"— and two galleries for changing exhibitions on contemporary native culture and materials from its collections. The museum has the largest and most comprehensive archaeological research collection of Anasazi (Ancient Puebloan) materials in the world. It also has considerable holdings from throughout the Americas, Africa, Asia, Australia, and the Pacific Islands that sometimes are displayed in changing exhibitions.

Maxwell Museum of Anthropology, University of New Mexico, University Blvd., MSCO 1, Albuquerque, NM 87131–0001. Phone: 505/277–4405. Fax: 505/277–1547. E-mail: *maxwell@unm.edu.* Web site: *www.unm.edu/~maxwell.* Hours: 9–4 Tues.–Fri.; 10–4 Sat.; closed Sun.–Mon. and major holidays. Admission: free.

Millicent Rogers Museum of Northern New Mexico. See Hispanic Museums and Galleries section.

Milwaukee Public Museum. See Representative Other Museums with Extensive Ethnic Collections or Exhibits in Multicultural section.

Museum of Anthropology, University of Missouri-Columbia. The permanent exhibit gallery at the Museum of Anthropology at the University of Missouri-Columbia focuses on Native American cultures from across North America and Missouri history from 11,200 years ago to the present. Many of the museum's ethnographic artifacts from the Arctic, Southwest, Plains, Northwest Coast, and Eastern Woodlands are displayed in the gallery. They include such items as American Indian textiles, pottery, basketry, apparel, beadwork, dolls, moccasins, bags, bowls, rattles, cradleboards, arrows, and war clubs.

Museum of Anthropology, University of Missouri-Columbia, 100 Swallow Hall, Francis Quadrangle, Columbia, MO 65211–1440. Phones: 573/882–3573 and 573/882–3764. Fax: 573/884–1435. E-mail *frenchme@missouri.edu*. Web site: *http://missouri.edu/anthromuseum*. Hours: 9–4 Mon.-Fri.; closed Sat.-Sun. and university holidays. Admission: free.

Museum of Northern Arizona. The prize-winning "Native Peoples of the Colorado Plateau" exhibit is presented at the Museum of Northern Arizona in Flagstaff. It documents 12,000 years of ethnology (including nine living tribes) in the region. The museum also has a Hopi kiva room and exhibits of Indian jewelry, ceramics, and fine arts. Nearly 5 million items are in the museum's collections, including such ethnographic holdings as baskets, pottery, katsina dolls, jewelry, and textiles and such prehistoric (largely Puebloan) items as sandals, arrow points, and ceramic vessels.

Museum of Northern Arizona, 3101 N. Fort Valley Rd., Flagstaff, AZ 86001. Phone: 928/774–5213. Fax: 928/779–1527. E-mail: *info@mna.mus.az.us*. Web site: *www.musnaz.org*. Hours: 9–5 daily; closed New Year's Day, Thanksgiving, and Christmas. Admission: adults, $5; seniors, $4; students, $3; children 7–17, $2; children under 7, free.

Museum of Peoples and Cultures. See Multicultural Museums and Galleries section.

Museum of the American West. The Museum of the American West, a part of the Autry National Center in Griffith Park in Los Angeles, California, has a scattering of Indian artifacts and artworks in its western exhibits. Most of the center's American Indian collections and exhibits are at its related Southwest Museum of the American Indian (see separate listing in Museums and Galleries section), which currently is being is rehabilitated and eventually will be moving to the Griffith Park location.

Museum of the American West, Autry National Center, 4700 Western Heritage Way, Los Angeles, CA 90027–1462. Phone: 323/667–2000. Fax: 323/660–5721. Web sites: *www.museumoftheamericanwest.org* and *www.autrynationalcenter.org*. Hours: 10–5 Tues.-Sun. (also to 8 Thurs.); closed Thanksgiving and Christmas. Admission: adults, $7.50; seniors and students, $5; children 2–12, $3; children under 2, free; free 4–8 Thurs.

National Cowboy and Western Heritage Museum. The National Cowboy and Western Heritage Museum in Oklahoma City, Oklahoma, has a Native American Gallery with seven exhibit areas that reflect the mosaic of spiritual, social, economic, and cultural influences in Indian art over thousands of years. The gallery contains common utilitarian items and special ceremonial objects that provide information about tribal beliefs, historical events, and cosmological views of the universe, as well as the individual owner.

The museum also has the Silberman Gallery, where changing thematic exhibitions of Native American art are presented from the Arthur and Shifra Silberman Collection. The collection contains more than 2,500 artworks by over 150 artists, representing more than 50 different cultural affiliations. It spans the Native American fine arts movement from the late nineteenth century to the present.

National Cowboy and Western Heritage Museum, 1700 N.E. 63rd St., Oklahoma City, OK 73111. Phone: 405/478–2250. Fax: 405/478–4714. E-mail: *info@nationalcowboymuseum.org*. Web site: *www.nationalcowboymuseum.org*. Hours: 9–5 daily; closed New Year's Day, Thanksgiving, and Christmas. Admission: adults, $8.50; seniors, $7; children 6–12, $4; children under 6, free.

Natural History Museum of Los Angeles County. The Lando Hall of California History at the Natural History Museum of Los Angeles County traces the history of the Southwest from the 1500s through the development of downtown Los Angeles in 1940. The gallery features 12 themes, including the role of American Indians. The museum also operates the William S. Hart Museum and Ranch, in the former movie cowboy's home in Newhall, which is filled with American Indian artifacts, western art, and early Hollywood memorabilia.

Natural History Museum of Los Angeles County, 900 Exposition Blvd., Los Angeles, CA 90007. Phones: 213/763–3412 and 213/763–3466. Fax: 213/743–4843. E-mail: *info@nhm.org*. Web site: *www.nhm.org*. Hours: 9:30–5 Mon.-Fri., 10–5 Sat.-Sun. and holidays; closed New Year's Day, Independence Day, Thanksgiving, and Christmas. Admission: adults, $9; seniors, students, and children 13–17, $6.50; children 5–12, $2; children under 5, free.

Northwest Museum of Arts and Culture. The Northwest Museum of Arts and Culture in Spokane, Washington, has collections and exhibits representing American Indian cultural groups throughout the Americas. It features one of the leading collections of Plateau material culture in the nation. The museum has more than 68,000 objects in its collections representing material culture and fine art from the Americas, Europe, and Asia.

Northwest Museum of Arts and Culture, 2316 W. 1st Ave., Spokane, WA 99204. Phones: 509/456–3931 and 509/363–5336. Fax: 509/363–5303. E-mail: *themac@northwestmuseum.org*. Web site: *www.northwestmuseum.org*. Hours: 11–5 Tues.-Sun.; closed Mon. and major holidays. Admission: adults, $7; seniors and students, $5; children under 6, free; open 5–8 1st Fri. of month by donation.

Oakland Museum of California. The Cowell Hall of California History at the Oakland Museum of California includes the early role of American Indians in the state. The museum has about 6,000 artifacts relating to North American Indians, with the largest group of objects from the native peoples of northern California. They include raw and processed materials used by indigenous cultures, and one of the finest collections of California baskets.

Oakland Museum of California, 1000 Oak St., Oakland, CA 94607. Phone: 510/238–2200. Fax: 510/238–2258. E-mail: *dmpower@museumca.org*. Web site: *www.museumca.org*. Hours: 10–5 Wed.-Sat.; 12–5 Sun.; closed Mon.-Tues., New Year's Day, Independence Day, Thanksgiving, and Christmas. Admission: adults, $8; seniors and students, $5; children under 6, free; 2nd Sun. of month free.

Peabody Museum of Archaeology and Ethnology. The Peabody Museum of Archaeology and Ethnology, founded in 1866 at Harvard University in Cambridge, Massachusetts, is one of the oldest museums in the world devoted to anthropology and houses one of the most comprehensive records of human cultural history in the Western Hemisphere. The museum had about 5 million objects in its collections, with artifacts from North America comprising nearly half of the archaeological and ethnographic holdings. Some of the artifacts are displayed in the Hall of the North American Indian and the adjoining gallery featuring "From Nation to Nation: Examining Lewis and Clark's Indian Collection."

The archaeological materials range from the Paleo-Indian to Historic periods. The native collections come from excavations in the Northeast, Southeast, Southwest, and Arctic regions and include such objects as Mimbres pottery and artifacts from Mississippian and Ohio River Valley mound sites. The ethnographic collection dates from the seventeenth to the twentieth centuries and has such holdings as Navajo rugs and textiles, Zuñi and other Pueblo ceramics, Hopi katchinas and pottery, Seminole textiles and garments, Cherokee and Chitimacha baskets, Chilkat blankets, and Inuit masks. In addition to North American holdings, the ethnographic collection includes objects from Asia, Europe, and Central and South America, such as cuneiform tablets from Nuzi and other sites, Iron Age artifacts from Slovenia and Italy, pottery from Cyprus and Iberia, artifacts from Maya sites, Aztec figurines, and Inca and Chimu metalwork.

Peabody Museum of Archaeology and Ethnology, Harvard University, 11 Divinity Ave., Cambridge, MA 02138. Phone: 617/496–1027. Fax: 617/495–7535. Web site: *www.peabody.harvard.edu*. Hours: 9–5 daily; closed New Year's Day, Thanksgiving, and Christmas Eve and Day. Admission: adults, $9; seniors and students, $7; children 3–18, $6; children under 3, free.

Peabody Museum of Natural History. The Peabody Museum of Natural History at Yale University in New Haven, Connecticut, has a Hall of Native American Cultures among its exhibits. The exhibit displays 360 objects from its extensive collections in sections relating to Plains, Southwest, Northwest Pacific Coast, and Arctic cultures. They include such materials as Blackfoot, Apache, and Sioux clothing; Cheyenne games; Navajo blankets; Zuñi and Hopi pottery; and Pima basketry. The museum has more than 11 million specimens and objects in its collections.

Peabody Museum of Natural History, Yale University, 170 Whitney Ave., PO Box 208118, New Haven, CT 06511–8118. Phone: 203/432–5050. Fax: 303/432–9816. E-mail: *peabody.webmaster@yale.edu*. Web site: *www.peabody.yale.edu*. Hours: 10–5 Mon.-Sat.; 12–5 Sun.; closed major holidays. Admission: adults, $7; seniors, $6; college students and children 3–18, $5; children under 3, free.

Philbrook Museum of Art. The Philbrook Museum of Art in Tulsa, Oklahoma, has American Indian paintings, baskets, pottery, costumes, and artifacts among its collections and exhibits. The museum also has the Roberta Campbell Lawson Collection of Indian books and conducts research on American Indian art.

Philbrook Museum of Art, 2727 S. Rockford Rd., Tulsa, OK 74114–4104 (mailing address: PO Box 52510, Tulsa, OK 74152–0510). Phones: 918/748–5300 and 918/748–5321. Fax: 918/743–4230. E-mail: *mwintas@philbrook.org*. Web site: *www.philbrook.org*. Hours: 10–5 Tues.-Sun. (also to 8 Thurs.); closed Mon. and major holidays. Admission adults, $7.50; seniors and students, $5.50; children under 19, free.

Phoebe A. Hearst Museum of Anthropology. The Phoebe A. Hearst Museum of Anthropology at the University of California at Berkeley has 3.8 million objects in its collections, with the largest share being California ethnological and archaeological artifacts and other materials. Many of the artifacts can be seen in the "Native California Cultures" permanent exhibit, which shows the historical similarities and differences of the Indian tribes that lived in the state. The museum also has another long-term exhibit, "From the Maker's Hand: Selections from the Permanent Collection," which uses objects from the collection to interpret the living and historical cultures of China, Africa, and the ancient civilizations of Egypt, Peru, Mediterranean, and North America.

Phoebe A. Hearst Museum of Anthropology, University of California at Berkeley, 103 Kroeber Hall, Berkeley, CA 94720–3712. Phone: 510/642–3682. Fax: 510/642–6271. E-mail: *pahma@berkeley.edu*. Web site: *http://hearstmuseum.berkeley.edu*. Hours 10–4:30 Wed.-Sat.; 12–4 Sun.; closed Mon.-Tues. and national holidays. Admission: adults, $4; seniors, $3; students, $1; children under 13, free; free on Thurs.

Rockwell Museum of Western Art. The Rockwell Museum of Western Art in the restored 1893 City Hall of Corning, New York, has the largest collection of American western art in eastern United States. The collection, which includes western artworks from 1820 to the 1940s, includes art by and about American Indians, as well as native artifacts from the Southwest and Great Plains. Among the artists represented are George Catlin, Alfred Jacob Miller, Frederic Remington, Charles M. Russell, and Joseph Henry Sharp. The museum also has a collection of antique firearms and the world's largest collection of Carder Steuben glass.

Rockwell Museum of Western Art, 111 Cedar St., Corning, NY 14830–2694. Phone: 607/937–5386. Fax: 607/974–4895. E-mail: *info@rockwellmuseum. org*. Web site: *www.rockwellmuseum.org*. Hours: Memorial Day-Labor Day — 9–8 daily; remainder of year — 9–5 daily; closed New Year's Day, Thanksgiving, and Christmas Eve and Day. Admission: adults, $6.50; seniors and students, $5.50; children under 18, free; families, $20.

Sam Noble Oklahoma Museum of Natural History. The story of Native Americans in Oklahoma over 15,000 years is told in the McCasland Family Hall of the People of Oklahoma at the Sam Noble Oklahoma Museum of Natural History at the University of Oklahoma in Norman. The gallery displays such Indian artifacts as a 10,000-year-old red hematite on a bison skull (the oldest painted art in North America), 1,000-year-old artifacts from the Mississippian culture, and various ethnographic objects from Oklahoma tribes. It also has a family arbor that depicts contemporary Indian cultures

living in western regions of the state. The Native American artifacts are only part of the museum's collection of over 5 million specimens and objects.

Sam Noble Oklahoma Museum of Natural History, University of Oklahoma, 2401 S. Chautauqua Ave., Norman, OK 73072–7029. Phone: 405/325–8978. Fax: 405/325–7699. E-mail: *snomnh@ou.ed*. Web site: *www.snomnh.ou.edu*. Hours: 10–5 Tues.-Sat.; 1–5 Sun.; closed Mon. and major holidays. Admission: adults, $5; seniors, $4; children 6–17, $3; children under 6, free.

San Diego Museum of Man. See Multicultural Museums and Galleries section.

School of Nations Museum. See Multicultural Museums and Galleries section.

Sid Richardson Museum. The Sid Richardson Museum in Fort Worth, Texas, displays a collection of western art (including American Indian scenes) acquired largely by the late oilman and philanthropist. Among its highlights are 55 paintings of the American West by Frederic Remington and Charles M. Russell. Other artists represented are William Robinson Leigh, Oscar E. Berninghaus, Edwin Willard Deming, Charles Schreyvogel, Charles Francis Browne, Frank Tenny Johnson, and Peter Moran.

Sid Richardson Museum, 309 Main St., Fort Worth, TX 76102. Phones: 817/332–6554 and 888/332–6554. Fax: 817/332–8671. E-mail: *info@sidrmuseum.org*. Web site: *www.sidrmuseum.org*. Hours: 9–5 Mon.-Thurs.; 9–8 Fri.-Sat.; 12–5 Sun.; closed major holidays. Admission: free.

Spurlock Museum. See Multicultural Museums and Galleries section.

UCLA Fowler Museum of Cultural History. See Multicultural Museums and Galleries section.

University of Pennsylvania Museum of Archaeology and Anthropology. See Representative Other Museums with Extensive Ethnic Collections or Exhibits in Multicultural section.

University of Texas Institute of Texan Cultures. See Multicultural Museums and Galleries section.

Woolaroc Museum and Native American Heritage Center. The Woolaroc Museum, located at the 3,700-acre Woolaroc Ranch and wildlife preserve near Bartlesville, Oklahoma, has American Indian displays among its five main exhibit halls and in the Native American Heritage Center, an interpretive center with exhibits and a multimedia presentation on American Indians of the past and present. The museum, founded by Mr. and Mrs. Frank Phillips (he was founder of the Phillips Petroleum Company) on their retreat ranch in 1929, also contains paintings and sculptures by many of the early masters of western art, including Frederic Remington, Charles M. Russell, and William R. Leigh.

The five exhibit halls in the main exhibition building cover eras or time periods in a broad chronological pattern and contain Indian artifacts, art, and exhibits ranging from prehistoric to recent times. The exhibits depict Indian history and ways of life and display early pottery, baskets, apparel, blankets, beadwork, masks, war bonnets, artworks, and other materials. The museum's collection includes objects from approximately 40 tribes.

Woolaroc Museum and Native American Heritage Center, State Hwy. 123, Rte. 3, Box 2100, Bartlesville, OK 74003. Phones: 918/336-0307 and 888/966-5276. Fax: 918/336-0084. Web site: *www.woolaroc.org*. Hours: Memorial Day-Labor Day—10-5 Tues.-Sun.; closed Mon.; remainder of year—10-5 Wed.-Sun.; closed Mon.-Tues., Thanksgiving, and Christmas. Admission: adults, $8; seniors, $6; children under 12, free.

NORWEGIAN (*also see* Scandinavian)

Museums and Galleries

Boynton Chapel. Boynton Chapel, located on the grounds of Björklunden vid Sjön, Lawrence University's northern campus along Lake Michigan in Door County, Wisconsin, is a small wooden chapel replica built in the style of a late twelfth-century Norwegian stave church. It has 41 hand-painted frescoes and fine carved wood furnishings. The chapel, a popular site for weddings, is open for tours during the summer.

Boynton Chapel, Björklunden vid Sjön, Lawrence University, PO Box 10, Baileys Harbor, WI 54202. Phone: 920/839-2216. Fax: 920/839-2688. E-mail: *mark.d.breseman@lawrence.edu*. Web site: *www.lawrence.edu/dept/bjork/chapel.shtml*. Hours: mid-June-late Aug.—1-4 Mon. and Wed.; closed remainder of week and year. Tour fee: $4 per person.

Heritage-Hjemkomst Interpretive Center. The Heritage-Hjemkomst Interpretive Center in Moorhead, Minnesota, has three parts—a replica of a Viking ship, a replica of a Norwegian stave church, and exhibits about local Norwegian heritage. The focal point is the *Hjemkomst* (which means "homecoming" in Norwegian) Viking ship, built in 1974 to 1980 by junior high school guidance councilor Robert Asp, who dreamed of sailing to Norway. When he died of leukemia, his family and friends

fulfilled his goal by making a 72-day voyage to Norway in 1982. When the ship was returned, the center was built to house it and interpretive exhibits, with the theme "Dare to Dream." The center also has exhibits of the Red River Valley cultural heritage.

The Norwegian stave church, located outside the center, is a full-scale replica of the Hopperstad Church in Vik, Norway. Norwegian stave churches were built after the Viking Age in Scandinavia in the 1100s and 1200s. The technique of using vertical staves (posts) had been modified over time to become wooden architectural works of art. The 72-feet-high church replica, constructed of cedar, redwood, and pine, was dedicated in 1998 and features the wood carvings of Guy Paulson.

Heritage-Hjemkomst Interpretive Center, 202 1st Ave. North, Moorhead, MN 56560 (mailing address: PO Box 157, Moorhead, MN 56561). Phone: 218/299-5511. Fax: 218/299-5510. E-mail: *dean.sather@ci.moorhead.mn.us*. Web site: *www.hjemkomst-center.com*. Hours: 9-5 Mon.-Sat. (also to 8 Tues.); 12-5 Sun.; closed major holidays. Admission: adults, $6; seniors and college students, $5; children 5-17, $4; children under 5, free.

Little Norway. See Historic Sites section.

Norskedalen Nature and Heritage Center and Skumsrud Heritage Farm. See Historic Sites section.

Norwegian-American Historical Association Archives. The Norwegian-American Historical Association, housed on the St. Olaf College campus in Northfield, Minnesota, has archives with stories, records, and illustrations of Norwegian immigration and settlement throughout the nation since 1825. The archives, located in Rolvaag Library, includes such materials as letters, diaries, book manuscripts, ledgers, journals, photographs, films, clippings, and other ephemera related to Norwegians in America.

Norwegian-American Historical Association Archives, St. Olaf College, 1510 St. Olaf Ave., Northfield, MN 55057-1097. Phone: 507/646-3221. Fax: 507/646-3734. E-mail: *naha@stolaf.edu*. Web site: *www.naha.stolaf.edu*. Hours: by appointment. Admission: $20.

Runestone Museum. The Runestone Museum, a local history museum in Alexandria, Minnesota, is Viking oriented. In addition to tracing the history of the largely Norse community, the museum contains the controversial 202-pound Kensington Runestone, with carvings that tell the alleged tragic journey of a band of Vikings in 1362; a collection of fourteenth-century Viking implements; a 28-foot Viking statue, and a 40-foot three-fourths replica of the Viking ship *Snorri*.

The museum is named for the Kensington Rune-stone, discovered in 1898 buried in the roots of an aspen tree on Olaf Ohman's farm in nearby Kens-ington. Carvings on the Runestone indicate that 10 Viking men were found dead at an encampment while other members of the party were out fishing in 1362. The Vikings are believed to have come to the area through Hudson Bay, Nelson River, Lake Winnipeg, and Red River of the North to nearby Cormorant Lake. Studies by runic scholars have confirmed the authenticity of the Runestone, but the controversy continues.

Among the other attractions at the museum are an adjacent replica of the 1860s Fort Alexandria and a reconstructed cabin, general store, church, and schoolhouse. The museum also has a re-created 1800s main street, 1900 to 1920s period rooms, and Native American, military, wildlife, and children's exhibits.

Runestone Museum, 206 N. Broadway, Alexan-dria, MN 56308. Phone: 320/763-3160. Fax: 320/763-9705. E-mail: *bigole@rea-alp.com*. Web site: *www.runestonemuseum.org*. Hours: Memorial Day-Labor Day — 9-5 Mon.-Fri.; 9-4 Sat.; 11-4 Sun.; re-mainder of year —10-5 Mon.-Fri.; 10-4 Sat.; closed Sun. and major holidays. Admission: adults, $6; sen-iors, $5; students 5-17, $3; children under 5, free; families, $15.

Vesterheim Norwegian-American Museum. The Vesterheim Norwegian-American Museum in Dec-orah, Iowa, is one of the nation's oldest, largest, and most comprehensive museums dedicated to a single immigrant group. Its collections began in 1877 at Luther College, were moved to the present site in 1933, and became an independent museum in 1964. It now has 16 historic buildings that occupy almost an entire block, plus two other sites, and hold over 24,000 artifacts.

The museum's main building contains such ob-jects as Norwegian textiles and traditional dress, decorative painting called rosemaling, pioneer fur-niture and housewares, and Norwegian-American fine art. Among the other structures are an 1851 re-stored stone mill with tools and machines, a house and grist mill from Norway, a blacksmith shop, a log parochial school, a Norwegian storage build-ing, a shed for drying hops, a Lutheran church, and such dwellings as two pioneer log houses, a prairie house, and a house of unusual stovewood construction.

Vesterheim Norwegian-American Museum, 523 W. Water St., PO Box 379, Decorah, IA 52101. Phone: 563/382-9681. Fax: 563/382-8828. E-mail: *info@vesterheim.org*. Web site: *www.vesterheim.org*. Hours: May-Oct.— 9-5 daily; remainder of year — 10-4 Tues.-Sun.; closed Mon., New Year's Day, Easter,

Thanksgiving, and Christmas. Admission: adults, $4; seniors, $3; children 7-18, $2; children under 7, free.

Museums Honoring Individuals

Swensson Farm Museum. The Swensson Farm Museum east of Montevideo, Minnesota, is located on the 1890s farm developed by Olof Swensson, a Norwegian immigrant who once ran for governor of the state. He became known for his innovations in building the 22-room brick farmhouse and large timber-framed barn, his religious activities (con-ducting services in a second-floor chapel in his home), writing about his convictions, and his po-litical activities.

The museum site now includes a 17-acre farm-stead, farmhouse, barn, grist mill remnants, fam-ily burial plot, and Moehring Building built by the Chippewa County Historical Society, which oper-ates the site. The Moehring Building houses a col-lection of early agricultural equipment, including such items as a walking plow, walk-behind cultiva-tor, handseeder, corn picker and shellers, fanning mill, foot-operated jigsaw, and tractors. The farm also is the site of an annual threshing show in Au-gust.

Swensson Farm Museum, State Hwy. 7, Monte-video, MN 56265 (mailing address: Chippewa County Historical Society, PO Box 303, Montevideo, MN 56265). Phone: 320/269-7636. Web site: *www.mon-techamber.com/cchs/swensson.htm*. Hours: Memorial Day-Labor Day —1-5 Sun. and by appointment. Ad-mission: adults, $4; children 6-17, $2; children under 6, free.

Historic Sites

Ephraim Village Museums. The village of Ephraim, Wisconsin, has had a strong Norwegian influence since it was founded by the Rev. Andreas Iverson, a Norwegian Moravian minister, and his followers in 1853. The Village Hall, a stone struc-ture with gables, was designed and built in the early 1920s to honor both the area and the Norwegian heritage. Some of the community's early Norwe-gian buildings now are among the historic struc-tures that are part of the Ephraim Village Muse-ums, featuring buildings preserved and operated by the Ephraim Village Foundation.

The historic buildings include the 1853 Goodlet-son Cabin, 1854 Iverson House, 1858 Anderson Store, 1880 Anderson Barn, and 1890s Svalhus (named for its overhanging second story used to keep the house cool). The principal summer event in town is the Fyr-Bal Fest, a mid-June re-creation of the Norwegian tradition of celebrating Midsum-mer's Eve. Among its highlights are an arts and crafts fair, fish boil, Norwegian dancers, and the lighting of lakefront bonfires to burn the Winter Witch and usher in the long sunny summer days.

Ephraim Village Museums, Ephraim Village Foundation, 3060 Anderson Lane, PO Box 165, Ephraim, WI 54211. Phone: 920/854–9688. Fax: 920/854–7232. E-mail: *info@ephraim.org*. Web site: *www.ephraim.org*. Hours: late June-Labor Day — 10:30–4 Mon.-Sat.; closed Sun.; after Labor Day-Columbus Day weekend — 10:30–4 Fri.-Sat.; closed remainder of week and year. Admission: adults, $5; students 6–18, $2; children under 6, free.

Little Norway. Little Norway is located at an 1856 Norwegian pioneer homestead near Blue Mounds, Wisconsin. It consists of a cluster of original log farm buildings of Norse architecture. Among the 14 structures are one with a sod roof and a spring house peaked by three cupolas. Little Norway also has a replica of a twelfth-century Norwegian stave church, complete with dragon heads at the peak of the gables. It was built in Norway for the 1893 World's Columbian Exposition in Chicago and now contains a collection of Norwegian folk objects from Scandinavia and America.

Little Norway, 3576 County Hwy. JG North, Blue Mounds, WI 53517. Phone: 608/437–8211. Fax: 608/437–7827. Web site: *www.littlenorway.com*. Hours: May-June and Sept.-Oct. — 9–5 daily; July-Aug. — 9–7 daily; closed remainder of year. Admission: adults, $12; seniors, $11; children 5–12, $5; children under 5, free.

Norskedalen Nature and Heritage Center and Skumsrud Heritage Farm. Collections of turn-of-the-twentieth-century buildings of Norwegian settlers are featured at Norskedalen Nature and Heritage Center and Skumsrud Heritage Farm near Coon Valley, Wisconsin. Norskedalen is a 400-acre Norwegian-oriented educational and research site with 12 restored 1880 to 1910 buildings, including an 1890s pioneer homestead, gardens, nature trails, and a visitor center. Skumsrud Heritage Farm, 3.5 miles west of Norskedalen, is an open-air museum with 11 restored historic buildings, with the oldest being an 1853 log cabin. Skumsrud is operated from Norskedalen and both sites are part of a combination ticket.

Norskedalen Nature and Heritage Center, W455 Ophus Rd., PO Box 235, Coon Valley, WI 54623-0225. Phone: 608/452–3424. Fax: 608/452–3157. E-mail: *info@norskedalen.org*. Web site: *www.norsekedalen.org*. Hours: May-Oct. — 9–6 Mon.-Fri.; 10–6 Sat.; 12–6 Sun.; remainder of year — 8–4 Mon.-Fri.; 12–4 Sun.; closed Sat. and major holidays. Admission (includes both sites): adults, $5; children 5–12, $2; children under 5, free; families, $12.

Skumsrud Heritage Farm, U.S. Hwy. 14/61, Coon Valley, WI 54623. Phone: 608/452–3424. Fax: 608/452–3157. E-mail: *info@norskedalen.org*. Web site: *www.norskedalen.org*. Hours: June-Aug. — 12–6 Mon.-Fri.; 10–5 Sat.; 12–5 Sun.; closed remainder of year. Admission: included in Norskedalen admission.

Runestone Museum. See Museums and Galleries section.

Vesterheim Norwegian-American Museum. See Museums and Galleries section.

OCEANIC PEOPLES (*also see* Hawaiian)

Museums and Galleries

Bishop Museum. See Hawaiian Museums and Galleries section.

Commonwealth of the Northern Mariana Islands Museum of History and Culture. The Commonwealth of the Northern Mariana Islands Museum of History and Culture in Saipan has archaeological, historical, and cultural materials reflecting the influence of the many ethnic groups found in the Northern Marianas Islands, a chain of 14 islands in the western Pacific. The museum, housed in a renovated 1926 former Japanese hospital, also has two special collections — gold, pottery vessels, and metal artifacts recovered from the 1638 shipwreck of a Spanish galleon south of Saipan and the original illustrations from the 1819 French expedition to the Marianas by Louis Claude de Saulses (Baron de Freycinet).

Commonwealth of the Northern Mariana Islands Museum of History and Culture, PO Box 504570, Saipan, Mariana Islands 96950. Phone: 670/664–2160. Fax: 670/664–2170. E-mail: *cnmimuseum@saipan.com*. Web site: *www.cnmimuseum.org*. Hours: 9–4:30 Mon.-Fri.; 9–12 Sat.; closed Sun. and major holidays. Admission: adults, $3; students, $1; children under 12, free.

Guam Museum. The Guam Museum in Adelup, Guam, is devoted to the history and culture of the Pacific island. It has artifacts from the 1500 B.C. Spanish colonial period and the seventeenth-nineteenth centuries, as well as exhibits of handicrafts and photographs. The museum, housed in the 1776 Garden House in the Ricardo J. Bordallo Governors' Complex, currently is closed for repairs while plans for a new site are under development.

Guam Museum, Faninadahen Kosas Guahan, Ricardo J. Bordallo Governors' Complex, Adelup, Guam 96932 (mailing address: PO Box 2950, Hagatina, Guam 96932). Phones: 671/475–4229 and 671/475–4230. Fax: 671/475–6727. E-mail: *airamire@ns.gpv/*

gu. Web site: *www.guam.net/gov/museum*. Hours: 9–4 Mon.-Fri.; 9–2 Sat.; closed Sun. and major holidays. Admission: adults, $3 suggested donation; students, $1 suggested donation; seniors and children under 12, free.

Isla Center for the Arts. The Isla Center for the Arts at the University of Guam in Mangilao is an art museum with Micronesian paintings, prints, sculpture, and artifacts. The contents range from stone tools to lithographs to folk art.

Isla Center for the Arts, University of Guam, House 15, Deansá Circle, PO Box 5230, Mangilao, Guam 96923. Phones: 671/735–2965 and 671/735–2966. Fax: 671/715–2967. E-mail: *isla@uog9.uog.edu*. Web site: *www.uog.edu/isla*. Hours: 10–5 Mon.-Fri.; 10–2 Sat.; closed Sun. and national and territorial holidays. Admission: free.

Jean P. Haydon Museum. Samoan history, culture, and art are the focus of the Jean P. Haydon Museum in the village of Fagatogo near Pago Pago, American Samoa. The museum is housed in a 1900s former post office building that served as a U.S. Navy commissary during World War II.

Jean P. Haydon Museum, Village of Fagatogo, PO Box 1540, Pago Pago, American Samoa 96799. Phone: 684/633–4347. Fax: 684/633–2059. E-mail: *ascach@samoatelco.com*. Hours: 10–4 Mon.-Fri.; 10–12 Sat.; closed Sun. and major holidays. Admission: free.

Pacific Asia Museum. See Asian Museums and Galleries section.

Pacific Heritage Museum. See Asian Museums and Galleries section.

Polynesian Cultural Center. The Polynesian Cultural Center in Laie, Oahu, Hawaii, is a 42-acre cultural entertainment park with re–created villages, exhibits, performances, and hands-on activities pertaining to South Pacific islands. Visitors can see the customs, arts, crafts, dances, and sports of the region, which includes Samoa, Aotearoa (Maori New Zealand), Fiji, Hawaii, Marquesas, Tahiti, Tonga, and Rapa Nui (Easter Island). The center, operated by the Mormon Church, has a large lagoon, waterfalls, tropical flora, erupting volcano, canoe pageant, Hawaiian luau, buffets, shops, Imax large-screen theater, and an elaborate evening show. Tickets vary from general admission to various special packages.

Polynesian Cultural Center, 55–370 Kamehameha Hwy., Laie, Oahu, HI 96762. Phones: 808/293–3333 and 800/367–7060. Fax: 888/722–7339. E-mail: *internetrez@polynesia.com*. Web site: *www.polynesia.com*. Hours: 12:30–6:30 Mon.-Sat.; closed Sun., Thanksgiving, and Christmas. General admission: adults, $40; children 3–11, $30; children under 3, free.

POLISH
Museums and Galleries

American Center of Polish Culture. The American Center of Polish Culture in Washington, D.C., seeks to preserve and interpret Polish American history, culture, art, and traditions through guided tours of the center, art gallery exhibitions, performances, and lectures. It is located in a restored townhouse near Embassy Row.

American Center of Polish Culture, 2025 O St., N.W., Washington, DC 20036–5913. Phone: 202/785–2320. Fax: 202/785–2159. E-mail: *director@polishcenterdc.org*. Web site: *www.polishcenterdc.org*. Hours: 10–4 Mon.-Fri.; Sat.-Sun. by appointment. Admission: free.

American Council for Polish Culture. The American Council for Polish Culture, a cultural and educational organization in Bethesda, Maryland, that represents the interests of some 25 affiliated Polish organizations across the nation, has displays and circulates traveling truck exhibits with materials on Polish history and customs. It also has a library and archives and engages in other activities to further Polish language, art, history, and cultural involvement and awareness.

American Council for Polish Culture, 5205 Sangamore Rd., Bethesda, MD 20816. Phone: 301/320–5688. Fax: 202/785–2159. Web site: *www.polishcultureacpc.org*. Hours: by appointment. Admission: free.

Galeria. The Galeria in Orchard Lake, Michigan, presents permanent and changing exhibitions of Polish and Polish American art, with the emphasis on contemporary art. The art gallery, which seeks to preserve Polish culture and further the arts, is housed in the former Michigan Military Academy. It also offers lectures and performing arts.

Galeria, 3535 Indian Trail, Orchard Lake, MI 48324. Phones: 248/683–0345, 248/583–0345, and 248/683–0425. Web site: *www.orchardlakeschools.org*. Hours: 1–5 Sat.-Sun.; Mon.-Fri. by appointment; closed major holidays. Admission: free.

Lemko Association Museum. See Ukrainian Museums and Galleries section.

National Polish-American Sports Hall of Fame. More than 100 outstanding Polish American athletes, coaches, and sports journalists are honored in the National Polish-American Sports Hall of Fame, housed in the Dombrowski Fieldhouse at St. Mary's College in Orchard Lake, Michigan. The hall contains plaques, information, and memorabilia about such inductees as Stan Musial in baseball, Mike Ditka in football, coach Mike Krzyzewski in basketball, Tony Zale in boxing, and Janet Lynn in figure skating.

National Polish-American Sports Hall of Fame, St. Mary's College, Dombrowski Fieldhouse, Orchard Lake, MI 48324 (mailing address: 11727 Gallagher, Hamtramck, MI 48212). Phones: 313/407–3300 and 248/683–0401. Fax: 313/876–7724. E-mail: *info@polishsportshof.com*. Web site: *www.polishsportshof.com*. Hours: by appointment; closed major holidays. Admission: free.

PIASA Gallery. The Polish Institute of Arts and Sciences of America, which seeks to inform the American public about Poland and its cultural heritage, displays changing exhibitions of contemporary Polish paintings, drawings, and sculpture in the PIASA Gallery and its outdoor garden in New York City.

PIASA Gallery, Polish Institute of Arts and Sciences of America, 208 E. 30th St., New York, NY 10016. Phone: 212/686–4164. Web site: *www.piasa.org/piasagallery.html*. Hours: 10–3 Mon.-Thurs.; closed Fri.-Sun. and major holidays. Admission: free.

Polish American Cultural Center and Museum. The Polish American Cultural Center and Museum in Philadelphia, Pennsylvania, seeks to preserve and display Polish history and culture for the general public. It celebrates the lives and accomplishments of distinguished people of Polish descent. Among those honored are musicians Frederic Chopin and Ignacy Jan Paderewski, scientists Nicholas Copernicus and Madame (Sklodowska) Curie, Revolutionary War military figures Thaddeus Kosciuszko and Casimir Pulaski, and modern leaders Lech Walesa and Pope John Paul II. Other exhibits are devoted to Polish folk art, Polish military experience in World War II, and the contributions of Pope John Paul II as the first Polish pope in the history of the Catholic Church.

Polish American Cultural Center and Museum, 308 Walnut St., Philadelphia, PA 19106. Phone: 215/922–1700. Web site: *www.polishamericancenter.org*. Hours: May-Dec.—10–4 Mon.-Sat.; closed Sun.; remainder of year—10–4 Mon.-Fri.; closed Sat.-Sun.; closed major holidays. Admission: free.

Polish American Museum. The Polish American Museum in Port Washington, New York, contains artifacts, documents, paintings, and exhibits that illustrate the achievements of people of Polish heritage. It highlights Polish contributions to such fields as medicine, education, art, science, and political theory. The museum also has displays on such important historical events as the Christening of Poland in 966, as well as paintings and drawings by Polish artists of Polish writers and political, military, and patriotic leaders who helped Poland, America, and other countries in gaining and maintaining independence. A research library and archives also are located at the site.

Polish American Museum, 16 Belleview Ave., Port Washington, NY 11050. Phones: 516/883–6542 and 516/767–1936 (also fax). E-mail: *polishmuseum@aol.com*. Hours: 10–2 Tues.-Fri.; 1–4 Sat.-Sun.; closed Mon. and major holidays. Admission: free.

Polish Falcons Museum of America. The Polish Falcons Museum of America in Pittsburgh, Pennsylvania, traces the history of the Polish Falcons of America fraternal life insurance organization. It is closed temporarily as a result of a move of the organization's headquarters.

Polish Falcons Museum of America, 615 Iron City Dr., Pittsburgh, PA 15205–4397. Phones: 412/922–2244 and 800/535–2071. Fax: 412/922–5029. Web site: *www.polishfalcons.org*. Hours: closed temporarily. Admission: free.

Polish Heritage Association of the Southeast-Aiken. The Polish Heritage Association of the Southeast in Aiken, South Carolina, has displays and a library related to Polish history and culture and the contributions made by Poles and Polish Americans. The materials include artifacts, artworks, pictorial materials, manuscripts, personal papers and correspondence, studies, records, and oral histories.

Polish Heritage Association of the Southeast-Aiken, 1080 Hayne Ave., S.W., Aiken, SC 29801. Phone: 803/648–9172. Fax: 803/648–4049. Hours: by appointment. Admission: free.

Polish Heritage Center. The Polish Heritage Center in Ashton, Nebraska, was founded in 1997 to preserve the ancestral culture, traditions, and language of Polish residents in the area. The center, housed in the former convent of St. Francis Catholic Church, contains museum displays, cultural artifacts, photographs, art, music, books, and local genealogical records. The highlight of the year is an annual Polish Festival in early September.

Polish Heritage Center, 226 Carlton Ave., PO Box 3, Ashton, NE 68817. Phones: 308/738–2249 and 308/738–2260. E-mail: *phc@cornhusker.net*. Web site: *www.polishheritagecenter.com*. Hours: 2–4 Sun. and by appointment. Admission: $3.

Polish Immigrant Museum. The Polish Immigrant Museum in Riverhead, New York, depicts the immigration and assimilation of Poles on Long Island since 1880. The museum also has displays on the contributions of Polish Americans.

Polish Immigrant Museum, Lincoln and Hallet Sts., Riverhead, NY 11901. Phone: 631/369–1616. Hours: varies. Admission: free.

Polish Museum of America. Founded in 1935, the Polish Museum of America in Chicago, Illinois, is one of the oldest ethnic museums in the nation. It seeks to further knowledge of Polish history, culture, and contributions to America. It contains artworks by Polish and Polish American artists, religious artifacts, folk costumes, photographs, manuscripts, books, and memorabilia of outstanding Polish Americans. It also has a library with 60,000 volumes, 250 periodicals, and collections of Polish music, and an archive with documents relating to Polish history and culture. The museum also presents lectures, concerts, movies, and theater performances.

Polish Museum of America, 984 N. Milwaukee Ave., Chicago, IL 60622. Phone: 773/384–3352. Fax: 773/384–3799. E-mail: *pma@prcua.org*. Web site: *www.prcua.org/pma*. Hours: 11–4 Mon.-Wed. and Fri.-Sun.; closed Thurs. and major holidays. Admission: adults, $5; seniors and students over 12, $4; children under 13, $3.

Polish Union of America Museum. The Polish Union of America, a fraternal life insurance organization in Buffalo, New York, has a museum with displays on its history and Polish history and culture.

Polish Union of America Museum, 761 Fillmore Ave., Box 97, Buffalo, NY 14212. Phone: 716/893–1365. Fax: 716/893–9782. Hours: by appointment. Admission: free.

Ukrainian Lemko Museum. See Ukrainian Museums and Galleries section.

PORTUGUESE

Museums and Galleries

Hispanic Society of America. See Hispanic Museums and Galleries section.

Portuguese Union of the State of California Museum. The museum of the Portuguese Union of the State of California in San Leandro is devoted to the history of the fraternal benefit society and the history and culture of the Portuguese.

Portuguese Union of the State of California Museum, 1120 E. 14th St., San Leandro, CA 94577. Phone: 510/483–7676. Hours: 9–4:30 Mon.-Fri.; closed Sat.-Sun. and major holidays. Admission: free.

PUERTO RICAN (*also see* Hispanic)

Museums and Galleries

El Museo del Barrio. El Museo del Barrio was founded in New York City in 1969 by a group of Puerto Rican educators, artists, parents, and community activists in East Harlem's Spanish-speaking El Barrio. Since then, it has evolved into a major institution representing the art and culture of all the Caribbean and Latin America. It still retains its strong community roots as a place of cultural pride and self-discovery, while presenting a wide array of art exhibitions and programs and developing a diverse collection of works on paper, paintings, prints, sculptures, films, photographs, santos, and pre–Columbian artifacts.

El Museo del Barrio, 1230 5th Ave., New York, NY 10029. Phone: 212/831–7272. Fax: 212/831–7927. E-mail: *info@elmuseo.org*. Web site: *www.elmuseo.org*. Hours: 11–5 Wed.-Sun.; closed Mon.-Tues. Admission: adults, $7 suggested donation; seniors and students, $5 suggested donation; children under 12, free.

Museo de Arte de Ponce. The Museo de Arte de Ponce in Ponce, Puerto Rico, is an art museum, sponsored by the Luis A. Ferre Foundation, that has over 3,500 pieces of paintings, sculpture, pre–Columbian ceramics, and other works, primarily by Puerto Rican and Latin American artists. It also has a fine collection of early European art.

Museo de Arte de Ponce, Luis A. Ferre Foundation, 2325 Ave. Las Americas, Ponce, Puerto Rico 00717 (mailing address: PO Box 9027, Ponce, PR 00732–9027). Phones: 787/848–0505 and 787/840–1510. Fax: 787/841–7309. E-mail: *map@museoarteponce.org*. Web site: *www.museoarteponce.org*. Hours: 10–5 daily; closed major holidays. Admission: adults, $5; children under 12, $2.50.

Museo de Arte de Religioso Porta Coeli. Sixteenth- to nineteenth-century religious paintings and sculpture from different churches in Puerto Rico can be seen in the Museo de Arte Religioso Porta Coeli, housed in the restored seventeenth-century chapel of the Convent of Santo Domingo de Guzmán in San German. The museum is affiliated with the Institute of Puerto Rican Culture.

Museo de Arte de Religioso Porta Coeli, Catte Ramas 2, Esq. Dr. Veve, PO Box 1160, San German, Puerto Rico 00683. Phone: 787/892–5845. Fax: 787/892–5695. E-mail: *guido@centroweb.com*. Web site: *www.netdial.cavive.net/~gation/portada.html*. Hours: 8:30–4:30 Wed.-Sun.; closed Mon.-Tues. and major holidays. Admission: adults, $1; children under 12, free.

Museo Fuerte Conde de Mirasol de Vieques. The Museo Fuerte Conde de Mirasol de Vieques in Vieques, Puerto Rico, has island history and art exhibits in the last Spanish fort built in America between 1845 and 1855. The fort once housed Spanish troops and was used as a jail until it was restored between 1989 and 1991 by the Institute of Puerto Rican Culture for the museum.

Museo Fuerte Conde de Mirasol de Vieques, PO Box 71, Vieques, Puerto Rico 00765. Phone and fax: 787/741–1717. E-mail: *bicke@prdigital.com.* Web site: *www.enchanted–isle.com/elfortin.* Hours: 10–4 Wed.-Sun; closed Mon.-Tues., Good Friday, Mother's Day, and Father's Day. Admission: adults, $2; children, $1.

Museum and Center for Humanistic Studies. The Museum and Center for Humanistic Studies at Turabo University in Gurabo, Puerto Rico, has a museum of archaeology, history, and ethnography and engages in archaeological excavations and folklore history studies of the eastern region of the island. It has permanent exhibits in archaeology and presents changing exhibitions of paintings, sculpture, photographs, and folk arts and crafts.

Museum and Center for Humanistic Studies, Turabo University, PO Box 3030, Gurabo, Puerto Rico 00778. Phone: 787/741–7979, Ext. 4135. Fax: 787/743–7979. E-mail: *jpasto@caribe.net.* Hours: Aug.-May — 8–12 and 1–5 daily; closed Jun.-July and major holidays. Admission: free.

Museum of Art of Puerto Rico. Puerto Rican paintings, sculpture, prints, and drawings from the eighteenth to twenty-first centuries are collected and exhibited by the Museum of Art of Puerto Rico, which opened in Santurce in 2000. The museum has 41,962 square feet of exhibit space in 15 galleries.

Museum of Art of Puerto Rico, 299 De Diego Ave., Stop 22, Santurce, Puerto Rico 00910 (mailing address: PO Box 41209, San Juan, PR 00940). Phone: 787/977–6277. Fax: 787/977–4444. Web site: *www. mapr.org.* Hours: 10–5 Tues.-Sat. (also to 8 Wed.); 11–6 Sun.; closed New Year's Day, Good Friday, Election Day, Thanksgiving, and Christmas. Admission: adults, $6; children and students, $3; seniors, $2.50.

Museum of Contemporary Art of Puerto Rico. The Museum of Contemporary Art of Puerto Rico in Santurce features contemporary art produced by Puerto Rican and Latin American artists since 1940.

Museum of Contemporary Art of Puerto Rico, Ponce de Leon Ave., Esq. Roberto H. Todd, Stop 18, Santurce, Puerto Rico 00909 (mailing address: PO Box 362377, San Juan, PR 00936–2377). Phone: 787/977–4030. Fax: 787/727–7996. E-mail: *macdpr@ caribe.net.* Web site: *www.museocontemporaneopr.org.* Hours: 8–12 and 1–5 Mon.-Fri.; 9–5 Sat.; closed Sun., New Year's Day, Constitution Day, Independence Day, and Christmas. Admission: free.

Museum of History, Anthropology, and Art (University of Puerto Rico). The Museum of History, Anthropology, and Art at the University of Puerto Rico in San Juan preserves and interprets Puerto Rico's historic, anthropological, and artis-

tic legacy. It has more than 30,000 objects of archaeological artifacts, paintings, drawings, prints, sculpture, posters, folk art, historical documents, pilatelics, and numismatics. The museum has six galleries, including exhibit halls for indigenous cultures, contemporary art, Egyptian cultures, and changing thematic exhibitions.

Museum of History, Anthropology, and Art, University of Puerto Rico, PO Box 21908, San Juan, Puerto Rico 00931–1908. Phones: 787/764–0000, Ext. 2452, and 787/763–3939. Fax: 787/763–4799. E-mail: *fmaricha@rrpac.clu.edu.* Web site: *http://rrpac. upr.clu.edu/-humanity/museo.* Hours: 9–4:30 Mon.-Fri.; 9–3 Sat.-Sun. and major holidays. Admission: free.

Popular Arts Museum. Folk art by Puerto Rican artisans is exhibited at the Popular Arts Museum in San Juan, Puerto Rico. The museum is operated by the Institute of Puerto Rican Culture.

Popular Arts Museum, Calle Cristo 253, San Juan, Puerto Rico 00901 (mailing address: Instituto de Cultura Puertorriquena, Apartado 9024184, Div. Artes Populares, San Juan, PR 00902–4184). Phone: 787/ 722–0621. Fax: 787/723–2320. Web site: *www. icp.gobierno.pr.* Hours: 10–5 Tues.-Fri.; 12–5 Sat.-Sun.; closed Mon. and major holidays. Admission: free.

Puerto Rican Cultural Center Juan Antonio Corretjer. See Museums Honoring Individuals section.

Puerto Rican Workshop/Taller Boricua. The Puerto Rican Workshop/Taller Boricua in New York City offers art exhibitions, lectures, and symposia on American-based artists.

Puerto Rican Workshop/Taller Boricua, 1680 Lexington Ave., New York, NY 10029. Phone: 212/833–4333. Fax: 212/831–6274. Hours: 12–6 Tues.-Wed. and Fri.-Sat.; 1–7 Thurs.; closed Sat.-Sun. and major holidays. Admission: free.

Museums Honoring Individuals

Dr. José Celso Barbosa Museum and Library. The home of Dr. José Celso Barbosa, noted physician, humanitarian, and political leader, in Bayamon, Puerto Rico, now is a historic house museum. The Dr. Jose Celso Barbosa Museum and Library, affiliated with the Institute of Puerto Rican Culture, contains his documents, furniture, and personal objects.

Dr. José Celso Barbosa Museum and Library, Calle Barbosa 16, Bayamon, Puerto Rico 00901 (mailing address: Instituto de Cultura Puertorriquena, Apartado 9024184, San Juan, PR 00902). Phone: 787/977–2700. Fax: 787/723–7837. Web site: *www.icp.prstar.net.* Hours: 9–4:30 Tues.-Sat.; closed Sun.-Mon. and major holidays. Admission: free.

Luis Muñoz Rivera Library and Museum. The birthplace and mausoleum of Puerto Rican liberal politician, journalist, orator, and writer Luis Muñoz Rivera is the site of the Luis Muñoz Rivera Library and Museum in Barranquitas, Puerto Rico. The museum, a one-story rectangular wood house with zinc roof characteristic of nineteenth-century architecture, contains Rivera's articles, documents, photographs, and other materials. A mural also shows his civic and political life and death. The house was restored in 1959 and converted into a museum by the Institute of Puerto Rican Culture.

Luis Muñoz Rivera Library and Museum, Calle Padre Berrios 9, Barranquitas, Puerto Rico 00794. Phone: 787/857–0230. Fax: 787/857–0230. Hours: 8:30–4:20 Tues.-Sun.; closed Mon. and major holidays. Admission: free.

Pablo Casals Museum. The Pablo Casals Museum in Old San Juan, Puerto Rico, honors the Spanish-born cellist and humanist who lived in Puerto Rico, where his mother and wife were born, from 1956 until his death in 1973. The museum contains original manuscripts of his music, his cello and piano, recordings and video tapes, memorabilia, and information about his life.

Pablo Casals Museum, Plaza San José, Old San Juan, Puerto Rico 00901 (mailing address: PO Box 41227, San Juan, PR 00940–1227). Phone: 787/723–9185. Faxes: 787/722–3338 and 787/722–5843. E-mail: *ecolon@cam-gobierno.pr.* Hours: 9:30–5 Tues.-Sat.; closed Sun.-Mon. and major holidays. Admission: adults, $1; seniors and children under 12, 50¢.

Puerto Rican Cultural Center Juan Antonio Corretjer. The Puerto Rican Cultural Center in Chicago is named for Juan Antonio Corretjer, poet, journalist, and political activist. The center is dedicated to preserving and interpreting Puerto Rican history and culture through exhibits and such programs as guided tours, lectures, films, crafts classes, and school presentations.

Puerto Rican Cultural Center Juan Antonio Corretjer, 2739–41 W. Division St., Chicago, IL 60622. Phone: 773/342–8023. Fax: 773/342–6609. E-mail: *webjefe@prcc-chgo.org.* Web site: *www.prcc-chgo.org.* Hours: 9:30–3:30 Sat., Mon.-Fri. by appointment; closed Sun. Admission: free.

Historic Sites

Caparra Museum and Historic Park. The Caparra Museum and Historic Park in Guaynabo,

Puerto Rico, is the site of the first colonization of Puerto Rico. It contains the ruins of one of the oldest Puerto Rican cities colonized during Spanish rule. A museum has objects related to the history and settlement of Puerto Rico.

Caparra Museum and Historic Park, Villa Caparra, 212 Carretera Rd. 2, Guaynabo, Puerto Rico 00901–1914 (mailing address: Instituto de Cultura Puertorriquena, Apartado 9024184, San Juan, PR 00902–4184). Phone 787/781–4795. Fax: 787/723–7837. Web site: *www.icp.gobierno.pr.* Hours: 9–4 Mon.-Fri.; closed Sat.-Sun. and major holidays. Admission: free.

Caquana Indian Ceremonial Park and Museum. See Native American Prehistoric Sites and Museums section.

Casa Blanca Museum. The Casa Blanca Museum in San Juan, Puerto Rico, is where Spanish explorer Juan Ponce de León built a home in ca. 1521, but died before living there. The structure was destroyed by a hurricane two years later and then replaced by one constructed by a son-in-law. It was inhabited by descendants until the mid–eighteenth century. The building now houses a museum of Puerto Rican domestic life during the first three centuries of Spanish colonization.

Casa Blanca Museum, Calle San Sebastian 1, San Juan, Puerto Rico 00901 (mailing address: Instituto de Cultura Puertorriquena, Apartado 9024184, San Juan, PR 00902–4184). Phones: 787/977–2700 and 787/977–2701. Fax: 787/723–7837. Web site: *www.icp.qobierno.pr.* Hours: 8:30–12 and 1–4 Tues.-Sat.; closed Sun.-Mon. and major holidays. Admission: adults, $2; children, $1; seniors, free.

Hacienda Buena Vista. The restored 1833 Hacienda Buena Vista north of Ponce in southern Puerto Rica is considered one of the island's best remaining examples of a coffee plantation. It is an 87-acre agricultural complex with a manor house, carriage house, stables, caretaker's house-office, hurricane shelter, coffee and corn mills, slave quarters, and two warehouses. During its height, the Hacienda Buena Vista produced and processed more than 10,000 pounds of coffee annually for shipment to Europe. The site, which can be seen only as part of guided tours upon reservation, was purchased from the Vives family in 1984 and restored by the Conservation Trust of Puerto Rico.

Hacienda Buena Vista, Rte. 123, Km. 16.8, Ponce, Puerto Rico 00731 (mailing address: Conservation Trust of Puerto Rico, PO Box 9023554, San Juan, PR 00902–3554). Phones: 787/284–7020 and 787/722–5834. Fax: 787/841–5997. E-mail: *fideicomiso@fideicomiso.org.* Web site: *www.fideicomiso.org.* Tour hours: individuals and small groups — 8:30, 10:30, 1:30, and 3:30 Sat.-Sun.; groups of 15 or

The Castille de San Felipe del Morro (known as El Morro), part of the San Juan National Historic Site in Puerto Rico, is a Spanish military fort started in 1539 and built over 250 years to protect the walled city of Old San Juan. Over 2 million people visit the historic site each year. *Courtesy San Juan National Historic Site and National Park Service.*

more — Wed.-Thurs. by appointment; closed remainder of week, New Year's Day, Epiphany, Good Friday, Independence Day, Thanksgiving, and Christmas. Admission: adults, $7; seniors and children under 12, $4; students, $2.

Museo Fuerte Conde de Mirasol de Vieques. See Museums and Galleries section.

San Juan National Historic Site. The San Juan National Historic Site includes three sixteenth to nineteenth-century Spanish forts, bastions, powder houses, and three-fourths of the city wall at Old San Juan, Puerto Rico. The best known and most visited fortress is the Castille de San Felipe del Morro (known as El Morro), constructed to keep seaborne enemies out of San Juan. Over 2 million people now visit the fort annually. The other two forts are San Cristóbal and San Juan de la Cruz, also called El Cañuelo. All three defensive fortifications surround the old colonial portion of San Juan, but only El Morro and San Cristóbal, both UNICEF world heritage sites, can be visited.

El Morro, which sits atop a high promontory at the entrance to San Juan Bay, was built over nearly 250 years and is one of the largest forts constructed by the Spaniards in the Caribbean. The foundation was laid and a tower built in 1539, but it was not completed until 1787. Fort San Cristóbal, at the eastern gate to the walled city of Old San Juan, was started in 1634 and finished in 1790. It was designed to protect the city from attacks by land. Among the artifacts at the national historic site are old Spanish uniforms, weapons, ceramics, coins, furnishings, maps, manuscripts, documents, construction plans, and photographs.

San Juan National Historic Site, 501 Norzagaray St., San Juan, Puerto Rico 00901. Phones: 787/729-6960 and 787/729-6777. Fax: 787/289-7972. E-mail: *doris_diaz@nps.gov.* Web site: *www.nps.gov/saju.* Hours: June-Nov.—9–5 daily; remainder of year—9–6 daily; closed Christmas. Admission: adults, $3 for one fort and $5 for two forts; children under 16, free.

ROMANIAN

Museums and Galleries

Romanian Cultural Center. Changing exhibitions of Romanian culture and arts are presented at the

Romanian Cultural Center in New York City. The center, operated by the Romanian foreign and cultural ministries, also offers lectures, films, and drama and concert performances.

Romanian Cultural Center, 200 E. 38th St., New York, NY 10016. Phone: 212/687–0180. Fax: 212/678–0181. Hours: 11–5 Mon.-Fri. and by appointment; closed major holidays. Admission: free.

Romanian Ethnic Art Museum. The Romanian Ethnic Art Museum, located in a school building adjoining the St. Mary's Romanian Orthodox Cathedral in Cleveland, Ohio, has collections and exhibits of folk costumes, textiles, wood crafts, paintings, Easter eggs, and photographs of traditional regions of Romania.

Romanian Ethnic Art Museum, St. Mary's Romanian Orthodox Cathedral, 3256 Warren Rd., Cleveland, OH 44111 (mailing address: 3256 Warren Rd., Cleveland, OH 44111). Phone: 216/941–5550. Fax: 216/356–7316. E-mail: *dobreaart@aol.com*. Web site: *www.communityconsultinggroup.org/ream*. Hours: by appointment (8:30–4:30 Mon.-Fri.; 10–1 Sun. and holidays). Admission: free.

Romanian Museum in Chicago. The virtual Romanian Museum in Chicago has had an Internet exhibit of folk costumes of Romania for a number of years and had planned to establish a museum facility featuring a Transylvanian peasant household. It no longer intends to build a walk-in museum, but continues to display 112 styles of ethnic costumes of people in six regions and 90 ethnographic zones who live in Romania.

Romanian Museum in Chicago, Chicago, IL. Phone: 773/545–8423. E-mail: *romania@romanian-museum.com*. Web site: *www.romanianmuseum.com*.

RUSSIAN (*also see* Ukrainian; German)

Museums and Galleries

Alutiiq Museum and Archaeological Repository. See Arctic Peoples Museums and Galleries section.

American Historical Society of Germans from Russia (Central California Chapter). See German Museums and Galleries section.

American Historical Society of Germans from Russia Cultural Heritage Research Center. See German Museums and Galleries section.

American Historical Society of Germans from Russia Library-Museum. See German Museums and Galleries section.

Freeman Museum and Archives. See German Museums and Galleries section.

Germans from Russian Heritage Society. See German Museums and Galleries section.

Heritage Village. See German Museums and Galleries section.

Kuban Education and Welfare Association. The Kuban Education and Welfare Association in Buena, New Jersey, seeks to preserve the history and culture of the Cossack people. It has collections and displays of records, personal papers and correspondence, manuscripts, and pictorial materials regarding the Cossacks, descendents from Russian and Poles who settled along the Dnieper and Don rivers in the fifteenth and sixteenth centuries. However, they lost their autonomy and were integrated into the Russian military because they took part in the seventeenth- and eighteenth-centuries peasant revolts. Most Cossacks fought against the Red Army in the 1918 to 1920 civil war and their communities later were collectivized, but many of their traditions have survived.

Kuban Education and Welfare Association, 228 Don Rd., Buena, NJ 08310. Phone: 856/697–2255. Hours: by appointment Admission: free.

Lemko Association Museum. See Ukrainian Museums and Galleries section.

Mennonite Heritage Museum. See German Museums and Galleries section.

Museum of Russian Art. The Museum of Russian Art in Minneapolis, Minnesota, was founded in 2002 by art dealer Raymond E. Johnson to preserve and interpret examples of Russian twentieth-century Realist painting of the 1934 to 1975 Soviet era. In addition to such works, the museum has a collection of Russian art from the late nineteenth century to 1991 period and displays changing exhibitions of other Russian art.

Museum of Russian Art, 5500 Stevens Ave. South, Minneapolis, MN 55419. Phone: 612/821–9045. Fax: 612/821–4392. E-mail: *behinkle@tmora.org*. Web site: *www.museumofrussianart.com*. Hours: 10–5 Mon.-Fri. (also to 8 Thurs.); 10–4 Sat.; closed Sun. and major holidays. Admission: adults, $5; seniors and students, donation.

Museum of Russian Culture. The Museum of Russian Culture is located in the Russian Center of San Francisco that was founded in 1939 by Russian immigrants for the preservation and advancement of their culture. Founded in 1948, the museum has exhibits about Russian history, culture, and immigration and collections of Russian documents, manuscripts, newspapers, books, numismatics, and ethnographic, military, and other materials.

Museum of Russian Culture, Russian Center of San Francisco, 2450 Sutter St., San Francisco, CA 94115. Phone and fax: 415/921–4082. Web site: *www.russiancentersf.com.* Hours: 10:30–2:30 Wed. and Sat.; closed remainder of week and major holidays. Admission: free.

Museum of Russian Icons. The Museum of Russian Icons in Clinton, Massachusetts, has the largest collection of Russian icons in North America and one of the largest outside of Russia. Its collection of 260 icons spans six centuries and includes some dating from the earliest periods of icon painting.

Museum of Russian Icons, 203 Union St., Clinton, MA 01510. Phone: 978/598–5005. Website: *www.museumofrussianicons.org.* Hours: 11–3 Tues.-Sat.; closed Sun.-Mon. and major holidays. Admission: adults, $5; seniors, students, and children, donation.

Ukrainian Lemko Museum. See Ukrainian Museums and Galleries section.

Historic Sites

Baranov Museum. See Arctic Peoples Museums and Galleries section.

Fort Ross State Historic Park. The Fort Ross State Historic Park north of Jenner, California, preserves the site of a thriving Russian-American Company trading post and settlement during 1812 to 1841. It was the southernmost penetration of Russian colonization in North America. It served as an agricultural base to supply Alaska (which it controlled then) and was the site of California's first windmills and shipbuilding activities. Russian scientists also were the first to record California's cultural and natural history. The only surviving structure is the Rotchev House, named for the last manager who renovated it in 1836. Among the buildings renovated are the first Russian Orthodox chapel south of Alaska, the stockade, and four other buildings, including the Kuskov House, the officials' barracks, and two corner blockhouses.

Fort Ross State Historic Park, 19005 Coast Hwy. 1, Jenner, CA 95450. Phone: 707/847–3286. Web site: *www.parks.ca.gov/default.asp?page_id=449.* Hours: dawn-dusk daily; closed Thanksgiving and Christmas. Admission: $6 per car; $5 for seniors.

Pioneer Adobe House Museum. See Mennonite Settlement Museum in German Museums and Galleries section.

Russian Bishop's House. The Russian Bishop's

House, one of the few surviving examples of Russian colonial architecture in North America, is part of the Sitka National Historical Park (see separate listing in Arctic Peoples Historic Sites section) in Sitka, Alaska. It was completed in 1842 and served as the center of the Russian Orthodox Church diocese from California to Siberian Kamchatka until closed in 1969. Imperial Russia was the dominant power in the North Pacific, including Alaska, for more than 125 years and Sitka was the Russian colonial capital. The National Park Service acquired the Bishop's House, located in downtown Sitka about a half mile from the park, in 1973 and restored and refurbished the building to its 1853 appearance. It now contains exhibits on Russian America. Tours are given by rangers.

Russian Bishop's House, Sitka National Historical Park, Lincoln St., Sitka, AK 99835 (mailing address: 103 Monastery St., Sitka, AK 99835). Phone: 907/747–0110. Fax: 907/747–5938. E-mail: *sitk_administration@nps.gov.* Web site: *www.nps.gov/sitk.* Hours: mid–May-Sept. — 9–5 daily; remainder of year — by appointment. Admission: adults, $4; children under 13, free.

Sitka National Historical Park. See Arctic Peoples Historic Sites section.

SCANDINAVIAN (*also see* Danish; Finnish; Icelandic; Norwegian; Swedish)

Museums and Galleries

Nordic Heritage Museum. The Nordic Heritage Museum in Seattle, Washington, is the only museum in the United States dedicated to the legacy of immigrants from the five Nordic countries (Denmark, Finland, Iceland, Norway, and Sweden). The museum, housed in a 1907 former schoolhouse, is devoted largely to Scandinavian cultural contributions to life in the Pacific Northwest from the eighteenth century to the present. Exhibits trace the Nordic immigrants' journeys to America, re–create their early small settlements, describe their role in the lumber and fishing industries, and highlight the contributions of each of the five Nordic groups.

Nordic Heritage Museum, 3014 N.W. 67th St., Seattle, WA 98117. Phone: 206/789–5707. Fax: 296/789–3271. E-mail: *nordic@nordicmuseum.org.* Web site: *www.nordicmuseum.org.* Hours: 10–4 Tues.-Sat.; 12–4 Sun.; closed Mon., New Year's Eve, Thanksgiving, and Christmas Eve and Day. Admission: adults, $6; seniors and college students, $5; children over 5, $4; children under 6, free.

Runestone Museum. See Norwegian Museums and Galleries section.

Scandia Museum. The Scandia Museum is a local history museum in Scandia, Kansas, devoted to the community's Scandinavian heritage. It traces the town's history from 1857 when it was settled by Swedish, Norwegian, and Danish homesteaders and features approximately 10,000 artifacts, many from pioneer days. The first settlers came from the Scandinavian Agricultural Society of Chicago. The museum has a replica Colony House kitchen (Scandinavian pioneers lived in such houses as protection from Indians until their homes could be built); an early post office, drugstore fountain, dentist's office, and hairdresser's shop; and collections of carriages, farm implements, clothing, household items, and other artifacts.

Scandia Museum, Main St. (off Hwy. 36), PO Box 153, Scandia, KS 66966. Phones: 785/335–2271 and 785/335–2561. Hours: May- Labor Day — 2–4 Mon.-Sat., closed Sun.; remainder of year — by appointment. Admission: free.

Scandinavia House: The Nordic Center in America. Scandinavia House: The Nordic Center in America in New York City houses the headquarters of the American-Scandinavian Foundation and serves as a leading educational and cultural link between the United States and the Nordic countries of Denmark, Finland, Iceland, Norway, and Sweden. It provides a forum for the exchange of ideas and cultural understanding; presents grants and fellowships to students, scholars, professionals, and artists; supports public projects involving cultural exchanges in the arts; and operates a library, children's learning center, and an exhibition galley.

Scandinavia House: The Nordic Center in America, American-Scandinavian Foundation, 58 Park Ave., New York, NY 10016. Phone: 212/879–9779. E-mail: *info@amscan.org*. Web site: *www.scandinaviahouse.org*. Gallery hours: 12–6 Tues.-Sat.; closed Sun.-Mon. and major holidays. Admission: adults, $3 suggested donation; seniors and students, $2 suggested donation.

Scandinavian American Cultural Center. A Scandinavian American Cultural Center is being developed by the Scandinavian Heritage Foundation in Portland, Oregon, to preserve and pass along Nordic culture to future generations. The cultural center is seen as a source of pride and promise for Scandinavians in Oregon and southwestern Washington. In addition to having a historical museum, it will be the site of educational programs, festivals, lectures, touring events, a library, and a genealogical research service.

Scandinavian American Cultural Center, Scandinavian Heritage Foundation, 8800 S.W. Oleson Rd., Portland, OR 97223. Phone: 503/977–0275. Fax: 503/977–0177. Web site: *www.scanheritage.org*. Hours and admission: still to be determined.

Scandinavian Cultural Center and Scandinavian Immigrant Experience Collection. Scandinavian immigrants and their descendants have had a major influence on Pacific Lutheran University in Tacoma, Washington, as evidenced by the numerous buildings with Scandinavian names, works of art reflecting the university's Nordic heritage, Scandinavian studies program, faculty and student exchange program with Scandinavian universities, and Scandinavian Cultural Center and Scandinavian Immigrant Experience Collection on the campus. The cultural center with Scandinavian materials is located in the University Center, while the Scandinavian collection with Nordic immigrant records, memoirs, and books are housed in the Robert A. L. Mortvedt Library.

Scandinavian Cultural Center and Scandinavian Immigrant Experience Collection, Pacific Lutheran University, 122nd and S. Park Ave., Tacoma, WA 988447. Phone: 253/535–7532. E-mail: *scancntr@plu.edu*. Web site: *www.plu.edu/~scancntr*. Hours: varies. Admission: free.

Scandinavian Heritage Park. The Scandinavian Heritage Park in Minot, North Dakota, is a historic park that celebrates the area's Nordic culture. The park has a 1771 Norwegian House, a Danish windmill, a Finnish sauna, a 25-foot-high Swedish dala horse, a replica of an early Norwegian church, statues of noted Scandinavians, a museum, and other attractions.

Scandinavian Heritage Park, 1020 S. Broadway, PO Box 862, Minot, ND 58702. Phone: 701/852–9161. Fax: 701/857–8228. Hours: Memorial Day-Labor Day — 8–7 Mon.-Fri.; 10–4 Sat.; 12–4 Sun.; remainder of year: 10–4 Mon.-Fri.; closed Sat.-Sun. and major holidays. Admission: free.

SCOTTISH (*also see* British)

Museums and Galleries

Center of Scottish Heritage at Rural Hill. See Historic Sites section.

Ellen Payne Odom Genealogy Library. The Ellen Payne Odom Genealogy Library, located in the Moultrie/Colquitt County Library in Moultrie, Georgia, houses the archives of 115 Scottish clans and genealogical materials about families that migrated from the eastern seaboard to the West. It also has a number of exhibits, including Civil War, Cherokee, and other documents and artifacts.

Ellen Payne Odom Genealogy Library, Moultrie/ Colquitt County Library, 204 5th St., S.E., Moultrie, GA 31768 (mailing address: PO Box 2828, Moultrie, GA 31776–2828). Phone: 912/985–6640. Fax: 912/985–0936. Hours: 8:30–5:30 Mon.-Sat.; closed Sun., Dec. 19-Jan. 2, and major holidays. Admission: free.

St. Andrews Presbyterian College Art Gallery. St. Andrews Presbyterian College in Laurinburg, North Carolina, has an art gallery in DeTamble Library with historic quilts of Scotland, etchings of North Carolina by Louis Orr, and changing exhibitions of Scottish and other artworks.

St. Andrews Presbyterian College Art Gallery, De-Tamble Library, 1700 Dogwood Mile, Laurinburg, NC 28352. Phone: 910/277–5264. Web site: *www. sapc.edu/detamble*. Hours: 9–4:30 Mon.-Fri.; closed Sat.-Sun., Easter, Good Friday, Memorial Day, and Dec. 24-Jan.1. Admission: free.

Scottish Heritage Center. The Scottish Heritage Center in the DeTamble Library of St. Andrews Presbyterian College in Laurinburg, North Carolina, contains documents, photographs, research, music, and books relating to Scottish-American history. Among its features are exhibits and artifacts pertaining to Scottish settlement in southeastern North Carolina and the largest collection of Celtic music in the United States. The center also hosts the annual Scottish Heritage Weekend and sponsors the St. Andrews College Pipe Band. The college archives and an art gallery (see separate listing) also are located in the library.

Scottish Heritage Center, St. Andrews Presbyterian College, DeTamble Library, 1700 Dogwood Mile, Laurinburg, NC 28352–5598. Phone: 910/277–5236. Fax: 910/277–5050. Web site: *www.sapc.edu/detamble*. Hours: mid–Aug.-mid–May — 9–5 Mon.-Fri.; closed Sat.-Sun., Easter, Good Friday, and Dec. 24-Jan.1; remainder of year — by appointment; closed Memorial Day. Admission: free.

Scottish Tartans Museum. The Scottish Tartans Museum in Franklin, North Carolina, is devoted to the origin, history, development, and display of tartans and Highland dress. Over 500 tartans, ranging from early clan tartans to Victorian styles that are still popular today, can be seen at the museum, which functions as a Scottish heritage center. It also gives weaving demonstrations and has a collection of kilts from the sixteenth century and a replica of a seventeenth-century weaver's cottage. The museum is an extension of the Scottish Tartans Society in Scotland.

Scottish Tartans Museum, 86 E. Main St., Franklin, NC 28734. Phone: 828/524–7472. E-mail: *tartans@scottishtartans.org*. Web site: *www.scottishtartans.org*. Hours: 10–5 Mon. Sat.; closed Sun. and

major holidays. Admission: adults, $1; children under 11, free.

Historic Sites

Center of Scottish Heritage at Rural Hill. Rural Hill Plantation, the 1760s colonial homestead of John and Violet Davidson in Huntersville, North Carolina, is a historic site being developed into a Scottish heritage center for the region. Major Davidson, a descendant of Scottish immigrants, served in American Army in the Revolutionary War and was a signer of the Mecklenburg Declaration of Independence. Six generations of the Davidson family lived at the 2,000-acre Rural Hill for more than 230 years as the plantation became one of the most prosperous in the Piedmont Carolinas.

The plantation, which now consists of 265 acres and 11 historic and reconstructed buildings, is being restored and converted to the Center of Scottish Heritage by the Catawba Valley Scottish Society. The society provides educational programs about the Davidson family and presents Scottish heritage and cultural events throughout the year, including the Loch Norman Highland Games, the premiere event held in April.

Center of Scottish Heritage at Rural Hill, 4431 Neck Rd., PO Box 1009, Huntersville, NC 28070–1009. Phone: 704/875–3113. Fax: 704/875–3193. E-mail: *office@ruralhillfarm.org*. Web site: *www.ruralhillfarm.org*. Hours: 9–5 Mon.-Sat.; closed Sun., Easter, Thanksgiving, and Dec. 20-Jan. 2. Admission: adults, $5; seniors and military, $4; students, $3; children under 7, free.

SERBIAN
Museums and Galleries

Serbian Heritage Museum and Library. The Serbian Heritage Museum and Library, located at the headquarters of the Serb National Federation in Pittsburgh, Pennsylvania, traces the history of Serbian people in America and displays Serbian art, artifacts, and memorabilia. Among the objects exhibited are folk costumes, musical instruments, and weapons. SNF is a fraternal life insurance organization.

Serbian Heritage Museum and Library, Serb National Federation, 1 5th Ave., Pittsburgh, PA 15222. Phones: 412/642–7372 and 800/538–7372. Fax: 412/642–1372. E-mail: *snf@snfonline.org*. Web site: *www.snfonline.org*. Hours: 10–12 and 2–4 daily; closed major holidays. Admission: free.

SLOVAK (*also see* Czech)
Museums and Galleries

Baine/Cincebeaux Collection of Slovak Folk

Dress and Folk Art. More than 2,000 folk dress items, 500 works of folk art, and 2,500 artifacts are among the objects in the Baine/Cincebeaux Collection of Slovak Folk Dress and Folk Art in Rochester, New York. The collection also includes books, periodicals, and an archives with photographs, slides, records, and personal papers and correspondence.

Baine/Cincebeaux Collection of Slovak Folk Dress and Folk Art, 151 Colebrook Dr., Rochester, NY 14617–2215. Phone: 716/342–9383. Hours: by appointment. Admission: donation.

Czech and Slovak Sokol Minnesota Museum. See Czech Museums and Galleries section.

Czech Cultural Center Houston. See Czech Museums and Galleries section.

Czech Memorial Center. See Czech Museums and Galleries section.

Czechoslovak Heritage Museum. See Czech Museums and Galleries section.

National Czech and Slovak Museum and Library. See Czech Museums and Galleries section.

National Slovak Society of the USA Museum. The National Slovak Society of the USA, a fraternal life insurance organization in McMurray, Pennsylvania, has a museum with artifacts, artworks, memorabilia, and other materials pertaining to the history and culture of Slovaks.

National Slovak Society of the USA Museum, 351 Valley Brook Rd., McMurray, PA 15317–3337. Phone: 724/731–0094. Web site: *www.nsslife.com*. Hours: 7:30–4 Mon.-Thurs.; 7:30–12:30 Fri.; closed Sat.-Sun. and major holidays. Admission: free.

Slovak Cultural Center Library and Museum. The Slovak Cultural Center Library and Museum is located at a retirement and cultural center in Winter Park, Florida. It contains artifacts, folk costumes, books, and other materials relating to Slovak history, culture, and immigration.

Slovak Cultural Center Library and Museum, 3110 Howell Branch Rd. 1, Winter Park, FL 32792. Phone 407/677–6894. Fax: 407/677–8442. Web site: *www.iarelative.com/flslovak*. Hours: 10–5 Mon.-Fri.; closed Sat-Sun. and major holidays. Admission: free.

Sokol South Omaha Czechoslovak Museum. See Czech Museums and Galleries section.

SLOVENIAN

Museums and Galleries

Slovenian Heritage Museum. The Slovenian Her-

itage Museum, operated by the Slovenian Women's Union of America in Joliet, Illinois, contains artifacts, art, memorabilia, photographs, books, and other materials pertaining to Slovenian history and culture and to Slovenian settlement in America.

Slovenian Heritage Museum, 431 N. Chicago St., Joliet, IL 60432. Phone: 815/727–1926. E-mail: *swu home@msn.com*. Web site: *www.swua.org/museum. htm*. Hours: by appointment. Admission: free.

SNPJ Slovenian Heritage Center. Slovenian costumes, household items, and arts and crafts are featured at the SNPJ Slovenian Heritage Center, operated by the Slovene National Benefit Society, in Enon Valley, Pennsylvania. The center is dedicated to preserving and interpreting customs and traditions Slovene immigrants brought to America. Among the items on display are Slovene embroidery, cipka lace, splatter cloths, decorated wooden plates, and ethnic costumes.

SNPJ Slovenian Heritage Center, Slovene National Benefit Society, 270 Martin Rd., Enon Valley, PA 16120. Phones: 724/336–5180 and 877/767–5732. Fax: 724/336–6716. E-mail: *snpj@snpjheritage.com*. Web site: *http://snpjheritage.org*. Hours: Apr.-Sept.— 1–5 Sun.; closed remainder of week and year. Admission: free.

SPANISH (*also see* Basque; Cuban; Hispanic; Mexican; Puerto Rican)

Museums and Galleries

Basque Museum and Cultural Center. See Basque Museums and Galleries section.

Colonial Spanish Quarter Museum. The Colonial Spanish Quarter Museum in St. Augustine, Florida, is a re–created 1700s colonial Spanish village that is a municipal living-history museum. It illustrates the life of Spanish soldiers and their families in 1740 in St. Augustine, where Spanish explorer Ponce de León searched for the fountain of youth in 1513. Costumed tradesmen demonstrate their blacksmithing, carpentering, leatherworking, candlemaking, and other skills.

The two-block outdoor museum includes 26 restored and reconstructed colonial buildings from the eighteenth and nineteenth centuries, including the ca. 1740 to 1760 DeMesa-Sanchez House. Exhibits and artifacts can be seen at the Government House Museum and a film about colonial life — *Struggle to Survive*—is shown at the visitor center.

Colonial Spanish Quarter Museum, 29 St. George

St., St. Augustine, FL 32084 (mailing address: PO Box 210, St. Augustine, FL 32085–1002). Phone: 904/825–6830. Fax: 904/825–6874. E-mail: *sqmuse@aug.com*. Web site: *www.historicstaugustine.com*. Hours: 9–5:30 daily; closed Christmas. Admission: site — adults, $6.89; seniors and military, $5.83; students 6–18, $4.24; children under 6, free; families, $13.78; Government House — adults, $2.50; children, $1.50; children under 6, free.

Hispanic Society of America. See Hispanic Museums and Galleries section.

Museum of Spanish Colonial Art. The Museum of Spanish Colonial Art in Santa Fe, New Mexico, preserves and exhibits Spanish colonial art forms produced in New Mexico and southern Colorado since the region was colonized by Spain in 1598. Among the various media featured are santos, retablos, textiles, tinwork, ceramics, silverwork, straw appliqué, ironwork, furniture, and books. The museum also displays some comparative objects from Spain, Latin America, and other regions to illustrate the influences that converged to inspire artists and art forms during the colonial era.

Museum of Spanish Colonial Art, 750 Camino Lejo, Santa Fe, NM 87505 (mailing address: Spanish Colonial Arts Society, PO Box 5378, Santa Fe, NM 87502–5378). Phone: 505/982–2226. Fax: 505/982–4585. E-mail: *museum@spanishcolonial.org*. Web site: *www.spanishcolonial.org*. Hours: 10–5 Tues.-Sun.; closed Mon. Admission: adults, $6; state residents, $3; children under 16, free; free on Sun. to state residents; 4-day pass to museum and four state museums, $18.

Oldest House Museum Complex. See Historic Sites section.

Queen Sofia Spanish Institute. The Queen Sofia Spanish Institute, formerly the Spanish Institute, in New York City seeks to promote public understanding of past and present Spanish culture and its influence upon the Americas through exhibitions, lectures, symposia, meetings, language instruction, and cultural events. Its gallery presents changing exhibitions of art, tradition, and history related to Spain and Latin America.

Queen Sofia Spanish Institute, 684 Park Ave., New York, NY 10021. Phone: 212/628–0420. Fax: 212/734–4177. E-mail: *information@queensofiasi.org*. Web site: *www.spanishinstitute.org*. Hours: 10–6 Mon.-Fri. (also to 8 Fri.); 11–5 Sat.; closed Sun. and major holidays. Admission: free.

Museums Honoring Individuals

Cabrillo National Monument. The Cabrillo National Monument in San Diego, California, honors Juan Rodriguez Cabrillo, the Spanish explorer who led the first European expedition to land on the West Coast of the United States in 1542. The memorial overlooks the city and the harbor. A statue and exhibits in the visitor center commemorate Cabrillo's landing in San Diego Bay and his exploration of the California coast. Also located in the park are the 1854 Old Point Loma Lighthouse and an exhibit in a former Army building that tells the story of the coast artillery.

Cabrillo National Monument, 1800 Cabrillo Memorial Dr., Point Loma, San Diego, CA 92106–3601. Phone: 615/557–5450. Fax: 619/226–6311. Web site: *www.nps.gov/cabr*. Hours: July 4-Labor Day — 9–6 daily; remainder of year — 9–5:15 daily. Admission: $5 per car or $3 per person; seniors, disabled, and children under 17, free.

Coronado National Monument. In 1540, Spanish explorer Francisco Vásquez de Coronado traveled through Arizona and New Mexico and then searched in vain in Texas, Oklahoma, and Kansas for the supposedly fabulous Seven Cities of Cibola for their gold, which did not exist. However, smaller exploring parties sent out by Coronado discovered the Grand Canyon and the mouth of the Colorado River.

The national monument, located in southeastern Arizona along the Mexican border, was established in 1952 after efforts to create an international monument at the border failed when Mexico did not develop a monument in a comparable adjoining area. The monument has a visitor center with exhibits about Coronado's exploits and Spanish exploration of the Southwest from 1540 to 1542 and such artifacts as mid–sixteenth-century Spanish costumes, documents, and weapons.

Coronado National Monument, 4101 E. Montezuma Canyon Rd., Hereford. AZ 85615. Phone: 520/366–5515. Fax: 520/366–5705. Web site: *www.nps.gov/coro*. Hours: 9–5 daily; closed Thanksgiving and Christmas. Admission: free.

Coronado-Quivira Museum. The Coronado-Quivira Museum in Lyons, Kansas, contains exhibits and artifacts pertaining to Spanish explorer Francisco Vásquez de Coronado and the Quivira Indians. It is located near where Coronado ended his futile search for the imaginary Seven Cities of Cibola in 1541. Instead of gold, Coronado found the serene Quivira (later known as the Wichita Indians). The museum, operated by the Rice County Historical Society in the 1910 to 1911 Carnegie Library building, also has exhibits on the Santa Fe Trail and early settlers.

Coronado-Quivira Museum, 105 W. Lyon St., Lyons, KS 67554. Phone: 620/257–3941. E-mail: *cq museum@hotmail.com.* Hours: 9–5 Mon.-Sat.; 1–5 Sun.; closed major holidays. Admission: adults, $2; children 6–12, $1; county residents and children under 6, free.

Coronado State Monument. See Native American Prehistoric Sites and Museums section.

Oñate Monument and Visitor Center. Juan de Oñate, first Spanish governor of New Mexico and former governor of the San Juan Pueblo, is honored at the Oñate Monument and Visitor Center in Alcalde, New Mexico. The site features a bronze statue of Oñate on horseback and exhibits on the El Camino Real and the Hispanic and Pueblo heritage of Española Valley and Arriba County.

Oñate Monument and Visitor Center, State Hwy. 68, PO Box 370, Alcalde, NM 87511. Phone: 505/852–4639. Fax: 505/852–2848. Hours: 8–5 Mon.-Sat.; closed Sun. and major holidays. Admission: free.

Pablo Casals Museum. See Puerto Rican Museums Honoring Individuals section.

Salvador Dalí Museum. The world's most comprehensive collection of artworks by renowned Spanish artist Salvado Dalí is at the Salvador Dalí Museum in St. Petersburg, Florida. The museum has 96 Dalí oil paintings, over 100 watercolors and drawings, and 1,300 graphics, sculptures, photographs, and art objects collected by A. Reynolds and Eleanor Morse over 45 years. It includes the Impressionist and Cubist styles of Dalí's early period, abstract work from his transition to Surrealism, and examples of his preoccupation with religion and science in his later years. The works are rotated in the galleries and shown in special exhibitions at the museum.

Salvador Dalí Museum, 1000 3rd St. South, St. Petersburg, FL 33701–4901. Phone: 727/823–3767. Fax: 727/894–6068. E-mail: *info@salvadordalimuseum.org.* Web site: *www.salvadordalimuseum.org.* Hours: 9:30–5:30 Mon.-Wed. and Sat.; 9:30–8 Thurs.; 9:30–6:30 Fri.; 12–5:30 Sun.; closed Thanksgiving and Christmas Eve and Day. Admission: adults, $15; seniors, $13.50; students over 9, $10; children 5–9, $4; children under 5, free; admission 5–8 Thurs., $5.

Serra Museum. See Historic Sites section.

Historic Sites

The Alamo. See Mexican Historic Sites section.

Anasazi Heritage Center. See Native American Prehistoric Sites and Museums section.

Ancient Spanish Monastery of St. Bernard de Clairvaux Cloisters. The Monastery of St. Bernard de Clairvaux originally was built in the Province of Segovia, Spain, between 1133 and 1141. Cistencian monks occupied the monastery until the 1830s, when the cloisters were seized, sold, and converted into a granary and stable during a social revolution in the area. In 1925, newspaper publisher William Randolph Hearst purchased the cloisters and the monastery's outbuildings and shipped the complex to America.

Almost as the shipment arrived, Hearst's financial problems forced him to sell much of the monastery collection at auction, and the structure's stones remained in a Brooklyn warehouse for 26 years. After Hearst's death in 1952, the stones were purchased and the monastery building was reassembled as a tourist attraction and then used as a church in New York City. In 1964, the monastery stones came to Florida when Bishop Henry Louttit purchased the property for the Diocese of South Florida, later merged into the Dioceses of Central, Southeast, and Southwest Florida. Because of a financial crisis, it was feared that the property would be sold again. But banker Robert Pentland, Jr., a benefactor of many Episcopal churches, purchased the cloisters for the parish of St. Bernard de Clairvaux in North Miami Beach. The structure now is known as the Ancient Spanish Monastery of St. Bernard de Clairvaux Cloisters. It contains religious artifacts and examples of Spanish art and culture.

Ancient Spanish Monastery of St. Bernard de Clairvaux Cloisters, 16711 W. Dixie Hwy., North Miami Beach, FL 33160. Phone: 305/945–1462. Fax: 305/945–6986. E-mail: *spanishmonastery@bellsouth.net.* Web site: *www.spanishmonastery.com.* Hours: 9–5 Mon.-Fri.; by appointment Sat.-Sun. Admission: adults, $5; seniors, $2.50; students and children under 13, $1.

Caparra Museum and Historic Park. See Puerto Rican Historic Sites section.

Capilla de la Lomita. The Capilla de la Lomita (Chapel of the Little Hill) near Mission, Texas, is one of the oldest and smallest missions still in use in Texas. Originally constructed in 1865, it was rebuilt in 1889. The adobe structure, which measures only 12 by 25 feet, first was an overnight way station for Oblate padres who traveled on horseback between Brownsville and Roma. It now is the center of a seven-acre park and is used primarily for private services, such as weddings. It still has its original brick floors, rough beamed ceiling, beehive outdoor ovens, and water well.

Capilla de la Lomita, Farm Rd. 1016, Mission, TX 78572 (contact: Mission Parks and Recreation Dept., 900 Doherty St., Mission, TX 78572). Phone:

956/580–8760. Fax: 956/580–8761. Hours: dawn-dusk daily. Admission: free.

Casa Blanca Museum. See Puerto Rican Historic Sites section.

Castillo de San Marcos National Monument. The Castillo de San Marcos is a restored 1672 to 1695 Spanish fort built as part of the outer defenses to St. Augustine, Florida, that now is a national monument. It was constructed when coastal Florida was a major field of conflict as European nations fought for control of the New World.

The fort, which never was defeated in battle, defended Spain's claim to Florida and other parts of the region. Its history is closely intertwined with nearly Fort Matanzas, which now also is a national monument (see separate listing). The fort's visitor center contains exhibits about the historic site, which also has guided tours, historical weapons demonstrations, and living-history re–enactments.

Castillo de San Marcos National Monument, 1 S. Castillo Dr., St. Augustine, FL 32084. Phone: 904/829–6506. Fax: 904/823–9388. Web site: *www.nps.gov/casa.* Hours: 8:45–5:15 daily; closed Christmas. Admission: adults, $6; children under 16, free.

Cathedral Basilica of St. Francis of Assisi. The Cathedral Basilica of St. Francis of Assisi in Santa Fe, New Mexico, began as a small Franciscan parish in the Spanish colony of San Gabriel in 1598. When the colony moved to higher ground in Santa Fe in 1610, the parish also relocated and had five other church sites before becoming a cathedral in 1886. It was the first church between Durango, Mexico, and St. Louis to become a cathedral. The Archdiocese of Santa Fe now has responsibility for over 300 historic churches in the region. A small museum near the cathedral has historical exhibits with artifacts, documents, and other materials relating to the cathedral's history.

Cathedral Basilica of St. Francis of Assisi, 223 Cathedral Pl., Santa Fe, NM 87501. Phones: 505/982–5619 and 505/983–3811. Fax: 505/992–0341. Hours: cathedral — 6–6 daily; museum — 9–4:30 Mon.-Fri.; closed Sat.-Sun. Admission: donation.

Corpus Christi de la Isleta Mission (Ysleta Mission). See Ysleta del Sur Cultural Art Center in Native American Museums and Galleries section.

Dominquez and Escalante Pueblos. See Anasazi Heritage Center in Native American Prehistoric Sites and Museums section.

El Morro National Monument. See Native American Prehistoric Sites and Museums section.

El Presidio de Santa Barbara State Historic Site.

The 1782 Spanish presidio in Santa Barbara, California, served as the military and government headquarters for the lands between Los Angeles and San Luis Obispo until 1846. It now is the site of the El Presidio de Santa Barbara State Historic Park. Two original structures have been restored, including El Cuartel, the oldest existing building in Santa Barbara and the second oldest in California. The other is the Canedo Adobe, which was deeded to a soldier after the presidio no longer was active. Five other buildings have been reconstructed.

The presidio was the last of four royal military fortresses built by the Spanish along the wilderness frontier. The fort was a fully enclosed quadrangle around a parade ground and had an outer defense wall with two cannon bastions. Earthquakes over the last 100 years have destroyed many of the original buildings. Among the structures that have been reconstructed are the commandant's office, chapel, and living and padre's quarters. Many of the artifacts on display are from archaeological digs surrounding the park.

El Presidio de Santa Barbara State Historic Park, 123 E. Canon Perdido St., PO Box 388, Santa Barbara, CA 93102. Phones: 805/966–9719 and 805/965–0093 (for tours). Fax: 805/568–1999. Web site: *www.sbthp.org.* Hours: 10:30–4:30 daily; closed major holidays. Admission: free.

El Pueblo de Los Angeles Historical Monument. See Mexican Historic Sites section.

El Pueblo History Museum. The El Pueblo History Museum in Pueblo, Colorado, features a full-size reproduction of an 1842 Spanish fur-trading post, an adobe quadrangle with two round bastions. The fort was located at the crossroads for Ute, Cheyenne, Arapaho, and Kiowa Indians, as well as mountain men, trappers, traders, and Spanish soldiers. It was abandoned in 1855 after a Ute attack and continued unrest along the Arkansas River. The building served as a shelter for passing travelers before falling into ruins. The museum, operated by the Colorado Historical Society, has exhibits on Spanish, Indian, Mexican, and early American frontier life; the trapping and trade era; and immigrant settlement and industrialization of the area.

El Pueblo History Museum, 301 N. Union Ave., Pueblo, CO 81003. Phone: 719/583–0453. Fax: 719/583–8214. E-mail: *deborahhespinosa@qwest.net.* Web site: *www.coloradohistory.org.* Hours: 10–4 Tues.-Sat.; closed Sun.-Mon., New Year's Day, and Christmas. Admission: adults, $4; seniors, $3; students and children 6–12, $3; children under 6, free; children under 13 free on Sat.

El Rancho de las Golondrinas. The El Rancho

de las Golondrinas (the Ranch of the Swallows) near Santa Fe, New Mexico, is a living-history museum that depicts Spanish colonial life in New Mexico. The ranch, which was a stop on the El Camino Real (the Royal Road) from Mexico City to early Santa Fe, has been restored with replicas of structures built on their early 1700s original foundations. The site, which resembles an early northern New Mexico colonial mountain village, includes a hacienda with a defensive tower, working water mills, wheelwright and blacksmith shops, winery, country store, schoolhouse, threshing grounds, and Penitente meetinghouse.

El Rancho de las Golondrinas, 334 Los Pinos Rd., Santa Fe, NM 87507. Phone: 505/471–2261. Fax: 505/471–5623. E-mail: *mail@golondrinas.org*. Web site: *www.golondrinas.org*. Hours: June-Sept.—10–4 Wed.-Sun.; closed Mon.-Tues.; tours Apr.-Oct. by appointment; closed remainder of year. Admission: adults, $5; seniors, military, and children 13–18, $4; children 5–12, $2; children under 5, free.

El Santuario de Chimayò. The El Santuario de Chimayò in Chimayò, New Mexico, has been called "the Lourdes of America," although no one seems to know for certain how it came about. People have been coming to the legendary shrine to pray, meditate, and experience peace of mind since it was built between 1814 and 1816. At the same time, many have come to the chapel to seek assistance with their ailments by touching the earth in a pit in the chapel, believing that it has curative powers. The chapel now is lined with cast-off crutches and braces.

The adobe chapel was built after a farmer had a vision to dig beneath his plow for dirt with healing powers. When he did so, it is said that he found a cross and cloth belonging to two priests martyred at the site. The chapel was constructed near the site and the cross placed in it. Since then, thousands have made pilgrimage to the chapel in search of cures.

El Santuario de Chimayò, Fantuario Rd., PO Box 235, Chimayò, NM 87522. Phone: 505/351–4889. E-mail: *cradigan@archdiocesesantafe.org*. Hours: June-Sept.— 9–5 daily; Oct.-Apr. — 9–4 daily; closed May, New Year's Day, Thanksgiving, and Christmas. Admission: free.

Fort Matanzas National Monument. Historic Fort Matanzas was a 1742 Spanish fortification that guarded the southern river approach to St. Augustine, Florida, when European nations fought for control of the New World. The park commemorates one of the earliest conflicts between European countries over land and ideals in the emerging continent. It led to the killing of nearly 250 French Huguenots by the Spanish, which gave the river

and inlet the name of Matanzas (Spanish for "slaughter").

The fort is located on barrier islands along the shores of the Atlantic Ocean and the Matanzas estuary and its history is closely related to that of the Castillo de San Marcos (see separate listing), another Spanish fort protecting St. Augustine. Fort Matanzas once guarded against attacks by enemies from the south, but now is a historic site that also protects almost 300 acres of pristine salt marsh, dunes, scrub, and maritime forest, as well as their plants and wildlife. The park has a visitor center that tells of the fort's past and present roles and has guided tours, living-history demonstrations, and free ferry service to the fort.

Fort Matanzas National Monument, 8635 A1A South, St. Augustine, FL 32080. Phone: 904/471–0116. Fax: 904/471–7605. Web site: *www.nps.gov/foma*. Hours: 9–5:30 daily; closed Christmas. Admission: free.

Fort Yuma Quechan Indian Museum. See Native American Museums and Galleries section.

Historic Taos Pueblo. See Native American Historic Sites section.

La Hacienda de los Martinez. The La Hacienda de los Martinez is a fortress-like trading post built in 1804 in the late Spanish colonial period in Taos, New Mexico. The historic structure, constructed by Severino Martin (later changed to Martinez), became an important trade center for the northern boundaries of the Spanish colonial empire and the headquarters for an extensive ranching and farming operation.

The building, which has massive adobe walls and 21 rooms surrounding two courtyards, was the final terminus for the Camino Real, which connected northern New Mexico to Mexico City. The hacienda also was the birthplace of Father Antonio Martinez, a social reformer who fought with French-born Archbishop Jean Baptiste Lamy to preserve the Hispanic character of the Catholic Church, created the first coeducational school in New Mexico, and brought the first printing press to Taos.

La Hacienda de los Martinez, Lower Ranchitos Rd., PO Drawer CCC, Taos, NM 87571. Phone: 505/758–0505. Fax: 758–0330. Hours: May-Sept.— 9–5 daily; remainder of year —10–4 daily; closed New Year's Day, Easter, Thanksgiving, and Christmas. Admission: adults, $6; children 6–15, $3; children under 6, free; combination pass for five Taos museums, $20.

La Purísima Mission State Historic Park. The La Purísima Mission State Historic Park northeast of Lompoc, California, contains one of the most fully restored of the 21 original Spanish missions established in the state. The Misión la Purisima Concepción de Maria Santisima was founded in 1787 by Father Fermín Francisco de Lasuén as the eleventh of the chain of Spanish missions in California. Its original buildings, however, were destroyed by an earthquake in 1812. Chumash Indians under the direction of Franciscan priests rebuilt the buildings between 1813 and 1822, but the site was abandoned after the Mexican government removed the Catholic Church from control of the missions and turned them over to civil authorities.

The site and buildings of the La Purisima Mission were sold to John Temple in 1845 and later acquired by Union Oil Company, which gave the property to the state of California. The state restored and refurnished the 10 adobe buildings as they looked in 1820 and made the site a state historic park. It also rebuilt the mission gardens and an original aqueduct and pond system, and added livestock of the period and a visitor center with exhibits and artifacts.

La Purisima Mission State Historic Park, 2295 Purisima Rd., Lompoc , CA 93436. Phone: 805/733-3713. Fax: 805/733-2497. E-mail: *lapurmis@sbceo.org*. Web site: *www.lapurisimamission.org*. Hours: 9–4 daily; closed New Year's Day, Thanksgiving, and Christmas. Admission: $4 per car.

Lorenzo de Picuris Mission. See Picuris Pueblo Museum in Native American Museums and Galleries section.

Los Encinos State Historic Park. The five-acre Los Encinos State Historic Park in Encino, California, was the center of human habitation in the southern San Fernando Valley until the late nineteenth century. The site, which features a natural spring, originally was the home of Indians, now called Gabrielino, Fernandeno, or Tongva, for hundreds or possibly thousands of years. The property then passed to mission, Californio, French, and Basque control. The land now is a state historic park and the water produced by the spring is a popular duck pond. The De la Ossa Museum was opened in 2007 in a historic house at the site.

Los Encinos State Historic Park, 16756 Moorpark St., Encino, CA 91436. Phone: 818/784-4849. Fax: 818/784-0621. E-mail: *ranger@los-encinos.org*. Web site: *www.los-encinos.org*. Hours: 10–5 Wed.-Sun.; closed Mon.-Tues. Admission: free.

Mission Basilica San Diego de Alcala. The 1769 Mission Basilica San Diego de Alcala was the first of 21 Spanish missions in California and the first church in San Diego, the initial European settlement in the state. The mission was founded by Father Junípero Serra at Presido Hill and then moved to its present site in Mission Valley in 1774. Father Serra, who was a strong defender of Indians, went on to establish numerous other missions in California between 1770 and 1782.

The San Diego mission was destroyed by earthquakes in 1803 and 1812, but subsequently rebuilt. The mission was designated a minor basilica in 1976 by Pope Paul VI. It has a visitor center with artifacts from Spanish colonial and early American periods, ecclesiastical objects, archaeological findings, and American Indian blankets.

Mission Basilica San Diego de Alcala, 10818 San Diego Mission Rd., San Diego, CA 92108. Phone: 619/283-7319. Fax: 619/283-7762. E-mail: *info@missionsandiego.com*. Web site: *www.missionsandiego.com*. Hours: 9–4:45 daily; closed Thanksgiving and Christmas. Admission: adults, $3 suggested donation; seniors, $2 suggested donation; children, $1 suggested donation.

Mission Nuestra Señora de la Soledad. The Mission Nuestra Señora de la Soledad south of Soledad, California, was founded in 1791 by Father Fermín Francisco del Lasuén. It was the thirteenth of the 21 early California missions. Despite its location on a dry, windy plain, three floodings by the Salinas River, and health difficulties of the early padres (nearly 30 different ones in a short span), the mission eventually prospered with irrigation from the river. But after secularization of California's missions in 1834, the mission was abandoned and fell into ruins over 100 years. It was not until 1954 that the Native Daughters of the Golden West began restoring what was left of the mission. The original quadrangle now is gone, but a wing of seven rooms and a small chapel have been recreated and a museum has been added in one of the rebuilt rooms.

Mission Nuestra Señora de la Soledad, 36641 Fort Romie Rd., PO Box 515, Soledad, CA 93960. Phone: 831/678-2586. Web site: *www.missiontour.org/soledad/index.htm*. Hours: 10–4 daily; closed New Year's Day, Easter, Independence Day, Thanksgiving, and Christmas. Admission: donation.

Mission Nuestra Señora del Espíritu Santo de Zuñiga and Goliad State Park. The partially restored 1749 to 1830 Mission Nuestra Señora del Espíritu Santo de Zuñiga (usually called Mission Espíritu Santo) is located at the Goliad State Park near Goliad, Texas. The restored mission buildings include the chapel, granary, workshop, and adjacent schoolhouse. The park commemorates the Texans slain during the 1836 Battle of Coleto Creek against the Mexican army. It was at nearby Presidio la Bahía that 342 Texan prisoners of war were executed in the Goliad Massacre (see Presidio la Bahía). The park has archaeological and Indian ar-

The first of the 21 early Spanish missions in California was the Mission Basilica San Diego de Alcala, founded in San Diego in 1769. It was destroyed by earthquakes in 1803 and 1812, but subsequently rebuilt and later designated a minor basilica. It now has a visitor center with artifacts from Spanish colonial and early American periods and other historical materials. *Courtesy Mission San Diego de Alcala.*

tifacts and exhibits on the mission, Spanish colonial and early Texas history, quarry ruins, and old brick and tile kilns.

Mission Nuestra Señora del Espíritu Santo de Zuñiga, Goliad State Park, 108 Park Rd. 6, Goliad. TX 77963. Phone: 361/645–3405. Fax: 361/645–8538. E-mail: *elizabeth.livingston@tpwd.state,tx.us.* Web site: *www.tpwd.state.tx.us.* Hours: 8–5 daily; closed Christmas. Admission: adults, $2; children under 12, free.

Mission San Antonio de Padua. The Mission San Antonio de Padua is the most off-the-beaten-path of the 21 early Spanish missions in California. It was founded by Father Junípero Serra as the third mission in 1771. Two years later, the mission was relocated three miles north in the Los Robles Valley to be closer to a better water supply. The San Antonio River was dammed and a long aqueduct brought water to a reservoir and was used to turn California's first gristmill. The site now is in the middle of Fort Hunter Liggett Military Reservation near Jolon. Although abandoned from 1882

to 1928, the mission, gristmill, and parts of the aqueduct have been restored to their 1813 appearance. The mission has a museum with Indian relics, a Spanish colonial wine press, manuscripts, and other historical materials.

Mission San Antonio de Padua, Mission Creek Rd., PO Box 803, Jolon, CA 93928. Phone: 831/385–4478. Fax: 831/386–9332. E-mail: *san1771@redshift. com.* Web site: *www.sanantoniomission.org.* Hours: Memorial Day-Labor Day — 8–6 daily; remainder of year — 8–5 daily. Admission: $1 suggested donation.

Mission San Antonio de Pala. The Mission San Antonio de Pala on the Pala Indian Reservation in Pala, California, is the only one of the 21 Spanish missions that still primarily serves American Indians (also see Cupa Cultural Center Museum in Native American Museums and Galleries section). It was founded in 1816 by Father Antonio Payri as an *asistencia* (branch) of the Mission San Luis Rey de Francia west of Pala. It still serves the Luiseño and Cupeño people on the reservation.

The mission has a chapel with Indian paintings on its walls, a bell tower, a courtyard garden, shrines, an old cemetery, and a museum that displays Indian artifacts, early statues, and other historical materials from the Pala mission and the mission period. An early aqueduct and an olive grove also are located on the grounds.

Mission San Antonio de Pala, Pala Indian Reservation, Pala Mission Rd. (off State Hwy. 76), PO Box 70, Pala, CA 92059. Phone: 760/742-3317. Hours: 10-5 daily. Admission: mission — free; museum — adults, $2; children under 12, $1.

Mission San Buenaventura. Mission San Buenaventura in Ventura was the last mission founded by Father Junipero Serra, who started the network of 21 Spanish colonial missions in California in the eighteenth century. Founded in 1782, it was the ninth of the missions. Father Serra turned the mission project over to Father Pedro Benito Cambon, who oversaw the construction of the mission and a seven-mile aqueduct from the Ventura River which made San Buenaventura one of the most productive of the missions.

The first mission building was destroyed by fire, the second fell apart, and the third, built in 1809, survived but was damaged by three earthquakes and a tidal wave and looted by pirates. The mission property was broken up and sold as part of the secularization of the missions, but then returned to the church by President Abraham Lincoln's proclamation in 1862. A major restoration of the mission took place in 1956 and 1957. The mission museum contains religious and Indian artifacts and other historical materials.

Mission San Buenaventura, 225 E. Main St. Ventura, CA 93001-2622 (mailing address: 211 E. Main St., Ventura, CA 93001-2622). Phone: 805/643-4318. Fax: 805/643-7831. E-mail: *mission@sanbuenaventuramission.org*. Web site: *www.sanbuenaventuramission.org*. Hours: 10-5 Mon.-Sat.; 10-4 Sun. Admission: $1 suggested donation.

Mission San Carlos Borromeo del Rio Carmelo. The Mission San Carlos Borromeo del Rio Carmelo, the second of the 21 Spanish museums in California, was founded by Father Junípero Serra in Monterey in 1770 and then moved to Carmel the following year. It was secularized in 1834 and returned to the church in 1859. The present mission was built between 1793 and 1797, but fell into ruin and was restored in 1884, 1924, and 1931 to 1939. The church was designated a minor basilica in 1960 by Pope John XXIII. Its museum contains Spanish colonial art and artifacts, including one of the most extensive mission period statue and silver collections.

Mission San Carlos Borromeo del Rio Carmelo, 3080 Rio Rd., Carmel, CA 93923. Phone: 831/624-3600. Fax: 831/624-0658. Web site: *www.carmelmission.org*. Hours: June-Aug. — 9:30-7:30 Mon.-Sat.; 10:30-7:30 Sun.; remainder of year — 9:30-4:30 Mon.-Sat.; 10:30-4:40 Sun.; closed Thanksgiving and Christmas. Admission: $2 suggested donation.

Mission San Fernando Rey de España. The Mission San Fernando Rey de España was founded north of Los Angeles (now Mission Hills, California) by Father Fermín Francisco del Lasuén in 1797. It was the seventeenth of the 21 Spanish missions in California. It became a major source of food for the pueblo of Los Angeles, producing olives, dates, wheat, barley, and corn and having 7,000 sheep and other livestock.

The mission was damaged by the 1812 and 1971 earthquakes and nearly fell into disrepair when the church floor was dug up by gold prospectors after gold was discovered in California in the 1848. Among the mission buildings that have been restored are the church, monastery, and some structures around the quadrangle with early furniture, vestments, bells, paintings, and other materials. The mission's museum has mission baskets, pottery, santos, and trade and commerce items, and an archival center contains documents, manuscripts, letters, and memorabilia associated with the Catholic Church in southern California.

Mission San Fernando Rey de España, 15151 San Fernando Mission Blvd., Mission Hills, CA 91345-1109. Phone: 818/361-0186. Fax: 818/361-3276. Hours: mission/museum — 9-4:30 daily; closed Thanksgiving and Christmas; archival center — 1-3 Mon. and Thurs.; other times by appointment; closed national holidays. Admission: mission and museum — adults, $4; children 7-15, $3; children under 7, free; archival center — free.

Mission San Francisco de Asís (Mission Dolores). The Mission San Francisco de Asís, popularly known as Mission Dolores, is the oldest intact building in San Francisco and one of the oldest original church buildings in California. The sixth of the 21 Spanish missions established in California was founded in San Francisco in 1776 by Father Francisco Palóu after San Francisco Bay was discovered accidentally by Gaspar de Portal's expedition while looking for Monterey Bay. However, because the seashore climate was severe and thousands of Indians died from measles and other diseases brought by the Spanish, the mission was moved to its present site in 1791.

The new adobe church was built so well that it withstood the 1906 earthquake. The mission is 114 feet long and 22 feet wide, has walls four feet thick, an ornate decorative altar, and a ceiling with Ohlone Indian designs done with vegetable dyes. It now also contains a covered walkway depicting the history of the mission, remains of the original cemetery, a museum with sacred and other items, and the 1918 parish church, which was designated a basilica — called Church of the Pope — in 1952.

Mission San Francisco de Asís, 3321 16th St., San Francisco, CA 94114. Phone: 415/621–8203. Fax: 415/621–2294. Web site: *www.missiondolores.org.* Hours: 9–4 daily; closed Thanksgiving and Christmas. Admission: adults, $2; children, free.

Mission San Francisco Solano and Sonoma State Historic Park. The Mission San Francisco Solano, the last and northernmost of the 21 Spanish missions in California, is one of the principal attractions at the Sonoma State Historic Park in Sonoma. The mission was founded in 1823 by Father José Altimira, but burned during a native uprising three years later. An 1825 adobe wing of the original wood building has been restored and now is the oldest building in the park. A discouraged Father Altimira returned to Spain, but Father Buenaventura Fortuny then built a church between 1827 and 1833, only to have it severely damaged by a rainstorm. In 1840 and 1841, a chapel was constructed by General Mariano Guadalupe Vallejo, military commander and colonization director of the northern frontier. The mission no longer is active, but it houses the Jorgensen watercolors of the early missions and other historical materials.

The Sonoma State Historic Park consists of six sites at several locations in Sonoma. In addition to the mission facilities, the park contains a number of other historic structures from the Vallejo period, such as an 1836 adobe barracks, a ca. 1843 three-story adobe tower, a ca. 1870 hotel, and two of Vallejo's homes — the 1840 La Casa Grande and his 1852 Lachryma Montis (Mountain Tear), which serves as a museum and interpretive center for the Vallejo home portion of the park.

Mission San Francisco Solano, Sonoma State Historic Park, 114 E. Spain St., Sonoma, CA 95476. Phones: 707/938–9580 and 707/938–1519. Web site: *http://missiontour.org.* Hours: 10–5 daily; closed New Year's Day, Thanksgiving, and Christmas. Admission: included in park admission.

Sonoma State Historic Park, 363 3rd St. West, Sonoma, CA 95476, Phone: 707/938–1519. Fax: 707/938–1406. Web site: *www.parks.ca.gov/default. asp?page_id=479.* Hours: 10–5 daily closed New Year's Day, Thanksgiving, and Christmas. Admission: adults, $2; children under 17, free.

Mission San Gabriel Arcángel. The Mission San Gabriel Arcángel in San Gabriel, California, is one of several missions known as the "Queen of the Missions." The mission, the fourth of the 21 Spanish missions in California, was founded in 1771 by Father Junípero Serra. After being moved from its original site because of disruptions by the Spanish military, the new site got the nickname for being so prosperous. The mission tower was damaged in the 1812 earthquake and was forced to close until 1993 after the 1987 earthquake. The mission's museum contains early Bibles, church furnishings, manuscripts, paintings, vestments, statues, and photographs.

Mission San Gabriel Arcángel, 428 S. Mission Dr., San Gabriel, CA 91776. Phone: 626/457–3035. Fax: 626/282–5308. E-mail: *alsgml@aol.com.* Web site: *www.sangabrielmission.org.* Hours: 9–4:30 daily; closed Easter, Thanksgiving, Christmas, and after noon on Good Friday and Christmas Eve. Admission: adults, $5; seniors, $4; children 6–17, $2; children under 6, free.

Mission San José. The Mission San José, which has the full name of Mission of the Glorious Patriarch San José, was the first of five missions built to fill the gap and serve the hostile and sometimes unpredictable Indians in the Fremont area between San Diego and San Francisco. It was founded in 1797 by Father Fermín Francisco del Lasuén as the fourteenth of the 21 Spanish missions in California.

The mission started in a temporary thatched roof structure, moved to an adobe building in 1809, was severely damaged by earthquakes in 1836 and 1868, and then replaced by a white frame church and rectory. In the early days the mission became known for its accomplished Indian orchestra of 30 musicians, and later for serving miners during the 1848 to 1855 California gold rush. In 1985, a new adobe building was rededicated with interior decorations similar to that of the prosperous times of the early 1830s before secularization. The mission now has a museum with Ohlone Indian artifacts, period furnishings, and sacred items.

Mission San José, 43300 Mission Blvd., PO Box 3314, Fremont, CA 94539. Phone: 510/657–1797. Hours: 10–5 daily; closed New Year's Day, Easter, Thanksgiving, and Christmas. Admission: adults, $1; children, 50¢.

Mission San Juan Capistrano. The Mission San Juan Capistrano once was the most magnificent of the 21 Spanish missions in California in San Juan Capistrano — known for the swallows that return each year to nest and raise their young. The mission was built between 1796 and 1805 and called the Great Stone Church, constructed of stone in the shape of a cross with a 120-foot bell tower. But the building was destroyed and 40 persons were killed when an earthquake struck during a mass six years later. Only the ruins remain today.

The mission originally was founded by Father Fermín Francisco del Lasuén in 1775, but abandoned after eight days because of the threat of an Indian attack. The church bells were buried and everyone fled to the San Diego Presidio. Father Juniper Serra returned to the area the following year, found the bells, and built a chapel with seven domes and a 104-foot bell tower between 1776 and 1778. It still stands today and is the oldest original church building in California. The building was restored in the 1890s and again after the 1987 earthquake. In addition to 13 acres with flowers from 60 countries, the mission has a museum with sacred items, ca. 1800 Spanish rancho artifacts, and local Indian collections.

Mission San Juan Capistrano, 31522 Camino Capistrano, San Juan Capistrano, CA 92675 (mailing address: PO Box 697, San Juan Capistrano, CA 92693). Phone: 949/234-1300. Fax: 949/443-2061. E-mail: *mission@fia.net*. Web site: *www.missionsjc.com*. Hours: 8:30–5 daily; closed New Year's Day, Good Friday, Thanksgiving, and Christmas. Admission: adults, $6; seniors and children 3–12, $5; children under 3, free.

Mission San Luis Obispo de Tolosa. The Mission San Luis Obispo de Tolosa in San Luis Obispo was the fifth Spanish museum founded in California by Father Junípero Serra. It was established in 1771 in what was called the Valley of the Bears because of the abundance of bears during the early years. Father José Cavallar was left to oversee the development of the mission. By 1794, the church and priest's residences were built by Spanish soldiers, missionaries, and Chumash Indians. Other buildings were added later, but all declined after the 1834 secularization. A number of improvements were made in the buildings in the second half of the nineteenth century. It was not until the 1930s, however, that the original buildings were restored. A museum now traces the mission's history and contains numerous religious materials, Chumash Indian artifacts, and memorabilia from early settlers.

Mission San Luis Obispo de Tolosa, 751 Palm St., PO Box 1461, San Luis Obispo, CA 93401. Phones: 805/543-6850 and 805/781-8220. Fax: 805/781-8214. Web site: *www.missionsanluisobispo.org*. Hours: Memorial Day-Labor Day — 9–5 daily; remainder of year — 9–4 daily; closed New Year's Day, Easter, Thanksgiving, and Christmas. Admission: $2 suggested donation.

Mission San Luis Rey. Mission San Luis Rey in Oceanside is the largest of the 21 Spanish missions built in California in the late eighteenth and early nineteenth centuries. It was founded by Father Fer-

mín Francisco de Lasuén in 1798 as the eighteenth in the chain of 21 California missions. The mission, built in the shape of a cross, has an arched colonnade, sunken gardens, retreats, gift shop, and a museum among its facilities and offers guided and unguided tours. The museum contains Spanish, Mexican, and Indian religious items; early Spanish decorative and fine arts; and Native American blankets.

Mission San Luis Rey, 4050 Mission Ave., Oceanside, CA 92057. Phone: 760/757-3651. Fax: 760/757-4613. E-mail: *museum@sanluisrey.org*. Web site: *www.sanluisrey.org*. Hours: 10-4 daily; closed New Year's Day, Easter, Thanksgiving, and Christmas. Admission: adults, $5; youth, $3; children under 6, free.

Mission San Miguel Arcángel. The Mission San Miguel Arcángel reopened in San Miguel at the end of 2006 after being closed for three years as result of extensive damage inflicted by the 2003 California earthquake. The mission was founded in 1797 by Father Fermín Francisco del Lasuén as the sixteenth of the 21 Spanish missions. Phase 1 of a seven-part restoration has been completed, opening the mission church, museum, and gift shop. The second phase — restoring the original convento that housed quarters of friars — currently is under way. The mission still contains the original paintings created by Indian artisans under the direction of Esteban Munras. The museum features artifacts of the old mission days and early murals and paintings.

Mission San Miguel Arcángel, 775 Mission St., PO Box 69, San Miguel, CA 93451. Phone: 805/467-3256. Fax: 805/467-2448. E-mail: *friars@missioinsanmiguel.org*. Web site: *www.missionsanmiguel.org*. Hours: 9:30-4:15 daily; closed New Year's Day, Easter, Thanksgiving, and Christmas. Admission: $1 suggested donation.

Mission San Rafael Arcángel. The Mission San Rafael Arcángel in San Rafael, California, began in 1817 as an *asistencia* (a branch of the Mission San Francisco de Asis) to serve as a hospital to treat sick Indians (the first sanitarium in California). Founded by Father Vicente de Sarría as the twentieth of the 21 early Spanish missions in California, it grew to full mission status in 1822.

After secularization, the buildings were sold to General Mariano Vallejo, the commandant of the San Francisco Presidio and a rancher, who later had the Mission Indians destroy their own church. During the 1846 to 1848 war with Mexico, John C. Frémont used the mission as his headquarters in the struggle to make California part of the United States. In 1861, a new parish church was built at the site of the old adobe hospital and the ruins were removed. However, a replica of the original mission chapel was built in 1949 next to the parish church of St. Raphael. It functions as a museum with religious artifacts and early photographs.

Mission San Rafael Arcángel, 1104 5th Ave., San Rafael, CA 94901–2916. Phone: 415/454–8141. Fax: 415/454–8193. Web site: *www.saintraphael.com.* Hours: 11–4 Mon.-Sat.; 10–4 Sun.; closed major holidays. Admission: donation.

Mission Santa Barbara. The Mission Santa Barbara on a hill overlooking Santa Barbara, California, has been called the "Queen of the Missions" because of its beauty. It was the first mission founded by Father Fermín Francisco de Lasuén, who succeeded Father Junípero Serra as head of the California missions. Founded in 1786, it was the tenth of 21 Franciscan missions in California. The first buildings were put up by Father Antonio Paterna, who made the initial converts. The original purpose of the mission was the Christianization of the Chumash Indians, but now it reflects the cultural diversity of California's heritage. The mission had three adobe churches—each larger than the other—before the present church opened in 1820 and the complex was finished in 1870. It was damaged considerably by a 1925 earthquake, but restored in 1927 and towers were added in 1953.

The large mission complex began with a quadrangle and rows of over 200 dwellings for mission natives. They were followed by a second quadrangle, a succession of larger adobe churches and support structures, and a water system that was the most elaborate of all the missions and parts are still used by the city of Santa Barbara. Five units of the extensive waterworks built by Chumash Indians are preserved, including a filter house, grist mill, sections of aqueducts, and two reservoirs. Ruins of the pottery kiln and tannery vats also remain, as well as the fountain and lavadero in front of the historic mission. The museum features religious artifacts and period furniture, and the archives contain documents of the entire California mission chain (resulting from the headquarters move by Father Narciso Duran, then president of the California missions, from Mission San José to Santa Barbara) and a large collection of sheet music from the mission era.

Mission Santa Barbara, 2201 Laguna St., Santa Barbara, CA 93105. Phone: 805/682–4713. Fax: 805/687–7841. Web site: *www.sbmission.org.* Hours: 9–5 daily; closed Easter, Thanksgiving, and Christmas. Admission: free; guided tours, $4 per adult.

Mission Santa Clara de Asis. The Mission Santa Clara de Asis on the campus of Santa Clara University in Santa Clara was the first of the 21 Califor-

nia missions to be named for a woman (Saint Clare, founder of the Order of the Poor Clares). Founded by Father Junípero Serra in 1777, it was the eighth of the early Spanish missions. During its peak, the mission had the largest number of Indians among the missions. After the Jesuit order of priests assumed control of the mission, Father John Nobili began a college on the mission site in 1851 that grew into Santa Clara University. It is the only mission to become part of a university and now is the oldest university in the state. Every evening the mission bells are rung—keeping a promise to King Charles IV of Spain when he sent the original bells to the mission in 1777. The university's de Saisset Museum has a mission gallery with historical displays and religious artifacts.

Mission Santa Clara de Asis, Santa Clara University, 500 El Camino Real, Santa Clara, CA 95053. Phone: 408/554–4023. Web site: *www.scu.edu/visitors/mission.* Hours: mission—8–6 daily; museum—11–4 Tues.-Sun.; closed Mon. and major holidays. Admission: free.

Mission Santa Cruz and Santa Cruz Mission State Historic Park. The Mission Santa Cruz—called the Misión la Exaltación de la Santa Cruz in Spanish—was founded by Father Fermín Francisco de Lasuén in 1791 as the twelfth of 21 Spanish missions in California. But it was badly damaged by several earthquakes and severe weather and finally collapsed in 1857, with only a partial wall now remaining on the Holy Cross Church grounds in Santa Cruz, California. The church also has a half-scale replica of the mission in its gallery. The site of a complex of buildings erected around the Santa Cruz Mission is now the Santa Cruz Mission State Historic Park. The restored Neary-Rodriquez Adobe built in 1791 is the last of the mission's many buildings to survive. The park is located in downtown Santa Cruz.

Mission Santa Cruz, Holy Cross Church, 126 High St., Santa Cruz, CA 95060. Phone: 831/426–5686. Fax: 831/423–1043. E-mail: *bpedrazzi@sbcglobal.net.* Hours: 10–4 Tues.-Sat.; 10–2 Sun.; closed Mon. and major holidays. Admission: free.

Santa Cruz State Historic Park, 144 School St., Santa Cruz, CA 95060. Phone: 831/425–5849. Fax: 831/429–2870. Web site: *www.parks.ca.gov/?page_id= 548.* Hours: 10–4 Thurs.-Sun.; closed major holidays. Admission: free.

Mission Santa Cruz de San Sabá and Presido San Luis de las Amarillas. The Mission Santa Cruz de San Sabá was founded by Franciscan missionaries near Menard, Texas, in 1757 to Christianize the eastern Apache Indians, and the Presidio San Luis de las Amarillas (known as Presidio de

San Saba) was built nearby to protect and support the mission. The Indian resistance was greater than expected, and both sites were virtually destroyed the following year after attacks by Apache, Comanche, and other Indians believed to have been supplied with guns by the French who opposed Spanish moves into the region. The mission and presidio then were consolidated about a mile upstream of Menard, but the site was abandoned in 1768 and the Indian menace eventually led to the Spanish withdrawal from Texas to settlements along the Rio Grande River. Only stones from the various San Sabá River area structures remain today.

Mission Santa Cruz de San Sabá and Presidio San Luis de las Amarillas, near Menard, TX 76859. No facilities.

Mission San Xavier del Bac. The Mission San Xavier del Bac on the Tohono O'odham Indian Reservation south of Tucson, Arizona, is known as the "White Dove of the Desert" because of its impressive white domes, carvings, arches, and flying buttresses. It is considered to be one of the finest examples of Spanish mission architecture in the Southwest. The mission was founded by Father Eusebio Francisco Kina near a Pima Indian village while traveling to California in 1692, but the present whitewashed church was not built until 1782.

During the secularization period, when the Mexican government demanded loyalty from all Spanish priests, many priests, including the one serving San Xavier, refused and were sent home to Spain. The church, which was vacant from 1828 to 1858, began to decay and was taken over by birds. Local Indians concerned about the church took furnishings home as a way of preserving them. The church was activated and largely restored after the 1859 Gadsden Purchase added Arizona to the Santa Fe Diocese. There are no registered members of the parish, but the Sunday services usually are packed. An attached museum has historical exhibits and many artifacts of the church, including early gowns, dishes, and books.

Mission San Xavier del Bac, Tohono O'odham Indian Reservation, 1950 W. San Xavier Rd., Tucson, AZ 85746. Phone: 520/294–2624. Hours: 9:30–5:30 daily. Admission: donation.

Mission Tejas State Park. The Mission Tejas State Park near Weches, Texas, was established in 1934 and 1935 as a commemorative representation of the 1690 Mission San Francisco de los Tejas, one of the first Spanish missions in Texas. The mission was moved to San Antonio in 1731 and now is part of the San Antonio Missions Historical Park (see separate listing). It originally was built to stem the tide of French settlement in the region. When the

French threat was gone, the mission and others in west Texas were relocated to San Antonio The park also contains the Rice Family Log Home, built between 1828 and 1838 and restored in 1974. It served as a stopover for travelers on the Old San Antonio Road across early Texas.

Mission Tejas State Park, State Hwy. 21, Rural Rte. 2, Box 108, Grapeland, TX 75844. Phone: 936/687–2394. Hours: 8–10 daily. Admission: adults and children over 12, $2; children under 13, free.

Museo Fuerte Conde de Mirasol de Vieques. See Puerto Rican Museums and Galleries section.

Nuestra Señora de la Limpia Concepción del Socorro Mission. The Nuestra Señora de la Limpia Concepción del Socorro Mission in Socorro, Texas, was located in Mexico until an 1829 flood changed the course of the Rio Grande River and left the village and the mission on the Texas side. Originally located near the Guadalupe Mission at Paso del Norte, the mission was moved by Spanish missionaries and the Piro, Thano, and Jeme Indian tribes to Socorro to escape the massacres occurring during the 1680 Pueblo Revolt period. It is one of the oldest missions in Texas.

Nuestra Señora de la Limpia Concepción del Socorro Mission, 328 Nevarez Rd., Socorro, TX 79927. Phone: 915/859–7718. Fax: 915/850–9452. Hours: 9–3 daily. Admission: free.

Old Mission San Juan Bautista and San Juan Bautista State Historic Park. The Old Mission San Juan Bautista in San Juan Bautista, California, was one of the largest of the 21 Spanish missions established in California. It was founded in 1797 by Father Fermín Francisco de Lasuén as the fifteenth of the early missions. The mission once had nine bells in recognition of its importance. Only three remain today. A historic cemetery next to the church contains the remains of over 4,000 Native Americans and Europeans.

The mission, located near the San Andreas Fault, was struck by a violent earthquake in 1906, collapsing the side walls of the church. The convento wing, which now houses the museum, is all that remains of the quadrangle. However, the church and the original Guadalupe Chapel were restored as part of the 1976 bicentennial observance. The museum now contains early vestments, artworks, books, and other historical materials. The six-acre San Juan State Historic Park, which is adjacent to the mission, has exhibits on life in the mission and Mexican and early American periods and a number of structures built in the 1800s, including the Castro Breen adobe, Plaza Hotel, Plaza Hall and stable, blacksmith shop, granary, and jail.

Old Mission San Juan Bautista, 2nd and Mariposa Sts., PO Box 400, San Juan Bautista, CA 95045–0400. Phone: 831/623–2127. Fax: 831/623–2433. Web site: *www.oldmissionsjb.org.* Hours: 9:30–4:45 daily; closed New Year's Day, Good Friday, Thanksgiving, and Christmas. Admission: adults, $2 suggested donation; seniors and students, $1 suggested donation; children under 6, free.

San Juan Bautista State Historic Park, 2nd St. (Washington and Mariposa Sts.), PO Box 787, San Juan Batista, CA 95045–0787. Phones: 831/623–4881 and 831/623–4526. Fax: 831/621–4612. Web site: *www.parks.ca.gov/?page_id=563.* Hours: 10–4:30 daily; closed New Year's Day, Thanksgiving, and Christmas. Admission: adults, $2; children under 17, free.

Old Mission Santa Inés. The Old Mission Santa Inés in Solvang, California, has been called the "Mission of the Passes" because of its proximity to the Santa Ynez and San Rafael mountain ranges. It was founded in 1804 by Father Estevan Tapis as the nineteenth of the 21 Spanish missions. An earthquake in 1812 partially destroyed the adobe mission building, but it was rebuilt in 1817 and has been in continuous service since then.

Eleven of the original 22 arches and over one-third of the original quadrangle still remain, as well as murals painted by Indian artists, a hand-crafted copper baptismal font, and works of European art and sculpture. The museum contains many mission-era artifacts, including pottery, silver, crucifixes, musical instruments, adobe bricks and tiles, and original altarpiece. Originally a Spanish-oriented village, Solvang became a Danish enclave starting in 1911 and is known today principally for its Danish-style buildings, windmills, bakeries, and, celebrations.

Old Mission Santa Inés, 1760 Mission Dr., Solvang, CA 93463 (mailing address: PO Box 408, Solvang, CA 93464). Phone: 805/688–4815. Fax: 805/686–4468. E-mail: *info@missionsantaines.org.* Web site: *www.missionsantaines.org.* Hours: 9–5 daily; closed major holidays. Admission: adults, $3; children under 16, free.

Old San Miguel Mission. The Old San Miguel Mission in Socorro, New Mexico, began as a little church in 1598 which was replaced with a much larger church between 1815 and 1826 with massive walls five feet in width and huge carved vigas and supporting corbel arches. It still is the current church building, although a wing was added in 1853. The mission flourished until the Pueblo Revolt of 1680, when the priests and Indian followers abandoned the church and retreated to El Paso. When Spanish and Mexican settlers returned to the area, they found the church in dilapidated condi-

tion and worked to restore it. The mission has four sub–floors, where some of the priests and prominent residents of the past are buried. A number of artifacts from the early years are displayed in the mission office.

Old San Miguel Mission, 403 Camino Real, Socorro, NM 87801. Phone: 505/835–1620. Hours: 7–7 daily. Admission: free.

Old Spanish Fort Museum. The Old Spanish Fort Museum in Pascagoula, Mississippi, is a former military site that became the oldest residential building in the state. The ca. 1718 building was a Spanish outpost in the Mississippi Valley and later occupied by the same family (Lapointe-Krebs) from at least 1768 to 1914. The historic house museum is preserved and operated by the Jackson County Historical Society.

Old Spanish Fort Museum, 4602 Fort St., Pascagoula, MS 39567. Phone: 228/769–1505. E-mail: *oldspanishfort@netscape.net.* Hours: 9:30–4:30 Mon.-Sat.; closed Sun. and national holidays. Admission: adults, $4; seniors, $3; children, $2.

Old Town and San Filipe de Neri Church. Old Town in Albuquerque, New Mexico, is where the first Spanish families settled in 1706. It was a colonial farming village and a military outpost along the Camino Real between Chihuahua and Santa Fe. It developed around a traditional Spanish pattern of a central plaza surrounded by a church, houses, and government buildings.

The San Filipe de Neri Church, also established in 1706, and many old adobe homes are still there, some of which have been converted to over 130 shops, galleries, and restaurants. They now constitute Albuquerque's Old Town. The original church building was destroyed in a flood and replaced with the current still-active adobe structure in 1793. Walking tours of Old Town are given Tuesday through Sunday from mid–May to mid–December, departing at 11 A.M. from the neighboring Albuquerque Museum.

Old Town, 1 block north of 200 block of Central Ave. N.W., Albuquerque, NM (contact: Old Town Merchants Association, PO Box 7483, Albuquerque, NM 87014). Phone: 505/338–2399. Web site: *www.albuquerqueoldtown.com.* Hours: open 24 hours. Admission: free.

San Filipe de Neri Church, 2005 N. Plaza St. N.W., Albuquerque, NM 87014. Phone: 505/243–4628. Fax: 505/224–9495. Hours: dawn-dusk daily. Admission: free.

Oldest House Museum Complex. The Oldest House Museum Complex in St. Augustine, Florida, features the early 1700s Gonzáles-Alvarez House, the oldest surviving Spanish colonial

The oldest continuously occupied public building in the United States is the Palace of the Governors, built by Spain in Santa Fe, New Mexico, in 1610. It originally was the headquarters for the Spanish regional government in the Southwest, and later occupied by Pueblo Indians, Mexican and American territorial governments, and Confederate forces before being restored and converted into a part of the Museum of New Mexico system. This photograph shows the building's portal where artists from the Native American Artisans Program sell their wares. *Courtesy Palace of the Governors, Museum of New Mexico, and photographer Blair Clark.*

dwelling in Florida. The house shows evidence of Spanish, British, and American occupation of St. Augustine and how the residents lived. The site has been occupied since the 1600s. The house contains artifacts and interpretive exhibits.

Oldest House Museum Complex, 14 St. Francis St., St. Augustine, FL 32084. Phone: 904/824–2873. Fax: 904/824–2569. E-mail: *sahsdirector@bellsouth.net*. Web site: *www.oldesthouse.org*. Hours: 9–5 daily; closed Christmas. Admission: adults, $8; seniors and military, $7; students, $4; children under 6, free.

Olivas Adobe Historic Park. See Mexican Historic Sites section.

Our Lady of Assumption Church. See Zia Cultural Center in Native American Museums and Galleries section.

Our Lady of Guadalupe Mission. See A:shiwi A:wan Museum and Heritage Center in Native American Museums and Galleries section.

Palace of the Governors. The Palace of the Governors, built by the Spanish in Santa Fe, New Mexico, in 1610, is the oldest continuously occupied public building in the United States. It first served as the seat of the Spanish government for what today is the American Southwest, but was abandoned by colonial officials during the Pueblo Revolt of 1680, only to be occupied by Pueblo Indians for 13 years. The building then housed the Mexican and American territorial governments, and even Confederate forces for a few weeks during the Civil War. When threatened with demolition in 1909, the adobe structure was converted to a museum and part of the newly established Museum of New Mexico system.

The Palace of the Governors has exhibits and archives on New Mexico and Southwest history dating from the colonial period, collections of over 15,000 artifacts and 380,000 historical photographs, and a 12,000-volume library relating to the history of southwestern America. The exhibits contain such historical objects as pottery, silver, furniture, decorative arts, firearms, and religious art.

The building also is known for the Indian artisans who sell their handmade goods daily to tourists near the entrance facing the Santa Fe Plaza.

Palace of the Governors, 105 W. Palace Ave., Santa Fe, NM 87504. Phone: 505/476–5100. Fax: 505/476–5104. E-mail: *rene.harris@state.nm.us*. Web site: *www.palaceofthegovernors.org*. Hours: 10–5 Tues.-Sun.; closed Mon., New Year's Day, Easter, Thanksgiving, and Christmas. Admission: adults, $6 for New Mexico residents and $8 for non–residents; children under 17, free; also free on Wed. for New Mexico seniors, Sun. for New Mexico residents; and 5–8 Fri. for all visitors; four-day museum pass to five museums, $18; one-day museum pass to two museums, $12.

Pecos National Historical Park. See Native American Historic Sites section.

Presidio la Bahía. The 1749 Presidio la Bahía near Goliad, Texas, was the most fought-over military post in Texas history. Nine flags have flown over the fort, which is considered the finest example of a Spanish frontier fort in the state. The presidio, which has been restored to its 1836 appearance, and two nearby missions constitute one of the best examples of a Spanish colonial mission-presidio complex in the nation. The presidio has massive 10-foot-high walls and other structures of the fort, including officers' quarters, barracks, and a chapel. The presidio's Our Lady of Loreto Chapel has served as a community church since 1779. A museum contains artifacts found during the restoration, memorabilia of the Texas Revolution, and exhibits on the history of the presidio.

The Presidio la Bahía grew into one of the most important forts on the Spanish and later Mexican frontiers. Spanish soldiers from the presidio fought the British during the Revolutionary War. It was the site of the first offensive action against Mexico in the 1836 Texas Revolution, and the Goliad Massacre where 342 Texans were taken as prisoners of war, including Colonel James W. Fannin, Jr., and were executed on orders from General Santa Ana (also see Mission Nuestra Señora del Espíritu Santo de Zuñiga and Goliad State Park). The Fannin Memorial Monument is located nearby and a re-enactment of the massacre and latter battle at Coleto Creek is held every March.

Presidio la Bahía, Refugio Hwy., PO Box 57, Goliad, TX 77963. Phone: 512/645–3752. Fax: 512/645–1706. E-mail: *presidioofbahia@tisd.net*. Web site: *www.presidiolabahia.org*. Hours: 9–5 daily; closed major holidays. Admission: adults, $3; seniors, $2.50; children under 12, $1.

Presidio San Luis de las Amarillas (Presidio de San Sabá). See Mission Santa Cruz de San Sabá and Presidio San Luis de las Amarillas.

Rancho los Alamitos. The Rancho los Alamitos in Long Beach, California, is one of the oldest continuously occupied places in southern California. The mesa on which the ranch is located was home to the Tongva (Gabrielino) Indians from approximately 500 to 1806. During the eighteenth century, Corporal José Manuel Perez Nieto, one of the soldiers who marched north with the Spanish priests and pioneers in 1769, began raising horses and cattle in the San Diego area and convinced his commander to give him land grants totaling 300,000 acres, including the Tongva land near the pueblo of Los Angeles. The grant was reduced to 167,000 acres after protests by Mission San Gabriel priests who said they needed the land to feed the Indians. Despite the reduction, it was the largest land grant given by Spain or Mexico in California.

Nieto had between 15,000 and 20,000 cattle on the land at the time of his death in 1804. After he died, his widow and children continued to operate the ranch. In 1834, the land was subdivided among family members into five large ranchos and one small ranch, including the 28,500-acre Rancho los Alamitos. In the years that followed, it was sold to Governor José Figueroa, merchant-rancher Abel Stearns, and John and Susan Bixby. The Bixby working ranch and dairy farm was downsized over the years by the growth of the Los Angeles metropolitan area, and the remains eventually given to the city of Long Beach in 1968 by descendants of the Bixbys. The Rancho los Alamitos now is an eight-acre historic ranch and gardens that reflects the early days with a ca. 1800 house, five early barns, a blacksmith shop, and four acres of lush gardens.

Rancho los Alamitos, 6400 Bixby Hill Rd., Long Beach, CA 90815. Phone: 562/431–3541. Fax: 562/430–9694. E-mail: *info@rancholosalamitos.com*. Web site: *www.rancholosalamitos.com*. Hours: 1–5 Wed.-Sun.; closed Mon.-Tues. and national holidays. Admission: free.

Rancho los Cerritos Historic Site. The Rancho los Cerritos Historic Site in Long Beach, California, is located on part of the 167,000 acres of land given to José Manuel Perez Nieto in land grants in the late eighteenth century (also see Rancho los Alamitos). It was one of the five large ranchos and a small ranch that were divided among Nieto family members in 1834. The oceanfront 27,000-acre Rancho los Cerritos went to Nieto's only surviving daughter, Maria Manuel Antonia, who sold it to John and Rafaela Temple in 1844. The Temples built a two-story, U-shaped, veranda-fronted adobe house which now is the centerpiece of the historic site.

The ranch was sold to Flint, Bixby & Company in the 1860s. Jotham Bixby raised sheep on the land and began subdividing the shore section of Los

Cerritos into what became Long Beach. More sales followed by Bixby and other family members, resulting in the founding of such other communities as Lakewood, Signal Hill, Bellflower, Paramount, and portions of South Gate and Downey. The city-operated historic site now covers 4.7 acres of landscaped grounds and features the Temple adobe house with period rooms and exhibits on the lifestyle at the Bixby ranch in the late nineteenth century. A visitor center also has an orientation exhibit on the history of the ranch.

Rancho los Cerritos Historic Site, 4600 Virginia Rd., Long Beach, CA 90807. Phone: 562/570-1755. Fax: 562/570-1893. E-mail: *ellen_calomiris@long-beach.gov.* Web site: *www.rancholoscerritos.org.* Hours: 1-5 Wed.-Sun.; closed Mon.-Tues. and major holidays. Admission: free.

Salinas Pueblo Missions National Monument. The Salinas Pueblo Missions National Monument near Mountainair, New Mexico, contains the ruins of three 1100 to 1670 American Indian pueblos and four Spanish missions. The 1,100-acre monument was established in 1980 by combining two New Mexico state monuments and the former Gran Quivira National Monument. The area originally was inhabited by Tiwa- and Tompiro-speaking puebloans. In the seventeenth century, Spanish missionaries came to Christianize the Indians and built missions. But by the late 1670s, the natives and the Spanish abandoned the area because of cultural and environmental pressures. Only the ruins of pueblos and missions remain at the sites of Abó, Quarai, and Gran Quivira.

The Abó Pueblo, a Timpiro village, once was the largest of the pueblos in the Southwest. The Mission San Gregorio de Abó, with a 40-foot buttressed curtain wall, was founded there in 1622. It is one of the few surviving examples of medieval architecture in the nation. The Quarai Pueblo has 10 large pueblo house mounds and ruins of the 1629 Mission Nuestra Señora de la Purísima Concepción de Cuara. The remains of Gran Quivira, which had 1,500 inhabitants at one time, include 21 limestone house mounds, 300 rooms, six kivas, and two missions — the 1629 Mission San Isidro and 1659 Mission San Buenaventura.

The national monument has a museum and three visitor centers. The museum at the Quarai site features a scale model of the mission, exhibits, and pottery and other artifacts. Exhibits also are presented at Gran Quivira and the monument headquarters visitor centers, but not at the Abó visitor center.

Salinas Pueblo Missions National Monument, 102 S. Ripley St., PO Box 517, Mountainair, NM 87036. Phone: 505/847-2585. Fax: 505/847-2441. E-mail: *tobin_roop@nps.gov.* Web site: *www.nps.gov/sapu.* Hours: Memorial Day-Labor Day — 9-6 daily; remainder of year — 9-5 daily; closed New Year's Day, Thanksgiving, and Christmas. Admission: free.

San Agustin de la Isleta Mission. The heavily buttressed San Agustin de la Isleta Mission on the Isleta Pueblo south of Albuquerque, New Mexico, originally was built in 1613 by Father Juan de Salas. It was burned and badly damaged during the Pueblo Revolt of 1680, then rebuilt using the surviving walls of the church following the reconquest of New Mexico by the Spanish in 1692 and 1693. It has since been renovated several times and the present appearance dates from the early 1960s.

San Agustin de la Isleta Mission, Isleta Pueblo, Tribal Rd. 45, PO Box 1270, Isleta, NM 87022. Phone: 505/869-3398. Hours: 9-6 daily; closed on some religious and ceremonial days. Admission: free.

San Antonio Missions National Historical Park. The San Antonio Missions National Historical Park in San Antonio, Texas, has the nation's largest concentration of Spanish colonial resources. Four seventeenth- and eighteenth-century Spanish frontier missions are preserved at the historical park, as well as an aqueduct, dam, ranch, flour mill, and several miles of irrigation ditches constructed by mission Indians under the direction of Franciscan friars.

Three of the missions were transferred from east Texas in 1731 during turbulent Indian times and territorial competition with the French. They are the 1690 Mission San Francisco de la Espada, which was named the San Francisco de los Tejas before being moved to the San Antonio River area; 1716 Mission San Juan Capisrano, formerly the San Juan de los Nazonis; and 1731 to 1755 Mission Nuestra Señora de la Purísima Concepción, believed to be the oldest unrestored stone church in the nation. The only mission founded at the site is the Mission San José y San Miguel de Aguayo, which has a compound that includes an outer wall with Indian dwellings, a granary, and a 1790 flour mill. All the missions still have active parishes. Another San Antonio mission was the 1718 Mission San Antonio de Valero, which became the Mission del Alamo del Parras in 1803 and later simply called The Alamo (see separate listing in Mexican Historic Sites section).

The historical park also has the remains of a 15-mile irrigation system; the 1745 Expada Dam which still diverts river water into the mother ditch; the Espada Aqueduct, the oldest Spanish aqueduct in the United States; and the ruins of the Rancho de Las Cabras, built after 1758 as part of the Mission Espada. Historical exhibits, art, and a film can be seen in the visitor center, located in the Mission San José.

San Antonio Missions National Historical Park, 6701 San José Dr., San Antonio, TX 78214 (mailing address: 2202 Roosevelt Ave., San Antonio, TX 78210–4919). Phone: 210/534–8633. Fax: 210/534–1106. E-mail: *saan_administration@nps.gov*. Web site: *www.nps.gov/saan*. Hours: 9–5 daily; closed New Year's Day, Thanksgiving, and Christmas. Admission: free.

San Elizario Presidio Chapel. The San Elizario Presidio Chapel was founded in 1777 to serve a Spanish military garrison in San Elizario, Texas. The Rio Grande River washed away the original mission, but it was rebuilt at the same site and now functions as a Catholic village church. The chapel preserves a type of architecture that replaced the more austere styles of such missions as the Ysleta Mission in El Paso and Nuestra Señora de la Concepción in Socorro (see separate listings).

San Elizario Presidio Chapel, 156 San Elizario Rd., PO Box 910, San Elizario, TX 79849. Phone: 915/851–2333. Hours: 9–5 daily. Admission: free.

San Estéban del Rey Mission. The San Estéban del Rey Mission, the largest and one of the earliest Spanish missions in the Southwest, was founded in 1629 on the Ácoma Pueblo (see Sky City Cultural Center and Haak'u Museum in Native American Museums and Galleries section) in New Mexico. The pueblo, dating from at least 1150, is one of the oldest continuously inhabited sites in the nation. It is located on a steep 370-foot-high mesa, which provided protection against enemies until the Spanish arrived with their superior weapons and numbers to overwhelm the Ácoma tribe. To construct the mission, it was necessary to carry the sand from below the mesa and to bring the log beams from forests 30 miles away. The mission has an unusual altar and contains early religious paintings and images of saints. It can be seen only as part of guided tours of the pueblo.

San Estéban del Rey Mission, Ácoma Pueblo, State Hwy. 23 (off Interstate 40 West, Exit 102), PO Box 448, Ácoma, NM 87034. Phones: 505/470–6403 and 800/747–0181. Fax: 505/552–7204. Web site: *www.skycity.com*. Hours: May-Oct.— 8–6 daily; remainder of year — 8–5 daily; closed during tribal ceremonials in mid–July. Admission: part of guided tour — adults, $10; seniors, $9; children 6–17, $7; children under 6, free.

San Filipe de Neri Church. See Old Town and San Filipe de Neri Church.

San Francisco de Asis Mission Church. The ca. 1772 San Francisco de Asis Mission Church in Ranchos de Taos, New Mexico, is one of the most impressive early Franciscan churches in the state. The 120-foot-long fortress-like church has adobe walls four feet thick, enormous buttresses, and twin bell towers. It contains images of saints, a large figure of Christ, and a huge carved altar screen divided into painted panels, believed to date from the time of the mission's founding. The rectory features Henry Ault's unusual painting *The Shadow of the Cross*, which shows Christ carrying or without the cross, depending on the lighting. The church, still used for services, is one of the best known and most photographed churches in New Mexico.

San Francisco de Asis Mission Church, 60 St. Francis Plaza, Ranchos de Taos, NM 87557. Phone: 505/758–2754. Fax: 505/751–3923. Hours: church — 6–6:30 Mon.-Fri.; 9–4 Sat.; 6–12:30 Sun.; rectory — 9–4 daily; closed first weeks in June. Admission: church — free; rectory — adults, $2; children under 13, free.

San Juan National Historic Site. See Puerto Rican Historic Sites section.

San Miguel Mission Church. The San Miguel Mission Church in Santa Fe, New Mexico, is the oldest church still in use in the United States. The adobe structure was built between 1610 and 1628 during Santa Fe's founding years by Tlaxcalan Indians of Mexico who came with the Spanish as servants. The church was burned and badly damaged during the Pueblo Revolt of 1680, but rebuilt in 1710 and a sacristy added on the south side in 1714.

In addition to repairs over the years, the 1798 altar screen and artwork were restored in 1955. Archaeological investigations made that year also found evidence under the foundation that American Indians occupied the site as early as 1300. Since its founding, San Miguel has served as a chapel and shrine to St. Michael (for whom the mission is named), a military chapel, an oratory for the Christian Brothers, a school chapel, and a barrio church. Today, it still serves as a shrine to St. Michael and a chapel where mass is celebrated weekly. It contains Spanish colonial and American Indian art, religious artifacts, early pottery, and what is believed to be the oldest bell in the nation (said to have been cast in Spain in 1356 and used in Spain and Mexico before coming to Santa Fe).

San Miguel Mission Church, 401 Old Santa Fe Trail, Santa Fe, NM 87501. Phone: 505/983–3974. E-mail: *sanmiguel1610@yahoo.com*. Hours: May-Oct.— 9–5 Mon.-Sat.; 10–4 Sun.; remainder of year — 10–4 Mon.-Sat.; 1:30–4:30 Sun.; closed New Year's Day, Good Friday, Easter, Thanksgiving, and Christmas. Admission: donation.

Santuario de Nuestra Señora de Guadalupe. The ca. 1780 Santuario de Nuestra Señora de Guadalupe built by the Franciscans in Santa Fe, New Mexico, is believed to be the oldest shrine in the nation honoring the Virgin of Guadalupe, the patron saint of Mexico. The shrine, known as Santuario de Guadalupe, contains the Archdiocese of Santa Fe's collection of New Mexican santos (carved images of saints), Italian Renaissance paintings, and Mexican baroque paintings. One of its most famous artworks is the oil painting *Our Lady of Guadalupe*, created in 1783 by José de Alzibar, the renowned Mexican artist.

Santuario de Nuestra Señora de Guadalupe, 100 S. Guadalupe St., Santa Fe, NM 87501. Phone: 505/ 988–2027. Hours: May-Oct.—9–4 Mon.-Sat.; closed Sun.; remainder of year—9–4 Mon.-Fri.; closed Sat.-Sun. Admission: free.

Serra Museum. The Serra Museum in San Diego, California, commemorates the site where Father Junípero Serra and Captain Gaspar de Portola established the first mission and military outpost on the West Coast of the United States and Canada in 1769. Father Serra founded the first nine of the 21 Spanish missions in California in the early eighteenth century and Captain Portola led the initial Spanish military force that created the first fortified settlement in what is now Presidio Park. The museum, housed in a 1929 mission-style building, features historical exhibits and such artifacts as early furniture, housewares, tools, and a cannon from the American Indian, Spanish, Mexican, and American periods through 1929.

Serra Museum, 2727 Presidio Dr., Presidio Park, San Diego, CA 92103 (mailing address: San Diego Historical Society, 1649 El Prado, San Diego, CA 92101). Phone: 619/297–3258. Fax: 619/232–6203. E-mail: *egan@sandiegohistory.org*. Web site: *www. sandiegohistory.org*. Hours: 10–4:30 daily; closed New Year's Day, Thanksgiving Day and day after, and Christmas Eve and Day. Admission: adults, $5; seniors, military, and students, $4; children 6–17, $2; children under 6, free.

Spanish Governor's Palace. The Spanish Governor's Palace in San Antonio is the only remaining example of an early aristocratic Spanish house in Texas. The 10-room adobe building was the residence of the commander of the Presidio de San Antonio de Béjar. The presidio was built to protect the Mission San Antonio de Valero, which later became known as The Alamo (see Mexican Historic Sites section). The palace, which was called the Commandancia, evolved into the seat of the government in 1722 when San Antonio was made the capital of the Spanish province of Texas.

After Spanish rule ended in 1822, the building was used for various other purposes before being purchased by the city of San Antonio in 1929. The Spanish Governor's Palace then was restored with its thick walls, room arrangements, fireplaces, brick

ovens, and antique furniture from the early 1700s. It also has an engraved keystone with a double-headed eagle over the front door, hand-carved doors, low beam ceilings, and a mosaic-tiled patio typical of colonial Spain.

Spanish Governor's Palace, 105 Military Plaza, San Antonio, TX 78205 (mailing address: 105 Plaza de Armas, San Antonio, TX 78205). Phone: 210/ 224–0601. Fax: 210/223–5562. E-mail: *nward@ sanantonio.gov*. Web site: *www.sanantoniocvb.com*. Hours: 9–5 Mon.-Sat.; 10–5 Sun.; closed New Year's Day, Fiesta Parade Day, Thanksgiving, and Christmas. Admission: adults, $1.50; children 7–13, 50¢; children under 7, free.

Tubac Presidio State Historic Park. The Tubac Presidio State Historic Park in Tubac, Arizona, was the site of a Spanish military post that became Arizona's first European settlement in 1752. The military base was established after the Pima Indians revolted against Spanish encroachment, but was relocated to Tucson in 1776. The site, however, was reoccupied by the Spanish and then the Mexicans before being abandoned in 1848. The park site now contains the ruins of the presidio commandant's 1752 house, a restored 1885 schoolhouse and 1914 community house, historical materials, and a museum with Indian, Spanish, Mexican, and territorial artifacts.

Tubac Presidio State Historic Park, 1 Burruel St., PO Box 1296, Tubac, AZ 85646–1296. Phone: 520/ 398–2252. Fax: 520/398–2685. Web site: *www.azstateparks.com*. Hours: 8–5 daily; closed Christmas. Admission: adults, $3; children under 14, free.

Tumacácori National Historical Park. The ruins of three Spanish colonial adobe missions are preserved at the Tumacácori National Historical Park in the upper Santa Cruz River Valley north of Nogales, Arizona. The park is located on 360 acres in three separate units near Tumacácori. The San José de Tumacácori and Los Santos Angeles de Guevavi missions, established in 1691 by Jesuit father Eusebio Francisco Kino, are the oldest missions in Arizona. The third mission, San Cayetano de Calabazas, was founded in 1757. The Tumacácori mission, which never was completed because of Apache raids and severe weather, has a visitor center which depicts the history and life of the mission and the area. The other two missions can be visited only as part of reserved ranger guided tours during the fall and winter months.

Tumacácori National Historical Park, 1891 E. Frontage Rd. (off Interstate 19, Exit 290, PO Box 67, Tumacácori, AZ 85640. Phone: 520/398–2341. Fax: 520/398–9271. Web site: *www.nps.gov/tuma*. Hours: 8–5 daily; closed Thanksgiving and Christmas. Admission: adults, $3; children under 17, free.

Ysleta Mission. The Ysleta Mission on the Tigua Indian Reservation in El Paso, Texas, is the oldest Spanish mission in Texas and the second oldest continuously used church in the nation. It has had a number of names over the years. Founded as the Mission Nuestra Señora del Carmen in 1681, its name was changed to Mission Corpus de la Isleta in 1690 and to Mission San Antonio de los Tiguas in 1980. Now it goes by simply Ysleta Mission. The mission was established to serve Tigua refugees after the Pueblo Revolt of 1680, and still is the focal point of the Indian community (also see Ysleta del sur Pueblo Cultural Center in Native American Museums and Galleries section).

The mission was destroyed in 1742 and 1829 when the Rio Grande River overflowed and was rebuilt on higher ground in 1851. The mission originally was located on the Mexican side of the river, but became part of Texas when river channel changed. The mission also was severely damaged by a fire in 1907. When reconstructed, a three-story tower incorporating Mission Revival decorations was added.

Ysleta Mission, Tigua Indian Reservation, 131 S. Zaragosa Rd., El Paso, TX 79907. Phone: 915/859–9848. Web site: *http://ysletamission.org*. Hours: 9–5 daily. Admission: free.

SWEDISH (*also see* Scandinavian)

Museums and Galleries

American Swedish Historical Museum. The American Swedish Historical Museum in Philadelphia, Pennsylvania, is dedicated to preserving and promoting the history and contributions of Swedes and Swedish Americans in the United States. Founded in 1926, the museum has 12 galleries with exhibits on such topics as a replicated Stuga, an idealized rendering of a nineteenth-century Swedish farmhouse interior; Alfred Nobel and the Nobel Prizes; Swedish maps; the daily life of Swedish colonists among the Lenape Indians; and a timeline and artifacts of the Swedish colonists and later immigrants. It also presents changing exhibitions.

The museum has artifacts, memorabilia, and a library relating to the Swedish colonial and immigrant experience from 1638. The museum building's design is based on Eriksberg, a seventeenth-century manor house in Södermanland, Sweden. It is located on a seventeenth-century Queen Christina land grant.

American Swedish Historical Museum, 1900 Pattison Ave., Philadelphia, PA 19145. Phone: 215/389–1776. Fax: 215/389–7701. E-mail *info@american swedish.org*. Web site: *www.americanswedish.org*. Hours: 10–4 Tues.-Fri.; 12–4 Sat.-Sun.; closed Mon. and major holidays. Admission: adults, $6; seniors, students, and children over 11, $5; children under 12, free.

American Swedish Institute. The permanent exhibit at the American Swedish Institute in Minneapolis, Minnesota, features immigrant artifacts, diaries, photographs, and vintage recordings that tell the story of early Swedish settlers in the Twin Cities. It also has collections of Swedish glass, decorative and fine arts, textiles, and other items from Sweden, and presents changing exhibitions relating to the Swedish American experience.

The institute is housed in the 1908 former mansion of newspaper publisher Swan J. Turnbald, who founded the museum and cultural center. The restored 33-room castle-like building has intricately carved woodwork, decorative plaster sculpted ceilings, early furnishings, artwork, and personal family materials.

American Swedish Institute, 2600 Park Ave., Minneapolis, MN 55407. Phone: 612/781–4907. Fax: 512/871–8682. E-mail: *info@americanswedishinst.org*. Web site: *www.americanswedishinst.org*. Hours: Jan.-Oct.—12–4 Tues.-Sat. (also to 8 Wed.); 1–5 Sun.; closed Mon. and national holidays; remainder of year —12–4 Tues.-Fri (also to 8 Wed.); 10–5 Sat.; 1–5 Sun.; closed Mon. and national holidays. Admission: adults, $5; seniors, $4; children 6–18, $3; children under 5, free.

Bishop Hill Heritage Museum. Bishop Hill Heritage Museum is devoted to the history of the 1846 Swedish communal settlement of religious dissenters in Bishop Hill, Illinois. It is housed in the 1854 Steeple Building, a three-story Greek Revival building with a clock tower that is part of the Bishop Hill State Historic Site (see separate listing in Historic Sites section). The museum, operated by the Bishop Hill Heritage Association, has historical exhibits and artifacts relating to Swedish immigration and Bishop Hill's settlement, communal life, and colony life. It also offers a film on Bishop Hill's history, workshops and demonstrations of traditional folk crafts, and costume-guided tours.

Bishop Hill Heritage Museum, Steeple Bldg., 103 N. Bishop Hill St., PO Box 92, Bishop Hill, IL 61419. Phone: 309/927–3899. Fax: 309/927–3010. E-mail: *bhha@winco.net*. Web site: *www.bishophill.com*. Hours: Apr.-Oct.—10–5 Mon.-Sat.; 12–5 Sun.; Nov.-Dec 10—10–4 Mon.-Sat.; 12–4 Sun; closed major holidays; remainder of year — by appointment. Admission: free.

Gammelgården Museum. The Gammelgården (small farm) Museum in Scandia, Minnesota, seeks to preserve, present, and promote Swedish immigrant heritage and history. The museum, owned by the Elim Lutheran Church, features six historic log cabins built by Swedish immigrant settlers between 1850 and 1879. They include an 1855 log cabin, 1856 church, 1868 pastor's house, and 1879 barn — all furnished with period artifacts. The 11-acre park also has a welcome house built in the style of an 1850s Swedish farmhouse. The historic buildings can be seen only as part of guided tours. The museum celebrates all Swedish holidays and hosts a Swedish fiddling festival and painting competition.

Gammelgården Museum, 20880 Olinda Trail, Scandia, MN 55073 (postal address: 9885 202nd St., Forest Lake, MN 550250). E-mail: *imoratzk@luth ersem.edu*. Web site: *www.scandiamn.com/gammelgarden*. Hours: May-mid–Dec.—10–4 Mon.-Sat.; 1–4 Sun.; closed Memorial Day, Independence Day, Labor Day, Thanksgiving, and remainder of year. Admission: adults and children over 12, $3; children under 13, free.

New Sweden Farmstead Museum. Seven log replicas of a seventeenth-century Swedish farmstead are featured at the New Sweden Farmstead Museum, an outdoor museum in the city park in Bridgeton, New Jersey. Tour guides take visitors to a farmhouse, bath-smokehouse, storehouse, blacksmith shop, stable, cow and goat barn, and threshing barn.

New Sweden Farmstead Museum, City Park, Mayor Aitken Dr., Bridgeton, NJ 08302 (mailing address: City Hall Annex, 181 E. Commerce St., Bridgeton, NJ 08302). Web site: *www.biderman.net/nj/new.htm*. Hours: by appointment. Admission: adults, $3; seniors, $2.50; children 6–12, $2; children under 6, free.

New Sweden Museum and Historic Area. New Sweden, founded as a Swedish colony in Maine in 1870, is known for its original and replica Swedish historic buildings. New Sweden Historical Society operates the New Sweden Museum in the Capitolium, a replica of the Swedish colony capitol building which burned in 1971. It preserves Swedish culture and traditions in America by documenting the lives of early Swedish settlers in the area.

Other nearby buildings include the ca. 1894 Lindsten Stuga, a restored typical immigrant log cabin moved next to the Capitolium, and three early churches—1880 Gustaf Adolph Lutheran Church, 1891 Evangelical Covenant, and 1892 First Baptist Church. Three historic buildings in the care of Maine's Swedish Colony are part of the town's historic area. They are the ca. 1871 Larsson-Ostlund Log Home, ca. 1900 Lars Noak Blacksmith Shop, and ca. 1926 one-room Capitol School.

New Sweden Museum, New Sweden Historical Society, 116 Station Rd., New Sweden, ME 04762. Phone: 207/896–3018. Hours: June-Aug.—12–4 Mon.-Fri.; 1–4 Sat.-Sun.; remainder of year — by appointment. Admission: free.

Lars Noak Blacksmith Shop, Larsson-Ostlund Log Home, and Capitol School, Station Rd., PO Box 50, New Sweden, ME 04762. Phone and fax: 207/896–3199. E-mail: *rmhme@mix.net*. Web site: *www.aroostook.me.us/newsweden/historical.html*. Hours: June-Aug.—12–4 Wed.-Sat.; 2–5 Sun.; other times — by appointment. Admission: free.

Sail Loft Museum. The Sail Loft Museum in Wilmington, Delaware, is devoted to the history and craftsmanship of the *Kalmar Nyckel*, a replica of the Swedish tall ship that landed nearby in 1638. A visit to the museum also includes a tour of the ship in the shipyard along the Christina River. The *Kalmar Nyckel* also has other berths along Wilmington's riverfront, participates in various festivals, and makes educational visits to such historic towns as New Castle and Lewes.

Sail Loft Museum, Kalmar Nyckel Foundation, 1124 E. 7th St., Wilmington, DE 19801. Phones: 302/429–7447 and 888/783–7247. Web site: *www.kalmarnyckel.org*. Hours: 10–4 Sat.-Sun.; closed Mon.-Fri. and major holidays. Admission: adults, $5; children 5–15, $3; children under 5, free.

Swedish American Museum. The Swedish American Museum in Swedesburg, Iowa, portrays Swedish immigrant family life, farming practices, social life, business activities, and major events in the history of the community. It occupies four buildings.

Swedish American Museum, 107 James Ave., PO Box 74, Swedesburg, IA 52652. Phones: 319/254–2317 and 319/254–2494. Hours: 9–4 Mon.-Tues. and Thurs.-Sat.; closed Wed.., Sun., New Year's Day, Thanksgiving, and Christmas. Admission: free.

Swedish American Museum Center. The Swedish American Museum Center in Chicago, Illinois, celebrates and interprets Swedish-American history and culture. King Carl XVI Gustaf of Sweden participated in the opening of the museum in 1976 and for its move to its expanded 24,000-square-foot site in the largely Swedish neighborhood of Andersonville.

The museum's permanent exhibit uses artifacts, memorabilia, and arts and crafts in telling the story of Swedes who immigrated to Chicago. Changing exhibitions also are presented on such subjects as contemporary Swedish art, famous Swedes in the United States, and furniture and woodcarvings by Swedish-Americans. A Children's Museum of Immigration with exhibits and programs for children ages 3–12 is located on the third floor of the building. The center also has classrooms, workshops, and a library, and offers lecture, performing arts, and film programs and Swedish crafts, folk dancing, and language classes.

Swedish American Museum Center, 5211 N. Clark St., Chicago, IL 60640. Phone: 773/728–8111. Fax: 773/728–8870. E-mail: *museum@samac.org*. Web site: *www.samac.org*. Hours: 10–4 Tues.-Fri; 11–4 Sat.-Sun.; closed Mon. Admission: adults, $4; seniors, students, and children, $3; families, $10; second Tues. of month, free (admission also includes Children's Museum of Immigration).

Swedish Heritage and Cultural Center. The Swedish Heritage and Cultural Center in Stanton, Iowa, relates the history and culture of the Halland Settlement, a group of communities in Montgomery and Page counties whose ancestors were immigrants from Sweden. The Swedish area is named for the Rev. Bengt Magnus Halland, an immigrant who founded the Stanton and Lutheran congregations of Bethesda, Nyman, Essex, and Red Oak and worked with officials of the B&M Railroad to acquire land for Swedish homesteads. The museum contains artifacts, documents, photographs, a video, and other materials in tracing the area's Swedish heritage and history since 1870.

Swedish Heritage and Culture Center, 410 Hilltop Ave., PO Box 231, Stanton, IA 51573. Phone: 712/829–2840. Hours: Apr.-Nov.—1–4 Tues.-Sun.; closed Mon. and major holidays; remainder of year — by appointment. Admission: adults and children over 11, $2; children under 12, free.

Swedish Heritage Center. The Swedish Heritage Center in Oakland, Nebraska, has exhibits on the area's Swedish history, typical period rooms of early Swedish American homes, and collections of Swedish crystal, linens, and needlework. The museum is housed in the former Swedish Covenant Mission Church building.

Swedish Heritage Center, 301 N. Chard Ave., Oakland, NE 68045. Phone: 402/685–6161. Hours: May-Sept.—1–4 Tues.-Sun.; closed Mon.; remainder of year—1–4 Sat.-Sun.; closed Mon.-Fri. and major holidays. Admission: free.

Vasa Museum. The Vasa Museum in Vasa, Minnesota, preserves, interprets, and displays artifacts and other materials related to Swedish history, culture, life, and religious traditions, as well as the history and activities of the sponsoring Vasa Lutheran Church.

Vasa Museum, County Rd. 7, Rural Rte. 1, Vasa, MN 55089–9801. Phone: 651/258–4281. Hours: May-Sept.—1–5 Sun.; closed Mon.-Sat.; remainder of year — by appointment. Admission: free.

Museums Honoring Individuals

Birger Sandzen Memorial Gallery. The Birger Sandzen Memorial Gallery at Bethany College in Lindsborg, Kansas, is named for the Swedish painter and printmaker who came to teach for two years and stayed for the rest of his life. The gallery, dedicated in 1957, honors Sandzen's memory as an artist, teacher, and early practitioner of outreach programs. The gallery contains collections of his oils, watercolors, and prints, as well as works by other artists.

Birger Sandzen Memorial Gallery, Bethany College, 421 N. 1st St., Lindsborg, KS 67456–1897. Phone: 785/227–2220. Fax: 785/227–4170. E-mail: *fineart@sandzen.org*. Web site: *www.sandzen.org*. Hours: 1–5 Tues.-Sun.; closed Mon. and major holidays. Admission: free.

Historic Sites

Bishop Hill State Historic Site. Over 1,000 Swedish immigrants came to Bishop Hill, Illinois, in 1846 to establish their "utopia on the prairie" under the leadership of Erik Jansson. They were religious dissidents who believed that the Bible was the only true book of God and that simplicity was the way to salvation. These beliefs were in conflict with Sweden's state church and led to the imprisonment of their leader. Jansson and his followers then pooled their resources and emigrated to the United States to form a communal community on the Illinois prairie that now is the Bishop Hill Historic State Site.

The Bishop Hill colony remained a religious communal community until 1861. It initially was quite successful, with more settlers arriving, permanent buildings erected, 12,000 acres of land put into production, and remarkable economic gains. Although the religious unity of the colonists was disrupted by Jansson's murder in 1850, Bishop Hill continued to thrive, with the colonists producing virtually everything needed and marketed, including fine linen, furniture, brooms, wagons, and farm products. However, the Civil War and financial mismanagement led to the dissolution of the colony in 1861, with the property being divided among the members. Public interest in restoring Bishop Hill resulted in much of the colony becoming a state historic site in 1946 and a national historic landmark in 1984.

Fifteen of the colony's 21 buildings still stand and are included in the Bishop Hill State Historic Site that commemorates the Swedish settlement. Among the restored buildings are five museums and 25 shops where the skills of colony life are demonstrated. The historic buildings include the 1847

Colony Church, the colony's first permanent structure that now serves as a museum with colony artifacts; the 1854 Steeple Building, a three-story Greek Revival building with a clock tower that houses the Bishop Hill Heritage Museum (see separate listing in Museums and Galleries section); and the Bishop Hill Museum, which features the early paintings of Bishop Hill by folk artist Olof Krans. Among the other historic buildings are the Colony Hotel, a blacksmith shop, a general store, and a building housing the Henry County Historical Museum. The historic site also contains the 1853 village park with two monuments — to the settlers of Bishop Hill and to those who responded to the Union call for troops at the outset of the Civil War.

Bishop Hill State Historic Site, 8 Bishop Hill St., PO Box 104, Bishop Hill, IL 61419. Phone: 309/927–3345. Fax: 309/927–3343. E-mail: *bishophill@winco.net*. Web site: *www.bishophill.com*. Hours: Memorial Day weekend-Labor Day — 9–5 daily; Mar.-late May — 9–5 Wed.-Sun.; closed Mon.-Tues.; remainder of year — 9–4 Wed.-Sun.; closed Mon.-Tues. and major holidays. Admission: adults, $2 suggested donation; children under 18, $1 suggested donation.

Erlander Home Museum. The Swedish Historical Society of Rockford, Illinois, operates the Erlander Home Museum and provides cultural programs that promote the city's Swedish American heritage. The historic Erlander Home, built in 1871 by industrialist John Erlander, contains Rockford-made furniture, Charlotte Weibull doll collection, and many artifacts regarding Swedish heritage and settlement in the area.

Erlander Home Museum, 404 S. 3rd St., Rockford, IL 61104. Phone: 815/963–5559. Fax: 612/871–8682. Web site: *www.swedishhistorical.org*. Hours: 1–4 Tues.-Fri.; 2–4 Sun.; closed Mon., Sat., and major holidays. Admission: adults, $5; seniors, $4; children 1–17, $3; children under 1, free.

Holy Trinity (Old Swedes) Church and Hendrickson House Museum. The 1698 to 1699 Holy Trinity Church (known as Old Swedes Church) in Wilmington, Delaware, is the nation's oldest church still standing as originally built and still used for religious services. It was founded as the Swedish Lutheran Church and placed under the jurisdiction of the Protestant Episcopal Church in 1791. The church was designated a national historic landmark in 1963. Tours now are given of the church and the adjacent 1690 Hendrickson House, believed to be the oldest stone house in America.

The Hendrickson House, originally built for Andrew Hendrickson, a Swedish farmer, and his bride near Chester, Pennsylvania, passed through a succession of owners before being donated to the church in 1958. It then was moved to Wilmington and restored by the church. The Hendrickson House now serves as a museum and the headquarters for the Holy Trinity Church Foundation and principal meeting place of the Delaware Swedish Colonial Society. It contains artifacts and other materials related to early colonial life and Swedish culture. The furniture in the house dates from 1690 to 1800.

Holy Trinity (Old Swedes) Church and Hendrickson House Museum, 606 Church St., Wilmington, DE 19801. Phone: 302/652–5629. Fax: 302/652–8615. E-mail: *oldswedes@aol.com*. Web site: *www.oldswedes.org*. Hours: 10–4 Wed.-Sat.; closed Sun-Tues. Admission: adults, $2; children, free.

Kingsburg Historical Park. The Swedish heritage of Kingsburg, California, can be seen at the Kingsburg Historical Park and throughout the community in the Central Valley. Swedish emigrants settled in the farming area in 1886 and quickly influenced much of the town's customs and architecture. Today, Kingsburg resembles a Swedish village, featuring many restored early buildings with steep wood-shingled roofs, dormer windows, and half-timbers. A historical park features such early structures as a windmill, schoolhouse, firehouse, grocery, service station, and medical building, and contains historic items like period farm tools, clothing, appliances, photographs, and a printing press.

Kingsburg Historical Park, 2321 Sierra St., PO Box 282, Kingsburg, CA 93631. Phones: 559/897–5795 and 559/859–1111. Fax: 559/897–4621. Web site: *www.kingsburgchamber.com/historical_park.html*. Hours: 1–4 Mon.-Sat.; other times by appointment; closed major holidays. Admission: adults and students, $3; children under 12, 50¢; families, $6.

1904 World's Fair Swedish Pavilion. The Swedish Pavilion from the 1904 World's Fair in St. Louis, Missouri, now is located at the McPherson County Old Mill Museum in Lindsborg, Kansas. The building, which is similar to a traditional Swedish manor house, was designed by Ferdinand Boberg, one of Sweden's premier architects at the turn of the century. When the Swedish government would not fund the return of the pavilion to Sweden, W. W. Thomas, the U.S. minister to Sweden and Norway, purchased the building and gave it to Bethany College in Lindsborg as a memorial to a friend. It served as a classroom, library, museum, and home to the art department for more than 60 years under Swedish-born artist Birger Sandzen. In 1969, the structure was moved to the McPherson County Old Mill Museum and now is used for cultural heritage events. The museum also has an 1879 railroad depot, 1898 flour mill, 1898 roller mill, and other historic buildings.

McPherson County Old Mill Museum, 120 Mill St., PO Box 94, Lindsborg, KS 67456. Phone: 785/227–3595. Fax: 785/227–2810. E-mail: *oldmillmuseum@hotmail.com*. Web site: *www.oldmillmuseum.org*. Hours: 9–5 Mon.-Sat.; 1–5 Sun.; closed New Year's Day, Thanksgiving, and Christmas. Admission: adults, $2; children 6–12, $1; children under 6, free.

Turnblad Mansion. See American Swedish Institute in Museums and Galleries section.

SWISS (*also see* German)
Museums and Galleries

Alpine Hills Historical Museum. Swiss history and culture are featured at the Alpine Hills Historical Museum in Sugarcreek, Ohio, which is called the "Little Switzerland of Ohio." The exhibits depict the early days of the community and its Swiss and Amish heritage. Among the displays are traditional Swiss musical instruments, a typical Amish kitchen, a replica of an 1890 cheese house, an early woodworking shop, a print shop where an Amish newspaper was published, and a large collection of horse-drawn farm machinery. The museum also serves as a tourist information center.

Alpine Hills Historical Museum, 106 W. Main St., PO Box 1776, Sugarcreek, OH 44681. Phones: 330/852–4113 and 888/609–7592. Hours: July-Sept.—9–4:30 Mon.-Sat.; closed Sun; Apr.-June and Oct.-Nov.—10–4:30 Mon.-Sat.; closed Sun.; remainder of year—closed. Admission: donation.

Amish and Mennonite Heritage Center. See German Museums and Galleries section.

Brethren in Christ Historical Library and Archives. See German Museums and Galleries section.

Chalet of the Golden Fleece. The Chalet of the Golden Fleece in New Glarus, Wisconsin, is a municipal museum housed in a 1937 replica of a Swiss Bernese mountain chalet decorated with items from Switzerland and around the world. Among its displays are Swiss period furniture, carvings, dolls, and prints, as well as early American furniture, glass, china, jewelry, and weapons.

Chalet of the Golden Fleece, 618 2nd St., New Glarus, WI 53574–9776.. Phone: 608/527–2614. Fax: 608/527–2062. Hours: May-Oct.—10–4:30 daily. Admission: adults, $5; children, 6–17, $2; children under 6, free.

German Culture Museum. See German Museums and Galleries section.

Hartzler Library Art Gallery. See German Museums and Galleries section.

Helvetia Museum. The history and culture of the Swiss in Helvetia, West Virginia, is the focus of the Helvetia Museum. The museum, housed in the 1871 Betler Cabin, contains immigrant memorabilia, early agricultural tools, and furniture of Swiss design.

Helvetia Museum, Historical Sq., PO Box 42, Helvetia, WV 26224. Phone: 304/924–6435. Hours: May-Sept.—12–4 Sat.-Sun.; other times by appointment. Admission: donation.

Illinois Mennonite Museum and Archives. See German Museums and Galleries section.

Imperial Valley Swiss Museum. The Imperial Valley Swiss Museum in Holtville, California, depicts Swiss history and culture in the area.

Imperial Valley Swiss Museum, 1585 E. Worthington Rd., Holtville, CA 92250. No phone. Hours: varies. Admission: free.

Iowa Mennonite Museum and Archives. See German Museums and Galleries section.

Juniata District Mennonite Historical Society. See German Museums and Galleries section.

Kauffman Museum. See German Museums and Galleries section.

Kidron-Sonnenberg Heritage Center. See German Museums and Galleries section.

Lancaster Mennonite Historical Society. See German Museums and Galleries section.

Menno-Hof Mennonite-Amish Visitors Center. See German Museums and Galleries section.

Mennonite Heritage Center. See German Museums and Galleries section.

Mennonite Heritage Museum. See German Museums and Galleries section.

Mennonite Information Center and Biblical Taberacle Reproduction. See German Museums and Galleries section.

Mennonite Library and Archives. See German Museums and Galleries section.

Mennonite Settlement Museum. See German Museums and Galleries section.

People's Place Quilt Museum. See German Museums and Galleries section.

Swiss Center of North America. The Swiss Center of North America, a research and cultural center, is being developed in New Glarus, Wisconsin, which has a large population of Swiss immigrants and their descendents. When completed, it will have exhibits, collections, a research library, and a research center. It will be the permanent home for the "Sister Republics" exhibit, which highlights Swiss immigration to North America and Swiss involvement in the American Revolutionary and Civil wars, and various collections of Swiss artifacts, artworks, and other materials.

Swiss Center of North America, 507 Durst Rd., New Glarus, WI 53574. Phone: 608/527–6565. Web site: *www.swisscenterna.com*. Hours and admission: still to be determined.

Swiss Historical Village. The Swiss Historical Village in New Glarus, Wisconsin, traces the history of the area from its founding as a Swiss colony in 1845 to its development as an ethnically oriented dairy farming community, known as "America's Little Switzerland." The Swiss founders came from Glarus, Switzerland, during a period of difficult economic conditions and unemployment.

The museum, operated by the New Glarus Historical Society, is a collection of 14 buildings that provide a look into the life of Swiss settlers in the region in the nineteenth century. It has artifacts and exhibits on Swiss immigration and colonization, life in the first colony, American Indian culture, and county history. The museum also presents changing exhibitions on Swiss history and New Glarus.

Swiss Historical Village, 612 7th Ave., PO Box 745, New Glarus, WI 53574. Phone: 608/527–2317. Fax: 608/527–2302. Web site: *www.swisshistoricalvillage. org*. Hours: May-Oct.—10–4 daily; closed remainder of year. Admission: adults, $7; children 6–13, $2; children under 6, free.

Swiss Institute-Contemporary Art. The Swiss Institute in New York City promotes cultural exchange between the United States and Switzerland and presents exhibitions of Swiss creative efforts. Changing exhibitions of Swiss and European paintings, drawings, and photographs are displayed in its contemporary art gallery on the third floor.

Swiss Institute-Contemporary Art, 495 Broadway, New York, NY 10012. Phone: 212/759–0606. Fax: 212/925–2040. E-mail: *info@swissinstitute.net*. Web site: *www.swissinstitute.net*. Hours: 10–6 Tues.-Sat.; closed Sun.-Mon. and major holidays. Admission: free.

Museums Honoring Individuals

1719 Hans Herr House and Museum. See German Museums Honoring Individuals section.

Sutter's Fort State Historic Park. The Sutter's Fort State Historic Park in Sacramento, California, is named for John Sutter, a Swiss immigrant who founded a flourishing agricultural empire and called it New Helvetia (New Switzerland). He immigrated to the United States in 1834, moved to California in 1839, received a Mexican land grant of 47,827 acres for New Helvetia (and had a second grant of 96,800 acres later declared invalid by the United States), built a major trading post and vast agricultural interests, and became the richest man in California at the time. But less than a decade after they were established, Sutter's properties were overrun by gold seekers and only the restored fort remains today.

Sutter became known for his hospitality and providing temporary refuge to travelers after sending aid to the Donner Party, a group of immigrants trapped in a winter storm in the Sierra Nevada Mountains in 1847. As a result, New Helvetia became a destination for many early immigrants to California. When gold was discovered by foreman James W. Marshall at Sutter's sawmill along the American River at Coloma in 1848, thousands of prospectors came looking for gold. Squatters took over much of Sutter's land, and swindlers acquired other holdings. As a result, Sutter sold the property in 1849, retired with his family, and spent the rest of his life — without success — trying to obtain compensation from the federal government for his aid to emigrants, helping colonizing California, and the land grant that was invalid. Sutter and his wife moved to Lititz, Pennsylvania, in 1871 and died and were buried in the Moravian Brotherhood's Cemetery in 1880. Sutter's Fort eventually was rebuilt as a state park and opened for tours.

Sutter's Fort State Historic Park, 2701 L St., Sacramento, CA 95816. Phone: 916/445–4422. Fax: 916/442–8613. Web site: *www.parks.ca.gov/?page_ id=485*. Hours: 10–5 daily; closed New Year's Day, Thanksgiving, and Christmas. Admission: Memorial Day-Labor Day — adults, $4; children 6–12, $1; children under 6, free; remainder of year — adults, $2; children under 13, free.

Warkentin House. See German Museums Honoring Individuals section.

Historic Sites

Pioneer Adobe House Museum. See Mennonite Settlement Museum in German Museums and Galleries section.

Swiss Historical Village. See Museums and Galleries section.

TIBETAN

Museums and Galleries

Jacques Marchais Museum of Tibetan Art. The

Jacques Marchais Museum of Tibetan Art was founded in 1945 by Jacques Marchais, the adopted name of Edna Coblentz, in Staten Island, New York. In the 1930s, after pursuing a career in the theater, she established the Asian Art Gallery in New York City. She wanted to share her passionate interest in Tibetan art and culture with the public.

The museum, which collects Tibetan art, photographs, and books and makes them available through exhibitions and educational programs, is housed in two fieldstone buildings that resemble a Himalayan mountain temple. The collection includes art from Tibet, Mongolia, and northern China from the fifteenth through the early twentieth centuries. It includes bronze and other metal statues of buddhas, arhats, and protector deities; thangka paintings; ornate ritual objects; and musical instruments.

Jacques Marchais Museum of Tibetan Art, 338 Lighthouse Ave., Staten Island, NY 10306. Phone: 718/987-3500. Fax: 718/351-0402. E-mail: *mventrudo@tibetanmuseum.org.* Web site: *www.tibetanmuseum.org.* Hours: 1–5 Wed.-Sun.; other times by appointment. Admission: adults, $5; seniors and students, $3; children under 13, $2.

UKRAINIAN (*also see* Russian)

Museums and Galleries

Diocesan Cultural Museum. The Diocesan Cultural Museum, part of the Byzantine Catholic Eparchy of Parma in Parma, Ohio, has artifacts, artworks, books, and historical materials relating to the Byzantine Catholic Church in the United States and its followers and their folk arts, crafts, customs, and traditions.

Diocesan Cultural Museum, 1900 Carlton Rd., Parma, OH 44134-3129. Phone: 216/741-8773. Fax: 216/741-9356. Web site: *www.parma.org.* Hours: by appointment. Admission: free.

Lemko Association Museum. The Lemko Association national headquarters in Yonkers, New York, has a historical display relating to the culture and traditions of Lemko immigrants, also known as Carpatho-Ruthenians. The Lemkos inhabited the Lower Beskid Range of the Carpathian Mountains until 1947 when the majority was deported from the southeastern corner of Poland to the Ukraine.

Lemko Association Museum, 556 Yonkers Ave., Yonkers, NY 19704. Phone: 609/758-1115. Fax: 609/758-7301. Web site: *http://lemko.org.* Hours: not open to public.

Museum of the Ukrainian Orthodox Memorial

Church. The Ukrainian Orthodox Church of the United States has a museum and mausoleum beneath the St. Andrew Memorial Church at Metroplia Center in Somerset, New Jersey. It contains artifacts and other materials of Ukrainian historical, cultural, social, religious, literary, and political life. The museum also has a temporary historical exhibition in the Ukrainian Cultural Center on the grounds. Plans call for a new 16,000-square-foot museum that will be attached to the Consistory-Library-Bookstore Complex near the Ukrainian Cultural Center and Seminary.

Museum of the Ukrainian Orthodox Memorial Church, St. Andrew Memorial Church, Metroplia Center, 135 Davidson Ave., Somerset, NJ 08873 (mailing address: PO Box 495, South Bound Brook, NJ 08880). Phone: 732/356-0090. Fax: 732/356-9437. E-mail *consistory@uocofusa.org.* Web site: *www.ukrainianorthodoxchurchusa.org.* Hours: by appointment. Admission: donation.

St. Nicholas Ukrainian Orthodox Church Museum. History of the local Ukrainian community is preserved in displays at the St. Nicholas Ukrainian Orthodox Church in Troy, New York.

St. Nicholas Ukrainian Orthodox Church Museum, 376 3rd St., Troy, NY 12180. Phone: 518/274-5482. E-mail: *tanyapetroff@yahoo.com.* Web site: *www.stnicholasuoc.org.* Hours: Sun. mornings. Admission: free.

Ukrainian American Archives and Museum of Detroit. The history, culture, and art of Ukrainian Americans are the focal points of the Ukrainian American Archives and Museum of Detroit, located in the suburb of Hamtramck, Michigan. The museum traces Ukrainian immigration and contributions; displays artifacts and artworks; and maintains an archive of documents and other historical materials.

Ukrainian American Archives and Museum of Detroit, 11756 Charest St., Hamtramck, MI 48212. Phone: 313/366-9764. Web site: *www.ukrainianmuseumdetroit.org.* Hours: 9–5 Mon.-Sat. and by appointment; closed Sun. and major holidays. Admission: free.

Ukrainian-American Museum and Archives. The Ukrainian-American Museum and Archives, located on the second floor of a cultural center in Warren, Michigan, has exhibits and collections pertaining to Ukrainian and Ukrainian American history and culture.

Ukrainian-American Museum and Archives, Ukrainian Cultural Center, 26601 Ryan Rd., Warren, MI 48091. Phone: 248/757-1052. Fax: 810/757-8684. Hours: by appointment. Admission: free.

Ukrainian Diocesan Museum. Ukrainian art, costumes, sculpture, and other cultural treasures can be seen at the Ukrainian Diocesan Museum at St. Basil College Seminary in Stamford, Connecticut. The museum is located in the historic Chateau building, a local landmark.

Ukrainian Diocesan Museum, St. Basil College Seminary, 161 Glenbrook Rd., Stamford, CT 06902. Phones: 203/324–0488 and 203/324–4578. Fax: 203/967–9948. Web site: *www.stbasilcollegesem.net.* Hours: by appointment. Admission: donation.

Ukrainian Eko Art Gallery. The Ukrainian Eko Art Gallery in Warren, Michigan, presents permanent and changing exhibits of Ukrainian art and cultural artifacts.

Ukrainian Eko Art Gallery, 26795 Ryan Rd., Warren, MI 48091–4073. Phone: 586/755–3535. Hours: varies; closed major holidays. Admission: free.

Ukrainian Heritage Studies Center. The Ukrainian Heritage Studies Center at Manor Junior College in Jenkintown, Pennsylvania, preserves and interprets Ukrainian culture, heritage, and folk arts. It has cultural exhibits and collections of folk arts, art, music, and films. The center also offers craft classes and presents conferences, workshops, an Easter egg expo, and an annual Ukrainian festival with dance and music performances, art displays, craft demonstrations, a folk market, and ethnic foods.

Ukrainian Heritage Studies Center, Manor Junior College, 700 Fox Chase Rd., Jenkintown, PA 19046–3399. Phone: 215/885–2360. Fax: 215/576–6564. Hours: by appointment. Admission: free.

Ukrainian Institute of Modern Art. Five to six major exhibitions of contemporary art are presented each year in the main gallery at the Ukrainian Institute of Modern Art in Chicago, Illinois. Three other galleries largely feature the works of Chicago artists of Ukrainian descent. The museum was founded in the Ukrainian Village neighborhood in 1972 by Dr. Achilles Chretowsky, who transformed three storefronts into a viable museum.

Ukrainian Institute of Modern Art, 2320 W. Chicago Ave., Chicago, 60622–4722. Phone: 773/227–5522. Web site: *www.uima-art.org.* Hours: 12–4 Wed-Sun. and by appointment during exhibitions; closed Mon.-Tues. and major holidays. Admission: varies.

Ukrainian Lemko Museum. Artifacts of the Lemko culture are featured at the Ukrainian Lemko Museum in Stamford, Connecticut. Among the historical objects are folk costumes, wood carvings, and artworks. The museum, originally located in Syracuse, New York, was moved to Stamford in 1981. It is located in the same building as the Ukrainian Diocesan Museum at St. Basil College Seminary.

Ukrainian Lemko Museum, 161 Glenbrook Rd., Stamford, CT 06902. Phone: 203/762–5912. Hours: by appointment. Admission: donation.

The Ukrainian Museum. The emphasis at The Ukrainian Museum in New York City is on the cultural legacy of the Ukrainians. Its exhibits, programs, and other activities seek to further understanding and appreciation of the scope and diversity of Ukrainian culture. The museum's folk art collection includes wedding and festive attire, ritual cloths, embroidered and woven textiles, ceramics, metalwork, brass and silver jewelry, decorative wood objects, and Easter eggs, while the fine arts collection features paintings, drawings, graphic works, and sculptures by leading Ukrainian artists. The archival holdings contain documents, photographs, and other materials relating to Ukrainian immigration and the cultural, social, and political life of the Ukraine. The museum is planning a new 25,000-square-foot home.

The Ukrainian Museum, 222 E. 6th St., New York, NY 10003–8201. Phone: 212/228-0110. Fax: 212/228-1947. E-mail: *info@ukrainianmuseum.org.* Web site: *www.ukrainianmuseum.org.* Hours: 11:30–5 Wed.-Sun.; closed Mon.-Tues. and major holidays. Admission: adults, $8; seniors and students, $6; children under 12, free.

Ukrainian Museum-Archives. The Ukrainian Museum-Archives in Cleveland, Ohio, contains artifacts, documents, artworks, photographs, books, and other materials pertaining to Ukrainian history and culture, particularly in Ohio and the United States. The museum was founded in 1953 in the Tremont neighborhood of Cleveland.

Ukrainian Museum-Archives, 1202 Kenilworth Ave., Cleveland, OH 44113. Phone: 216/781-4329. Fax: 216/781-5844. E-mail: staff@umacleveland.org. Web site: www.umacleveland.org. Hours: by appointment. Admission: free.

Ukrainian National Museum of Chicago. Historical, art, and folk arts and crafts exhibits related to Ukrainian cultural heritage are presented at the Ukrainian National Museum of Chicago. The museum, founded in 1952, traces the history of Ukrainian immigration to Chicago and the nation and displays examples of Ukrainian weaving, textiles, woodworking, embroideries, beadwork, paintings, sculpture, and other works. A library featuring rare books and an archive with documents, photographs, music, and other historical materials also are located at the site.

Ukrainian National Museum of Chicago, 721 N. Oakley Blvd., Chicago, IL 60612. Phone: 312/421–8020. Fax: 773/722–2883. E-mail: *info@ukrntlmuseum.org.* . Web site: www.ukrntlmuseum.org. Hours: 11–4 Thurs.-Sun.; Mon.-Wed. by appointment; closed Easter and Christmas. Admission: adults, $5; students and children, $2.

WELSH (*also see* British)

Museums and Galleries

Great Plains Welsh Heritage and Culture Center. The Great Plains Welsh Heritage and Culture Center in Wymore, Nebraska, interprets the story of Welsh Americans and the early Welsh settlers of the Great Plains through interactive exhibits, artifacts, and oral histories. A Hall of Heroes also honors Welshmen who have made contributions to their adopted country. In addition, the Great Plains Welsh Project, which founded the cultural center, also operates the 1906 one-room Pleasantview country schoolhouse, where programs are given twice a year. Teachers dressed in Welsh attire lead classes in 1929 subjects and give instruction in the Welsh language.

Great Plains Welsh Heritage and Culture Center, PO Box 253, Wymore, NE 68466. Phone: 402/645–3186. E-mail: *gpwhp@galaxycable.net.* Web site: *www.welshheritage.org.* Hours: by appointment. Admission: free.

Welsh-American Heritage Museum. Welsh heritage and culture are preserved and displayed at the Welsh-American Heritage Museum, housed in the Old Welsh Congregational Church in Oak Hill, Ohio.

Welsh-American Heritage Museum, Old Welsh Congregational Church, E. Main St., Oak Hill, OH 45656. Phones: 740/682–6515 and 740/682–7057. Hours: May-Oct.—1–4 Tues., Thurs., Sat.-Sun; other times by appointment. Admission: free.

Bibliography

Buttlar, Lois J., and Lubomyr R. Wynar (compiler). *Guide to Information Resources in Ethnic Museum, Library, and Archival Collections in the United States*. Westport, CT: Greenwood Press, 1996.

Carrier, Jim. *A Traveler's Guide to the Civil Rights Movement*. Orlando, FL: Harcourt, 2003.

Curtis, Nancy C. *Black Heritage Sites: An African American Odyssey and Finder's Guide*. Chicago: American Library Association, 1994.

_____. *Black Heritage Sites: The North*. New York: New Press, 1998.

_____. *Black Heritage Sites: The South*. New York: New Press, 1998.

Davalos, Karen Mary. *Exhibiting Mestizaje: Mexican (American) Museums in the Diaspora*. Albuquerque: University of New Mexico Press, 2005.

Eichstedt, Jennifer, and Stephen Small. *Representations of Slavery: Race and Ideology in Southern Plantation Museums*. Washington: Smithsonian Press, 2002.

Graham, Joe Stanley. *Hispanic-American Material Culture: An Annotated Directory of Collections, Sites, Archives and Festivals in the United States*. Westport, CT: Greenwood Press, 1989.

Grossman, Grace Cohen. *Jewish Museums of the World*. Westport, CT: Hugh Lanter Levin Associates, 2003.

Halliday, Jan. *Native Peoples of Alaska: A Traveler's Guide to Land, Art, and Culture*. Seattle: Sasquatch Books, 1998.

_____. *Native Peoples of the Northwest: A Traveler's Guide to Land, Art, and Culture*. Seattle: Sasquatch Books, 2000.

Jacoby, Tamar, and William Frucht (eds.). *Reinventing the Melting Pot: The New Immigrants and What It Means to Be American*. New York: Basic Books, 2004.

Marquis, Arnold. *A Guide to America's Indians, Ceremonials, Reservations, and Museums*. Norman: University of Oklahoma Press, 1974.

The Official Museum Directory 2008. New Providence, NJ: National Register Publishing, 2007.

West, W. Richard. *The Changing Presentation of the American Indian: Museums and Native Cultures*. Seattle: University of Washington Press, 1999.

Wynar, Lubomyr Roman. *Slavic Ethnic Libraries, Museums, and Archives in the United States: A Guide and Directory*. Kent, OH: Kent State University, 1980.

Index